Lecture Notes in Artificial Intelligence   4371

Edited by J. G. Carbonell and J. Siekmann

Subseries of Lecture Notes in Computer Science

Katsumi Inoue   Ken Satoh
Francesca Toni (Eds.)

Computational Logic
in Multi-Agent Systems

7th International Workshop, CLIMA VII
Hakodate, Japan, May 8-9, 2006
Revised Selected and Invited Papers

 Springer

Series Editors

Jaime G. Carbonell, Carnegie Mellon University, Pittsburgh, PA, USA
Jörg Siekmann, University of Saarland, Saarbrücken, Germany

Volume Editors

Katsumi Inoue
Ken Satoh
National Institute of Informatics
Foundations of Information Research Division
2-1-2 Hitotsubashi, Tokyo 101-8430, Japan
E-mail: {ki,ksatoh}@nii.ac.jp

Francesca Toni
Imperial College London
Department of Computing
South Kensington Campus, Huxley Building, London SW7 2AZ, UK
E-mail: ft@doc.ic.ac.uk

Library of Congress Control Number: 2006939322

CR Subject Classification (1998): I.2.11, I.2, C.2.4, F.4

LNCS Sublibrary: SL 7 – Artificial Intelligence

ISSN   0302-9743
ISBN-10   3-540-69618-0 Springer Berlin Heidelberg New York
ISBN-13   978-3-540-69618-6 Springer Berlin Heidelberg New York

Springer is a part of Springer Science+Business Media

springer.com

© Springer-Verlag Berlin Heidelberg 2007
Printed in Germany

Typesetting: Camera-ready by author, data conversion by Scientific Publishing Services, Chennai, India
Printed on acid-free paper   SPIN: 11972709   06/3142   5 4 3 2 1 0

Preface

Multi-agent systems are communities of problem-solving entities that can perceive and act upon their environment to achieve their individual goals as well as joint goals. The work on such systems integrates many technologies and concepts in artificial intelligence and other areas of computing as well as other disciplines. Over recent years, the agent paradigm gained popularity, due to its applicability to a full spectrum of domains, from search engines to educational aids to electronic commerce and trade, e-procurement, recommendation systems, simulation and routing, to cite only some.

Computational logic provides a well-defined, general and rigorous framework for studying syntax, semantics and procedures for various tasks by individual agents, as well as interaction amongst agents in multi-agent systems, for implementations, environments, tools and standards, and for linking together specification and verification of properties of individual agents and multi-agent systems.

The CLIMA (Computational Logic in Multi-Agent Systems) workshop series aims at identifying synergies between computational logic and multi-agent systems, whereby computational logic methods, tools and techniques are used for representing, programming and reasoning about agents and multi-agent systems in a formal way.

The first workshop in this series took place in Las Cruces, New Mexico, USA, in 1999, under the designation Multi-Agent Systems in Logic Programming (MASLP 1999), and was affiliated with ICLP 1999. In the following year, the name of the workshop changed to Computational Logic in Multi-Agent Systems, and CLIMA 2000 took place in London, UK, affiliated with CL 2000. Further information about the CLIMA workshop series, with links to past and future events, is available at http://centria.di.fct.unl.pt/~clima.

The seventh edition of CLIMA (CLIMA VII) took place in Hakodate, Japan, on May 8–9, 2006, affiliated with AAMAS 2006. It received 29 regular submissions, of which only 14 were selected for presentation and inclusion in the preproceedings. About 30 delegates from 12 countries registered for the event, and many more AAMAS 2006 participants attended. More details about the event can be found at the workshop Web site http://research.nii.ac.jp/climaVII/

CLIMA VII also hosted the Second CLIMA Contest, following the first such contest at CLIMA VI. This competition is an attempt to stimulate research in the area of multi-agent systems by identifying key problems and collecting suitable benchmarks that can serve as milestones for testing new approaches and techniques from computational logics. Three groups participated in the second edition, and the winner was team brazil consisting of Rafael Bordini, Jomi Huebner, and Daniel Tralamazza. All results can be checked at http://agentmaster.in.tu-clausthal.de/.

This volume contains improved and revised versions of the 14 papers presented at CLIMA VII, as well as papers describing the 3 contest entries and a paper by the contest organizers presenting the contest and assessing its outcomes. All papers went through a thorough revision, with three to six reviews over two rounds.

The topics of the regular papers include agent reasoning, such as deontic reasoning, probabilistic reasoning, contextual reasoning, decision making and abduction, agent communication, such as argumentation and dialogue, agent architecture and verification of multi-agent systems. The contest papers describe implemented agent architectures solving the gold mining domain.

Our thanks go to the authors who responded to our initial call with very high quality submissions and revised their contribution thoroughly for inclusion in this volume. We are also grateful to the members of the CLIMA VII Program Committee for their valuable work in reviewing, discussing and re-reviewing the submitted articles. Further, we thank the organizers of the contest, Mehdi Dastani from Utrecht University, Jürgen Dix and Peter Novak from Clausthal University of Technology, for their efforts in creating a server architecture and a nice framework for the whole contest. Finally, we are grateful to our sponsor, the National Institute of Informatics, Tokyo, Japan, for providing support for some of the CLIMA VII participants.

October 2006

Katsumi Inoue
Ken Satoh
Francesca Toni

Organization

CLIMA VII took place in Hakodate, Japan.

Workshop Chairs

Katsumi Inoue, National Institute of Informatics, Japan
Ken Satoh, National Institute of Informatics, Japan
Francesca Toni, Imperial College London, UK

Contest Organizers

Mehdi Dastani, Utrecht University, The Netherlands
Jürgen Dix, Technical University of Clausthal, Germany
Peter Novak, Technical University of Clausthal, Germany

CLIMA Steering Committee

Jürgen Dix, Technical University of Clausthal, Germany
Michael Fisher, University of Manchester, UK
João Leite, New University of Lisbon, Portugal
Francesca Toni, Imperial College London, UK
Fariba Sadri, Imperial College London, UK
Ken Satoh, National Institute of Informatics, Japan
Paolo Torroni, University of Bologna, Italy

Program Committee

José Júlio Alferes, New University of Lisbon, Portugal
Rafael H. Bordini, University of Durham, UK
Gerhard Brewka, University of Leipzig, Germany
Stefania Costantini, University of L'Aquila, Italy
Jürgen Dix, Technical University of Clausthal, Germany
Patrick Doherty, Linköping University, Sweden
Phan Ming Dung, AIT, Thailand
Thomas Eiter, Vienna University of Technology, Austria
Klaus Fischer, DFKI, Germany
Michael Fisher, The University of Liverpool, UK
Michael Gelfond, Texas Technical University, USA
James Harland, RMIT, Australia
Hisashi Hayashi, Toshiba, Japan

Wiebe van der Hoek, The University of Liverpool, UK
Antonis Kakas, University of Cyprus, Cyprus
João Leite, New University of Lisbon, Portugal
Fangzhen Lin, Hong Kong University of Science and Technology, Hong Kong
Paola Mello, University of Bologna, Italy
John-Jules Ch. Meyer, Utrecht University, The Netherlands
Leora Morgenstern, IBM T.J. Watson Research Center, USA
Naoyuki Nide, Nara Women's University, Japan
Maurice Pagnucco, University of New South Wales, Australia
Wojciech Penczek, Polish Academy of Sciences, Poland
Enrico Pontelli, New Mexico State University, USA
Fariba Sadri, Imperial College London, UK
Chiaki Sakama, Wakayama University, Japan
Abdul Sattar, Griffith University, Australia
Hajime Sawamura, Niigata University, Japan
Renate Schmidt, University of Manchester, UK
Tran Cao Son, New Mexico State University, USA
Kostas Stathis, City University London, UK
Michael Thielscher, Dresden University of Technology, Germany
Satoshi Tojo, Japan Advanced Institute of Science and Technology, Japan
Paolo Torroni, University of Bologna, Italy
Marina de Vos, University of Bath, UK
Cees Witteveen, Delft University of Technology, The Netherlands

Referees

Marco Alberti	Wojciech Jamroga	Krzysztof Trojanowski
Martin Caminada	Beata Konikowska	Mathijs de Weerdt
Tristan Caulfield	Jonty Needham	Yingqian Zhang
Guido Governatori	Dmitry Tishkovsky	

Sponsoring Institution

The National Institute of Informatics, Tokyo, Japan.

Table of Contents

Contest Papers

Acts of Commanding and Changing Obligations

Tomoyuki Yamada

Graduate School of Letters, Hokkaido University
Nishi 7, Kita 10, Kita-ku, Sapporo, Hokkaido, 060-0810, Japan
yamada@LET.hokudai.ac.jp

Abstract. If we are to take the notion of speech act seriously, we must be able to treat speech acts as acts. In this paper, we will try to model changes brought about by various acts of commanding in terms of a variant of update logic. We will combine a multi-agent variant of the language of monadic deontic logic with a dynamic language to talk about the situations before and after the issuance of commands, and the commands that link those situations. Although the resulting logic inherits various inadequacies from monadic deontic logic, some interesting principles are captured and seen to be valid nonetheless. A complete axiomatization and some interesting valid principles together with concrete examples will be presented, and suggestions for further research will be made.

1 Introduction

Consider the following example:

Example 1. Suppose you are reading an article on logic in the office you share with your boss and a few other colleagues. While you are reading, the temperature of the room rises, and it is now above 30 degrees Celsius. There is a window and an air conditioner. You can open the window, or turn on the air conditioner. You can also concentrate on the article and ignore the heat. Then, suddenly, you hear your boss's voice. She commanded you to open the window. What effects does her command have on the current situation?

Your boss's act of commanding does not affect the state of the window directly. Nor does it affect the number of alternatives you have. It is still possible for you to turn on the air conditioner, to ignore the heat, or to open the window. But it has now become impossible for you to choose alternatives other than that of opening the window without going against your obligation. It is now obligatory upon you to open the window, although it was not so before.

If the notion of speech acts, or more specifically that of illocutionary acts, is to be taken seriously, it must be possible to see utterances not only as acts of uttering words but also as acts of doing something more. But speech acts do not seem to affect so called brute facts directly, except for those various physical and physiological conditions involved in the production and perception of sounds or written symbols. What differences can they bring about in our life?

In attempting to answer this question, it is important to be careful not to blur the distinction between illocutionary acts and perlocutionary acts. Since Grice [10], many philosophers, linguists, and computer scientists have talked about utterers' intentions

K. Inoue, K. Satoh, and F. Toni (Eds.): CLIMA VII, LNAI 4371, pp. 1–19, 2007.

to produce various changes in the attitudes of addressees in their theories of communication. But utterers' intentions usually go beyond illocutionary acts by involving perlocutionary consequences, while illocutionary acts can be effective even if they do not produce intended perlocutionary consequences. Thus, in the above example, even if you refuse to open the window in question, that will not make her command void. Your refusal would not constitute disobedience if it could make her command void. Her command is effective in a sense even if she has failed to get you to form the intention to open the window. In order to characterize effects of illocutionary acts adequately, we need to be able to isolate them from perlocutionary consequences of utterances.

It is interesting to note, in this connection, that some illocutionary acts such as commanding, forbidding, permitting, and promising seem to affect our social life by bringing about changes in the deontic status of various alternative courses of actions. Thus, in the above example, before the issuance of your boss's command, none of your three alternatives were obligatory upon you, but after the issuance, one of them has become obligatory. In what follows, we will model changes acts of commanding bring about in terms of a new update logic. We will combine a multi-agent variant of the language of monadic deontic logic with a dynamic language to talk about the situations before and after the issuance of commands, and the commands that link those situations. Although the resulting language inherits various inadequacies from the language of monadic deontic logic, some interesting principles are captured and seen to be valid nonetheless.

The idea of update logic of acts of commanding is inspired by the update logics of public announcements and private information transmissions developed in Plaza [16], Groeneveld [11], Gerbrandy & Groeneveld [9], Gerbrandy [8], Baltag, Moss, & Solecki [2], and Kooi & van Benthem [13] among others. In van Benthem [4], the logics of such epistemic actions are presented as exemplars of a view of logic as "the analysis of general informational processes: knowledge representation, giving or receiving information, argumentation, communication", and used to show "how using a 'well-known' system as a vehicle, viz. standard epistemic logic, leads to totally *new issues* right from the start"(p.33). The basic idea of the update logic of acts of commanding is to capture the workings of acts of commanding by using deontic logic instead of epistemic logic as a vehicle. This may lead to a significant extension of the range of the kind of logical analysis advocated in van Benthem [4], since acts of commanding exemplify a kind of speech acts radically different from those discussed in the logics of epistemic actions.

2   A Static Base Language $\mathcal{L}_{MDL^+}$ and a Static Logic MDL$^+$

Let's go back to Example 1. In the situation before the command is given, it was neither obligatory upon you to open the window, nor was it so not to open it. But in the situation after your boss's act of commanding, it has become obligatory upon you to open it. In order to describe these situations, we use a language $\mathcal{L}_{MDL^+}$, the Language of Multi-agent monadic Deontic Logic With an alethic modal operator, MDL$^+$. We represent the two situations by two models M and N with a world s for $\mathcal{L}_{MDL^+}$. Thus, we can describe the difference between these situations as follows:

$$M, s \models_{\mathsf{MDL}^+} \neg O_a p \wedge \neg O_a \neg p \tag{1}$$

$$N, s \models_{\mathsf{MDL}^+} O_a p \ , \tag{2}$$

where the proposition letter p stands for the proposition that the window is open at such and such a time, say t_1. The operator O_a here is indexed by a given finite set $I = \{a, b, c, \ldots, n\}$ of agents, and the index a represents you. Intuitively, a formula of form $O_i \varphi$ means that it is obligatory upon the agent i to see to it that φ. Thus:

Definition 1. *Take a countably infinite set* Aprop *of proposition letters and a finite set I of agents, with p ranging over* Aprop *and i over I. The multi-agent monadic deontic language $\mathcal{L}_{\mathsf{MDL}^+}$ is given by:*

$$\varphi ::= \top \mid p \mid \neg\varphi \mid \varphi \wedge \psi \mid \Box\varphi \mid O_i\varphi$$

The set of all well formed formulas (sentences) of $\mathcal{L}_{\mathsf{MDL}^+}$ is denoted by S_{MDL^+} and operators of the form O_i are called deontic operators. For each $i \in I$, we call a sentence i-free if no O_i's occur in it. We call sentence alethic if no deontic operators occur in it, and boolean if no modal operators occur in it. For each $i \in I$, the set of all i-free sentences is denoted by $S_{i\text{-free}}$. The set of all alethic sentences and the set of all boolean sentences are denoted by S_{Aleth} and S_{Boole} respectively.

$\bot$, $\vee$, $\rightarrow$, $\leftrightarrow$, and $\Diamond$ are assumed to be introduced by standard definitions. We also abbreviate $\neg O_i \neg \varphi$ as $P_i \varphi$, and $O_i \neg \varphi$ as $F_i \varphi$. Note that Aprop $\subset S_{\mathrm{Boole}} \subset S_{\mathrm{Aleth}} \subset S_{i\text{-free}} \subset S_{\mathsf{MDL}^+}$ for each $i \in I$.[1]

Definition 2. *By an $\mathcal{L}_{\mathsf{MDL}^+}$-model, we mean a quadruple $M = \langle W^M, R_A^M, R_I^M, V^M \rangle$ where:*

(i) W^M *is a non-empty set (heuristically, of 'possible worlds')*

(ii) $R_A^M \subseteq W^M \times W^M$

(iii) R_I^M *is a function that assigns a subset $R_I^M(i)$ of R_A^M to each agent $i \in I$*

(iv) V^M *is a function that assigns a subset $V^M(p)$ of W^M to each proposition letter $p \in$ Aprop .*

We usually abbreviate $R_I^M(i)$ as R_i^M.

Note that for any $i \in I$, R_i^M is required to be a subset of R_A^M. Thus we assume that whatever is permitted is possible.

Definition 3. *Let M be an $\mathcal{L}_{\mathsf{MDL}^+}$-model and w a point in M. If $p \in$ Aprop, φ, $\psi \in S_{\mathsf{MDL}^+}$, and $i \in I$, then:*

(a) $M, w \models_{\mathsf{MDL}^+} p$ *iff $w \in V^M(p)$*

(b) $M, w \models_{\mathsf{MDL}^+} \top$

---

[1] Formally there is no difference between S_{MDL^+} and $\mathcal{L}_{\mathsf{MDL}^+}$ since a formal language can be identified with the set of its sentences. Thus we have two names for the same thing here.

(c) $M, w \models_{\text{MDL}^+} \neg\varphi$ iff it is not the case that $M, w \models_{\text{MDL}^+} \varphi$ (hereafter, $M, w \not\models_{\text{MDL}^+}\varphi$)

(d) $M, w \models_{\text{MDL}^+} (\varphi \wedge \psi)$ iff $M, w \models_{\text{MDL}^+} \varphi$ and $M, w \models_{\text{MDL}^+} \psi$

(e) $M, w \models_{\text{MDL}^+} \Box\varphi$ iff for every v such that $\langle w, v \rangle \in R_A^M$, $M, v \models_{\text{MDL}^+} \varphi$

(f) $M, w \models_{\text{MDL}^+} O_i\varphi$ iff for every v such that $\langle w, v \rangle \in R_i^M$, $M, v \models_{\text{MDL}^+} \varphi$.

A formula φ is true in an $\mathcal{L}_{\text{MDL}^+}$-model M at a point w of M if $M, w \models_{\text{MDL}^+} \varphi$. We say that a set Σ of formulas of $\mathcal{L}_{\text{MDL}^+}$ is true in M at w, and write $M, w \models_{\text{MDL}^+} \Sigma$, if $M, w \models_{\text{MDL}^+} \psi$ for every $\psi \in \Sigma$. If $\Sigma \cup \{\varphi\}$ is a set of formulas of $\mathcal{L}_{\text{MDL}^+}$, we say that φ is a semantic consequence of Σ, and write $\Sigma \models_{\text{MDL}^+} \varphi$, if for every $\mathcal{L}_{\text{MDL}^+}$-model M and every point w such that $M, w \models_{\text{MDL}^+} \Sigma$, $M, w \models_{\text{MDL}^+} \varphi$. We say that a formula φ is valid, and write $\models_{\text{MDL}^+} \varphi$, if $\emptyset \models_{\text{MDL}^+} \varphi$.

Intuitively, $\langle w, v \rangle \in R_i^M$ means that the world v is compatible with i's obligations at w in M. Thus, according to this semantics, it is obligatory upon i to see to it that φ at w in M iff φ holds at every world compatible with i's obligations at w in M.

Note that it is not standard to relativize obligation to agents. In dealing with moral or legal obligations, for example, it is natural to work with un-relativized obligations. But we are here trying to capture the effects of acts of commanding, and commands can be, and usually are, given to some specific addressees. In order to describe how such commands work in a situation where their addressees and non-addressees are present, it is necessary to work with a collection of accessibility relations relativized to various agents. In such multi-agent settings, we may have to talk about commands given to every individual agent in a specified group, as distinct not only from commands given to a single agent but also from commands meant for every agent, e.g. "Thou shalt not kill". And even among commands given to a group of agents, we may have to distinguish commands to be executed jointly by all the members of the group from commands to be executed individually by each of them. Although we will only consider commands given to a single agent in this paper, it doesn't seem impossible to extend our analysis to commands given to more than one agents.

A word about the use of monadic deontic operators here may be in order. Monadic deontic logics are known to be inadequate to deal with conditional obligations and R. M. Chisholm's contrary-to-duty imperative paradox; dyadic deontic logics are better in this respect. But there are still other problems which are unsolved even by dyadic deontic logics, and Åqvist [1], for example, stresses the importance of temporal and quantificational machinery to viable deontic logics. The use of the language of monadic deontic logic here does not reflect any substantial theoretical commitment. It is used to keep things as simple as possible as we are in such an early stage of the development. We will discuss some shortcomings resulting from the static nature of this language and the possibility of using different languages as vehicles later.

A word about the use of alethic modal operator may also be in order. It can be used to describe unchanging aspects of the changing situations. As we have seen in the above example, even after your boss's act of commanding, it was still possible for you to turn on the air conditioner or to ignore the heat. Thus we have:

$$M, s \models_{\mathsf{MDL^+}} \Diamond p \wedge \Diamond q \wedge \Diamond(\neg p \wedge \neg q) \tag{3}$$

$$N, s \models_{\mathsf{MDL^+}} \Diamond p \wedge \Diamond q \wedge \Diamond(\neg p \wedge \neg q) , \tag{4}$$

where p is to be understood as before, and q as meaning that the air conditioner is running at t_1. Note that the notion of possibility here is that of alethic (or metaphysical) possibility, and not that of epistemic possibility. Suppose, for example, you obeyed your boss's command by opening the window by t_1. Then we have $N, s \models_{\mathsf{MDL^+}} p$. But we may still have, for some world w alethically accessible from s, $N, w \models_{\mathsf{MDL^+}} \neg p$. Thus, even after all the people in the office came to know that you had opened it, some of your colleagues, without noticing that you had been commanded to do so, might complain that if you hadn't opened it, they wouldn't have been disturbed by the outside noises. [2]

Now we define proof system for $\mathsf{MDL^+}$.

Definition 4. *The proof system for* $\mathsf{MDL^+}$ *contains the following axioms and rules:*

(Taut)   *all instantiations of propositional tautologies over the present language*

($\Box$-Dist) $\Box(\varphi \to \psi) \to (\Box\varphi \to \Box\psi)$ ($\Box$-distribution)

(O_i-Dist) $O_i(\varphi \to \psi) \to (O_i\varphi \to O_i\psi)$ *for each* $i \in I$ (O_i-distribution)

(Mix) $P_i\varphi \to \Diamond\varphi$ *for each* $i \in I$ (Mix Axiom)

(MP) $\dfrac{\varphi \quad \varphi \to \psi}{\psi}$ (Modus Ponens)

($\Box$-Nec) $\dfrac{\varphi}{\Box\varphi}$ ($\Box$-necessitation)

(O_i-Nec) $\dfrac{\varphi}{O_i\varphi}$ *for each* $i \in I$.   (O_i-necessitation)

An $\mathsf{MDL^+}$*-proof of a formula* φ *is a finite sequence of* $\mathcal{L}_{\mathsf{MDL^+}}$*-formulas having* φ *as the last formula such that each formula is either an instance of an axiom, or it can be obtained from formulas that appear earlier in the sequence by applying a rule. If there is a proof of* φ, *we write* $\vdash_{\mathsf{MDL^+}} \varphi$. *If* $\Sigma \cup \{\varphi\}$ *is a set of* $\mathcal{L}_{\mathsf{MDL^+}}$*-formulas, we say that* φ *is deducible in* $\mathsf{MDL^+}$ *from* Σ *and write* $\Sigma \vdash_{\mathsf{MDL^+}} \varphi$ *if* $\vdash_{\mathsf{MDL^+}} \varphi$ *or there are formulas* $\psi_1, \ldots, \psi_n \in \Sigma$ *such that* $\vdash_{\mathsf{MDL^+}} (\psi_1 \wedge \cdots \wedge \psi_n) \to \varphi$.

The above rules obviously preserve validity, and all the axioms are easily seen to be valid. Thus this proof system is sound.[3]

The completeness of this proof system can be proved in a completely standard way by building a canonical model. Thus we have:

Theorem 1 (Completeness of $\mathsf{MDL^+}$). *Let* $\Sigma \cup \{\varphi\} \subseteq S_{\mathsf{MDL^+}}$. *Then, if* $\Sigma \models_{\mathsf{MDL^+}} \varphi$ *then* $\Sigma \vdash_{\mathsf{MDL^+}} \varphi$.

---

[2] The notion of alethic possibility may be said to be too weak to capture the kind of possibility involved in the notion of possible alternative courses of actions. Although the possibility of interpreting $\Diamond$ and $\Box$ in terms of notions of possibility and necessity stronger than those of alethic ones is tempting, we will not pursue it in this paper.

[3] Strictly speaking, O_i-necessitation is redundant since it is derivable. It is included here just to record the fact that $\mathsf{MDL^+}$ is normal.

3   A Dynamic Language $\mathcal{L}_{CL}$ and a Dynamic Logic ECL

As is clear from the above example, formulas of $\mathcal{L}_{MDL^+}$ can be used to describe the situations before and after the issuance of your boss's command. But note that your boss's act of commanding, which change M into N, is talked about not in $\mathcal{L}_{MDL^+}$ but in the meta-language. In order to have an object language in which we can talk about acts of commanding, we introduce expressions of the form $!_i\varphi$ for each $i \in I$. An expression of this form denotes the type of an act of commanding in which someone commands an agent i to see to it that φ. Let a and p be understood as before. Then your boss's act of commanding was of type $!_a p$, where a represents not your boss but you. The static base language $\mathcal{L}_{MDL^+}$ shall be expanded by introducing new modalities indexed by expressions of this form. Then, in the resulting language, the language $\mathcal{L}_{CL}$, of Command Logic, we have formulas of the form $[!_i\varphi]\psi$, which is to mean that after every successful act of commanding of type $!_i\varphi$, ψ holds. Thus we define:

Definition 5. *Take the same countably infinite set* Aprop *of proposition letters and the same finite set* I *of agents as before, with* p *ranging over* Aprop *and* i *over* I*. The language of command logic $\mathcal{L}_{CL}$ is given by:*

$$\varphi ::= \top \mid p \mid \neg\varphi \mid \varphi \wedge \psi \mid \Box\varphi \mid O_i\varphi \mid [\pi]\varphi$$
$$\pi ::= \ !_i\varphi$$

Terms of the form $!_i\varphi$ and operators of the form $[!_i\varphi]$ are called command type terms and command operators, respectively. The set of all well formed formulas of $\mathcal{L}_{CL}$ is referred to as S_{CL}, and the set of all the well formed command type terms as Com.

$\bot$, $\vee$, $\rightarrow$, $\leftrightarrow$, $\Diamond$, P_i, F_i , and $\langle !_i\varphi \rangle$ are assumed to be introduced by definition in the obvious way. Note that $S_{MDL^+} \subset S_{CL}$.

Now, in order to give truth definition for this language, we have to specify how acts of commanding change models. As we have observed earlier, in the situation before the issuance of your boss's command, we have $\neg O_a p$ at s. This means that in M, at some point v such that $\langle s, v \rangle \in R_a^M$, $\neg p$ holds. Let t be such a point. Now in the updated situation N we have $O_a p$ at s, and this means that in N, there is no point w such that $\langle s, w \rangle \in R_a^N$ and $N, w \models_{MDL^+} \neg p$. But since we have $M, t \models_{MDL^+} \neg p$, we also have $N, t \models_{MDL^+} \neg p$. As we have remarked, her command does not affect the state of the window directly. This means that in N, $\langle s, t \rangle$ is not in R_a^N.

A bit of terminology is of some help here. If a pair of points $\langle w, v \rangle$ is in some accessibility relation R, the pair will be referred to as the R-arrow from w to v. Thus we will talk about R_A^M-arrows, R_i^N-arrows, and so on. We will sometimes omit superscripts for models when there is no danger of confusion. Then the above consideration suggests that an act of commanding of the form $!_i\varphi$, if performed at w in M, eliminates from R_i^M every R_i^M-arrow that terminates in a world where φ doesn't hold. Thus, the updated model N differs from the original only in that it has $R_a^M - \{\langle w, v \rangle \in R_a^M \mid M, v \not\models_{MDL^+} \varphi\}$, or equivalently $\{\langle w, v\rangle \in R_a^M \mid M, v \models_{\mathsf{MDL}^+} \varphi\}$, in place of R_a^M as the deontic accessibility relation for the agent a.[4]

A command is said to be eliminative if it always works in this way — that is, never adds arrows. Then, the truth definition for the sentences of $\mathcal{L}_{\mathsf{CL}}$ that incorporates this conception of an eliminative command can be given with reference to $\mathcal{L}_{\mathsf{MDL}^+}$-models. Note that the subscript "ECL" in the following definition is different from the subscript "CL" used in the name of the language. We use "ECL" instead of "CL" just to indicate that the logic to be studied below is based on this conception of an eliminative command.[5]

Definition 6. Let $M = \langle W^M, R_A^M, R_I^M, V^M \rangle$ be an $\mathcal{L}_{\mathsf{MDL}^+}$-model, and $w \in W^M$. If $p \in$ Aprop, $\varphi, \psi, \chi \in S_{\mathsf{CL}}$, and $i \in I$, then:

(a) $M, w \models_{\mathsf{ECL}} p$ iff $w \in V^M(p)$

(b) $M, w \models_{\mathsf{ECL}} \top$

(c) $M, w \models_{\mathsf{ECL}} \neg\varphi$ iff $M, w \not\models_{\mathsf{ECL}} \varphi$

(d) $M, w \models_{\mathsf{ECL}} (\varphi \wedge \psi)$ iff $M, w \models_{\mathsf{ECL}} \varphi$ and $M, w \models_{\mathsf{ECL}} \psi$

(e) $M, w \models_{\mathsf{ECL}} \Box\varphi$ iff $M, v \models_{\mathsf{ECL}} \varphi$ for every v such that $\langle w, v\rangle \in R_A^M$

(f) $M, w \models_{\mathsf{ECL}} O_i\varphi$ iff $M, v \models_{\mathsf{ECL}} \varphi$ for every v such that $\langle w, v\rangle \in R_i^M$

(g) $M, w \models_{\mathsf{ECL}} [!_i\chi]\varphi$ iff $M_{!_i\chi}, w \models_{\mathsf{ECL}} \varphi$,

where $M_{!_i\chi}$ is an $\mathcal{L}_{\mathsf{MDL}^+}$-model obtained from M by replacing R_I^M with the function $R_I^{M_{!_i\chi}}$ such that:

(i) $R_I^{M_{!_i\chi}}(j) = R_I^M(j)$, for each $j \in I$ such that $j \neq i$

(ii) $R_I^{M_{!_i\chi}}(i) = \{\langle x, y\rangle \in R_i^M \mid M, y \models_{\mathsf{ECL}} \chi\}$.

We abbreviate $\{\langle x, y\rangle \in R_i^M \mid M, y \models_{\mathsf{ECL}} \chi\}$ as $R_i^M \restriction \chi^{\downarrow}$. A formula φ is true in an $\mathcal{L}_{\mathsf{MDL}^+}$-model M at a point w of M if $M, w \models_{\mathsf{ECL}} \varphi$. We say that a set Σ of formulas of $\mathcal{L}_{\mathsf{CL}}$ is true in M at w, and write $M, w \models_{\mathsf{ECL}} \Sigma$, if $M, w \models_{\mathsf{ECL}} \psi$ for every $\psi \in \Sigma$. If $\Sigma \cup \{\varphi\}$ is a set of formulas of $\mathcal{L}_{\mathsf{CL}}$, we say that φ is a semantic consequence of Σ, and write $\Sigma \models_{\mathsf{ECL}} \varphi$, if for every $\mathcal{L}_{\mathsf{MDL}^+}$-model M and every point w of M such that $M, w \models_{\mathsf{ECL}} \Sigma$, $M, w \models_{\mathsf{ECL}} \varphi$. We say that a formula φ is valid, and write $\models_{\mathsf{ECL}} \varphi$, if $\emptyset \models_{\mathsf{ECL}} \varphi$.

---

[4] We can think of a more restricted, or local, variant of update operation, namely, that of replacing R_i^M with $R_i^M - \{\langle w, v\rangle \in R_i^M \mid w = s$ and $M, v \not\models_{\mathsf{MDL}^+} \varphi\}$ when an act of commanding of the form $!_i\varphi$ is performed at s in M. It is much harder to work with this operation than with the one we use in this paper, though.

[5] The subscript "CL" in "$\mathcal{L}_{\mathsf{CL}}$", on the other hand, is used to emphasize the fact that the definition of $\mathcal{L}_{\mathsf{CL}}$ does not by itself preclude the possibility of giving truth definition based on some non-eliminative operation. In personal communications, some people have shown interest in using some operation which sometimes adds arrows to interpret command operators. Some arrow adding operation may well be necessary when we deal with acts of permitting. But whether any arrow adding operation is necessary for interpreting command operators is not so clear as it may seem. For more on this, see Section 5.

The crucial clause here is (g). The truth value of $[!_i\chi]\varphi$ at w in M is defined in terms of the truth value of φ at w in the updated model $M_{!_i\chi}$.[6] Note that $M_{!_i\chi}$ has the same domain (the set of the worlds), the same alethic accessibility relation, and the same valuation as M. Since we always have $R_i^M \restriction \chi^\downarrow \subseteq R_i^M$, we also have $R_i^M \restriction \chi^\downarrow \subseteq R_A^M$ as required in the clause (iii) of Definition 2. Thus $M_{!_i\chi}$ is guaranteed to be an $\mathcal{L}_{\mathsf{MDL}^+}$-model. [7]

Also note that the remaining clauses in the definition reproduce the corresponding clauses in the truth definition for $\mathcal{L}_{\mathsf{MDL}^+}$. Obviously, we have:

Corollary 1. *Let M be an $\mathcal{L}_{\mathsf{MDL}^+}$-model and w a point of M. Then for any $\varphi \in S_{\mathsf{MDL}^+}$, $M, w \models_{\mathsf{ECL}} \varphi$ iff $M, w \models_{\mathsf{MDL}^+} \varphi$.*

The following corollary can be proved by induction on the length of ψ:

Corollary 2. *Let $\psi \in S_{i\text{-}free}$. Then, for any $\varphi \in S_{\mathsf{CL}}$, $M, w \models_{\mathsf{ECL}} \psi$ iff $M_{!_i\varphi}, w \models_{\mathsf{ECL}} \psi$.*

This means that acts of commanding will not affect deontic status of possible courses of actions of agents other than the addressee. This may be said to be a simplification. We will return to this point later.

Another thing the above corollary means is that acts of commanding will not affect brute facts and alethic possibilities in any direct way. Thus, in our example, if s in M is the actual world before the issuance of your boss's command, then s in $M_{!_ip}$ is the actual world after the issuance, and we have:

$$M_{!_ip}, s \models_{\mathsf{ECL}} \Diamond p \wedge \Diamond q \wedge \Diamond(\neg p \wedge \neg q) , \tag{5}$$

since we have $M, s \models_{\mathsf{ECL}} \Diamond p \wedge \Diamond q \wedge \Diamond(\neg p \wedge \neg q)$. But note that we also have:

$$M, s \models_{\mathsf{ECL}} [!_ip]O_ip . \tag{6}$$

Your boss's command eliminates all the R_i^M-arrows $\langle w, v \rangle$ such that $M, v \not\models_{\mathsf{ECL}} p$, and consequently we have $M_{!_ip}, s \models_{\mathsf{ECL}} O_ip$.

In fact this is an instantiation of the following principle:

---

[6] This notation for updated models is derived from the notation of van Benthem & Liu [5], in which the symbol of the form $\mathcal{M}_{\varphi!}$ denotes the model obtained by updating $\mathcal{M}$ with a public announcement of the form $\varphi!$ and that of the form $\mathcal{M}_{\Uparrow\varphi}$ denotes the model obtained by "upgrading" $\mathcal{M}$ by a suggestion of the form $\Uparrow\varphi$. This notation is adapted for deontic updates here in order to avoid the rather baroque notation used in Yamada [20], in which the model $M_{!_i\varphi}$ of the present article was denoted by the symbol of the form $[R_i^M/R_i^M \restriction \varphi^\downarrow]M$.

[7] If we impose additional restrictions on deontic accessibility relations by adding extra axioms to the proof system of MDL^+, however, the above model updating operation may yield models which violate these conditions. Thus we will have to impose matching constraints upon updating operation, but it might not always be possible. For example, the so-called D Axiom cannot be added to MDL^+ as will be observed in the discussion on Dead End Principle in Section 6. Model updating operations has been used and studied in dynamic epistemic logics, and a useful general discussion can be found in van Benthem & Liu [5].

Proposition 1 (CUGO Principle). *If $\varphi \in S_{i\text{-free}}$, then $\models_{\mathsf{ECL}} [!_i\varphi]O_i\varphi$.*

The restriction on φ here is motivated by the fact that the truth of φ at a point v in M does not guarantee the truth of φ at v in $M_{!_i\varphi}$ if φ involves deontic modalities for the agent i. Thus, $[!_iP_iq]O_iP_iq$ is not valid, as is seen in the following example:

Example 2. Let $I = \{i\}$, and $M = \langle W^M, R_A^M, R_I^M, V^M \rangle$ where $W^M = \{s, t, u\}$, $R_A^M = \{\langle s, t \rangle, \langle t, u \rangle\}$, $R_I^M(i) = \{\langle s, t \rangle, \langle t, u \rangle\}$, and $V^M(q) = \{u\}$. Then we have $M, u \models_{\mathsf{ECL}} q$. Hence we have $M, t \models_{\mathsf{ECL}} P_iq$ but not $M, u \models_{\mathsf{ECL}} P_iq$. This in turn means that $\langle s, t \rangle$ is, but $\langle t, u \rangle$ is not, in $R_i^M \upharpoonright P_iq^{\downarrow}$. Thus we have $M_{!_iP_iq}, t \not\models_{\mathsf{ECL}} P_iq$. This in turn means that we have $M_{!_iP_iq}, s \not\models_{\mathsf{ECL}} O_iP_iq$. Therefore we have $M, s \not\models_{\mathsf{ECL}} [!_iP_iq]O_iP_iq$.

As this example shows, the model updating operation used to interpret $[!_i\varphi]$ may eliminate R_i^M-arrows on which the truth of φ at a world accessible from the current world in M depends.[8]

Now, CUGO principle characterizes (at least partially) the effect of an act of commanding; though not without exceptions, commands usually generate obligations. The workings of an act of commanding of the form $!_i\varphi$ can be visualized by imagining $R_{!_i\varphi}$-arrows, so to speak. If an act of commanding $!_i\varphi$ is performed in M at a point w, it will take us to w in $M_{!_i\varphi}$ along an $R_{!_i\varphi}$-arrow. Thus $R_{!_i\varphi}$-arrows could be used to interpret acts of commanding. R_A^M-arrows, in contrast, only take us to points within M since they only connect points in M. While ordinary actions affect brute facts, acts of commanding affect deontic aspects of situations in our life. This difference is reflected in the difference between R_A-arrows and $R_{!_i\varphi}$-arrows. Different choices of different alternative actions are represented by different worlds within one and the same $\mathcal{L}_{\mathsf{MDL}^+}$-model and these worlds are connected by R_A-arrows of that model. In contrast, different $\mathcal{L}_{\mathsf{MDL}^+}$-models are used to represent situations differing from each other in deontic aspects, and only $R_{!_i\varphi}$-arrows connect those situations. Thus it seems that the difference between R_A-arrows and $R_{!_i\varphi}$-arrows exemplifies the difference between usual acts and illocutionary acts. Illocutionary acts affects institutional facts while usual acts affect brute facts.[9]

4   Proof System for ECL

Now we define proof system for ECL.

Definition 7. *The proof system for ECL contains all the axioms and all the rules of the proof system for MDL$^+$, and in addition the following reduction axioms and rules:*

(RAt)	$[!_i\varphi]p \leftrightarrow p \quad$ *where $p \in Aprop$*	(Reduction to Atoms)
(RVer)	$[!_i\varphi]\top \leftrightarrow \top$	(Reduction to Verum)
(FUNC)	$[!_i\varphi]\neg\psi \leftrightarrow \neg[!_i\varphi]\psi$	(Functionality)

---

[8] Let S_{CGO} be the set of sentences φ such that $\models_{\mathsf{ECL}} [!_i\varphi]O_i\varphi$. Since $O_i\psi \to O_i\psi \in S_{\mathsf{CGO}}$, we have $S_{i\text{-free}} \subset S_{\mathsf{CGO}} \subset S_{\mathsf{CL}}$. But exactly how large S_{CGO} is is an interesting open question.

[9] CUGO principle may raise some worry. If p is an immoral proposition, for example, do we still have $[!_ip]O_ip$? For more on the conditions of successful issuance of commands, see Section 5.

([!$_i\varphi$]-Dist) [!$_i\varphi$]($\psi \wedge \chi$) $\leftrightarrow$ ([!$_i\varphi$]$\psi \wedge$ [!$_i\varphi$]χ)   ([!$_i\varphi$]-Distribution)

(RAleth) [!$_i\varphi$]$\Box\psi \leftrightarrow \Box$[!$_i\varphi$]$\psi$ (Reduction for Alethic Modality)

(RObl)) [!$_i\varphi$]$O_i\psi \leftrightarrow O_i(\varphi \rightarrow$ [!$_i\varphi$]ψ)   (Reduction for Obligation)

(RInd) [!$_i\varphi$]$O_j\psi \leftrightarrow O_j$[!$_i\varphi$]$\psi$ where $i \neq j$ (Independence)

([!$_i\varphi$]-Nec) $\dfrac{\psi}{[!_i\varphi]\psi}$ for each $i \in I$.   ([!$_i\varphi$]-necessitation)

An ECL-*proof of a formula φ is a finite sequence of $\mathcal{L}_{CL}$-formulas having φ as the last formula such that each formula is either an instance of an axiom, or it can be obtained from formulas that appear earlier in the sequence by applying a rule. If there is a proof of φ, we write* $\vdash_{ECL} \varphi$. *If $\Sigma \cup \{\varphi\}$ is a set of $\mathcal{L}_{CL}$-formulas, we say that ϕ is deducible in* ECL *from Σ and write $\Sigma \vdash_{ECL} \varphi$ if $\vdash_{ECL} \varphi$ or there are formulas $\psi_1, \ldots, \psi_n \in \Sigma$ such that $\vdash_{ECL} (\psi_1 \wedge \cdots \wedge \psi_n) \rightarrow \varphi$.*

It is easy to verify that all these axioms are valid and the rules preserve validity. Hence the proof system for ECL is sound. Obviously the following condition holds:

Corollary 3. *Let $\Sigma \cup \{\varphi\} \subseteq S_{MDL^+}$. Then, if $\Sigma \vdash_{MDL^+} \varphi$, then $\Sigma \vdash_{ECL} \varphi$.*

Note that the form of RObl axiom is very closely similar to, though not identical with, that of the following axiom of the logic of public announcements:

$$[\varphi!]K_i\psi \leftrightarrow (\varphi \rightarrow K_i [\varphi!]\psi) .$$

The similarity of the forms reflects the similarity of updating mechanisms; both of them are eliminative. The difference between the forms reflects the difference between the preconditions. Since a public announcement that φ is supposed to produce mostly the knowledge that φ, φ has to be true.[10] But in the case of an act of commanding of form !$_i\varphi$, φ need not be true in order for the command to be effective.

RAt and RVer axioms enable us to eliminate any command operator prefixed to a propositional letter and $\top$ respectively, and other reduction axioms enable us to reduce the length of any sub-formula to which a command operator is prefixed step by step. Thus these axioms enable us to translate any sentence of $\mathcal{L}_{CL}$ into a sentence of $\mathcal{L}_{MDL^+}$ that is provably equivalent to it. This means that the completeness of the dynamic logic of eliminative commands ECL is derivable from the completeness of the static deontic logic MDL$^+$.

The use of translation based on reduction axioms has been a standard method in the development of the dynamic logics of public announcements. Where a complete set of reduction axioms is available, it enables us to have an easy proof of the completeness.[11] We now present the outline of the proof of the completeness of ECL here.

First, we define translation from $\mathcal{L}_{CL}$ to $\mathcal{L}_{MDL^+}$.

---

[10] The epistemic analogue of the unrestricted form of CUGO principle, namely $[\varphi!]K_i\varphi$, is not valid as is seen in the puzzle of the muddy children. See, for example, Gerbrandy & Groeneveld [9], p.163.

[11] Van Benthem & Liu [5] proved that every relation changing operation that is definable in PDL without iteration has a complete set of reduction axioms in dynamic epistemic logic.

Definition 8 (Translation). *The translation function t that takes a formula from $\mathcal{L}_{CL}$ and yields a formula in $\mathcal{L}_{MDL^+}$ is defined as follows:*

$$
\begin{array}{llll}
t(p) & = p & t([!_i\varphi]p) & = p \\
t(\top) & = \top & t([!_i\varphi]\top) & = \top \\
t(\neg\varphi) & = \neg t(\varphi) & t([!_i\varphi]\neg\psi) & = \neg t([!_i\varphi]\psi) \\
t(\varphi \wedge \psi) & = t(\varphi) \wedge t(\psi) & t([!_i\varphi](\psi \wedge \chi)) & = t([!_i\varphi]\psi) \wedge t([!_i\varphi]\chi) \\
t(\Box\varphi) & = \Box t(\varphi) & t([!_i\varphi]\Box\psi) & = \Box t([!_i\varphi]\psi) \\
t(O_i\varphi) & = O_i t(\varphi) & t([!_i\varphi]O_i\psi) & = O_i(t(\varphi) \rightarrow t([!_i\varphi]\psi)) \\
& & t([!_i\varphi]O_j\psi) & = O_j t([!_i\varphi]\psi) & \text{where } i \neq j \\
& & t([!_i\varphi][!_j\psi]\chi) & = t([!_i\varphi]t([!_j\psi]\chi)) & \text{for any } j \in I \ .
\end{array}
$$

The following corollary can be proved by induction on the length of η:

Corollary 4 (Translation Effectiveness). *For any formula $\eta \in S_{CL}$, $t(\eta) \in S_{MDL^+}$.*

With the help of Corollary 4 and reduction axioms, the following lemma is proved by induction on the length of η:

Lemma 1 (Translation Correctness). *Let M be an $\mathcal{L}_{MDL^+}$-model, and w a point of M. Then for any formula $\eta \in S_{CL}$, $M, w \models_{ECL} \eta$ iff $M, w \models_{ECL} t(\eta)$.*

The following corollary is an immediate consequence of this lemma and Corollary 1:

Corollary 5. *Let M be an $\mathcal{L}_{MDL^+}$-model, and w a point of M. Then for any formula $\eta \in S_{CL}$, $M, w \models_{ECL} \eta$ iff $M, w \models_{MDL^+} t(\eta)$.*

Reduction axioms and Corollary 4 enable us to prove the following lemma by induction on the length of η:

Lemma 2. *For any formula $\eta \in S_{CL}$, $\vdash_{ECL} \eta \leftrightarrow t(\eta)$.*

Finally, the completeness of **ECL** can be proved with the help of Corollary 3, Corollary 5 and Lemma 2.

Theorem 2 (Completeness of ECL). *Let $\Sigma \cup \{\varphi\} \subseteq S_{CL}$. Then, if $\Sigma \models_{ECL} \varphi$, then $\Sigma \vdash_{ECL} \varphi$.*

5 Three Built-In Assumptions

The semantics of $\mathcal{L}_{CL}$ defined in this paper incorporates a few assumptions. Firstly, as is mentioned earlier, it incorporates the conception of an eliminative command. Thus commands are assumed to be eliminative; we have $R_i^{M}\lceil\varphi^{\downarrow} \subseteq R_i^{M}$ for any model M, any agent $i \in I$ and any formula φ. This might be said to be a simplification on the ground that some acts of commanding seem to add arrows. Consider the following example:

Example 3. Suppose you are in a combat troop and now waiting for your captain's command to fire. Then you hear the command, and it has become obligatory upon you to fire. But before that, you were not permitted to fire. This forbiddance is now no longer in force. Thus it seems that after his command, you are permitted to fire, at least in the sense of lack of forbiddance.

Does your captain's command in this example add arrows? Note that the forbiddance in force before the issuance of your captain's command is not an absolute one; although you were forbidden to fire without his command, it was not forbidden that you should fire at his command. Unfortunately, we have no systematic way of expressing these facts in $\mathcal{L}_{CL}$. Since a command type term of the form $!_i\varphi$ is not a sentence, it cannot be used to state the fact that you are commanded to see to it that φ, and no sentence we can build with $!_i\varphi$ and other expressions can be used to do so, either. Furthermore, a world in which you fire at his command is not simply a world in which he has commanded you to fire and you fire, but a world in which you fire because he has commanded you to do so. Thus even if we postulate that p and q express the proposition that your captain has commanded you to fire and the proposition that you fire, respectively, $p \wedge q$ doesn't fully characterize a world to be a world in which you fire at his command. We can say, however, that a world in which you fire at his command is also a world in which you fire. Thus at least one world in which you fire is among permissible possible worlds with respect to you in the initial situation. This fact can be expressed in $\mathcal{L}_{CL}$. Let M be your initial situation, and t the current world in that situation. Then we have $M, t \models_{ECL} P_i q$. We also have $M, t \models_{ECL} F_i(\neg p \wedge q) \wedge [!_i q]P_i q$. This formula can be read as saying that you are forbidden to fire without your captain's command and that you are permitted to fire after someone successfully command you to fire. Moreover, we have:

Proposition 2. *For any $\varphi \in S_{CL}$, $\models_{ECL} [!_i\varphi]P_i\varphi \rightarrow P_i\varphi$.*

This principle closely parallels the above discussion. This consideration suggests that whether an arrow-adding operation is necessary or not is not so clear as it may seem.

Secondly, as is noted in Corollary 2, commands of the form $!_i\varphi$ are assumed to have no effect on the deontic accessibility relations for any agents other than i. This might also be said to be a simplification. For example, suppose one of your colleague b was in your office in Example 1. Let p and q be understood as in earlier discussions of this example. We have $M, s \models_{ECL} P_b p \wedge P_b q \wedge P_b(\neg p \wedge \neg q)$. Then by our semantics, we have $M_{!_a p}, s \models_{ECL} P_b p \wedge P_b q \wedge P_b(\neg p \wedge \neg q)$. But if b turns on the air conditioner just after your boss's command, he would go against your boss's intention in a sense; his doing so will undermine the condition under which your opening the window would contribute to your boss's plan, and thereby prevent your boss's goal from being achieved as intended. Moreover, even b's opening the window could possibly be problematic in that it will preclude the possibility of your opening it.

One possible way of dealing with phenomena of this kind is to interpret your boss's command as meant to be heard by all the people in the office, and to obligate them to see to it that you see to it that p. But again, we have no systematic way of expressing this in $\mathcal{L}_{CL}$. In order to do so, we need to extend our language by allowing deontic operators and actions terms to be indexed by groups of agents, and by introducing construction that enables us to have a formula which can expresses that you see to it that p. Although such an extension will be of much interest, it is beyond the scope of the present paper.

Thirdly, commands we talk about in ECL are assumed to be issued successfully. Although this assumption may be said to be unrealistic, it is not harmful. One obvious condition for successful issuance of a command is the condition that the commanding agent has authority to do so. Such conditions will be of central importance, for example, when we try to decide, given an particular utterance of an imperative sentence by an agent in a particular context, whether a command is successfully issued in that utterance or not. But it is important to notice that there is another more fundamental question to ask, namely that of what a successfully issued command accomplishes. This question requires us to say what an act of commanding is. It is this question that ECL is developed to address, and when we use ECL to answer it, we can safely assume that the commands we are talking about are issued by suitable authorities.

Another natural candidate for the precondition for the act of commanding i to do A is the requirement that it should be possible for i to do A. But we have no direct way of requiring this, since we have no way of talking about actions other than commanding. Thus, the best we could do might be to require that $\Diamond\varphi$ holds, for example, as the precondition for the successful issuance of a command of the form $!_i\varphi$. But even if we do so, there remains a real possibility of conflicting commands coming from different authorities. We will return to this point in the next section.

6 Some Interesting Validities and Non-validities

Here are a few more interesting principles our semantics validates.

Proposition 3. *The following principles are valid:*

(DE) $[!_i(\varphi \wedge \neg\varphi)]O_i\psi$ (Dead End)

(RSC) $[!_i\varphi][!_i\psi]\chi \leftrightarrow [!_i(\varphi \wedge \psi)]\chi$ *where* $\varphi, \psi \in S_{i\text{-free}}$
                                                     (Restricted Sequential Conjunction)

(ROI) $[!_i\varphi][!_i\psi]\chi \leftrightarrow [!_i\psi][!_i\varphi]\chi$ *where* $\varphi, \psi \in S_{i\text{-free}}$.   (Restricted Order Invariance)

Dead End Principle states that a self-contradictory command leads to a situation where everything is obligatory. Such a situation is an obligational dead end. Whatever choice you may make, you will go against some of your obligations. The absurdity of such a situation is nicely reflected in the updated model. Since $\varphi \wedge \neg\varphi$ is not true at any world in any model, $R_i^M \upharpoonright (\varphi \wedge \neg\varphi)^{\downarrow}$ is empty for any model M. Thus, if a command of the form $!_i(\varphi \wedge \neg\varphi)$ is given to an agent i at some world w in M, every world will become $R_i^{M_{!_i(\varphi \wedge \neg\varphi)}}$- inaccessible from any world in the updated model $M_{!_i(\varphi \wedge \neg\varphi)}$. Hence every world in $M_{!_i(\varphi \wedge \neg\varphi)}$ will be a dead end with respect to $R_i^{M_{!_i(\varphi \wedge \neg\varphi)}}$- accessibility.

Restricted Sequential Conjunction Principle states that commands given in a sequence usually, though not always, add up to a command with a conjunctive content. Unrestricted form of sequential conjunction principle is not valid because $(R_i^M \upharpoonright \varphi^{\downarrow}) \upharpoonright \psi^{\downarrow}$ can be distinct from $R_i^M \upharpoonright (\varphi \wedge \psi)^{\downarrow}$. Similarly, Restricted Order Invariance Principle states that the order of issuance usually doesn't matter. Unrestricted form of this principle is not valid because $(R_i^M \lceil \varphi^{\downarrow}) \lceil \psi^{\downarrow}$ can be distinct from $(R_i^M \lceil \psi^{\downarrow}) \lceil \varphi^{\downarrow}$. [12]

As a consequence of Dead End Principle, right-unboundedness is not generally preserved with respect to deontic accessibility relations. Hence it is not possible for us to add the so-called D Axiom, i.e. $O_i\varphi \rightarrow P_i\varphi$, to our proof system. For example, for any M and w, we have:

$$M_{!_i(p \wedge \neg p)}, w \models_{\text{ECL}} O_i(p \wedge \neg p) \wedge \neg P_i(p \wedge \neg p) \ . \tag{7}$$

Moreover, as an instance of Restricted Sequential Conjunction Principle, we have:

$$[!_i p][!_i \neg p]\chi \leftrightarrow [!_i(p \wedge \neg p)]\chi \ . \tag{8}$$

Hence, by Dead End Principle, we have:

$$[!_i p][!_i \neg p]O_i\varphi \ . \tag{9}$$

Although no boss might be silly enough to give you a command to see to it that $p \wedge \neg p$, you might have two bosses and after one of them gives you a command to see to it that p, the other one might give you a command to see to it that $\neg p$. Unless both of them belong to the same hierarchy, neither command might be overridden by the other. Whichever command you may choose to obey, you will have to disobey the other.

If we require $\Diamond\varphi$ to hold as the precondition for successful issuance of a command of the form $!_i\varphi$, every command of the form $!_i(\psi \wedge \neg\psi)$ will be precluded. But even if we do this, there may be a situation M such that $\Diamond p \wedge \Diamond\neg p$ holds at w in M. In such a situation, a command of the form $!_i p$ can be issued. In the resulting situation, $\Diamond p \wedge \Diamond\neg p$ still holds at w, and hence it remains possible to issue a command of the form $!_i\neg p$.

One way of avoiding obligational dead end of this kind could be to require φ in $!_i\varphi$ to be in Aprop. But it would not be a real solution, and even if we do this, you might still find yourself in a contingent analogue of an obligational dead end. Consider the following example:

Example 4. Suppose the boss of your department commanded you to attend an international one-day conference on logic to be held in São Paulo next month. Also suppose that soon after that your political guru commanded you to join an important political

---

[12] Note that our notation for models and deontic accessibility relations involves a record of updates. For example, $(M_{!_i\varphi})_{!_i\psi}$ is the model obtained by updating $M_{!_i\varphi}$ with a command of form $!_i\psi$, and the model $M_{!_i\varphi}$ in turn is the model obtained by updating M with a command of form $!_i\varphi$. Such records might be utilized to answer the interesting question raised by Ken Satoh at CLIMA VII workshop. He asked whether authorities can change their minds in ECL. Although we haven't incorporated action types for acts of canceling in ECL, it seems possible to extend it to include them. For example, if the earlier act of commanding of form $!_i\varphi$ performed at w in M is canceled at w in $(M_{!_i\varphi})_{!_i\psi}$, then, it seems, the resulting situation will be represented by $M_{!_i\psi}$. Whether this strategy turns out to be fruitful or not is yet to be seen.

demonstration to be held on the very same day in Tokyo. It is possible for you to obey either command, but it is transportationally impossible for you to obey both. Even after you decide which command to obey, you might still regret not being able to obey the other command.

As no logical inconsistency is involved in the combination of obligations generated by these commands, we may say, for example, that it would be possible for you to obey both command if a sufficiently fast means of transportation were available. But the metaphysical possibility of such a fast means of transportation is of no help to you in the real world. You are in a situation very closely similar to those in which you are said to be in real moral dilemmas. As Marcus [14] has argued, they can be real even if the moral rules involved are logically consistent.

In this example, each of your boss and your guru can be assumed to have suitable authority for the issuance of his or her command. Moreover, it is really possible for you to obey one or the other of the two commands. Still, their commands are in conflict with each other. Such conflicts can be sometimes extremely difficult to avoid in real life as conflicts can arise due to some unforeseen contingencies of the real world.

If we allow deontic accessibility relations, deontic operators, and command type terms to be indexed by the Cartesian product of a given set of agents and a given set of command issuing authorities, then your situation can be represented as a situation which may be suitably called an obligational dilemma. In the extended language, we can use expressions of the form $!_{(i,j)}\varphi$ to denote the type of an act of commanding in which an authority j commands an agent i that he or she should see to it that φ. Let a, b and c represent you, your boss and your guru, respectively. Let the model-world pair (M, s) represent the situation before the issuance of your boss's command, and p represent the proposition that you will attend the conference in São Paulo. Then, after your boss's command you are in $(M_{!_{(a,b)}p}, s)$. Now, let q represent the proposition that you will join the the demonstration in Tokyo. Then, after the issuance of your guru's command, you are in $((M_{!_{(a,b)}p})_{!_{(a,c)}q}, s)$. In this situation, from the real world s, only the worlds in which you attend the conference in São Paulo will be $R_{(a,b)}$-accessible, only the worlds in which you join the demonstration in Tokyo will be $R_{(a,c)}$-accessible, and s can be either among the $R_{(a,b)}$-accessible worlds or among the $R_{(a,c)}$-accessible worlds, though it cannot be among the worlds that are both $R_{(a,b)}$-accessible and $R_{(a,c)}$-accessible. Contingent facts about the present state of our system of transportation prevent it from being both $R_{(a,b)}$-accessible and $R_{(a,c)}$-accessible. It is obligatory upon you with respect to your boss that you attend the the conference in São Paulo, and it is obligatory upon you with respect to your guru that you join the demonstration in Tokyo. You can respect one or the other of these obligations, but you are not able to respect both. If you obey your boss's command, you will disobey your guru's command, and if you obey your guru's command, you will disobey your boss's command.

This refinement will also enable us to represent the situation you will be in if a command of the form $!_{(a,c)}\neg p$ is issued after a command of the form $!_{(a,b)}p$ is issued as an obligational dilemma. It is not difficult to incorporate this refinement into $\mathcal{L}_{MDL^+}$ and $\mathcal{L}_{CL}$.[13]

---

[13] This refinement is incorporated in Yamada [21].

7 Related Works and Further Directions

As is noted in the introduction, the idea of ECL is inspired by the logics of epistemic actions developed in Plaza [16], Groeneveld [11], Gerbrandy & Groeneveld [9], Gerbrandy [8], Baltag, Moss, & Solecki [2], and Kooi & van Benthem [13] among others. In the field of deontic reasoning, van der Torre & Tan [18] and Žarnić [22] extended the update semantics of Veltman [19] so as to cover normative sentences and natural language imperatives, respectively. Apart from the fact that the languages they used are stronger than $\mathcal{L}_{MDL^+}$, the main difference between their systems and ECL consists in that the former deal with the interpretation of sentences while the latter deals with the dynamics of acts of commanding. Broadly speaking, the relation between their systems and ECL is analogous to that between Veltman's update semantics and the logics of epistemic actions.

In this respect, PDL based systems of Pucella & Weissman [17], and Demri [6] are closer to the present work in spirit. Their systems dynamified DLP of van der Meyden [15]. DLP is obtained from test-free PDL by introducing operators which have semantics that distinguish permitted (green) transitions from forbidden (red) ones. The set of green transitions of each model is the so-called policy set. In Pucella & Weissman [17], DLP is dynamified so that in the resulting system DLP_{dyn} the policy set can be updated by adding or deleting transitions, and in Demri [6], DLP_{dyn} is extended to DLP^+_{dyn} by adding test operator "?" and allowing the operators for updating policy sets to be parameterized by the current policy set. One important difference between these PDL-based systems and ECL lies in the fact that in these PDL-based systems, we can talk about permitted or forbidden actions as well as obligatory state of affairs whereas we can only talk about permitted, forbidden or obligatory state of affairs in ECL.

Another interesting related work is stit theory developed in Belnap, Perloff, & Xu [3] and Horty [12]. As the wording in this paper might have already suggested, agentive sentences can be utilized to capture the contents of commands. But the language of monadic deontic logic lacks the resource for distinguishing agentives from non-agentives. This defect can be removed by using a language of stit theory. In order to do so, however, we have to rethink our update operation, as we talk about "moments" in stead of possible worlds in stit theory. Since moments are partially ordered in a tree like branching temporal structure, we have to take their temporal order into account. But the update operation of this paper is not sensitive to temporal order. Thus when we think of the points in our model not as possible worlds but as stages of some language game, for example, it might look a bit problematic, since it can eliminate deontic arrows that connect stages earlier than the stage at which the command is issued. Although this does not mean that the update operation of this paper could affect the past state of affairs, it means that deontic status of the past state of affairs can be affected afterward. As it is possible to define different update operations even with respect to $\mathcal{L}_{MDL^+}$-models, one immediate task for us is to examine the logics obtained by replacing the update operation.

Finally, the most closely related work in this field is that of van Benthem & Liu [5]. They proposed what they call "preference upgrade" as a counter part to information update. According to them, my "command operator for propositions A can be modeled exactly as an upgrade sending R to $R;?A$ " in their system, and their paper "provides a much more general treatment of possible upgrade instructions"([5]). Although their preference upgrade clearly has much wider application than the deontic update of the present paper, the notion of preference upgrade seems to be connected with perlocutionary consequences, while the notion of deontic update is meant to be used to capture a differential feature of an act of commanding as a specific kind of illocutionary acts. They can be seen as mutually complementary.

8   Conclusion

We have shown that commands can be considered as deontic updators. Since the base language $\mathcal{L}_{\mathsf{MDL^+}}$ we dynamified is a variant of monadic deontic logic, our extended language $\mathcal{L}_{\mathsf{CL}}$ inherits various inadequacy of the language of monadic deontic logic. But the fact that even such a simple language can be used to capture some interesting principles may be said to suggest the possibility of further research, including dynamifying stronger deontic languages. Moreover, the possibilities of update logics of various other kinds of illocutionary acts suggest themselves. For example, an act of promising can be considered as another updator of obligations, and an act of asserting as an updator of propositional commitments. Logics of such acts may provide us with a fairly fine-grained picture of social interactions when combined not only with each other but also with logics of perlocutionary acts that update systems of knowledge, beliefs and preferences of agents.

In this paper, logic of acts of commanding is not yet combined with logics of other speech acts. There are many things yet to be done before it becomes possible to address various interesting issues relating to interactions among agents. But in order to combine logics, we need logics to combine. And even already within ECL, we can talk about the effects of a sequence of acts of commanding as Restricted Sequential Conjunction Principle and Restricted Order Invariance Principle exemplify. Furthermore, the refinement suggested in the last part of Section 6 will enable us to distinguish between the effects of a sequence of commands issued exclusively by one and the same authority and the effects of a sequence of commands involving commands issued by different authorities, and thereby raise interesting questions of preference management for agents who have roles to play in more than one organizations. The same kind of question can also arise when a command is issued which conflicts with a promise already made. Thus one of our immediate tasks is to extend ECL to deal with the interactions among agents involved in such a situation. Although the development of ECL is a small step towards the development of richer logics of acts of commanding, it can be part of the beginning of the explorations into the vast area of the logical dynamics of social interactions.

Acknowledgments. I thank Johan van Benthem, Fenrong Liu, John Perry, Keith Devlin, Edward Zalta, Koji Nakatogawa, and the anonymous reviewers as well as the participants of CLIMA VII workshop for their helpful comments on earlier versions of this paper. Special thanks go to Johan van Benthem for his constant encouragements.

References

1. Åqvist, L: Deontic Logic. In: Gabbay & Guentner [7] (2002) 147–264
2. Baltag, A., Moss, L. S., Solecki, S.: The Logic of Public Announcements, Common Knowledge, and Private Suspicions. Technical Report, TR534. Department of Computer Science (CSCI), Indiana University (1999)
3. Belnap, N., Perloff, M., Xu, M.: Facing the Future: Agents and Choices in Our Indeterminist World. Oxford University Press, Oxford (2001)
4. van Benthem, J.: Update Delights. An Invited Lecture. ESSLLI 2000 (Birmingham). A manuscript. Institute of Logic, Language and Computation, University of Amsterdam (2000)
5. van Benthem, J., Liu, F.: Dynamic Logic of Preference Upgrade. Journal of Applied Non-Classical Logics (to appear)
6. Demri, S.: A Reduction from DLP to PDL. Journal of Logic and Computation, 15-5 (2005), 767–785
7. Gabbay, D. M., Guenthner, F.(eds.): Handbook of Philosophical Logic. 2nd Edition, Volume 8. Kluwer Academic Publishers, Dordrecht / Boston / London (2002)
8. Gerbrandy, J.: Bisimulations on Planet Kripke. Ph. D. Thesis. ILLC Dissertation Series DS-1999-01, University of Amsterdam (1999)
9. Gerbrandy, J., Groeneveld, W.: Reasoning about Information Change. Journal of Logic, Language, and Information, Vol.6 (1997) 147–169
10. Grice, H. P.: Meaning (1948). Reprinted in: Grice, H. P., Studies in the Way of Words. Harvard University Press, Cambridge, Massachusetts / London, England (1989), 213–223
11. Groeneveld, W.: Logical Investigations into Dynamic Semantics. Ph. D. Thesis. ILLC Dissertation Series, DS-1995-18, University of Amsterdam (1995)
12. Horty, J. F.: Agency and Deontic Logic. Oxford University Press, Oxford (2001)
13. Kooi, B., van Benthem, J.: Reduction Axioms for Epistemic Actions. In: Schmidt, R., Pratt-Hartmann, I., Reynolds, M., Wansing, H. (eds): Preliminary Proceedings of AiML-2004. Department of Computer Science, University of Manchester (2004) 197–211
14. Marcus, R. B.: Moral Dilemmas and Consistency. Journal of philosophy, LXXVII, 3 (1980) 121–136. Reprinted in: Marcus, R. B., Modalities: Philosophical Essays. Oxford University Press, New York/Oxford (1993) 125–141
15. van der Meyden, R.: The Dynamic Logic of Permission. Journal of Logic and Computation, Vol. 6, No. 3 (1996) 465–479
16. Plaza, J. A.: Logics of public communications. In: Emrich, M. L., Pfeifer, M. S., Hadzikadic, M., Ras, Z. W. (eds.): Proceedings of the 4th International Symposium on Methodologies for Intelligent Systems (1989), 201–216
17. Pucella, R., Weissman, V.: Reasoning about Dynamic Policies. In: Walukiewicz (ed.): FOS-SACS 2004. Lecture Notes in Computer Science, Vol. 2987, Springer-Verlag, Berlin / Heidelberg / New York (2004) 453-467
18. van der Torre, L. W. N., Tan, Yao-Hua: An Update Semantics for Deontic Reasoning. In: McNamara, P., Prakken, H. (eds.): Norms, Logics and Information Systems. New Studies on Deontic Logic and Computer Science. Frontiers in Artificial Intelligence and Applications, Volume 49. IOS Press (1999) 73–90
19. Veltman, F.: Defaults in Update Semantics. Journal of Philosophical Logic, 25 (1996), 221–261
20. Yamada, T.: Completeness of the Logic of Eliminative Commands. In: Tanaka, H. (ed.): Language Understanding and Action Control. Annual Project Report. Grant-in-Aid for Creative Basic Research (13NP0301). Tokyo Institute of Technology (2006) 9-20

21. Yamada, T.: Logical Dynamics of Commands and Obligations. In: McCready, E. (ed.): Preliminary Proceedings of the Third International Workshop on Logic and Engineering of Natural Language Semantics (LENLS2006), Tokyo, Japan, June 5-6. The Japanese Society for Artificial Intelligence (2006) 43–55
22. Žarnić, B.: Imperative Change and Obligation to Do. In: Segerberg, K., Sliwinski (eds.): Logic, Law, Morality: Thirteen Essays in Practical Philosophy in Honour of Åqvist. Uppsala Philosophical Studies 51. Department of Philosophy, Uppsala University, Uppsala (2003) 79–95

Hierarchical Decision Making in Multi-agent Systems Using Answer Set Programming

Davy Van Nieuwenborgh[1,*], Marina De Vos[2], Stijn Heymans[3], and Dirk Vermeir[1]

[1] Dept. of Computer Science
Vrije Universiteit Brussel, VUB
Pleinlaan 2, B1050 Brussels, Belgium
{dvnieuwe,dvermeir}@vub.ac.be
[2] Dept. of Computer Science
University of Bath
Bath, BA2 7AY, UK
mdv@cs.bath.ac.uk
[3] Digital Enterprise Research Institute (DERI)
University of Innsbruck, Austria
stijn.heymans@deri.org

Abstract. We present a multi-agent formalism based on extended answer set programming. The system consists of independent agents connected via a communication channel, where knowledge and beliefs of each agent are represented by a logic program. When presented with an input set of literals from its predecessor, an agent computes its output as an extended answer set of its program enriched with the input, carefully eliminating contradictions that might occur.

It turns out that while individual agents are rather simple, the interaction strategy makes the system quite expressive: essentially a hierarchy of a fixed number of agents n captures the complexity class Σ_n^P, i.e. the n-th level of the polynomial hierarchy. Furthermore, unbounded hierarchies capture the polynomial hierarchy $\mathcal{PH}$. This makes the formalism suitable for modelling complex applications of MAS, for example cooperative diagnosis. Furthermore, such systems can be realized by implementing an appropriate control strategy on top of existing solvers such as DLV and SMODELS.

1 Introduction

In *answer set programming* ([30]) a logic program is used to intuitively describe the requirements that must be fulfilled by the solutions of a certain problem. The answer sets of the program, usually defined through (a variant/extension of) the stable model semantics [25], then correspond to the solutions of the problem. This technique has been successfully applied in problem areas such as planning [18, 30], configuration and verification [36], superoptimisation [3], diagnosis [17, 43], game theory [15] and multi-agent systems[2, 7, 16, 6, 10] where [6, 10] use answer set programming to reason about the behaviour of a group of agents, [2, 7, 16] use the formalism to model the reasoning capabilities, knowledge and beliefs of a single agent within a multi-agent

* Supported by the Flemish Fund for Scientific Research (FWO-Vlaanderen).

K. Inoue, K. Satoh, and F. Toni (Eds.): CLIMA VII, LNAI 4371, pp. 20–40, 2007.
© Springer-Verlag Berlin Heidelberg 2007

system. While [2] and [7] use the basic answer set semantics to represent an agent's domain knowledge, [16] applies an extension of the semantics incorporating preferences among choices in a program.

The traditional answer set semantics, even in the absence of constraints, is not universal, i.e. some programs may not have any answer set at all. While natural, this poses a problem in cases where there are no exact solutions, but one would appreciate to obtain approximate ones, even if they violate some rules. For example, it is not acceptable that an airplane's auto-pilot agent fails to work just because it has some contradictory readings regarding the outside temperature. To achieve this, the extended answer set semantics ([42]) allows problematic rules to be *defeated*: the rules $a \leftarrow$, $b \leftarrow$ and $\neg a \leftarrow b$ are clearly inconsistent and have no classical answer set, while both $\{a, b\}$ and $\{\neg a, b\}$ will be recognized as extended answer sets. In $\{a, b\}$, $\neg a \leftarrow b$ is defeated by $a \leftarrow$, while in $\{\neg a, b\}$, $a \leftarrow$ is defeated by $\neg a \leftarrow b$.

In this paper we use the extended answer set semantics to model the knowledge and beliefs of a single agent. Each agent reasons over two languages, one public and one private. This allows agents to dynamically decide which information they wish to share with others, with only public information being made available. Agents may then cooperate to select among the various possible solutions (extended answer sets) that are presented to them. In the case that an agent, using the extended answer set semantics, has a number of (approximate) solutions to a certain problem, it can rely upon other agents to sort out which solutions are the better ones. In the absence of any extended answer sets, the agent relies completely on the information received from the others. E.g., when a company has to make up an emergency evacuation plan for a building, one of the employees will make up all strategies that could be implemented for that building. However, as she is probably not aware of all current regulations about such strategies, her solutions are forwarded to the emergency services, who will only select those plans that are conforming to all legal requirements. These legal candidate plans are then presented to the firm's management to select an optimal one (e.g. the cheapest) for implementation.

To deal with problems like the one described above, we propose a multi-agent framework that is capable of modelling hierarchical decision problems. To this end, we consider a sequence of agents $A_1 \ldots A_n$, each having their private knowledge described by a logic program. Intuitively, an agent A_i communicates a solution she finds acceptable to the next agent A_{i+1} in the hierarchy. For such an A_i-acceptable solution, A_{i+1} computes a solution S that adds her knowledge to the given information. Provided that this new knowledge does not conflict with the information she received from her predecessor A_i, she passes this solution to the following agent in line, i.e. A_{i+2}. In case agent A_{i+1} is unable to provide any solutions of her own, she will simply pass on information she obtained from the previous agents higher up in the hierarchy. When her solution S conflicts with the solution offered by her predecessors, she sends S for verification to her predecessor A_i. If A_i is able to find another possible solution T that is consistent with S, the communication from A_i to A_{i+1} starts over again with T as a new input. In the case that none of the solutions of A_{i+1} survive the verification step, A_{i+1} has no other option than accepting the input from A_i and send it to A_{i+2}.

It turns out that, although the agents are relatively simple in complexity terms, such sequences of agents are rather expressive. More specifically, we show that such agent systems can capture the polynomial hierarchy, which make them suitable for encoding complex applications.

Computing the extended answer set semantics is located at the first level of the polynomial hierarchy. Problems located at this first level can be directly solved using the DLV [24] and SMODELS [34] answer set solvers. On the second level, only DLV remains to perform the job directly. However, by using a "guess and check" fixpoint procedure, SMODELS can indirectly be used to solve problems at the second level [4, 22, 45]. Beyond the second level, there are still interesting problems, such as the most expressive forms of diagnostic reasoning, i.e. subset-minimal diagnosis on disjunctive system descriptions [17] or preference-based diagnosis on ordered theories [43]. These are located at the third level of the polynomial hierarchy, together with sequences of weak constraints[1] on disjunctive programs. For these problems, and problems located even higher in the polynomial hierarchy, no direct computational vehicle is available. The framework presented in this paper provides a means to effectively compute solutions for such problems with each agent using SMODELS or DLV to compute better solutions combined with an appropriate control strategy for the communication.

The remainder of the paper is organized as follows. In Section 2, we review the extended answer set semantics. Section 3 presents the definitions for hierarchical agents and agent systems. Section 4 discusses the complexity of the proposed semantics, while Section 5 compares it with related approaches from the literature. Finally, we conclude with directions for further research in Section 6.

2   Extended Answer Sets

In this section we provide a short overview of extended answer set semantics for simple logic programs [41]. A *term* is a constant or a variable, where the former will be written lower-case and the latter upper-case. An *atom* is of the form $p(t_1, \ldots, t_n)$, $0 \leq n < \infty$, where p is an n-ary[2] predicate name and t_i, $1 \leq i \leq n$, are terms. A *literal* is an atom a or a negated atom $\neg a$.

A *simple logic program* (SLP) is a finite set of *simple rules* of the form $\alpha \leftarrow \beta$ with $\alpha \cup \beta$ a set of literals and $|\alpha| \leq 1$. If $\alpha = \emptyset$, we call the rule a *constraint*. The set α is the *head* of the rule while β is called the *body*.

A *ground* atom, literal, rule, or SLP does not contain variables. Substituting every variable in a SLP P with every possible constant in P yields the ground SLP $gr(P)$. In what follows, we always assume ground SLPs and ground literals; to obtain the definitions for ungrounded SLPs, replace every occurrence of a SLP P by $gr(P)$, e.g., an extended answer set of an ungrounded SLP P is an extended answer set of $gr(P)$.

For a set of literals X, we use $\neg X$ to denote the set $\{\neg p \mid p \in X\}$ where $\neg\neg a \equiv a$. Further, X is said to be *consistent* if $X \cap \neg X = \emptyset$, i.e. X does not contain contradictory literals a and $\neg a$.

---

[1] A weak constraint is a constraint that is "desirable" but may be violated if there are no other options to obtain an answer set.

[2] We thus allow for 0-ary predicates, i.e., *propositions*.

The *Herbrand base* $\mathcal{B}_P$ of a SLP P is the set of all ground atoms that can be formed using the language of P. The set of all literals that can be formed with P, i.e. $\mathcal{B}_P \cup \neg\mathcal{B}_P$, is denoted by $\mathcal{L}_P$. An *interpretation* I of P is any consistent subset of $\mathcal{L}_P$.

A rule $r = a \leftarrow \beta \in P$ is *satisfied* by an interpretation I, denoted $I \models r$, if $a \in I$ whenever $\beta \subseteq I$, i.e. if r is *applicable* ($\beta \subseteq I$), then it must be *applied* ($\beta \cup \{a\} \subseteq I$). On the other hand, a constraint $\leftarrow \beta$ is satisfied if $\beta \not\subseteq I$, i.e. the constraint is not applicable. The rule r is said to be *defeated* w.r.t. I iff there exists an applied *competing rule* $\neg a \leftarrow \beta' \in P$. We use $P_I \subseteq P$ to denote the *reduct* of P w.r.t. I, i.e. $P_I = \{r \in P \mid I \models r\}$, the set of rules satisfied by I.

If an interpretation I satisfies all rules in P, i.e. $P_I = P$, I is called a *model* of P. A model I is a minimal model or *answer set* of P iff no other model J of P exists such that $J \subset I$. An *extended answer set* of P is any interpretation I such that I is an answer set of P_I and each unsatisfied rule in $P \setminus P_I$ is defeated. The set of all extended answer sets of a program P is denoted by $\mathcal{AS}(P)$.

Example 1. Consider the following SLP P about diabetes.

$$hypoglycemia \leftarrow \qquad sugar \leftarrow hypoglycemia \qquad coke \leftarrow sugar$$
$$diabetes \leftarrow \qquad \neg sugar \leftarrow diabetes \qquad diet\_coke \leftarrow \neg sugar$$

Clearly, while this program has no traditional answer sets, it does have two extended answer sets $I = \{diabetes, hypoglycemia, sugar, coke\}$ and $J = \{diabetes, diet\_coke, hypoglycemia, \neg sugar\}$.

Note that the extended answer set semantics is universal for simple programs containing no constraints [41]. This is not the case for general, constraint allowing, simple programs, due to the fact that constraints cannot be defeated.

3 Hierarchical Agents

If humans want to share information or to have discussions in an effective manner they typically use the same language; without it, it would be nearly impossible to establish any communication. So it is only natural to assume that all agents in our framework "speak the same language" which we denote as $\mathcal{AL}$. Modeling an agent's knowledge and beliefs, it might not always be a good idea to pass on the entire answer set, e.g., a manager is certainly not going to tell her employee that she cannot have a meeting on Monday because she wants to have an extended weekend in Paris. Instead she will simply say that Monday is out of the question. To allow this we need to perform some filtering on the answer set before it is passed to the next agent. Thus we consider agents that use two languages: a public language $\mathcal{AL}$ used for communication and a private language $\mathcal{AL}'$ for private reasoning purposes. The latter allows the manager in our example to tell her employee she cannot have the meeting on Monday, without giving her the underlying reason that she is in Paris for a trip. On the other hand, if it is a business trip, she could choose to communicate the reason. Information received from other agents will be assumed private by default. If it needs to be passed on, one simply adds a rule $l \leftarrow l'$ for each literal l' that could be received from the other agent. Summarizing, an agent will receive input in the form of literals from $\mathcal{L}_{\mathcal{AL}}$, reason with a program over $\mathcal{L}_{\mathcal{AL}} \cup \mathcal{L}_{\mathcal{AL'}}$ and only communicate the part over $\mathcal{L}_{\mathcal{AL}}$ to the other agents. We will use $l' \in \mathcal{L}_{\mathcal{AL'}}$ to denote the private version of the literal $l \in \mathcal{L}_{\mathcal{AL}}$ and we have for $l' \in \mathcal{L}_{\mathcal{AL'}}$ that $l'' = l$ with $l \in \mathcal{L}_{\mathcal{AL}}$. We extend the notation as usual to a set $X \subseteq \mathcal{L}_{\mathcal{AL}} \cup \mathcal{L}_{\mathcal{AL'}}$, i.e. $X' = \{l' \mid l \in X\}$.

Definition 1. *For an agent language $\mathcal{AL}$, a **hierarchical agent** A is a SLP such that $\mathcal{B}_A \subseteq \mathcal{AL} \cup \mathcal{AL'}$. For such an agent A and a set of literals $I \subseteq \mathcal{L}_{\mathcal{AL}}$, the **agent input**, we use $A(I)$ to denote the SLP $A \cup \{l' \leftarrow \mid l \in I\}$.*

*An interpretation $S \subseteq \mathcal{L}_{\mathcal{AL}}$ is an **agent answer set** w.r.t. the agent input I if*
- *$S = M \cap \mathcal{L}_{\mathcal{AL}}$ with $M \in \mathcal{AS}(A(I))$, or*
- *$S = I$ when $\mathcal{AS}(A(I)) = \emptyset$.*

We use $\mathcal{AS}(A, I)$ to denote the set of all agent answer sets of A w.r.t. input I.

The first condition of the agent answer set definition ensures that the agent only communicates public information. The second condition makes the agent answer set semantics universal. In case our agent cannot produce an answer set, because of constraints being violated, she will assume the input as the solution. This makes sense in the context of hierarchical agents. E.g., as an employee, one should reschedule previously arranged meetings if one's boss cannot make it on the agreed time. The person with the least power to make changes should concede.

Example 2. Take $\mathcal{AL} = \{hypoglycemia, diabetes, sugar, coke, diet\_coke\}$ and consider the following diabetes agent A.

$$sugar' \leftarrow hypoglycemia' \qquad \neg sugar' \leftarrow diabetes'$$
$$diet\_coke \leftarrow \neg sugar' \qquad coke \leftarrow sugar'$$

Intuitively, the above agent is set up to use information from a doctor agent concerning hypoglycemia and diabetes to decide if a patient needs to have diet coke or normal coke. In order to do so, she determines if the patient needs sugar or should not have sugar. The patient only needs to be told that she can have either a diet coke or a normal coke, hence diet coke and coke are the only literals in the public language.

Let $I_1 = \emptyset$, $I_2 = \{diabetes\}$ and $I_3 = \{hypoglycemia\}$ be three agent inputs. One can check that A has only one agent answer set w.r.t. I_1 which is $S_1 = \emptyset$. Similar, feeding both I_2 and I_3 as input to A results in a single agent answer set, i.e. $S_2 = \{diet\_coke\}$ and $S_3 = \{coke\}$ respectively.

As mentioned before, information can be easily made public by adding a rule $l \leftarrow l'$ for each literal one wants to make public. Depending on the agent, a large number of such rules may be needed. To shorten the programs, we introduce the shorthand **pass**(S) for $\{l \leftarrow l' \mid l \in S\}$, with $S \subseteq \mathcal{AL}$ the set of literals that need to be made public if derived in the private part.

Using a combination of public and private information, it is possible to easily encode that for example certain input information should be considered more important than the agent's own knowledge or vice versa.

Example 3. Consider the following employee agent A_1:

$$\textbf{pass}(\{pay\_rise, overworked\})$$

$overworked \leftarrow$ $dislike\_boss' \leftarrow overworked$
$happy \leftarrow \neg dislike\_boss', pay\_rise'$ $\neg dislike\_boss' \leftarrow pay\_rise'$

Obviously the agent will never publicly admit disliking her boss. Given $\{pay\_rise\}$ as input, the agent produces two answer sets: $\{overworked, pay\_rise\}$ and $\{overworked, pay\_rise, happy\}$.

Now that we have defined a single hierarchical agent and the semantics that comes with it, we can start connecting them. As mentioned previously, we are interested in multi-agent systems where some agents have more authority than others, yet require information from others in order to make correct decisions. In the introduction, we discussed the situation of a company that needs to implement an emergency evacuation plan. Although a manager needs to approve the emergency plan, she does not need to verify legal issues or draw up the plans herself. She will stipulate the requirements that need to be fulfilled for her approval. So, in this case we have the employee being on top of the hierarchy generating all possible plans, followed by the legal office rejecting those plans which are not safe. Finally, these plans will be matched against the criteria set out by the manager. Since a plan is needed, she will be unable to reject them all.

We have a different situation when a head of department needs to arrange a meeting with her staff. Obviously she will allow her staff to have a say in the organisation, but at the end of the day her diary will take precedence over that of her staff. Here the head of department will be on top of the hierarchy to generate all possible dates she can have the meeting, which can then be verified by her staff.

The above two examples demonstrate that there can be a difference between the agent hierarchy and the hierarchy of the people/things modeled by the agents. The agent with the greatest power is the one generating all the candidate models. The effect of the other agents is inversely proportional to their distance to this initial (generator) agent.

In this paper, we restrict to linearly connected agents, since such systems are already capable of representing the most common forms of hierarchy.

Formally, a *hierarchical agent system (HAS)* is a linear sequence of hierarchical agents $A = (A_1, \ldots, A_n)$, where A_1 is the source agent, i.e. the agent that starts all communication. For a HAS A, we refer to the i-th agent as A_i, while we use $A_{<i}$ to denote the HAS consisting of the predecessors of A_i, i.e. $A_{<i} = (A_1, \ldots, A_{i-1})$.

We assume for our theoretical model that agents are fully aware of the agents that they can communicate with (as the communication structure is fixed) and that they can communicate by passing sets of literals over the communication channels. When put to practice in an open multi-agent environment, an agent would first engage in establishing a community and the appropriate hierarchy before collaborating on establishing a consensus on the answer sets. Furthermore, one would expect the set of literals encapsulated in a communication protocol.

Each agent in a HAS is a separate entity with its own reasoning skills, knowledge and beliefs. Each agent has the right to remove or add information to the input as she sees fit. To reflect this, we introduce an *interpretation* for a HAS $A = (A_1, \ldots, A_n)$ as a sequence of interpretations $I = (I_1, \ldots, I_n)$, one for each agent, denoting the public knowledge of each individual agent. For interpretations, we introduce the same notation I_i and $I_{<i}$ as we did for hierarchical agent systems. An interpretation I is consistent iff $\bigcup_{1 \leq i \leq n} I_i$ is consistent. Given a sequence I and a set S, we will write (I, S) to denote the new sequence obtained from concatenating I and S.

Example 4. Consider the HAS $A = (A_1, A_2)$ with $A_1 = \{meeting \leftarrow\}$ and $A_2 = \{out\_of\_office \leftarrow meeting'\}$. Then, $(\{meeting\}, \{out\_of\_office\})$ is an interpretation.

The solutions of such a hierarchical agent system, called hierarchical answer sets, are defined inductively. For a HAS A, we will use $\mathcal{AG}(A)$ to denote the set of all hierarchical answer sets of A.

Definition 2. *Let $\mathcal{AL}$ be an agent language.*
- *A **hierarchical answer set** of a HAS $A = (A_1)$ is a consistent interpretation $S = (S_1)$ such that $S_1 \in \mathcal{AS}(A_1, \emptyset)$.*
- *A **hierarchical answer set** of a HAS $A = (A_1, \ldots, A_n)$ is a consistent interpretation $S = (S_1, \ldots, S_n)$ such that $S_{<n}$ is a hierarchical answer set of $A_{<n}$, i.e. $S_{<n} \in \mathcal{AG}(A_{<n})$, and*
  1. *$S_n \in \mathcal{AS}(A_n, S_{n-1})$; or*
  2. *$S_n = S_{n-1}$ iff $\forall S' \in \mathcal{AG}(A_{<n}) \cdot \forall T \in \mathcal{AS}(A_n, S_{n-1}) \cdot (S', T)$ inconsistent.*

The case of a single agent HAS is simple: hierarchical answer sets equal the agent's agent answer sets with empty input. The two conditions of the general case are the encoding of the principle that an agent either has to be able to augment the input in a consistent manner (condition 1) or convince itself that all the alternatives it can propose are inconsistent with solutions that are acceptable by its predecessors. In that case, the input will be accepted (condition 2). If not, the candidate will be rejected.

Example 5. Consider the following simple HAS $A = (A_1, A_2, A_3)$ with:
- the general director A_1 of a company containing the following rules[3]:

$$monday \oplus tuesday \oplus friday \leftarrow \qquad \neg wednesday \leftarrow \qquad \neg thursday \leftarrow$$

- the head of research A_2 containing the rules:

$$monday \oplus thursday \leftarrow \qquad \neg tuesday \leftarrow \qquad \neg wednesday \leftarrow \qquad \neg friday \leftarrow$$

- the project manager A_3 containing the rules:

$$friday \oplus wednesday \leftarrow \qquad \neg monday \leftarrow \qquad \neg tuesday \leftarrow \qquad \neg thursday \leftarrow$$

who attempt to arrange a meeting. The director agent produces three possible hierarchical answer sets for the HAS (A_1), i.e.
- $(M_1) = (\{monday, \neg tuesday, \neg wednesday, \neg thursday, \neg friday\})$
- $(M_2) = (\{\neg monday, tuesday, \neg wednesday, \neg thursday, \neg friday\})$
- $(M_3) = (\{\neg monday, \neg tuesday, \neg wednesday, \neg thursday, friday\})$

---

[3] In the following we will use rules of the form $a \oplus b \oplus c \leftarrow$ to denote the set of rules $\{a \leftarrow ;$ $b \leftarrow ; c \leftarrow ; \neg a \leftarrow ; \neg b \leftarrow ; \neg c \leftarrow ; \leftarrow a, b ; \leftarrow a, c ; \leftarrow b, c ; \leftarrow \neg a, \neg b, \neg c\}$, i.e. an exclusive choice between a, b and c.

Let us now consider $A_{<3} = (A_1, A_2)$. When we feed A_2 with M_1, we notice that M_1 is accepted. This means that (M_1, M_1) is a hierarchical answer set for $A_{<3}$. Any other answer set from A_2 with input M_1 leads to contradiction. When we use M_2 as input we have that $M_1 \in \mathcal{AS}(A_2, M_2)$ is clearly inconsistent with M_2, but which is consistent with an acceptable solution of the predecessors, i.e. (M_1). This implies that there is no hierarchical answer with M_2 as input for A_2. The same is true when M_3 is used as input. As a result, we have $\mathcal{AG}(A_{<3}) = \{(M_1, M_1)\}$.

Now that we have the hierarchical answer sets for $A_{<3}$, we can define those of A. When we compute the answer sets of A_3 with M_1 as input, we obtain two answer sets: one assuming friday to be true and the other wednesday to be true. Both are inconsistent with (M_1, M_1), so our project manager has no other option than to conform to M_1 herself, resulting in $\mathcal{AG}(A) = \{(M_1, M_1, M_1)\}$.

Now consider the rearranged HAS $B = (A_1, A_3, A_2)$, e.g. because A_3 has prior arrangements with customers who do not appreciate changes to their schedule. This change would result in a different hierarchical answer set, namely (M_3, M_3, M_3).

Although we request that hierarchical answer sets are consistent, this does not mean that internal inconsistencies cannot appear. Further, the system also allows for cheating and/or lying.

Example 6. Consider the following HAS $A = (A_1, A_2)$ with $A_1 = \{a \leftarrow\}$ and $A_2 = \{b \leftarrow; \neg a' \leftarrow b; c \leftarrow \neg a'; a \leftarrow a'\}$. This HAS produces two hierarchical answer sets: $(\{a\}, \{a, b\})$ and $(\{a\}, \{b, c\})$. In the latter case, the agent A_2 knows that there would be a contradiction if she would admit $\neg a$, so she decides to ignore what she knows about $\neg a$ and only states the implication of $\neg a'$, i.e. the conclusion c.

Example 7. Consider the job selection procedure of a company. The first agent A_1 corresponds with the possible profiles of the applicants. Thus, each agent answer set of the agent below corresponds with a possible applicant's profile.

$$male \oplus female \leftarrow \qquad old \oplus young \leftarrow \qquad experienced \oplus inexperienced \leftarrow$$

The decision which applicant gets the job goes through a chain of decision makers. First, the agent A_2 of the human resources department implements company policy which stipulates that experienced persons should be preferred over inexperienced ones. Therefore, the agent passes through all of its input, except when it encounters a profile containing *inexperienced*, which it changes to *experienced*, intuitively implementing that an applicant with the same profile but *experienced* instead of *inexperienced* would be preferable. Further, the department is convinced that younger employees are ambitious.

$$\mathbf{pass}(\{male, female, old, young, experienced\})$$
$$\mathbf{pass}(\{\neg male, \neg female, \neg old, \neg young, \neg inexperienced\})$$
$$experienced \leftarrow inexperienced'$$
$$\neg inexperienced \leftarrow inexperienced'$$
$$ambitious \leftarrow young'$$

On the next level of the decision chain, the financial department reviews the remaining candidates. As young and inexperienced persons tend to cost less, it has a strong desire to hire such candidates, which is implemented in the following agent A_3.

$$\textbf{pass}(\{male, female, young, inexperienced\})$$
$$\textbf{pass}(\{\neg male, \neg female, \neg old, \neg experienced\})$$

$inexperienced \leftarrow young', experienced'$	$\neg experienced \leftarrow young', experienced'$
$young \leftarrow young', experienced'$	$\neg old \leftarrow young', experienced'$
$young \leftarrow old', inexperienced'$	$\neg old \leftarrow old', inexperienced'$
$inexperienced \leftarrow old', inexperienced'$	$\neg experienced \leftarrow old', inexperienced'$
$inexperienced \leftarrow old', experienced'$	$\neg inexperienced \leftarrow old', experienced'$
$experienced' \leftarrow old', experienced'$	$\neg experienced' \leftarrow old', experienced'$
$young \leftarrow old', experienced'$	$\neg young \leftarrow old', experienced'$
$old \leftarrow old', experienced'$	$\neg old \leftarrow old', experienced'$
$\leftarrow old, experienced$	$cheaper \leftarrow inexperienced$
	$cheaper \leftarrow young$

Intuitively, this agent handles the four possible cases: when the input profile is from a young and inexperienced person, nothing will be changed, indicating that the input cannot be improved. On the other hand, if only one of the properties is not as desired, e.g. *young* and *experienced*, then the only improvement would be a profile containing both *young* and *inexperienced*. Finally, a profile containing *old* and *experienced* has three possible improvements: the contradictory rules together with the constraint ensure that the agent answer sets proposed by A_3 will contain *young* or *inexperienced*, or both.

Finally, the management has the final call in the selection procedure. As the current team of employees is largely male, the management prefers the new worker to be a woman, as described by the next agent A_4, which is similar to A_2.

$$\textbf{pass}(\mathcal{AL} \setminus \{male, \neg female, ambitious, cheaper\})$$
$$female \leftarrow male' \qquad \neg male \leftarrow \neg female' \qquad \leftarrow female'$$

One can check that the system (A_1) has eight hierarchical answer sets, among them are

$$(M_1) = (\{experienced, \neg inexperienced, male, \neg female, young, \neg old\}) \ ,$$
$$(M_2) = (\{experienced, \neg inexperienced, male, \neg female, old, \neg young\}) \ ,$$
$$(M_3) = (\{experienced, \neg inexperienced, female, \neg male, young, \neg old\}) \ ,$$
$$(M_4) = (\{experienced, \neg inexperienced, female, \neg male, old, \neg young\}) \ ,$$
$$(M_5) = (\{inexperienced, \neg experienced, female, \neg male, young, \neg old\}) \ .$$

However, only four of these will survive agent A_2, i.e. $\mathcal{AG}((A_1, A_2)) = \{(M_1, M_1 \cup \{ambitious\}), (M_2, M_2), (M_3, M_3 \cup \{ambitious\}), (M_4, M_4)\}$, which fits the human resource policy to drop inexperienced people. Feeding M_5 as input to A_2 yields one agent answer set $M_3 \cup \{ambitious\}$, which is consistent with $(M_3) \in \mathcal{AG}((A_1))$, making (M_5, M_5) unacceptable as a solution for the system. Similarly, when agent A_3 is taken into account, only $(M_1, M_1 \cup \{ambitious\}, M_1 \cup \{cheaper\})$ and $(M_3, M_3 \cup \{ambitious\}, M_3 \cup \{cheaper\})$ are contained in $\mathcal{AG}((A_1, A_2, A_3))$. Considering the last agent A_4, the HAS (A_1, A_2, A_3, A_4) yields a single hierarchical answer set,

$$(M_3, M_3 \cup \{ambitious\}, M_3 \cup \{cheaper\}, M_3) \ ,$$

which fits our intuition that, if possible, a woman should get the job.

4   Complexity

We briefly recall some relevant notions of complexity theory (see [31] for an introduction). The class $\mathcal{P}$ ($\mathcal{NP}$) represents the problems that are deterministically (nondeterministically) decidable in polynomial time, while $co\mathcal{NP}$ contains the problems whose complements are in $\mathcal{NP}$. The polynomial hierarchy, denoted $\mathcal{PH}$, is made up of three classes of problems, i.e. Δ_k^P, Σ_k^P and Π_k^P, $k \geq 0$, which are defined as follows:

1. $\Delta_0^P = \Sigma_0^P = \Pi_0^P = \mathcal{P}$; and
2. $\Delta_{k+1}^P = \mathcal{P}^{\Sigma_k^P}, \Sigma_{k+1}^P = \mathcal{NP}^{\Sigma_k^P}, \Pi_{k+1}^P = co\Sigma_{k+1}^P$.

The class $\mathcal{P}^{\Sigma_k^P}$ ($\mathcal{NP}^{\Sigma_k^P}$) represents the problems decidable in deterministic (nondeterministic) polynomial time using an oracle for problems in Σ_k^P, where an oracle is a subroutine capable of solving Σ_k^P problems in unit time. Note that $\Delta_1^P = P$, $\Sigma_1^P = \mathcal{NP}$ and $\Pi_1^P = co\mathcal{NP}$. The class $\mathcal{PH}$ is defined by $\mathcal{PH} = \bigcup_{k=0}^{\infty} \Sigma_k^P$. Finally, the class $PSPACE$ contains the problems that can be solved deterministically by using a polynomial amount of memory and unlimited time.

A decision problem D is called *hard* in a complexity class C of the polynomial hierarchy if any other problem from this class can be reduced to it by a polynomial time reduction[4]. A decision problem D is called *complete* in a complexity class C if both D is in C and D is hard in C.

A quantified boolean formula (QBF) is an expression of the form $Q_1 X_1 Q_2 X_2 \ldots Q_k X_k \cdot G$, where $k \geq 1$, G is a Boolean expression over the atoms of the pairwise nonempty disjoint sets of variables $X_1, \ldots, X_k$ and the Q_i's, for $i = 1, \ldots, k$ are alternating quantifiers from $\{\exists, \forall\}$. When $Q_1 = \exists$, the QBF is k-existential, when $Q_1 = \forall$ we say it is k-universal. We use $QBF_{k,\exists}$ ($QBF_{k,\forall}$) to denote the set of all valid k-existential (k-universal) QBFs.

Deciding, for a given k-existential (k-universal) QBF ϕ, whether $\phi \in QBF_{k,\exists}$ ($\phi \in QBF_{k,\forall}$) is a Σ_k^P-complete (Π_k^P-complete) problem. When we drop the bound k on the number of quantifiers, i.e. considering $QBF_\exists = \bigcup_{i \in \mathbb{N}} QBF_{i,\exists}$, we have a hard problem for $PSPACE$.

The following results shed some light on the data complexity of the hierarchical answer set semantics for hierarchical agent systems, i.e. we measure the complexity with respect to the size of the facts, while the rules in the different hierarchical agents are fixed. Note that in the case of data complexity, for an ungrounded hierarchical agent P, the size of $gr(P)$ is polynomial in terms of the size of the facts.

First, we consider the case where the number of agents in the hierarchy is fixed by some number n.

Theorem 1. *The problem of deciding, given a HAS $(A_i)_{i=1,\ldots,n}$, with n fixed, and a literal $l \in \mathcal{L}_{\mathcal{AL}}$, whether there exists a hierarchical answer set I containing l is Σ_n^P-complete. On the other hand, deciding whether every hierarchical answer set contains l is Π_n^P-complete.*

---

[4] The only exception is $\mathcal{P}$-hardness, where logarithmic space reductions have to be used.

Proof Sketch. Membership Σ_n^P: It is shown, by induction, in [38] that checking if an interpretation I for A is not a hierarchical answer set of A, i.e. $I \notin \mathcal{AG}(A)$, is in Σ_{n-1}^P. The main result follows by

- guessing an interpretation I containing l; and
- checking that it is not the case that $I \notin \mathcal{AG}(A)$.

As the latter is in Σ_{n-1}^P, the problem itself can be done by an $\mathcal{NP}^{\Sigma_{n-1}^P}$ algorithm, i.e. the problem is in Σ_n^P.

Hardness in Σ_n^P: To prove this, we provide a reduction of deciding validity of QBFs by means of a HAS . Let $\phi = \exists X_1 \forall X_2 \ldots Q X_n \cdot G \in QBF_{n,\exists}$, where $Q = \forall$ if n is even and $Q = \exists$ otherwise. We assume, without loss of generality [37], that, if n is even, G is in disjunctive normal form, i.e. $G = \vee_{c \in C} C$ where C is a set of sets of literals over $X_1 \cup \ldots \cup X_n$ and each $c \in C$ has to be read as a conjunction; or that, if n is odd, G is in conjunctive normal form, i.e. $G = \wedge_{c \in C} C$ where C is a set of sets of literals over $X_1 \cup \ldots \cup X_n$ and each $c \in C$ has to be read as a disjunction.

In what follows, we will use the following shorthand notations for certain sets of rules. To check satisfiability of G in case n is even, we use P_{even}^{sat} to denote the set of rules $\{sat' \leftarrow c' \mid c \in C\}$. On the other hand, satisfiability of G in case n is odd is checked by using P_{odd}^{sat}, which contains the rules[5]

- $\{notsat' \leftarrow c'_\neg \mid c \in C\}$,
- $\{\leftarrow c'_\neg, \neg notsat' \mid c \in C\}$,
- $\neg notsat' \leftarrow$,
- $sat' \leftarrow \neg notsat'$,

where $c_\neg$ denotes the version of c where the literals are negated and read conjunctively, i.e. $c = a \vee b \vee \neg d$ results in $c_\neg = \neg a \wedge \neg b \wedge d$. One can check that in both P_{even}^{sat} and P_{odd}^{sat} only sat' is derived iff G is valid w.r.t. the chosen truth values for $X_1 \cup \ldots \cup X_n$.

Further, we use $P_\forall^i$ to denote the program containing the rules

- **pass**$(\{x, \neg x \mid x \in X_j \wedge 1 \le j < i\})$,
- $\{x' \leftarrow \ ; \ \neg x' \leftarrow \mid x \in X_j \wedge i \le j \le n\}$,
- P_{even}^{sat} or P_{odd}^{sat},
- $\{\leftarrow sat' \ ; \ \neg sat \leftarrow \ ; \ \leftarrow \neg sat\}$.

Similarly, we use $P_\exists^i$ to denote the program

- **pass**$(\{x, \neg x \mid x \in X_j \wedge 1 \le j < i\})$,
- $\{x' \leftarrow \ ; \ \neg x' \leftarrow \mid x \in X_j \wedge i \le j \le n\}$,
- P_{even}^{sat} or P_{odd}^{sat},
- $\{\neg sat' \leftarrow \ ; \ \leftarrow \neg sat' \ ; \ \leftarrow sat\}$.

The HAS $A_\phi = (A_1, \ldots, A_n)$ corresponding to ϕ is defined by the following hierarchical agents:

- A_1 contains the rules $\{x' \leftarrow \ ; \ \neg x' \leftarrow \mid x \in X_j \wedge 1 \le j \le n\}$ and either P_{even}^{sat} or P_{odd}^{sat};

---

[5] The rules use an encoding in the extended answer set semantics for negation as failure [39].

- if n is even, then $A_i = P_\forall^{n+2-i}$ when i even and $A_i = P_\exists^{n+2-i}$ when $i > 1$ odd;
- if n is odd, then $A_i = P_\exists^{n+2-i}$ when i even and $A_i = P_\forall^{n+2-i}$ when $i > 1$ odd.

Obviously, the above construction can be done in polynomial time. Intuitively, the hierarchical agent A_1 has agent answer sets for every possible combination of the X_i's and if such a combination makes G valid, then the corresponding agent answer set also contains the atom sat. The intuition behind the hierarchical agent $P_\forall^i$ is that it tries to disprove, for the received input, the validity of the corresponding $\forall$, i.e. for a given input combination over the X_j's making G satisfied, the hierarchical agent $P_\forall^i$ will try to find a combination, keeping the X_j's with $j < i$ fixed, making G false. On the other hand, the hierarchical agent $P_\exists^i$ will try to prove the validity of the corresponding $\exists$, i.e. for a given combination making G false it will try to compute a combination, keeping the X_j's with $j < i$ fixed, making G satisfied.

Instead of giving the formal proof for the above construction, we illustrate, for clarity, the construction and the working of the HAS A_ϕ on an example and refer the reader to [38] for the actual proof.

Consider

$$\phi = \exists x \cdot \forall y \cdot \exists z \cdot \forall w \cdot (x \wedge \neg y \wedge z) \vee (y \wedge \neg z) \vee w \ .$$

The hierarchical agent A_1 contains the following rules.

$x' \leftarrow$	$\neg x' \leftarrow$	$y' \leftarrow$	$\neg y' \leftarrow$
$z' \leftarrow$	$\neg z' \leftarrow$	$w' \leftarrow$	$\neg w' \leftarrow$
$sat' \leftarrow x', \neg y', z'$	$sat' \leftarrow y', \neg z'$	$sat' \leftarrow w'$	

We have 16 possible agent answer sets for $A_1(\emptyset)$, i.e. $I_1 = \{x, y, z, w, sat\}$, $I_2 = \{x, y, z, \neg w\}$, $I_3 = \{x, y, \neg z, w, sat\}$, $I_4 = \{x, y, \neg z, \neg w, sat\}$, $I_5 = \{x, \neg y, z, w, sat\}$, $I_6 = \{x, \neg y, z, \neg w, sat\}$, $I_7 = \{x, \neg y, \neg z, w, sat\}$, $I_8 = \{x, \neg y, \neg z, \neg w\}$, $I_9 = \{\neg x, y, z, w, sat\}$, $I_{10} = \{\neg x, y, z, \neg w\}$, $I_{11} = \{\neg x, y, \neg z, w, sat\}$, $I_{12} = \{\neg x, y, \neg z, \neg w, sat\}$, $I_{13} = \{\neg x, \neg y, z, w, sat\}$, $I_{14} = \{\neg x, \neg y, z, \neg w\}$, $I_{15} = \{\neg x, \neg y, \neg z, w, sat\}$ and $I_{16} = \{\neg x, \neg y, \neg z, \neg w\}$.

Clearly, for $1 \le i \le 16$, (I_i) is a hierarchical answer set of (A_1).

The second hierarchical agent A_2 is defined by $P_\forall^4$ and thus contains the following rules.

$\mathbf{pass}(\{x, \neg x, y, \neg y, z, \neg z\}) \leftarrow$	$w' \leftarrow$	$\neg w' \leftarrow$
$sat' \leftarrow x', \neg y', z'$	$sat' \leftarrow y', \neg z'$	$sat' \leftarrow w'$
$\leftarrow sat'$	$\neg sat \leftarrow$	$\leftarrow \neg sat$

Now, feeding I_1 to A_2 yields I_2 as the single agent answer set, which is clearly inconsistent with I_1, yielding that (I_1, I_2) cannot be a hierarchical answer set of the HAS (A_1, A_2). Further, for I_2 we have that $I_2 \in \mathcal{AG}(A_1)$, yielding that (I_2, I_2) is clearly consistent, which implies that (I_1, I_1) is neither a hierarchical answer set of (A_1, A_2).

On the other hand, $A_2(I_3)$ yields I_3 as the single agent answer set which is clearly consistent with itself, yielding that (I_3, I_3) is a hierarchical answer set of (A_1, A_2), i.e. A_2 passes the input I_3 as a result as it cannot disprove $\forall w \cdot (x \wedge \neg y \wedge z) \vee (y \wedge \neg z) \vee w$ for the chosen truth value of x, y, z in I_3.

In case of the input I_2, the agent program $A_2(I_2)$ has no extended answer sets and I_2 is returned as the single agent answer set. As I_2 is consistent with itself, (I_2, I_2) is a hierarchical answer set of (A_1, A_2).

One can check in similar ways that $\mathcal{AG}((A_1, A_2))$ contains 11 interpretations, i.e. $\mathcal{AG}((A_1, A_2)) = \{(I_2, I_2), (I_3, I_3), (I_4, I_4), (I_5, I_5), (I_6, I_6), (I_8, I_8), (I_{10}, I_{10}),$ $(I_{11}, I_{11}), (I_{12}, I_{12}), (I_{14}, I_{14}), (I_{16}, I_{16})\}$. It is not difficult to see that for each of these hierarchical answer sets it holds that $\forall w \cdot (x \wedge \neg y \wedge z) \vee (y \wedge \neg z) \vee w$ when x, y and z are taken as in the interpretation iff the literal sat is contained in the hierarchical answer set.

The third hierarchical agent A_3 is given by $P_{\exists}^3$ and thus contains the following rules.

$$\textbf{pass}(\{x, \neg x, y, \neg y\}) \leftarrow \qquad z' \leftarrow \qquad \neg z' \leftarrow \qquad sat' \leftarrow x', \neg y', z'$$
$$w' \leftarrow \qquad \neg w' \leftarrow \qquad sat' \leftarrow y', \neg z'$$
$$\neg sat' \leftarrow \qquad \leftarrow \neg sat' \qquad \leftarrow sat \qquad sat' \leftarrow w'$$

When providing A_3 with the input I_2, we have $\mathcal{AS}(A_3, I_2) = \{I_1, I_3, I_4\}$, none of them consistent with I_2. However, for both I_3 and I_4 there is a $T \in \mathcal{AG}((A_1, A_2))$ such that I_3 and I_4 is consistent with T, i.e. $T = (I_3, I_3)$ and $T = (I_4, I_4)$ respectively. As a result $(I_2, I_2, I_2) \notin \mathcal{AG}((A_1, A_2, A_3))$.

On the other hand, feeding I_3 as input to A_3 will yield the single agent answer set I_3, implying that $(I_3, I_3, I_3) \in \mathcal{AG}((A_1, A_2, A_3))$.

In case of the input I_{14}, we have $\mathcal{AS}(A_3, I_{14}) = \{I_{13}, I_{15}\}$ and none of them consistent with I_{14}. Further, neither for I_{13} nor I_{15} there is a $T \in \mathcal{AG}((A_1, A_2))$ such that I_{13} or I_{15} is consistent with T, yielding that (I_{14}, I_{14}, I_{14}) is a hierarchical answer set of (A_1, A_2, A_3) in this case, i.e. A_3 passes the input I_{14} as a result because it proved that $\exists z \cdot \forall w \cdot (x \wedge \neg y \wedge z) \vee (y \wedge \neg z)$ does not hold for the chosen truth value of x and y in I_14. In a similar way one can check that also $(I_3, I_3, I_3) \in \mathcal{AG}((A_1, A_2, A_3))$.

One can check in similar ways that $\mathcal{AG}((A_1, A_2, A_3))$ contains 8 interpretations, i.e. $\mathcal{AG}((A_1, A_2)) = \{(I_3, I_3), (I_4, I_4), (I_5, I_5), (I_6, I_6), (I_{11}, I_{11}), (I_{12}, I_{12}), (I_{14}, I_{14}),$ $(I_{16}, I_{16})\}$. Again, it is not difficult to see that for each of these hierarchical answer sets it holds that $\exists z \cdot \forall w \cdot (x \wedge \neg y \wedge z) \vee (y \wedge \neg z) \vee w$ when x and y are taken as in the interpretation iff the literal sat is contained in the hierarchical answer set.

The final hierarchical agent A_4 is given by $P_{\forall}^2$, and by similar reasoning as we did for A_2, one can check that $\mathcal{AG}((A_1, A_2, A_3, A_4))$ contains 6 interpretations, i.e. $\mathcal{AG}((A_1, A_2)) = \{(I_3, I_3), (I_4, I_4), (I_5, I_5), (I_6, I_6), (I_{14}, I_{14}), (I_{16}, I_{16})\}$. Again, for each hierarchical answer set in $\mathcal{AG}((A_1, A_2, A_3, A_4))$ it holds that $\forall y \cdot \exists z \cdot \forall w \cdot (x \wedge \neg y \wedge z) \vee (y \wedge \neg z)$ for x taken as in the interpretation iff the literal sat is contained in the hierarchical answer set. From this it follows that ϕ is valid iff there exists a hierarchical answer set $I \in \mathcal{AG}((A_1, A_2, A_3, A_4))$ such that the literal sat is contained in the interpretation. In our example, I_3 is such a hierarchical answer set and one can check that ϕ holds when assuming x is true.

Π_n^P-*completeness:* To show this result, we consider in [38] the complementary decision problem and show that it is Σ_n^P-complete, from which the result follows.   □

While the previous result handles the cases where the number of agents in the hierarchy is fixed, we can generalize the results to arbitrary hierarchies.

Theorem 2. *Given a HAS $(A_i)_{i=1,...,n}$ and a literal $l \in \mathcal{L}_{AC}$, the problem of deciding whether there exists a hierarchical answer set I containing l is PSPACE-complete.*

Proof Sketch. Membership PSPACE: Intuitively, each agent in the hierarchy needs the space to represent a single HAS-interpretation (used for computing the agent answer sets), while the HAS itself needs the space to represent a hierarchical answer set. Now, the algorithm will place a possible solution in the latter allocated space, and will use the former allocated space to check if it is indeed a hierarchical answer set. Thus, an algorithm for a hierarchy of n programs, needs maximum $n + 1$ times the space to represent a HAS-interpretation, which is clearly polynomial in space, from which membership to *PSPACE* follows.

Hardness PSPACE: Clearly, the hardness proof of Theorem 1 can be generalized to validity checking of arbitrary quantified boolean formulas, from which hardness readily follows.   □

While the previous results describe the complexity of reasoning with the presented framework, they do not give a clear picture on the expressiveness [27] of the system, i.e. whether each problem that belongs to a certain complexity class can be expressed in the framework. This is because a formalism F being complete for a particular class only implies that each instance of a problem in that class can be reduced in polynomial time to an instance of F such that the yes/no answer is preserved.

However, completeness does not imply that the polynomial time reduction itself from an instance of the problem to an instance in F is expressible in F[6].

In this context, one says that a formalism *captures* a certain complexity class iff the formalism is in the class and every problem in that class can be expressed in the formalism. The latter part is normally proved by taking an arbitrary expression in a normal (or general) form[7] for the particular complexity class and by showing that it can be expressed in the formalism.

By using the results from [21, 20], the following normal forms for the complexity classes Σ_k^P, with $k \geq 2$ and k even, and Π_k^P, with $k \geq 2$ and k odd, can be obtained. First, we have to consider a signature $\sigma = (O, F, P)$, with O finite and $F = \emptyset$, i.e. we do not allow function symbols. A finite database over σ is any finite subset of the Herbrand Base over σ. Secondly, we have three predicates that do not occur in P, i.e. *succ, first* and *last*. Enumeration literals are literals over the signature $(O, \emptyset, \{succ, first, last\})$ that satisfy the conditions:

- *succ* describes an enumeration of the elements in O; and
- *first* and *last* contain the first and last element in the enumeration respectively.

Intuitively, *succ* is a binary predicate such that $succ(x, y)$ means that y is the successor of x. Further, *first* and *last* are unary predicates.

---

[6] A good example of this fact is the query class *fixpoint*, which is $PTIME$-complete but cannot express the simple query $even(R)$ to check if $|R|$ is even. See e.g. [12, 1] for a more detailed explanation on the difference between completeness and expressiveness (or capturing).

[7] A normal (or general) form of a complexity class is a form to which every problem in the class can be reduced [27]. E.g. the polynomial hierarchy is the set of languages expressible by second-order logic, i.e. each problem of the polynomial hierarchy can be reduced to a second-order logical formula. Note that not every complexity class necessarily has a general form.

A collection S of finite databases over the signature $\sigma = (O, \emptyset, P)$ is in Σ_k^P, with $k \geq 2$ and k even, iff there is a second order formula of the form

$$\phi = Q_1 U_{1,\ldots,m_1}^1 Q_2 U_{1,\ldots,m_2}^2 \cdots Q_k U_{1,\ldots,m_k}^k \exists \overline{x} \cdot \theta_1(\overline{x}) \vee \ldots \vee \theta_l(\overline{x}) \ ,$$

where $Q_i = \exists$ if i is odd, $Q_i = \forall$ if i is even, $U_{1,\ldots,m_i}^i$ $(1 \leq i \leq k)$ are finite sets of predicate symbols and $\theta_i(\overline{x})$ $(1 \leq i \leq l)$ are conjunctions of enumeration literals or literals involving predicates in $P \cup \{U_{1,\ldots,m_1}^1, U_{1,\ldots,m_2}^2, \ldots, U_{1,\ldots,m_k}^k\}$ such that for any finite database w over σ, $w \in S$ iff w satisfies ϕ.

Similarly, a collection S of finite databases over the signature $\sigma = (O, \emptyset, P)$ is in Π_k^P, with $k \geq 2$ and k odd, iff there is a second order formula of the form

$$\phi = Q_1 U_{1,\ldots,m_1}^1 Q_2 U_{1,\ldots,m_2}^2 \cdots Q_k U_{1,\ldots,m_k}^k \exists \overline{x} \cdot \theta_1(\overline{x}) \vee \ldots \vee \theta_l(\overline{x}) \ ,$$

where $Q_i = \forall$ if i is odd, $Q_i = \exists$ if i is even, $U_{1,\ldots,m_i}^i$ $(1 \leq i \leq k)$ are finite sets of predicate symbols and $\theta_i(\overline{x})$ $(1 \leq i \leq l)$ are conjunctions of enumeration literals or literals involving predicates in $P \cup \{U_{1,\ldots,m_1}^1, U_{1,\ldots,m_2}^2, \ldots, U_{1,\ldots,m_k}^k\}$ such that for any finite database w over σ, $w \in S$ iff w satisfies ϕ.

Again, we first consider the case in which the number of agents in the hierarchy is fixed by a number $n \in \mathbb{N}$.

Theorem 3. *The hierarchical answer set semantics for hierarchical agent systems with a fixed number n of agents captures Σ_n^P.*

Proof Sketch. Membership Σ_n^P: The result follows directly from the membership part of the proof of Theorem 1.

Capture Σ_n^P: This proof is a generalization of the technique used in the hardness proof of Theorem 1. Further, the construction of the agents, especially the first one, is based on the proofs in [21], where it is shown that disjunctive logic programming under the brave semantics captures Σ_2^P.

However, we first have to consider the case where $n = 1$ separately, as the general form discussed above only holds for $n \geq 2$. In [39] we have shown that the extended answer set semantics coincides with the classical answer set semantics. As the latter is already proven in the literature (e.g. in [1]) to capture $\Sigma_1^P = \mathcal{NP}$, the same holds for the former, yielding that also the hierarchical answer set semantics for hierarchies of a single agent captures $\mathcal{NP}$.

To prove that any problem of Σ_n^P, with $n \geq 2$, can be expressed in a HAS of n agents under the hierarchical answer set semantics, we consider two cases, i.e. one where n is even and from which the result follows directly; and one where n is odd and the result follows from the fact that we solve the complementary problem (and $\Sigma_k^P = co\Pi_k^P$).

In case n is even, we show a construction of a HAS $\langle A_i \rangle_{i=1,\ldots,n}$ such that a finite database w satisfies the formula

$$\phi = \exists U_{1,\ldots,m_1}^1 \forall U_{1,\ldots,m_2}^2 \cdots \forall_n U_{1,\ldots,m_n}^n \exists \overline{x} \cdot \theta_1(\overline{x}) \vee \ldots \vee \theta_l(\overline{x}) \ ,$$

with everything defined as in the general form for Σ_n^P described before, iff $\langle A_i \rangle_{i=1,\ldots,n}$ has a hierarchical answer set containing *sat*.

The first agent A_1 in the hierarchy contains, beside the facts that introduce the database w (as w'), the following rules:

- For the enumeration of the predicates $U^1_{1,\dots,m_1}, U^2_{1,\dots,m_2}, \dots, U^n_{1,\dots,m_n}$, we have, for $1 \leq i \leq n$ and $1 \leq k \leq m_i$, the rules:

$$U^{i\,'}_k(\overline{w^i_k}) \leftarrow \qquad\qquad \neg U^{i\,'}_k(\overline{w^i_k}) \leftarrow$$

- To introduce the linear ordering, we need a set of rules similar to the ones used in Section 2.1.13. of [1] (see the technical report [38] for a detailed description). This set of rules has the property that when a linear ordering is established, the literal *linear'* is derived.
- To check satisfiability, we use, for $1 \leq i \leq l$, the rules $sat' \leftarrow \theta_i{}'(\overline{x})$, *linear'* .

The other agents of the hierarchy are defined, similar to the hardness proof of Theorem 1 by using two skeletons $P^i_\forall$ and $P^i_\exists$. First, both skeletons have the following set of rules P^i in common

- **pass**($\{ U^j_k(\overline{w^j_k}), \neg U^j_k(\overline{w^j_k}) \mid (1 \leq j < i) \wedge (1 \leq k \leq m_i) \}$) ,
- **pass**($\{$*facts of the linear ordering*$\}$) ,
- **pass**(w) ,
- $\{ U^{j\,'}_k(\overline{w^j_k}) \leftarrow \; ; \; \neg U^{j\,'}_k(\overline{w^j_k}) \leftarrow \; \mid (i \leq j \leq n) \wedge (1 \leq k \leq m_i) \}$, and
- $\{ sat' \leftarrow \theta_i{}'(\overline{x}), linear' \mid 1 \leq i \leq l \}$.

Now, we define the programs $P^i_\forall$ and $P^i_\exists$ as $P^i_\forall = P^i \cup \{ \leftarrow sat' \; ; \; \neg sat \leftarrow \; ; \; \leftarrow \neg sat \}$ and $P^i_\exists = P^i \cup \{ \neg sat' \leftarrow \; ; \; \leftarrow \neg sat' \; ; \; \leftarrow sat \}$ respectively.

Besides A_1, the remaining agents in the hierarchy are defined by: $A_i = P^{n+2-i}_\forall$ when i even and $A_i = P^{n+2-i}_\exists$ when $i > 1$ odd.

It is not difficult to see (similar to the hardness proof of Theorem 1 that the above constructed HAS will only generate, for a given input database w, hierarchical answer sets that contain *sat* iff ϕ is satisfied.

Finally, for the case where n is odd, we can reuse the agents defined above for the even case, i.e. the HAS $\langle A_i \rangle_{i=1,\dots,n}$ is defined, besides A_1, as $A_i = P^{n+2-i}_\exists$ when i even and $A_i = P^{n+2-i}_\forall$ when $i > 1$ odd.

This time, it is not so hard to see that ϕ is satisfied iff all hierarchical answer sets of the above constructed HAS, for a given input database w, contain *sat*. As this proves capturing of Π^P_n for the complementary problem we want to show expressiveness for, the result follows.   □

When we drop the fixed number of agents in the hierarchy, the above result can be easily generalized to arbitrary HAS.

Corollary 1. *The hierarchical answer set semantics for hierarchical agent systems captures[8] $\mathcal{PH}$, i.e. the polynomial hierarchy.*

The above result yields that the presented framework is able to encode each problem in the polynomial hierarchy, making the framework useful for complex knowledge reasoning tasks by agents.

---

[8] Note that while the semantics captures $\mathcal{PH}$, it can never be complete for it as the hierarchy would then collapse.

5 Relationships to Other Approaches

In [5], answer set optimization (ASO) programs are presented. Such ASO programs consist of a generator program and a sequence of optimizing programs. To perform the optimization, the latter programs use rules of the form $c_1 < \ldots < c_n \leftarrow \beta$ which intuitively read: when β is true, making c_1 true is the most preferred option and only when c_1 cannot be made true, the next best option is to make c_2 true, ... Solutions of the generator program that are optimal w.r.t. the first optimizing program and, among those, are optimal w.r.t. the second optimizing program, and so on, are called preferred solutions for the ASO program.

The framework of ASO programming can be simply adapted to the setting of agents, i.e. just consider the generator program as agent A_1 and the optimizing programs as agents $A_2, \ldots, A_n$. The resulting semantics is very similar to our approach. However, ASO programs are far more limited w.r.t. their expressiveness. It turns out that the expressiveness of an ASO program does not depend on the length of the sequence of optimizing programs, but it is always Σ_2^P-complete. This yields that ASO programs can easily be captured by the presented agent systems in this paper using two single agents. How these two agents simulating ASO programs can be constructed is subject to further research.

Weak constraints were introduced in [8] as a relaxation of the concept of a constraint. Intuitively, a weak constraint is allowed to be violated, but only as a last resort, meaning that one tries to minimize the number of violated constraints. Additionally, weak constraints are allowed to be hierarchically layered by means of a sequence of sets of weak constraints. Intuitively, one first chooses the answer sets that minimize the number of violated constraints in the first set of weak constraints in the sequence, and then, among those, one chooses the answer sets that minimize the number of violated constraints in the second set, etc.

Again, this approach can be "agentized" in a straightforward manner and will look similar to our approach. This time the complexity of such a system, independent of the number of sets of weak constraints, is at most Δ_3^P-complete. Thus, using the presented agent system from Section 3 with three single agents will suffice to capture the most expressive form of that formalism.

In [26, 40], hierarchies of preferences on a single program are presented. The preferences are expressible on both the literals and the rules in that program. It is shown that for a sequence of n agents the complexity of the system is Σ_{n+1}^P-complete. The semantics proposed in Section 3 is a generalization of that approach: instead of using one global program with agents only using preferences on that program, we equip each agent with her own, in general different, program and let her implement whatever optimizing strategy she wants. To simulate a hierarchy of n preference relations, we need $n + 1$ optimizing agents: the first one will correspond with the global program, while the rest will correspond to the n preference relations. The system described in Example 7 can be seen as a translation of such a preference hierarchy. Intuitively, agent A_2 describes the preference relation[9] $experienced < inexperienced$, while A_3 implements the relation $young < old$; $inexperienced < experienced$. Finally, A_4 corresponds to

---

[9] The expression $a < b$ means a is preferred upon b.

the single preference *female* < *male*. Further, the current approach also allows each agent to express its program by using any syntactical and semantical extension of answer set programming (not only preferences, but e.g. cardinality constraints), as long as the extension can be transformed into the (extended) answer set semantics[10]. Finally, [26, 40] only contained complexity results for the given semantics, while the current work also shows important expressiveness results.

In [33], a theory for coordinating agents is presented. When two agents A and B, which are represented by extended disjunctive programs, coordinate their answer sets, they can either opt for generating the union of their answer sets or the intersection. Their coordination act results in a new program that has the desired answer sets as outcome. Our approach is very different, our aim is to compromise on answer sets without changing the internal knowledge of our agents, i.e. the programs. Our agents share answer sets and not programs. Furthermore, in HAS a hierarchy is established, giving more power to some agents while in [33] agents are considered equal.

[14, 16] also present a multi-agent framework, LAIMA, were the agents are represented as logic programs. LAIMA allows agents to be connected in any sort of way, including loops. The HAS system presented in this paper places the most influential agents at the start of the sequence of agents, providing a top-down approach, while in LAIMA more power is given to agents were communication ends, as they can completely change the answer set even if this causes a contradiction. A more important difference is the absence of failure feedback in LAIMA. It is exactly this feedback that provides the increase in complexity for HAS .

In the Minerva architecture [29], the authors build their agents out of subagents that work on a common knowledge base written as a MDLP (Multi-Dimensional Logic Programs) which is an extension of Dynamic Logic Programming. Our agents do not work with a common knowledge base; each agent decides what she wants to keep private or make available. Minerva does not restrict itself to modeling the beliefs of agents, but allows for full BDI-agents that can plan towards a certain goal. It would be interesting to see if this can also be incorporated in HAS . The complexity of the language used for representing the knowledge is similar. MDLP can be translated to extended logic programs. The procedure given [13] for DLP can easily be extended to MDLP. It is the failure feedback between agents that gives HAS its expressive power, not the expressiveness of the representation language. It would be very interesting to see MDLP used as the representation language of the agent HAS , giving users more flexibity in expressing preferences.

6   Conclusions and Directions for Further Research

We presented a framework suitable for solving hierarchical decision problems using simple logic programming agents that cooperate via a sequential communication channels. The resulting semantics turns out to be very expressive, as it essentially captures the polynomial hierarchy, thus enabling further complex applications. The framework

---

[10] Due to the results in [39], normal answer set programming can be reduced to extended answer set programming.

could be used to develop implementations for diagnostic systems at the third level of the polynomial hierarchy [17, 19, 43].

Future work comprises the development of a dedicated implementation of the approach, using existing answer set solvers, e.g. DLV [24] or SMODELS [34], possibly in a distributed environment. Such an implementation will use a control structure that communicates candidate solutions between consecutive agents. For the implementation of this control loop and the communication between the agents, we foresee the use of JADE [28] and Protégé [32] in much the same way as it is been done for the LAIMA system [14].

In the context of an implementation, it is also interesting to investigate which conditions an agent has to fulfil in order for it not to lift the complexity up one level in the polynomial hierarchy, yielding possible optimizations of the computation and communication processes.

Once the system is implemented we will have the opportunity to work on larger applications. One of our goals, is to try to incorporate the ALIAS [9] system, an agent architecture for legal reasoning based on abductive logic, into ours. The Carell multi-agent system [44] for allocation organs and tissue would be an interesting test case.

In terms of integration it would be nice to see how HAS could possibly work together with agents written for the Dali [11] or Socs [23, 35] platforms, two agent platforms using logic programming languages to model the agents.

At present, we only work with a linear sequence of communication channels. We plan to look into a broader class of communication structures, like for example trees or more generally, a (strict) partial ordering of agents.

Finally, we would like to experiment with the language(s) used for our agents. The definitions of hierarchical agent system and the corresponding hierarchical answer set do not rely on the formalisms used to represent the agents but on the generation of answer sets. Even the generation of these can be debated, as it suffices that agents communicate sets of literals.

References

[1] C. Baral. *Knowledge Representation, Reasoning and Declarative Problem Solving*. Cambridge Press, 2003.

[2] C. Baral and M. Gelfond. Reasoning agents in dynamic domains. In *Logic-based artificial intelligence*, pages 257–279. Kluwer Academic Publishers, 2000.

[3] M. Brain, T. Crick, M. De Vos, and J. Fitch. Toast: Applying answer set programming to superoptimisation. In *Proceedings of the 22nd International Conference on Logic Programming (ICLP2006)*, volume 4079 of *LNCS*, pages 270–284. Springer, 2006.

[4] G. Brewka, I. Niemela, and T. Syrjanen. Implementing ordered disjunction using answer set solvers for normal programs. In *Proceedings of the 8th European Conference on Logics in Artificial Intelligence (JELIA 2002)*, volume 2424 of *LNAI*, pages 444–455. Springer, 2002.

[5] G. Brewka, I. Niemelä, and M. Truszczynski. Answer set optimization. In G. Gottlob and T. Walsh, editors, *IJCAI*, pages 867–872. Morgan Kaufmann, 2003.

[6] F. Buccafurri and G. Caminiti. A social semantics for multi-agent systems. In C. Baral, G. Greco, N. Leone, and G. Terracina, editors, *LPNMR*, volume 3662 of *Lecture Notes in Computer Science*, pages 317–329. Springer, 2005.

[7] F. Buccafurri and G. Gottlob. Multiagent compromises, joint fixpoints, and stable models. In *Computational Logic: Logic Programming and Beyond, Essays in Honour of Robert A. Kowalski, Part I*, volume 2407 of *LNCS*, pages 561–585. Springer, 2002.

[8] F. Buccafurri, N. Leone, and P. Rullo. Strong and weak constraints in disjunctive datalog. In *Proceedings of the 4th International Conference on Logic Programming (LPNMR '97)*, pages 2–17, 1997.

[9] A. Ciampolini and P. Torroni. Using abductive logic agents for modeling the judicial evaluation of crimimal evidence. *Applied Artificial Intelligence*, 18:251–275, 2004.

[10] O. Cliffe, M. De Vos, and J. Padget. Specifying and analysing agent-based social institutions using answer set programming. In *Selected revised papers from the workshops on Agent, Norms and Institutions for Regulated Multi-Agent Systems (ANIREM) and Organizations and Organization Oriented Programming (OOOP) at AAMAS'05*, volume 3913 of *LNCS*, pages 99–113. Springer, 2006.

[11] S. Costantini and A. Tocchio. Context-based Commmonsense Reasoning in the DALI Logic Programmming Language. In *Proceedings of the 4th International and Interdisciplinary Conference, Context 2003*, volume 2680 of *LNAI*. Springer, 2003.

[12] E. Dantsin, T. Eiter, G. Gottlob, and A. Voronkov. Complexity and expressive power of logic programming. *ACM Computing Surveys*, 33(3):374–425, 2001.

[13] M. De Vos. Implementing Ordered Choice Logic Programming using Answer Set Solvers. In *Third International Symposium on Foundations of Information and Knowledge Systems (FoIKS'04)*, volume 2942, pages 59–77, Vienna, Austria, Feb. 2004. Springer Verlag.

[14] M. De Vos, T. Crick, J. Padget, M. Brain, O. Cliffe, and J. Needham. A Multi-agent Platform using Ordered Choice Logic Programming. In *Declarative Agent Languages and Technologies (DALT'05)*, 2005.

[15] M. De Vos and D. Vermeir. Choice Logic Programs and Nash Equilibria in Strategic Games. In J. Flum and M. Rodríguez-Artalejo, editors, *Computer Science Logic (CSL'99)*, volume 1683 of *LNCS*, pages 266–276, Madrid, Spain, 1999. Springer Verslag.

[16] M. De Vos and D. Vermeir. Extending Answer Sets for Logic Programming Agents. *Annals of Mathematics and Artifical Intelligence*, 42(1–3):103–139, Sept. 2004. Special Issue on Computational Logic in Multi-Agent Systems.

[17] T. Eiter, W. Faber, N. Leone, and G. Pfeifer. The diagnosis frontend of the dlv system. *AI Communications*, 12(1-2):99–111, 1999.

[18] T. Eiter, W. Faber, N. Leone, G. Pfeifer, and A. Polleres. The DLV^k planning system. In *Proceedings of the 8th European Conference on Logics in Artificial Intelligence (JELIA 2002)*, volume 2424 of *LNAI*, pages 541–544. Springer, 2002.

[19] T. Eiter and G. Gottlob. The complexity of logic-based abduction. *Journal of the Association for Computing Machinery*, 42(1):3–42, 1995.

[20] T. Eiter, G. Gottlob, and Y. Gurevich. Normal forms for second-order logic over finite structures, and classification of np optimization problems. *Annals of Pure and Applied Logic*, 78(1-3):111–125, 1996.

[21] T. Eiter, G. Gottlob, and H. Mannila. Disjunctive datalog. *ACM Transactions on Database Systems*, 22(3):364–418, 1997.

[22] T. Eiter and A. Polleres. Towards automated integration of guess and check programs in answer set programming. In *Proceedings of the 7th International Conference on Logic Programming and Nonmonotonic Reasoning (LPNMR 2004)*, volume 2923 of *LNCS*, pages 100–113. Springer, 2004.

[23] U. Endriss, N. Maudet, F. Sadri, and F. Toni. Logic-based agent communication protocols. In *Advances in Agent Communication*, volume 2922 of *LNAI*, pages 91–107. Springer, 2004.

[24] W. Faber and G. Pfeifer. dlv homepage. http://www.dbai.tuwien.ac.at/proj/dlv/.

[25] M. Gelfond and V. Lifschitz. The stable model semantics for logic programming. In *Proceedings of the Fifth International Conference and Symposium on Logic Programming*, pages 1070–1080. The MIT Press, 1988.

[26] S. Heymans, D. Van Nieuwenborgh, and D. Vermeir. Hierarchical decision making by autonomous agents. In *Proceedings of 9th European Conference on Logics in Artificial Intelligence (JELIA2004)*, volume 3229 of *LNCS*, pages 44–56. Springer, 2004.

[27] N. Immerman. *Descriptive Complexity*. Springer, 1999.

[28] Jade:. http://jade.tilab.com/.

[29] J. A. Leite, J. J. Alferes, and L. M. Pereira. Minerva - a dynamic logic programming agent architecture. In *Intelligent Agents VIII*, number 2002 in LNAI, pages 141–157. Springer, 2002.

[30] V. Lifschitz. Answer set programming and plan generation. *Journal of Artificial Intelligence*, 138(1-2):39–54, 2002.

[31] C. H. Papadimitriou. *Computational Complexity*. Addison Wesley, 1994.

[32] Protégé. http://protege.stanford.edu/.

[33] C. Sakama and K. Inoue. Coordination between logical agents. In *Proceedings of the 5th International Workshop on Computational Logic in Multi-Agent Systems (CLIMA-V)*, volume 3487 of *LNAI*, pages 161–177. Springer, 2005.

[34] P. Simons. smodels homepage. http://www.tcs.hut.fi/Software/smodels/.

[35] SOCS:. http://lia.deis.unibo.it/research/socs/.

[36] T. Soininen and I. Niemelä. Developing a declarative rule language for applications in product configuration. In *Proceedings of the First International Workshop on Practical Aspects of Declarative Languages (PADL '99)*, LNCS, San Antonio, Texas, 1999. Springer.

[37] L. Stockmeyer and A. Meyer. Word problems requiring exponential time. In *Proceedings of the 5th ACM Symposium on Theory of Computing (STOC '73)*, pages 1–9, 1973.

[38] D. Van Nieuwenborgh, M. De Vos, S. Heymans, and D. Vermeir. Hierarchical decision making in multi-agent systems using answer set programming. Technical report, Vrije Universiteit Brussel, Dept. of Computer Science, 2005.

[39] D. Van Nieuwenborgh, S. Heymans, and D. Vermeir. Approximating extended answer sets. In *Proceedings of the 17th European Conference on Artificial Intelligence (ECAI 2006)*. IOS Press.

[40] D. Van Nieuwenborgh, S. Heymans, and D. Vermeir. On programs with linearly ordered multiple preferences. In *Proceedings of 20th International Conference on Logic Programming (ICLP 2004)*, number 3132 in LNCS, pages 180–194. Springer, 2004.

[41] D. Van Nieuwenborgh and D. Vermeir. Preferred answer sets for ordered logic programs. In *Proceedings of the 8th European Conference on Logics in Artificial Intelligence (JELIA 2002)*, volume 2424 of *LNAI*, pages 432–443. Springer, 2002.

[42] D. Van Nieuwenborgh and D. Vermeir. Order and negation as failure. In *Proceedings of the 19th International Conference on Logic Programming*, volume 2916 of *LNCS*, pages 194–208. Springer, 2003.

[43] D. Van Nieuwenborgh and D. Vermeir. Ordered diagnosis. In *Proceedings of the 10th International Conference on Logic for Programming, Artificial Intelligence, and Reasoning (LPAR2003)*, volume 2850 of *LNAI*, pages 244–258. Springer, 2003.

[44] J. Vázquez-Salceda, J. Padget, U. Cortés, A. López-Navidad, and F. Caballero. Formalizing an electronic institution for the distribution of human tissues. *Artificial Intelligence in Medicine*, 27(3):233–258, 2003. published by Elsevier.

[45] T. Wakaki, K. Inoue, C. Sakama, and K. Nitta. Computing preferred answer sets in answer set programming. In *Proceedings of the 10th International Conference on Logic for Programming, Artificial Intelligence, and Reasoning (LPAR2003)*, volume 2850 of *LNAI*, pages 259–273. Springer, 2003.

On a Linear Framework for Belief Dynamics in Multi-agent Environments

Akira Fusaoka, Katsunori Nakamura, and Mitsunari Sato

Department of Human and Machine Intelligence, Ritsumeikan University
Nojihigashi, Kusatsu-city, SIGA, 525-8577, Japan
fusaoka@ci.ritsumei.ac.jp

Abstract. In this paper, we discuss the dynamics of multi-agent belief change in the framework of linear algebra. We regard an epistemic state of each agent as an element in the vector space spanned by the basis of possible worlds, so that belief change corresponds to a linear transformation on this vector space. The compound belief states of multi-agents are treated by using the product tensor of the vector for each agent. In this formulation, the reasoning in the process of belief change can be reduced to the matrix and tensor calculation.

1 Introduction

In this paper, we present a framework of the linear algebra to deal with the dynamics of belief change under multi-agent environment. An epistemic state of each agent is represented by using the vector of subjective probability that she conceives for each possible world. The information that causes the belief change is treated as the operator on this vector space. The observation of a new fact about the current world is characterized as a projection matrix and time evolution (world change) is treated by a stochastic matrix. The compound belief states in the multi-agent environment are represented by using a tensor structure on this vector space.

Belief dynamics has been studied intensively and there have been a lot of work in the fields of AI, philosophy and game theory. Roughly speaking, these works deal with the following characteristics or difficulties of multi-agent belief change.

C1: Since the belief change contains reasoning about knowledge or linguistic information, the logical formulation is indispensable. On the other hand, agent's beliefs and information are sometimes uncertain so that the strength of belief (probability or plausibility grading) is also necessary. The essential problem is that these types of epistemic attitudes should be integrated in a unified framework since we use the mixture of the logical and probabilistic beliefs and information in a daily life such as " *if prob(A|B) > r and P then Q*". Gärdenfores and his colleagues introduce the axiomatic method for the belief dynamics and give the characterization of the belief revision in the form of the postulates, which is the common foundation to logical and probabilistic belief change (AGM-Theory)[1,8].

K. Inoue, K. Satoh, and F. Toni (Eds.): CLIMA VII, LNAI 4371, pp. 41–59, 2007.
© Springer-Verlag Berlin Heidelberg 2007

C2: There are two flows of time, one for the mental process and another for the world change. Katsuno and Mendelzon extend AGM-Theory to the belief change forced by the change of the world (KM-Theory) [11,12]. Therefore, we need a general framework again to deal with two types of dynamics for belief change: one for belief update caused by ontic actions (time evolution) and another for belief revision caused by epistemic actions.

C3: In the multi-agent environment, it is necessary to deal with the revision or update of beliefs about other agents and the belief change caused by the higher-order beliefs (beliefs about the other agents' beliefs about the other agents' belief $\cdots$), and also revision or update of common knowledge. There have been a lot of significant works for this problem from the logical standpoint [2,3,9,10]. Although AGM-Theory and KM-Theory give a firm basis for the multi-agent belief change, there seems to be some difficulties in the straightforward extension of these theories to the multi-agent case [14].

In the previous work [7], we introduced a linear theory for the belief change in the case of a single agent. In this paper, we present a linear framework to deal with multi-agent belief change based on the previous work. Our method seems to be rather standard formulation of the general dynamics in other fields but radically different from the existing approaches of belief change. However, it can be regarded as a representation or model of the AGM-Theory and KM-Theory because every axiomatic requirement in these theories holds in this linear theory of belief dynamics for the case of non-introspective single agent.

The following four principles are the basis of our method.

P1: the epistemic state (internal) is a vector
    We represent an epistemic state of an agent by a vector of the subjective probability which she holds for each possible world. This is called a pure state. We consider that a set of the epistemic states constitutes a vector space spanned by the basis of possible worlds, which is called the belief space.

P2: Information is an operator
    The information about the state of the world (observation) is treated as a projection matrix. Let A be a factual knowledge and u be an epistemic state in a belief space W. The state $u \in W$ transfers to $Au \in W$ after A is learned.

    The information about the change of the world is also treated by the operator(the stochastic matrix) which transforms a belief space W to another space W'. Namely, each possible world shifts to other possible worlds with some probability by an (nondeterministic) action.

P3: the belief state (external) is a tensor
    The belief state of an agent a is observed as a tensor of the pure epistemic states from the outside of a. We call it an ensemble. The ensemble represents a's beliefs at each possible world. An introspective agent sometimes treats her own epistemic state as an object in the mental process. This objected epistemic state is also represented by an ensemble.

P4: the compound belief space is a product tensor
   We deal with the compound beliefs of multi-agent by using the tensor product of the ensembles of each agent. When a group of agents holds a common
   belief, they share the same belief space.

   Through the introduction of the linear formulation to the belief dynamics,
we aim at to present a general, unified and efficient treatment for belief change.
Namely, it is motivated by the following reasons.

M1: The linear model covers the principal operations of both the logical and
   the probabilistic belief change: the belief expansion, the belief revision and
   the belief update. And it also covers the probabilistic belief change such as
   Bayesian conditioning and Lewis's imaging [13].
M2: We can give a matrix representation for any information as a linear approximation. The linearity is not necessarily a strong constraint for the broader
   class of knowledge such as the factual knowledge, conditionals, and the information about other's belief [7].
M3: Since various procedures for reasoning in the belief change can be reduced
   to matrix and tensor calculation in our linear framework, we can present
   a simple and unified method to deal with the belief change. Although the
   matrix representation of knowledge seems to be redundant, the efficient
   implementation is possible because it is usually sparse.

2 Linear Framework for Belief

2.1 An Epistemic State

Let $\mathcal{L}_P$ be a propositional language. Throughout this paper, we deal the sentences of $\mathcal{L}_P$. Also we often use the modal operators $K_a\varphi, B_a\varphi$ to represent "an
agent a knows φ" and "an agent a believes φ", which satisfy the axiom system
KT45, KD45 respectively. We denote this language by $\mathcal{L}_D$.

Definition 1 (Possible world). *Let $\{e_1, e_2, \cdots, e_n\}$ be a set of possible worlds.
We write $e_i \models_P \varphi$ if a sentence $\varphi \in \mathcal{L}_P$ is true in e_i, namely e_i is φ-world.*

Definition 2 (A space of epistemic space)

*(1) Let $W(e_1, e_2, \cdots, e_n)$ be a vector space spanned by the basis $\{e_1, e_2, \cdots, e_n\}$.
   We assume that $\{e_1, e_2, \cdots, e_n\}$ gives the orthonormal basis of W. The point
   $u \in W$ is a superposition of the basis, that is $u = \alpha^1 e_1 + \alpha^2 e_2 + \cdots + \alpha^n e_n$,
   which we denote by $u = (\alpha^1, \alpha^2, \cdots, \alpha^n)$ where $0 \leq \alpha^i \leq 1$ and $\sum_{i=1}^{n} \alpha^i =
   1$. Intuitively, α^i means the subjective probability for the possible world e_i,
   namely the strength of the belief that e_i actually coincides with the real world.*
*(2) We denote the dual vector space of $W(e_1, e_2, \cdots, e_n)$ by $W^*(e^1, e^2, \cdots, e^n)$
   where $(e^1, e^2, \cdots, e^n)$ is the dual basis to $(e_1, e_2, \cdots, e_n)$. Mathematically,
   W^* is the vector space of a linear mapping $x : W \to \mathbb{R}$ such that $x(u) =
   x_1\alpha^1 + x_2\alpha^2 + \cdots + x_n\alpha^n$ for $x = (x_1, x_2, \cdots, x_n)$ and $u = (\alpha^1, \alpha^2, \cdots, \alpha^n)$.*

We define the epistemic state of an agent as a contravariant vector $u \in W$. This is called the pure epistemic state. On the other hands, the dual (covariant) vector of $v^* \in W^*$ is introduced to deal with the belief states of other agents. Each possible world e_i is also regarded as a vector in W of which i-th element is 1 and all other elements are 0.

(3) When the superindex and subindex with the same letter appear, we often omit the symbol $\sum$ according to the Einstein's notation such a way that

$$u = \sum_i \alpha^i e_i = \alpha^i e_i, v = \sum_k x_k e^k = x_k e^k.$$

(4) For any $u = (\alpha^1, \alpha^2, \cdots, \alpha^n)$, $u \models \varphi$ if and only if $e_i \models_P \varphi$ for all e_i such that $\alpha^i \neq 0$.

We define the formula $Bel(u)$ associated with u by

$$Bel(u) = \bigwedge \varphi \text{ where } u \models \varphi.$$

For any sentence φ, the strength of belief for a sentence φ at a state u is given by

$$prob(\varphi, u) = \Sigma_i \alpha^i \text{ for } e_i \models_P \varphi.$$

Note that $prob(\varphi, u) = 1$ if and only if $u \models \varphi$. The vectors u, v are said to be qualitatively equivalent if and only if $Bel(u) = Bel(v)$.

Definition 3 (Normalization). A vector $u = (\alpha^1, \alpha^2, \cdots, \alpha^n)$ is a provability distribution so that it must be normalized. We denote the normalization operator by ν. Namely,

$$(\nu(u))_i = \frac{\alpha^i}{\alpha^1 + \alpha^2 + \cdots + \alpha^n}.$$

2.2   Time Evolution

Definition 4 (Action). An action or a change of world is a mapping from $W(e_1, e_2, \cdots, e_n)$ to $W'(e_1', e_2', \cdots, e_n')$ where $Bel(e_i) = Bel(e_i')$ for all i. When an action is performed at some world e_j, it is transferred to the other worlds. We assume that action is non-deterministic, so that e_j is transferred to $e_1', e_2', \cdots, e_n'$ with the probability p_{ij}. Therefore, $\Sigma_i p_{ij} = 1$, namely, the matrix $A = (p_{ij})$ is a stochastic matrix. If A is regular, we can regard this transaction as the basis transformation.

2.3   Operator for Information

The information which changes the agent's beliefs is represented by an operator in this epistemic space, which transforms one epistemic state to another. We assume that this transformation is linear. And also it must be a projection since the epistemic state is invariant for the given information if it is already known. Namely, the operator must be represented by the projection matrix which satisfies the condition $A^2 = A$, which we call " the knowledge operator".

Definition 5 (Knowledge operator). *Let A be an $n \times n$ matrix. A is called a knowledge operator if A is a projection, namely $A^2 = A$.*

When an agent learns information A at the state u, her state is transferred to Au. Because $A(Au) = Au$, the eigenvalue of the knowledge operator is 1 and the result state Au is the eigenvector of A. Namely, when an agent knows A, her epistemic state is dropped into the eigenstate of A.

Let $S(A) = \{Ax \mid x \in W\}$ and $Ker(A) = \{y \mid Ay = 0$ for $y \in W\}$. It is known that W is separated to two subspace $S(A)$ and $Ker(A)$ by a projection A, that is, $W = S(A) \oplus Ker(A)$. Also, for every subspace U, there is a projection A such that $S(A) = U$.

$S(A)$ is a set of states in which A is known. On the other hand, $Ker(A)$ is a set of states in which A is believed to be false. The projection $E - A$ generates a subspace $Ker(A)$ so that $E - A$ is regarded as a negation of A. We represent the negation $E - A$ by $\bar{A}$. Also we can introduce the AND, OR operations of projections formally. Namely, AND: $A \cap B$ is defined by $S(A \cap B) = S(A) \cap S(B)$ and OR: $A \cup B$ is given by the condition that $S(A \cup B)$ is the largest subspace such that $S(A \cup B) \subseteq S(A) \cup S(B)$. However, these logical operations $\bar{A}, A \cap B, A \cup B$ do not necessarily form propositional logic (generally, they satisfy the axioms of quantum logic). Moreover, "B is learned after A" is not necessarily equivalent to "A is learned after B", that is $AB \neq BA$ in general. When A, B are commutative, AB becomes the projection matrix such that $S(AB) = S(BA) = S(A) \cap S(B)$. This means that we can't learn A and B simultaneously unless $AB = BA$. This is one of the reasons why the iteration of the revision or the update is so complicated.

Definition 6 (Diagonal projection). *An $n \times n$ matrix Δ is called a diagonal projection if and only if its diagonal entries are 0 or 1, and all other entries are 0. A diagonal projection is regarded as a matrix form for the sentence of $\mathcal{L}_P$. Namely, a sentence φ corresponds to the diagonal projection Δ_φ such that $\Delta_\varphi(ii) = 1$ if $e_i \models \varphi$ else $\Delta_\varphi(ii) = 0$, and also $\Delta_\varphi(ij) = 0$ if $i \neq j$.*

The following theorem is the characterization of the projection [16].

Theorem 1. *For any projection P, there exists a regular matrix T such that $P = T^{-1}\Delta T$, where Δ is a diagonal projection.*

By this theorem, we can introduce a partition of the set of all projections such that the logical operations $\bar{A}, A \cap B, A \cup B$ satisfies the axioms of propositional logic in each class.

Definition 7 (Knowledge class). *For any regular matrix T, a set of projection K_T is defined as*

$$K_T = \{P \mid P = T^{-1}\Delta T \text{ for some } \Delta\}.$$

Each class K_T forms a propositional logic by the operations $\bar{A}, A \cap B, A \cup B$.

Theorem 2
(1) For any $A, B \in K_T, AB = BA$.
(2) Assume that $A = T^{-1}\Delta_\varphi T, B = T^{-1}\Delta_\psi T$. Then,
$\bar{A} = E - A = T^{-1}\Delta_{\neg\varphi} T$,
$A \cap B = AB = T^{-1}\Delta_{\varphi\wedge\psi} T$,
$A \cup B = A + B - AB = T^{-1}\Delta_{\varphi\vee\psi} T$.
K_T forms a propositional logic with these operations.

Theorem 2 means that for any regular matrix T, there exists a knowledge class K_T in which the logical reasoning is possible. Note that it is not necessary that $AB = BA$ if A, B belong to the different classes.

3   The Belief Change of the Single Agent

3.1   The Operators for the Belief Change

We review how the belief change can be formulated in this linear framework. The detailed discussion is given in [7].

(1) **Belief Expansion:** When the knowledge φ is consistent with the epistemic state u, the new state is given by eliminating the $\neg\varphi$-world and by normalizing the remaining probability. This is called the belief expansion that is the belief change in accordance with Bayes' rule. A diagonal projection Δ_φ is a knowledge operator corresponding to the belief expansion by φ. Since it is an element of K_E for the identity matrix E, the expansion by ψ after the expansion φ is equivalent to the expansion by $\psi \wedge \varphi$. Namely,

$$\Delta_\varphi \Delta_\psi u = \Delta_{\psi\wedge\varphi} u \text{ if } \psi \wedge \varphi \text{ is consistent with } Bel(u).$$

(2) **Belief Revision:** When the knowledge φ is learned which conflicts with the epistemic state u, all-nonzero values of u must be reset to 0 and at least one of φ-world must have nonzero probability. Although there have been a lot of revision methods concerning how to determine the probability of the φ-world, we use the belief revision defined by AGM postulates [8]. We can define it as a matrix by using the Pearl's ε-theory [4]. Let H be a matrix such that $H_{ij} = \varepsilon^{\mu_{ij}}$ for $i \neq j$ and $H_{ii} = 0$ where μ_{ij} is a distance from e_i to e_j and ε is a very small number, namely an infinitesimal. The revision matrix R_φ is a projection given by $R_\varphi = \Delta_\varphi + \Delta_\varphi H \Delta_{\neg\varphi}$.

Theorem 3. *The revision operator R_φ satisfies the AGM postulates for probabilistic belief revision [8] (the proof is given in [7]).*

1. *$prob(\varphi, R_\varphi) = 1$.*
2. *If $\vdash \varphi \equiv \psi$ then $R_\varphi = R_\psi$.*
3. *$R_\varphi = O$ (zero matrix) if and only if $\vdash \neg\varphi$.*
4. *If $prob(\varphi, u) > 0$ then $R_\varphi u = \Delta_\varphi u$ for all u such that $u \neq 0$*
5. *if $prob(\psi, R_\varphi u) > 0$ then $R_\psi R_\varphi u = R_{\varphi\wedge\psi} u$.*

(3) **Belief Update:** When an agent receives in the state u the information that φ becomes to be true after some unspecified change of the world, she imagines a set of φ-worlds after the minimal change of the world(KM-Theory). This thinking process can be implemented by a matrix which is a projection and is also stochastic. Let D be an $n \times n$ regular matrix such that

$$d_{ii} = 0; \quad d_{ij} = \rho^{\mu_{ij}} \text{ for all } i, j$$

where ρ is a real number such that $0 < \rho < 1$ and $\Sigma_i \rho^{\mu_{ij}} = 1$ for each j. Intuitively, d_{ij} represents the quantity of probability shifted from the world i to the world j so that $\sum_i d_{ij} = 1$.

For any sentence φ and the matrix D, the belief update operator on φ is given by

$$M_\varphi = \Delta_\varphi + \Gamma_\varphi \text{ where } \Gamma_\varphi = \Delta_\varphi D \Delta_{\neg\varphi}(E - \Delta_{\neg\varphi} D \Delta_{\neg\varphi})^{-1}.$$

Theorem 4. *The update operator M_φ satisfies the KM postulates for belief update [11] (the proof is given in [7]).*

1. $M_\varphi u \models \varphi$.
2. *If* $u \models \varphi$ *then* $M_\varphi u = u$.
3. *If* $\vdash \varphi \equiv \psi$ *then* $M_\varphi = M_\psi$.
4. $M_\varphi = O$ *(zero matrix) if and only if* $\vdash \neg\varphi$.
5. *If* $M_\varphi \models \psi$ *and* $M_\psi \models \varphi$ *then* $M_\varphi = M_\psi$.

3.2 Example

We give an simple example of the belief change in AGM-Theory, KM-Theory and our formulation for comparison.

Example 1 (The book and the magazine). [12]
We consider the language with only two propositional letters P, Q where P means the book is on the table and Q means the magazine is on the table. The possible world is given by

$$W = \{e_1 = \{P \wedge Q\}, e_2 = \{\neg P \wedge Q\}, e_3 = \{P \wedge \neg Q\}, e_4 = \{\neg P \wedge \neg Q\}\}.$$

Assume that an agent a believes that $\psi \equiv \neg P \wedge Q \vee P \wedge \neg Q$.

(1) belief expansion
When the agent a observes that "the book is on the table", she changes her belief according to the belief expansion since this information is consistent with ψ. In AGM-Theory, her epistemic state is represented by a propositional formula $\neg P \wedge Q \vee P \wedge \neg Q$. This state is changed to $\psi \circ \mu$ by the information $\mu = P$ where $\psi \circ \mu$ denotes the revision of ψ by μ. By using the AGM postulates, $\psi \circ \mu = P \wedge \neg Q$ [1].

In our formulation, the epistemic state is given by $u = (0, \alpha_1, \alpha_2, 0)$ and the revision operator for the information μ is given by a matrix Δ_P

$$\Delta_P = \begin{pmatrix} 1&0&0&0 \\ 0&0&0&0 \\ 0&0&1&0 \\ 0&0&0&0 \end{pmatrix}.$$

The result is given by

$$u' = \Delta_P u = \begin{pmatrix} 1&0&0&0 \\ 0&0&0&0 \\ 0&0&1&0 \\ 0&0&0&0 \end{pmatrix}\begin{pmatrix} 0 \\ \alpha_1 \\ \alpha_2 \\ 0 \end{pmatrix} = \begin{pmatrix} 0 \\ 0 \\ \alpha_2 \\ 0 \end{pmatrix} \to \begin{pmatrix} 0 \\ 0 \\ 1 \\ 0 \end{pmatrix} \text{ (by normalization)}.$$

(2) belief revision

Assume that the agent a observes that "both the book and the magazine are on the table", namely $\mu = P \wedge Q$. Since μ contradicts to her belief ψ, she must revise her belief in order to maintain consistency. In AGM theory, we have $\psi \circ \mu = P \wedge Q$ by using the AGM postulates [1].

In our formulation, however, the revision (and also update) operators depends on the distance between possible worlds. In order to calculate the revision and update operators, we use the distance of two worlds that is measured by the number of propositional letters in which they differ. Then the revision operator for μ is given by a matrix

$$R_{P \wedge Q} = \Delta_{P \wedge Q}(E + H\Delta_{\neg(P \wedge Q)}) = \begin{pmatrix} 1 & \varepsilon & \varepsilon & \varepsilon^2 \\ 0&0&0&0 \\ 0&0&0&0 \\ 0&0&0&0 \end{pmatrix} \text{ where } H = \begin{pmatrix} 0 & \varepsilon & \varepsilon & \varepsilon^2 \\ \varepsilon & 0 & \varepsilon^2 & \varepsilon \\ \varepsilon & \varepsilon^2 & 0 & \varepsilon \\ \varepsilon^2 & \varepsilon & \varepsilon & 0 \end{pmatrix}.$$

$$R_{P \wedge Q} u = \begin{pmatrix} (\alpha_1 + \alpha_2)\varepsilon \\ 0 \\ 0 \\ 0 \end{pmatrix} \to \begin{pmatrix} 1 \\ 0 \\ 0 \\ 0 \end{pmatrix} \text{ (normalization)}.$$

Although $(\alpha_1 + \alpha_2)\varepsilon$ is apparently close to 0 because ε is an infinitesimal, it gives the standard values 1 via the normalization.

Therefore, our formulation gives the same result as AGM-Theory.

(3) belief update

If the agent learned that "someone put the book on the table", she changes her belief according to the belief update. In KM-Theory, the state ψ is changed to $\psi \diamond \mu$ by the information $\mu = P$ where $\psi \diamond \mu$ denotes the update of ψ by μ. By the postulates of KM-Theory, $\psi \diamond \mu = P$ [12]. In our formulation, the update operator $M_{P \wedge Q}$ is given by

$$M_P = \Delta_P + \Delta_P D \Delta_{\neg P}(E - \Delta_{\neg P} D \Delta_{\neg P})^{-1}$$

where the stochastic matrix $D = (\rho^{\mu_{ij}})$ is

$$D = \begin{pmatrix} 0 & \rho & \rho & \rho^2 \\ \rho & 0 & \rho^2 & \rho \\ \rho & \rho^2 & 0 & \rho \\ \rho^2 & \rho & \rho & 0 \end{pmatrix}.$$

Since $2\rho + \rho^2 = 1$, $\rho = \sqrt{2} - 1$. Therefore, we have

$$M_P = \begin{pmatrix} 1 & 2 - \sqrt{2} & 0 & \sqrt{2} - 1 \\ 0 & 0 & 0 & 0 \\ 0 & \sqrt{2} - 1 & 1 & 2 - \sqrt{2} \\ 0 & 0 & 0 & 0 \end{pmatrix}.$$

So that the state u is changed to

$$M_P u = ((2 - \sqrt{2})\alpha_1, 0, (\sqrt{2} - 1)\alpha_1 + \alpha_2, 0).$$

This is qualitatively equivalent to the result of KM-Theory. Namely, $Bel(M_P u) = P$.

4 The Multi-agent Belief Space

In the case of a multi-agent environment or even in the introspective single-agent case, agents treat the higher-order beliefs such as beliefs about other agent's beliefs or beliefs about their own beliefs in addition to factual knowledge. In order to represent the higher-order beliefs, we introduce two concepts: the tensor product of pure epistemic states and the ensemble.

4.1 The Compound Belief Space for Multi-agent

We use the concept of product tensor to deal with the belief dynamics in the multi-agent environment, in which each agent has beliefs about both the real world and the other's beliefs, and also shares some beliefs via communications. In the following, we deal with the case of two agents. The extension to the case of more agents is straightforward.

Let $W_a(e_1, e_2, \cdots, e_n), W_b(e'_1, e'_2, \cdots, e'_n)$ be vector spaces of the agents a, b. The compound belief space of a, b is given by the product tensor $W_a \otimes W_b$.

Definition 8. *Let $W_a(e_1, e_2, \cdots, e_n), W_b(e'_1, e'_2, \cdots, e'_n)$ be vector spaces of the agents a, b.*

(1) a product tensor of pure states
For the pure epistemic states $u = (\alpha^1, \alpha^2, \cdots, \alpha^n)$ and $v = (\beta^1, \beta^2, \cdots, \beta^n)$, the product tensor $u \otimes v$ is defined by

$$u \otimes v = \alpha^i \beta^j e_i \otimes e_j$$
$$= (\alpha^1 \beta^1, \alpha^1 \beta^2, \cdots, \alpha^2 \beta^1, \alpha^2 \beta^2, \cdots, \alpha^n \beta^1, \alpha^n \beta^2, \cdots, \alpha^n \beta^n).$$

$u \otimes v$ is a contravariant tensor of rank 2. It informally means the mixed belief state of u and v.
(2) a tensor product of vector spaces
The compound belief space of a, b is given by the tensor product $W_a \otimes W_b$ which is regarded as the vector space with the $n \times n$ basis $e_i \otimes e'_j$.
  Note that an element of $W_a \otimes W_b$ is not necessarily a product tensor $u \otimes v$ of $u \in W_a$ and $v \in W_b$.

Definition 9 (a tensor of the operators). *Let the linear operators A, B operate on W_a and W_b respectively. Then the tensor product $A \otimes B$ is a linear operator on $W_a \otimes W_b$ such that*

$$(A \otimes B)(u \otimes v) = Au \otimes Bv \text{ for } u \in W_a, v \in W_b.$$

$A \otimes B$ means that the agent a learns A and the agent b learns B. When the agent a learns A after C and the agent b learns B after D, the successive operations satisfy

$$(A \otimes B)(C \otimes D) = (AC) \otimes (BD).$$

4.2   The Ensemble

We introduce here a mixed tensor $\varepsilon \in W \otimes W^*$ for $W(e_1, e_2, \cdots, e_n)$ and $W^*(e^1, e^2, \cdots, e^n)$ to deal with higher-order beliefs. An epistemic state itself is represented by using a vector of W, but the external view for the epistemic state of an agent depends on which possible world she actually resides in.

Definition 10 (ensemble)

1. *An ensemble ε_a for the agent a is a mixed tensor*

$$\varepsilon_a = \alpha_i^j e_j \otimes e^i$$

   where $\alpha_i^j \geq 0$. The ensemble ε_a means that the agent a appears to have an subjective probability α_i^j for the possible world e_j when she is in e_i.

2. *We introduce two sets of possible worlds:*

$$domain(\varepsilon_a) = \{e^i | \alpha_i^j \neq 0 \text{ for some } j\},$$
$$support(\varepsilon_a) = \{e_j | \alpha_i^j \neq 0 \text{ for some } i\}.$$

3. *matrix representation*
   An ensemble ε_a is a 2-rank mixed tensor. We usually represent the ensemble by a vector of the elements of W. Namely,

$$\varepsilon_a = (u_1, u_2, \cdots, u_n) \text{ where } u_i = (\alpha_i^1, \alpha_i^2, \cdots, \alpha_i^n) \in W.$$

   It can be also interpreted as a linear mapping $W \to W$ with the matrix form

$$\begin{pmatrix} \alpha_1^1 & \alpha_2^1 & \cdots & \alpha_n^1 \\ \alpha_1^2 & \alpha_2^2 & \cdots & \alpha_n^2 \\ & \cdots & \\ \alpha_1^n & \alpha_2^n & \cdots & \alpha_n^n \end{pmatrix}.$$

Note that $\sum_j \alpha_i^j = 1$. Namely, it is a stochastic matrix so that it also works as an operator on W. For $v = (\beta^1, \beta^2, \cdots, \beta^n) \in W$,

$$\varepsilon_a \cdot v = \mathcal{C}(2\ 3)(\alpha_i^j e_j \otimes e^i \otimes (\beta^k e_k)) = \mathcal{C}(2\ 3)(\alpha_i^j \beta^k e_j \otimes e^i \otimes e_k) = \alpha_i^j \beta^i e_j.$$

where $\mathcal{C}(2\ 3)$ is a contract operator which means to contract 2nd superindex and 3rd subindex. Namely $(\sum_k \alpha_k^j \beta^k) e_j$. The contraction is corresponding to the matrix product [15].

4. *a product of ensembles*

Let $\varepsilon_a = (u_1, u_2, \cdots, u_n), \varepsilon_b = (v_1, v_2, \cdots, v_n) \in W^n$. *Then the product of ensembles is given by*

$$\varepsilon_a \otimes \varepsilon_b = (u_1 \otimes v_1, u_1 \otimes v_2, \cdots, u_2 \otimes v_1, \cdots, u_n \otimes v_1, \cdots, u_n \otimes v_n).$$

When we can assume that both agent a and b reside in the same world, we have a simplified version:

$$\varepsilon_a \otimes \varepsilon_b = (u_1 \otimes v_1, u_2 \otimes v_2, \cdots, u_n \otimes v_n) \in (W \otimes W)^n.$$

We give an example of how the ensemble is used.

Example 2 (Ensemble)
Let P denote "it is raining" and $e_1 = \{P\}, e_2 = \{\neg P\}$. Suppose that an agent a, b have no information whether P, but the agent a knows that the agent b is very sensitive to the low atmospheric pressure, so that a believes
b has a subjective probability $\frac{2}{3}$ for e_1 and $\frac{1}{3}$ for e_2 if she is in e_1,
b has a subjective probability $\frac{1}{3}$ for e_1 and $\frac{2}{3}$ for e_2 if she is in e_2.
Namely the agent a holds the ensemble for b

$$\varepsilon_b = \frac{2}{3}e_1 \otimes e^1 + \frac{1}{3}e_2 \otimes e^1 + \frac{1}{3}e_1 \otimes e^2 + \frac{2}{3}e_2 \otimes e^2.$$

When a has a biased belief $v = (\frac{1}{4}, \frac{3}{4})$, he estimates the belief state of agent b to be

$$\varepsilon_b \cdot v = \mathcal{C}(2\ \ 3)(\tfrac{2}{3}e_1 \otimes e^1 + \tfrac{1}{3}e_2 \otimes e^1 + \tfrac{1}{3}e_1 \otimes e^2 + \tfrac{2}{3}e_2 \otimes e^2) \otimes (\tfrac{1}{4}e_1 + \tfrac{3}{4}e_2)$$
$$= \tfrac{5}{12}e_1 + \tfrac{7}{12}e_2.$$

Note that the ensemble can be regarded as the quantitative version of the Kripke model under the interpretation that the pair (e^i, e_i) corresponds to the possible world e_i of the kripke model and $\alpha_i^j \neq 0$ means the accessibility relation from the possible world e^i to e_j. Therefore, ε must satisfy the following properties for the language **KD45** and **KT45** from the corresponding theorem of the normal modal logic.

(1) Serial relation: $support(\varepsilon_a) \subseteq domain(\varepsilon_a)$.
(2) Transitive relation: $\forall i, j, k[\alpha_i^j \neq 0 \wedge \alpha_j^k \neq 0 \to \alpha_i^k \neq 0]$.
(3) Euclidean relation: $\forall i, j, k[\alpha_i^j \neq 0 \wedge \alpha_i^k \neq 0 \to \alpha_j^k \neq 0]$.
(4) Reflexive relation: $\forall i[\alpha_i^i \neq 0]$ for **KT45**. Namely, $support(\varepsilon_a) = domain(\varepsilon_a)$.

We call ε_a **KD45**-frame if it has the serial, transitive, and Euclidean relation. Also ε_a is called **KT45**-frame if $\alpha_{ij} \neq 0$ is an equivalence relation.

Definition 11 (logical valuation). *Let $W(e_1, e_2, \cdots, e_n)$ be a vector space and $\varepsilon_a, \varepsilon_b$ be ensembles of agents a, b. We extend the valuation $\models$ for $\mathcal{L}_P$ to $\mathcal{L}_D$.*

The concepts of validity in **KD45** *and* **KT45**-*frame are defined in [6] for the sentences of* $\mathcal{L}_D$.

$e_i \models \varphi$ *iff* $e_i \models_P \varphi$ *if* $\varphi \in \mathcal{L}_P$.

$e_i \models \neg\varphi$ *iff* $e_i \not\models \varphi$.

$e_i \models \varphi \supset \psi$ *iff* $e_i \not\models \varphi$ *or* $e_i \models \psi$.

$e_i \models K_a\varphi$ *iff* $\varphi \in \mathcal{L}_D$ *is a valid sentence in* **KD45**-*frame*$\mathcal{L}_D$ *or* $\alpha_i^i \neq 0 \wedge u_i \models \varphi$.

$e_i \models B_a\varphi$ *iff* φ *is a valid sentence in* **KT45**-*frame*$\mathcal{L}_D$ *or* $u_i \models \varphi$.

$u_i \models \varphi$ *iff* $\forall j[\alpha_i^j \neq 0 \supset e_j \models \varphi]$.

$e^i \models \varphi$ *is defined similarly. Note that* $e^i \models \varphi$ *if and only if* $e_i \models \varphi$

Definition 12. *We introduce the sets of* $\mathcal{L}_D$ *sentences such that*

$$Fom(e) = \{\varphi \in \mathcal{L}_D | e \models \varphi\},$$
$$Fom(u) = \{\varphi \in \mathcal{L}_D | u \models \varphi\},$$
$$Fom(\varepsilon_a) = \{\varphi \in \mathcal{L}_D | e \models \varphi \text{ for every } e \in domain(\varepsilon_a)\}.$$

4.3   Belief Structure of Agent

The belief space of an agent has a multi-layered structure which consists of the epistemic state, the belief state of her own belief, the beliefs about other's beliefs, the beliefs about other's beliefs about her beliefs, $\cdots$ and the common beliefs shared by other agents. The mental state in which the agent has some beliefs about the world is represented by the pure epistemic state (only one vector) because she knows unconsciously what she believes. On the other hand, she may hold the beliefs about her own beliefs consciously if she is an introspective agent. We distinguish strictly the pure state itself in which she believes something from the state for beliefs extracted from the pure state by the awareness or reflection. For an epistemic state u, the beliefs about u are represented by $u \otimes 1^*$. Note that this is the ensemble which gives an external view for her own epistemic state. The belief structure of other agent's beliefs is represented by using an ensemble because the agent may have an alternative candidate of the other's beliefs for each possible world. We need a distinct ensemble for each higher-order belief. In order to deal with this belief structure, we use a tensor product of each state. Therefore, if an introspective agent has an epistemic state u and the ensemble ε_b about other agent b, she conceives the belief structure $u \otimes (u \otimes 1^*) \otimes \varepsilon_b$. If agent a learns that φ is true but the agent b believes $\neg\varphi$, the operator $R_\varphi \otimes R_\varphi \otimes R_{\neg\varphi}$ is applied to $u \otimes (u \otimes 1^*) \otimes \varepsilon_b$.

Lindström and Rabinowicz gives the introspective belief change which shows some insufficiency in **AGM** postulate [14]. We gives our formulation for the belief change in the following example.

Example 3 (Rainy Uppsala)
Let P denote "it is raining in Uppsala". Suppose that an agent a has no information whether P or not, but she believes that she does not believe P. Namely, she has a beliefs set $\{\neg B_a P\}$. Then she is announced that P is true. So that

she revises her beliefs to $\{P, \neg B_a P\}$. We can not eliminate $\neg B_a P$ by the standard **AGM** belief revision because $P \wedge \neg B_a P$ is consistent. Believing $P \wedge \neg B_a P$, however, leads to the contradiction $B_a(B_a P \wedge \neg B_a P)$ in **KD45**.

In our formulation, the agent belief state is represented by $u \otimes 1^*$ where

$$u = \begin{pmatrix} \alpha^1 \\ \alpha^2 \end{pmatrix}, \quad u \otimes 1^* = \begin{pmatrix} \alpha^1 & \alpha^1 \\ \alpha^2 & \alpha^2 \end{pmatrix} \quad \text{where } e_1 = \{P\}, e_2 = \{\neg P\}.$$

By the belief revision $\Delta_P \otimes \Delta_P$, it is changed to

$$u = \begin{pmatrix} \alpha_1 \\ 0 \end{pmatrix}, \quad u \otimes 1^* = \begin{pmatrix} \alpha_1 & \alpha_1 \\ 0 & 0 \end{pmatrix}.$$

Therefore, there is no contradiction in our formulation. In general, however, the belief about the agent's own epistemic state is not always equivalent to the original epistemic state since she may learn something unconsciously. The disagreement of two states does not necessarily mean inconsistency.

4.4 The Information About Other's Belief

Usually the information about other's belief is given by linguistic form, namely by an operator, via communication. When agent a receives the information that b believes φ, she changes her beliefs about b's beliefs ε_b to $R_\varphi \varepsilon_b$. And also she may update her own epistemic state u to $R_\varphi u$ if she believes that b's belief is correct. However, the other's belief can be learned also by acquiring the epistemic state itself via observation. When agent a learns that the agent b's epistemic state is u, a's ensemble ε_b about b's belief is changed to be u by applying the operator $u \otimes 1^*$, because for $u = (\alpha^1, \alpha^2, \cdots, \alpha^n)$ and any vector $v = (\beta^1, \beta^2, \cdots, \beta^n)$,

$$(u \otimes 1^*) \cdot v = \mathcal{C}(2\ 3)((\alpha^j e_j \otimes e^i) \otimes (\beta^k e_k)) = \mathcal{C}(2\ 3)(\alpha^j \beta^k e_j \otimes e^i \otimes e_k)$$
$$= \sum_i \alpha^j \beta^i e_j = \alpha^j \sum_i \beta^i e_j = \alpha^j e_j = u.$$

Also $u \otimes 1^*$ is projection because

$$(u \otimes 1^*) \cdot (u \otimes 1^*) = \mathcal{C}(2\ 3)(\alpha^j e_j \otimes e^i) \otimes (\alpha^k e_k \otimes e^m)$$
$$= \mathcal{C}(2\ 3)(\alpha^j \alpha^k e_j \otimes e^i \otimes e_k \otimes e^m) = \sum_k \alpha^j \alpha^k e_j \otimes e_m$$
$$= (\sum_k \alpha^k) \alpha^j e_j \otimes e_m = \alpha^j e_j \otimes e_m = u \otimes 1^*.$$

On the other hand, the agent a may revise her own belief after learning b's state u. To do so, the logical contents $Bel(u)$ of u must be extracted. The revision operator $\Delta_{Bel(u)}$ is generated from u by the expansion

$$\Delta_{Bel(u)} = \sum_{i=1}^n \left(\frac{1}{\alpha^i} e_i \otimes e^i \right) u.$$

Sometimes agents may receive information about the ignorance of others. When a hears b saying "I don't know whether φ or not", a must change her beliefs about b's beliefs if a believes b knows φ. This is done by the operation on the ensemble rather than the vectors.

Definition 13 (Ignorance). *Let $\{u_1, u_2, \cdots, u_n\}$ be an ensemble for a's beliefs and let $\Theta(\varphi)$ be the information that a does not know whether φ or not. $\Theta(\varphi)$ requires that*

$$\Delta_\varphi u_i \neq 0 \text{ and } \Delta_{\neg\varphi} u_i \neq 0 \text{ for all } u_i$$

because $\Delta_\varphi u_i = 0$ means that a believes $\neg\varphi$ and $\Delta_{\neg\varphi} u_i = 0$ means that a believes φ. Therefore we eliminate u_i if it satisfies $\Delta_\varphi u_i = 0$ or $\Delta_{\neg\varphi} u_i = 0$.

4.5   Example

We give an example to show how these operations can be used for multi-agent belief change.

Example 4 (The book and the magazine again)
We consider the similar problem to example 1. The agent a believes that $\neg P \wedge Q \vee P \wedge \neg Q$ and also she believes that the agent b has the same belief. Someone comes to a and tell that (1) I put them on the table and (2) I informed b of the only fact that both are on the table. Assume that a believes this announcement. So that she updates her epistemic state and revises her beliefs about b's beliefs. The epistemic space W of the agent a is given by $W = \{e_1 = \{P \wedge Q\}, e_2 = \{\neg P \wedge Q\}, e_3 = \{P \wedge \neg Q\}, e_4 = \{\neg P \wedge \neg Q\}\}$. The initial epistemic state of a is u where $u = (0, \alpha_1, \alpha_2, 0)$ and the ensemble ε_b is

$$\varepsilon_b = \begin{pmatrix} 0 & 0 & 0 & 0 \\ 0 & \beta_1 & \beta_3 & 0 \\ 0 & \beta_2 & \beta_4 & 0 \\ 0 & 0 & 0 & 0 \end{pmatrix}.$$

Formally we treat the belief state of the agent a by using a tensor $u \otimes \varepsilon_b$. So that a's belief change caused by the announcement can be formulated by $(M_{P \wedge Q} \otimes R_{P \wedge Q})(u \otimes \varepsilon_b)$.

(1) The update matrix $M_{P \wedge Q}$ is given by

$$M_{P \wedge Q} = \Delta_{P \wedge Q}(E + D\Delta_{\neg(P \wedge Q)}(E - \Delta_{\neg(P \wedge Q)}D\Delta_{\neg(P \wedge Q)})^{-1}) = \begin{pmatrix} 1 & 1 & 1 & 1 \\ 0 & 0 & 0 & 0 \\ 0 & 0 & 0 & 0 \\ 0 & 0 & 0 & 0 \end{pmatrix}.$$

a's new state is given by $u' = M_{P \wedge Q}u = ((\alpha_1 + \alpha_2), 0, 0, 0)$. By the normalization, $u' = (1, 0, 0, 0)$.
(2) The revision matrix $R_{P \wedge Q}$ is given in the example 1. Therefore, ε_b is revised to be ε_b' where

$$\varepsilon_b' = R_{P \wedge Q}\varepsilon_b = \begin{pmatrix} 0 & (\beta_1 + \beta_2)\varepsilon & (\beta_3 + \beta_4)\varepsilon & 0 \\ 0 & 0 & 0 & 0 \\ 0 & 0 & 0 & 0 \\ 0 & 0 & 0 & 0 \end{pmatrix} \rightarrow \begin{pmatrix} 0 & 1 & 1 & 0 \\ 0 & 0 & 0 & 0 \\ 0 & 0 & 0 & 0 \\ 0 & 0 & 0 & 0 \end{pmatrix} \text{ (normalization)}.$$

Thus the new belief state of agent a is $u' \otimes \varepsilon_b'$.

5   Common Belief

5.1   Shared Space

When agents a, b have their epistemic states in the same space $W(e_1, e_2, \cdots, e_n)$, we call $W \otimes W$ the shared space. Agents must share the space if they have a common belief.

Definition 14 (common belief, common knowledge)
Let C be the set of sentences in $\mathcal{L_D}$ which contains at least all valid sentences.

(1) For a group of agents (a, b), the set C is called the B-closure if and only if

$$\text{for all } \varphi[\varphi \in C \to B_a\varphi \in C \land B_b\varphi \in C].$$

Similarly, the set C is called K-closure if and only if

$$\text{for all } \varphi[\varphi \in C \to K_a\varphi \in C \land K_b\varphi \in C].$$

(2) For a B-closure C, agents a, b have a set of common beliefs C at a possible world e if and only if for all $\varphi \in C, e \models \varphi$. Also they have a set of common knowledge C at a possible world e if and only if for all $\psi \in C, e \models \psi$ if C is a K-closure.

*(3) Let $Fom(\varepsilon) = \{\varphi \in \mathcal{L_D} | u \models \varphi$ for every $u \in \varepsilon\}$. For the ensembles $\varepsilon_a, \varepsilon_b \in W$ of **KD45**-frame, we say that $\varepsilon_a \otimes \varepsilon_b \in W$ defines a common belief φ if a B-closure $C = \{\varphi, B_a\varphi, B_b\varphi, B_aB_b\varphi, B_bB_a\varphi, \cdots\} \subseteq Fom(\varepsilon_a) \cap Fom(\varepsilon_b)$. Similarly, $\varepsilon_a \otimes \varepsilon_b \in V$ of **KT45**-frame defines a common knowledge φ if a K-closure $C = \{\varphi, B_a\varphi, B_b\varphi, B_aB_b\varphi, B_bB_a\varphi, \cdots\} \subseteq Fom(\varepsilon_a) \cap Fom(\varepsilon_b)$.*

We give the necessary and sufficient condition for the existence of a common belief.

Lemma 1 (necessity). *If the ensembles of **KD45**-frame $\varepsilon_a \otimes \varepsilon_b$ have a common belief $\varphi \in \mathcal{L_D}$ then the following sharing world condition holds*

SWCB: $support(\varepsilon_a) \subseteq domain(\varepsilon_b)$ and $support(\varepsilon_b) \subseteq domain(\varepsilon_a)$.

Proof. Assume that $C = \{\varphi, B_a\varphi, B_b\varphi, B_aB_b\varphi, B_bB_a\varphi, \cdots\} \subseteq Fom(\varepsilon_a) \cap Fom(\varepsilon_b)$. Then for all $e^i \in domain(\varepsilon_a)$, $e^i \models B_aB_b\varphi$. Since $u_i \models B_b\varphi$ for all u_i, $e_j \models B_b\varphi$ for all i, j such that $\alpha_i^j \neq 0$. So that $v_j \models \varphi$ for all j such that $e_j \in support(\varepsilon_a)$. Therefore, $support(\varepsilon_a) \subseteq domain(\varepsilon_b)$. By symmetry, $support(\varepsilon_b) \subseteq domain(\varepsilon_a)$.

Lemma 2 (sufficiency). *Let $\varepsilon_a, \varepsilon_b$ be **KD45**-frame. If **SWCB** holds then $Fom(\varepsilon_a) \cap Fom(\varepsilon_b)$ is a B-closure.*

Proof. Assume $\varphi \in Fom(\varepsilon_a) \cap Fom(\varepsilon_b)$. Then for all $e^i \in domain(\varepsilon_a) \cup domain(\varepsilon_b)$, $e^i \models \varphi$. Since $support(\varepsilon_a) \subseteq domain(\varepsilon_a)$, for all $e_j \in support(\varepsilon_a), e_j \models \varphi$. So that $u_i \models \varphi$ for all $u_i \neq 0$. Namely, for all $e^i \in domain(\varepsilon_a), e^i \models B_a\varphi$. So $B_a\varphi \in Fom(\varepsilon_a)$. Also, for all $e_j \in support(\varepsilon_b), e_j \models \varphi$ from **SWCB**. So that $v_i \models \varphi$ for all $v_i \neq 0$. This means $B_a\varphi \in Fom(\varepsilon_a)$. By symmetry of a, b, We have $Fom(\varepsilon_a) \cap Fom(\varepsilon_b)$ is a B-closure.

From Lemma 1 and Lemma 2, we have the following theorem.

Theorem 5 (common belief). *Let W be a shared space of the agents a, b and $\varepsilon_a = \{u_1, u_2, \cdots, u_n\}, \varepsilon_b = \{v_1, v_2, \cdots, v_n\}$ be their ensembles respectively. $Fom(\varepsilon_a) \cap Fom(\varepsilon_b)$ is a B-closure if and only if* **SWCB** *holds. Namely, $\varepsilon_a \otimes \varepsilon_b$ define the common beliefs $C = Fom(\varepsilon_a) \cap Fom(\varepsilon_b)$.*

Theorem 6 (common knowledge). *Let W be a shared space of the agents a, b and $\varepsilon_a = \{u_1, u_2, \cdots, u_n\}, \varepsilon_b = \{v_1, v_2, \cdots, v_n\}$ be* **KT45**-*frame.*

(1) $Fom(\varepsilon_a) \cap Fom(\varepsilon_b)$ is K-closure if and only if $\varepsilon_a, \varepsilon_b$ satisfies the following sharing world condition

$$\mathbf{SWCK:}\ support(\varepsilon_a) = support(\varepsilon_b).$$

(2) If **SWCK** *holds then $Fom(\varepsilon_a) = Fom(\varepsilon_b)$.*
Namely, $\varepsilon_a \otimes \varepsilon_b$ have the common knowledge $Fom(\varepsilon_a)$ if and only if $\varepsilon_a, \varepsilon_b$ satisfies **SWCK**.

Proof. (1) **if part:** Since the common knowledge is a common belief, **SWCB** holds. Namely, $support(\varepsilon_b) \subseteq domain(\varepsilon_a)$ and $support(\varepsilon_a) \subseteq domain(\varepsilon_b)$ Also we have $support(\varepsilon_a) = domain(\varepsilon_a)$ and $support(\varepsilon_b) = domain(\varepsilon_b)$ because of **KT45**-frame. So that $support(\varepsilon_a) = support(\varepsilon_b)$
only if part: Assume that $support(\varepsilon_a) = support(\varepsilon_b)$.
Let $\varphi \in Fom(\varepsilon_a) \cap Fom(\varepsilon_b)$. Since $e_i \models \varphi$ for all $e_i \in domain(\varepsilon_a) = support(\varepsilon_a)$, $u_j \models \varphi$ for all u_j. So that $K_a\varphi \in Fom(\varepsilon_a)$. Namely, $e_i \models K_a\varphi$ for all $e_i \in domain(\varepsilon_b)$. This means $K_a\varphi \in Fom(\varepsilon_b)$ because $domain(\varepsilon_a) = domain(\varepsilon_b)$. Similarly, $K_b\varphi \in Fom(\varepsilon_a) \cap Fom(\varepsilon_b)$. Thus $Fom(\varepsilon_a) \cap Fom(\varepsilon_b)$ is K-closure.
(2) Assume **SWCK**. If $\varphi \in Fom(\varepsilon_a)$ then for all $e_i \in domain(\varepsilon_a), e_i \models \varphi$. This means for all $e_i \in domain(\varepsilon_b), e_i \models \varphi$ because $domain(\varepsilon_a) = domain(\varepsilon_b)$. So that $\varphi \in Fom(\varepsilon_b)$. Namely, $Fom(\varepsilon_a) \subseteq Fom(\varepsilon_b)$. By symmetry, we have $Fom(\varepsilon_a) = Fom(\varepsilon_b)$.

6   Example: The Muddy Children Puzzle

We treat the well known muddy children puzzle in the framework of linear dynamics of beliefs. This is a problem for common knowledge rather than common belief. To save space, we solve it for the case of only two children but the cases for the more children can be solved by the same method.

Definition 15 (the muddy children puzzle)

step 1. *Two children a, b may get mud on their foreheads during their play. Each can see the mud on another's but not his own forehead.*
step 2. *the father says "At least one of you has mud on your forehead".*
step 3. *the father asks "Does any of you know whether you have mud on your own forehead?" They answer "No".*

step 4. *the father repeats the question "Does any of you know whether you have mud on your own forehead?" Then they will answer "Yes".*

Assume that P, Q represent the facts "a has a mud on his forehead" and "b has a mud on his forehead", respectively. Let $\mathcal{L}_D$ denotes the language with two modal operators K_a and K_b. We denote the set of valid sentences in $\mathcal{L}_D$ by C_0. Thus we have 4 possible worlds such that

$$e_1 = \{P, Q\}, e_2 = \{\neg P, Q\}, e_3 = \{P, \neg Q\}, e_4 = \{\neg P, \neg Q\}.$$

Let W be a vector space of the children a, b spanned by the basis of possible worlds $\{e_1, e_2, e_3, e_4\}$.

step 1: From the condition that each can see the mud on partner's but not his own forehead, the ensembles for a, b are $\varepsilon_a = \{u_1, u_2, u_3, u_4\}, \varepsilon_b = \{v_1, v_2, v_3, v_4\}$ where

$u_1 = (\alpha_1, \alpha_2, 0, 0), u_2 = (\alpha_3, \alpha_4, 0, 0), u_3 = (0, 0, \beta_1, \beta_2), u_4 = (0, 0, \beta_3, \beta_4) \in W,$
$v_1 = (\gamma_1, 0, \gamma_2, 0), v_2 = (\gamma_3, 0, \gamma_4, 0), v_3 = (0, \delta_1, 0, \delta_2), v_4 = (0, \delta_3, 0, \delta_4) \in W.$
$support(\varepsilon_a) = support(\varepsilon_b) = \{e_1, e_2, e_3, e_4\}.$

By **SWCK**, there is the common knowledge $C_1 = Fom(\varepsilon_a) = Fom(\varepsilon_b)$ where

$$C_1 = C_0 \cup \{K_a Q \vee K_a \neg Q, K_b P \vee K_b \neg P, \neg(K_a P \vee K_a \neg P), \cdots\}.$$

The common belief space is given by the following 4 product tensors in $W \otimes W$:

$$\begin{aligned}
T_1 &= u_1 \otimes v_1 = (\alpha_1\gamma_1, 0, \alpha_1\gamma_2, 0, \alpha_2\gamma_1, 0, \alpha_2\gamma_2, 0, 0, 0, 0, 0, 0, 0, 0, 0), \\
T_2 &= u_2 \otimes v_2 = (0, \alpha_3\gamma_3, 0, \alpha_3\gamma_4, 0, \alpha_4\gamma_3, 0, \alpha_4\gamma_4, 0, 0, 0, 0, 0, 0, 0, 0), \\
T_3 &= u_3 \otimes v_3 = (0, 0, 0, 0, 0, 0, 0, 0, \beta_1\delta_1, 0, \beta_1\delta_2, 0, \beta_2\delta_1, 0, \beta_2\delta_2, 0), \\
T_4 &= u_4 \otimes v_4 = (0, 0, 0, 0, 0, 0, 0, 0, 0, \beta_3\delta_3, 0, \beta_3\delta_4, 0, \beta_4\delta_3, 0, \beta_4\delta_4).
\end{aligned}$$

step 2: The father's comment that "at least one of you has mud on your forehead" is represented by the diagonal projection $\Delta_{P\vee Q}$

$$\Delta_{P\vee Q} = \begin{pmatrix} 1 & 0 & 0 & 0 \\ 0 & 1 & 0 & 0 \\ 0 & 0 & 1 & 0 \\ 0 & 0 & 0 & 0 \end{pmatrix}.$$

This knowledge is shared by the children so that the operator $\Delta_{P\vee Q} \otimes \Delta_{P\vee Q}$ is applied to the tensor. By using

$$(\Delta_{P\vee Q} \otimes \Delta_{P\vee Q})(u \otimes v) = (\Delta_{P\vee Q} u) \otimes (\Delta_{P\vee Q} v)$$

we have $\beta_2 = 0, \beta_4 = 0, \delta_2 = 0, \delta_4 = 0$. Namely,

$$\begin{aligned}
T_1 &= (\alpha_1\gamma_1, 0, \alpha_1\gamma_2, 0, \alpha_2\gamma_1, 0, \alpha_2\gamma_2, 0, 0, 0, 0, 0, 0, 0, 0, 0), \\
T_2' &= (0, \alpha_3\gamma_3, 0, 0, 0, \alpha_4\gamma_4, 0, 0, 0, 0, 0, 0, 0, 0, 0, 0), \\
T_3' &= (0, 0, 0, 0, 0, 0, 0, 0, \beta_1\delta_1, 0, \beta_1\delta_2, 0, 0, 0, 0, 0), \\
T_4' &= (0, 0, 0, 0, 0, 0, 0, 0, 0, \beta_3\delta_3, 0, 0, 0, 0, 0, 0).
\end{aligned}$$

Here, $support(\varepsilon_a') = support(\varepsilon_b') = \{e_1, e_2, e_3\}.$

By **SWCK**, we have the common knowledge $C_2 = Fom(\varepsilon_a') = Fom(\varepsilon_b')$ where

$$C_2 = C_1 \cup \{P \vee Q, K_a(P \vee Q), K_b(P \vee Q), \cdots \}.$$

step 3: For the father's question "Does any of you know whether you have mud on your own forehead?", both a and b reply "No". This ignorance condition is given by $\Theta(P)$ for ε_a and $\Theta(Q)$ for ε_b. So that we must eliminate the vector u from ε_a which satisfies the condition $\Delta_P u = 0$ or $\Delta_{\neg P} u = 0$. And also we must eliminate the vector v from ε_b which satisfies the condition $\Delta_Q v = 0$ or $\Delta_{\neg Q} v = 0$. Namely, we eliminate the tensor T which satisfies at least one of the following conditions

$$(\Delta_P \otimes E)T = 0, (\Delta_{\neg P} \otimes E)T = 0, (E \otimes \Delta_Q)T = 0, (E \otimes \Delta_{\neg Q})T = 0.$$

Since $(\Delta_P \otimes E)T'3 = 0, (\Delta_P \otimes E)T'4 = 0$ and $(E \otimes \Delta_Q)T'2 = 0, (E \otimes \Delta_Q)T'4 = 0$, we have $\beta_1 = 0, \beta_3 = 0, \gamma_3 = 0, \delta_3 = 0$. Thus, only T_1 is left. Here, $\varepsilon_a'' = \{u_1\}, \varepsilon_b'' = \{v_1\}$. So that $support(\varepsilon_a'') = \{e_1, e_2\}, support(\varepsilon_b'') = \{e_1, e_3\}$. However, a, b must share nontrivial knowledge because they exists in the same world. Therefore, $e_2 \notin \varepsilon_b''$ and $e_3 \notin \varepsilon_a''$ are eliminated by **SWCK**. Namely, $\alpha_2 = \gamma_2 = 0$, so that we have $\varepsilon_a''' = \{u_1'\}, \varepsilon_b''' = \{v_1'\}$ and $support(\varepsilon_a''') = support(\varepsilon_b''') = \{e_1\}$, where $u_1' = v_1' = (1, 0, 0, 0)$. The common knowledge C_3 is

$$C_3 = C_1 \cup C_2 \cup \{P, Q, K_a P, K_a Q, K_b P, K_b Q, \cdots \}.$$

Therefore, both a and b reach the same conclusion $P \wedge Q$.

We can also prove this final step in the usual reasoning in which the belief about another's belief is used (without **SWCK**) [6]. Note that the children share the situation so that they can observe the partner's epistemic state and change their beliefs. Since b knows that a's epistemic state is only u_1, b gets the information $Bel(u_1) = Q$ by the following expansion.

$$\Delta_{Bel(u_1)} = \begin{pmatrix} 1 & 0 & 0 & 0 \\ 0 & 1 & 0 & 0 \\ 0 & 0 & 0 & 0 \\ 0 & 0 & 0 & 0 \end{pmatrix}.$$

The agent b changes her belief according to other's belief. Namely, $v_1' = \Delta_{Bel(u_1)} v_1 = (\gamma_1, 0, 0, 0)$. Similarly, $u_1' = \Delta_{Bel(v_1)} u_1 = (\alpha_1, 0, 0, 0)$. By normalization, $u_1' = v_1' = (1, 0, 0, 0)$. Therefore, both a and b recognize that they have mud on their own foreheads.

7 Concluding Remarks

In this paper, we have discussed the belief change in the framework of the linear algebra. For the simplicity, we have used the subjective probability itself as a basic entity. If we select a square root of the subjective probability, an equivalent but more mathematically elegant formulation will be possible. In such a theory, time evolution is represented by the orthogonal matrix rather than the stochastic matrix.

References

1. Alchourròn,C.E., Gärdenfors,P., and Makinson,D. (1985). On the logic of theory change: Partial meet functions for contraction and revision. *J. Symbolic Logic* 50:510-530.
2. Baltag,A., Moss,L.S., and Solecki,S. (1999). The Logic of Public Announcements, Common Knowledge, and Private Suspicions. In *Proc. 13th Int. Joint Conf. on Artificial Intelligence*, pp.519-525.
3. Cantwell,J. (2005). A formal model of multi-agent belief-interaction. *Journal of Logic, Language and Information* 14:397-422.
4. Darwiche,A., and Pearl,J. (1997). On the logic of iterated belief revision. *Artificial Intelligence* 89:1-29.
5. Engesser,K. and Gabbay,D.M. (2002). Quantum logic, Hilbert space, Revision theory. *Artificial Intelligence* 136:61-100.
6. Fagin,F., Halpern,J.Y., Moses,Y., and Vardi,M.Y. (1995). *Reasoning About Knowledge*. MIT Press.
7. Fusaoka ,A. (2002). On a Linear Representation Theory for Quantitative Belief Revision. In *Proc. 15th Australian.Conf.on Artificial Intelligence*, pp.48-59.
8. Gärdenfors,P. (1988). *Knowledge in flux*. MIT Press.
9. Gertbrandy,J., and Groeneveld,W. (1997). Reasoning about Information Change. *Journal of Logic, Language and Information.* 23:267-306.
10. Herzig,A., Lang, J., and Marquis, P. (2004) Revision and update in multi-agent belief structure. In *5th Conf.on Logic and the Foundation of Game and Decision Theory(Loft 6)*, Leipzig.
11. Katsuno,H., and Mendelzon,A. (1991). Propositional knowledge base revision and minimal change. *Artificial Intelligence* 52:263-294.
12. Katsuno,H., and Mendelzon,A. (1991). On the difference between updating a knowledge base and revising it. In *Proc. 2nd Inter.Conf.on Principles of Knowledge Representation and reasoning*, pp.383-394,1991.
13. Lewis,D.K. (1976). Probabilities of conditionals and conditional probabilities. *The Philosophical Review* 85:297-315.
14. Lindström,S., and Rabinowicz, W. (1999). DDL unlimited: Dynamic Doxastic Logic for introspective agents. *Erkenntnis* 50:353-385.
15. Ruiz-Tolosa,J.R., and Castillo,E. (2005). *From Vectors to Tensors*. Springer-Verlag.
16. Smith,L. (1984). *Linear algebra*. Springer-Verlag.

Answer Set Programming for Representing and Reasoning About Virtual Institutions

Owen Cliffe, Marina De Vos, and Julian Padget

Department of Computer Science
University of Bath,
BATH BA2 7AY, UK
{occ,mdv,jap}@cs.bath.ac.uk

Abstract. It is recognised that institutions are potentially powerful means for making agent interactions effective and efficient, but institutions will only really be useful when, as in other safety-critical scenarios, it is possible to prove that particular properties do or do not hold for all possible encounters. In contrast to symbolic model-checking, answer set programming permits the statement of problems and queries in domain-specific terms as executable logic programs, thus eliminating the gap between specification and verification language. Furthermore, results are presented in the same terms. In this paper we describe the use of answer set programs as an institutional modelling technique. We demonstrate that our institutional model can be intuitively be mapped into an answer set program such that the ordered event traces of the former can be obtained as the answer sets of the latter, allowing for an easy way to query properties of models.

1 Introduction

The case for institutions as mechanisms to structure and enable agent interactions has been made at length in numerous places over the last 10 years. Probably the most relevant fact for this paper is the recognition that it is the *institutional norms* [18] that hold the key, where norms are statements that serve to guide or regulate agent behaviour, ranging from the abstract ("treat others as you would wish to be treated yourself") through rules ("if this boat's catch of cod exceeds its annual quota then a fine is payable") to protocols defining sequences of (typically) speech acts.

This is not the place for a repetition of the arguments for institutions, but for the sake of making this paper self-contained, we give a brief introduction to the literature for the interested reader. The earliest presentation in the computer science literature is perhaps Noriega's thesis [35], followed by Rodriguez [37] and Vazquez-Salceda [38]. Alongside, there have been several attempts at finding tractable representations of institutional norms, starting from the original FishMarket paper [36] using automata [22], process algebra [29], symbolic model-checking with temporal logics [11], commitments [39], social institutions [41] action languages [2] and answer set programming [10]. Initial approaches were bottom-up, starting from protocols, but to date creating a verifiable relationship between protocols and higher level representations of norms has not proven fruitful. Thus more recent approaches such as [1, 16, 42] and including our own, have

K. Inoue, K. Satoh, and F. Toni (Eds.): CLIMA VII, LNAI 4371, pp. 60–79, 2007.

sought to address this problem by specifying normative behaviour at a level which is both easily expressed by designers and computationally executable and verifiable.

In this paper a top-down approach to virtual institutions is described, in which external normative concepts are represented in terms that at the same time designers may analyse (off-line) and about which agents may reason (on-line) using the answer set programming paradigm. In formalising the ideas set out in [10], this paper makes two further contributions: (i) a formal event-based model of the specification of institutions that captures all the essential properties, namely empowerment, permission, violation and obligation (ii) a verifiable translation to answer set programming, resulting in a decidable and executable model for institutions.

2 Virtual Institutions

To provide some context for the theory that follows, this section begins with a brief overview of institutions and the terms that we use. As outlined in the introduction the essential characteristics of an institution are captured in its norms with varying degrees of specificity. What agents do or say is constrained by a given institutional context, so that irrelevant actions or communications are filtered out, and relevant ones advance the interaction, cause an agent to acquire an obligation, or through a violation, invite a sanction. But while that serves to capture the agent's point of view, what about the (institutional) environment? How are actions to be observed, how are obligations to be recorded and their satisfaction enforced, and how are violations to be detected and the corresponding sanctions to be applied?

The model we propose is based on the concept of *Observable Events* that capture notions of the physical world — "shoot somebody" — and *Institutional Events* that are those generated by society — "murder" — but which only have meaning within a given social context. While observable events are clearly observable, institutional ones are not, so how do they come into being? Searle [28] describes the creation of an institutional state of affairs through *Conventional Generation*, whereby an event in one context *Counts As* the occurrence of another event in a second context. Taking the physical world as the first context and by defining conditions in terms of states, institutional events may be created that count as the presence of states or the occurrence of events in the institutional world.

Thus, we model an institution as a set of *institutional states* that evolve over time subject to the occurrence of *events*, where an institutional state is a set of *institutional fluents* that may be held to be true at some instant. Furthermore, we may separate such fluents into *domain* fluents, that depend on the institution being modelled, such as "A owns something", and *normative fluents* that are common to all specifications and may be classified as follows:

– **Institutional Power:** This represents the institutional capability for an event to be brought about meaningfully, and hence change some fluents in the institutional state. Without institutional power, the event may not be brought about and has no effect; for example, a marriage ceremony will only bring about the married state, if the person performing the ceremony is empowered so to do.

- **Permission:** Each permission fluent captures the property that some event may occur without violation. If an event occurs, and that event is not permitted, then a *violation event* is generated.
- **Obligation:** Obligation fluents are modelled as the dual of permission . An obligation fluent states that a particular event is obliged to occur before a given deadline event (such as a timeout) and is associated with a specified violation. If an obligation fluent holds and the obliged event occurs then the obligation is said to be satisfied. If the corresponding deadline event occurs then the obligation is said to be violated and the specified violation event is generated.

Events can be classified into: (i) a set of observable events, being those events external to the institution which may be brought about independently from the institution and (ii) a set of *institutional events* which may be broken down into *violation events* and *institutional actions*; these events may only be brought about if they are generated by the institutional semantics. Finally we have a set of institutional rules which associate the occurrence of events with some effects in the subsequent state. These can be divided into: (i) *generation rules* which account for the conventional generation of events. Each generation rule associates the satisfaction of some conditions in the current institutional state and the occurrence of an (observed or institutional) event with a generated institutional event. For example: "A wedding ceremony counts as civil marriage only if the couple have a licence". The generating and generated events are taken by the institution to have occurred simultaneously. (ii) *consequence rules*, each of which associates the satisfaction of some conditions in the current institutional state and the occurrence of an event in the institution or the world to the change in state of one or more fluents in the next institution state. For example: "Submitting a paper to a conference grants permission for the paper to be redistributed by the conference organisers".

Violation and sanction play an important role in the specification of institutions. Violations may arise either from explicit generation, from the occurrence of a non-permitted event, or from the failure to fulfil an obligation. In these cases sanctions that may include obligations on violating agents or other agents and/or changes in agents' permission to do certain actions, may then simply be expressed as consequences of the occurrence of the associated violation event in the subsequent institutional state.

2.1 The Institutional Model

From the introduction above, it can be seen that a definition of a institution is a quintuple $\mathcal{I} := \langle \mathcal{E}, \mathcal{F}, \mathcal{C}, \mathcal{G}, \mathcal{S}_0 \rangle$ consisting of institutional events ($\mathcal{E}$), fluents ($\mathcal{F}$), a consequence relation ($\mathcal{C}$), an event generation relation ($\mathcal{G}$) and an initial state ($\mathcal{S}_0$). We now describe each of these in more detail.

Institutional Events. Each institution defines a set of event signatures $\mathcal{E}$, to denote the types of events that may occur. $\mathcal{E}$ comprises two disjoint subsets, $\mathcal{E}_{obs}$ denoting *observable events* and $\mathcal{E}_{inst}$ denoting *institutional events*. We break institutional events down further into the disjoint subsets: *institutional actions*, $\mathcal{E}_{instact}$ and *violation events* $\mathcal{E}_{viol}$. We define $\mathcal{E}_{viol}$ such that $\forall e \in \mathcal{E}_{instact} \cup \mathcal{E}_{obs} \cdot \text{viol}(e) \in \mathcal{E}_{viol}$ (i.e. each institutional action has a corresponding violation event $\mathrm{viol}(e)$ in $\mathcal{E}_{viol}$ which may arise from the performance of e when it is not permitted).

Institutional Fluents. Each institution comprises the union of four distinguished sets of fluents: one defines a set of *Domain Fluents* denoted $\mathcal{D}$ that account for the description of the domain the institution operates, while the remainder are sets of boolean fluents indicating different types of *normative fluents*:

$\mathcal{W}$ A set of institutional powers of the form $\mathrm{pow}(e) : e \in \mathcal{E}_{instact}$ where each power fluent denotes the capability of some event e to be brought about (generated) in the institution.

$\mathcal{M}$ A set of event permissions: $\mathrm{perm}(e) : e \in \mathcal{E}_{instact} \cup \mathcal{E}_{obs}$ where each permission fluent denotes that it is permitted for an event e to be brought about. An event is not explicitly forbidden, instead this is implicitly represented by the absence of permission for that event to be brought about.

$\mathcal{O}$ A set of obligations, of the form $\mathrm{obl}(e, d, v) : e \in \mathcal{E}, d \in \mathcal{E}, v \in \mathcal{E}_{inst}$ where each obligation fluent denotes that event e should be brought about before the occurrence of event d or be subject to the violation v.

Together, these disjoint sets of domain fluents and normative fluents form the *Institutional Fluents* $\mathcal{F}$ ($\mathcal{F} = \mathcal{W} \cup \mathcal{M} \cup \mathcal{O} \cup \mathcal{D}$).

The state of an institution at a certain time is determined by those institutional fluents that are valid at that time. The set of all possible *institutional states* is denoted as Σ with $\Sigma = 2^{\mathcal{F}}$. It is important to appreciate that not all those states will actually be used in an institution.

Events can have the same effect on multiple of states, not just one. Borrowing a book from a library will result in the obligation to bring it back regardless of how many books have been borrowed in the past. To facilitate this, we introduce the concept of *State Formula* as a collection of states that satisfy certain properties in that they either contain certain fluents or they do not. The set of all state formulae is denoted as $\mathcal{X}$ with $\mathcal{X} = 2^{\mathcal{F} \cup \neg \mathcal{F}}$, where $\neg \mathcal{F}$ is the negation of each fluent in $\mathcal{F}$.

Consequences. Each institution defines a function $\mathcal{C}$ that describes which fluents are initiated and terminated by the occurrence of a certain event in a state matching some criteria. The function is expressed as $\mathcal{C} : \mathcal{X} \times \mathcal{E} \to 2^{\mathcal{F}} \times 2^{\mathcal{F}}$. Given $X \in \mathcal{X}$ and $e \in events$, $C(X, e) = (\mathcal{C}^{\uparrow}(X, e), \mathcal{C}^{\downarrow}(X, e))$ with $\mathcal{C}^{\uparrow}(X, e)$ containing those fluents which are *initiated* by the event e in any state matching X and $\mathcal{C}^{\downarrow}(X, e)$ collecting those fluents which are *terminated* by event e in any state matching X.

Event Generation. Each institution defines an event generation function $\mathcal{G}$ which describes when the occurrence of one event *counts as* the occurrence of other events inside the institution: $\mathcal{G} : \mathcal{X} \times \mathcal{E} \to 2^{\mathcal{E}_{inst}}$.

As a consequence there could be a cascading of events. As we will see later, we require the transitive closure to obtain all generated events from one initial observable event.

Initial State. Each institution defines the set $\mathcal{S}_0 \subseteq \mathcal{F}$ that denotes the set of fluents that hold when the institution is created.

2.2 Semantics

During the lifetime of an institution, its state changes due to events taking place. Each observable event possibly generates more events which in turn could create further events. Each of these events could affect the current state, while their confluence determines the next state.

States. We define the semantics of an institution over a set of states Σ. Each state comprises a set of fluents in $\mathcal{F}$ which are held to be true at a given time (see for example Figure 7). We say that a state $S \in \Sigma$ satisfies fluent $f \in \mathcal{F}$, denoted $S \models f$, when $f \in S$. It satisfies its negation $\neg f$, when $f \notin S$. This notation can be extended to sets $X \subseteq \mathcal{X}$ in the following way: $S \models X$ iff $\forall x \in X \cdot S \models x$.

Event Generation. In order to account for event generation we define a function that describes which events to generated in a given state. $\mathrm{GR} : \Sigma \times 2^{\mathcal{E}} \to \mathcal{E}$ ($\mathcal{E}$ is the set of all institutional events). In some state S subject to a set of events E, $\mathrm{GR}(S, E)$ includes all of the events which must be generated by the occurrence of events E in state S and is defined as follows:

$$
\begin{aligned}
\mathrm{GR}(S, E) = \{ e \in \mathcal{E} \mid\ & e \in E && \text{or} \\
& \exists e' \in E, \phi \in \mathcal{X}, e \in G(\phi, e') \cdot S \models \mathrm{pow}(e) \wedge S \models \phi\ \text{or} \\
& \exists e' \in E, \phi \in \mathcal{X}, e \in G(\phi, e') \cdot e \in \mathcal{E}_{viol} \wedge S \models \phi && \text{or} \\
& \exists e' \in E \cdot e = viol(e'), S \models \neg \mathrm{perm}(e') && \text{or} \\
& \exists e' \in \mathcal{E}, d \in E \cdot S \models \mathrm{obl}(e', d, e) \}
\end{aligned}
$$

1. The first condition ensures that events remain generated (inertia).
2. The second condition defines event generation to be explicitly specified by the institutional relation G. One event generates another event in a given state, when (i) the generation was specified by the institution, (ii) the current state satisfies the conditions for the generation and (iii) the generated event is empowered.
3. The third condition deals with violations generated as specified by the institution rather that violations resulting from events that were not permitted. Violations do not require empowerment.
4. The fourth condition considers the generation of violation events as the result of the occurrence of non-permitted events.
5. The last condition deals with the generation of violation events as the result of the failure to bring about an obliged event. For all asserted obligation fluents, the occurrence of the deadline event d generates the corresponding violation event e.

The parallel generation of events, means it is possible for an event which fulfils an obligation to be generated simultaneously with the obligation's deadline (that is, the deadline counts as the fulfilment of the obligation or the obligation counts as the fulfilment of the deadline or another action counts as both the fulfilment of the deadline and the fulfil lent of the obligation). While we consider this situation undesirable we do not prohibit its specification, but say that when it does occur the obligation is considered as not to have been fulfilled.

It is easy to see that $\mathrm{GR}(S, E)$ is a monotonic function. This implies that for any given state and a set of events, we can obtain a fixpoint $\mathrm{GR}^{\omega}(S, E)$. In our institutional model, generated events come about from the performance of one *observable event* $e_{obs} \in \mathcal{E}_{obs}$ in a given state S. So, to obtain all events that originate from this one event in this state, we simply need $\mathrm{GR}^{\omega}(S, \{e_{obs}\})$.

Event Effects. Each fluent in $\mathcal{F}$ may either be asserted or not in each state in S. The status of these fluents changes over time according to which generated events have occurred in the previous transition.

Events can have two sorts of effects: fluents can be initiated (they become true in the next state) or they can be terminated (they cease to be true in the next state). The combination of all effects generated in a state defines the state transition. The state transition function captures inertia, so all fluents that are not affected in the current state remain valid in the next state.

As mentioned above, given an observable event e_{obs} all events that could have an effect on the state S, are obtained by $\mathrm{GR}^{\omega}(S, \{e_{obs}\})$.

The set of all *initiated fluents* $\mathrm{INIT}(S, e_{obs}) \subseteq \mathcal{F}$ for some state $S \in \Sigma$ and an observable event $e_{obs} \in \mathcal{E}_{obs}$ is defined as:

$$\mathrm{INIT}(S, e_{obs}) = \{p \in \mathcal{F} \mid \exists e \in \mathrm{GR}^{\omega}(S, \{e_{obs}\}), X \in \mathcal{X} \cdot p \in \mathcal{C}^{\uparrow}(X, e) \wedge S \models X\}$$

A fluent will be initiated if an event is generated in the current state for which $\mathcal{C}$ specifies, that in current state, this event has the consequence that the fluent is initiated.

We go on to define which fluents are terminated in a given state by the occurrence of a given event:

$$\begin{aligned}
\mathrm{TERM}(S, e_{obs}) = \{p \in \mathcal{F} \mid & \exists e \in \mathrm{GR}^{\omega}(S, \{e_{obs}\}), X \in \mathcal{X} \cdot p \in \mathcal{C}^{\downarrow}(X, e), S \models X \text{ or} \\
& p = \mathrm{obl}(e, d, v) \wedge p \in S \wedge e \in \mathrm{GR}^{\omega}(S, \{e_{obs}\}) \qquad \text{or} \\
& p = \mathrm{obl}(e, d, v) \wedge p \in S \wedge d \in \mathrm{GR}^{\omega}(S, \{e_{obs}\})\}
\end{aligned}$$

A fluent is terminated if an event is generated in the current state for which $\mathcal{C}$ specifies that it needs terminating. Furthermore, an obligation fluent is terminated if either its deadline or the obliged event are in the set of generated events.

Now that we know which fluents need adding or deleting we can define the transition function $\mathrm{TR} : \Sigma \times \mathcal{E}_{obs} \to \Sigma$ as:

$$\begin{aligned}
\mathrm{TR}(S, e_{obs}) = \{p \in \mathcal{F} \mid & p \in S, p \notin \mathrm{TERM}(S, e_{obs}) \text{ or} \\
& p \in \mathrm{INIT}(S, e_{obs})\}
\end{aligned}$$

The first condition models inertia: all fluents which are asserted in the current state persist into the next state, unless they are terminated. The second condition includes fluents which are initiated in the current state.

Ordered Traces. Now that we have defined how states may be generated from a previous state and a single observable event, we are able to define traces and their state evaluations:

– An *ordered trace* is defined as a sequence of observable events

$$\langle e_0, e_1, \ldots, e_n \rangle \quad e_i \in \mathcal{E}_{obs}, 0 \leq i \leq n$$

$$\mathcal{E}_{obs} = \{\texttt{shoot}, \texttt{startwar}, \texttt{declaretruce}, \texttt{callup}, \texttt{provoke}\} \tag{1}$$

$$\mathcal{E}_{instact} = \{\texttt{conscript}, \texttt{murder}\} \tag{2}$$

$$\mathcal{E}_{viol} = \{\text{viol}(\texttt{shoot}), \text{viol}(\texttt{startwar}), \text{viol}(\texttt{declaretruce}),$$
$$\text{viol}(\texttt{callup}), \text{viol}(\texttt{provoke}), \text{viol}(\texttt{conscript}), \text{viol}(\texttt{murder})\} \tag{3}$$

$$\mathcal{D} = \{\texttt{atwar}\} \tag{4}$$

$$\mathcal{W} = \{\text{pow}(\texttt{conscript}), \text{pow}(\texttt{murder})\} \tag{5}$$

$$\mathcal{M} = \{\text{perm}(\texttt{shoot}), \text{perm}(\texttt{startwar}), \text{perm}(\texttt{declaretruce}),$$
$$\text{perm}(\texttt{callup}), \text{perm}(\texttt{provoke}), \text{perm}(\texttt{conscript}), \text{perm}(\texttt{murder})\} \tag{6}$$

$$\mathcal{O} = \{\text{obl}(\texttt{startwar}, \texttt{shoot}, \texttt{murder})\} \tag{7}$$

$$\mathcal{C}^{\uparrow}(\mathcal{X}, \mathcal{E}): \quad \langle\{\neg atwar\}, \texttt{startwar}\rangle \;\rightarrow\; \{atwar\} \tag{8}$$

$$\langle\{\neg atwar\}, \texttt{provoke}\rangle \;\rightarrow\; \{\text{obl}(\texttt{startwar}, \texttt{shoot}, \texttt{murder})\} \tag{9}$$

$$\langle\emptyset, \texttt{conscript}\rangle \;\rightarrow\; \{\text{perm}(shoot)\} \tag{10}$$

$$\langle\emptyset, \texttt{startwar}\rangle \;\rightarrow\; \{\text{pow}(conscript)\} \tag{11}$$

$$\mathcal{C}^{\downarrow}(\mathcal{X}, \mathcal{E}): \langle\{atwar\}, \texttt{declaretruce}\rangle \rightarrow \{atwar\} \tag{12}$$

$$\langle\emptyset, \texttt{declaretruce}\rangle \;\rightarrow\; \{\text{perm}(shoot)\} \tag{13}$$

$$\langle\emptyset, \texttt{declaretruce}\rangle \;\rightarrow\; \{\text{pow}(conscript)\} \tag{14}$$

$$\mathcal{G}(\mathcal{X}, \mathcal{E}): \quad \langle\emptyset, \texttt{callup}\rangle \;\rightarrow\; \{conscript\} \tag{15}$$

$$\langle\emptyset, \texttt{viol}(\texttt{shoot})\rangle \;\rightarrow\; \{murder\} \tag{16}$$

$$S_0 = \{\text{perm}(callup), \text{perm}(startwar), \text{perm}(conscript), \text{perm}(provoke),$$
$$\text{pow}(murder), \text{perm}(murder)\} \tag{17}$$

Fig. 1. The War Institution

- The *evaluation of an ordered trace* for a given starting state S_0 is a sequence $\langle S_0, S_1, \ldots S_{n+1}\rangle$ such that $S_{i+1} = \text{TR}(S_i, e_i)$
- Ordered traces and their evaluations allow us to monitor or investigate the evolution of an institution over time. They also provide us with the data necessary to answer most queries one might have about the dynamic evolution of institutional state.

2.3 An Example: War

A country is constantly swinging between war and peace with its neighbour. The countries have agreed that when they are at peace, the act of a citizen of the first shooting a citizen of the second counts as murder. But, when they are at war and a citizen has been conscripted into the army it is permitted to shoot. When one country is provoked, it is obliged to start war first before it is allowed to shoot.

The institutional model is depicted in Figure 1. (1) shows that a country can observe a shooting, that either party has started the war or declared a truce, that the citizenry have been called up and that a country has been provoked, while the institution as a whole can acknowledge that conscription has taken place and somebody has been murdered, as stated by (2). (3) indicates all the violations that could occur. (4) contains one domain fluent stating that the country is at war, while (5–7) indicate the empowerments, permissions and obligation the countries can hold.

The decision to start a war in time of peace results in the institutional state changing to war, as shown in (8). (9) generates the obligation to start a war first before shooting to avoid committing a murder whenever being provoked during a period of peace. (10) provides the permission to shoot whenever conscription has taken place, which is empowered when a war is started, as indicated by (11). Declaring a truce will end the state of war (12) when at war and revoke the permission to shoot (13) and the power to conscript (14). When a country issues the *callup* command, the institution will generate conscription when empowered (15). When a shooting violation occurs, the institution will raise the murder event (16). Initially (17), the institution declares a number of permissions and empowerments.

3 Modelling Institutions Using Answer Set Programming

By encoding institutions as declarative specifications it becomes possible to reason computationally about the consequences of "real world" actions such as message exchanges, on social states. This allows agents participating in an institution to take account of events up to given point in time and to execute the specification in order to determine the social state at that time. Similarly agents may reason about the social effects of future actions and act accordingly.

In this section we discuss the use of answer set programming (ASP) [4] to model and reason about institutions, the agents that participate in them and the norms that govern them. ASP is a logic programming language that has the advantage that specification and implementation are identical, the language is easy to understand yet very powerful and expressive, it comes with efficient algorithms, called solvers, to provide the solution to the encoded problem and the availability of different types of negation: classical negation and negation-as-failure[1], the latter giving rise to non-deterministic outcomes.

3.1 Answer Set Programming

In *answer set programming* ([4, 24]) a logic program is used to describe the requirements that must be fulfilled by the solutions of a certain problem. The answer sets of the program, usually defined through (a variant/extension of) the stable model semantics [24], then correspond to the solutions of the problem. This technique has been successfully applied in domains such as planning [20, 33], configuration and verification [40], super-optimisation [6], diagnosis [19], game theory [14] and multi-agent systems[5, 8, 15, 7, 10] where [7, 10] use answer set programming to reason about the behaviour of a group of agents, while [5, 8, 15] use the formalism to model the reasoning capabilities, knowledge and beliefs of a single agent within a multi-agent system.

The smallest building block of an answer set program is an atom or predicate, e.g owns(X, Y) stating that X owns Y. X and Y are variables which can be grounded with constants, e.g. owns(me, book). Each ground atom can be assigned the truth value *true*

---

[1] For classical negation one expects a proof that something is indeed false, while for negation-as-failure it is sufficient that no proof exists that something is true.

```
          guilty ← evidence.
        evidence ← trusted_witness.
 trusted_witness ← not lying, witness.
         witness.
         believe ← not disbelieve.
      disbelieve ← not believe.
           lying ← disbelieve.
```

Fig. 2. Program for jury example

or *false*. Answer set programs uses two types of negation: ¬ and **not**. The former is classical negation, indicating that something is know to be false because a proof exists. The latter denotes negation as failure, stating that something should be assumed false due to the failure of proving it to be true. A literal is an atom a or its negation ¬a. An *extended* literal is either a literal l or its negation **not** l.

An answer set programs consist of a set of statements, called rules. Each rule $l ← B$ is made of two parts namely the body B, which is a set of extended literals, and a head literal l. It should be read as: "if all the elements of B are true, so is the head l" or "l" is *supported* if all elements of B are considered to be true. An assignment of truth values to all literals in the program, without causing contradiction, is called an interpretation. Often only those literals that are considered true are mentioned, as all the others are false by default (negation as failure).

Obviously, we only assume those literals to be true that are actually supported. This form of reasoning is referred to as the minimal model semantics. Unfortunately, in the presence of negation-as-failure this approach is insufficient. Negation-as-failure gives us no guarantee that something is indeed false and that information derived from it is actually correct. To obtain intuitive solutions, we need to verify this. This is done by reducing the program to a simpler program containing no instances of negation-as-failure. Given an interpretation, all rules that contain **not** l that are considered false are removed while the remaining rules only retain their literals. This reduction is often referred to as the Gelfond-Lifschitz transformation. When this program gives the same supported literals as the ones with which we began, we have found an answer set.

Definition 1. *Let P be a ground program.*
*The Gelfond-Lifschitz transformation of P w.r.t S, a set of ground literals, is the program P^S containing the rules $l ← B$ such that $l ← B$, **not** $C \in P$ with $C \cap S = \emptyset$, with B and C sets of literals.*

A set of ground literals S is an answer set of P iff S is the minimal model of P^S.

The uncertain nature of negation-as-failure gives rise to several answer sets, which are all acceptable solutions to the problem that has been modelled. It is in this non-determinism that the strength of answer set programming lies.

Example 1. Consider the following situation. A jury member has to decide if the accused is guilty or not based on evidence provided by a witness. The only problem for the jury member is to decide whether they trust this witness or not. This situation can be represented by the following program shown in Figure 2, which has two answer sets:

- {guilty, evidence, trusted_witness, witness, believe}
- {witness, lying, disbelieve}

These two answer sets indicate clearly that the jury member has to decide on the credibility of the witness and her decision is vital for her judgement of the accused.

Algorithms and implementations for obtaining answer sets of logic programs are referred to as *answer set solvers*. The most popular and widely used solvers are DLV[21] and SMODELS[34]. An alternative is CMODELS[26], a solver based on translating the program to a SAT problem.

Each solver has two phases. First the program is grounded, that is the variables are substituted for constants. Within this phase, rules which are obviously leading to nothing are eliminated. Take for example the program:

```
ifluent(atwar).
event(shoot).
holdsat(P, 2) ← holdsat(P, 1), not terminated(P, 1), ifluent(P).
```

this last rule has two grounded instances:

```
holdsat(atwar, 2) ← holdsat(atwar, 1), not terminated(atwar, 1), ifluent(atwar)
holdsat(shoot, 2) ← holdsat(shoot, 1), not terminated(shoot, 1), ifluent(shoot).
```

The parser will eliminate the second ground instance as no rules are provided to derive ifluent(shoot). The second phase is the actual solver where a grounded program is taken and the set of its answer sets is produced.

For this paper we have opted to use SMODELS as our solver and hence we use the SMODELS syntax in the examples that follow. This will also allow us to use the distributed PLATYUS solver[27], which uses SMODELS as a back-end, for larger implementations of institutions.

3.2   Translation into Answer Set Programs

In order to reason about traces over a given institution, we define the following translation from the institution $\mathcal{I} = \langle \mathcal{E}, \mathcal{F}, \mathcal{C}, \mathcal{G}, \mathcal{S}_0 \rangle$ into an answer set program. We use instances of time to indicate the state transitions of an institution.

The mapping uses the following atoms: ifluent(P) to identify fluents, evtype(E, T) to describe the type of an event, event(E) to denote the events, instant(I) for time instances, final(I) for the last time instance in a trace, next(I1, I2) to establish time ordering, occurred(E, I) to indicate that the event happened at time I, observed(E, I) that the event was observed at that time, holdsat(P, I) to state that the institutional fluent holds at I, initiated(P, I) and terminated(P, I) for fluents that are initiated and terminated at I.

Since we are using SMODELS, we can take advantage of some of its syntactic constructs. In our mapping we use their choices syntax, symbolic functions and the built-in compute statement:

- Choices written $L\{l_1, \ldots l_n\}M$ are a convenient construct to express that any number of literals between L and M from the set $\{l_1 \ l_n\}$ need to be true in order to satisfy the construct. When omitted L is considered 0 and M to be n.

$$\text{occurred}(E, I) \leftarrow \text{observed}(E, I). \tag{18}$$

$$\begin{aligned}\text{holdsat}(P, I2) \leftarrow\ &\text{holdsat}(P, I1), \text{not terminated}(P, I1),\\ &\text{next}(I1, I2), \text{instant}(I1; I2),\\ &\text{ifluent}(P).\end{aligned} \tag{19}$$

$$\begin{aligned}\text{holdsat}(P, I2) \leftarrow\ &\text{initiated}(P, I1), \text{ifluent}(P),\\ &\text{next}(I1, I2), \text{instant}(I1; I2),\end{aligned} \tag{20}$$

$$\begin{aligned}\text{occurred}(\text{viol}(E), I) \leftarrow\ &\text{occurred}(E, I),\\ &\text{not holdsat}(\text{perm}(E), I),\\ &\text{event}(E), \text{event}(\text{viol}(E)), \text{instant}(I).\end{aligned} \tag{21}$$

$$\begin{aligned}\text{occurred}(V, I) \leftarrow\ &\text{holdsat}(\text{obl}(E, D, V), I), \text{occurred}(D, I),\\ &\text{event}(E; D; V), \text{instant}(I).\end{aligned} \tag{22}$$

$$\begin{aligned}\text{terminated}(\text{obl}(E, D, V), I) \leftarrow\ &\text{occurred}(E, I),\\ &\text{holdsat}(\text{obl}(E, D, V), I),\\ &\text{event}(E; D; V), \text{instant}(I).\end{aligned} \tag{23}$$

$$\begin{aligned}\text{terminated}(\text{obl}(E, D, V), I) \leftarrow\ &\text{occurred}(D, I),\\ &\text{holdsat}(\text{obl}(E, D, V), I),\\ &\text{event}(E; D; V), \text{instant}(I).\end{aligned} \tag{24}$$

Fig. 3. The institution base program

- A symbolic function $f(X, Y)$ defines a new constant that is the value of the function. It is used as a shorthand to group sets of variables together in a meaningful way. We use this represent obligations $\text{obl}(E, D, V)$ and violations $\text{viol}(R)$.
- The compute statement is used to generate only those answer sets that satisfy certain properties. The statement $\text{compute number}\{l_1, \ldots l_n\}$. makes sure that only answer sets that satisfy every extended literal l_i for $1 \leq i \leq n$ are computed. The number of generated answers is controlled by number.
- We also use facility for passing multiple argument lists to literals: when used in the body of a rule $a(\text{args}_1; \ldots; \text{args}_n)$ is replaced by $\{a(\text{args}_1), \ldots, a(\text{args}_n)\}$.

Each mapping of each institution $\mathcal{I}$ consists of two parts: P_{base} which is identical for each interpretation and $P_{\mathcal{I}}^*$ specific for the institution being modelled. Together they form the program $P_{\mathcal{I}}$.

The base program P_{base} (Figure 3) consists of rules responsible for the occurrence of observed events and dealing with obligations and inertia. The first rule (18) assures that each observed event ($\text{observed}(E, I)$) will be marked as occurred, as all observable events are valid events. Rules (19) encode standard inertia, using negation as failure: any fluent which is currently valid ($\text{holdsat}(I_1)$) and will not be terminated in this state ($\text{not terminated}(P, I_1)$) needs still to be valid in the next state ($\text{holdsat}(P, I_2)$). The atoms $\text{next}(I_1, I_2)$ and $\text{instant}(I_1; I_2)$ are responsible for obtaining the next time instance and for restricting the grounding domain. The rule (20) ensures that fluents that are initiated ($\text{initiated}(P, I_1)$) become valid ($\text{holdsat}(P, I_2)$) in the next state. Rule (21) is responsible for the generation of violations that are caused by non-permitted

$$\{\text{observed}(E, I)\} \leftarrow \text{evtype}(E, \text{obs}), \text{event}(E), \text{instant}(I), \text{not final}(I). \qquad (25)$$

$$\text{ev}(I) \leftarrow \text{observed}(E, I), \text{event}(E), \text{instant}(I). \qquad (26)$$

$$\leftarrow \text{not ev}(I), \text{instant}(I), \text{not final}(I). \qquad (27)$$

$$\leftarrow \text{observed}(E1, I), \text{observed}(E2, I), E1! = E2,$$

$$\text{instant}(I), \text{event}(E1), \text{event}(E2). \qquad (28)$$

Fig. 4. Rules for ensuring observable traces

events. Whenever an event occurs (occurred(E, I)) for which no permission exists in that state (not holdsat(perm(E), I)) a violation is raised (occurred(viol(E), I)). The last three rules deal with obligations. (22) is responsible for raising a violation (occurred(V, I)) whenever the deadline expires (occurred(D, I)). The other atoms in the body of this rule guarantee appropriate grounding of this rule. The rules (23) and (24) regulate the end of obligations (terminated(obl(E, D, V), I)) when either the obligation is fulfilled (occurred(E, I)) or the deadline expires (occurred(D, I)).

To constrain the answer set to those containing observable traces we add the rules in Figure 4 to P_{base}. Rule (25) is responsible for the generation of observed(E, I) atoms. For each combination of an event (event(E)) which is observable (evtype(E, obs)) and non-final (not final(I)) at time instance (instance(i)) an {observed(E, I)}-choice is created, indicating that you can either use this observed(E, I) atom or not. (26) creates for each choice of observed(E, I) atom an ev(I) atom, which will be used by (27) to restrict the answer sets to observable traces, that is an observable event occurs at each time instance. The last constraint (28) assures that each answer set has only one observable event at every time instance.

To make the program $P_{\mathcal{I}}^*$ more readable we introduce the shorthand $EX(\_, I)$ to denote the translation of expression $X \in \mathcal{X}$ into the body of an ASP rule referring to time I. $EX(x_1 \wedge x_2 \wedge \ldots x_n, I)$, with $x_i \in X$, is translated into an ASP conjunction $EX(x_1, I), EX(x_2, I), \ldots, EX(x_n, I)$. $EX(\neg p, I)$ is translated using negation as failure into not $EX(p, I)$. $EX(p, I)$ is translated into holdsat(p, I).

With these syntactic rules $P_{\mathcal{I}}^*$ becomes the program shown in Figure 5. By (29), all the fluents are encoded as facts ifluent(p) in the program. The main purpose of these facts is to facilitate grounding. Each event e in the institution is responsible for the creation of two facts: (30) generates event(e). facts while (31–33) record the types of events with facts of the form evtype(e, X) with X equal to obs, act, viol to indicate observable, institutional actions and violations. (34) and (35) produce the rules for consequence generation. Whenever a fluent needs to be initiated/terminated a rule will be created with the occurrence of the responsible event (occurred(e, I)) and the conditions on the state (EX(X, I) in the body and the initiation/termination atom in the head (initiated(p, I)/terminated(p, I)). Event generation is dealt with by (36). For each event that could be generated a rule is produced containing the occurrence of the triggering event (occurred(e, I)), the permission to execute this triggering event (holdsat(pow(e), I)) and the conditions for the generation in the body and the occurrence of the generated event in the head (occurred(g, I)). Finally, the encoding of the

$$p \in \mathcal{F} \Leftrightarrow \texttt{ifluent(p)}. \tag{29}$$

$$e \in \mathcal{E} \Leftrightarrow \texttt{event(e)}. \tag{30}$$

$$e \in \mathcal{E}_{obs} \Leftrightarrow \texttt{evtype(e, obs)}. \tag{31}$$

$$e \in \mathcal{E}_{instact} \Leftrightarrow \texttt{evtype(e, act)}. \tag{32}$$

$$e \in \mathcal{E}_{viol} \Leftrightarrow \texttt{evtype(e, viol)}. \tag{33}$$

$$\mathcal{C}^{\uparrow}(X, e) = P \Leftrightarrow \forall p \in P \cdot \texttt{initiated(p, I)} \leftarrow \texttt{occurred(e, I)}, EX(X, I). \tag{34}$$

$$\mathcal{C}^{\downarrow}(X, e) = P \Leftrightarrow \forall p \in P \cdot \texttt{terminated(p, I)} \leftarrow \texttt{occurred(e, I)}, EX(X, I). \tag{35}$$

$$\mathcal{G}(X, e) = E \Leftrightarrow g \in E, \texttt{occurred(g, I)} \leftarrow \texttt{occurred(e, I)},$$
$$\texttt{holdsat(pow(e), I)}, EX(X, I). \tag{36}$$

$$p \in S_0 \Leftrightarrow \texttt{holdsat(p, i}_0\texttt{)}. \tag{37}$$

Fig. 5. Rules for translation into SMODELS

initial state is taken care of by (37), each fluent p in the initial state is transformed into a fact $\texttt{holdsat(p, i}_0\texttt{)}$.

Note that P_i^* is only ungrounded with respect to the time instances. The constants for these are provided by a third program P^n. It is this program that determines the length of the traces. This modularisation into three programs allows for easy reuse.

$$0 < k < n : \texttt{instant(i}_k\texttt{)}. \tag{38}$$

$$0 < k < n - 1 : \texttt{next(i}_k, \texttt{i}_{k+1}\texttt{)}. \tag{39}$$

$$\texttt{final(i}_n\texttt{)}. \tag{40}$$

The facts produced by (38) provide the program with all available time instances, while the facts from (39) give order time necessary to go from one state to the other. Since we cannot have an observable event occurring at the final time instance, we need a fact indicating the final state. This fact is produced by (40).

Together P_{base}, $P_{\mathcal{I}}^*$ and P^n generate $P_{\mathcal{I}}^n$, an answer set program capable of providing all ordered traces of length n for the institution $\mathcal{I}$.

Theorem 1. *Let* $\mathcal{I} = \langle \mathcal{E}, \mathcal{F}, \mathcal{C}, \mathcal{G}, \mathcal{S}_0 \rangle$ *be an institution with* $P_{\mathcal{I}}^n$ *its corresponding answer set program. Then, a one-to-one mapping exists between the ordered traces of length* n *and the answer sets of* $P_{\mathcal{I}}^n$.

Given such a mapping we can add the necessary rules that allow us to produce those traces that fulfil certain requirements. We will demonstrate this in the next section by means of our war institution.

3.3   An Example: War in ASP

When we translate the War institution $\mathcal{I}$ from §2.3 for traces of length 3, we obtain for $P_{\mathcal{I}}^* \cup P^3$ the program shown in Figure 6. From left to right and top to bottom, the

ifluent(atwar).	ifluent(obl(startwar, shoot, murder)).
event(shoot). event(startwar). event(declaretruce). event(callup). event(conscript). event(murder). event(provoke). event(viol(shoot)). event(viol(startwar)). event(viol(declaretruce)). event(viol(callup)). event(viol(conscript)). event(viol(provoke)).	evtype(shoot, obs). evtype(startwar, obs). evtype(declaretruce, obs). evtype(callup, obs). evtype(conscript, inst). evtype(murder, inst). evtype(provoke, obs). evtype(viol(shoot), viol). evtype(viol(startwar), viol). evtype(viol(declaretruce), viol). evtype(viol(callup), viol). evtype(viol(conscript), viol). evtype(viol(murder), viol). evtype(viol(provoke), viol).

$$
\begin{aligned}
\text{initiated(obl(startwar, shoot, murder), I)} &\leftarrow \text{occurred(provoke, I), instant(I),} \\
&\quad \text{not holdsat(atwar, I).} \\
\text{initiated(atwar, I)} &\leftarrow \text{occurred(startwar, I), instant(I),} \\
&\quad \text{not holdsat(atwar, I).} \\
\text{initiated(perm(shoot), I)} &\leftarrow \text{occurred(conscript, I), instant(I).} \\
\text{initiated(pow(conscript), I)} &\leftarrow \text{occurred(startwar, I), instant(I).}
\end{aligned}
$$

$$
\begin{aligned}
\text{terminated(atwar, I)} &\leftarrow \text{occurred(declaretruce, I), instant(I)} \\
&\quad \text{, holdsat(atwar, I).} \\
\text{terminated(perm(shoot), I)} &\leftarrow \text{occurred(declaretruce, I), instant(I).} \\
\text{terminated(pow(conscript), I)} &\leftarrow \text{occurred(declaretruce, I), instant(I).}
\end{aligned}
$$

$$
\begin{aligned}
\text{occurred(conscript, I)} &\leftarrow \text{occurred(callup, I), instant(I),} \\
&\quad \text{holdsat(pow(conscript), I).} \\
\text{occurred(murder, I)} &\leftarrow \text{occurred(viol(shoot), I), instant(I).}
\end{aligned}
$$

| instant(i0; i1; i2; i3).
next(i0, i1).
next(i1, i2).
next(i2, i3).
final(i3). | holdsat(perm(callup), i0).
holdsat(perm(startwar), i0).
holdsat(perm(conscript), i0).
holdsat(perm(declaretruce), i0).
holdsat(perm(murder), i0).
holdsat(perm(provoke), i0).
holdsat(pow(murder)), i0. |

Fig. 6. War in ASP

first two boxes encode the two non auto-generated facts produced by (29). For clarity, we omit the encodings of permissions and power for each institutional event. The two following boxes show the encodings of the events and the event types, as prescribed by (30–33). The initiating consequence generation rules of (34) are in box five, while box six has the terminating consequence rules of (35). The event generation rules (36) are in the next box. The program P^3 is in box eight and box nine has the initial state (37).

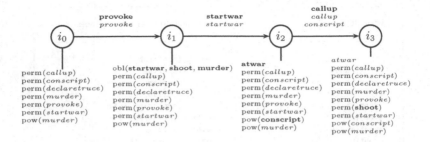

i_0: The initial state, wherein all the initial fluents are initiated. The institution observes that a country is provoked. From the event generation function (15 and 16) we know that no further events are generated. The consequence relation (9) is responsible for initiating the obligation obl(**startwar**, **shoot**, **murder**) in the next state.

i_1: As of this state the obligation obl(**startwar**, **shoot**, **murder**) holds. The institution observes startwar event. This event does not generate any further events. Since the obligation has been fulfilled it can be terminated in the next state. The consequence relation (8 and 11) indicate that **atwar** and pow(**conscript**) have to be initiated in the next state.

i_2: In this state the obligation no longer holds and **atwar** and pow(**conscript**) have been initiated. The institution now observes the **callup** event. The event generation function (15) thus generates the conscription event, since conscription is now empowered. This results in the consequence relation (10) to order perm(**shoot**) to be initiated in the next state.

i_3: This leads us to the final state in which the institution has the permission to shoot.

Fig. 7. Answer set illustrating the obligation satisfied

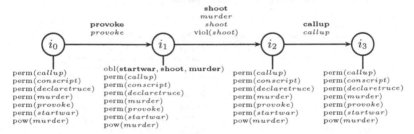

i_0: As for i_0 of Figure 7

i_1: As of this state the obligation obl(**startwar**, **shoot**, **murder**) holds. The institution observes the event **shoot**. The events indicates that the deadline of the obligation has passed, so event generation will produce the corresponding violation, in this case **murder**. Furthermore, since the event shoot was not permitted, the violation viol(**shoot**) is generated, which in turn is responsible for the event **murder** by (17). Since the obligation is violated, it will be terminated in the next state. None of the events cause any state change.

i_2: After the violation of the obligation, the institution is returned to its original state. In this state the institution observes the callup event. Because the institution is not empowered to conscript, no other events are generated and no state changes are considered.

i_3: The institution has not changed.

Fig. 8. Answer set illustrating the obligation violated

Once we have this basic program P_I we can start to query for specific results, like "Is it possible to have a wartime murder?", "Will provocation always lead to shooting?". In order to do this, two rules have to be added to the program: one to represent the query and one to indicate to the solver that we are only interested in those ordered traces that satisfy the condition. The following ASP rules encode the query "Will the country ever have the obligation to start the war before shooting?":

```
condition←holdsat(obl(startwar, shoot, murder), I), instant(I).
compute all {condition}.
```

The Figures 7 and 8 provide a graphical representation of two of the answer sets from running the program with this query. The former demonstrates that the obligation can be satisfied while the latter shows that there exists at least one trace in which the obligation is broken. The circles represent the time instances. The observable events are given in bold above the arrows linking the time instances together with the result of event generation. Below the circles, we list all the institutional fluents that hold in the current state with the new fluents in bold.

4   Related Work

Much recent and contemporary work on modelling norms and violations has chosen temporal logics as a starting point, as we now discuss.

Colombetti et al in [12] outline an abstract model for agent institutions based on social commitments, where institutions comprise a set of *registration rules* that capture agents' entry into and exit from institutions, a set of *interaction rules* that govern commitment creation and satisfaction, a set of *authorisations* that describe agents' capabilities and an *internal ontology* that describes a model for the interpretation of terms relevant to the institution. Their approach (outlined in [23, 13, 41]) builds on the CTL± extension of CTL[9], which includes past tense modalities for reasoning about actions which have already occurred. Dignum in [17] also uses an extension of CTL to describe her language for representing contracts in the building of agent organisations.

The Event Calculus (EC) [31, 32] is a declarative logic that reinterprets the Situation Calculus to capture when and how states change in response to external events. EC has been used to model both the behaviour of commitments [42] among agents in order to build interaction protocols, corresponding to the regulatory aspects of the work described above, as well as more general social models such as those described in [30]. From a technical point of view, our approach essentially has a kind of duality compared to EC, in that the basis for the model is events rather than states. In itself, this offers no technical advantage although we believe that being able to express violations in terms of events rather than states better captures their nature. More significant are the consequences of the grounding in ASP:

- For the most part the state and event models are equivalent with respect to properties such as induction and abduction, but non-monotonicity is inherent in ASP and so resort to the tricky process of circumscription is avoided.
- Likewise, reasoning about defaults requires no special treatment in ASP.

- The consequence rules of our specification have equivalents in EC, but the event generation rules do not.
- The state of a fluent is determined by its truth-value in the ASP interpretation, whereas EC (typically) has to encode this explicitly using two predicates.
- Inertia in EC is axiomatic, whereas in our approach it follows from the application of the TR operator—although there is a strong syntactic similarity (perhaps compounded by using the same terminology!) the philosophy is different.
- ASP allows a wider variety of queries than is typically provided in EC implementations but space constraints do not allow the full illustration of this aspect here.

Artikis et al. in [1, 2, 3, 30] describe a system for the specification of normative social systems in terms of power, empowerment and obligation. This is formalized using both the event calculus [31] and a subset of the action language $C+$ [25]. The notions of power and empowerment are equivalent in both systems, but additionally we introduces violation as events and our modelling of obligations differs in that (i) they are deadline-sensitive, and (ii) can raise a violation if they are not met in time. Violations greatly improve the capacity to model institutions, but it should be remembered that institutional modelling was (apparently) not Artikis's goal. Likewise, although the interpretation of $C+$ using the CCalc tool gives rise to similar reasoning capabilities (with similar complexity) to ASP, we believe our approach, including violations, provides a more intuitive and natural way of expressing social constraints involving temporal aspects. A further advantage is in the formulation of queries, where ASP makes it possible to encode queries similar to those found in (bounded) temporal logic model checking, whereas, as noted above, queries on action languages are constrained by the action language implementation. The other notable difference is once again, our focus on events rather than states, which we have discussed at some length above.

In [7], Buccafurri et al. address the problem of specifying normative properties through the use of *Social Logic Programs* which discriminate between states considered to be acceptable or unacceptable by particular agents. For a given society and situation these social logic programs can be combined and solved under the stable models semantics to give the set of states which are considered to be socially acceptable by group as a whole. In our work we intentionally view the internal models of agents' attitudes as unknown (and hence that all actions which *might* be chosen by are included in possible models of our programs). From the perspective of our work, in the case where it is known that for instance some actions will never be performed by some agents because those actions are considered unacceptable by the agent performing them, it would be desirable to remove these actions from the set of possible models for a given institution. Resolving this automatically represents an interesting area for future research.

5   Conclusions and Directions for Future Research

We have described a formal specification for institutions for the purpose of modelling obligations, permissions and violations, while interactions between agents create traces that record their actions. We demonstrate how the specification may be translated into ASP and subsequently executed producing an answer set. Through the careful specification of the institutional state manipulation operations, this answer set has a one-to-one relationship with the institutional event traces of the formal model. In consequence, we arrive at an executable institutional specification that agents may dynamically compute and query to establish both how the current institutional state was reached and which actions will have what consequences in the future of the current state. Tools are currently being prototyped to automate these processes and aid in their visualization.

The ability to reason about and query time-related information is a strong point for using ASP. In our current model of time is discrete, yet we would also like to reason about durations, for examples when dealing with obligations. The DLV[21] system already provides a limited set of aggregates, which would appear to offer a solution and we will experiment with them in the near future.

The current approach does not deal with the effectiveness of sanctions since we do not encode the agent's utility. One solution to this problem would be to encode it as an atom $utility(Agent, X, T)$ and to use an extension of the ASP language we currently use that allows preference. In such a language one would be able to express that $utility(Agent, 10, T)$ is more preferred than $utility(Agent, 5, T)$ for any given Agent at any time.

References

[1] A. Artikis. *Executable Specification of Open Norm-Governed Computational Systems*. PhD thesis, Department of Electrical & Electronic Engineering, Imperial College London, Sept. 2003.

[2] A. Artikis, M. Sergot, and J. Pitt. An executable specification of an argumentation protocol. In *Proceedings of conference on artificial intelligence and law (icail)*, pages 1–11. ACM Press, 2003.

[3] A. Artikis, M. Sergot, and J. Pitt. Specifying electronic societies with the Causal Calculator. In F. Giunchiglia, J. Odell, and G. Weiss, editors, *Proceedings of Workshop on Agent-Oriented Software Engineering III (AOSE)*, LNCS 2585. Springer, 2003.

[4] C. Baral. *Knowledge Representation, Reasoning and Declarative Problem Solving*. Cambridge Press, 2003.

[5] C. Baral and M. Gelfond. Reasoning agents in dynamic domains. In *Logic-based artificial intelligence*, pages 257–279. Kluwer Academic Publishers, 2000.

[6] M. Brain, T. Crick, M. De Vos, and J. Fitch. Toast: Applying answer set programming to superoptimisation. In *International Conference on Logic Programming*, LNCS. Springer, Aug. 2006.

[7] F. Buccafurri and G. Caminiti. A social semantics for multi-agent systems. In C. Baral, G. Greco, N. Leone, and G. Terracina, editors, *LPNMR*, volume 3662 of *Lecture Notes in Computer Science*, pages 317–329. Springer, 2005.

[8] F. Buccafurri and G. Gottlob. Multiagent compromises, joint fixpoints, and stable models. In A. C. Kakas and F. Sadri, editors, *Computational Logic: Logic Programming and Beyond, Essays in Honour of Robert A. Kowalski, Part I*, volume 2407 of *Lecture Notes in Computer Science*, pages 561–585. Springer, 2002.

[9] E. M. Clarke, E. A. Emerson, and A. P. Sistla. Automatic verification of finite-state concurrent systems using temporal logic specifications. *ACM Transactions on Programming Languages and Systems*, 8(2):244–263, 1981.

[10] O. Cliffe, M. De Vos, and J. Padget. Specifying and analysing agent-based social institutions using answer set programming. In O. Boissier, J. Padget, V. Dignum, G. Lindemann, E. Matson, S. Ossowski, J. Sichman, and J. Vazquez-Salceda, editors, *Selected revised papers from the workshops on Agent, Norms and Institutions for Regulated Multi-Agent Systems (ANIREM) and Organizations and Organization Oriented Programming (OOOP) at AAMAS'05*, volume 3913 of *LNCS*, pages 99–113. Springer Verlag, 2006. ISBN: 3-540-35173-6.

[11] O. Cliffe and J. Padget. Towards a framework for checking agent interraction within institutions. In *Model Checking and Artificial Intelligence Workshop (MoChArt 02)*, Lyon, France, 2002.

[12] M. Colombetti, N. Fornara, and M. Verdicchio. The role of institutions in multiagent systems. In *Proceedings of the Workshop on Knowledge based and reasoning agents, VIII Convegno AI*IA 2002, Siena, Italy*, 2002.

[13] M. Colombetti and M. Verdicchio. An analysis of agent speech acts as institutional actions. In *The First International Joint Conference on Autonomous Agents and Multiagent Systems (AAMAS '02)*, pages 1157–1164, New York, NY, USA, 2002. ACM Press.

[14] M. De Vos and D. Vermeir. Choice Logic Programs and Nash Equilibria in Strategic Games. In J. Flum and M. Rodríguez-Artalejo, editors, *Computer Science Logic (CSL'99)*, volume 1683 of *Lecture Notes in Computer Science*, pages 266–276, Madrid, Spain, 1999. Springer Verslag.

[15] M. De Vos and D. Vermeir. Extending Answer Sets for Logic Programming Agents. *Annals of Mathematics and Artifical Intelligence*, 42(1–3):103–139, Sept. 2004. Special Issue on Computational Logic in Multi-Agent Systems.

[16] V. Dignum. *A Model for Organizational Interaction Based on Agents, Founded in Logic*. PhD thesis, Utrecht University, 2004.

[17] V. Dignum, J.-J. Meyer, F. Dignum, and H. Weigand. Formal Specification of Interaction in Agent Societies. In *Formal Approaches to Agent-Based Systems (FAABS-02)*, volume 2699 of *Lecture Notes in Computer Science*, pages 37–52, Oct. 2003.

[18] Douglass C. North. *Institutions, Institutional Change and Economic Performance*. Cambridge University Press, 1991.

[19] T. Eiter, W. Faber, N. Leone, and G. Pfeifer. The diagnosis frontend of the dlv system. *AI Communications*, 12(1-2):99–111, 1999.

[20] T. Eiter, W. Faber, N. Leone, G. Pfeifer, and A. Polleres. The DLV^k planning system. In S. Flesca, S. Greco, N. Leone, and G. Ianni, editors, *European Conference, JELIA 2002*, volume 2424 of *Lecture Notes in Artificial Intelligence*, pages 541–544, Cosenza, Italy, September 2002. Springer Verlag.

[21] T. Eiter, N. Leone, C. Mateis, G. Pfeifer, and F. Scarcello. The KR system dlv: Progress report, comparisons and benchmarks. In A. G. Cohn, L. Schubert, and S. C. Shapiro, editors, *KR'98: Principles of Knowledge Representation and Reasoning*, pages 406–417. Morgan Kaufmann, San Francisco, California, 1998.

[22] M. Esteva, J. Padget, and C. Sierra. Formalizing a language for institutions and norms. In M. Tambe and J.-J. Meyer, editors, *Intelligent Agents VIII*, Lecture Notes in Artificial Intelligence. Springer Verlag, 2001.

[23] N. Fornara and M. Colombetti. Operational specification of a commitment-based agent communication language. In *AAMAS '02: Proceedings of the first international joint conference on Autonomous agents and multiagent systems*, pages 536–542, New York, NY, USA, 2002. ACM Press.

[24] M. Gelfond and V. Lifschitz. The stable model semantics for logic programming. In R. A. Kowalski and K. A. Bowen, editors, *Logic Programming, Proceedings of the Fifth International Conference and Symposium*, pages 1070–1080, Seattle, Washington, August 1988. The MIT Press.

[25] E. Giunchiglia, J. Lee, V. Lifschitz, N. McCain, and H. Turner. Nonmonotonic causal theories. *Artificial Intelligence, Vol. 153, pp. 49-104*, 2004.

[26] E. Giunchiglia, Y. Lierler, and M. Maratea. SAT-Based Answer Set Programming. In *Proceedings of the 18th National Conference on Artificial Intelligence (AAAI-04)*, pages 61–66, 2004.

[27] J. Gressmann, T. Janhunen, R. Mercer, T. Schaub, S. Thiele, and R. Tichy. Platypus: A Platform for Distributed Answer Set Solving. In *Proceedings of the 8th International Conference on Logic Programming and Nonmonotonic Reasoning (LPNMR'05)*, pages 227–239, 2005.

[28] John R. Searle. *The Construction of Social Reality*. Allen Lane, The Penguin Press, 1995.

[29] Julian Padget. Modelling simple market structures in process algebras with locations. *Artificial Intelligence and Simulation of Behaviour Journal*, 1(1):87–108, 2001. ISSN 1476-3036.

[30] L. Kamara, A. Artikis, B. Neville, and J. Pitt. Simulating computational societies. In P. Petta, R. Tolksdorf, and F. Zambonelli, editors, *Proceedings of workshop on engineering societies in the agents world (esaw)*, LNCS 2577, pages 53–67. Springer, 2003.

[31] R. Kowalski and M. Sergot. A logic-based calculus of events. *New Gen. Comput.*, 4(1):67–95, 1986.

[32] R. A. Kowalski and F. Sadri. Reconciling the event calculus with the situation calculus. *Journal of Logic Programming*, 31(1–3):39–58, Apr.–June 1997.

[33] V. Lifschitz. Answer set programming and plan generation. *Journal of Artificial Intelligence*, 138(1-2):39–54, 2002.

[34] I. Niemelä and P. Simons. Smodels: An implementation of the stable model and well-founded semantics for normal LP. In J. Dix, U. Furbach, and A. Nerode, editors, *Proceedings of the 4th International Conference on Logic Programing and Nonmonotonic Reasoning*, volume 1265 of *LNAI*, pages 420–429, Berlin, July 28–31 1997. Springer.

[35] P. Noriega. *Agent mediated auctions: The Fishmarket Metaphor*. PhD thesis, Universitat Autonoma de Barcelona, 1997.

[36] J.-A. Rodríguez, P. Noriega, C. Sierra, and J. Padget. FM96.5 A Java-based Electronic Auction House. In *Proceedings of 2nd Conference on Practical Applications of Intelligent Agents and MultiAgent Technology (PAAM'97)*, pages 207–224, London, UK, Apr. 1997. ISBN 0-9525554-6-8.

[37] J. A. Rodriguez-Aguilar. *On the Design and Construction of Agent-mediated Institutions*. PhD thesis, Universitat Autonoma de Barcelona, 2001.

[38] J. V. Salceda. *The role of Norms and Electronic Institutions in Multi-Agent Systems applied to complex domains*. PhD thesis, Technical University of Catalonia, 2003.

[39] M. P. Singh. A social semantics for agent communication languages. In F. Dignum and M. Greaves, editors, *Issues in Agent Communication*, pages 31–45. Springer-Verlag: Heidelberg, Germany, 2000.

[40] T. Soininen and I. Niemelä. Developing a declarative rule language for applications in product configuration. In *Proceedings of the First International Workshop on Practical Aspects of Declarative Languages (PADL '99)*, LNCS, San Antonio, Texas, 1999. Springer.

[41] M. Verdicchio and M. Colombetti. A logical model of social commitment for agent communication. In *AAMAS '03: Proceedings of the second international joint conference on Autonomous agents and multiagent systems*, pages 528–535, New York, NY, USA, 2003. ACM Press.

[42] P. Yolum and M. P. Singh. Flexible protocol specification and execution: applying event calculus planning using commitments. In *AAMAS '02: Proceedings of the first international joint conference on Autonomous agents and multiagent systems*, pages 527–534. ACM Press, 2002.

A Complete Probabilistic Belief Logic*

Zining Cao

Department of Computer Science and Engineering
Nanjing University of Aero. & Astro., Nanjing 210016, China
caozn@nuaa.edu.cn

Abstract. In this paper, we propose the logic for reasoning about probabilistic belief, called PBL_f. Our language includes formulas that essentially express "agent i believes that the probability of φ is at least p". We first provide an inference system of PBL_f, and then introduce a probabilistic semantics for PBL_f. The soundness and finite model property of PBL_f are proven.

1 Introduction

The study of knowledge and belief has a long tradition in philosophy. An early treatment of a formal logical analysis of reasoning about knowledge and belief came from Hintikka's work [14]. More recently, researchers in such diverse fields as economics, linguistics, artificial intelligence and theoretical computer science have become increasingly interested in reasoning about knowledge and belief [1,6,7,8,9,10,11,13,17,18,22]. In wide areas of application of reasoning about knowledge and belief, it is necessary to reason about uncertain information. Therefore the representation and reasoning of probabilistic information in belief is important.

There has been a lot of works in the literatures related to the representation and reasoning of probabilistic information, such as evidence theory [24], probabilistic logic [7], probabilistic dynamic logic [3], probabilistic nonmonotonic logic [19], probabilistic knowledge logic [6] and etc.

A distinguished work was done by Fagin and Halpern [6], in which a probabilistic knowledge logic was proposed. It expanded the language of knowledge logic by adding formulas like "$w_i(\varphi) \geq 2w_i(\psi)$" and "$w_i(\varphi) < 1/3$", where φ and ψ are arbitrary formulas. These formulas mean "φ is at least twice probable as ψ" and "φ has probability less than $1/3$". The typical formulas of their logic are "$a_1w_i(\varphi_1) + ... + a_kw_i(\varphi_k) \geq b$", "$K_i(\varphi)$" and "$K_i^b(\varphi)$", the latter formula is an abbreviation of "$K_i(w_i(\varphi) \geq b)$". Here formulas may contain nested occurrences of the modal operators w_i and K_i, and the formulas in [7] do not contain nested occurrences of the modal operators w_i. On the basis of knowledge logic, they added axioms of reasoning about linear inequalities and probabilities. To provide semantics for such logic, Fagin and Halpern introduced a probability space

* This work was supported by the National Natural Science Foundation of China under Grant 60473036.

on Kripke models of knowledge logic, and gave some conditions about probability space, such as *OBJ, SDP* and *UNIF*. At last, Fagin and Halpern concluded by proving the soundness and weak completeness of their probabilistic knowledge logic.

Kooi's work [17] combined the probabilistic epistemic logic with the dynamic logic yielding a new logic, *PDEL*, that deals with changing probabilities and takes higher-order information into account. The syntax of *PDEL* is an expansion of Fagin and Halpern's logic by introducing formula "$[\varphi_1]\varphi_2$", which can be read as "φ_2 is the case, after everyone simultaneously and commonly learns that φ_1 is the case". The semantics of *PDEL* is essentially same as Fagin and Halpern's semantics, which is based on a combination of Kripke structure and probability functions. Kooi proved the soundness and weak completeness of *PDEL*.

In [20], the authors also presented a probabilistic belief logic, called *PEL*, which is essentially a restricted version of the logic proposed by Fagin and Halpern. But the inference system was not given and the corresponding properties such as soundness and completeness of *PEL* were not studied.

In [15], Hoek investigated a probabilistic logic $P_F D$. This logic is enriched with operators $P_r^>, (r \in [0,1])$ where the intended meaning of $P_r^> \varphi$ is "the probability of φ is strictly greater than r". The author gave a completeness proof of $P_F D$ by the construction of a canonical model for $P_F D$ considerably. Furthermore, the author also proved finite model property of the logic by giving a filtration-technique for the intended models. Finally, the author proved the decidability of the logic. In [15], the logic $P_F D$ is based on a set F, where F is a finite set and $\{0,1\} \subseteq F \subseteq [0,1]$. The completeness of $P_F D$ was not proven in [15] for the case that F is infinite. Hoek presented this problem as an open question and considered it as a difficult task. He thought this problem may be tackled by introducing infinitary rules. In [5], a temporal epistemic logic was presented, which is essential a combinational logic of $P_F D$ and temporal logic. This logic was used to represent and verify some properties in multi-agent systems.

In this paper, we propose a probabilistic belief logic. There is no axiom and rule about linear inequalities and probabilities in the inference system of probabilistic belief logic. Hence the inference system looks simpler than Fagin and Halpern's logic. We also propose a simpler semantics for probabilistic belief logic, where is no accessible relation and can be generalized to description semantics of other probabilistic modal logics. Moreover, we present the new completeness proofs for our probabilistic belief logic.

The remainder of the paper is organized as follows: In Section 2, we propose a probabilistic belief logic, called PBL_f. We provide the probabilistic semantics of PBL_f, and prove the soundness and finite model property of PBL_f with respect to the semantics. From the finite model property, we obtain the weak completeness of PBL_f. Note that a logic system has the compactness property if and only if the weak completeness is equivalent to the completeness in that logic. The compactness property does not hold in PBL_f. For example, $\{B_i(1/2, \varphi), B_i(2/3, \varphi), ..., B_i(n/n + 1, \varphi),...\} \cup \{\neg B_i(1, \varphi)\}$ is not satisfied in any PBL_f-model, but any finite subset of it has a model. Therefore the weak completeness of PBL_f is not equivalent to the completeness. PBL_f is proven to be weak complete. In Section 3, we compare our logic with the logic in [6] in terms of their syntax, inference system, semantics and proof technique. The paper is concluded in Section 4.

2 PBL_f and Its Inner Probabilistic Semantics

In this section, we first review the standard belief logic system and the standard Kripke semantics. Some examples are given to illustrate why it is necessary to extend belief to probabilistic belief. Then we introduce a probabilistic belief logic PBL_f.

In belief logic, the formula $B_i\varphi$ says that agent i believes φ. Consider a system with n agents, say $1, ..., n$, and we have a nonempty set Φ of primitive propositions about which we wish to reason. We construct formulas by closing off Φ under conjunction, negation and modal operators B_i, for $i = 1, ..., n$ (where $B_i\varphi$ is read as "agent i believes φ").

The semantics to these formulas is given by means of Kripke structure. A Kripke structure for belief (for n agents) is a tuple $(S, \pi, R_1, ..., R_n)$, where S is a set of states, $\pi(s)$ is a truth assignment to the primitive propositions of Φ for each state $s \in S$, and R_i is an accessible relation on S, which satisfies the following conditions: Euclideanness ($\forall s \forall s' \forall s''(sR_is' \wedge sR_is'' \rightarrow s'R_is'')$), transitivity ($\forall s \forall s' \forall s''(sR_is' \wedge s'R_is'' \rightarrow sR_is'')$) and definality ($\forall s \exists s'(sR_is')$).

We now assign truth values to formulas at each state in the structure. We write $(M, s) \models \varphi$ if the formula φ is true at state s in Kripke structure M.

$(M, s) \models p$ (for $p \in \Phi$) iff $\pi(s)(p) = true$
$(M, s) \models \neg\varphi$ iff $(M, s) \not\models \varphi$
$(M, s) \models \varphi \wedge \psi$ iff $(M, s) \models \varphi$ and $(M, s) \models \psi$
$(M, s) \models B_i\varphi$ iff $(M, t) \models \varphi$ for all $t \in R_i(s)$ with $R_i(s) = \{s' | (s, s') \in R_i\}$

The last clause in this definition captures the intuition that agent i believes φ in world (M, s) exactly if φ is true in all worlds that i considers possible.

It is well known that the following set of axioms and inference rules provides a sound and complete axiomatization for the logic of belief with respect to the class of Kripke structures for belief:

All instances of propositional tautologies and rules.

$(B_i\varphi \wedge B_i(\varphi \rightarrow \psi)) \rightarrow B_i\psi$
$B_i\varphi \rightarrow \neg B_i\neg\varphi$
$B_i\varphi \rightarrow B_iB_i\varphi$
$\neg B_i\varphi \rightarrow B_i\neg B_i\varphi$
$\vdash \varphi \Rightarrow \vdash B_i\varphi$

There are examples of probabilistic belief in daily life. For example, one may believe that the probability of "it will rain tomorrow" is less than 0.4; in a football game, one may believe that the probability of "team A will win" is no less than

0.7 and so on. In distribute systems, there may be the cases that "agent i believes that the probability of 'agent j believes that the probability of φ is at least a' is no less than b". Suppose there are two persons communicating by email, agent A sends an email to agent B. Since the email may be lost in network, A does not know whether B has received the email. Therefore A may believe that the probability of "B has received my email" is less than 0.99, or may believe that the probability of "B has received my email" is at least 0.8, and so on. On the other hand, B may believe that the probability of "A believes that the probability of 'B has received my email' is at least 0.9" is less than 0.8. In order to reply to A, B sends an acknowledgement email to A, A receives the email, and sends another acknowledgement email to B, now B believes that the probability of "A believes that the probability of 'B has received my first email' is equal to 1" is equal to 1. In order to represent and reason with probabilistic belief, it is necessary to extend belief logic to probabilistic belief logic. In following, we propose a probabilistic belief logic PBL_f, the basic formula in PBL_f is $B_i(a, \varphi)$, which says agent i believes that the probability of φ is no less than a. In the semantics of PBL_f, we assign an inner probability space to every possible world in the model, here "inner" means the measure does not obey the additivity condition, but obeys some weak additivity conditions satisfied by inner probability measure.

2.1   Language of PBL_f

Throughout this paper, we let L^{PBL_f} be a language which is just the set of formulas of interest to us.

Definition 1. The set of formulas in PBL_f, called L^{PBL_f}, is given by the following rules:

(1) If $\varphi \in$ Atomic formulas set $Prop$, then $\varphi \in L^{PBL_f}$;
(2) If $\varphi \in L^{PBL_f}$, then $\neg\varphi \in L^{PBL_f}$;
(3) If $\varphi_1, \varphi_2 \in L^{PBL_f}$, then $\varphi_1 \wedge \varphi_2 \in L^{PBL_f}$;
(4) If $\varphi \in L^{PBL_f}$ and $a \in [0,1]$, then $B_i(a, \varphi) \in L^{PBL_f}$, where i belongs to the set of agents $\{1, ..., n\}$. Intuitively, $B_i(a, \varphi)$ means that agent i believes the probability of φ is no less than a.

2.2   Semantics of PBL_f

We will describe the semantics of PBL_f, that is, a formal model that we can use to determine whether a given formula is true or false. We call the formal model inner probabilistic model, roughly speaking, at each state, each agent has an inner probability on a certain set of states.

Definition 2. An inner probabilistic model PM of PBL_f is a tuple $(S, P_1, ..., P_n, \pi)$, where
(1) S is a nonempty finite set whose elements are called possible worlds or states.
(2) P_i is a mapping, it maps every possible world s to a PBL_f-probability space $P_i(s) = (S, X, \mu_{i,s})$, here $X = \wp(S)$;

$\mu_{i,s}$ is a PBL_f-inner probability measure assigned to the set X, which means that $\mu_{i,s}$ satisfies the following conditions:

(a) $0 \le \mu_{i,s}(A) \le 1$ for all $A \in X$.

(b) $\mu_{i,s}(\emptyset) = 0$ and $\mu_{i,s}(S) = 1$.

(c) If $A_1, A_2 \in X$ and $A_1 \subseteq A_2$, then $\mu_{i,s}(A_1) \le \mu_{i,s}(A_2)$;

(d) If $A_1, A_2 \in X$ and $A_1 \cap A_2 = \emptyset$, then $\mu_{i,s}(A_1 \cup A_2) \ge \mu_{i,s}(A_1) + \mu_{i,s}(A_2)$;

(e) If $A_1, A_2 \in X$, then $\mu_{i,s}(A_1 \cap A_2) \ge \mu_{i,s}(A_1) + \mu_{i,s}(A_2) - 1$;

(f) Let $\Lambda_{i,s} = \{s' | P_i(s) = P_i(s')\}$, then $\mu_{i,s}(\Lambda_{i,s}) = 1$.

(3) π is a mapping: $S \times Prop \to \{true, false\}$, where $Prop$ is an atomic formulas set.

Remark: It is easy to see that the conditions (d) and (e) in Definition 2 are weaker than the finite additivity condition in probability measure. One can check that if μ is a probability measure, then inner measure μ^* (here $\mu^*(A) = sup(\{\mu(B) | B \subseteq A\})$) induced by μ obeys the conditions (d) and (e) in Definition 2, i.e., the reason we call $\mu_{i,s}$ inner probability measure.

The notation $\Lambda_{i,s}$ in the condition (f) represents the set of states whose probability space is same as the probability space of state s. Therefore the condition (f) means that for agent i who is in state s, the probability space of almost all states is the same as the probability space of s. We introduce the condition (f) for the reason of soundness and completeness. In the standard belief logic, modal operator B_i satisfies the some axioms such as: $B_i\varphi \to \neg B_i \neg \varphi$ and $B_i\varphi \to B_i B_i \varphi$. To make the Kripke semantics of belief logic coincide with these axioms, the accessible relation R_i is assumed to satisfy the conditions: Euclideanness ($\forall s \forall s' \forall s''(sR_is' \land sR_is'' \to s'R_is'')$), transitivity ($\forall s \forall s' \forall s''(sR_is' \land s'R_is'' \to sR_is'')$) and definality ($\forall s \exists s'(sR_is')$). In our PBL_f logic, there are also some axioms such as $B_i(a, \varphi) \to B_i(1, B_i(a, \varphi))$ and $\neg B_i(a, \varphi) \to B_i(1, \neg B_i(a, \varphi))$. These axioms are probabilistic generalization of $B_i\varphi \to \neg B_i\neg\varphi$ and $B_i\varphi \to B_iB_i\varphi$. Similar to the case of standard belief logic, to assure the probabilistic semantics of PBL_f logic coincide with the axioms of PBL_f, the condition (f) is introduced. we will see in the following that the proof of soundness and completeness in the cases of $B_i(a, \varphi) \to B_i(1, B_i(a, \varphi))$ and $\neg B_i(a, \varphi) \to B_i(1, \neg B_i(a, \varphi))$ relies on the condition (f).

As an example, we consider a PBL_f-model such that $PM = (S, \pi, P_1)$. Here $S = \{s_1, s_2, s_3\}$; $\pi(s_1, p) = false$, $\pi(s_2, p) = false$, $\pi(s_3, p) = true$, $\pi(s_1, q) = true$, $\pi(s_2, q) = true$, $\pi(s_3, q) = true$; P_1 is defined as follows: for every $s \in S$, $P_1(s) = (S, X, \mu_{1,s})$, where $X = \wp(S)$, $\mu_{1,s_1}(\emptyset) = \mu_{1,s_2}(\emptyset) = \mu_{1,s_3}(\emptyset) = 0$, $\mu_{1,s_1}(\{s_1\}) = \mu_{1,s_2}(\{s_1\}) = 1/2$, $\mu_{1,s_3}(\{s_1\}) = 0$, $\mu_{1,s_1}(\{s_2\}) = \mu_{1,s_2}(\{s_2\}) = 1/2$, $\mu_{1,s_3}(\{s_2\}) = 0$, $\mu_{1,s_1}(\{s_3\}) = \mu_{1,s_2}(\{s_3\}) = 0$, $\mu_{1,s_3}(\{s_3\}) = 1$, $\mu_{1,s_1}(\{s_1, s_2\}) = \mu_{1,s_2}(\{s_1, s_2\}) = 1$, $\mu_{1,s_3}(\{s_1, s_2\}) = 0$, $\mu_{1,s_1}(\{s_1, s_3\}) = \mu_{1,s_2}(\{s_1, s_3\}) = 1/2$, $\mu_{1,s_3}(\{s_1, s_3\}) = 1$, $\mu_{1,s_1}(\{s_2, s_3\}) = \mu_{1,s_2}(\{s_2, s_3\}) = 1/2$, $\mu_{1,s_3}(\{s_2, s_3\}) = 1$, $\mu_{1,s_1}(S) = \mu_{1,s_2}(S) = \mu_{1,s_3}(S) = 1$. It is easy to check that the above model satisfies the conditions in Definition 2. In this model, it is clear that inner probability measure $\mu_{1,s}$ varies with s, and consequently the probability space also varies with s, hence we index probability space by s.

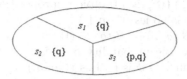

Fig. 1. The states of PM

In Figure 1, we shows PM in the above example.
We also give the value of μ_{1,s_1}, μ_{1,s_2} and μ_{1,s_3} in Table 1:

Table 1. The value of μ_{1,s_1}, μ_{1,s_2} and μ_{1,s_3}

	$\emptyset$	$\{s_1\}$	$\{s_2\}$	$\{s_3\}$	$\{s_1, s_2\}$	$\{s_1, s_3\}$	$\{s_2, s_3\}$	$\{s_1, s_2, s_3\}$
μ_{1,s_1}	0	1/2	1/2	0	1	1/2	1/2	1
μ_{1,s_2}	0	1/2	1/2	0	1	1/2	1/2	1
μ_{1,s_3}	0	0	0	1	0	1	1	1

Definition 3. Probabilistic semantics of PBL_f
$(PM, s) \models p$ iff $\pi(s, p) = true$, where p is an atomic formula;
$(PM, s) \models \neg\varphi$ iff $(PM, s) \not\models \varphi$;
$(PM, s) \models \varphi_1 \wedge \varphi_2$ iff $(PM, s) \models \varphi_1$ and $(PM, s) \models \varphi_2$;
$(PM, s) \models B_i(a, \varphi)$ iff $\mu_{i,s}(ev_{PM}(\varphi)) \geq a$, where $ev_{PM}(\varphi) = \{s' | (PM, s')$ $\models \varphi\}$.

2.3 Inference System of PBL_f

Now we list a number of valid properties of probabilistic belief, which form the
inference system of PBL_f.

Axioms and inference rules of proposition logic

Axiom 1. $B_i(0, \varphi)$ (For any proposition φ, agent i believes that the probability
of φ is no less than 0.)

Axiom 2. $B_i(a, \varphi) \wedge B_i(b, \psi) \to B_i(max(a+b-1, 0), \varphi \wedge \psi)$ (For any φ and ψ,
if agent i believes that the probability of φ is no less than a, and believes that
the probability of ψ is no less than b, then agent i believes that the probability
of $\varphi \wedge \psi$ is no less than $max(a + b - 1, 0)$.)

Axiom 3. $B_i(a, \varphi) \to B_i(1, B_i(a, \varphi))$ (If agent i believes that the probability
of φ is no less than a, then agent i believes that the probability of his belief
being true is no less than 1.)

Axiom 4. $\neg B_i(a, \varphi) \to B_i(1, \neg B_i(a, \varphi))$ (If agent i believes that the probability
of φ is less than a, then agent i believes that the probability of his belief being
true is no less than 1.)

Axiom 5. $B_i(a, \varphi) \to B_i(b, \varphi)$, where $1 \geq a \geq b \geq 0$. (If agent i believes that
the probability of φ is no less than a, and $1 \geq a \geq b \geq 0$, then agent i believes
that the probability of φ is no less than b.)

Rule 1. $\vdash \varphi \Rightarrow \vdash B_i(1, \varphi)$ (If φ is a tautology proposition, then agent i believes that the probability of φ is no less than 1.)

Rule 2. $\vdash \varphi \rightarrow \psi \Rightarrow \vdash B_i(a, \varphi) \rightarrow B_i(a, \psi)$ (If $\varphi \rightarrow \psi$ is a tautology proposition, and agent i believes that the probability of φ is no less than a, then agent i believes that the probability of ψ is no less than a.)

Rule 3. $\vdash \neg(\varphi \wedge \psi) \Rightarrow \vdash \neg(B_i(a, \varphi) \wedge B_i(b, \psi))$ for any $a, b \in [0, 1]$ such that $a + b > 1$. (If φ and ψ are incompatible propositions, then it is impossible that agent i believes that the probability of φ is no less than a, and believes that the probability of ψ is no less than b, where $a + b > 1$.)

Rule 4. $\vdash \neg(\varphi \wedge \psi) \Rightarrow \vdash B_i(a, \varphi) \wedge B_i(b, \psi) \rightarrow B_i(a + b, \varphi \vee \psi)$, where $a + b \leq 1$. (If φ and ψ are incompatible propositions, agent i believes that the probability of φ is no less than a, and believes that the probability of ψ is no less than b, where $a + b \leq 1$, then agent i believes that the probability of $\varphi \vee \psi$ is no less than $a + b$.)

Rule 5. $\Gamma \vdash B_i(a_n, \varphi)$ for all $n \in M \Rightarrow \Gamma \vdash B_i(a, \varphi)$, where M is an arbitrary index set, $a = sup_{n \in M}(\{a_n\})$. (If agent i believes that the probability of φ is no less than a_n, where n is any element in the index set M, then agent i believes that the probability of φ is no less than a, where $a = sup_{n \in M}(\{a_n\})$.)

In many epistemic logics, the consistency property of beliefs is written as $B_i\varphi \rightarrow \neg B_i\neg\varphi$. In this logic, we can write $B_i(1, \varphi) \rightarrow \neg B_i(1, \neg\varphi)$, and $B_i(1, \varphi) \rightarrow \neg B_i(0.1, \neg\varphi)$, and so on, these rules are the generialization of $B_i\varphi \rightarrow \neg B_i\neg\varphi$. So that the consistency of beliefs can be represented in this logic.

In the following sections, we will show that in a precise sense these properties completely characterize the formulas of PBL_f that are valid with respect to probabilistic model.

We first consider the notion of provability. Inference system PBL_f consists of a collection of axioms and inference rules. We are actually interested in (substitution) instances of axioms and inference rules (so we in fact think of axioms and inference rules as schemes). For example, the formula $B_i(0.7, \varphi) \wedge B_i(0.8, \psi) \rightarrow B_i(0.5, \varphi \wedge \psi)$ is an instances of the propositional tautology $B_i(a, \varphi) \wedge B_i(b, \psi) \rightarrow B_i(max(a + b - 1, 0), \varphi \wedge \psi)$, obtained by substituting $B_i(0.7, \varphi)$, $B_i(0.8, \psi)$ and $B_i(0.5, \varphi \wedge \psi)$ for $B_i(a, \varphi)$, $B_i(b, \psi)$ and $B_i(max(a + b - 1, 0), \varphi \wedge \psi)$ respectively. A proof in PBL_f consists of a sequence of formulas, each of which is either an instance of an axiom in PBL_f or follows from an application of an inference rule. (If "$\varphi_1, ..., \varphi_n$ infer ψ" is an instance of an inference rule, and if the formulas $\varphi_1, ..., \varphi_n$ have appeared earlier in the proof, then we say that ψ follows from an application of an inference rule.) A proof is said to be from Γ to φ if the premise is Γ and the last formula is φ in the proof. We say φ is provable from Γ in PBL_f, and write $\Gamma \vdash_{PBL_f} \varphi$, if there is a proof from Γ to φ in PBL_f.

2.4   Soundness of PBL_f

We will prove that PBL_f characterizes the set of formulas that are valid with respect to probabilistic model. Inference system of PBL_f is said to be sound with respect to probabilistic models if every formula provable in PBL_f is valid with respect to probabilistic models. The system PBL_f is complete with respect to probabilistic models if every formula valid with respect to probabilistic models is provable in PBL_f. We think of PBL_f as characterizing probabilistic models if it provides a sound and complete axiomatization of that class; notationally, this amounts to saying that for all formulas set Γ and all formula φ, we have $\Gamma \vdash_{PBL_f} \varphi$ if and only if $\Gamma \models_{PBL_f} \varphi$. The soundness and completeness provide a tight connection between the syntactic notion of provability and the semantic notion of validity.

Now we first prove the soundness of PBL_f. The completeness of PBL_f is proven in Section 2.5.

Proposition 1. (Soundness of PBL_f) If $\Gamma \vdash_{PBL_f} \varphi$, then $\Gamma \models_{PBL_f} \varphi$.

Proof. We show each axiom and each rule of PBL_f is sound, respectively.

Axiom 1: By the definition of PBL_f-probability measure, for any s, if $A \in X_{i,s}$ then $\mu_{i,s}(A) \geq 0$. Since by the definition of $X_{i,s}$, for any φ, $ev_{PM}(\varphi) = \{s'|(PM, s') \models \varphi\} \in X_{i,s}$, we have $\mu_{i,s}(ev_{PM}(\varphi)) \geq 0$, therefore $B_i(0, \varphi)$ holds.

Axiom 2: Suppose $(PM, s) \models B_i(a, \varphi) \wedge B_i(b, \psi)$, so $\mu_{i,s}(ev_{PM}(\varphi)) \geq a$ and $\mu_{i,s}(ev_{PM}(\psi)) \geq b$. For $\mu_{i,s}$ is PBL_f-probability measure, we get $\mu_{i,s}(ev_{PM}(\varphi \wedge \psi)) = \mu_{i,s}(ev_{PM}(\varphi) \cap ev_{PM}(\psi)) \geq \mu_{i,s}(ev_{PM}(\varphi)) + \mu_{i,s}(ev_{PM}(\psi)) - 1 \geq a + b - 1$, which implies $(PM, s) \models B_i(max(a + b - 1, 0), \varphi \wedge \psi)$.

Axiom 3: Suppose $(PM, s) \models B_i(a, \varphi)$, therefore $\mu_{i,s}(ev_{PM}(\varphi)) \geq a$. Let $\Lambda_{i,s} = \{s'|P_i(s) = P_i(s')\}$, then $\Lambda_{i,s} \in X$ and $\mu_{i,s}(\Lambda_{i,s}) = 1$. Let $\Xi = \{s'|\mu_{i,s'}(ev_{PM}(\varphi)) \geq a\}$. Since $s' \in \Lambda_{i,s}$ implies $s' \in \Xi$, it is clear $\Lambda_{i,s} \subseteq \Xi$, since $\mu_{i,s}(\Lambda_{i,s}) = 1$, so $\mu_{i,s}(\Xi) = 1$. If $s' \in \Xi$, then $s' \in ev_{PM}(B_i(a, \varphi))$, therefore $\mu_{i,s}(ev_{PM}(B_i(a, \varphi))) = 1$, we get $(PM, s) \models B_i(1, B_i(a, \varphi))$ as desired.

Axiom 4: Suppose $(PM, s) \models \neg B_i(a, \varphi)$, so $\mu_{i,s}(ev_{PM}(\varphi)) < a$. Let $\Lambda_{i,s} = \{s'|P_i(s) = P_i(s')\}$, then $\Lambda_{i,s} \in X$ and $\mu_{i,s}(\Lambda_{i,s}) = 1$. Let $\Xi = \{s'|\mu_{i,s'}(ev_{PM}(\varphi)) < a\}$, for $s' \in \Lambda_{i,s}$ implies $s' \in \Xi$, it is clear $\Lambda_{i,s} \subseteq \Xi$, since $\mu_{i,s}(\Lambda_{i,s}) = 1$, so $\mu_{i,s}(\Xi) = 1$. If $s' \in \Xi$, then $s' \in ev_{PM}(B_i(a, \varphi))$, therefore $\mu_{i,s}(ev_{PM}(\neg B_i(a, \varphi))) = 1$, we get $(PM, s) \models B_i(1, \neg B_i(a, \varphi))$ as desired.

Axiom 5: Suppose $(PM, s) \models B_i(a, \varphi)$, so $\mu_{i,s}(ev_{PM}(\varphi)) \geq a$. If $1 \geq a \geq b \geq 0$, then $\mu_{i,s}(ev_{PM}(\varphi)) \geq b$, so $(PM, s) \models B_i(b, \varphi)$, therefore $B_i(a, \varphi) \rightarrow B_i(b, \varphi)$ holds.

Rule 1: Since $\models \varphi$, so for any possible world s, $\mu_{i,s}(ev_{PM}(\varphi)) \geq 1$, therefore $\models B_i(1, \varphi)$ holds.

Rule 2: Since $\models \varphi \rightarrow \psi$, so $ev_{PM}(\varphi) \subseteq ev_{PM}(\psi)$. Suppose $(PM, s) \models B_i(a, \varphi)$, therefore $\mu_{i,s}(ev_{PM}(\varphi)) \geq a$, by the property of PBL_f-probability space, we get $\mu_{i,s}(ev_{PM}(\varphi)) \leq \mu_{i,s}(ev_{PM}(\psi))$. So $\mu_{i,s}(ev_{PM}(\psi)) \geq a$. Therefore $(PM, s)| = B_i(a, \psi)$, and *Rule* 2 of PBL_f holds.

Rule 3: Suppose $\models \neg(\varphi \wedge \psi)$, so $ev_{PM}(\varphi) \cap ev_{PM}(\psi) = \emptyset$. By the property of PBL_f-probability space, for any possible world s, we get $\mu_{i,s}(ev_{PM}(\varphi) \cup ev_{PM}(\psi)) = \mu_{i,s}(ev_{PM}(\varphi)) + \mu_{i,s}(ev_{PM}(\psi))$ and $\mu_{i,s}(ev_{PM}(\varphi) \cup ev_{PM}(\psi)) \leq 1$, therefore $\mu_{i,s}(ev_{PM}(\varphi)) + \mu_{i,s}(ev_{PM}(\psi)) \leq 1$. Assume $(PM, s) \models (B_i(a, \varphi) \wedge B_i(b, \psi))$ where $a + b > 1$, then $\mu_{i,s}(ev_{PM}(\varphi)) \geq a$, $\mu_{i,s}(ev_{PM}(\psi)) \geq b$, but $a + b > 1$, it is a contradiction.

Rule 4: Suppose $\models \neg(\varphi \wedge \psi)$ and for possible world s, $(PM, s) \models B_i(a, \varphi) \wedge B_i(b, \psi)$, so $ev_{PM}(\varphi) \cap ev_{PM}(\psi) = \emptyset$, $\mu_{i,s}(ev_{PM}(\varphi)) \geq a$, and $\mu_{i,s}(ev_{PM}(\psi)) \geq b$. By the property of PBL_f-probability space, for any possible world s, we get $\mu_{i,s}(ev_{PM}(\varphi) \cup ev_{PM}(\psi)) = \mu_{i,s}(ev_{PM}(\varphi)) + \mu_{i,s}(ev_{PM}(\psi))$. Hence, $\mu_{i,s}(ev_{PM}(\varphi)) + \mu_{i,s}(ev_{PM}(\psi)) \geq a + b$ and $\mu_{i,s}(ev_{PM}(\varphi) \cup ev_{PM}(\psi)) \geq a + b$, which means $(PM, s) \models B_i(a + b, \varphi \vee \psi)$.

Rule 5: Suppose $\Gamma \models B_i(a_n, \varphi)$ for all $n \in M$, therefore for every s, if $(PM, s) \models \Gamma$, then $(PM, s) \models B_i(a_n, \varphi)$ for all $n \in M$, so $\mu_{i,s}(ev_{PM}(\varphi)) \geq a_n$ for all $n \in M$. We get $\mu_{i,s}(ev_{PM}(\varphi)) \geq sup_{n \in M}(\{a_n\})$. Therefore, $(PM, s) \models B_i(a, \varphi)$ and $a = sup_{n \in M}(\{a_n\})$, we get $\Gamma \models B_i(a, \varphi)$ and $a = sup_{n \in M}(\{a_n\})$ as desired.

2.5   Finite Model Property of PBL_f

We now turn our attention to the finite model property of PBL_f. It needs to show that if a formula is PBL_f-consistent, then it is satisfiable in a finite structure. The idea is that rather than considering maximal consistent formulas set when trying to construct a structure satisfying a formula φ, we restrict our attention to sets of subformulas of φ.

Definition 4. Suppose ζ is a consistent formula with respect to PBL_f, $Sub^*(\zeta)$ is a set of formulas defined as follows: let $\zeta \in L^{PBL_f}$, $Sub(\zeta)$ is the set of subformulas of ζ, then $Sub^*(\zeta) = Sub(\zeta) \cup \{\neg\psi|\psi \in Sub(\zeta)\}$. It is clear that $Sub^*(\zeta)$ is finite.

Definition 5. The model PM_ζ with respect to formula ζ is $(S_\zeta, P_{\zeta,1}, ..., P_{\zeta,n}, \pi_\zeta)$.

(1) Here $S_\zeta = \{\Gamma|\Gamma$ is a maximal consistent formulas set with respect to PBL_f and $\Gamma \subseteq Sub^*(\zeta)\}$.

(2) For any $\Gamma \in S_\zeta$, $P_{\zeta,i}(\Gamma) = (S_\zeta, X_\zeta, \mu_{\zeta,i,\Gamma})$, where $X(\varphi) = \{\Gamma'| \Gamma' \vdash_{PBL_f} \varphi\}$ and $X_\zeta = \{X(\varphi)| \varphi$ is a Boolean combination of formulas in $Sub^*(\zeta)\}$; $\mu_{\zeta,i,\Gamma}$ is a mapping: $X_\zeta \to [0,1]$, and $\mu_{\zeta,i,\Gamma}(X(\varphi)) = sup(\{a|B_i(a, \varphi)$ is provable from Γ in $PBL_f\})$.

(3) π_ζ is a truth assignment as follows: For any atomic formula p, $\pi_\zeta(p, \Gamma) = true \Leftrightarrow p \in \Gamma$.

We mainly need to show that the above model PM_ζ is a PBL_f-inner probabilistic model. The following lemmas from Lemma 1 to Lemma 13 contribute to this purpose. Furthermore, Lemma 14 states that PM_ζ is "canonical", i.e., for any consistent formula $\varphi \in Sub^*(\zeta)$, there is a state s, such that $(PM_\zeta, s) \models \varphi$. Since we can prove that PM_ζ is a finite model, these lemmas imply the finite model property of PBL_f.

Lemma 1. S_ζ is a nonempty finite set.

Proof. Since the rules and axioms of PBL_f are consistent, S_ζ is nonempty. For $Sub^*(\zeta)$ is a finite set, by the definition of S_ζ, the cardinality of S_ζ is no more than the cardinality of $\wp(Sub^*(\zeta))$.

Lemma 2. X_ζ is the power set of S_ζ.

*Proof.*Firstly, since $Sub^*(\zeta)$ is finite, so if $\Gamma \in S_\zeta$ then Γ is finite. We can let φ_Γ be the conjunction of the formulas in Γ. Secondly, if $A \subseteq S_\zeta$, then $A = X(\vee_{\Gamma \in A}\varphi_\Gamma)$. By the above argument, we have that X_ζ is the power set of S_ζ.

Lemma 3. If φ is consistent (here φ is a Boolean combination of formulas in $Sub^*(\zeta)$), then there exists Γ such that φ can be proven from Γ, here Γ is a maximal consistent set with respect to PBL_f and $\Gamma \subseteq Sub^*(\zeta)$.

Proof. For φ is a Boolean combination of formulas in $Sub^*(\zeta)$, therefore by regarding the formulas in $Sub^*(\zeta)$ as atomic formulas, φ can be represented as disjunctive normal form. Since φ is consistent, so there is a consistent disjunctive term in disjunctive normal form expression of φ, let such term be $\psi_1 \wedge ... \wedge \psi_n$, then φ can be derived from the maximal consistent set Γ which contains $\{\psi_1, ..., \psi_n\}$.

Lemma 4. For any $\Gamma \in S_\zeta$, $P_{\zeta,i}(\Gamma)$ is well defined.

Proof. It suffices to prove the following claim: if $X(\varphi) = X(\psi)$, then $\mu_{\zeta,i,\Gamma}(X(\varphi)) = \mu_{\zeta,i,\Gamma}(X(\psi))$. If $X(\varphi) = X(\psi)$, it is clear that $\vdash \varphi \leftrightarrow \psi$. For suppose not, then $\varphi \wedge \neg\psi$ is consistent, by Lemma 3, there is Γ' such that $\varphi \wedge \neg\psi$ can be proven from Γ', therefore $\Gamma' \in X(\varphi)$ and $\Gamma' \notin X(\psi)$, it is a contradiction. Thus $\vdash \varphi \leftrightarrow \psi$. By rule: $\vdash \varphi \to \psi \Rightarrow \vdash B_i(a,\varphi) \to B_i(a,\psi)$, we get $\vdash B_i(a,\varphi) \leftrightarrow B_i(a,\psi)$, which means $\mu_{\zeta,i,\Gamma}(X(\varphi)) = \mu_{\zeta,i,\Gamma}(X(\psi))$.

Lemma 5. Let $Pro_{\zeta,i,\Gamma}(\varphi) = \{a|B_i(a,\varphi)$ can be proven from Γ in $PBL_f\}$, then $sup(Pro_{\zeta,i,\Gamma}(\varphi)) \in Pro_{\zeta,i,\Gamma}(\varphi)$.

Proof. Suppose $Pro_{\zeta,i,\Gamma}(\varphi) = \{a|B_i(a,\varphi)$ can be proven from Γ in $PBL_f\}$, therefore $\Gamma \vdash B_i(a_n,\varphi)$ for all $a_n \in Pro_{\zeta,i,\Gamma}(\varphi)$, by *Rule 5* of PBL_f, $\Gamma \vdash B_i(a,\varphi)$, where $a = sup_{n \in M}(\{a_n\}) = sup(Pro_{\zeta,i,\Gamma}(\varphi))$, so we get $sup(Pro_{\zeta,i,\Gamma}(\varphi)) \in Pro_{\zeta,i,\Gamma}(\varphi)$ as desired.

Lemma 6. If $A \in X_\zeta$, then $0 \leq \mu_{\zeta,i,\Gamma}(A) \leq 1$. Furthermore, $\mu_{\zeta,i,\Gamma}(\emptyset) = 0$, $\mu_{\zeta,i,\Gamma}(S_\zeta) = 1$.

Proof. By the definition, if $B_i(a,\varphi)$ is a well formed formula, then $0 \leq a \leq 1$; furthermore, check the axioms and rules of PBL_f, any formula derived from well formed formulas is also a well formed formula, so $0 \leq \mu_{\zeta,i,\Gamma}(X(\varphi)) \leq 1$. Therefore, if $A \in X_\zeta$, then $0 \leq \mu_{\zeta,i,\Gamma}(A) \leq 1$.

By rule: $\vdash \varphi \Rightarrow \vdash B_i(1,\varphi)$, therefore we have $\mu_{\zeta,i,\Gamma}(S_\zeta) = 1$ as desired. By axiom: $B_i(0,\varphi)$, we get $B_i(0,false)$, so $\mu_{\zeta,i,\Gamma}(\emptyset) \geq 0$. By rule: $\vdash \neg(\varphi \wedge \psi) \Rightarrow \vdash B_i(a,\varphi) \wedge B_i(b,\psi) \to B_i(a+b,\varphi \vee \psi)$, where $a+b \leq 1$, we have $\vdash B_i(a,false) \wedge B_i(b,true) \to B_i(a+b,false \vee true)$, hence $\mu_{\zeta,i,\Gamma}(S_\zeta) \geq \mu_{\zeta,i,\Gamma}(S_\zeta) + \mu_{\zeta,i,\Gamma}(\emptyset)$. Since $\mu_{\zeta,i,\Gamma}(S_\zeta) = 1$, so $1 \geq 1 + \mu_{\zeta,i,\Gamma}(\emptyset)$, therefore $\mu_{\zeta,i,\Gamma}(\emptyset) = 0$ as desired.

Lemma 7. If $A_1, A_2 \in X_\zeta$ and $A_1 \subseteq A_2$, then $\mu_{\zeta,i,\Gamma}(A_1) \leq \mu_{\zeta,i,\Gamma}(A_2)$.

Proof. Since $A_1, A_2 \in X_\zeta$, assume $A_1 = X(\varphi)$, $A_2 = X(\psi)$. If $X(\varphi) \subseteq X(\psi)$, by rule: $\vdash \varphi \to \psi \Rightarrow \vdash B_i(a,\varphi) \to B_i(a,\psi)$, we have $\mu_{\zeta,i,\Gamma}(X(\varphi)) \leq \mu_{\zeta,i,\Gamma}(X(\psi))$. Therefore if $A_1, A_2 \in X_\zeta$ and $A_1 \subseteq A_2$, then $\mu_{\zeta,i,\Gamma}(A_1) \leq \mu_{\zeta,i,\Gamma}(A_2)$ holds.

Lemma 8. If $A_1, A_2 \in X_\zeta$ and $A_1 \cap A_2 = \emptyset$, then $\mu_{\zeta,i,\Gamma}(A_1 \cup A_2) \geq \mu_{\zeta,i,\Gamma}(A_1) + \mu_{\zeta,i,\Gamma}(A_2)$.

Proof. Since $A_1, A_2 \in X_\zeta$, assume $A_1 = X(\varphi)$, $A_2 = X(\psi)$, by rule: $\vdash \neg(\varphi \wedge \psi) \Rightarrow \vdash B_i(a, \varphi) \wedge B_i(b, \psi) \rightarrow B_i(a + b, \varphi \vee \psi)$, where $a_1 + a_2 \leq 1$, we have $\mu_{\zeta,i,\Gamma}(X(\varphi) \cup X(\psi)) \geq \mu_{\zeta,i,\Gamma}(X(\varphi)) + \mu_{\zeta,i,\Gamma}(X(\psi))$. Therefore if $A_1, A_2 \in X_\zeta$ and $A_1 \cap A_2 = \emptyset$, then $\mu_{\zeta,i,\Gamma}(A_1 \cup A_2) \geq \mu_{\zeta,i,\Gamma}(A_1) + \mu_{\zeta,i,\Gamma}(A_2)$.

Lemma 9. For any $C, D \in X_\zeta$, $\mu_{\zeta,i,\Gamma}(C \cap D) \geq \mu_{\zeta,i,\Gamma}(C) + \mu_{\zeta,i,\Gamma}(D) - 1$.

Proof. Since $C, D \in X_\zeta$, assume $C = X(\varphi)$, $D = X(\psi)$, by axiom: $B_i(a, \varphi) \wedge B_i(b, \psi) \rightarrow B_i(max(a + b - 1, 0), \varphi \wedge \psi)$, we get $\mu_{\zeta,i,\Gamma}(X(\varphi) \cap X(\psi)) \geq \mu_{\zeta,i,\Gamma}(X(\varphi)) + \mu_{\zeta,i,\Gamma}(X(\psi)) - 1$.

Lemma 10. Let $B_i^-(\Gamma) = \{\Gamma' | \{\varphi : B_i(1, \varphi) \in \Gamma\} \subseteq \Gamma'\}$, then $\mu_{\zeta,i,\Gamma}(B_i^-(\Gamma)) = 1$.

Proof. For Γ is a finite formulas set, therefore $B_i^-(\Gamma) = X(\wedge_{B_i(1,\varphi_n) \in \Gamma} \varphi_n)$, by axiom: $B_i(a, \varphi) \wedge B_i(b, \psi) \rightarrow B_i(max(a + b - 1, 0), \varphi \wedge \psi)$, we have that $\wedge B_i(1, \varphi_n) \rightarrow B_i(1, \wedge \varphi_n)$, so $B_i(1, \wedge_{B_i(1,\varphi_n) \in \Gamma} \varphi_n)$ can be proven from Γ in PBL_f, so $\mu_{\zeta,i,\Gamma}(B_i^-(\Gamma)) = 1$.

Lemma 11. Let $\Lambda_{i,\Gamma} = \{\Gamma' | P_{\zeta,i}(\Gamma) = P_{\zeta,i}(\Gamma')\}$, then $\mu_{\zeta,i,\Gamma}(\Lambda_{i,\Gamma}) = 1$.

Proof. Suppose $\Gamma' \in B_i^-(\Gamma)$. If $B_i(a, \varphi) \in \Gamma$, by rule: $B_i(a, \varphi) \rightarrow B_i(1, B_i(a, \varphi))$, we get $B_i(1, B_i(a, \varphi)) \in \Gamma$, for $\Gamma' \in B_i^-(\Gamma)$, hence $B_i(a, \varphi) \in \Gamma'$. If $\neg B_i(a, \varphi) \in \Gamma$, by rule: $\neg B_i(a, \varphi) \rightarrow B_i(1, \neg B_i(a, \varphi))$, we get $B_i(1, \neg B_i(a, \varphi)) \in \Gamma$, for $\Gamma' \in B_i^-(\Gamma)$, hence $\neg B_i(a, \varphi) \in \Gamma'$. Therefore $B_i(a, \varphi) \in \Gamma$ iff $B_i(a, \varphi) \in \Gamma'$, which means for any $A \in X_\zeta$, $\mu_{\zeta,i,\Gamma}(A) = \mu_{\zeta,i,\Gamma'}(A)$, so $\Gamma' \in \Lambda_{i,\Gamma}$, and furthermore $B_i^-(\Gamma) \subseteq \Lambda_{i,\Gamma}$. By Lemma 10, $\mu_{\zeta,i,\Gamma}(B_i^-(\Gamma)) = 1$, we get $\mu_{\zeta,i,\Gamma}(\Lambda_{i,\Gamma}) = 1$ as desired.

Lemma 12. For any $\Gamma \in S_\zeta$, $P_{\zeta,i}(\Gamma)$ is a PBL_f-inner probability space.

Proof. By Lemma 6 to Lemma 11, we can get the claim immediately.

Lemma 13. The inner probabilistic model PM_ζ is a finite model.

Proof. By the definition of S_ζ, the cardinality of S_ζ is no more than the cardinality of $\wp(Sub^*(\zeta))$, which means $|S_\zeta| \leq 2^{|Sub^*(\zeta)|}$.

The above lemmas show that PM_ζ is a finite PBL_f-model and the following lemma states that PM_ζ is canonical.

Lemma 14. For the finite canonical model PM_ζ, for any $\Gamma \in S_\zeta$ and any $\varphi \in Sub^*(\zeta)$, $(PM_\zeta, \Gamma) \models \varphi \Leftrightarrow \varphi \in \Gamma$.

Proof. We argue by cases on the structure of φ, here we only give the proof in the case of $\varphi \equiv B_i(a, \psi)$:

It suffices to prove: $(PM_\zeta, \Gamma) \models B_i(a, \psi) \Leftrightarrow B_i(a, \psi) \in \Gamma$.

If $B_i(a, \psi) \in \Gamma$, by the definition of PM_ζ, $\mu_{\zeta,i,\Gamma}(X(\psi)) = b \geq a$, therefore $(PM_\zeta, \Gamma) \models B_i(a, \psi)$.

If $B_i(a, \psi) \notin \Gamma$, by Lemma 5, there exists $b = sup(\{c | B_i(c, \psi) \in \Gamma\})$ such that $B_i(b, \psi) \in \Gamma$ and $a > b$. By the definition of PM_ζ, $\mu_{\zeta,i,\Gamma}(X(\psi)) = b$, therefore $(PM_\zeta, \Gamma) \not\models B_i(a, \psi)$.

From the above lemmas, we know that PM_ζ is a finite PBL_f-model that is canonical. Now it is no difficult to get the following proposition.

Proposition 2 (Finite model property of PBL_f). If Γ is a finite set of consistent formulas, then there is a finite PBL_f-model PM such that $PM \models_{PBL_f} \Gamma$.

Proof. By Lemma 14, there exists a finite PBL_f-model $PM_{\wedge\Gamma}$ such that Γ is satisfied in $PM_{\wedge\Gamma}$.

Proposition 3 (Weak completeness of PBL_f). If Γ is a finite set of formulas, φ is a formula, and $\Gamma \models_{PBL_f} \varphi$, then $\Gamma \vdash_{PBL_f} \varphi$.

Proof. Suppose not, then $(\wedge\Gamma) \wedge \neg\varphi$ is consistent with respect to PBL_f, by Proposition 2, there exists an inner probabilistic model $PM_{(\wedge\Gamma)\wedge\neg\varphi}$ such that $(\wedge\Gamma) \wedge \neg\varphi$ is satisfied in $PM_{(\wedge\Gamma)\wedge\neg\varphi}$, but this contradicts our assumption that $\Gamma \models_{PBL_f} \varphi$, thus the proposition holds.

3   Comparison of Fagin and Halpern's Logic with Our Logic

The probabilistic knowledge logic proposed by Fagin and Halpern in [6] is a famous epistemic logic with probability. In this section, we mainly compare the logic in [6] with our logic in terms of their syntax, inference system, semantics and proof technique of completeness.

Syntax. The basic formulas of logic in [6] can be classified into two categories: the standard knowledge logic formula such as $K_i\varphi$, and the probability formula such as $a_1w_i(\varphi_1) + ... + a_kw_i(\varphi_k) \geq b$. The formula $K_i^b(\varphi)$ is an abbreviation for $K_i(w_i(\varphi) \geq b)$, intuitively, this says that "agent i knows that the probability of φ is greater than or equal to b". Except the difference of knowledge and belief operators, the formula $K_i^b(\varphi)$ is similar to the formula $B_i(b, \varphi)$ of this paper. But in this paper, $B_i(b, \varphi)$ is a basic formula, and there is no formula such as $a_1w_i(\varphi_1) + ... + a_kw_i(\varphi_k) \geq b$, because $a_1w_i(\varphi_1) + ... + a_kw_i(\varphi_k) \geq b$ contains non-logical symbols such as "$\times$", "$+$" and "$\geq$", and accordingly, the language and reasoning system have to deal with linear inequalities and probabilities.

On the contrary, in this paper the only basic formulas are of the form $B_i(b, \varphi)$, which makes the syntax and axioms of our logic system simpler.

Inference system. The inference system in [6] consists of four components: the first component includes axioms and rules for propositional reasoning; the second component includes the standard knowledge logic; the third component allows us to reason about inequalities (so it contains axioms that allow us to deduce, for example, that $2x \geq 2y$ follows from $x \geq y$); while the fourth is the only one that has axioms and inference rules for reasoning about probability. It is worthy noting that $W3$ $(w_i(\varphi \wedge \psi) + w_i(\varphi \wedge \neg \psi) = w_i(\varphi))$ in [6] corresponds to finite additivity, not countable infinite additivity, i.e., $\mu(A_1 \cup A_2 \cup ... \cup A_n ...) = \mu(A_1) + \mu(A_2) + ... + \mu(A_n) + ...$, if $A_1, ..., A_n, ...$ is a countable collection of disjoint measurable sets. As Fagin and Halpern indicated, they thought it is enough to introduce an axiom corresponding to finite additivity for most applications. They could not express countable infinite additivity in their language.

In this paper, there are two components in our inference systems: the first component includes axioms and rules for propositional reasoning; the second component includes axioms and rules for probabilistic belief reasoning. In our system, when one perform reasoning, one need not to consider different kinds of axioms and rules that may involve linear inequalities or probabilities.

In order to express the properties of probability (such as finite additivity, monotonicity or continuity) by probabilistic modal operator directly instead of by inequalities and probabilities, we introduce some new axioms and rules. While in Fagin and Halpern's paper, these properties are expressed by the axioms for linear inequalities or probabilities. Similar to Fagin and Halpern's logic system, we only express finite additivity, but not countable infinite additivity, because we cannot express such property in our language. In fact, we believe that this property cannot be expressed by finite length formula in reasoning system. On the other hand, we think the finite additivity property is enough for the most of meaningful reasoning about probabilistic belief.

Semantics. In [6], a Kripke structure for knowledge and probability (for n agents) is a tuple $(S, \pi, K_1, ..., K_n, P)$, where P is a probability assignment, which assigns to each agent $i \in \{1, ..., n\}$ and state $s \in S$ a probability space $P(i, s) = (S_{i,s}, X_{i,s}, \mu_{i,s})$, where $S_{i,s} \subseteq S$.

To give semantics to formulas such as $w_i(\varphi) \geq b$, the obvious way is $(M, s) \models w_i(\varphi) \geq b$ iff $\mu_{i,s}(S_{i,s}(\varphi)) \geq b$, here $S_{i,s}(\varphi) = \{s' \in S_{i,s} | (M, s') \models \varphi\}$. The only problem with this definition is that the set $S_{i,s}(\varphi)$ might not be measurable (i.e., not in $X_{i,s}$), so that $\mu_{i,s}(S_{i,s}(\varphi))$ might not be well defined. They considered two models. One model satisfies $MEAS$ condition (for every formula φ, the set $S_{i,s}(\varphi) \in X_{i,s}$) to guarantee that this set is measurable, and the corresponding inference system AX_{MEAS} has finite additivity condition $W3$. The other model does not obey $MEAS$ condition, and the corresponding inference system AX has no finite additivity condition $W3$. To deal with the problem in this case, they adopted the inner measures $(\mu_{i,s})^*$ rather than $\mu_{i,s}$, here $(\mu_{i,s})^*(A) = sup(\{\mu_{i,s}(B) | B \subseteq A\})$, $sup(A)$ is the least upper bound of A. Thus, $(M, s) \models w_i(\varphi) \geq b$ iff $(\mu_{i,s})^*(S_{i,s}(\varphi)) \geq b$.

The model of PBL_f are similar to the model of AX in [6]. There is an inner probability measure rather than probability measure in the model of PBL_f. In the model of AX, the semantics of formula is given by inner probability measure induced by probability measure. Meanwhile, in the model of PBL_f, we introduce inner probability measure directly, which satisfies some weaker additivity properties.

Since there is no accessible relation in our model, we need not to consider the conditions about accessible relations. The only conditions we have to consider are probability space at different states, which simplifies the description and construction of model.

Proof technique of completeness. In [6], they proved the weak completeness by reducing the problem to the existence of solution of a finite set of linear inequalities. But this method does not provide the value of measure assigned to every possible world, and just assures the existence of measure.

In this paper, the proof for completeness is significant different from the proof in [6]. There are no auxiliary axioms such as the probability axioms and linear inequality axioms, which are necessary in the proof of [6]. We prove the weak completeness by constructing the model that satisfies the given consistent formulas set. Furthermore, our proof can be generalized to get the completeness of other probabilistic logic systems because it depends very lightly on the concrete axioms and rules.

4   Conclusions

In this paper, we proposed probabilistic belief logic PBL_f, and gave the respective probabilistic semantics of this logic. We then presented an inference system of PBL_f. Furthermore we proved the soundness and finite model property of PBL_f. The above probabilistic belief logic allows the reasoning about uncertain information of agent in artificial intelligent systems. The probabilistic semantics of probabilistic belief logic can also be applied to describe other probabilistic modal logics by adding the respective restricted conditions on probability space. Furthermore, the completeness proof in this paper can be applied to prove the completeness of other probabilistic modal logics. Recently, to express the property of uncertain agents, some probabilistic epistemic temporal logics were proposed. Ferreira, Fisher and Hoek introduced probabilistic epistemic temporal logic $PRO\text{-}TEM$ in [4,5], which is a combination of temporal logic and probabilistic belief logic $P_F KD45$ [4]. For example, one can express statements such as "if it is probabilistic common knowledge in group of agents Γ that φ, then Γ can achieve a state satisfying ψ". Kooi's work [17] combined the probabilistic epistemic logic with the dynamic logic yielding a new logic, $PDEL$, that deals with changing probabilities and takes higher-order information into account. Our logic can also be combined with temporal logics to describe the property of uncertain agents. Furthermore, we are now developing a model checking algorithm for our logic, which can be used to verify automatically the property of uncertain agents.

References

1. F. Bacchus. Representing and reasoning with probabilistic knowledge: a logical approach to probabilities. Cambridge, Mass. : MIT Press, 1990.
2. M. Fattorosi-Barnaba and G. Amati. Modal Operators with Probabilistic Interpretations i. Studia Logica, 1987, XLVI(4):383-393.

3. Y. Feldman. A decidable prepositional probabilistic dynamic logic with explicit probabilities. Information and Control, 1984, 63: 11-38.
4. N. de C. Ferreira, M. Fisher, W. van der Hoek: Practical Reasoning for Uncertain Agents. Proc. JELIA-04, LNAI 3229, pp82-94.
5. N. de C. Ferreira, M. Fisher, W. van der Hoek: Logical Implementation of Uncertain Agents. Proc. EPIA-05, LNAI 3808, pp536-547.
6. R. Fagin and J. Y. Halpern. Reasoning about knowledge and probability. J. ACM, 1994, 41(2): 340-367.
7. R. Fagin, J. Y. Halpern and N. Megiddo. A logic for reasoning about probabilities, Information and Computation. 1990, 87(1/2): 78-128.
8. R. Fagin, J. Y. Halpern, Y. Moses and M. Y.Vardi. Reasoning about knowledge. Cambridge, Massachusetts: The MIT Press, 1995.
9. J. Y. Halpern. The relationship between knowledge, belief, and certainty. Annals of Mathematics and Artificial Intelligence 1991, 4: 301-322.
10. J. Y. Halpern. Lexicographic probability, conditional probability, and nonstandard probability. In Proceedings of the Eighth Conference on Theoretical Aspects of Rationality and Knowledge, 2001, 17-30.
11. J. Y. Halpern and Y. Moses. Knowledge and common knowledge in a distributed environment. J ACM, 1990, 37(3): 549-587.
12. S. Hart and M. Sharir. Probabilistic temporal logics for finite and bounded models. In Proceedings of the 16th ACM Symposium on Theory of Computing, 1984, ACM, New York, 1-13.
13. J. Y. Halpern and M. R. Tuttle. Knowledge, probability, and adversaries,. J.ACM, 1993, 40(4): 917-962.
14. J. Hintikka. Knowledge and belief. Ithaca, NY: Cornell University Press, 1962.
15. W. van der Hoek. Some considerations on the logic PFD: A logic combining modality and probability. J. Applied Non-Classical Logics, 7(3):287-307, 1997.
16. N. Ikodinovic, Z. Ognjanovic: A Logic with Coherent Conditional Probabilities. Proc. ECSQARU 2005: pp726-736.
17. B. P. Kooi. Probabilistic Dynamic Epistemic Logic. Journal of Logic, Language and Information 2003, 12: 381-408.
18. A. Laux and H. Wansing. (eds) Knowledge and belief in philosophy and artificial intelligence, Akademie Verlag GmbH, Berlin, 1995.
19. T. Lukasiewicz. Weak nonmonotonic probabilistic logics, KR2004, Whistler, Canada, 2004.
20. B. Milch and D. Koller. Probabilistic Models for Agent's Beliefs and Decisions. Proc. 16th Conference on Uncertainty in Artificial Intelligence 2000: 389-396.
21. J. Pearl. Probabilistic reasoning in intelligent systems: Networks of plausible inference. Morgan Kaufmann, San Mateo, CA, USA, 1988.
22. A. S. Rao and M. P. Georgeff. Modeling rational agents within a BDI-architecture. Proceeding of KR-91, 1991, San Mateo, CA, USA, 473-484.
23. M. Raskovic, Z. Ognjanovic, Z. Markovic: A Logic with Conditional Probabilities. Proc. JELIA-04 (LNAI 3229), pp226-238.
24. G. Shafer. A mathematical theory of evidence. Princeton University Press, Princeton, N.J, 1976.

Prototyping 3APL in the Maude Term Rewriting Language

M. Birna van Riemsdijk[1], Frank S. de Boer[1,2,3], Mehdi Dastani[1],
and John-Jules Ch. Meyer[1]

[1] ICS, Utrecht University, The Netherlands
[2] CWI, Amsterdam, The Netherlands
[3] LIACS, Leiden University, The Netherlands

Abstract. This paper presents an implementation of (a simplified version of) the cognitive agent programming language 3APL in the Maude term rewriting language. Maude is based on the mathematical theory of rewriting logic. The language has been shown to be suitable both as a logical framework in which many other logics can be represented, and as a semantic framework, through which programming languages with an operational semantics can be implemented in a rigorous way. We explore the usage of Maude in the context of agent programming languages, and argue that, since agent programming languages such as 3APL have both a logical and a semantic component, Maude is very well suited for prototyping such languages. Further, we show that, since Maude is reflective, 3APL's meta-level reasoning cycle or deliberation cycle can be implemented very naturally in Maude. Moreover, although we have implemented a simplified version of 3APL, we argue that Maude is very well suited for implementing various extensions of this implemented version. An important advantage of Maude, besides the fact that it is well suited for prototyping agent programming languages, is that it can be used for verification as it comes with an LTL model checker. Although this paper does not focus on model checking 3APL, the fact that Maude provides these verification facilities is an important motivation for our effort of implementing 3APL in Maude.

1 Introduction

An important line of research in the agent systems field is research on agent programming languages [3]. This type of research is concerned with an investigation of what kind of programming constructs an agent programming language should contain, and what exactly the meaning of these constructs should be. In order to test whether these constructs indeed facilitate the programming of agents in an effective way, the programming language has to be implemented.

This can be done using Java, which was for example used for implementing the agent programming language 3APL [13]. Java has several advantages, such as its platform independence, its support for building graphical user interfaces, and the extensive standard Java libraries. A disadvantage is however that the

K. Inoue, K. Satoh, and F. Toni (Eds.): CLIMA VII, LNAI 4371, pp. 95–114, 2007.
© Springer-Verlag Berlin Heidelberg 2007

translation of the formal semantics of an agent programming language such as 3APL into Java is not very direct. It can therefore be difficult to ascertain that such an implementation is a faithful implementation of the semantics of the agent programming language, and experimenting with different language constructs and semantics can be quite cumbersome.

As an alternative to the use of Java, we explore in this paper the usage of the Maude term rewriting language [6] for prototyping 3APL. Maude is based on the mathematical theory of rewriting logic. The language has been shown to be suitable both as a *logical* framework in which many other logics can be represented, and as a *semantic* framework, through which programming languages with an operational semantics can be implemented in a rigorous way [17]. We argue that, since agent programming languages such as 3APL have both a logical and a semantic component, Maude is very well suited for prototyping such languages (see Section 5.1). Further, we show that, since Maude is reflective, 3APL's meta-level reasoning cycle or deliberation cycle can be implemented very naturally in Maude (Section 4.2).

An important advantage of Maude is that it can be used for verification as it comes with an LTL model checker [12]. This paper does not focus on model checking 3APL using Maude, for reasons of space and since the usage of Maude's model checker is relatively easy, given the implementation of 3APL in Maude. The fact that Maude provides these verification facilities however, is an important, and was in fact, our original, motivation for our effort of implementing 3APL in Maude.

The outline of this paper is as follows. We present (a simplified version of) 3APL in Section 2, and we briefly explain Maude in Section 3. We explain how we have implemented this simplified version of 3APL in Maude in Section 4. In Section 5, we discuss in more detail the advantages of Maude for the implementation of agent programming languages such as 3APL, and we address related work.

2   3APL

In this section, we present the version of 3APL that we have implemented in Maude. This version comes closest to the one presented in [26]. It is single-agent and builds on propositional logic. We refer to [9,10] for first order, multi-agent, and otherwise extended versions. We have implemented this simple version of 3APL to serve as a proof-of-concept of the usage of Maude for prototyping languages such as 3APL. In Section 5.2, we discuss the possible implementation of various extensions of the version of 3APL as defined in this section, although implementing these is left for future research. It is beyond the scope of this paper to elaborate on the motivations for the various language constructs of 3APL. For this, we refer to the cited papers, which also include example programs.

3APL, which was first introduced by Hindriks [13], is a cognitive agent programming language. This means that it has explicit constructs for representing the high-level mental attitudes of an agent. A 3APL agent has beliefs, a plan, and goals. Beliefs represent the current state of the world and information internal to the agent. Goals represent the desired state of the world, and plans are the means to achieve the goals. Further, a 3APL agent has rules for selecting a plan to achieve a certain goal given a certain belief, and it has rules for revising its plan during execution. Sections 2.1 and 2.2 formally define the syntax and semantics of the language constructs.

2.1 Syntax

The version of 3APL as presented in this paper takes a simple language, consisting of a set of propositional atoms, as the basis for representing beliefs and goals.

Definition 1 *(base language)*. The base language is a set of atoms Atom.

As specified in Definition 7, the belief base and goal base are sets of atoms from Atom.

Below, we define the language of plans. A plan is a sequence of basic actions. Informally, basic actions can change the beliefs of an agent if executed. This simple language of plans could be extended with, e.g., if-then-else and while constructs as was done in [26], but these are straightforward extensions and the language as given here suffices for the purpose of this paper. Abstract plans can be modeled as basic actions that are never executable, i.e., that have a precondition that is always false.

Definition 2 *(plan)*. Let BasicAction with typical element a be the set of basic actions. The set of plans Plan with typical element π is then defined as follows.

$$\pi ::= a \mid \pi_1; \pi_2$$

We use ϵ to denote the empty plan and identify $\epsilon; \pi$ and $\pi; \epsilon$ with π.

In order to be able to test whether an agent has a certain belief or goal, we use belief and goal query languages. These languages are built from the atoms $\mathbf{B}(p)$ and $\mathbf{G}(p)$ for expressing that the agent believes p and has p as a goal, respectively, and negation, disjunction and conjunction. Implication could be defined in terms of these, but this is not used a lot in practice. Therefore, we omit it here.

Definition 3 *(belief and goal query language)*. Let $p \in$ Atom. The belief query language $\mathcal{L}_\mathsf{B}$ with typical element β, and the goal query language $\mathcal{L}_\mathsf{G}$ with typical element κ, are then defined as follows.

$$\beta ::= \top \mid \mathbf{B}(p) \mid \neg\beta \mid \beta_1 \wedge \beta_2 \mid \beta_1 \vee \beta_2$$
$$\kappa ::= \top \mid \mathbf{G}(p) \mid \neg\kappa \mid \kappa_1 \wedge \kappa_2 \mid \kappa_1 \vee \kappa_2$$

The actions of an agent's plan update the agent's beliefs, if executed. In order to specify how actions should update the beliefs, we use so-called action specifications. In papers on 3APL, often a belief update function $\mathcal{T}$ is assumed for this purpose, i.e., the exact definition of $\mathcal{T}$ is usually omitted. Since in this paper we are concerned with implementing 3APL, we also have to be specific about the implementation of belief update through actions.

An action specification is of the form $\{\beta\}a\{Add, Del\}$. Here, a represents the action name, β is a belief query that represents the precondition of the action, and Add and Del are sets of atoms, that should be added to and removed from the belief base, respectively, if a is executed. This way of specifying how actions update beliefs corresponds closely with the way it is implemented in the Java version of 3APL.

Definition 4 *(action specification).* The set of action specifications $\mathcal{AS}$ is defined as follows: $\mathcal{AS} = \{\{\beta\}a\{Add, Del\} \ : \ \beta \in \mathcal{L}_B, a \in \mathsf{BasicAction}, Add \subseteq \mathsf{Atom}, Del \subseteq \mathsf{Atom}\}.$[1]

Plan selection rules are used for selecting an appropriate plan for a certain goal. A plan selection rule is of the form $\beta, \kappa \Rightarrow \pi$. This rule represents that it is appropriate to select plan π for the goals as represented through κ, if the agent believes β.[2]

Definition 5 *(plan selection rule).* The set of plan selection rules $\mathcal{R}_{\mathsf{PS}}$ is defined as follows: $\mathcal{R}_{\mathsf{PS}} = \{\beta, \kappa \Rightarrow \pi \ : \ \beta \in \mathcal{L}_B, \kappa \in \mathcal{L}_G, \pi \in \mathsf{Plan}\}.$

Plan revision rules are used to revise an agent's plan during execution. These rules facilitate the programming of flexible agents which can operate in dynamic domains. A plan revision rule $\pi_h \mid \beta \rightsquigarrow \pi_b$ represents that in case the agent believes β, it can replace the plan π_h by the plan π_b.

Definition 6 *(plan revision rule).* The set of plan revision rules $\mathcal{R}_{\mathsf{PR}}$ is defined as follows: $\mathcal{R}_{\mathsf{PR}} = \{\pi_h \mid \beta \rightsquigarrow \pi_b \ : \ \beta \in \mathcal{L}_B, \pi_h, \pi_b \in \mathsf{Plan}\}.$

The notion of a configuration is used to represent the state of a 3APL agent at each point during computation. A configuration consists of a belief base σ and a goal base γ which are both sets of atoms, a plan, and sets of plan selection rules, plan revision rules, and action specifications.

Definition 7 *(configuration).* A 3APL configuration is a tuple $\langle \sigma, \pi, \gamma, \mathsf{PS}, \mathsf{PR}, \mathsf{AS} \rangle$ where $\sigma \subseteq \mathsf{Atom}$ is the belief base, $\pi \in \mathsf{Plan}$ is the plan, $\gamma \subseteq \mathsf{Atom}$ is the goal base, $\mathsf{PS} \subseteq \mathcal{R}_{\mathsf{PS}}$ is a set of plan selection rules, $\mathsf{PR} \subseteq \mathcal{R}_{\mathsf{PR}}$ is a set of plan revision rules, and $\mathsf{AS} \subseteq \mathcal{AS}$ is a set of action specifications.

Programming a 3APL agent comes down to specifying its initial configuration.

---

[1] We use the notation $\{\ldots \ : \ \ldots\}$ instead of $\{\ldots \mid \ldots\}$ to define sets, to prevent confusing usage of the symbol $\mid$ in Definition 6.

[2] Note that it is up to the programmer to specify appropriate plans for a certain goal. 3APL agents do not do planning from first principles.

2.2   Semantics

The semantics of 3APL agents is defined by means of a transition system [22]. A transition system for a programming language consists of a set of axioms and derivation rules for deriving transitions for this language. A transition is a transformation of one configuration into another and it corresponds to a single computation step. In the configurations of the transitions below, we omit the sets of plan revision rules PR, plan selection rules PS, and action specifications AS for reasons of presentation, i.e., we use configurations of the form $\langle \sigma, \pi, \gamma \rangle$ instead of $\langle \sigma, \pi, \gamma, \mathsf{PS}, \mathsf{PR}, \mathsf{AS} \rangle$. This is not problematic, since these sets do not change during execution of the agent.

Before moving on to defining the transition rules for 3APL, we define the semantics of belief and goal queries. The satisfaction relations $\models_{\mathcal{L}_B}$ and $\models_{\mathcal{L}_G}$ are used for this purpose. Belief and goal queries are evaluated in a configuration. A formula $\mathbf{B}(p)$ is true in a configuration iff p is in the belief base, and $\mathbf{G}(p)$ is true iff p is in the goal base. The semantics of negation, disjunction, and conjunction are defined in the obvious way, which we omit for reasons of space.

Definition 8 *(belief and goal queries)*

$$\langle \sigma, \pi, \gamma \rangle \models_{\mathcal{L}_B} \mathbf{B}(p) \Leftrightarrow p \in \sigma$$
$$\langle \sigma, \pi, \gamma \rangle \models_{\mathcal{L}_G} \mathbf{G}(p) \Leftrightarrow p \in \gamma$$

The first transition rule as specified below is used to derive a transition for action execution. An action a that is the first action of the plan, can be executed if there is an action specification for a, and the precondition of this action as specified in the action specification holds. The belief base σ is updated such that the atoms of *Add* are added to, and the atoms of *Del* are removed from σ. Further, the atoms that have been added to the belief base should be removed from the goal base, as the agent believes these goals to be achieved. Also, the action is removed from the plan.

Definition 9 *(action execution).* The transition for action execution is defined as follows:

$$\frac{\{\beta\}a\{Add, Del\} \in \mathsf{AS} \qquad \langle \sigma, a; \pi, \gamma \rangle \models_{\mathcal{L}_B} \beta}{\langle \sigma, a; \pi, \gamma \rangle \to \langle \sigma', \pi, \gamma' \rangle}$$

where $\sigma' = (\sigma \cup Add) \setminus Del$, and $\gamma' = \gamma \setminus Add$.

An agent can apply a plan selection rule $\beta, \kappa \Rightarrow \pi$ if it has an empty plan. The idea is that the agent can only select a new plan, if it has completed the execution of a previous plan. Further, the conditions β and κ have to hold in order for the rule to be applicable. If the rule is applied, the plan π becomes the plan of the agent.

Definition 10 *(plan selection rule application)*

$$\frac{\beta, \kappa \Rightarrow \pi \in \mathsf{PS} \qquad \langle \sigma, \epsilon, \gamma \rangle \models_{\mathcal{L}_B} \beta \qquad \langle \sigma, \epsilon, \gamma \rangle \models_{\mathcal{L}_G} \kappa}{\langle \sigma, \epsilon, \gamma \rangle \to \langle \sigma, \pi, \gamma \rangle}$$

The transition below specifies the application of a plan revision rule of the form $\pi_h \mid \beta \Rightarrow \pi_b$ to a plan of the form $\pi_h; \pi$. The rule can be applied if β holds. If the rule is applied, the plan π_h is replaced by the body of the rule, yielding the plan $\pi_b; \pi$.

Definition 11 *(plan revision rule application)*

$$\frac{\pi_h \mid \beta \rightsquigarrow \pi_b \in \mathsf{PR} \quad \langle \sigma, \pi_h; \pi, \gamma \rangle \models_{\mathcal{L}_\mathsf{B}} \beta}{\langle \sigma, \pi_h; \pi, \gamma \rangle \rightarrow \langle \sigma, \pi_b; \pi, \gamma \rangle}$$

3   Maude

We cite from [21]: "Maude is a formal declarative programming language based on the mathematical theory of rewriting logic [18]. Maude and rewriting logic were both developed by José Meseguer. Maude is a state-of-the-art formal method in the fields of algebraic specification [28] and modeling of concurrent systems. The Maude language specifies rewriting logic theories. Data types are defined algebraically by equations and the dynamic behavior of a system is defined by rewrite rules which describe how a part of the state can change in one step."

A rewriting logic specification consists of a *signature*, a set of *equations*, and a set of *rewrite rules*. The signature specifies the *terms* that can be rewritten using the equations and the rules. Maude supports membership equational logic [19], which is an extension of order-sorted equational logic, which is in turn an extension of many-sorted equational logic. For this paper, it suffices to treat only the many-sorted subset of Maude. A signature in many-sorted equational logic consists of a set of *sorts*, used to distinguish different types of values, and a set of *function symbols* declared on these sorts.

In Maude, sorts are declared using the keyword `sort`, for example as follows: `sort List`. Function symbols can be declared as below, using the keywords `op` and `ops`.

```
op app : Nat List -> List .
ops 0 1 2 3 : -> Nat .
op nil : -> List .
```

The function `app`, expressing that natural numbers can be appended to form a list, takes an argument of sort `Nat` and an argument of sort `List`, and the resulting term is again of sort `List`. The functions 0, 1, 2 and 3 are nullary functions, i.e., constants, of sort `Nat`. The nullary function `nil` represents the empty list. An example of a term (of sort `List`) over this signature is `app(1,app(2,app(3,nil)))`.

In order to define functions declared in the signature, one can use equations. An equation in Maude has the general form `eq ⟨Term-1⟩ = ⟨Term-2⟩`. Assume a function declaration `op sum : List -> Nat`, and a function + for adding natural numbers (declared as `op _+_ : Nat Nat -> Nat`, in which the underscores are used express infix use of +). Further, assume variable declarations `var N : Nat` and `var L : List`, expressing that `N` and `L` are variables of sorts `Nat` and `List` respectively. The equations `eq sum(app(N,L)) = N + sum(L)` and `eq sum(nil) = 0` can then be used to define the function `sum`.

Maude also supports conditional equations, which have the following general form.

$$\texttt{ceq } \langle\texttt{Term-1}\rangle = \langle\texttt{Term-2}\rangle$$
$$\texttt{if } \langle\texttt{EqCond-1}\rangle \texttt{ /\textbackslash } \ldots \texttt{ /\textbackslash } \langle\texttt{EqCond-n}\rangle$$

A condition can be either an ordinary equation of the form `t = t'`, a matching equation of the form `t := t'`, or an abbreviated boolean equation of the form `t`, which abbreviates `t = true`. An example of the use of a matching equation as the condition of a conditional equation is `ceq head(L) = N if app(N,L') := L`. This equation defines the function `head`, which is used to extract the first element of a list of natural numbers. The matching equation `app(N,L') := L` expresses that `L`, as used in the lefthand side of the equation, has to be of the form `app(N,L')`, thereby binding the first element of `L` to `N`, which is then used in the righthand side of the equation.

Operationally, equations can be applied to a term from left to right. Equations in Maude are assumed to be terminating and confluent,[3] i.e., there is no infinite derivation from a term `t` using the equations, and if `t` can be reduced to different terms `t1` and `t2`, there is always a term `u` to which both `t1` and `t2` can be reduced. This means that any term has a *unique normal form*, to which it can be reduced using equations in a finite number of steps.

Finally, we introduce rewrite rules. A rewrite rule in Maude has the general form `rl [⟨Label⟩] : ⟨Term-1⟩ => ⟨Term-2⟩`, expressing that term `Term-1` can be rewritten into term `Term-2`. Conditional rewrite rules have the following general form.

$$\texttt{crl } [\langle\texttt{Label}\rangle] \ \langle\texttt{Term-1}\rangle \texttt{ => } \langle\texttt{Term-2}\rangle$$
$$\texttt{if } \langle\texttt{Cond-1}\rangle \texttt{ /\textbackslash } \ldots \texttt{ /\textbackslash } \langle\texttt{Cond-n}\rangle$$

Conditions can be of the type as used in conditional equations, or of the form `t => t'`, which expresses that it is possible to rewrite term `t` to term `t'`. An example of a rewrite rule is `rl [duplicate] : app(N,L) => app(N,app(N,L))`, which expresses that a list with head `N` can be rewritten into a new list with `N` duplicated. The term `app(1,app(2,app(3,nil)))` can for example be rewritten to the term `app(1,app(1,app(2,app(3,nil))))` using this rule. The former term can however also be rewritten into `app(1,app(2,app(2,app(3,nil))))`, because rewrite rules (and equations alike) can be applied to subterms.

The way the Maude interpreter executes rewriting logic specifications, is as follows [21]. Given a term, Maude tries to apply equations from left to right to this term, until no equation can be applied, thereby computing the normal form of a term. Then, an applicable rewrite rule is arbitrarily chosen and applied (also from left to right). This process continues, until no rules can be applied.

---

[3] If this is not the case, the operational semantics of Maude does not correspond with its mathematical semantics.

Equations are thus applied to reduce each intermediate term to its normal form before a rewrite rule is applied.

Finally, we remark that in Maude, rewriting logic specifications are grouped into modules with the following syntax: mod ⟨Module-Name⟩ is ⟨Body⟩ endm. Here, ⟨Body⟩ contains the sort and variable declarations and the (conditional) equations and rewrite rules.

4   Implementation of 3APL in Maude

In this section, we describe how we have implemented 3APL in Maude. We distinguish the implementation of 3APL as defined in Section 2, which we will refer to as object-level 3APL (Section 4.1), and the implementation of a meta-level reasoning cycle (Section 4.2).

4.1   Object-Level

The general idea of the implementation of 3APL in Maude, is that 3APL configurations are represented as terms in Maude, and the transition rules of 3APL are mapped onto rewrite rules of Maude. This idea is taken from [27], in which, among others, implementations in Maude of the operational semantics of a simple functional language and an imperative language are discussed. In this section we describe in some detail how we have implemented 3APL, thereby highlighting 3APL-specific issues.

Syntax. Each component of 3APL's syntax as specified in Definitions 1 through 6 is mapped onto a module of Maude. As an example, we present the definition of the module for the belief query language, corresponding with Definition 3.

```
mod BELIEF-QUERY-LANGUAGE is
    including BASE-LANGUAGE .

    sort BQuery .

    op B : LAtom -> BQuery .
    op top : -> BQuery .
    op ~_ : BQuery -> BQuery .
    op _/\_ : BQuery BQuery -> BQuery .
    op _\/_ : BQuery BQuery -> BQuery .

endm
```

The module BELIEF-QUERY-LANGUAGE imports the module used to define the base language of Definition 1. A sort BQuery is declared, representing elements from the belief query language. The sort LAtom is declared in the module BASE-LANGUAGE, and represents atoms from the base language. Five operators

are defined for building belief query formulas, which correspond with the operators of Definition 3. The other syntax modules are defined in a similar way. Note
that only sort and function declarations are used in syntax modules. None of the
syntax modules contain equations or rewrite rules.

The notion of configuration as specified in Definition 7 is also mapped onto
a Maude module. This module imports the other syntax modules, and declares
a sort `Conf` and an operator op `<_,_,_,_,_,_>` : `BeliefBase Plan GoalBase`
`PSbase PRbase ASpecs -> Conf`.

Semantics. The implementation of the semantics of 3APL in Maude can be
divided into the implementation of the *logical* part, i.e., the belief and goal
queries as specified in Definition 8, and the *operational* part, i.e., the transition
rules of Definitions 9 through 11. The logical part, i.e., the semantics of the
satisfaction relations $\models_{\mathcal{L}_B}$ and $\models_{\mathcal{L}_G}$, is modelled as equational specifications,
whereas the transition rules of the operational part are translated into rewrite
rules.

As an example of the modeling of the logical part, we present part of the module for the semantics of $\models_{\mathcal{L}_B}$ below. Here [owise] is a built-in Maude construct
that stands for "otherwise".

```
mod BELIEF-QUERY-SEMANTICS is
    including BELIEF-QUERY-LANGUAGE .


    op  _|=LB_  : BeliefBase BQuery -> Bool .


    var p : LAtom .
    vars BB BB' : BeliefBase .
    vars BQ : BQuery .


    ceq BB |=LB B(p) = true if p BB' := BB .
    eq BB |=LB B(p) = false [owise] .


    ceq BB |=LB ~BQ = true if not BB |=LB BQ .
    eq BB |=LB ~BQ = false [owise] .
    ...


endm
```

The relation $\models_{\mathcal{L}_B}$ is modeled as a function `|=LB`, which takes a belief base of
sort `BeliefBase` (a sort from the base language module), and a belief query
of sort `BQuery`, and yields a boolean, i.e., `true` or `false`. Although the semantics of belief queries as specified in Definition 8 is defined on configurations rather than on belief bases, it is in fact only the belief base part of
the configuration that is used in the semantic definition. For ease of spec-
ification we thus define the function `|=LB` on belief bases, rather than on
configurations.

The first pair of (conditional) equations defines the semantics of a belief query
B(p). Belief bases are defined as associative and commutative space-separated
sequences of atoms. The matching equation p BB' := BB expresses that belief
base BB is of the form p BB' for some belief base BB', i.e., that the atom p is
part of BB. The second pair of (conditional) equations specifies the semantics of
a negative query ~BQ. The term not BB |=LB BQ is an abbreviated boolean equa-
tion, i.e., it abbreviates not BB |=LB BQ = true, and not is a built-in boolean
connective. The module for the semantics of goal query formulas is defined in a
similar way.

We now move on to the implementation of the operational part. Below, we
present the rewrite rule for action execution, corresponding with the transition
rule of Definition 9. The variables B, B' and B'' are of sort BeliefBase, A is
of sort Action, P is of sort Plan, and G and G' are of sort GoalBase. Moreover,
PSB, PRB, and AS are respectively of sorts PSbase, PRbase, and ASpecs. Further,
Pre is of sort BQuery and Add and Del are of sort AtomList.

```
crl [exec] : < B, A ; P, G, PSB, PRB, AS > =>
               < B', P, G', PSB, PRB, AS >
    if {Pre} A {Add,Del} AS' := AS  /\  B |=LB Pre /\  B'' := B U Add  /\
       B' := B'' \ Del  /\  G' := G \ Add .
```

The transition as specified in the conclusion of the transition rule of Definition
9 is mapped directly to the rewrite part of the conditional rewrite rule.[4] The
conditions of the transition rule, and the specification of how belief base and goal
base should be changed, are mapped onto the conditions of the rewrite rule.

The first condition of the rewrite rule corresponds with the first condition of
the transition rule. It specifies that if action A is to be executed, there should
be an action specification for A in the set of action specifications AS. The second
condition of the rewrite rule corresponds with the second condition of the transition rule, and specifies that the precondition of the action should hold. Note
that the previously defined satisfaction relation |=LB is used here.

The third and fourth conditions of the rewrite rule specify how the belief base
is changed, if the action A is executed. For this, a function U (union) has been
defined using equations, which we omit here for reasons of space. This function
takes a belief base and a list of atoms, and adds the atoms of the list to the
belief base, thereby making sure that no duplicate atoms are introduced in the
belief base. The function \ for deleting atoms is defined in a similar way, and is
also used for updating the goal base as specified in the last condition.

The translation of the transition rules for plan selection and plan revision rule
application is done in a similar way. As an illustration, we present the rewrite
rule for plan revision, corresponding with the transition rule of Definition 11.
The variables Ph and Pb are of sort Plan, and PRB' is of sort PRbase. The
syntax (Ph | BQ -> Pb) is used for representing a plan revision rule of the
form $\pi_h \mid \beta \rightsquigarrow \pi_b$.

---

[4] Recall that the plan selection and plan revision rule bases and the action specifications were omitted from Definitions 9 through 11 for reasons of presentation.

```
crl [apply-pr] : < B, Ph ; P, G, PSB, PRB, AS > =>
                   < B, Pb ; P, G, PSB, PRB, AS >
      if (Ph | BQ -> Pb) PRB' := PRB /\ B |=LB BQ .
```

As was the case for action execution, the transition as specified in the conclusion
of the transition rule of Definition 11 is mapped directly onto the rewrite part
of the conditional rewrite rule. The conditions of the transition rule furthermore
correspond to the conditions of the rewrite rule.

Above, we have discussed the Maude modules for specifying the syntax and
semantics of 3APL. In order to run a concrete 3APL program using Maude,
one has to create another module for this program. In this module, one needs
to specify the initial belief base, goal base, etc. For this, the atoms as can be
used in, e.g., the belief base have to be declared as (nullary) operators of sort
LAtom. Also, the possible basic actions have to be declared. Then, the initial
configuration has to be specified. This can be conveniently done by declaring an
operator for each component of the configuration, and specifying the value of
that component using an equation. An initial belief base containing the atoms
p and q can for example be specified using eq bb = p q, where bb is a nullary
operator of sort BeliefBase, and p and q are atoms. In a similar way, the
initial plan, goal base, rule bases, and action specifications can be defined. The
3APL program as thus specified can be executed by calling Maude with the
command rewrite <bb, plan, gb, psb, prb, as>, where <bb, plan, gb,
psb, prb, as> is the initial configuration.

4.2   Meta-level

Given the transition system of 3APL as defined in Section 2.2, different possible
executions might be derivable, given a certain initial configuration. It might for
example be possible to execute an action in a certain configuration, as well as to
apply a plan revision rule. The transition system does not specify which transition to choose during the execution. An implementation of 3APL corresponding
with this transition system might non-deterministically choose a possible transition. The implementation of 3APL in Maude does just this, as Maude arbitrarily
chooses an applicable rewrite rule for application.

In some cases however, it can be desirable to have more control over the
execution. This can be achieved by making it possible to specify more precisely
which transition should be chosen, if multiple transitions are possible. In the case
of 3APL, meta-level languages have been introduced for this purpose (see [13,8]).
These meta-languages have constructs for specifying that an action should be
executed or that a rule should be applied. Using a meta-language, various so-
called *deliberation cycles* can be programmed.

A deliberation cycle can for example specify that the following process should
be repeated: first apply a plan selection rule (if possible), then apply a plan
revision rule, and then execute an action. Alternatively, a deliberation cycle
could for example specify that a plan revision rule can only be applied if it is

not possible to execute an action. It might depend on the application which is an appropriate deliberation cycle.

It turns out that this kind of meta-programming can be modeled very naturally in Maude, since rewriting logic is *reflective* [7]. "Informally, a reflective logic is a logic in which important aspects of its metatheory can be represented at the object level in a consistent way, so that the object level representation correctly simulates the relevant metatheoretic aspects." [6, Chapter 10]

In order to perform meta-level computation, terms and modules of the object-level have to be represented as Maude terms on the meta-level, i.e., they have to be *meta-represented*. For this, Maude has predefined modules, that include the functions upTerm and upModule for meta-representing terms and modules, and the function metaXapply which defines the meta-level application of a rewrite rule[5].

The function upTerm takes an (object-level) term and yields the meta-representation of this term, i.e., a term of sort Term. The function upModule takes the meta-representation of the name of a module, i.e., the name of a module with a quote prefixed to it, and yields the meta-representation of the module with this name, i.e., a term of sort Module. The function metaXapply takes the meta-representation of a module, the meta-representation of a term, the meta-representation of a rule label (i.e., the rule label with a quote prefixed to it), and some more arguments which we do not go into here, as they are not relevant for understanding the general idea. The function tries to rewrite the term represented by its second argument using the rule as represented by its third argument. A rule with the label as given as the third argument of the function, should be part of the module as represented by the function's first argument. The function returns a term of sort Result4Tuple?. If the rule application was successful, i.e., if the rule could be applied to the term, the function returns a 4-tuple of sort Result4Tuple,[6] which contains, among other information, the term resulting from the rule application. This term can be retrieved from the tuple using the function getTerm, which returns the meta-representation of the term of sort Term resulting from the rewrite rule application.

Meta-level function calls, such as the application of a certain rewrite rule through metaXapply, can be combined to form so-called *strategies* [6]. These strategies can be used to define the execution of a system at the meta-level. Deliberation cycles of 3APL can be programmed as these strategies.

An example of a deliberation cycle implemented in Maude is specified below using the function one-cycle. It first tries to apply a plan selection rule, then to execute an action and then to apply a plan revision rule. The function one-cycle only specifies one sequence of applications of reasoning rules and action executions. It is repeated to form a deliberation cycle using the function cycle, which is specified below.

---

[5] Maude also has a function metaApply for this purpose with a slightly different meaning [6]. It is however beyond the scope of this paper to explain the difference.

[6] Note that the difference with the sort Result4Tuple? is the question mark. The sort Result4Tuple is a subsort of the sort Result4Tuple?

```
ceq one-cycle(Meta-Conf, Meta-Prog) = Meta-Conf'
    if Meta-Conf' := try-meta-apply-pr(try-meta-exec(try-meta-apply-ps(
                     Meta-Conf, Meta-Prog), Meta-Prog), Meta-Prog) .
```

Here, Meta-Conf and Meta-Conf' are variables of sort Term which stand for the meta-representations of 3APL configurations, and Meta-Prog is a variable of sort Module, which should be instantiated with the meta-representation of the module with Maude code of a 3APL program[7]. The variable Meta-Conf is input to the function one-cycle, and Meta-Conf' represents the result of applying the function one-cycle to Meta-Conf and Meta-Prog. This module imports the syntax and semantics modules, which are also meta-represented in this way. The functions try-meta-apply-pr, try-meta-exec, and try-meta-apply-ps try to apply the (object-level) rewrite rules for plan revision, action execution, and plan selection, respectively. In the definitions of these functions, the pre-defined function metaXapply is called, with the names of the respective object-level rewrite rules as one of its arguments, i.e., with, respectively, apply-pr, exec, and apply-ps.

Before giving an example of these functions, we show how the function one-cycle can be iterated to form a deliberation cycle. The function cycle applies the function one-cycle repeatedly to Meta-Conf and Meta-Prog, until the application of one-cycle does not result in a change to the configuration Meta-Conf, which means the 3APL program has terminated.

```
ceq cycle(Meta-Conf, Meta-Prog) = cycle(Meta-Conf', Meta-Prog)
    if Meta-Conf' := one-cycle(Meta-Conf, Meta-Prog)  /\
                     Meta-Conf' =/= Meta-Conf .

eq cycle(Meta-Conf,Meta-Prog) = Meta-Conf [owise] .
```

As an example of the functions for applying object-level rewrite rules, we present the definition of the function try-meta-apply-pr.

```
ceq try-meta-apply-pr(Meta-Conf, Meta-Prog) =
        if Result? :: Result4Tuple
        then getTerm(Result?)
        else Meta-Conf
        fi
    if Result? := metaXapply(Meta-Prog, Meta-Conf, 'apply-pr, ...) .
```

The variable Result? is of sort Result4Tuple?. The function metaXapply takes the meta-representation of a module representing a 3APL program,[8] the meta-representation of a configuration, and the meta-representation of the label of

---

[7] Note that by "3APL program", we mean the Maude representation of a concrete 3APL program, i.e., consisting of specific sets of plan selection rules, plan revision rules, etc.

[8] The modules defining the syntax and semantics of 3APL are imported by this module, and are therefore also meta-represented.

the plan revision rewrite rule, i.e., 'apply-pr, and yields the result of applying the plan revision rewrite rule to the configuration. If the rule application was successful, i.e., if Result? is of sort Result4Tuple, the term of the resulting 4-tuple which meta-represents the new configuration, is returned. Otherwise, the original unmodified configuration is returned. Note that there is only one object-level rule for plan revision (see Section 4.1), and that this is the one referred to in the definition of the function try-meta-apply-pr. Nevertheless, there might be multiple ways of applying this rule, since potentially multiple plan revision rules are applicable in a configuration. The function metaXapply then takes the first instance it finds.

A 3APL program can be executed through a deliberation cycle by calling Maude with the command.[9]

```
rewrite cycle(upTerm(conf),upModule('3APL-PROGRAM))  .
```

The term conf represents the initial configuration of the 3APL program, and '3APL-PROGRAM is the meta-representation of the name of the module containing the 3APL program.

5   Discussion and Related Work

5.1   Experiences in Using Maude

Based on our experience with the implementation of 3APL in Maude as elaborated on in Section 4, we argue in this section that Maude is well suited as a prototyping and analysis tool for logic based cognitive agent programming languages.

Advantages of Maude. In [17], it is argued that rewriting logic is suitable both as a *logical* framework in which many other logics can be represented, and as a *semantic* framework.[10] The paper shows how to map Horn logic and linear logic in various ways to rewriting logic, and, among other things, it is observed that operational semantics can be naturally expressed in rewriting logic. The latter has been demonstrated from a more practical perspective in [27], by demonstrating how simple functional, imperative, and concurrent languages can be implemented in Maude.

In this paper, we show how (a simple version of) 3APL can be implemented in Maude. We observe that cognitive agent programming languages such as 3APL have a logical *as well as* a semantic component: the logical part consists of the belief and goal query languages (together with their respective satisfaction relations), and the semantic part consists of the transition system. Since Maude supports both the logical and the semantic component, the implementation of languages like 3APL in Maude is very natural, and the integration of the two components is seamless.

---

[9] We omit some details for reasons of clarity.

[10] Obviously, logics often have semantics, but the notion of a *semantic framework* used in the cited paper refers to semantics of programming languages.

We observe that the direct mapping of transition rules of 3APL into rewrite rules of Maude ensures a *faithful* implementation of the operational semantics of 3APL in Maude. This direct mapping is a big advantage compared with the implementation of a 3APL interpreter in a general purpose language such as Java, in which the implementation is less direct. In particular, in Java one needs to program a mechanism for applying the specified transition rules in appropriate ways, whereas in the case of Maude the term rewriting engine takes care of this. As another approach of implementing a cognitive agent programming language in Java, one might consider to implement the plans of the agent as methods in Java, which is for example done in the Jadex framework [23]. Since Java does not have support for revision of programs, implementing 3APL plans as methods in Java is not possible. We refer to [25] for a theoretical treatment of the issues with respect to semantics of plan revision.

A faithful implementation of 3APL's semantics in Maude is very important with regard to our main original motivation for this work, i.e., to use the Maude LTL model checker to do formal verification for 3APL. The natural and transparent way in which the operational semantics of 3APL can be mapped to Maude, is a big advantage compared with the use of, e.g., the PROMELA language [14] in combination with the SPIN model checker [15].

SPIN is a generic verification system which supports the design and verification of asynchronous process systems. SPIN verification models are focused on proving the correctness of process interactions, and they attempt to abstract as much as possible from internal sequential computations. The language PROMELA is a high level language for specifying abstractions of distributed systems which can be used by SPIN, and it's main data structure is the message channel. In [4], an implementation of the cognitive agent programming language AgentSpeak(F) - the finite state version of AgentSpeak(L) [20] - in PROMELA is described, for usage with SPIN. Most of the effort is devoted to translating AgentSpeak(F) into the PROMELA data structures. It is shown how to translate the data structures of AgentSpeak(F) into PROMELA channels. It is however not shown that this translation is correct, i.e., that the obtained PROMELA program correctly simulates the AgentSpeak(F) semantics. In contrast with the correctness of the implementation of 3APL in Maude, the correctness of the AgentSpeak(F) implementation in PROMELA is not obvious, because of the big gap between AgentSpeak(F) data structures and semantics, and PROMELA data structures and semantics.

In [12], it is demonstrated that the performance of the Maude model checker "is comparable to that of current explicit-state model checkers" such as SPIN. The cited paper evaluates the performance of the Maude model checker against the performance of SPIN by taking a number of given systems specified in PROMELA, and implementing these in Maude. Then, for a given model checking problem, the running times as well as memory consumptions of SPIN and of the Maude model checker were compared on the respective specifications.

A further important advantage of Maude is that deliberation cycles can be programmed very naturally as strategies, using reflection. A related advantage is that a clear separation of the object-level and meta-level semantics can be maintained in Maude *because* the meta-level reasoning cycle can be implemented separately from the object-level semantics, using reflection. A 3APL program can be executed without making use of a deliberation cycle, while it can equally easily be executed *with* a deliberation cycle.

Finally, we have found that learning Maude and implementing this simplified version of 3APL in Maude can be done in a relatively short amount of time (approximately two weeks). We cannot compare this effort with the implementation of the 3APL platform in Java where the implementation time is concerned. This is because the platform in Java implements an interpreter for full 3APL [9] and provides a number of other features, such as graphic user interfaces. Nevertheless, we believe that the implementation of the simplified version of 3APL in Maude can be extended very naturally in various ways. This is discussed in Section 5.2.

Advantages of Java Over Maude. As stated in the introduction, Java has several advantages over Maude such as its platform independence, its support for building graphical user interfaces, and the extensive standard Java libraries. Support for building, e.g., graphical user interfaces, is very important when it comes to building a platform of which the most important aim is to allow the implementation of agent systems in a certain (agent programming) language. Such a platform should ideally implement a (relatively) stable version of a programming language. However, in the process of designing a language, it is important to be able to implement it rapidly in order to be able to test it. Maude is very well suited for this, since logics as well as operational semantics can be translated naturally into Maude, providing a prototype that faithfully implements the designed language.

We thus advocate the usage of Maude primarily for rapid prototyping of cognitive agent programming languages. Once the agent programming language has reached a point where it is reasonably stable, it might be desirable to implement a supporting platform in a language such as Java. While such a platform should be well suited for *testing* an agent program, one may again want to use Maude with its accompanying model checker when it comes to *verifying* this program. One might have to abstract over certain aspects of the agent programming language as implemented in Java, such as calls to Java from plans in the case of 3APL, although there is recent work describing an implementation of an operational semantics of Java in Maude [1].

5.2   Extending the Implementation

As was explained in Section 2, this paper presents an implementation of a simplified version of 3APL in Maude. We however argue that the features of Maude are very well suited to support the implementation of various extensions of this version of 3APL. Implementing these extensions is left for future research.

In particular, an extension of a single-agent to a *multi-agent* version will be naturally implementable, since, from a computational point of view, rewriting logic is intrinsically concurrent [17]. It was in fact the search for a general concurrency model that would help unify the heterogenity of existing models, that provided the original impetus for the first investigations on rewriting logic [18].

Further, a more practically useful implementation will have to be *first-order*, rather than propositional. Although the implementation of a first-order version will be more involved, it can essentially be implemented in the same way as the current version, i.e., by mapping transition rules to rewrite rules. In [9], the transition rules for a first-order version of 3APL are presented. Configurations in this setting have an extra substitution component, which records the assignment of values to variables. An implementation of this version in Maude will involve extending the notion of a configuration with such a substitution component, as specified in the cited paper.

Finally, we aim to extend the *logical part* in various ways, for which, as already pointed out, Maude is very well suited. Regarding this propositional version, one could think of extending the belief base and goal base to arbitrary sets of propositional formulas, rather than just sets of atoms. Also, the belief and goal query languages could be extended to query arbitrary propositional formulas. The satisfaction relations for queries could then be implemented using, e.g., tableau methods as suggested in [17], for checking whether a propositional formula follows from the belief or goal base. Further, when considering a first-order version of 3APL, the belief base can be implemented as a set of Horn clauses, or even as a Prolog program. In the current Java implementation of 3APL, the belief base is implemented as a Prolog program. How to define standard Prolog in rewriting logic has been described in [16]. Finally, we aim to experiment with the implementation of more sophisticated specifications of the goals of 3APL agents and their accompanying satisfaction relations, such as proposed in [24].

An aspect of 3APL as implemented in Java that is not easily implemented in Maude, are the actions by means of which a Java method can be called from the plan of a 3APL agent. The execution of a method may return a value to the 3APL program. A similar mechanism could be implemented in Maude by introducing the ability to access built-in Maude functions from the plans of the agent.

5.3   Related Work

Besides the related work as already discussed in Sections 5.1 and 5.2, we mention a number of papers on Maude and agents. To the best of our knowledge, Maude has not been used widely in the agent community, and in particular not in the area of agent programming languages. Nevertheless, we found a small number of papers describing the usage of Maude in the agent systems field, which we will briefly discuss in this section.

A recent paper describes the usage of Maude for the specification of DIMA multi-agent models [5]. In that paper, the previously not formalized DIMA model of agency is formalized using Maude. This work thus differs from our approach in that it does not implement an agent *programming language* which already has a formal semantics, independent of Maude. Consequently, its techniques for implementation are not based on the idea that transition rules can be translated into rewrite rules.

Further, Maude has been used in the mobile agent area for checking fault-tolerant agent-based protocols used in the DaAgent system [2]. Protocols in the DaAgent system are related to mobility issues, such as detection of node failure. The authors remark that the Java implementation for testing their protocols has proved to be "extremely time-consuming and inflexible". Using Maude, the protocol specifications are formalized and they can be debugged using the Maude model checker. Another example of the usage of Maude in the mobile agent area is presented in [11]. In that paper, Mobile Maude is presented, which is a mobile agent language extending Maude, and supporting mobile computation.

References

1. W. Ahrendt, A. Roth, and R. Sasse. Automatic validation of transformation rules for Java verification against a rewriting semantics. In G. Sutcliffe and A. Voronkov, editors, *Proceedings, 12th International Conference on Logic for Programming, Artificial Intelligence and Reasoning, Montego Bay, Jamaica*, volume 3835 of *LNCS*, pages 412–426. Springer, Dec 2005.
2. J. V. Baalen, J. L. Caldwell, and S. Mishra. Specifying and checking fault-tolerant agent-based protocols using Maude. In *FAABS '00: Proceedings of the First International Workshop on Formal Approaches to Agent-Based Systems-Revised Papers*, volume 1871 of *LNCS*, pages 180–193, London, UK, 2001. Springer-Verlag.
3. R. H. Bordini, M. Dastani, J. Dix, and A. El Fallah Seghrouchni. *Multi-Agent Programming: Languages, Platforms and Applications*. Springer, Berlin, 2005.
4. R. H. Bordini, M. Fisher, C. Pardavila, and M. Wooldridge. Model checking AgentSpeak. In *Proceedings of the second international joint conference on autonomous agents and multiagent systems (AAMAS'03)*, pages 409–416, Melbourne, 2003.
5. N. Boudiaf, F. Mokhati, M. Badri, and L. Badri. Specifying DIMA multi-agent models using Maude. In *Intelligent Agents and Multi-Agent Systems, 7th Pacific Rim International Workshop on Multi-Agents (PRIMA 2004)*, volume 3371 of *LNCS*, pages 29–42. Springer, Berlin, 2005.
6. M. Clavel, F. Durán, S. Eker, P. Lincoln, N. Martí-Oliet, J. Meseguer, and C. Talcott. Maude manual (version 2.1.1). 2005.
7. M. Clavel and J. Meseguer. Reflection and strategies in rewriting logic. *Electronic Notes in Theoretical Computer Science*, 4:125–147, 1996.
8. M. Dastani, F. S. de Boer, F. Dignum, and J.-J. Ch. Meyer. Programming agent deliberation – an approach illustrated using the 3APL language. In *Proceedings of the second international joint conference on autonomous agents and multiagent systems (AAMAS'03)*, pages 97–104, Melbourne, 2003.
9. M. Dastani, M. B. van Riemsdijk, F. Dignum, and J.-J. Ch. Meyer. A programming language for cognitive agents: goal directed 3APL. In *Programming multiagent systems, first international workshop (ProMAS'03)*, volume 3067 of *LNAI*, pages 111–130. Springer, Berlin, 2004.

10. M. Dastani, M. B. van Riemsdijk, and J.-J. Ch. Meyer. Programming multi-agent systems in 3APL. In R. H. Bordini, M. Dastani, J. Dix, and A. El Fallah Seghrouchni, editors, *Multi-Agent Programming: Languages, Platforms and Applications*. Springer, Berlin, 2005.
11. F. Durán, S. Eker, P. Lincoln, and J. Meseguer. Principles of mobile Maude. In *ASA/MA 2000: Proceedings of the Second International Symposium on Agent Systems and Applications and Fourth International Symposium on Mobile Agents*, volume 1882 of *LNCS*, pages 73–85, London, UK, 2000. Springer-Verlag.
12. S. Eker, J. Meseguer, and A. Sridharanarayanan. The Maude LTL model checker. In F. Gaducci and U. Montanari, editors, *Proceedings of the 4th International Workshop on Rewriting Logic and Its Applications (WRLA 2002)*, volume 71 of *Electronic Notes in Theoretical Computer Science*. Elsevier, 2002.
13. K. V. Hindriks, F. S. de Boer, W. van der Hoek, and J.-J. Ch. Meyer. Agent programming in 3APL. *Int. J. of Autonomous Agents and Multi-Agent Systems*, 2(4):357–401, 1999.
14. G. Holzmann. *Design and Validation of Computer Protocols*. Prentice Hall, New Jersey, 1991.
15. G. Holzmann. The model checker SPIN. *IEEE Trans. Software Engineering*, 23(5):279–295, 1997.
16. M. Kulas and C. Beierle. Defining standard Prolog in rewriting logic. In *Electronic Notes in Theoretical Computer Science*, volume 36. Elsevier Science Publishers, 2000.
17. N. Martí-Oliet and J. Meseguer. Rewriting logic as a logical and semantic framework. In J. Meseguer, editor, *Electronic Notes in Theoretical Computer Science*, volume 4. Elsevier Science Publishers, 2000.
18. J. Meseguer. Conditional rewriting logic as a unified model of concurrency. *Theoretical Computer Science*, 96:73–155, 1992.
19. J. Meseguer. Membership algebra as a logical framework for equational specification. In *WADT '97: Selected papers from the 12th International Workshop on Recent Trends in Algebraic Development Techniques*, pages 18–61, London, UK, 1997. Springer-Verlag.
20. A. Moreira and R. Bordini. An operational semantics for a BDI agent-oriented programming language. In *Proceedings of the Workshop on Logics for Agent-Based Systems (LABS'02)*, 2002.
21. P. C. Ölveczky. Formal modeling and analysis of distributed systems in Maude. Lecture Notes, 2005.
22. G. D. Plotkin. A Structural Approach to Operational Semantics. Technical Report DAIMI FN-19, University of Aarhus, 1981.
23. A. Pokahr, L. Braubach, and W. Lamersdorf. Jadex: a BDI reasoning engine. In R. H. Bordini, M. Dastani, J. Dix, and A. El Fallah Seghrouchni, editors, *Multi-Agent Programming: Languages, Platforms and Applications*. Springer, Berlin, 2005.
24. M. B. van Riemsdijk, M. Dastani, and J.-J. Ch. Meyer. Semantics of declarative goals in agent programming. In *Proceedings of the fourth international joint conference on autonomous agents and multiagent systems (AAMAS'05)*, pages 133–140, Utrecht, 2005.
25. M. B. van Riemsdijk, J.-J. Ch. Meyer, and F. S. de Boer. Semantics of plan revision in intelligent agents. In C. Rattray, S. Maharaj, and C. Shankland, editors, *Proceedings of the 10th International Conference on Algebraic Methodology And Software Technology (AMAST04)*, volume 3116 of *LNCS*, pages 426–442. Springer-Verlag, 2004.

26. M. B. van Riemsdijk, W. van der Hoek, and J.-J. Ch. Meyer. Agent programming in Dribble: from beliefs to goals using plans. In *Proceedings of the second international joint conference on autonomous agents and multiagent systems (AAMAS'03)*, pages 393–400, Melbourne, 2003.
27. A. Verdejo and N. Martí-Oliet. Executable structural operational semantics in Maude. Technical report, Universidad Complutense de Madrid, Madrid, 2003.
28. M. Wirsing. Algebraic specification. In J. van Leeuwen, editor, *Handbook of Theoretical Computer Science*, volume B: Formal Models and Semantics, pages 675–788. Elsevier, Amsterdam, 1990.

Dialogue Game Tree with Nondeterministic Additive Consolidation

Yoshitaka Suzuki

Research Center for Trustworthy e-Society, Japan Advanced Institute of Science and Technology
syoshita@jaist.ac.jp

Abstract. In this paper, we will show that theory-based legal argumentation can be formalized as a dialogue game tree. In [37], a variation of Olsson's additive consolidation [29] is used for the formalization, but this dialogue game was not treed, because, in each move on the dialogue, the consolidation must construct a unique coherent theory, but not several coherent theories. Therefore, we abandon the requirement that rational consolidation must be unique, and we allow the consolidation to generate plural outputs. Such an operator will be applied for a dialogue game tree with Bench-Capon and Sartor's example.

1 Introduction

Argumentation is one of the important studies for the logic of multiagent system, and it is mainly performed by two players who purchase the own purposes. For example, Kraus et al. [25] showed the model of the argumentation through the negotiation with the BDI logic and implementation. In the model, each player persuades and threatens the other side, and increases the personal utility. Brewka [7] also developed the meta-logic for the argumentation with situation calculus, and it can be used for the formalization of the procedure that performs the argumentation.

Especially, legal argumentation is performed by the two players, the plaintiff and defendant. Each of them argues the legal remedy dialectically and rebuts the opposite side. Usually, the framework of a model of legal argumentation is inference-based [32]. "[T]he argumentation process is viewed as consisting in the exchange of arguments, i.e., of inferences supporting or attacking contested propositions" [36]. Such inferences can be described by argumentation approach (c.f. [10]) with nonmonotonic reasoning. However, the study of inference-based legal argumentation concentrate a research on the static *theory,* where theory is a set of rules intended to explain a legal domain, and it neglects how to construct such a theory dynamically. Thus, legal argumentation also has theory-based aspect, the study of which concentrate the dynamic theory change, and it is performed by "dialectical exchange of competing theories, which support opposed outcomes by explaining the same evidence and appealing to the same values" [36]. In the presentation, our purpose is to propose rational operators that perform theory-based legal argumentation, where 'rational' means that operators should be analized by mathematical postulates. Prakken and Sartor [34] consider that legal argumentation has theory-based defeasibility. "This results from the evaluation and the choice of theories which explain and systematise the available input information: when a better theory

K. Inoue, K. Satoh, and F. Toni (Eds.): CLIMA VII, LNAI 4371, pp. 115–133, 2007.
© Springer-Verlag Berlin Heidelberg 2007

becomes available, inferior theories are to be abandoned" [34]. According to them, this study is inspired by theories of the development of science centered upon the idea of competition between alternative theories. Most approaches to the study adopt *belief revision* [1,11], which is the formal study about theory change. In the research of belief revision, it is important to propose the rational postulates, which should be satisfied by operational functions of belief revision, and to prove the equivalence between the postulates and the functions. However, because Prakken and Sartor [34] think that belief revision is not useful to capture the legal domain, they do not suppose the rational postulates. In our consideration, it has a problem, since they do not argue that theory change is arbitrary. We should discuss the rational criteria about theory-based defeasibility unless it is not arbitrary. Our aim is to show that a variation of belief revision can be applied to theory-based argumentation, the rational postulates for it can be proposed, and the representation theorem between the variational functions and the rational postulates can be proved.

We consider that the theory-based argumentation is performed as follows. At first, the proponent constructs a plausible theory, which derives the winning statement for him. Second, because the opponent cannot accept the first theory as plausible, he adds some information to this theory, and constructs a plausible theory, which defeats the winning statement for the proponent. Third, because the proponent cannot accept the second theory as plausible, he adds some information to this theory, and constructs a plausible theory, which derives the winning statement for him, and so on. Such a framework for theory-based argumentation was studied by Bench-Capon and Sartor [36,4,5]. They considered that plausible theories developed by the participants should be coherent (e.g., background knowledge may be introduced, analogical reasoning with precedents can be recommended, etc.). However, when one player can construct several plausible coherent theories, there may be a conflict between them. Therefore, they assumed that the participant had an ability to compare the coherent theories (e.g., more cases should be covered, more factors should be considered, simpler theories should be choiced, etc.), and resolve the conflict. Therefore, to explain theory-based aspect of legal argumentation, they took into account how to construct coherent theories and compare them with some criteria of choice, i.e., they studied the model of *theory construction* and *theory comparison*. Thus, theory-based legal argumentation is performed by amalgamation of theory construction and theory comparison. First, theory construction adds some information to a given theory, and makes a coherent theory. Second, theory comparison selects some best coherent theories. However, they still have not supplied sufficient formal account of theory-based legal argumentation. In [36,4,5], the outline of dialogue game with theory construction and comparison was discussed, but there was no mathematical definition of the dialogue game. Moreover, there was no rational postulates, which theory construction and comparison should satisfy. We consider that Olsson's *additive consolidation* [29] is available to the problem, which is a variation of Hansson's *belief consolidation* [19] in the field of belief revision, and applied it to the formalization of a dialogue game about Bench-Capon and Sartor's example [36,4,5]. Originally, belief revision was developed by AGM [1]. AGM's belief revision eliminates some information from some knowledge, which is inconsistent with some external input, makes the knowledge be consistent with the input, and incorporates the input. However, Hansson's consolidation [19] is a variation of belief revision, which subtracted parts of inconsistent knowledge and made the knowledge consistent. Olsson [29] abstract his subtractive consolidation from Hansson's one. Instead of consistency, coherence is important for his subtractive consolidation, i.e., this operation subtracted parts of incoherent knowledge and made the knowledge coherent. Besides it, he supposed additive consolidation. It is very different from the above belief change operators, because it does not perform the subtraction from an original belief, but the addition to the one. That is to say, this operation adds some information to incoherent knowledge and makes the knowledge coherent[1]. He quoted Klein and Warfield's example [23] about additive consolidation.

> A detective has gathered a large body of evidence that provide a good basis for pinning a murder on Mr.Dunnit. In particular, the detective believes that Dunnit had a motive for the murder and that several credible witnesses claim to have seen Dunnit do it. However, because the detective also believes that a credible witness claims that she saw Dunnit two hundred miles away from the crime scene at the time the murder was committed, her belief set is incoherent (or at least somewhat incoherent). Upon further checking, the detective discovers some good evidence that Dunnit has an identical twin whom the witness providing the alibi mistook for Dunnit.

We considered that theory construction and comparison in law (and theory-based argumentation) implicitly assumed such a consolidating process. That is to say, each of the parties consolidates a theory constructed by the opposite side, and make the theory coherent in each turn of the dialogue game. However, Olsson [29] made the following three assumptions, which were shared by the usual study for the coherentist belief revision [11,12,20,21].

1. Coherent epistemic state must be consistent.
2. Logic is monotonic. Thus, when x is deduced by A that is a subset of B, x is also deduced by B. Moreover, it must be supraclassical, i.e., if x is deduced by A with classical logic, x is also deduced by A with the assumed logic.
3. Language includes the usual connective $\wedge$, $\vee$, $\rightarrow$, and $\neg$.

Prakken and Sartor [34] considered that these were the reason why the study of belief revision was not applicable to legal argumentation. Legal theory may be inconsistent. It is obvious from the conflict of parties in judiciary proceedings. Legal reasoning seems to be nonmonotonic, and it is not resemble with classical logic [32,30,17]. It may be described by extended logic programming, which does not include the disjunctive connective $\vee$ [32]. Thus, when we use the additive consolidation for the dialogue game, these assumptions must be eliminated. In Suzuki and Tojo[37], this game consisted of two additive consolidations, *positive consolidation* and *negative consolidation*, where

---

[1] Additive consolidation does not modify any agent's old beliefs. Olsson [29] assumed that $K \subseteq K <$ is a rational postulate, where K is a set of sentences and $<$ is an additive consolidation operator. Such an operation is very different from the base revision in [14] and the refinement in [28].

we did not define any particular logic and language, and the criteria of the coherent theories were arbitrary. Positive one was the consolidation for the proponent, which added some sentences to the original theory, and constructed a coherent theory that deduced the proponent's win. Negative one was the consolidation for the opponent, which added some sentences to the original theory, and constructed a coherent theory that did *not* deduced the proponent's win. We could propose the rational postulates for positive and negative consolidation, and prove the representation theorems between the operational functions and the rational postulates. When we assumed Prakken and Sartor's argumentation logic [32], such a dialogue game could be applied to Bench-Capon and Sartor's example [36,4,5].

However, in the conclusion of [37], a problem is indicated, i.e., these consolidations must choose a unique result, and could not select plural best coherent theories. This restriction meant that this dialogue game could not be treed, and a back-tracking process of selection did not be admitted.

Now we will accept Doyle's discussion about belief revision [9] and solve the problem about the uniqueness. He proposed a variation of AGM's original belief revision [1] and emphasized the difference between his revision and the original revision as follows. "[S]ince there may be several alternatives of maximal preferability, our theory does not make the strong assumption of unique revisions [9]". That is to say, whereas AGM's revision is a deterministic function, which accepts an original theory and an incorporated external information, and generates a unique revised theory, his belief revision is a nondeterministic function, which accepts an original theory and an incorporated external information, and generates a set of the best alternative revised theories. In the same way, we will repair the two deterministic consolidations in Suzuki and Tojo [37], which accept an original theory and proponent's winning statement, and generate a unique consolidated theory, and introduce the two nondeterministic consolidations, which accept an original theory and proponent's winning statement, and generate a set of the best alternative consolidated theories. Such an expansion of the consolidations will enable us to formalize a dialogue game tree about Bench-Capon and Sartor's example [36,4,5].

However, we must admit that our discussion is different from Doyle's one [9] with respect to two important points. First, he did not assume the principle of *minimal change*, while we do, because there might be various criteria of theory comparison apart from the minimal change. This principle is a central dogma for the study of belief revision, and it means that we do not want to change our beliefs unnecessarily, and then, it is equal to Occam's razor in the context of theory comparison [4,5], i.e., we should not increase our beliefs unnecessarily. Thus, this principle is independent of the other criteria for theory comparison, e.g., more cases should be explained, more factors should be considered, etc. In the following discussion, we will assume that the constructed theories must satisfy the principle of minimal change, and this principle prevails the other criteria, because we want to follow the conventional tradition of belief revision. Second, according to the normative theory of economic rationality, he required that the selection mechanism of the theories depended on a total preference preordering, whereas we do not. We consider that many researchers of AI and law (e.g., Chorley and Bench-Capon [8]) agree with his supposition, and therefore, we shall improve our framework in the future work. We will explain the reason of our consideration in the concluding section.

This paper's organization is as follows. Bench-Capon and Sartor's example is introduced in Section 2. We will use this example through the rest of the paper. Two nondeterministic consolidation functions are introduced in Section 3. We will call the functions *selective consolidations*. A dialogue game is formalized with positive and negative nondeterministic consolidations, and the introduced example is applied, in Section 4. As already discussed, the usual issues about belief revision prove the equivalence between operational function and some rational postulates, i.e., they show that the supposed operator does not have irregular behavior, and therefore, rational postulates of positive and negative nondeterministic consolidation are proposed, and representation theorems about selective consolidations and rational postulates are proved, in Section 5. Finally, we discuss the relationship between our framework and Doyle's one [9], and indicate our future works, in Section 6. By the way, whereas many issues about belief revision use the word 'consolidation' as the deterministic one, we will not develop it in this paper. Therefore, in the following discussion, this word will be used as the nondeterministic one.

2 Bench-Capon and Sartor's Example

In the section, we introduce Bench-Capon and Sartor's example, because they refer to the concept of coherence, logic, and language, and it helps our discussion about theory-based legal argumentation. For details, see their publications [36,4,5]. We use this example through the rest of the paper, but we do not want the reader to think that the definition of coherence, logic, and language for the example is essential to our dialogue game, because our two consolidations and dialogue game can be defined with arbitrary definition of coherence, logic, and language. Therefore, we can regard some theories, which are constructed from some procedure for speech acts, as coherent like Gordon's pleadings game [15]. However, we do not discuss how to convert the pleadings game into our framework, and we will study it in our future works.

Their example, originally discussed in [6], is as follows:

> In the first, Pierson v Post, the plaintiff was hunting a fox in the traditional manner using horse and hound when the defendant killed and carried off the fox. The plaintiff was held to have no right to the fox because he had gained no possession of it. In the second case, Keeble v Hickeringill, the plaintiff owned a pond and made his living by luring wild ducks there with decoys and shooting them. Out of malice the defendant used guns to scare the ducks away from the pond. Here the plaintiff won. In a third case, Young v Hitchens, both parties were commercial fisherman. While the plaintiff was closing his nets, the defendant sped into the gap, spread his own net and caught the fish. In this case the defendant won [36].

"In all those cases, the plaintiff π was chasing an animal. The defendant δ intervened stopping the chase, so defeating the objective of π. π is arguing for the conclusion that he has a legal remedy against δ, while δ is arguing that no such remedy exists" [36]. Our purpose is to explain "how the decision in Young v Hitchens can be justified on the basis of the previous decisions in Pierson v Post and in Keeble v Hickeringill" [36]. However, such an explanation may not only depend on previous cases, as Ashley's HYPO [3], but also social values, underlying the cases. Therefore, when Sartor [36] attempted to formalize the theory constructor with Prakken and Sartor's logical tool [32], he composed some language with value preferences and promotions. In Ashley [3], factors are important components for the judgements in previous cases. Therefore, his language must include the representations about both factors and values. The components of this language are as follows[2].

Factors: $\pi Liv = \pi$ was pursuing his livelihood.

                $\pi Land = \pi$ was on his own land.

                $\pi Nposs = \pi$ was not in possession of the animal.

                $\delta Liv = \delta$ was pursuing his livelihood.

Outcomes: $\Pi = \pi$ has a legal remedy against δ.

                $\Delta = \delta$ has a legal remedy against π.

Values: $LLit$ =Less Litigation.

                $MProd$ =More productivity.

                $MSec =$ More security of possession.

Connectives: $\Rightarrow, >, \triangleright$.

Our language $\mathcal{L}$ is composed as follows.

1. F is a nonempty set of factors and x is an outcome iff $F \Rightarrow x$ is a rule.
2. ρ_1 and ρ_2 are rules iff $\rho_1 > \rho_2$ is a rule-preference.
3. V_1 and V_2 are nonempty sets of values iff $V_1 > V_2$ is a value-preference.
4. ρ is a rule and V is a nonempty set of values iff $\rho \triangleright V$ is a promotion.
5. x is a sentence iff x is a(n) factor, outcome, rule, rule-preference, value-preference, or promotion.

It is obvious that our language, the set of all sentences, is finite. After the definition of our language, we can define our logic. We use the argumentation logic of Prakken and Sartor [32]. At first, we introduce the notion of an *argument*. Given a set of sentences S, we say that a subset $A \subseteq S$ is an argument in S iff for any rule $F \Rightarrow x \in A$, each element in F is the factor, or the consequent of some rule, in A. All consequences of rules in A are conclusions of A. Since an argumentation has a dialectical aspect, we also define the notion of a *counterargument*. Given two arguments A_1 and A_2 in some S, A_1 is an counterargument of A_2 iff for some rule $F_1 \Rightarrow x_1 \in A_1$, there is some rule $F_2 \Rightarrow x_2 \in A_2$ such that x_1 and x_2 conflict each other, e.g., if $x_1 = \Pi$, then $x_2 = \Delta$, else if $x_1 = \Delta$, then $x_2 = \Pi$. When conflicting arguments are given, we must determine whether an argument *defeats* another argument. Given an argument A_1 and a counterargument A_2 of A_1 in some S, A_1 defeats A_2 iff for some conflicting rules $\rho_1 \in A_1$ and $\rho_2 \in A_2$, $\rho_2 > \rho_1 \notin A_2$. When A_1 defeats A_2, but A_2 does not defeat A_1, A_1 *strongly defeats* A_2. Prakken and Sartor divided all arguments into three categories, justified, defensible, and overruled ones. However, our interests are only *justified* arguments. "[A]n argument is shown to be justified if the proponent can make the opponent run out of moves in whatever way the opponent attacks" [32]. Now we will

---

[2] However, '$\triangleright$' was denoted as 'promotes' in [36].

not explain the definition of justified argument for details. The following definition is sufficient for only the case of one step arguments. Given an argument A_1 in some S, A_1 is justified when for each counterargument A_2 of A_1 in S, A_1 strongly defeats A_2. For the case of multiple steps, see [32]. Finally, we define our inference operation. Given a set S of sentences, $x \in Inf(S)$ iff for some justified argument A in S, $F \Rightarrow x \in A$.

We defined the logic and language for the example. Here, we will define the concept of coherence. Before we discuss what is a coherent theory, we introduce the notion of background knowledge, current situation, and precedent cases, which are necessary for constructing any coherent theories. Background knowledge (BGK) is the set of primitive rules and promotions for constructing coherent theories.

$$BGK = \{ \pi Liv \Rightarrow \Pi, \pi Land \Rightarrow \Pi, \pi Nposs \Rightarrow \Delta, \delta Liv \Rightarrow \Delta,$$
$$\lceil \pi Liv \Rightarrow \Pi \rceil \rhd MProd, \lceil \pi Land \Rightarrow \Pi \rceil \rhd MSec,$$
$$\lceil \pi Nposs \Rightarrow \Delta \rceil \rhd LLit, \lceil \delta Liv \Rightarrow \Delta \rceil \rhd MProd\}$$

Current situation (CS) is a set of factors which can be referred in the current Young case. All theories developed by parties must be constructed from CS.

$$CS = \{\pi Liv, \pi Nposs, \delta Liv\}.$$

$CASE$ is a set of precedent cases, i.e., $CASE = \{Pierson, Keeble\}$. Each case can be regarded as a set of factors and an outcome, which are considered in each case.

$$Pierson = \{\pi Nposs, \Delta\}$$
$$Keeble\ = \{\pi Liv, \pi Land, \pi Nposs, \Pi\}$$

For determining coherent theories, we define the notion of *explained case*. In the following discussion, let $F(T)$ be the set of all factors in T.

Definition 1. *A theory T explains a case $c \in CASE$ with factors $x_1, ..., x_n$ and an outcome y, iff*

$$y \in Inf(T \backslash F(T) \cup \{x_1, ..., x_n\}).$$

We also define *referred factor*. However, we do not use it in this section, and it will be utilized for the definition of selection function in Section 4.

Definition 2. *Suppose that a theory T explains a case $c \in CASE$. We call $Ref(T, c)$ a referred set of factors in c by T when for all factors $x \in c$, $x \in Ref(T, c)$ iff for some F and y, $x \in F$ and $F \Rightarrow y \in T$.*

Now we define our coherent theories. This definition is directly translated from Bench-Capon and Sartor's rules of theory construction [36,4,5]. These rules show that all coherent theories must be constructed from some existing coherent theories by some procedure. Moreover, they considered that these rules must be justified by precedent cases, or promote some social values, called the purpose of the law. Thus, they recommend some analogical reasonings: *factor-merging, value-merging, rule-preference-from-value-preference, rule-preference-from-case, value-ordering,* and *rule-broadening.* However, we eliminate the criterion of *arbitrary-rule-preference* in [36,4,5], because it leads us to incoherence[3]. In the following definition, F is a set of factors, V is a set of values, and ρ is a rule.

The set $\mathfrak{C}$ of coherent theories is defined as follows.

1. CS is coherent;
2. whenever T is coherent and $x \in BGK$, $T \cup \{x\}$ is also coherent.
3. (factor-merging) whenever T is coherent with $F_1 \Rightarrow x \in T$ and $F_2 \Rightarrow x \in T$,
   $T \cup \{F_1 \cup F_2 \Rightarrow x\}, T \cup \{\lceil F_1 \cup F_2 \Rightarrow x \rceil > \lceil F_1 \Rightarrow x \rceil\}$ and
   $T \cup \{\lceil F_1 \cup F_2 \Rightarrow x \rceil > \lceil F_2 \Rightarrow x \rceil\}$ are also coherent;
4. (value-merging) whenever T is coherent with $\lceil F_1 \Rightarrow x \rceil \rhd V_1 \in T$ and
   $\lceil F_2 \Rightarrow x \rceil \rhd V_2 \in T, T \cup \{\lceil F_1 \cup F_2 \Rightarrow x \rceil \rhd V_1 \cup V_2\}$ is also coherent;
5. (value-ordering) whenever T is coherent, $T \cup \{V_1 \cup V_2 > V_1\}$ is also coherent;
6. (rule-preference-from-value-preference) whenever T is coherent with
   $V_1 > V_2 \in T, \rho_1 \rhd V_1 \in T$, and $\rho_2 \rhd V_2 \in T, T \cup \{\rho_1 > \rho_2\}$ is also coherent;
7. (rule-broadening) whenever T is coherent with $F_1 \cup F_2 \Rightarrow x \in T, T \cup \{F_1 \Rightarrow x\}$
   is also coherent;
8. (rule-preference-from-case) whenever T is coherent such that
   (a) T does not explain $c_1, ..., c_n \in CASE$, and
   (b) $\{\rho_1 > \rho_2, ..., \rho_j > \rho_k\}$ is a minimal set of rule preferences such that
      $T \cup \{\rho_1 > \rho_2, ..., \rho_j > \rho_k\}$ explains $c_1, ..., c_n \in CASE$,
   $T \cup \{\rho_1 > \rho_2, ..., \rho_j > \rho_k\}$ is also coherent.
9. whenever T is coherent, it must be constructed from the above conditions.

For example, all of the following theories are coherent.

1. $T_1 = CS$.
2. $T_2 = T_1 \cup \{\pi Liv \Rightarrow \Pi, \pi Land \Rightarrow \Pi, \pi Nposs \Rightarrow \Delta, \delta Liv \Rightarrow \Delta\}$ from BGK.
3. $T_3 = T_2 \cup \{\lceil \pi Land \Rightarrow \Pi \rceil > \lceil \pi Nposs \Rightarrow \Delta \rceil\}$ from rule-preference-from-case, because T_2 cannot explain $Keeble$, but T_3 can.
4. $T_4 = T_3 \cup \{\lceil \pi Liv \Rightarrow \Pi \rceil \rhd MProd, \lceil \pi Land \Rightarrow \Pi \rceil \rhd MSec, \lceil \delta Liv \Rightarrow \Delta \rceil \rhd MProd\}$ from BGK.
5. $T_5 = T_4 \cup \{\lceil \{\pi Liv, \pi Land\} \Rightarrow \Pi \rceil \rhd \{MProd, MSec\}\}$ from value-merging.
6. $T_6 = T_5 \cup \{\{MProd, MSec\} > MProd\}$ from value-ordering.
7. $T_7 = T_6 \cup \{\lceil \{\pi Liv, \pi Land\} \Rightarrow \Pi \rceil > \lceil \delta Liv \Rightarrow \Delta \rceil\}$ from rule-preference-from-value-preference.

3 Selective Consolidations

In this section, we construct two consolidation functions for dialogue game. Usually, the issues about belief revision adopt *partial meet* approach for the definition of the operational function. This approach consists of three steps. First, all alternative results of

---

[3] Note that we don't question what is a coherent *argument* or *reasoning* like [32]. For example, you may think that factor-merging is very odd criteria, because Prakken [31] did not infer $F_1 \cup F_2 \Rightarrow x$ from $F_1 \Rightarrow x$ and $F_2 \Rightarrow x$. However, the coherence of theory change should not be confused with that of logic. In our definition, a sentence, which can be added to a theory by theory change, may not be derived from the theory by logic.

the revision are collected. Second, a selection function chooses several best alternatives from all possible alternatives. Third, the output of the revision function must be equal to the intersection of the best alternatives. Thus, according to the third step, the output of the revision function must be unique. However, since our consolidations are nondeterministic functions, we will utilize the first and second step, but will not use the third step, and define some nondeterministic consolidation functions. We call them *positive* and *negative selective consolidations*. We don't want the reader to think that these are few advances of the additive consolidation in Suzuki and Tojo [37], and therefore, it is very easy work, because we will prove the representation theorems between these operational functions and some rational postulates, and show the rationality of these operators. Such theorems were not shown in Doyle [9], and he only showed that his variation of belief revision satisfied AGM postulates of belief revision [1].

In the first step of the consolidation functions, we introduce the *minimal coherent supersets which deduce* (or *do not deduce*) *a sentence*. Given an original theory and the winning statement for the proponent, while these are the coherent supersets of the given theory, which can (not) deduce the given statement, we want theories to be *minimal* or *simple* as well as coherent. We consider that a desirable theory is not complicated and is too large to prohibit any refutation, but is simple to leave the room for the opposition. When there is no refutation, such a theory may be accepted by all the parties.

Definition 3. *The set of T's minimal coherent supersets which deduce x (w.r.t. $\mathfrak{C}$), noted by $T \uparrow_{\mathfrak{C}}^{+} x$, is the set such that $A \in T \uparrow_{\mathfrak{C}}^{+} x$ iff*

   (i) $T \subseteq A$,

   (ii) $A \in \mathfrak{C}$ and $x \in Inf(A)$, and

   (iii) if $T \subseteq B \subset A$, then $B \notin \mathfrak{C}$ or $x \notin Inf(B)$.

Definition 4. *The set of T's minimal coherent supersets which do not deduce x (w.r.t. $\mathfrak{C}$), noted by $T \uparrow_{\mathfrak{C}}^{-} x$, is the set such that $A \in T \uparrow_{\mathfrak{C}}^{-} x$ iff*

   (i) $T \subseteq A$,

   (ii) $A \in \mathfrak{C}$ and $x \notin Inf(A)$, and

   (iii) if $T \subseteq B \subset A$, then $B \notin \mathfrak{C}$ or $x \in Inf(B)$.

We can consider this definition as the theory constructing part of theory-based legal argumentation, i.e., theory construction is the process for adding some statements to the given theory and making the theory coherent. Besides it, this definition implies that the principle of minimal change precedes the other criteria for theory comparison. Note that this definition does not depend on the logic, language, and coherent theory in Section 2.

In Section 2, we assumed that our language was finite. However, because we want to generalize the representation theorem in Section 4, we make the following assumption. When our language is infinite, there may not be any minimal superset theory w.r.t. coherence and inference. For example, let logic and language be propositional, and suppose that $T \in \mathfrak{C}$ iff T is infinite. Then, there is no $X \in \{atom\} \uparrow_{\mathfrak{C}}^{+} atom$.

EXISTENCE ASSUMPTION 1. For every set $A \supseteq T$ such that $A \in \mathfrak{C}$ and $x \in Inf(A)$, there is a set $X \subseteq A$ with $X \in T \uparrow_{\mathfrak{C}}^{+} x$.

EXISTENCE ASSUMPTION 2. For every set $A \supseteq T$ such that $A \in \mathfrak{C}$ and $x \notin Inf(A)$, there is a set $X \subseteq A$ with $X \in T \uparrow_{\mathfrak{C}}^{-} x$.

In the second step of the consolidation functions, in order to select some best alternatives among the minimal coherent supersets, we introduce *positive* (or *negative*) *selection function*. Of course, we can consider this function as the theory comparison part of theory-based legal argumentation, although the principle of minimal change dominates the selection mechanism.

Definition 5. γ_T^+ *is a* positive selection function *iff* $\gamma_T^+(T \uparrow_{\mathfrak{C}}^+ x)$ *is a nonempty subset of* $T \uparrow_{\mathfrak{C}}^+ x$ *unless* $T \uparrow_{\mathfrak{C}}^+ x$ *is empty in which case* $\gamma_T^+(T \uparrow_{\mathfrak{C}}^+ x) = \{T\}$.

Definition 6. γ_T^- *is a* negative selection function *iff* $\gamma_T^-(T \uparrow_{\mathfrak{C}}^- x)$ *is a nonempty subset of* $T \uparrow_{\mathfrak{C}}^- x$ *unless* $T \uparrow_{\mathfrak{C}}^- x$ *is empty in which case* $\gamma_T^-(T \uparrow_{\mathfrak{C}}^- x) = \{T\}$.

From the above two components, we can define a *positive* or *negative selective consolidation*.

Definition 7. *An operation* C^+ *is a* positive selective consolidation *(w.r.t. $\mathfrak{C}$) iff for all* T *and* x,

$$C^+(T, x) = \gamma_T^+(T \uparrow_{\mathfrak{C}}^+ x).$$

Definition 8. *An operation* C^- *is a* negative selective consolidation *(w.r.t. $\mathfrak{C}$) iff for all* T *and* x,

$$C^-(T, x) = \gamma_T^-(T \uparrow_{\mathfrak{C}}^- x).$$

In Suzuki and Tojo [37], *positive* or *negative partial meet consolidation* $<^{+(-)}$ was introduced. These operations are equal to the intersection of positive and negative selective consolidations, i.e., $T <^{+(-)} x = \cap C^{+(-)}(T, x)$. However, these consolidations cannot generate multiple results.

4   Applying Consolidation to Dialogue Game

4.1   Formalization of Dialogue Game Tree

In this section, we formalize a dialogue game tree with two consolidations developed in the above discussion, and show how to apply our dialogue game to the example in Section 2. Firstly, we explain the intention of our formalization of dialogue game in the following discussion. We consider that given a current state and a formula, the players' purpose in a dialogue game is to construct a coherent theory interchangeably, which (does not) deduce(s) the given formula. Every move in a dialogue game consists of a theory constructed from the last move of the opposite player by a positive (or negative) consolidation. The type of consolidation in each move depends on who moves. The proponent wants the win to be deduced, whereas the opponent only wants to prevent it from being deduced. Therefore, the proponent's purpose is to consolidate the last opponent's theory positively, whereas the opponent's purpose is to consolidate the last proponent's theory negatively. A player wins the dialogue game when the opposite player can not move, i.e., can not construct any coherent theory, accomplishing his purpose. Now we can define the dialogue game as follows.

Definition 9. *Let C^+ and C^- be positive and negative consolidations. Given a set of sentences CS and a formula x, a dialogue game $\mathcal{D}_{CS,x}^{C^+,C^-}$ is a finite nonempty sequence of moves $move_i = (Player_i, T_i)$ for any $0 \le i \le n$, such that*

1. *$Player_i = P$ iff i is odd; and $Player_i = O$ iff i is even;*
2. *If $Player_i = P$, then $T_i \in C^+(T_{i-1}, x)$;*
3. *If $Player_i = O$,*
   (a) *if $i = 0$, then $T_i = CS$;*
   (b) *otherwise $T_i \in C^-(T_{i-1}, x)$;*
4. *for any $0 \le i \le n$, $T_i \ne T_{i-1}$;*
5. *If n is odd, then $C^-(T_n, x) = \{T_n\}$; and if n is even, then $C^+(T_n, x) = \{T_n\}$.*

P (or O) wins *a dialogue game $\mathcal{D}_{CS,x}^{C^+,C^-} = \{move_0, ..., move_n\}$ iff $Player_n = P$ (or O).*

Note that we do not consider the case of infinite moves. We already assume that the players can construct several coherent theories from the original theory. Therefore, we will define a dialogue game tree as follows.

Definition 10. *A dialogue game tree is a finite tree of moves such that*

1. *Each path from the root to the leaf is a dialogue game;*
2. *If $Player_i = P$, the children of $move_i$ are all theories in $C^-(T_i, x)$.*
3. *If $Player_i = O$, the children of $move_i$ are all theories in $C^+(T_i, x)$.*

P (or O) wins *a dialogue game tree iff it wins all paths from the root to all the leaves.*

Note that we can not decide the winner when both P and O win each of dialogue games in the tree. In such a case, we will consider that both players draw, and the winner may be decided by a trial game like [15], i.e., the court selects a dialogue game from the tree, and the winner of the selected game becomes that of the tree.

4.2 Application

In this subsection, we show that our dialogue game tree can be applied for the example in Section 2. For the application, we must define our selection function, which can select plural best alternatives. It chooses the best alternative theories by the criteria of *case-coverage* (e.g., more cases should be covered) and *factor-coverage* (e.g., more factors should be considered), according to [36], and returns the multiple results.

Procedure: $\gamma^{+(-)}(T, T \uparrow_{\mathfrak{C}}^{+(-)} x)$

1. If $T \uparrow_{\mathfrak{C}}^{+(-)} x$ is empty, then return T.
2. (case-coverage) For all $A \in T \uparrow_{\mathfrak{C}}^{+(-)} x$, if there is no $B \in T \uparrow_{\mathfrak{C}}^{+(-)} x$ such that
   (a) for all cases $c \in CASE$, if A explains c, then B also explains c, and
   (b) for some cases $c \in CASE$, A does not explain c, but B explains c,
   then let $A \in CC$.
3. (factor-coverage) For all $A \in CC$, if there is no $B \in CC$ such that

(a) for all cases $c \in CASE$ such that both A and B explain c,
    $Ref(B, c) \supseteq Ref(A, c)$, and
(b) for some cases $c \in CASE$ such that both A and B explain c,
    $Ref(B, c) \supset Ref(A, c)$,
then let $A \in FC$. Then, return FC.

Now, we formalize our dialogue game. Our two players, proponent P and opponent O, are the plaintiff π and the defendant δ. Our two selective consolidations C^+ and C^- are constructed by the inference operation Inf and the set $\mathfrak{C}$ of coherent theories in Section 2, and the selection function in this subsection. Given the current situation CS and the winning statement for the plaintiff Π, our dialogue game tree will consist of two dialogue games $\{move_0, move_1, move_2, move_3, move_4\}$ and $\{move_0, move_1, move'_2\}$, as follows. At first, $move_0 = (\delta, CS)$. $CS \uparrow^+_{\mathfrak{C}} \Pi$ has only the following one element T_1, where $\pi Liv \Rightarrow \Pi$ is introduced from BGK. Therefore, $T_1 \in C^+(CS, \Pi)$, and $move_1 = (\pi, T_1)$.

$$T_1 = \{\pi Liv, \pi Nposs, \delta Liv, \pi Liv \Rightarrow \Pi\}$$

$T_1 \uparrow^-_{\mathfrak{C}} \Pi$ has the following two elements T_2 and T'_2. Because the former does not explain Keeble, but Pierson, whereas the latter does not explain Pierson, but Keeble, we cannot select either of them with case-coverage and factor-coverage. Therefore, $T_2, T'_2 \in C^-(T_1, \Pi)$, and $move_2 = (\delta, T_2)$ and $move'_2 = (\delta, T'_2)$. Here, $C^+(T'_2, \Pi) = \{T'_2\}$, and hence, one of the dialogue games is over. The winner is the defendant.

$$T_2 = \{ \pi Liv, \pi Nposs, \delta Liv, \pi Liv \Rightarrow \Pi, \pi Nposs \Rightarrow \Delta\}$$
$$T'_2 = \{ \pi Liv, \pi Nposs, \delta Liv, \pi Liv \Rightarrow \Pi, \delta Liv \Rightarrow \Delta\}$$

$T_2 \uparrow^+_{\mathfrak{C}} \Pi$ has only the following one element T_3, where $\lceil \pi Liv \Rightarrow \Pi \rceil > \lceil \pi Nposs \Rightarrow \Delta \rceil$ is introduced by rule-preference-from-case. Therefore, $T_3 \in C^+(T_2, \Pi)$, and $move_3 = (\pi, T_3)$.

$$T_3 = \{ \pi Liv, \pi Nposs, \delta Liv, \pi Liv \Rightarrow \Pi, \pi Nposs \Rightarrow \Delta, \lceil \pi Liv \Rightarrow \Pi \rceil > \lceil \pi Nposs \Rightarrow \Delta \rceil\}$$

$T_3 \uparrow^-_{\mathfrak{C}} \Pi$ has only the following one element T_4, where $\delta Liv \Rightarrow \Delta$, $\lceil \pi Liv \Rightarrow \Pi \rceil \rhd MProd$, $\lceil \pi Nposs \Rightarrow \Delta \rceil \rhd LLit$, $\lceil \delta Liv \Rightarrow \Delta \rceil \rhd MProd$ are introduced from BGK, $\{\pi Nposs, \delta Liv\} \Rightarrow \Delta$ is introduced by factor-merging, $\lceil \{\pi Nposs, \delta Liv\} \Rightarrow \Delta \rceil \rhd \{LLit, MProd\}$ by value-merging, $\{LLit, MProd\} > MProd$ by value-ordering, and $\lceil \{\pi Nposs, \delta Liv\} \Rightarrow \Delta \rceil > \lceil \pi Liv \Rightarrow \Pi \rceil$ by rule-preference-from-value-preference. Therefore, $T_4 \in C^-(T_3, \Pi)$, and $move_4 = (\delta, T_4)$.

$$T_4 = \{ \pi Liv, \pi Nposs, \delta Liv, \pi Liv \Rightarrow \Pi, \pi Nposs \Rightarrow \Delta, \lceil \pi Liv \Rightarrow \Pi \rceil > \lceil \pi Nposs \Rightarrow \Delta \rceil,$$
$$\delta Liv \Rightarrow \Delta, \{\pi Nposs, \delta Liv\} \Rightarrow \Delta, \lceil \pi Liv \Rightarrow \Pi \rceil \rhd MProd, \lceil \pi Nposs \Rightarrow \Delta \rceil \rhd LLit,$$
$$\lceil \delta Liv \Rightarrow \Delta \rceil \rhd MProd, \lceil \{\pi Nposs, \delta Liv\} \Rightarrow \Delta \rceil \rhd \{LLit, MProd\},$$
$$\{LLit, MProd\} > MProd, \lceil \{\pi Nposs, \delta Liv\} \Rightarrow \Delta \rceil > \lceil \pi Liv \Rightarrow \Pi \rceil\}$$

$C^+(T_4, \Pi) = \{T_4\}$, and then, the other of the dialogue games is over. The winner of the game is the defendant. In all of the dialogue games, the winner is the defendant, and therefore, the winner of the dialogue game tree is the defendant.

5   Rational Postulates of Two Consolidations

As we have already discussed since Section 1, the issues about belief revision usually introduce some rational postulates of some revision operator, and show the representation theorem about them. Therefore, we will show that our consolidations have rational postulates, and we can prove that these postulates are equivalent with the operational functions in Section 3, i.e., selective consolidations.

Now, we do not assume the logic and language in Section 2. Instead, we can introduce arbitrary language $\mathcal{L}$ and arbitrary inference operation Inf, which takes an original theory and returns a deduced theory. We use the symbol $\mathfrak{C} \subseteq \mathcal{P}(\mathcal{L})$ as the set of coherent theories. Now, the set $\mathfrak{C}$ can be arbitrary, because our logic and language already may be arbitrary, and therefore, we can not decide what is coherent. Note that selective consolidations in Section 3 can be defined without any particular concept of logic, language, and coherence. We suppose that C^+ is a positive consolidation, which takes a theory and a sentence, and returns a set of theories. $C^+(T, x)$ means that "C^+ consolidates an original theory T, and constructs a set of coherent theories, each of which derives the proponent's win x." Similarly, we suppose that C^- is a negative consolidation, too. $C^-(T, x)$ means "C^- consolidates an original theory T, and constructs a set of coherent theories, each of which does not derive the proponent's win x."

We assumed arbitrary language, logic, and coherence. However, it does not mean that our positive and negative consolidations may be arbitrary. Although various components do not have particular criteria, we can show that our two consolidations have rational behavior. Thus, we introduce rational postulates of two consolidations. We suppose rational postulates of positive consolidation as follows.

(*Nonempty*$^+$) There is some $X \in C^+(T, x)$.
(*Inclusion*$^+$) For all $A \in C^+(T, x), T \subseteq A$.
(*C1*$^+$) If there is some $X \supseteq T$ such that $X \in \mathfrak{C}$ and $x \in Inf(X)$, then for all
    $A \in C^+(T, x), A \in \mathfrak{C}$ and $x \in Inf(A)$.
(*C2*$^+$) If there is no $X \supseteq T$ such that $X \in \mathfrak{C}$ and $x \in Inf(X)$, then $C^+(T, x) = \{T\}$.
(*Strond Relevance*$^+$) For all $A \in C^+(T, x)$, if $y \in A \setminus T$, then
    (a) $A \in \mathfrak{C}$ and $x \in Inf(A)$, and
    (b) $B \notin \mathfrak{C}$ or $x \notin Inf(B)$ for all B such that $T \subseteq B \subseteq A \setminus \{y\}$.

These are the nondeterministic versions of the rational postulates in Suzuki and Tojo [37]. We can explain the meaning of these postulates as follows. The result of consolidation should not be empty, even if there are no alternative consolidated theories (*Nonempty*$^+$). All alternatives should include an original theory (*Inclusion*$^+$). If it is possible to construct a coherent theory, which deduces the proponent's win, then positive consolidation must construct such theories (*C1*$^+$). Otherwise, it should give up constructing such theories, and the original theory must not be changed (*C2*$^+$). *Strong Relevance*$^+$ demands the principle of minimal change, i.e., we do not want to change our theory unnecessarily. Although Doyle [9] did not adopt this principle, it is important for the study of usual belief revision. Sentences added by positive consolidation must contribute to consolidate the original theory, and when a sentence can be deleted, and it does not affect the coherence of the consolidated theory nor the deduction of the proponent's win, it should not be added to the original theory.

We also suppose rational postulates of negative consolidation as follows.

(*Nonempty$^-$*) There is some $X \in C^-(T, x)$.
(*Inclusion$^-$*) For all $A \in C^-(T, x)$, $T \subseteq A$.
(*C1$^-$*) If there is some $X \supseteq T$ such that $X \in \mathfrak{C}$ and $x \notin Inf(X)$, then for all $A \in C^-(T, x)$, $A \in \mathfrak{C}$ and $x \notin Inf(A)$.
(*C2$^-$*) If there is no $X \supseteq T$ such that $X \in \mathfrak{C}$ and $x \notin Inf(X)$, then $C^-(T, x) = \{T\}$.
(*Strond Relevance$^-$*) For all $A \in C^-(T, x)$, if $y \in A \setminus T$, then
   (a) $A \in \mathfrak{C}$ and $x \notin Inf(A)$, and
   (b) $B \notin \mathfrak{C}$ or $x \in Inf(B)$ for all B such that $T \subseteq B \subseteq A\setminus\{y\}$.

We can prove the following representation theorem.

Theorem 1. *A positive (or negative) consolidation $C^{+(-)}$ is a positive (or negative) selective consolidation iff $C^{+(-)}$ satisfy Nonempty$^{+(-)}$, Inclusion$^{+(-)}$, C1$^{+(-)}$, C2$^{+(-)}$, and Strong Relevance$^{+(-)}$.*

Proof. We prove only the positive case.
   (Only-If-Part.) Suppose that $C^+(T, x) = \gamma_T^+(T \uparrow_{\mathfrak{C}}^+ x)$ for all T and x. *Nonempty$^+$*, *Inclusion$^+$*, and *C2$^+$* are trivial. We will show *C1$^+$* and *Strong Relevance$^+$*.
   (*C1$^+$*) Suppose that there is some $X \supseteq T$ such that $X \in \mathfrak{C}$ and $x \in Inf(X)$. From EXISTENCE ASSUMPTION, there is some $Y \in T \uparrow_{\mathfrak{C}}^+ x$. Therefore, $T \uparrow_{\mathfrak{C}}^+ x$ is nonempty, i.e. $\gamma_T^+(T \uparrow_{\mathfrak{C}}^+ x) \subseteq T \uparrow_{\mathfrak{C}}^+ x$. We want to show that for all $A \in C^+(T, x) = \gamma_T^+(T \uparrow_{\mathfrak{C}}^+ x)$, $A \in \mathfrak{C}$ and $x \in Inf(A)$. Suppose that $A \in \gamma_T^+(T \uparrow_{\mathfrak{C}}^+ x)$. Since $\gamma_T^+(T \uparrow_{\mathfrak{C}}^+ x) \subseteq T \uparrow_{\mathfrak{C}}^+ x$, $A \in T \uparrow_{\mathfrak{C}}^+ x$, and hence, $A \in \mathfrak{C}$ and $x \in Inf(A)$. It follows that for all $A \in C^+(T, x)$, $A \in \mathfrak{C}$ and $x \in Inf(A)$.
   (*Strong Relevance$^+$*) Let $A \in C^+(T, x)$, and $y \in A \setminus T$. We want to show that (a) $A \in \mathfrak{C}$ and $x \in Inf(A)$, and (b) $B \notin \mathfrak{C}$ or $x \notin Inf(B)$ for all B such that $T \subseteq B \subseteq A\setminus\{y\}$. Obviously, $A \neq T$. Therefore, $T \uparrow_{\mathfrak{C}}^+ x$ is nonempty, because if $T \uparrow_{\mathfrak{C}}^+ x$ is empty, then $C^+(T, x) = \gamma_T^+(T \uparrow_{\mathfrak{C}}^+ x) = \{T\}$, and $A = T$. Because $T \uparrow_{\mathfrak{C}}^+ x$ is nonempty, $\gamma_T^+(T \uparrow_{\mathfrak{C}}^+ x) \subseteq T \uparrow_{\mathfrak{C}}^+ x$. Since $C^+(T, x) = \gamma_T^+(T \uparrow_{\mathfrak{C}}^+ x)$, $A \in T \uparrow_{\mathfrak{C}}^+ x$. It follows that (a) $A \in \mathfrak{C}$ and $x \in Inf(A)$, and $B \notin \mathfrak{C}$ or $x \notin Inf(B)$ for all B such that $T \subseteq B \subset A$, i.e., (b) $B \notin \mathfrak{C}$ or $x \notin Inf(B)$ for all B such that $T \subseteq B \subseteq A\setminus\{y\}$.
   (If-Part.) Let C^+ be an operation which satisfies *Nonempty$^+$*, *Inclusion$^+$*, *C1$^+$*, *C2$^+$*, and *Strong Relevance$^+$*. Suppose that for every T and x, $\gamma_T^+(T \uparrow_{\mathfrak{C}}^+ x) = C^+(T, x)$. We will show that γ_T^+ is a selection function, i.e., (1) if $T \uparrow_{\mathfrak{C}}^+ x$ is empty, then $\gamma_T^+(T \uparrow_{\mathfrak{C}}^+ x) = \{T\}$, (2) otherwise, $C^+(T, x)$ is a nonempty subset of $T \uparrow_{\mathfrak{C}}^+ x$.
   First, we will show (1). Suppose that $T \uparrow_{\mathfrak{C}}^+ x$ is empty. Then, there is no minimal theories $X \supseteq T$ such that $X \in \mathfrak{C}$ and $x \in Inf(X)$. From EXISTENCE ASSUMPTION, there is no theories $T' \supseteq T$ such that $T' \in \mathfrak{C}$ and $x \in Inf(T')$. From *C2$^+$*, $C^+(T, x) = \{T\}$. Since $\gamma_T^+(T \uparrow_{\mathfrak{C}}^+ x) = C^+(T, x)$, $\gamma_T^+(T \uparrow_{\mathfrak{C}}^+ x) = \{T\}$. We proved that (1) if $T \uparrow_{\mathfrak{C}}^+ x$ is empty, then $\gamma_T^+(T \uparrow_{\mathfrak{C}}^+ x) = \{T\}$.
   Second, we will show (2). Suppose that $T \uparrow_{\mathfrak{C}}^+ x$ is nonempty. From *Nonempty$^+$*, $C^+(T, x)$ is nonempty. Therefore, it suffices to show $C^+(T, x) \subseteq T \uparrow_{\mathfrak{C}}^+ x$. Suppose that $A \in C^+(T, x)$. We will show $A \in T \uparrow_{\mathfrak{C}}^+ x$, i.e., (i) $T \subseteq A$, (ii) $A \in \mathfrak{C}$ and $x \in Inf(A)$, and (iii) $B \notin \mathfrak{C}$ or $x \notin Inf(B)$ for all B with $T \subseteq B \subset A$. By *Inclusion$^+$*, (i) $T \subseteq A$. Since $T \uparrow_{\mathfrak{C}}^+ x$ is nonempty, for some $X \supseteq T$, $X \in \mathfrak{C}$ and

$x \in Inf(X)$. By CI^{+}, (ii) $A \in \mathfrak{C}$ and $x \in Inf(A)$. It remains to show (iii). Suppose $T \subseteq B \subset A$. It follows that there is some $y \in A \setminus B$. Thus, $y \in A \setminus T$. By *Strong Relevance*$^{+}$, such that (a) $A \in \mathfrak{C}$ and $x \in Inf(A)$, and (b) $B \notin \mathfrak{C}$ or $x \notin Inf(B)$ for all B such that $T \subseteq B \subseteq A \setminus \{y\} \subset A$. Thus, we showed (iii). Therefore, (i), (ii), and (iii) are shown, i.e., $A \in T \Uparrow_{\mathfrak{C}}^{+} x$. We proved that (2) if $T \uparrow_{\mathfrak{C}}^{+} x$ is nonempty, then $C^{+}(T, x)$ is a nonempty subset of $T \uparrow_{\mathfrak{C}}^{+} x$. □

6 Conclusion

In [37], Suzuki and Tojo's aim was to provide a sufficient formal tool of theory-based legal argumentation. For the purpose, It was required that theory construction must accomplish coherence, the player's win, and minimal change. the idea of additive consolidation was used and a dialogue game was shown, which was based on theory construction, but the consolidated theories must be unique, and therefore, the selection mechanism for alternative consolidated theories was too rigid. Now we are released from the uniqueness, since our consolidation is changed from the deterministic function to the nondeterministic one, and we can formalize dialogue game tree with nondeterministic additive consolidation.

However, there are several problems, because we adopt a part of Doyle's idea [9], but do not accept all of it.

At first, he did not think that the principle of minimal change was the most important principle, but it might be one of the criteria of the selection for the alternatives. In our consolidations, this principle is as same as the principle of simplicity, i.e., Occam's razor. However, in Chorley and Bench-Capon's AGATHA [8], which is an automated system that constructs case law theories through A* algorithm, simplicity[4] is one of the criteria of coherence, but not superior to the other criteria, e.g., explanatory power, completion, etc. In future work, we will develop some consolidation functions without minimal change, and study the relationship between our rational postulates of nondeterministic consolidations and the operational functions.

Second, Doyle [9] assumed that there were some partial preference (or utility) orderings over the possible alternatives for the selection mechanism. "preferences may stem from many different motivations, such as computational costs or moral principles [9]". In the same way, preferences over legal theories may stem from many different motivations, such as simplicity, explanatory power, completion, case-coverage, factor-coverage, etc. However, several preference orderings may conflict. Therefore, we need an aggregation policy, which is a function that specifies the global order corresponding to any given set of partial preference orders. Thus, maximal theories w.r.t. the global order can be choiced by a selection function. However, given some properties, which are analogs of desiderata for social choice in [2], Doyle [9] indicated that there was some problem like Arrow's theorem [2], i.e., some reasonable aggregation policy cannot avoid the emergence of dictator. Although he proposed some possible ways around the problem, we feel that there is no unique result of the problem. None the less we

---

[4] Note that Chorley and Bench-Capon's simplicity means the number of rules in the theory, the number of arbitrary rule preferences and the number of rule preferences obtained from value preferences, while our simplicity means the minimality w.r.t. set inclusion.

should research how to decide a global order from various legal preference orders, because our approach is normative, defining rational postulates for legal argumentation through theory construction. While Chorley and Bench-Capon's approach [8] is cognitive, aimed at constructing the best explanatory theory with the previous cases through realistic adversarial dialogue, of course, it does not mean that all researchers about implemented system for realistic theory-based argumentation may neglect such rational criteria for aggregation policy.

We also should ask ourselves how to define good selection function. As Chorley and Bench-Capon [8] discussed, in theory-based legal argumentation, two parties do not intend to construct the best explanatory theory, but to prevent their opponent from reaching a better theory. Now good selection function must not only purchase the comparison about coherence, but also the strategy for the win of the dialogue game[5]. However, whether the proponent's strategy is good or not depends on the opponent's strategy, and vice versa. It means that we need game theoretical analysis for the definition of good selection function. Thus, we cannot avoid to study selection mechanism from the point of economic rationality, i.e., social choice, game theory, decision theory, etc.

To research such collective decision theories, the first thing we should do is to relate additive consolidation with rational choice. The microeconomic study, including social choice and game theory, usually assumes that a rational agent's decision is based on a total preorder over alternatives, called preference order, and he chooses maximal alternatives w.r.t. the preorder (the principle of utility maximization). Therefore, we expect theory comparison to be such a utility function based on the preference order. In Suzuki [38], a new additive consolidation is proposed, but this is very different from the ones in [37] and the present paper. For example, although we eliminate the three assumptions about logic, language, and coherence for the usual coherentist belief revision [11,12,20,21], i.e., coherent theory is consistent, logic is monotonic and supraclassical, and language includes propositional connectives, the study of the new consolidation adopts the old criteria in [11,12]. Thus, coherent theory is consistent and deductively closed w.r.t. classical logic, i.e., if x is classically deduced from a coherent theory A, x is an element in A. Of course, language must includes the connectives $\wedge$, $\vee$, $\rightarrow$, and $\neg$. Besides them, instead of minimal change, this new one depends on the principle of maximal change. In the study of belief revision, minimal change usually means conservatism, i.e., we do not want to eliminate our old belief unnecessarily. In the additive setting, however, it means "we should instead demand that no belief is *added* in the absence of good reasons to add it [29]." Therefore, maximal change means that an assumption should be added in the absence of bad reasons to add it. According to [38], when we use the old criteria of coherence and the principle of maximal change, and suppose that selection function is defined with total preorder over maximal coherent theories, which can be considered as possible worlds[6], such an additive consolidation is equivalent with a collection of the rational postulates for nonmonotonic reasoning

---

[5] However, it does not mean that we can neglect theory comparison for coherence, and persist the strategic aspect like [18].

[6] Such a total preorder over possible worlds is entirely the same as the semantic approach to belief revision [16,22].

[24,26,27,35]. This result is almost as same as Rott's study [35] between the rational postulates of nonmonotonic reasoning and rational choice function.

We consider that such a study is instructive to the theory-based legal argumentation. Prakken and Sartor [34] suppose that theory change in legal argumentation is defeasible, but they do not advocate that such a defeasible theory chage is not arbitrary. Let C be some theory change operator, which accepts an original theory and generates a constructed theory. Perhaps, they may not agree with monotonicity, i.e., if $A \subseteq B$, then $C(A) \subseteq C(B)$. However, do they agree with some weaker conditions of monotonicity? For example, they may agree with the cautious monotonicity, one of the rational postulates of nonmonotonic reasoning, i.e., if $A \subseteq B \subseteq C(A)$, then $C(A) \subseteq C(B)$. Thus, when we suppose that theory change is not arbitrary, we need to study the criteria of theory change. In Section 5, we enumerated the rational postulates, but we do not suppose the postulates about monotonicity or the weaker condition. It is interesting that we study the constraint on the selection function for the quasi-monotonicity. However, we cannot use the above consolidation in [38], because it assume consistency, propositional logic, and propositional language. Therefore, our problem is to study the relation between the rational postulate about quasi-monotonicity and the constraint on the selection function without consistency, propositional logic, and propositional language.

Finally, in this paper, we use only Bench-Capon and Sartor's example, whose theory construction depends on analogical reasoning like HYPO [3], but neglects the aspect of speech acts like Gordon's pleadings game [15]. It means that we do not explain the procedural layer in Prakken [30] sufficiently, while we will study the strategic layer in it. Prakken [30] considers that models of legal argument can be described in terms of four layers.

> The first, *logical* layer defines what arguments are, i.e., how pieces of information can be combined to provide basic support for a claim. The second, *dialectical* layer focuses on conflicting arguments: it introduces such notions as 'counterargument', 'attack', 'rebutal' and 'defeat', and it defines, given a set of arguments and evaluation criteria, which arguments prevail. The third, *procedural* layer regulates how an actual dispute can be conducted, i.e., how parties can introduce or challenge new information and state new arguments. In other words, this level defines the possible speech acts and the discourse rules governing them. Thus the procedural layer differs from the first two in one crucial respect. While those layers assume a fixed set of premises, at the procedural layer the set of premises is constructed dynamically, during a debate. This also holds for the final layer, the *strategic* or *heuristic* one, which provides rational ways of conducting a dispute within the procedural bounds of the third layer. [33]

Our dialogue game with additive consolidation is obviously related with the procedural layer. However, while we show that Bench-Capon and Sartor's example [36,4,5] can be formalized with the procedure based on the precedent cases and social values, we do not use any procedure based on speech act. Because our additive consolidation is very abstract framework, we consider that it is available to formalize the dialogue game with speech act. In future work, we will show that the pleadings game can be formalized with our developed tools for theory-based legal argumentation.

References

1. C.E. Alchourrón, P. Gärdenfors, and D. Makinson, "On the logic of theory change: partial meet contraction and revision functions," Journal of Symbolic Logic 50, pp. 510–530 (1985).
2. K.J. Arrow, Social Choice and Individual Values, Yale University Press, 2nd Edition (1963).
3. K.D. Ashley, Modeling Legal Argument, The MIT Press, Cambridge: MA (1990).
4. T. Bench-Capon and G. Sartor, "Theory Based Explanation of Case Law Domains," pp.12–21 in Proceedings of The Eighth International Conference on Artificial Intelligence and Law (ICAIL'01), New York: ACM (2001).
5. T. Bench-Capon and G. Sartor, "A model of legal reasoning with cases incorporating theories and values," Artificial Intelligence 150(1-2), pp. 97–143 (2003).
6. D.H. Berman and C.D. Hafner, "Representing Teleological Structure in Case Based Reasoning," pp. 50–59 in The Fourth International Conference on Artificial Intelligence and Law (ICAIL'93), New York: ACM (1993).
7. G. Brewka, "Dynamic argument systems: a formal model of argumentation processes based on situation calculus," Journal of Logic and Computation 11, pp. 257–282 (2001).
8. A. Chorley and T. Bench-Capon, "AGATHA: Automated Construction of Case Law Theories Through Heuristic Search," pp. 45–54 in Proceedings of The Tenth International Conference on Artificial Intelligence and Law (ICAIL'05), New York: ACM (2005).
9. J. Doyle, "Rational Belief Revision (Preliminary Report)," pp. 163–174 in Principles of Knowledge Representation and Reasoning: Proceedings of the Second International Conference (KR'91), J.Allen, R.Fikes, and E.Sandewall (eds.), Morgam Kaufmann (1991).
10. P.M. Dung, "On the acceptability of arguments and its fundamental role in nonmonotonic reasoning, logic programming, and n-person games," Artificial Intelligence 77 (2), pp. 321–357 (1995).
11. P. Gärdenfors, Knowledge in Flux: Modeling the Dynamics of Epistemic States, The MIT Press, Cambridge, MA (1988).
12. P.Gärdenfors,"The dynamics of belief systems: Foundations vs. coherence theories," Revue International de Philosopie 44, pp24-46 (1990).
13. H. Geffner and J. Pearl, "Conditional Entailment: Bridging Two Approaches to Default Reasoning," Artificial Intelligence 53 (2-3), pp. 209–244 (1992).
14. P.D. Giusto and G. Governatori, "A New Approach to Base Revision," pp. 327–341 in Progress in Artificial Intelligence: 9th Portuguese Conference on Artificial Intelligence, EPIA'99, Évora, Portugal, September 21-24, 1999, Proceedings, P. Barahona and J.J. Alferes (eds.), LNCS 1695, Springer, Berlin (1999).
15. T.F. Gordon, The Pleadings Game. An Artificial Intelligence Model of Procedural Justice, Kluwer Academic Publishers, Dordrecht (1995).
16. A.Grove,"Two modelings for theory change," Journal of Philosophical Logic 17, pp.157-170 (1988).
17. J.C. Hage, "Reasoning With Rules. An Essay on Legal Reasoning and Its Underlying Logic," Kluwer Academic Publishers, Dordrecht (1997).
18. A. Hamfelt, J. Eriksson, and J.F. Nilsson, "A Metalogical Formalization of Legal Argumentation as Game Trees with Defeasible Reasoning," pp. 250–251 in Proceedings of The Tenth International Conference on Artificial Intelligence and Law (ICAIL'05), New York: ACM (2005).
19. S.O. Hansson, "Taking belief bases seriously," pp. 13–28 in Logic and Philosophy of Science in Uppsala, D.Prawitz and D.Westerstahl (eds.), Dordrecht: Kluwer Academic Publishers (1994).
20. S.O.Hansson, A Textbook of Belief Dynamics. Theory Change and Database Updating,Dordrecht: Kluwer Academic Publishers (1999).

21. S.O. Hansson, "Coherentist Contraction," Journal of Philosophical Logic 29, pp.315-330 (2000)
22. H.Katsuno and A.Mendelzon, "Propositional knowledge base revision and minimal change," Artificial Intelligence 52,pp.263-294 (1991).
23. P. Klein and T.A. Warfield,"What price coherence?," Analysis 54, pp.129-132 (1994).
24. S.Kraus, D.Lehmann and M.Magidor,"Nonmonotonic reasoning, preferential models and cumulative logics," Artificial Intelligence 41,pp.167-207 (1990).
25. S. Kraus, K. Sycara, and A. Evenchik, "Reaching agreements through argumentation: a logical model and implementation," Artificial Intelligence 104, pp. 1–69 (1998).
26. D.Lehmann and M.Magidor,"What does a conditional knowledge base entail?" Artificial Intelligence 55,pp.1-60 (1992).
27. D.Makinson,"General Patterns in Nonmonotonic Reasoning," pp.35-110 in Handbook of Logic in Artificial Intelligence and Logic Programming Vol. 3:Nonmonotonic Reasoning and Uncertain Reasoning, D.Gabbay, C.J.Hogger, and J.A.Robinson, ed, Oxford: Oxford University Press (1994).
28. J. Maranhão, "Refinement. A tool to deal with inconsistencies," pp. 52-59 in Proceedings of The Eighth International Conference on Artificial Intelligence and Law (ICAIL'01), New York: ACM (2001).
29. E.J. Olsson, "Making Beliefs Coherent," Journal of Logic, Language, and Information 7, pp. 143–163 (1998).
30. H. Prakken, Logical Tools for Modelling Legal Argument. A Study of Defeasible Reasoning in Law, Kluwer Academic Publishers, Dordrecht (1997).
31. H. Prakken, "A study of Accrual of Arguments, with Applications to Evidential Reasoning," pp. 85–94 in Proceedings of The Tenth International Conference on Artificial Intelligence and Law (ICAIL'05), New York: ACM (2005).
32. H. Prakken and G. Sartor, "A dialectical model of assessing conflicting arguments in legal reasoning," Artificial Intelligence and Law 4, pp. 331–368 (1996).
33. H. Prakken and G. Sartor, "The role of logic in computational models of legal argument: a critical survey," pp. 342–380 in Computational Logic: Logic Programming and Beyond. Essays In Honour of Robert A. Kowalski, Part II, In A.Kakas and F.Sadri (eds.), LNCS 2048, Berlin: Springer (2002).
34. H. Prakken and G. Sartor, "The three faces of defeasibility in the law," Ratio Juris 17 (1), pp. 118–139 (2004).
35. H. Rott, Change, choice and inference : a study of belief revision and nonmonotonic reasoning, Oxford: Oxford University Press (2001).
36. G. Sartor, "Teleological Arguments and Theory-based Dialectics," Artificial Intelligence and Law 10, pp. 95–112 (2002).
37. Y. Suzuki and S. Tojo, "Additive Consolidation for Dialogue Game," pp. 105–114 in Proceedings of The Tenth International Conference on Artificial Intelligence and Law (ICAIL'05), New York: ACM (2005).
38. Y. Suzuki, "Additive Consolidation with Maximal Change," The 13th Workshop on Logic, Language, Information and Computation (WoLLIC'06), Stanford (To appear) (2006).

Representing and Verifying Temporal Epistemic Properties in Multi-Agent Systems*

Zining Cao

Department of Computer Science and Engineering,
Nanjing University of Aero. & Astro., Nanjing 210016, China
caozn@nuaa.edu.cn

Abstract. In this paper, we present a temporal epistemic logic, called μTEL, which generalizes μ-calculus by introducing knowledge modality and cooperation modality. Similar to μ-calculus, μTEL is a succinct and expressive language. It is showed that temporal modalities such as "always", "sometime" and "until", and knowledge modalities such as "everyone knows" and "common knowledge" can be expressed in such a logic. Furthermore, we study the model checking technique and its complexity. Finally, we use μTEL and its model checking algorithm to study the well-known trains and controller problem.

1 Introduction

The field of multi-agent systems (MAS) theories is traditionally concerned with the formal representation of the mental attitudes of autonomous entities, or agents, in a distributed system. For this task several modal logics have been developed in the past 20 years, the most studied being logics for knowledge, beliefs, desires, goals, and intentions.

These logics are seen as specifications of particular classes of MAS systems. Their aim is to offer a description of the macroscope mental properties (such as knowledge, belief and etc.) that a MAS should exhibit in a specific class of scenarios. Sometimes, interaction properties are studied. For example, in an epistemic and doxastic model of agency it often makes sense to impose that knowledge is "true belief". This leads to a logic with two families of modalities, $\{K_a\}_{a \in \Sigma}$, $\{B_a\}_{a \in \Sigma}$, where B_a is a $KD45$-modality, K_a is a $S5$-modality, and the interaction axiom $K_a\varphi \rightarrow B_a\varphi$ expresses the intended interplay between the two informational operators. A considerable number of these formal studies are available in the literature and temporal extensions of these (i.e., modal combinations of CTL or LTL with the modalities for the mental attitudes) have appeared recently [11,20,25]. The typical technical contribution of this line of work is to explore the metalogical properties of these logics, e.g., completeness, decidability, and computational complexity.

---

* This work was supported by the National Natural Science Foundation of China under Grant 60473036.

K. Inoue, K. Satoh, and F. Toni (Eds.): CLIMA VII, LNAI 4371, pp. 134–150, 2007.

Verification of reaction systems by means of model checking techniques is now a well-established area of research [10]. In this paradigm one typically models a system S in terms of automata (or by a similar transition-based formalism), builds an implementation P_S of the system by means of a model-checker friendly language such as the input for *SMV* or *PROMELA*, and finally uses a model-checker such as *SMV* or *SPIN* to verify some temporal property φ the system: $M_P \models \varphi$, where M_P is a temporal model representing the executions of P_S. As it is well known, there are intrinsic difficulties with the naive approach of performing this operation on an explicit representation of the states, and refinements of symbolic techniques (based on *OBDD*'s, and *SAT* translations) are being investigated to overcome these hurdles. Formal results and corresponding applications now allow for the verification of complex systems that generate more than 10^{20} states.

The field of multi-agent systems has also recently become interested in the problem of verifying complex systems. In *MAS*, modal logics representing concepts such as knowledge, belief, and intention. Since these modalities are given interpretations that are different from the ones of the standard temporal operators, it is not straightforward to apply existing model checking tools developed for *LTL\CTL* temporal logic to the specification of *MAS*. The recent developments of model checking *MAS* can broadly be divided into streams: in the first category standard predicates are used to interpret the various intensional notions and these are paired with standard model checking techniques based on temporal logic. Following this line is [29] and related papers. In the other category we can place techniques that make a genuine attempt at extending the model checking techniques by adding other operators. Works along these lines include [8,21] and so on.

To express the cooperation property in open systems, Alur and Henzinger introduced alternating-time temporal logic *ATL* in [6], which is a generalization of *CTL*. The main difference between *ATL* and *CTL* is that in *ATL*, path quantifies are replaced by cooperation modalities. For example, the *ATL* formula $\langle\langle \Gamma \rangle\rangle \bigcirc \varphi$, where Γ is a group of agents, expresses that the group Γ can cooperate to achieve a next state that φ holds. Thus, we can express some properties such as "agents 1 and 2 can ensure that the system never enters a fail state". An *ATL* model checking systems called *MOCHA* was developed [5]. In *MAS*, agents are intelligent, so it is not only necessary to represent the temporal properties but also necessary to express the mental properties. For example, one may need to express statements such as "if it is common knowledge in group of agents Γ that φ, then Γ can cooperate to ensure ψ". To represent and verify such properties, a temporal epistemic logic *ATEL* was presented in [21]. This logic extended *ATL* with knowledge modalities such as "every knows" and common knowledge. In [21], a model checking algorithm for *ATEL* was given, its complexity was also studied.

In this paper, we present a temporal epistemic logic μTEL, which is an extension of μ-calculus by adding cooperation modality $\langle\langle \Gamma \rangle\rangle \bigcirc$ and knowledge modality K_a. Although its syntax is very simple, we can show that temporal modalities such as "always", "sometime" and "until", and knowledge modalities such as "everyone knows" and "common knowledge" can be expressed in such a logic. In fact we prove that $ATEL$ is a sublogic of μTEL. A translating function from any $ATEL$ formula to an equivalent μTEL formula is given. For temporal logics, it is well known that almost all famous temporal logics, such as PDL, LTL, CTL and CTL^*, are sublogic of μ-calculus, hence the problems of model checking PDL, LTL, CTL and CTL^* can be uniformly reduced to model checking μ-calculus [9]. Model checking μ-calculus is a very active research area and there have been lots of algorithm for model checking μ-calculus [9]. Similarly, for temporal epistemic logics, μTEL plays on a role of μ-calculus. Almost all model checking problems for temporal epistemic logics such as $ATEL$ [21], CKL_n [20] and CTL_PK [25] can be reduced to model checking μTEL. Hence it is important to study model checking algorithms for μTEL. In fact, it is not difficult to extend μ-calculus model checking algorithm to μTEL. In this paper, we present a model checking algorithm for μTEL. We also studied the complexity of model checking μTEL.

The rest of the paper is organized as follows: In Section 2, we present a temporal epistemic logic μTEL, give its syntax, semantics and inference system. In Section 3, we study the expressivity of μTEL. $ATEL$ is showed to be a sublogic of μTEL. In Section 4, the approach to model checking μTEL is studied. Furthermore, the complexity of model checking μTEL is studied. In Section 5, we show that the properties of a well-known trains and controller problem can be represented in μTEL and these properties can be verified by our model checking algorithm. The paper is concluded in Section 6.

2   A Temporal Epistemic Logic μTEL

2.1   Syntax of μTEL

Throughout this paper, we let $L^{\mu TEL}$ be a language which is just the set of formulas of interest to us. In the following, we use Σ to denote the set of agents.

Definition 1. The set of formulas in μTEL, called $L^{\mu TEL}$, is given by the following rules:

(1) If $\varphi \in$ atomic formulas set Π, then $\varphi \in L^{\mu TEL}$.
(2) If $\varphi \in$ proposition variables set V, then $\varphi \in L^{\mu TEL}$.
(3) If $\varphi \in L^{\mu TEL}$, then $\neg\varphi \in L^{\mu TEL}$.
(4) If $\varphi_1, \varphi_2 \in L^{\mu TEL}$, then $\varphi_1 \wedge \varphi_2 \in L^{\mu TEL}$.
(5) If $\varphi \in L^{\mu TEL}$, $\Gamma \subseteq \Sigma$, then $\langle\langle \Gamma \rangle\rangle \bigcirc \varphi \in L^{\mu TEL}$. Intuitively, $\langle\langle \Gamma \rangle\rangle \bigcirc \varphi$ means that agents Γ can cooperate to ensure that φ is true in the next state.
(6) If $\varphi \in L^{\mu TEL}$, then $K_a\varphi \in L^{\mu TEL}$, where $a \in \Sigma$. Intuitively, $K_a\varphi$ means that agent a knows φ.
(7) If $\varphi(X) \in L^{\mu TEL}$, then $\mu X.\varphi(X) \in L^{\mu TEL}$, here X occurs positively in $\varphi(X)$, i.e., all free occurrences of X fall under an even number of negations.

2.2 Semantics of μTEL

We will describe the semantics of μTEL, that is, a formal model that we can use to determine whether a given formula is true or false.

Definition 2. A model S of μTEL is a concurrent game structure [6] $S = (\Sigma, Q, \Pi, \pi, e, d, \delta, \sim_a$ here $a \in \Sigma)$, where

(1) Σ is a finite set of agents, in the following, without loss of generality, we usually assume $\Sigma = \{1, ..., k\}$.

(2) Q is a finite, nonempty set, whose elements are called possible worlds or states.

(3) Π is a finite set of propositions.

(4) π is a map: $Q \rightarrow 2^\Pi$, where Π is a set of atomic formulas.

(5) e is an environment: $V \rightarrow 2^Q$, where V is a set of proposition variables.

(6) For each player $a \in \Sigma = \{1, ..., k\}$ and each state $q \in Q$, a natural number $d_a(q) \geq 1$ of moves available at state q to player a. We identify the moves of player a at state q with the numbers $1, ..., d_a(q)$. For each state $q \in Q$, a move vector at q is a tuple $\langle j_1, ..., j_k \rangle$ such that $1 \leq j_a \leq d_a(q)$ for each player a. Given a state $q \in Q$, we write $D(q)$ for the set $\{1, ..., d_1(q)\} \times ... \times \{1, ..., d_k(q)\}$ of move vectors. The function D is called move function.

(7) For each state $q \in Q$ and each move vector $\langle j_1, ..., j_k \rangle \in D(q)$, a state $\delta(q, j_1, ..., j_k)$ that results from state q if every player $a \in \Sigma = \{1, ..., k\}$ choose move j_a. The function is called transition function.

(8) $\sim_a$ is an accessible relation on Q, which is an equivalence relation.

Formally, a formula φ is interpreted as a set of states in which φ is true. We write such set of states as $[[\varphi]]_S^e$, where S is a model and $e: V \rightarrow 2^Q$ is an environment. We denote by $e[X \leftarrow W]$ a new environment that is the same as e except that $e[X \leftarrow W](X) = W$. The set $[[\varphi]]_S^e$ is defined recursively as follows:

Definition 3. Semantics of μTEL

$[[p]]_S^e = \{q \mid p \in \pi(q)\}$

$[[X]]_S^e = e(X)$

$[[\neg\varphi]]_S^e = Q - [[\varphi]]_S^e$

$[[\varphi \wedge \psi]]_S^e = [[\varphi]]_S^e \cap [[\psi]]_S^e$

$[[\langle\langle \Gamma \rangle\rangle \bigcirc \varphi]]_S^e = \{q \mid$ for every player $a \in \Gamma$, there exists a move $j_a \in \{1, ..., d_a(q)\}$ such that for all players $b \in \Sigma - \Gamma$ and moves $j_b \in \{1, ..., d_b(q)\}$, we have $\delta(q, j_1, ..., j_k) \in [[\varphi]]_S^e\}$.

$[[K_a\varphi]]_S^e = \{q \mid$ for all $r \in [[\varphi]]_S^e$ and $r \in_{\sim_a} (q)$ with $\sim_a (q) = \{q' \mid (q, q') \in_{\sim_a}$

$\}\}$

$[[\mu X.\varphi(X)]]_S^e = \cap\{W \subseteq Q \mid [[\varphi(X)]]_S^{e[X \leftarrow W]} \subseteq W\}$.

Let $S = (\Sigma, Q, \Pi, \pi, e, d, \delta, \sim_a$ here $a \in \Sigma)$ be a model. Notice that the set 2^Σ of all subsets of Σ forms a lattice under the set inclusion ordering. Each element Σ' of the lattice can also be thought of as a predicate on Σ, where the predicate is viewed as being true for exactly the states in Σ'. The least element in the lattice is the empty set, which corresponds to the predicate false, and the greatest element in the lattice is the set Σ, which corresponds to true. A function τ mapping 2^{Σ} to 2^{Σ} is called a predicate transformer. A set $\Sigma' \subseteq \Sigma$ is a fixed point of a function $\Sigma': 2^{\Sigma} \to 2^{\Sigma}$ if $\tau(\Sigma') = \Sigma'$. Whenever τ is monotonic (i.e., when $U \subseteq V$ implies $\tau(U) \subseteq \tau(V)$), τ has a least fixed point denoted by $\mu Z.\tau(Z)$, and a greatest fixed point, denoted by $\nu Z.\tau(Z)$. When τ is monotonic and $\cup$-continuous (i.e., when $W_1 \subseteq W_2 \subseteq \ldots$ implies $\tau(\cup_i W_i) = \cup_i \tau(W_i)$), then $\mu Z.\tau(Z) = \cup_i \tau^i(False)$. When τ is monotonic and $\cap$-continuous (i.e., when $W_1 \supseteq W_2 \supseteq \ldots$ implies $\tau(\cap_i W_i) = \cap_i \tau(W_i)$), then $\nu Z.\tau(Z) = \cap_i \tau^i(True)$.

In order to characterize the properties of knowledge and temporal, we will characterize the formulas that are always true. More formally, given a model S, we say that φ is valid in S, and write $S \models \varphi$, if $q \in [[\varphi]]_S^e$ for every state q in Q, and we say that φ is satisfiable in S, and write $S, q \models \varphi$, if $q \in [[\varphi]]_S^e$ for some q in Q. We say that φ is valid, and write $\models_{\mu TEL} \varphi$, if φ is valid in all models, and that φ is satisfiable if it is satisfiable in some model. We write $\Gamma \models_{\mu TEL} \varphi$, if φ is valid in all models in which Γ is satisfiable.

2.3 Inference System of μTEL

Now we list a number of valid properties of knowledge and temporal, which form the inference system of μTEL.

All instances of propositional tautologies and rules.

$K1$ $(K_a \varphi \wedge K_a(\varphi \to \psi)) \to K_a \psi$
$K2$ $K_a \varphi \to \varphi$
$K3$ $K_a \varphi \to K_a K_a \varphi$
$K4$ $\neg K_a \varphi \to K_a \neg K_a \varphi$
$KT1$ $\vdash \varphi \Rightarrow \vdash K_a \varphi$
$C1$ $\langle\langle \Gamma \rangle\rangle \bigcirc \top$
$C2$ $\langle\langle \Gamma \rangle\rangle \bigcirc \varphi \to \langle\langle \Gamma \cup \{a\} \rangle\rangle \bigcirc \varphi$
$C3$ $\langle\langle \Gamma \rangle\rangle \bigcirc \varphi \to \neg\langle\langle \Sigma - \Gamma \rangle\rangle \bigcirc \neg\varphi$
$C4$ $\langle\langle \emptyset \rangle\rangle \bigcirc \varphi \leftrightarrow \neg\langle\langle \Sigma \rangle\rangle \bigcirc \neg\varphi$
$C5$ $((\langle\langle \Gamma_1 \rangle\rangle \bigcirc \varphi \wedge \langle\langle \Gamma_2 \rangle\rangle \bigcirc \psi) \to \langle\langle \Gamma_1 \cup \Gamma_2 \rangle\rangle \bigcirc (\varphi \wedge \psi)$ for disjoint Γ_1 and Γ_2
$CT1$ $\vdash \varphi \to \psi \Rightarrow \vdash \langle\langle \Gamma \rangle\rangle \bigcirc \varphi \to \langle\langle \Gamma \rangle\rangle \bigcirc \psi$
$M1$ $\varphi(\mu X.\varphi(X)) \to \mu X.\varphi(X)$
$MT1$ $\vdash \varphi(\psi) \to \psi \Rightarrow \vdash \mu X.\varphi(X) \to \psi$

In this inference system, $K1$-$K4$, $KT1$ characterize knowledge modality. $C1$-$C5$, $CT1$ characterize cooperation modality. $M1$, $MT1$ characterize least fixpoint operator.

A proof in μTEL consists of a sequence of formulas, each of which is either an instance of an axiom in μTEL or follows from an application of an inference rule. (If "$\varphi_1, ..., \varphi_n$ infer ψ" is an instance of an inference rule, and if the formulas $\varphi_1, ..., \varphi_n$ have appeared earlier in the proof, then we say that ψ follows from an application of an inference rule.) A proof is said to be from Γ to φ if the premise is Γ and the last formula is φ in the proof. We say φ is provable from Γ in μTEL, and write $\Gamma \vdash_{\mu TEL} \varphi$, if there is a proof from Γ to φ in μTEL.

Inference system of μTEL is said to be sound with respect to concurrent game structures if every formula provable in μTEL is valid with respect to concurrent game structures. The system μTEL is complete with respect to concurrent game structures if every formula valid with respect to concurrent game structures is provable in μTEL. The soundness and completeness provide a tight connection between the syntactic notion of provability and the semantic notion of validity.

It is not difficult to prove that all axioms and rules in the inference system hold in any concurrent game structure S. Therefore we have the soundness of the inference system:

Proposition 1. The inference system of μTEL is sound, i.e., $\Gamma \vdash_{\mu TEL} \varphi \Rightarrow \Gamma \models_{\mu TEL} \varphi$.

It is well known that $K1$-$K4$, $KT1$ with propositional axioms and rules comprise a complete inference system for knowledge logic [14], and $M1$, $MT1$ with axioms and rules for minimal modal logic comprise a complete inference system for μ-calculus [28]. Therefore to give a complete inference system for μTEL, we only need to give a complete inference system for $\langle\langle\Gamma\rangle\rangle\bigcirc$ operator. In [17], $C1$-$C5$, $CT1$ were proven to be a complete inference system for $\langle\langle\Gamma\rangle\rangle\bigcirc$, then the inference system for μTEL is also complete.

Proposition 2. The inference system of μTEL is complete, i.e., $\Gamma \models_{\mu TEL} \varphi \Rightarrow \Gamma \vdash_{\mu TEL} \varphi$.

3   Expressivity of μTEL

Now we will discuss the express power of μTEL. As far as we know, most temporal epistemic logics in the literature are sublogics of μTEL. We demonstrate this by an example, i.e., $ATEL$, is a sublogic of μTEL. In the following, we first review the syntax and semantics of alternating time temporal epistemic logic $ATEL$ [21]. Then we give an inference system of $ATEL$. Finally, we prove that $ATEL$ is a sublogic of μTEL and give a function which can translates an $ATEL$ formula into an equivalent μTEL formula.

3.1   Syntax of $ATEL$

The well form formulas of $ATEL$ are defined as follows.

Definition 4. [21] The set of formulas in $ATEL$, called L^{ATEL}, is given by the following rules:

(1) If $\varphi \in$ atomic formulas set Π, then $\varphi \in L^{\mu TEL}$.
(2) If $\varphi \in$ proposition variables set V, then $\varphi \in L^{\mu TEL}$.
(3) If $\varphi \in L^{\mu TEL}$, then $\neg\varphi \in L^{\mu TEL}$.
(4) If $\varphi, \psi \in L^{\mu TEL}$, then $\varphi \wedge \psi \in L^{\mu TEL}$.
(5) If $\varphi, \psi \in L^{\mu TEL}$, $\Gamma \subseteq \Sigma$, then $\langle\langle\Gamma\rangle\rangle \bigcirc \varphi$, $\langle\langle\Gamma\rangle\rangle[]\varphi$, $\langle\langle\Gamma\rangle\rangle\varphi U\psi \in L^{\mu TEL}$.
Intuitively, [] means "always" and U means "until".
(6) If $\varphi \in L^{\mu TEL}$, then $K_a\varphi, E_\Gamma\varphi, C_\Gamma\varphi \in L^{\mu TEL}$, where $a \in \Sigma$, $\Gamma \subseteq \Sigma$. Intuitively, $E_\Gamma\varphi$ means that φ is known by every agent in Γ, $C_\Gamma\varphi$ means that φ is a common knowledge in Γ.

3.2   Semantics of $ATEL$

In order to give the semantics of $ATEL$, we first define computations and strategies of a concurrent game structure.

Computations. For two states $q, q' \in Q$ and an agent $a \in \Sigma$, we say that state q' is a successor to q if there exists $j_1, ..., j_k$ such that $q' = \delta(q, j_1, ..., j_k)$. Intuitively, if q' is a successor to q, then when the system is in state q, the agents Σ can cooperate to ensure that q' is the next state the system enters.

A computation of a concurrent game structure $S = (\Sigma, Q, \Pi, \pi, e, d, \delta, \sim_a$ here $a \in \Sigma)$ is an infinite sequence of states $\lambda = q_0, q_1, ...$ such that for all $u > 0$, the state q_u is a successor to q_{u-1}. A computation λ starting in state q is referred to as a q-computation; if $u \in N = \{0, 1, 2, ...\}$, then we denote by $\lambda[u]$ the u'th state in λ; similarly, we denote by $\lambda[0, u]$ and $\lambda[u, \infty]$ the finite prefix $q_0, q_1, ..., q_u$ and the infinite suffix $q_u, q_{u+1}, ...$ of λ respectively.

Strategies and their outcomes. Intuitively, a strategy is an abstract model of an agent's decision-making process; a strategy may be thought of as a kind of plan for an agent. By following a strategy, an agent can bring about certain states of affairs. Formally, a strategy f_a for an agent $a \in \Sigma$ is a total function f_a that maps every nonempty finite state sequence $\lambda \in Q^+$ to a natural number such that if the last state of λ is q, then $f_a(\lambda) \le d_a(q)$. Thus, the strategy f_a determines for every finite prefix λ of a computation a move $f_a(\lambda)$ for player a. Given a set $\Gamma \subseteq \Sigma$ of agents, and an indexed set of strategies $F_\Gamma = \{f_a \mid a \in \Gamma\}$, one for each agent $a \in \Gamma$, we define $out(q, F_\Gamma)$ to be the set of possible outcomes that may occur if every agent $a \in \Gamma$ follows the corresponding strategy f_a, starting when the system is in state $q \in Q$. That is, the set $out(q, F_\Gamma)$ will contain all possible q-computations that the agents Γ can "enforce" by cooperating and following the strategies in F_Γ. Note that the "grand coalition" of all agents in the system can cooperate to uniquely determine the future state of the system, and so $out(q, F_\Sigma)$ is a singleton. Similarly, the set $out(q, F_\emptyset)$ is the set of all possible q-computations of the system.

We can now turn to the definition of semantics of $ATEL$.

Definition 5. [21] Semantics of $ATEL$

$[[p]]_S = \{q \mid p \in \pi(q)\}$

$[[\neg\varphi]]_S = Q - [[\varphi]]_S$

$[[\varphi \wedge \psi]]_S = [[\varphi]]_S \cap [[\psi]]_S$

$[[\langle\langle\Gamma\rangle\rangle \bigcirc \varphi]]_S = \{q \mid$ there exists a set F_Γ of strategies, one for each player in Γ, such that for all computations $\lambda \in out(q, F_\Gamma)$, we have $\lambda[1] \in [[\varphi]]_S.\}$

$[[\langle\langle\Gamma\rangle\rangle[]\varphi]]_S = \{q \mid$ there exists a set F_Γ of strategies, one for each player in Γ, such that for all computations $\lambda \in out(q, F_\Gamma)$ and all positions $i \ge 0$, we have $\lambda[i] \in [[\varphi]]_S.\}$

$[[\langle\langle\Gamma\rangle\rangle\varphi U\psi]]_S = \{q \mid$ there exists a set F_Γ of strategies, one for each player in Γ, such that for all computations $\lambda \in out(q, F_\Gamma)$, there exists a position $i \ge 0$, such that $\lambda[i] \in [[\psi]]_S$ and for all positions $0 \le j < i$, we have $\lambda[j] \in [[\varphi]]_S.\}$

$[[K_a\varphi]]_S = \{q \mid$ for all $r \in [[\varphi]]_S$ and $r \in \sim_a (q)$ with $\sim_a (q) = \{q' \mid (q, q') \in \sim_a$
$\}\}$

$[[E_\Gamma\varphi]]_S = \{q \mid \text{for all } r \in [[\varphi]]_S \text{ and } r \in \sim^E_\Gamma(q) \text{ with } \sim^E_\Gamma(q) = \{q' \mid (q,q') \in \sim^E_\Gamma\}\}$, here $\sim^E_\Gamma = (\cup_{a\in\Gamma} \sim_a)$.

$[[C_\Gamma\varphi]]_S = \{q \mid \text{for all } r \in [[\varphi]]_S \text{ and } r \in \sim^C_\Gamma(q) \text{ with } \sim^C_\Gamma(q) = \{q' \mid (q,q') \in \sim^C_\Gamma\}\}$, here $\sim^C_\Gamma$ denotes the transitive closure of $\sim^E_\Gamma$.

Similarly, the notations of $S \models \varphi$, $S,q \models \varphi$, $\models_{ATEL} \varphi$ and $\Gamma \models_{ATEL} \varphi$ are defined as the case of μTEL.

3.3 Inference System of *ATEL*

In [21], some axioms and inference rules for *ATEL* were listed, but the completeness was not studied. The following set of axioms and inference rules adapted from [17] provides an inference system for the logic of knowledge, cooperation and temporal with respect to the class of Kripke structures for knowledge, cooperation and temporal:

All instances of propositional tautologies and rules.

$K1$ $(K_a\varphi \wedge K_a(\varphi \to \psi)) \to K_a\psi$

$K2$ $K_a\varphi \to \varphi$

$K3$ $K_a\varphi \to K_aK_a\varphi$

$K4$ $\neg K_a\varphi \to K_a\neg K_a\varphi$

$K5$ $E_\Gamma\varphi \leftrightarrow \wedge_{a\in\Gamma} K_a\varphi$

$K6$ $C_\Gamma\varphi \to E_\Gamma(\varphi \wedge C_\Gamma\varphi)$

$KT1$ $\vdash \varphi \Rightarrow \vdash K_a\varphi$

$KT2$ $\vdash \varphi \to E_\Gamma(\psi \wedge \varphi) \Rightarrow \vdash \varphi \to C_\Gamma\psi$

$C1$ $\neg\langle\langle\Gamma\rangle\rangle \bigcirc \bot$

$C2$ $\langle\langle\Gamma\rangle\rangle \bigcirc \top$

$C3$ $\neg\langle\langle\emptyset\rangle\rangle \bigcirc \neg\varphi \to \langle\langle\Sigma\rangle\rangle \bigcirc \neg\varphi$

$C4$ $(\langle\langle\Gamma_1\rangle\rangle \bigcirc \varphi \wedge \langle\langle\Gamma_2\rangle\rangle \bigcirc \psi) \to \langle\langle\Gamma_1 \cup \Gamma_2\rangle\rangle \bigcirc (\varphi \wedge \psi)$ for disjoint Γ_1 and Γ_2.

$C5$ $\langle\langle\Gamma\rangle\rangle[]\varphi \leftrightarrow \varphi \wedge \langle\langle\Gamma\rangle\rangle \bigcirc \langle\langle\Gamma\rangle\rangle[]\varphi$

$C6$ $\langle\langle\emptyset\rangle\rangle[](\theta \to (\varphi \wedge \langle\langle\Gamma\rangle\rangle \bigcirc \theta)) \to \langle\langle\emptyset\rangle\rangle[](\theta \to \langle\langle\Gamma\rangle\rangle[]\varphi)$

$C7$ $\langle\langle\Gamma\rangle\rangle\varphi U\psi \leftrightarrow \psi \vee (\varphi \wedge \langle\langle\Gamma\rangle\rangle \bigcirc \langle\langle\Gamma\rangle\rangle\varphi U\psi$

$C8$ $\langle\langle\emptyset\rangle\rangle[]((\psi \vee (\varphi \wedge \langle\langle\Gamma\rangle\rangle \bigcirc \theta)) \to \theta) \to \langle\langle\emptyset\rangle\rangle[](\langle\langle\Gamma\rangle\rangle\varphi U\psi \to \theta)$

$CT1$ $\vdash \varphi \to \psi \Rightarrow \vdash \langle\langle\Gamma\rangle\rangle \bigcirc \varphi \to \langle\langle\Gamma\rangle\rangle \bigcirc \psi$

$CT2$ $\vdash \varphi \Rightarrow \vdash \langle\langle\emptyset\rangle\rangle[]\varphi$

In [17], $C1$-$C8$, $CT1$-$CT2$ were proven to be a complete inference system of alternating-time temporal logic. Furthermore, $K1$-$K6$, $KT1$-$KT2$ comprise a complete inference system for knowledge logic with common knowledge operator [14]. Therefore the inference system for *ATEL* is also complete.

Proposition 3. The inference system of *ATEL* is sound and complete, i.e., $\Gamma \models_{ATEL} \varphi \Leftrightarrow \Gamma \vdash_{ATEL} \varphi$.

3.4 *ATEL* Is a Sublogic of μTEL

We have seen that the syntax of μTEL is very simple, it is just an extension of μ-calculus with cooperation modality $\langle\langle\Gamma\rangle\rangle\bigcirc$ and knowledge modality K_a. But its express power is strong. In this section, we will prove that temporal operators $\langle\langle\Gamma\rangle\rangle[]\cdot$ and $\langle\langle\Gamma\rangle\rangle(\cdot U\cdot)$, knowledge operators $E_\Gamma\cdot$ and $C_\Gamma\cdot$ all can be expressed in μTEL. This means that $ATEL$ is a sublogic of μTEL.

Proposition 4. [6] $\langle\langle\Gamma\rangle\rangle[]\varphi \models \nu X.(\varphi \wedge \langle\langle\Gamma\rangle\rangle \bigcirc X)$ and $\nu X.(\varphi \wedge \langle\langle\Gamma\rangle\rangle \bigcirc X) \models \langle\langle\Gamma\rangle\rangle[]\varphi$, here $\nu X.\varphi(X) \stackrel{def}{=} \neg\mu X.\neg\varphi(\neg X)$.

Proposition 5. [6] $\langle\langle\Gamma\rangle\rangle\varphi_1 U\varphi_2 \models \mu X.(\varphi_2 \vee (\varphi_1 \wedge \langle\langle\Gamma\rangle\rangle \bigcirc X))$ and $\mu X.(\varphi_2 \vee (\varphi_1 \wedge \langle\langle\Gamma\rangle\rangle \bigcirc X)) \models \langle\langle\Gamma\rangle\rangle\varphi_1 U\varphi_2$.
   Define $(F_\Gamma)^0\varphi = true$ and $(F_\Gamma)^{k+1}\varphi = E_\Gamma(\varphi \wedge (F_\Gamma)^k\varphi)$.
   Then we take $(S,s) \models C_\Gamma\varphi$ iff $(S,t) \models (F_\Gamma)^k\varphi$ for all $k \geq 1$.

Proposition 6. $C_\Gamma\varphi \models \nu X.E_\Gamma(\varphi \wedge X)$ and $\nu X.E_\Gamma(\varphi \wedge X) \models C_\Gamma\varphi$.

Proof : It is enough to prove that $C_\Gamma\varphi$ is the greatest fixpoint solution of the equation $X \leftrightarrow E_\Gamma(\varphi \wedge X)$.

Similar to the argument in [15]. We first show that $C_\Gamma\varphi$ is a fixed-point solution of the equation $X \leftrightarrow E_\Gamma(\varphi \wedge X)$, that is, that $C_\Gamma\varphi \leftrightarrow E_\Gamma(\varphi \wedge C_\Gamma\varphi)$ is valid. One implication is straightforward: if $E_\Gamma(\varphi \wedge C_\Gamma\varphi)$ holds at (S,s), then so does $E_\Gamma(\varphi \wedge (F_\Gamma)^k\varphi)$ for each k, since $C_\Gamma\varphi \to (F_\Gamma)^k\varphi$ is valid. That is, $(F_\Gamma)^{k+1}\varphi$ holds for each k at (S,s), and so $C_\Gamma\varphi$ holds at (S,s). As for the other implication, assume that $C_\Gamma\varphi$ holds at (S,s). Hence, $(F_\Gamma)^{k+1}\varphi$, that is, $E_\Gamma(\varphi\wedge(F_\Gamma)^k\varphi)$ holds at (S,s) for each k. For each agent i, let $A_{i,k}$ be the set of states in $S_{i,s} = K_i(s)$, where $\varphi \wedge (F_\Gamma)^k\varphi$ holds, for $k = 1,2....$ Since $(S,s) \models E_\Gamma(\varphi\wedge(F_\Gamma)^k\varphi)$, it follows that $s \in A_{i,k}$. It is straightforward to verify, by induction on k, that $(F_\Gamma)^{k+1}\varphi \to (F_\Gamma)^k\varphi$ is valid. (Proof. The case $k = 0$ is easy, since $(F_\Gamma)^0\varphi = true$. For the inductive step, note that the validity of $(F_\Gamma)^{k+1}\varphi \to (F_\Gamma)^k\varphi$ implies the validity of $E_\Gamma(\varphi \wedge (F_\Gamma)^{k+1}\varphi) \to E_\Gamma(\varphi \wedge (F_\Gamma)^k\varphi)$. But this last formula is precisely $(F_\Gamma)^{k+2}\varphi \to (F_\Gamma)^{k+1}\varphi$.) Thus, we have $A_{i,1} \supseteq A_{i,2}....$ It is easy to see that $s \in A_{i,\infty} = \cap_{k=1}^\infty A_{i,k}$. By construction, $\varphi \wedge C_\Gamma\varphi$ holds at $A_{i,\infty}$. It thus follows that $E_\Gamma(\varphi \wedge C_\Gamma\varphi)$ holds at (S,s), as desired.
   We now show that $C_\Gamma\varphi$ is the greatest fixpoint. Assume that ψ is a fixpoint in a structure S, that is, that $S \models \psi \leftrightarrow E_\Gamma(\varphi \wedge \psi)$. We want to show that $S \models \psi \to C_\Gamma\varphi$. We first show, by induction on k, that $S \models \psi \to (F_\Gamma)^k\varphi$. Since $(F_\Gamma)^0\varphi = true$ by definition, the result is immediate in the case of $k = 0$. For the induction step, suppose $S \models \psi \to (F_\Gamma)^m\varphi$. It follows easily that $S \models E_\Gamma(\varphi \wedge \psi) \to E_\Gamma(\varphi \wedge (F_\Gamma)^m\varphi)$. Hence, since $S \models \psi \leftrightarrow E_\Gamma(\varphi \wedge \psi)$, we must also have $S \models \psi \to E_\Gamma(\varphi \wedge (F_\Gamma)^m\varphi)$. But $(F_\Gamma)^{m+1}\varphi = E_\Gamma(\varphi \wedge (F_\Gamma)^m\varphi)$. So $S \models \psi \to (F_\Gamma)^{m+1}\varphi$. This completes the inductive step. It now follows that if $(S,s) \models \psi$, then $(S,s) \models (F_\Gamma)^k\varphi$ for all k, and hence that $(S,s) \models C_\Gamma\varphi$. Thus, $(S,s) \models \psi \to C_\Gamma\varphi$. This proves that $C_\Gamma\varphi$ is the greatest fixpoint solution of the equation $X \leftrightarrow E_\Gamma(\varphi \wedge X)$.
   By the above propositions, all modal operators of $ATEL$ can be expressed in μTEL.
   Now we can give a translating function from $ATEL$ formula to μTEL formula:

Definition 6. The translating function T is defined inductively as follows:

$T(p) = p$ for atomic proposition p

$T(\neg\varphi) = \neg T(\varphi)$

$T(\varphi_1 \wedge \varphi_2) = T(\varphi_1) \wedge T(\varphi_2)$

$T(\langle\langle\Gamma\rangle\rangle \bigcirc \varphi) = \langle\langle\Gamma\rangle\rangle \bigcirc T(\varphi)$

$T(\langle\langle\Gamma\rangle\rangle[]\varphi) = \nu X.(T(\varphi) \wedge \langle\langle\Gamma\rangle\rangle \bigcirc X)$

$T(\langle\langle\Gamma\rangle\rangle\varphi_1 U\varphi_2) = \mu X.(T(\varphi_2) \vee (T(\varphi_1) \wedge \langle\langle\Gamma\rangle\rangle \bigcirc X))$

$T(K_a\varphi) = K_a T(\varphi)$

$T(E_\Gamma\varphi) = \wedge_{a\in\Gamma} K_a T(\varphi)$

$T(C_\Gamma\varphi) = \nu X. \wedge_{a\in\Gamma} K_a(T(\varphi) \wedge X)$

The following proposition states the correctness of translating function T.

Proposition 7. For any $\varphi \in ATEL$, $T(\varphi) \in \mu TEL$ and $\models T(\varphi) \leftrightarrow \varphi$.

Proof : By Propositions 4, 5 and 6.

Since for 1-player game structures, the temporal part of μTEL is the same as μ-calculus, the temporal part of $ATEL$ is the same as CTL and μ-calculus is more expressive than CTL, we have that μTEL is more expressive than $ATEL$.

It is not difficult to see that other temporal epistemic logics in the literature are sublogics of μTEL too. It is well known that LTL and CTL are sublogics of μ-calculus [10], hence temporal epistemic logic CKL_n in [20], which is a combination of LTL and common knowledge logic, is also a sublogic of μTEL. Similarly, since computation tree logic of knowledge with past named $CTL_P K$ in [25] is essentially CTL with knowledge and past operators, this logic is a sublogic of the extension of μTEL with past operators.

Moreover, it is even possible to present other temporal epistemic logics which is a sublogic of μTEL. In [6], an extension of ATL, named ATL^*, is presented. ATL^* is more expressive than ATL and is a sublogic of μ-calculus with $\langle\langle\Gamma\rangle\rangle\bigcirc$ operator. Hence we can extend ATL^* with knowledge modality, and such a new temporal epistemic logic is still a sublogic of μTEL.

4   Model Checking for μTEL

4.1   A Model Checking Approach

The model checking problem for μTEL asks, given a game structure S and a μTEL formula φ, for the set of states in Q that satisfy φ.

There are lots of algorithms for μ-calculus model checking [10]. The only difference between the classical μ-calculus and μTEL is the $\langle\langle\Gamma\rangle\rangle\bigcirc$ operator and K_a operator. Hence almost all algorithms for μ-calculus model checking can be modified to handle μTEL by implementing the functions which compute $\langle\langle\Gamma\rangle\rangle\bigcirc$ operator and K_a operator. This means that we have in fact lots of algorithms for μTEL model checking.

In the following, we give a model checking algorithm for μTEL. We denote the desired set of states by $Eval(\varphi, e)$, where e is an environment.

For each φ' in $Sub(\varphi)$ do
   case $\varphi' = p : Eval(\varphi', e) := Reg(p)$
   case $\varphi' = X : Eval(\varphi', e) := e(X)$
   case $\varphi' = \neg\theta : Eval(\varphi', e) := Eval(true, e) - Eval(\theta, e)$
   case $\varphi' = \theta_1 \wedge \theta_2 : Eval(\varphi', e) := Eval(\theta_1, e) \cap Eval(\theta_2, e)$
   case $\varphi' = \langle\langle\Gamma\rangle\rangle \bigcirc \theta : Eval(\varphi', e) := Pre(\Gamma, Eval(\theta, e))$
   case $\varphi' = K_a\theta : Eval(\varphi', e) := \{q \mid Img(q, \sim_a) \subseteq Eval(\theta, e)\}$
   case $\varphi' = \mu X.\theta(X) :$
      $Eval(\varphi', e) := Eval(false, e)$
      repeat
         $\rho := Eval(\varphi', e)$
         $Eval(\varphi', e) := Eval(\theta(X), e[X \leftarrow Eval(\varphi', e)])$
      until $\rho = Eval(\varphi', e)$
   end case
return $Eval(\varphi, e)$

The algorithm uses the following primitive operations:

(1) The function Sub, when given a formula φ, returns a queue of syntactic subformulas of φ such that if φ_1 is a subformula of φ and φ_2 is a subformula of φ_1, then φ_2 precedes φ_1 in the queue $Sub(\varphi)$.

(2) The function Reg, when given a proposition $p \in \Pi$, returns the set of states in Q that satisfy p.

(3) The function Pre, when given a set $\Gamma \subseteq \Sigma$ of players and a set $\rho \subseteq Q$ of states, returns the set of states q such that from q, the players in Γ can cooperate and enforce the next state to lie in ρ. Formally, $Pre(\Gamma, \rho)$ contains state $q \in Q$ if for every player $a \in \Gamma$, there exists a move $j_a \in \{1, ..., d_a(q)\}$ such that for all players $b \in \Sigma - \Gamma$ and moves $j_b \in \{1, ..., d_b(q)\}$, we have $\delta(q, j_1, ..., j_k) \in \rho$.

(4) The function $Img : Q \times 2^{Q \times Q} \to Q$, which takes as input a state q and a binary relation $R \subseteq Q \times Q$, and returns the set of states that are accessible from q via R. That is, $Img(q, R) = \{q' \mid qRq'\}$.

(5) Union, intersection, difference, and inclusion test for state sets. Note also that we write $Eval(true, e)$ for the set Q of all states, and write $Eval(false, e)$ for the empty set of states.

Notice that for any given inputs, all of these functions may be easily computed in time polynomial in the size of the inputs and structure against which they are being computed. In the case of $\varphi' = \mu X.\theta(X)$, $Eval(\varphi', e)$ is computed by iterative evaluation: $[[\mu X.\varphi(X)]]_S^e = \cup_i \tau^i(\emptyset)$, where $\tau(W) = [[\varphi(X)]]_S^{e[X \leftarrow W]}$. In fact, the complexity of this algorithm mainly depends on the cost of computing fixpoint.

Partial correctness of the algorithm can be proved induction on the structure of the input formula φ. Termination is guaranteed, because the state space Q is finite. Therefore we have the following proposition:

Proposition 8. The algorithm given in the above terminates and is correct, i.e., it returns the set of states in which the input formula is satisfied.

A famous efficient model checking technique is symbolic model checking [27], which uses ordered binary-decision diagrams (*OBDDs*) to represent Kripke structures. Roughly speaking, if each state is a valuation for a set X of Boolean variables, then a state set ρ can be encoded by a Boolean expression $\rho(X)$ over the variables in X. For Kripke structures that arise from descriptions of closed systems with Boolean state variables, the symbolic operations necessary for *CTL* model checking have standard implementations. In this case, a transition relation R on states can be encoded by a Boolean expression $\underline{R}(X, X')$ over X and X', where X' is a copy of X that represents the values of the state variables after a transition. Then, the *pre-image* of ρ under R, i.e., the set of states that have R-successors in ρ, can be computed as $\exists X'(\underline{R}(X, X') \wedge \rho(X'))$. Based on this observation, symbolic model checkers for *CTL*, such as $S\overline{M}V$ [10], typically use *OBDDs* to represent Boolean expressions, and implement the Boolean and pre-image operations on state sets by manipulating *OBDDs*.

To apply symbolic techniques to our model checking algorithm, we should mainly give symbolic implementation of the computation of $Eval(\langle\langle\Gamma\rangle\rangle \bigcirc \theta, e)$ and $Eval(K_a\theta, e)$.

Since computing $Eval(\langle\langle\Gamma\rangle\rangle \bigcirc \theta, e)$ is reduced to computing $Pre(\Gamma, Eval (\theta, e))$, we only need to give a symbolic implementation of the *Pre* operator. For the game structure S, such a symbolic implementation was discussed in [6,2,4]. In this case, Boolean expression $\underline{R}(X, X')$ in Kripke structures should be replaced by an encoding of the move function and the transition function using Boolean expressions.

The computation of $Eval(K_a\theta, e)$ can also be done using standard symbolic techniques. When given an equivalence relation $\sim_a$ and a set ρ of states, suppose that $\underline{\sim_a}(X', X)$ is a Boolean expression that encodes the equivalence relation $\sim_a$ and $\rho(X')$ is a Boolean expression that encodes the set ρ of states, then $\{q \mid Img(q, \sim_a) \subseteq \rho\}$ can be computed as $\exists X'(\underline{\sim_a}(X', X) \wedge (X \rightarrow \underline{\rho}(X')))$.

4.2   The Complexity of Model Checking for μ*TEL*

The modal μ-calculus model checking problem is well known to be in the complexity class $NP \cap co - NP$ [12]. Moreover, since μ-calculus model checking is equivalent via linear time reductions to the problem of deciding the winner in parity game, in [23] the modal μ-calculus model checking problem was proved to be in $UP \cap co - UP$, where UP is unambiguous nondeterministic polynomial time class and obviously $P \subseteq UP \cap co - UP \subseteq NP \cap co - NP$. This is the best result for the complexity of μ-calculus model checking up to now. Since algorithms for μ-calculus model checking can be modified to handle μTEL by implementing the functions which compute $\langle\langle\Gamma\rangle\rangle\bigcirc$ operator and K_a operator. From a computational point of view, the complexity of μTEL model checking is the same as μ-calculus. Therefore we have the following proposition:

Proposition 9. The μTEL model checking problem is in $UP \cap co - UP$.

It is not known whether $UP \cap co - UP = P$ or not. There are relatively few natural problems known in $UP \cap co - UP$. As far as we known, some famous problems in $UP \cap co - UP$ were recently proved in P. For example, the problem of primality has been showed to belong to $UP \cap co - UP$ [16], and recently primality was further proved to belong to P [1]. This leads us to conjecture that the μTEL model checking problem is in P. Up to now, the best algorithm for μ-calculus model checking costs subexponential time in the worst case [24]. Since the complexity of μTEL model checking is the same as μ-calculus, we also have a subexponential time algorithm for μTEL model checking.

4.3   Model Checking for Other Temporal Epistemic Logics

In [20], a temporal epistemic logic CKL_n was presented. This logic is a combination of LTL and common knowledge logic. CKL_n model checking was showed to be reduced to LTL model checking. In [21], a model checking algorithm for $ATEL$ was given and its correctness and complexity were studied. In [25], authors presented a computation tree logic of knowledge with past named $CTL_P K$. Essentially, this logic is CTL with knowledge and past operators. The $CTL_P K$ model checking problem was reduced to SAT problem. But it was well known that SAT problem is NP-complete and most believe that SAT problem needs exponential time, therefore in this approach, the complexity of model checking is exponential time in the worst cases.

These temporal epistemic logics can be verified uniformly by μTEL model checking. For CKL_n, since LTL was showed to be a sublogic of μ-calculus [10], we can translate any CKL_n formula into a μTEL formula, then reduce CKL_n model checking to μTEL model checking. For $ATEL$, since $ATEL$ is a sublogic of μTEL, we can also reduce $ATEL$ model checking problem to μTEL model checking problem by translating function. For $CTL_P K$, since CTL is a sublogic of ATL [6], similarly, $CTL_P K$ model checking can also be reduced to a model checking algorithm for the extension of μTEL with past operators.

5   A Case Study

In this section we study an example of how μTEL can be used to represent and verify the properties in multi-agent systems. The system we consider is a train controller (adapted from [5]). The system consists of three agents: two trains and a controller—see Figure 1. The trains, one Eastbound, the other Westbound, occupy a circular track. At one point, both tracks need to pass through a narrow tunnel. There is no room for both trains to be in the tunnel at the same time, therefore the trains must avoid this to happen. Traffic lights are placed on both sides of the tunnel, which can be either red or green. Both trains are equipped with a signaller, that they use to send a signal when they approach the tunnel. The controller can receive signals from both trains, and controls the color of the traffic lights. The task of the controller is to ensure that trains are never both in the tunnel at the same time. The trains follow the traffic lights signals diligently, i.e., they stop on red.

In the following, we use in_tunnel_a to represent that agent a is in the tunnel, and use $\langle\langle \Gamma \rangle\rangle <> \varphi$ to abbreviate $\langle\langle \Gamma \rangle\rangle \top U \varphi$.

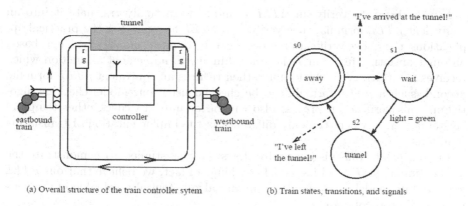

(a) Overall structure of the train controller sytem   (b) Train states, transitions, and signals

Fig. 1. The local transition structures for the two trains and the controller

Firstly, consider the property that "when one train is in the tunnel, it knows the other train is not the tunnel":

$\langle\langle\emptyset\rangle\rangle[](in\_tunnel_a \rightarrow K_a \neg in\_tunnel_b)$ $(a \neq b \in \{TrainE, TrainW\})$

This property can also be represented as the following μTEL formulas:

$\nu X.((in\_tunnel_a \rightarrow K_a \neg in\_tunnel_b) \wedge \langle\langle\emptyset\rangle\rangle \bigcirc X)$ $(a \neq b \in \{TrainE, TrainW\})$

To verify such formulas, we can check these formulas using our model checking algorithm for μTEL. The result shows that all states satisfy these formulas, hence the property is valid in the system.

We now consider the formula that express the fact that "it is always common knowledge that the grand coalition of all agents can cooperate to eventually get train a in the tunnel":

$\langle\langle\emptyset\rangle\rangle[]C_\Sigma\langle\langle\Sigma\rangle\rangle <>in\_tunnel_a$ $(a \in \{TrainE, TrainW\})$

Using the translating function, we get the following equivalent formula:

$\nu X.(\nu Y. \wedge_{a \in \Sigma} K_a(\mu Z.(in\_tunnel_a \vee (\top \wedge \langle\langle\Sigma\rangle\rangle \bigcirc Z)) \wedge \langle\langle\emptyset\rangle\rangle \bigcirc X) \wedge Y)$

Since $\top \wedge \langle\langle\Sigma\rangle\rangle \bigcirc Z \leftrightarrow \langle\langle\Sigma\rangle\rangle \bigcirc Z$, we have

$\nu X.(\nu Y. \wedge_{a \in \Sigma} K_a(\mu Z.(in\_tunnel_a \vee \langle\langle\Sigma\rangle\rangle \bigcirc Z) \wedge \langle\langle\emptyset\rangle\rangle \bigcirc X) \wedge Y)$

The following are valid fixpoint principles. Arnold and Niwinski call these "the golden lemma" of μ-calculus [7].

$\mu X.\mu Y.\varphi(X,Y) \leftrightarrow \mu X.\varphi(X,X) \leftrightarrow \mu Y.\mu X.\varphi(X,Y)$
$\nu X.\nu Y.\varphi(X,Y) \leftrightarrow \nu X.\varphi(X,X) \leftrightarrow \nu Y.\nu X.\varphi(X,Y)$

Using these lemmas, we can further simplify the formula.

$\nu X. \wedge_{a \in \Sigma} K_a(\mu Z.(in\_tunnel_a \vee \langle\langle\Sigma\rangle\rangle \bigcirc Z) \wedge \langle\langle\emptyset\rangle\rangle \bigcirc X) \wedge X$

Now this formula is checked by model checking algorithm for μTEL. The return is the whole set of states. Therefore this property is true.

We can also express that "agent can make itself know that the other is not in the tunnel":

$\langle\langle\emptyset\rangle\rangle[]\langle\langle a\rangle\rangle <> K_a(\neg in\_tunnel_b)$ $(a \neq b \in \{TrainE, TrainW\})$

Similarly, this can also be represented as follows:

$\nu X.(\mu Y.(K_a(\neg in\_tunnel_b) \vee \langle\langle a\rangle\rangle \bigcirc Y) \wedge \langle\langle\emptyset\rangle\rangle \bigcirc X)$ $(a \neq b \in \{TrainE, TrainW\})$

We can further verify these formulas using our model checking algorithm for μTEL, and result shows that the above property does not hold in the system.

In the above, to verify an $ATEL$ formula, we actually translate it into an equivalent μTEL formula, then verify this μTEL formula. For the practical applications, the above verification process can be done automatically: First, based on our translating function T, it is not difficult to implement a function which receives an arbitrary $ATEL$ formula, then returns an equivalent μTEL formula. Second, such a μTEL formula can be checked using our model checking algorithm. This verification process also can be adapted to check other temporal epistemic logics, where the only difference is the implementation of translating function.

In [20], a bit transmission protocol system was studied to demonstrate the application of CKL_n and its model checking. In fact, we believe that our μTEL logic and its model checking algorithm are also potentially valuable in the verification of protocol systems.

6   Conclusions

Recently, there has been growing interest in the logics for representing and reasoning temporal and epistemic properties in multi-agent systems [20,21,25,26,29]. In this paper, we present a temporal epistemic logic μTEL, which is a succinct and powerful language for expressing complex properties of multi-agent system. Similar to μ-calculus in temporal logics, almost all temporal epistemic logics appeared in the literatures can be translated into μTEL. As an example, $ATEL$ is showed to be a sublogic of μTEL. Moreover, since ATL generalizes CTL [6], modal combinations of CTL or LTL with the modalities for the mental attitudes [20,25] can also be represented in μTEL. Thus a model checking algorithm for μTEL can uniformly check various of temporal and epistemic properties. In this paper, the approach to model checking μTEL is studied. Finally we use μTEL and its model checking algorithm to represent and reason properties in a trains and controller system. It is also hopeful to apply such μTEL logic and its model checking algorithm to verify the correctness of protocol systems. In [26], a logic called $mv\ \mu K^+$ was presented, which combined three different logical frameworks: the logic of knowledge with interpreted system semantics, temporal logic and modal μ-calculus. The model checking algorithm for $mv\ \mu K^+$ was also studied. The work in [26] is similar to this wok. But there are still some superior points of this work over the above work. We give a comparison with [26] and this paper from the following points: (1) Our μTEL logic contains operator $\langle\langle \Gamma \rangle\rangle\bigcirc$, so μTEL can express the properties about cooperation and temporal. But mv μK^+ only contains temporal operator $\bigcirc$ and can not express the cooperation properties. It is well known that cooperation is an essential phenomenon in MAS. So it seems that thr expressive power of $mv\ \mu K^+$ is poor for MAS. Since $\bigcirc$ can be expressed by $\langle\langle \Gamma \rangle\rangle\bigcirc$, $mv\ \mu K^+$ is a sublogic of μTEL. (2) The semantics of μTEL is given by concurrent game structure. Whereas the semantics of $mv\ \mu K^+$ was given by Kripke structure. The concurrent game structure is more natural than the Kripke structure for modelling MAS. (3) We give the sound and complete inference systems for μTEL and $ATEL$. (4) We studied the symbolic model checking technique for μTEL. But the symbolic model checking technique for $mv\,\mu K^+$ was not discussed. (5) We show that the complexity of model checking for μTEL is in $UP \cap co - UP$. Whereas the complexity of model checking for $mv\,\mu K^+$ was not discussed. (6) Since $mv\,\mu K^+$ is a sublogic of μTEL, our model checking algorithm for μTEL can also be applied to $mv\,\mu K^+$. But the converse does not hold because $mv\,\mu K^+$ can not express operator $\langle\langle\Gamma\rangle\rangle \bigcirc$.

The further research direction may include the following aspects: (1) Since agents in an open system may have wrong information or probabilistic information, it is worth to extend μTEL with belief modality or probabilistic knowledge modality. (2) In some systems, predictable response times are essential for correctness. Such systems are called real-time systems. It is interesting to study whether μTEL can be extended to express real-time properties in real-time multi-agent systems. (3) In most literatures, model checking algorithm can only answer whether a state satisfies a property. But in practical areas, to help one can easily find the design error of system, it is more important to give some checking information when the state does not satisfy the property. It is necessary to study how to represent and generate such useful checking information.

References

1. Manindra Agrawal, Neeraj Kayal, Nitin Saxena, "PRIMES is in P." Annals of Mathematics 160(2): 781-793 (2004).
2. L. de Alfaro, T. A. Henzinger, F. Y. C. Mang. The Control of Synchronous Systems Part II. In CONCUR 01: Concurrency Theory, 12th International Conference, Lectures Notes in Computer Science, Springer-Verlag, 2001.
3. L. de Alfaro, T. A. Henzinger, R. Majumdar. From Verification to Control: Dynamic Programs for Omega-Regular Objectives. In LICS 01: 16th International IEEE Symposium on Logic in Computer Science, IEEE press, 2001.
4. L. de Alfaro, T. A. Henzinger, F. Y. C. Mang. The Control of Synchronous Systems. In CONCUR 00: Concurrency Theory, 11th International Conference, Lecture Notes in Computer Sciences, Springer Verlag, 2000.
5. R. Alur, L. de Alfaro, T. A. Henzinger, S. C. Krishnan, F. Y. C. Mang, S. Qadeer, S. K. Rajamni, and S. Tasiran, MOCHA user manual, University of Berkeley Report, 2000.
6. R. Alur and T. A. Henzinger. Alternating-time temporal logic. In Journal of the ACM, 49(5): 672-713.
7. A. Arnold and D. Niwinski. Rudiments of μ-calculus. Studies in Logic, Vol 146, North-Holland, 2001
8. M. Bourahla and M. Benmohamed. Model Checking Multi-Agent Systems. In Informatica 29: 189-197, 2005.
9. J. Bradfield and C. Stirling. Modal Logics and mu-Calculi: An Introduction. In Handbook of Process Algebra, Chapter 4. Elsevier Science B.V. 2001.
10. E. M. Clarke, J. O. Grumberg, and D. A. Peled. Model checking. The MIT Press, 1999.
11. H. van Ditmarsch, W van der Hoek, and B. P. Kooi. Dynamic Epistemic Logic with Assignment, in AAMAS05, ACM Inc, New York, vol. 1, 141-148, 2005.
12. E. A. Emerson, C. S. Jutla, and A. P. Sistla. On model checking for fragments of the μ-calculus. In CAV93, LNCS 697, 385-396, 1993.

13. R. Fagin and J. Y. Halpern. Reasoning about knowledge and probability, Journal of the ACM, 41(2): 340-367, 1994.
14. R. Fagin, J. Y. Halpern, Y. Moses, and M. Y. Vardi. Reasoning About Knowledge, The MIT Press: Cambridge, MA, 1995.
15. R. Fagin, J. Y. Halpern, Y. Moses, and M. Y. Vardi. Common knowledge revisited, Annals of Pure and Applied Logic 96: 89-105, 1999.
16. M. R. Fellows and N. Koblitz. Self-witnessing polynimial-time complexity and prime factorization. In Proceedings of the 7th Annal Conference on Structure in Complexity Theory, 107-110, IEEE Computer Society Press, 1992.
17. V. Goranko, G. van Drimmelen. Complete axiomatization and decidability of Alternating-time temporal logic. Theoretical Computer Science 353 (2006) 93-117.
18. J. Y. Halpern. Reasoning about knowledge: a survey, Handbook of Logic in Artificial Intelligence and Logic Programming, Vol. 4, D. Gabbay, C. J. Hogger, and J. A. Robinson, eds., 1-34, Oxford University, Press1995.
19. J. Y. Halpern and Y. Moses. Knowledge and common knowledge in a distributed environment, Journal of the ACM, 37(3): 549-587, 1990.
20. W. van der Hoek and M. Wooldridge. Model Checking Knowledge, and Time. In Proceedings of SPIN 2002 (LNCS 2318), 95-111, 2002.
21. W. van der Hoek and M. Wooldridge. Cooperation, Knowledge, and Time: Alternating-time Temporal Epistemic Logic and its Applications. Studia Logica, 75: 125-157, 2003.
22. W. van der Hoek and M. Wooldridge. On the Logic of Cooperation and Propositional Control. Artificial Intelligence, 64:1-2, 81-119, 2005.
23. M. Jurdzinski. Deciding the winner in parity games is in UP∩co-UP. Information Processing Letters, 68: 119-134, 1998.
24. M. Jurdzinski, M. Paterson and U. Zwick. A Deterministic Subexponential Algorithm for Solving Parity Games. In Proceedings of ACM-SIAM Symposium on Discrete Algorithms, SODA 2006, January 2006.
25. M. Kacprzak, A. Lomuscio and W. Penczek. Verification of multiagent systems via unbounded model checking. In Proceedings of the 3rd International Conference on Autonomous Agents and Multiagent Systems (AAMAS-04), 2004.
26. B. Konikowska and W. Penczek. Model Checking for Multivalued Logic of Knowledge and Time. AAMAS06, 169-176, 2006.
27. K. L. McMillan. Symbolic model checking: An Approach to the State Explosion Problem. Kluwer Academic, 1993.
28. I. Walukiewicz. Completeness of Kozen's axiomatisation of the propositional μ-calculus. Information and Computation 157, 142-182, 2000.
29. M. Wooldridge, M. Fisher, M. Huget, and S. Parsons. Model checking multiagent systems with mable. In Proceedings of the First International Conference on Autonomous Agents and Multiagent Systems (AAMAS-02), 2002.

A New Logical Semantics for Agent Communication

Jamal Bentahar[1], Bernard Moulin[2], John-Jules Ch. Meyer[3],
and Yves Lespérance[4]

[1] Concordia University, Concordia Institute for Information Systems Engineering
(CIISE), Canada
bentahar@encs.concordia.ca
[2] Laval University, Depart. of Computer Science and Software Engineering, Canada
bernard.moulin@ift.ulaval.ca
[3] University Utrecht, Depart. of Computer Science, The Netherlands
jj@cs.uu.nl
[4] York University, Depart. of Computer Science, Canada
lesperan@cs.yorku.ca

Abstract. In this paper we develop a semantics of our approach based
on commitments and arguments for conversational agents. We propose a
logical model based on CTL* (Extended Computation Tree Logic) and
on dynamic logic. Called Commitment and Argument Network (CAN),
our formal framework based on this hybrid approach uses three basic
elements: social commitments, actions that agents apply to these commitments and arguments that agents use to support their actions. The
advantage of this logical model is to gather all these elements and the existing relations between them within the same framework. The semantics
we develop here enables us to reflect the dynamics of agent communication. It also allows us to establish the important link between commitments as a deontic concept and arguments. On the one hand CTL*
enables us to express all the temporal aspects related to the handling of
commitments and arguments. On the other hand, dynamic logic enables
us to capture the actions that agents are committed to achieve.

1 Introduction

Recent years have seen an increasing interest in specifying and verifying multi-
agent systems (MAS) using computational logics [24]. Indeed, modeling agent
interactions in logic-based MAS has attracted the attention of several researchers
[7,16] (see [25] for a good synthesis). In this context, semantics of agent communication is one of the most important aspects, particularly in the current
state of open and interoperable MAS. Although a certain number of significant
proposals were done in this field, for example [1,12,17,23,26,27], the definition
of a clear and global semantics (i.e. dealing with the various aspects of agent
communication) is an objective yet to be reached.

The objective of this paper is to propose a general framework capturing semantic issues of an approach based on social commitments (SCs) and arguments

K. Inoue, K. Satoh, and F. Toni (Eds.): CLIMA VII, LNAI 4371, pp. 151–170, 2007.
© Springer-Verlag Berlin Heidelberg 2007

for agent communication. Indeed, this work is a continuation of our preceding research in which we developed this approach and addressed in detail the pragmatic aspects [6]. Pragmatics deals with the way of using the communicative acts correctly. It is related to the dynamics of agent interactions and to the way of connecting the isolated acts to build complete conversations. Thus, the paper highlights semantic issues of our approach and the link with pragmatic ones. The semantics we define here deals with all the aspects we use in our SC and argument approach. The purpose is to propose a complete, clear and unambiguous semantics for agent communication.

In addition to proposing a unified framework for pragmatic and semantic issues, this work presents two results: 1. it semantically establishes the link between SCs and arguments; 2. it uses both a temporal logic (CTL* with some additions) and a dynamic logic to define an unambiguous semantics. We notice here that the semantics presented in this paper is different from the one that we have developed in [8,9]. The logical model presented here is more expressive because the content of SCs are path formulae and not state formulae and their semantics is expressed in terms of satisfaction paths and not in terms of deadlines. This makes the semantics more clear and easy to verify. In addition, this semantics expresses explicitly the relation between SCs and actions by using the philosophical literature on actions and by introducing the new *Happens* operator.

Paper overview. In Section 2, we introduce the main ideas of our pragmatic approach based on commitments and arguments. In Section 3, we present the syntax and the semantics of our logical model for agent communication. In Section 4, we conclude the paper by comparing our approach to related work.

2   Commitment and Argument-Based Approach

2.1   Social Commitments

A social commitment SC is an engagement made by an agent (called the *debtor*), that some fact is true or that some action will be performed. This commitment is directed to a set of agents (called *creditors*). A commitment is an obligation in the sense that the debtor must respect and behave in accordance with this commitment. Commitments are social in the sense that they are expressed publicly and governed by some rules. This means that they are observable by all the participants. The main idea is that a speaker is committed to a statement when he made this statement or when he agreed upon this statement made by another participant and acts accordingly. What is important here is not that an agent agrees or disagrees upon a statement, but rather the fact that the agent expresses agreement or disagreement. Consequently, SCs are different from the agent's private mental states like beliefs, desires and intentions. This notion allows us to represent agent conversations as observed by the participants and by an external observant, and not on the basis of the internal agents' states.

We denote a SC as follows: $SC(Ag_1, A^*, t, \varphi)$ where Ag_1 is the debtor, A^* is the set of the creditors ($A^* = A \setminus \{Ag_1\}$, where A is the set of participants), t is the time associated with the commitment, and φ its content. Logically speaking, a commitment is a public propositional attitude. The content of a commitment can be a proposition or an action. A detailed taxonomy of SCs that we use in our approach will be discussed later. To simplify the notation, we suppose throughout this paper that $A = \{Ag_1, Ag_2\}$.

In order to model the dynamics of conversations, we interpret a *speech act* as an action performed on a commitment or on a commitment content. A speech act is an abstract act that an agent, the *speaker*, performs when producing an utterance Ut and addressing it to another agent, the *addressee*. According to speech act theory, the primary units of meaning in the use of language are not isolated propositions but rather speech acts of the type called *illocutionary acts*. Assertions, questions, orders and declarations are examples of these illocutionary acts. In our framework, a speech act can be defined as follows.

Definition 1 (Speech Acts). $SA(i_k, Ag_1, Ag_2, t_{ut}, Ut) =_{def}$
$$Act(Ag_1, t_{ut}, SC(Ag_1, Ag_2, t, \varphi))$$
$$|Act-cont(Ag_1, t_{ut}, SC(Ag_i, Ag_j, t, \varphi))$$
$$|Act-cont(Ag_1, t_{ut}, SC(Ag_1, Ag_2, t, \varphi)) \ \&$$
$$Act-cont(Ag_1, t_{ut}, SC(Ag_i, Ag_j, t, \varphi))$$

where SA is the abbreviation of "Speech Act", i_k is the identifier of the speech act, Ag_1 is the speaker, Ag_2 is the addressee, t_{ut} is the utterance time, Ut is the utterance, Act indicates the action performed by the speaker on the commitment: $Act \in \{Create, Withdraw, Violate, Satisfy\}$, $Act-cont$ indicates the action performed by the speaker on the commitment content: $Act-cont \in \{Accept-cont, Refuse-cont, Chal-cont, Justify-cont, Defend-cont, Attack-cont\}$, $i, j \in \{1, 2\}$, $i \neq j$, the meta-symbol "&" indicates the logical conjunction.

The definiendum $SA(i_k, Ag_1, Ag_2, t_{ut}, Ut)$ is defined by the definiens $Act(Ag_1, t_{ut}, SC(Ag_1, Ag_2, t, \varphi))$ as an action performed by the speaker on its SC. The definiendum is defined by the definiens $Act-cont(Ag_1, t_{ut}, SC(Ag_i, Ag_j, t, \varphi))$ as an action performed by the speaker on the content of its SC ($i = 1, j = 2$) or on the content of the addressee's SC ($i = 2, j = 1$). Finally, the definiendum is defined as an action performed by the speaker on its SC and as an action performed by the speaker on the content of its SC or on the content of the addressee's SC. These actions are similar to the moves proposed in [22]. The following example illustrates this idea.

Example 1. Let us consider the following utterances:
Ut_1: *Quebec is the capital of Canada*
Ut_2: *No, the capital of Canada is Ottawa*

The utterance Ut_1 leads to the creation of a new commitment:
$SA(i_0, Ag_1, Ag_2, t_{ut_1}, Ut_1) =_{def}$
$$Create(Ag_1, t_{ut_1}, SC(Ag_1, Ag_2, t_1, Capital(Canada, Quebec)))$$

The utterance Ut_2 leads at the same time to an action performed on the content of the commitment created following the utterance Ut_1 and to the creation of another commitment. Formally:

$$SA(i_1, Ag_2, Ag_1, t_{ut_2}, Ut_2) =_{def}$$
$$Refuse\text{–}cont(Ag_2, t_{ut_2}, SC(Ag_1, Ag_2, t_1, Capital(Canada, Quebec))) \&$$
$$Create(Ag_2, t_{ut_2}, SC(Ag_2, Ag_1, t_2, Capital(Canada, Ottawa)))$$

2.2 Taxonomy

The types of commitments we use in our agent communication framework are:

A. *Absolute Commitments (ABC)*. Absolute commitments are commitments whose fulfillment does not depend on any particular condition. Two types can be distinguished: *propositional commitments* and *action commitments*.

A1. *Propositional Commitments (PC)*. Propositional commitments are related to the state of the world. They are generally, but not necessarily, expressed by assertives. They can be directed towards the past, the present, or the future.

A2. *Action Commitments (AC)*. Action commitments (also called *commitments to a course of action*) are directed towards the present or the future and are related to actions that the debtor is committed to carry out. The fulfillment and the lack of fulfillment of such commitments depend on the performance of the underlying action. This type of commitment is typically conveyed by promises.

B. *Conditional Commitments (CC)*. Absolute commitments do not consider conditions that may make relative the need for their fulfillment. However, in several cases, agents need to make commitments not in absolute terms but under given conditions. Another commitment type is therefore required. These commitments are said to be conditional. We distinguish between *conditional commitments about propositions (CCP)* and *conditional commitments about actions (CCA)*. A conditional commitment about a proposition p' under the condition p expresses the fact that if the condition p is true, then the creditor commits that the content p' is true (there is an implication link between p and p').

C. *Commitment Attempts (CT)*. The commitments described so far directly concern the debtor who commits either that a certain fact is true or that a certain action will be performed. For example, these commitments do not allow us to explain the fact that an agent asks another one to be committed to carrying out an action (by a speech act of a directive type). To solve this problem, we propose the concept of commitment attempt. We consider a commitment attempt as a request made by a debtor to push a creditor to be committed. Thus, when an agent Ag_1 requests another agent Ag_2 to do something, we say that Ag_1 is trying to induce Ag_2 to make a commitment. We distinguish four types of commitment attempts: *propositional commitment attempts (PCT)*, *action commitment attempts (ACT)*, *conditional commitment attempts about propositions (CCTP)*, and *conditional commitment attempts about actions (CCTA)*.

2.3   Argumentation and Social Commitments

Contrary to monotonic logics, in a nonmonotonic logic, adding premises can lead to the withdrawal of conclusions. Argumentation systems are studied in the context of this kind of reasoning. Several models of defeasible argumentation have been proposed [13,14,19,21]. In these models, adding arguments can lead to the defeat of arguments. An argument is defeated if it is attacked successfully by a counterargument. A defeasible argumentation system essentially includes a logical language $\mathcal{L}$, a definition of the argument concept, a definition of the attack relation between arguments, and finally a definition of acceptability. Here Γ indicates a possibly inconsistent knowledge base with possibly no deductive closure (that is the deductive closure is not necessarily included in Γ), and $\vdash$ stands for classical inference. The propositions of the language $\mathcal{L}$ are denoted by $a, b, \ldots$

Definition 2 (Argument). *An argument is a pair (H, h) where h is a formula of $\mathcal{L}$ and H a subset of Γ such that: i) H is consistent, ii) $H \vdash h$ and iii) H is minimal, so that no subset of H satisfying both i and ii exists. H is called the support of the argument and h its conclusion.*

Example 2. Let $\Gamma = \{a, a \to b, c \to \neg b, c\}$. Then, $(\{a, a \to b\}, b)$ and $(\{a \to b\}, \neg a \vee b)$ are two arguments.

Definition 3 (Attack). *Let (H_1, h_1), (H_2, h_2) be two arguments. (H_1, h_1) attacks (H_2, h_2) iff $H_2 \vdash \neg h_1$. In other words, an argument is attacked if and only if there exists an argument for the negation of its conclusion.*

Example 3. Let $\Gamma = \{a, a \to b, c \to \neg b, c, \neg b \to \neg d, \neg c\}$. Then, the argument $(\{a, a \to b\}, b)$ attacks the argument $(\{c, c \to \neg b, \neg b \to \neg d\}, \neg d)$ and also the argument $(\{\neg c\}, \neg c)$ attacks the argument $(\{c, c \to \neg b, \neg b \to \neg d\}, \neg d)$.

The link between commitments and arguments enables us to capture both the public and reasoning aspects of agent communication. This link is explained as follows. Before committing to some fact h being true (i.e. before creating a commitment whose content is h), the speaker agent must use its argumentation system to build an argument (H, h). On the other side, the addressee agent must use its own argumentation system to select the answer it will give (i.e. to decide about the appropriate manipulation of the content of an existing commitment). For example, an agent Ag_1 accepts the commitment content h proposed by another agent Ag_2 if it is able to build an argument which supports this content from its knowledge base. If Ag_1 has an argument $(H', \neg h)$, then it refuses the commitment content proposed by Ag_2 by attacking the conclusion h. Now, if Ag_1 has an argument neither for h, nor for $\neg h$, then it must ask for an explanation. The social relationship that exists between agents, their reputations and trusts also influence the acceptance of the arguments by agents. However, this aspect will not be dealt with in this paper. The argumentation relations that we use in our model are thought of as actions applied to commitment contents. The set of these relations is: $\{Justify, Defend, Attack\}$.

We used this approach in [6] to propose a formal framework called Commitment and Argument Network (CAN). The idea of this formalism is to reflect the dynamics of agent communication by a network in which agents manipulate commitments and arguments. In the following section, we will propose a formal semantics of our framework in the form of a logical model. The elements that we use in our framework and in our logical model are: SCs, actions and arguments. These elements are separated in three levels. The first level includes SCs that agents use in their conversations. The second level includes actions that agents apply to the commitments. The third level is composed of arguments that agents use to support their actions applied to the commitments.

3   The Logical Model of Agent Communication

3.1   Syntax

In this section we specify the syntax of the different elements that we use in our agent communication framework. These elements are: propositional elements, actions, social commitments, actions applied to commitments and argumentation relations. Our formal language L (the object language) is based on an extended version of CTL* [15] and on dynamic logic [18]. We use a branching time for the future and we suppose that the past is linear. Each node in the branching time model is represented by a state s_i and a time point t_j. We also suppose that time is discrete. In our model, temporal logic enables us to express all the temporal aspects related to the handling of commitments and arguments. On one hand, we use the branching time in order to formalize the different choices that agents have when they participate in conversations. On the other hand, dynamic logic allows us to capture the actions that agents are committed to perform and the actions that agents perform on different commitments and commitment contents when they participate in these conversations. Indeed, from a philosophical point of view, action and branching time are logically related [4]. The agents' actions are not fully determined. Moreover, these actions can have many different possible future effects. For this reason, it is preferable to work out a logic of action that is compatible with indeterminism. According to indeterminism, several moments of time might follow the same moment in the future of the world. Any moment of time can belong to several paths representing possible courses of the world with the same past and present but different historic continuations of that moment.

Let Φ_p be the set of atomic propositions and Φ_{at} be the set of atomic actions. The set Φ_a denotes a set of complex actions (a complex action is composed of a number of atomic actions). The set of agents is denoted by A and the set of time points is denoted by TP. The agents' actions on commitments and on their contents and the argumentation relations are introduced as modal operators. In this paper, a commitment formula, independently of the SC type, is denoted by $SC(Ag_1, Ag_2, t, \varphi)$ where φ is a well-formed formula of L. When t is unknown (unspecified), we drop it from the commitment formula. In this case a commitment is denoted by $SC(Ag_1, Ag_2, *, \varphi)$. In this logical model we use the symbol $\wedge$ in the object language and the symbol & in the metalanguage for "and". For "or" we use the symbol $\vee$ in the object language and the symbol $|$ in the metalanguage. The language L can be defined by the following syntactic rules.

Propositional Elements

R1 (Atomic formula). $\forall \psi \in \Phi_p, \psi \in L$

R2 (Conjunction). $p, q \in L \Rightarrow p \wedge q \in L$

R3 (Negation). $p \in L \Rightarrow \neg p \in L$

R4 (Arguments). $p, q \in L \Rightarrow p \therefore q \in L$

R4 means that p is an argument for q. We can read this formula: p, so q. We notice that the difference between the operator $\therefore$ and the formal notation of an argument as a pair (see Definition 2) is that $\therefore$ is a language construct. In the notation $p \therefore q$, p is a formula of the language, however in the notation (H, h), H is a sub-set of a knowledge base.

Example 4. Let p and q be two formulae of L. Then, $(p \wedge p \rightarrow q) \therefore q$ is a formula of L saying that $p \wedge p \rightarrow q$ is an argument for q.

We notice that the property of defeasibility of arguments does not appear at this level. The reason is that R4 introduces only argumentation as a logical relation between propositions. As Prakken and Vreeswijk argued, argumentation systems are able to incorporate the monotonic notions of logical consequence as a special case in their definition of what an argument is [21]. In our model, we capture the property of defeasibility by the argumentation relations (attack, defense, justification).

R5 (Universal path-quantifier). $p \in L \Rightarrow Ap \in L$

R6 (Existential path-quantifier). $p \in L \Rightarrow Ep \in L$

R7 (Until). $p, q \in L \Rightarrow pU^+q \in L$

R8 (Next moment). $p \in L \Rightarrow X^+p \in L$

R9 (Since). $p, q \in L \Rightarrow pU^-q \in L$

R10 (Previous moment). $p \in L \Rightarrow X^-p \in L$

Informally, Ap means that p holds along all paths, Ep means that there is a path along which p holds, and pU^+q (p *until* q) means that on a given path from the given moment, there is some future moment in which q will eventually hold and p holds at all moments until that future moment. X^+p holds at the current moment, if p holds at the next moment. The intuitive interpretation of pU^-q (p *since* q) is that on a given path from the given moment, there is some past moment in which q eventually held and p holds at all moments since that past moment. X^-p holds at the current moment, if p held at the previous moment.

Actions

R11 (Action performance). $\alpha \in \Phi_{at} \Rightarrow Happens(\alpha) \in L$

R12 (Sequential composition). $\alpha \in \Phi_{at}, \alpha' \in \Phi_a \Rightarrow Happens(\alpha; \alpha') \in L$

R13 (Non-deterministic choice). $\alpha, \alpha' \in \Phi_a \Rightarrow Happens(\alpha|\alpha') \in L$

R14 (Test). $p \in L \Rightarrow Happens(p?) \in L$

$Happens(\alpha)$ is an operator from dynamic logic. It allows us to represent the actions that agents perform and the effects of these actions. It expresses the fact that the action symbol α happens. We also introduce constructors for action expression which are similar to the constructors used in dynamic logic. $Happens(\alpha; \alpha')$ allows us to combine two action symbols. It means that α is followed by α'. $Happens(\alpha|\alpha')$ means that α or α' happens. $Happens(p?)$ allows us to build action expressions that depend on the truth or falsity of p. This constructor is interesting to express the fact that by way of performing actions, agents bring about facts in the world [11]. This fact can be expressed as follows: $Happens(\alpha; p?)$. This formula says that after α is performed, p becomes true.

Creation of Social Commitments

In the rest of this paper we assume that $\{Ag_1, Ag_2\} \subseteq A$ and $t \in TP$

R15 (CrPC). $p \in L \Rightarrow Create(Ag_1, PC(Ag_1, Ag_2, t, p)) \in L$
R16 (CrAC). $\alpha \in \Phi_a \ \& \ p \in L \Rightarrow Create(Ag_1, AC(Ag_1, Ag_2, t, (\alpha, p))) \in L$
R17 (CrCCP). $p, p' \in L \Rightarrow Create(Ag_1, CCP(Ag_1, Ag_2, t, (p, p'))) \in L$
R18 (CrCCA). $\alpha \in \Phi_a \ \& \ p, p' \in L \Rightarrow$
$$Create(Ag_1, CCA(Ag_1, Ag_2, t, (p, (\alpha, p')))) \in L$$

$CrPC$ formula says that Ag_1 commits towards Ag_2 at the moment t that p is true. $CrAC$ formula says that Ag_1 commits towards Ag_2 to do α, and by doing α, p becomes true. $CrCCP$ formula says that if p is true, Ag_1 commits towards Ag_2 that p' is true. $CrCCA$ formula says that if p is true, Ag_1 commits towards Ag_2 to do α, and by doing α, p' becomes true.

Commitment attempts. In order to formally introduce the notion of commitment attempt (syntax and semantics) we introduce the following definition.

Definition 4 (some predicate). *Let x be a variable term and $c_1, \ldots, c_n$ be constant terms. A constant term can be a number, a name, etc.*
$some(x, \{c_1, , c_n\}, p(x)) =_{def} p(c_1) \vee \ldots \vee p(c_n)$

Example 5. Let PRC be a predicate indicating the price of a given car, for example $Mazda3$, and let x be a variable representing this price. Then,
$some(x, \{20K\$, 25K\$, 30K\$\}, PRC(Mazda3, x)) =_{def}$
$$PRC(Mazda3, 20K\$) \vee PRC(Mazda3, 25K\$) \vee PRC(Mazda3, 30K\$)$$

In this example, the predicate *some* indicates that the price of a $Mazda3$ is in the set $\{20K\$, 25K\$, 30K\$\}$.

We can define the syntax of propositional commitment attempts, action commitment attempts, conditional commitment attempts about propositions and conditional commitment attempts about actions as follows.

R19 (CrPCT). $p \in L \Rightarrow$
$$Create(Ag_1, PCT(Ag_1, Ag_2, t, some(x, \{c_1, \ldots, c_n\}, p(x)))) \in L$$
R20 (CrACT). $\alpha \in \Phi_a \ \& \ p \in L \Rightarrow Create(Ag_1, ACT(Ag_1, Ag_2, t, (\alpha, p))) \in L$

R21 (CrCCTP). $p, p' \in L \Rightarrow$
$$Create(Ag_1, CCTP(Ag_1, Ag_2, t, (p, some(x, \{c_1, \ldots, c_n\}, p'(x))))) \in L$$

R22 (CrCCTA). $\alpha \in \Phi_a \& p, p' \in L$
$$\Rightarrow Create(Ag_1, CCTA(Ag_1, Ag_2, t, (p, (\alpha, p')))) \in L$$

$CrPCT$ formula says that Ag_1 asks Ag_2 at the moment t to commit about $some(x, \{c_1, , c_n\}, p(x))$. $CrACT$ formula says that Ag_1 asks Ag_2 to commit to perform α, which makes p true. $CrCCTP$ and $CrCCTA$ formulae are conditional. Their meanings are intuitive.

Agent's Desire about a Commitment from the Addressee
R23 (Want PC). $p \in L \Rightarrow Want_P(Ag_1, PC(Ag_2, Ag_1, t, p)) \in L$

This formula means that Ag_1 wants that Ag_2 commits that p is true. The $Want_P$ modality will be used to define the semantics of open questions. In the same way we can define the $Want_P$ modality for the other commitment types.

Action Occurrences applied to Commitments
We use the abbreviation $SC(Ag_1, Ag_2, t, \varphi)$ to indicate a SC. The syntactical form of the commitment content φ depends of the commitment type. For example, for a PC, φ has the syntactical form of p, and for an AC, φ has the syntactical form of (α, p), etc.

R24 (Withdrawal). $\varphi \in L \Rightarrow Withdraw(Ag_1, SC(Ag_1, Ag_2, t, \varphi)) \in L$
R25 (Satisfaction). $\varphi \in L \Rightarrow Satisfy(Ag_1, SC(Ag_1, Ag_2, t, \varphi)) \in L$
R26 (Violation). $\varphi \in L \Rightarrow Violate(Ag_1, SC(Ag_1, Ag_2, t, \varphi)) \in L$
R27 (Non-persistence). $\varphi \in L \Rightarrow NPersist(SC(Ag_1, Ag_2, t, \varphi)) \in L$
R28 (Active). $\varphi \in L \Rightarrow Active(SC(Ag_1, Ag_2, t, \varphi)) \in L$

The notion of *non-persistence* is used to define the semantics of the withdrawal action. The commitment becomes not persistent after withdrawal. The notion of *active commitment* is defined in terms of the withdrawal. This notion is used to define the semantics of acceptation, refusal, and challenge. For example, a commitment cannot be accepted if it is not active.

Action Occurrences applied to Commitment Contents
R29 (Acceptation). $\varphi \in L \Rightarrow Accept-cont(Ag_2, SC(Ag_1, Ag_2, t, \varphi)) \in L$
R30 (Refusal). $\varphi \in L \Rightarrow Refuse-cont(Ag_2, SC(Ag_1, Ag_2, t, \varphi)) \in L$
R31 (Challenge). $\varphi \in L \Rightarrow Chal-cont(Ag_2, SC(Ag_1, Ag_2, t, \varphi)) \in L$

Argumentation Relations
R32 (Attack). $p, p' \in L \Rightarrow Attack-cont(Ag_2, PC(Ag_1, Ag_2, t, p), p') \in L$
R33 (Defense). $p, p' \in L \Rightarrow Defend-cont(Ag_1, PC(Ag_1, Ag_2, t, p), p') \in L$
R34 (Justification). $p, p' \in L \Rightarrow Justify-cont(Ag_1, PC(Ag_1, Ag_2, t, p), p') \in L$

Attack formula says that Ag_2 attacks the Ag_1's commitment by using the content p'. *Defense* and *justification* formulae are defined by the same way.

Agent's Desire about the Justification of a Commitment Content from the Addressee
R35 (Want Justify). $p \in L \Rightarrow$
$$Want_J(Ag_1, Justify - cont(Ag_2, PC(Ag_2, Ag_1, t, p))) \in L$$

This formula means that Ag_1 wants that Ag_2 justifies its commit content. This formula will be used to define the semantics of the challenge action.

3.2   Semantics

In this section, we define the formal model in which we evaluate the well-formed formulae of our framework. Thereafter, we give the semantics of the different elements that we specified syntactically in the previous section.

The Formal Model
Let S be a set of states and $R \subseteq S \times S$ be a transition relation indicating branching time. A path Pa is an infinite sequence of states $\langle s_0, s_1, \ldots \rangle$ where: $\forall i \in \mathbb{N}, (s_i, s_{i+1}) \in R$ and $T(s_{i+1}) = T(s_i) + 1$. The function T gives us for each state s_i the corresponding moment t (this function will be specified later). We use the notation $s_i[Pa$ to indicate that the state s_i belongs to the path Pa (i.e. s_i appears in the sequence $\langle s_0, s_1, \ldots \rangle$ that describes the path Pa). We denote the set of all paths by σ. The set of all paths traversing the state s_i are denoted by σ^{s_i}. We suppose that all paths start from s_0 $(T(s_0) = 0)$. In our vision of branching future, we can have several states at the same moment. Along a given path (for example the real path) there is one and only one state at one moment. Indeed, in our framework, s_i does not indicate (necessarily) the state at moment i.

The formal model for L is defined as follows: $M = \langle S, R, A, TP, Np, Fap, T, Gap, Rsc, Rw \rangle$ where: S is a nonempty set of states; $R \subseteq S \times S$ is the transition relation; A is a nonempty set of agents; TP is a nonempty set of time points; $Np : S \rightarrow 2^{\Phi_p}$ is a function relating each state $s \in S$ to the set of the atomic propositions that are true in this state; $Fap : S \times \Phi_{at} \rightarrow 2^S$ is a function that gives us the state transitions caused by the achievement of an action; $T : S \rightarrow TP$ is a function associating to any state s_i the corresponding time; $Gap : A \times S \rightarrow 2^{\Phi_a}$ is a function that gives us for each agent the set of performed actions in a given state; $Rsc : A \times A \times S \rightarrow \wp(\sigma)$ is a function producing the accessibility modal relations for SCs ($\wp(\sigma)$ is the powerset of paths); $Rw : A \times A \times S \rightarrow \wp(\sigma)$ is a function producing the accessibility modal relations for agent' desires about the commitments of the addressee.

The function Fap allows us to indicate the accessible states from a given state by transitions labeled with actions. This represents the Chellas' view [11]: to each moment m there corresponds the set of alternative moments which are compatible with all the actions that an agent performs at moment m. We notice that $s_j \in Fap(s_i, \alpha)$ does not necessarily imply that $(s_i, s_j) \in R$. The function Rsc associates to a state s_i the set of paths along which an agent commits towards another agent. These paths are conceived as merely "possible", and as paths where the contents of commitments made in a given state should be true. For example, if we have: $Pa \in Rsc(Ag_1, Ag_2, s_i)$, then this means that the commitments that are made in the state s_i by Ag_1 towards Ag_2 should be satisfied along the path Pa. The function Rw gives us the paths along which an agent wants that the addressee commits or justifies its commitment. These paths represent the agents' desires about the addressees' commitments. This accessibility modal relation will be used to define the semantics of the commitment attempts and the challenge of a commitment attempt. The logic of absolute and conditional commitments (using Rsc) is a KD4 modal logic and the logic of commitment attempts (using Rw) is a KD modal logic (see [5] for more details).

As in CTL*, we have in our model path formulae and state formulae. The notation $M, s_i \models \Psi$ indicates that the formula Ψ is evaluated in the state s_i of the model M. The notation $M, Pa, s_i \models \Psi$ indicates that the formula Ψ is evaluated at the state s_i along the path Pa where $s_i [Pa$ (we recall here that $s_i [Pa$ means that the state s_i belongs to the path Pa). We can now define the semantics of the elements of L in the model M. For space limit reasons, we only define the semantics of formulae that are not in CTL*. In addition, in the examples of this section, we suppose that the model M is given. Thus, we only illustrate the path along which a formula is satisfied.

Arguments

$M, s_i \models p \therefore q$ iff $M, s_i \models p$ & $(\forall M' \in \mathcal{M}$ & $\forall s_j \in S_{M'}$ $M', s_j \models p \Rightarrow M', s_j \models q)$
where $\mathcal{M}$ is the set of models, and $S_{M'}$ is the set of states of the model M'.

We add the first clause to capture the following aspect: when an agent presents an argument p for q for this agent p is true and if p is true then q is true.

Actions

$M, Pa, s_i \models Happens(\alpha)$ iff $\exists s_j : s_j [Pa$ & $s_j \in Fap(s_i, \alpha)$
$M, Pa, s_i \models Happens(\alpha; \alpha')$ iff
$\qquad \exists s_j : s_j [Pa$ & $s_j \in Fap(s_i, \alpha)$ & $M, Pa, s_j \models Happens(\alpha')$
$M, Pa, s_i \models Happens(\alpha | \alpha')$ iff $M, Pa, s_i \models Happens(\alpha) \vee Happens(\alpha')$
$M, Pa, s_i \models Happens(p?)$ iff $M, Pa, s_i \models p$

$Happens(\alpha)$ is satisfied in the model M iff there is an accessible state s_j from the current state s_i using the function Fap. Thus, this formula is satisfied iff there is a labeled transition with α between s_i and a state s_j. To express the fact that a formula becomes true only after the performance of an action, we introduce the following abbreviation: $Happens'(\alpha; p?) =_{def} \neg p \wedge Happens(\alpha; p?)$

Example 6. The formula $Happens(\alpha)$ is satisfied along the path Pa from the state s_i as illustrated in Fig. 1

Fig. 1. $Happens(\alpha)$ along the path Pa

Creation of Social Commitments

$M, s_i \models Create(Ag_1, PC(Ag_1, Ag_2, t, p))$ *iff*
$\qquad \exists \alpha \in Gap(Ag_1, s_i) :$
$\qquad \forall Pa \; Pa \in Rsc(Ag_1, Ag_2, s_i) \Rightarrow$
$\qquad\qquad \exists s_j [Pa : T(s_j) = T(s_i) \; \& \; M, Pa, s_j \models Happens(\alpha; p?) \; \& \; t = T(s_i)$

We notice here that we evaluate the formula $Happens(\alpha; p?)$ along an accessible path Pa at a state s_j that can be different from the current state s_i. This allows us to model agents' uncertainty about this current state. This means that we do not assume that agents know the current state. However, we assume that these agents know which time is associated to each state. The semantics of propositional commitments is defined in terms of accessible paths. The commitment is satisfied in a model at a state s_i iff there is an action α performed by Ag_1 and this performance makes true the commitment content along all accessible paths and if the commitment moment is equal to the time associated to the current state. This semantics highlights the fact that committing is an action in itself. Indeed, the action α corresponds to the agent's utterance which creates the commitment.

Example 7. The formula $Create(Ag_1, PC(Ag_1, Ag_2, t, p))$ is satisfied at the state s_i as illustrated in Fig. 2

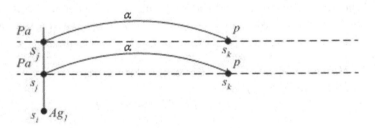

Fig. 2. $Create(Ag_1, PC(Ag_1, Ag_2, t, p))$ at the state s_i

$M, s_i \models Create(Ag_1, AC(Ag_1, Ag_2, t, (\alpha, p)))$ *iff*
$\qquad M, s_i \models Create(Ag_1, PC(Ag_1, Ag_2, t, F^+ Happens'(\alpha; p?))) \; \&$
$\qquad \forall Pa \; Pa \in Rsc(Ag_1, Ag_2, s_i) \Rightarrow \exists s_j [Pa : T(s_j) \geq T(s_i) \; \& \; \alpha \in Gap(Ag_1, s_j)$

This formula indicates that Ag_1 is committed towards Ag_2 to do α and that along all accessible paths Pa performing α makes p true. The semantics we give to the commitments requires their fulfillment. Thus, if it is created, a commitment must be held. This satisfaction-based semantics reflects the idea of "*prior*

possible choices of agents" that Belnap and Perloff used in their logic of agency
[3]. In this logic, agents make choices in time. In our model, these choices are
represented by the commitments created by these agents. The notion of acting or choosing at a moment m is thought of in Belnap and Perloff's logic as
constraining the course of events to lie within some particular subset of the possible histories available at that moment. This subset of the possible histories is
represented by the set of paths along which the commitment must be satisfied.
However, it is always possible to violate or withdraw such a commitment. For
this reason, these two operations are explicitly included in our framework.

$$M, s_i \models Create(Ag_1, CCP(Ag_1, Ag_2, t, (p, p'))) \ \textit{iff}$$
$$\forall Pa \in \sigma^{s_i} \ \& \ \forall s_j[Pa : T(s_j) \geq T(s_i)$$
$$(M, s_j \models p \Rightarrow M, s_j \models Create(Ag_1, PC(Ag_1, Ag_2, t, p')))$$

$$M, s_i \models Create(Ag_1, CCA(Ag_1, Ag_2, t, (p, (\alpha, p')))) \ \textit{iff}$$
$$\forall Pa \in \sigma^{s_i} \ \& \ \forall s_j[Pa : T(s_j) \geq T(s_i)$$
$$(M, s_j \models p \Rightarrow M, s_j \models Create(Ag_1, AC(Ag_1, Ag_2, t, (\alpha, p'))))$$

A conditional commitment about a proposition p' under condition p is satisfied in the model iff the debtor commits that p' is true if the condition p is true.

$$M, s_i \models Want_P(Ag_1, PC(Ag_2, Ag_1, t, p)) \ \textit{iff} \ \forall Pa \ Pa \in Rw(Ag_1, Ag_2, s_i) \Rightarrow$$
$$\exists s_j[Pa : T(s_j) = T(s_i) \ \& \ M, Pa, s_j \models Create(Ag_2, PC(Ag_2, Ag_1, t, p))$$

Ag_1's desire about a propositional commitment of Ag_2 whose content is p is
satisfied in the model iff along all accessible paths via Rw, Ag_2 commits towards
Ag_1 that p. In the same way we can define the semantics of an agent's desire
about the other commitment types.

By using this formula, we can define the semantics of propositional commitment attempts as follows:

$$M, s_i \models Create(Ag_1, PCT(Ag_1, Ag_2, t, some(x, \{c_1, \ldots, c_n\}, p(x)))) \ \textit{iff}$$
$$M, s_i \models Create(Ag_1, PC(Ag_1, Ag_2, t,$$
$$Want_P(Ag_1, PC(Ag_2, Ag_1, *, p(c_1) \vee \ldots \vee p(c_n)))))$$

The Ag_1's propositional commitment attempt towards Ag_2 is satisfied in the
model iff Ag_1 commits that it wants that Ag_2 commits at a certain moment,
which is not necessarily specified, that one of the propositions $p(c_i)$ is true. This
notion of commitment attempt captures open and yes/no questions. We recall
that the time argument is dropped from the propositional commitment formula
because the moment at which Ag_1 wants that Ag_2 commits is not specified.

Example 8. Let us consider the example of an agent Ag_1 asking an agent Ag_2
about the price of a *Mazda3*. This request is captured in our model as a commitment attempt created by Ag_1 towards Ag_2 whose content can be expressed using
the *some* predicate. If we assume that this price is in the set $\{20K\$, 25K\$, 30K\$\}$,
then we have:

$Create(Ag_1, PCT(Ag_1, Ag_2, t,$
$$some(x, \{20K\$, 25K\$, 30K\$\}, PRC(Mazda3, x)))) \equiv$$
$Create(Ag_1, PC(Ag_1, Ag_2, t, Want_P(Ag_1, PC(Ag_2, Ag_1, *,$
$$PRC(Mazda3, 20K\$) \vee PRC(Mazda3, 25K\$) \vee PRC(Mazda3, 30K\$)))))$$

According to the semantics of propositional commitment attempts, this example is interpreted as an Ag_1's propositional commitment that it wants that Ag_2 commits about the price of the $Mazda3$.

The semantics of action commitment attempts is also defined using the $Want_P$ formula as follows:

$M, s_i \models Create(Ag_1, ACT(Ag_1, Ag_2, t, (\alpha, p)))$ iff
$\quad M, s_i \models Create(Ag_1, PC(Ag_1, Ag_2, t, Want_P(Ag_1, AC(Ag_2, Ag_1, *, (\alpha, p)))))$

The Ag_1's action commitment attempt towards Ag_2 is satisfied in the model iff Ag_1 commits that it wants that Ag_2 commits at a certain moment to perform the action. In the same way we can define the semantics of conditional commitment attempts about propositions and about actions.

Example 9. Let us consider the example of an agent Ag_1 asking an agent Ag_2 to open the door. Formally:

$Create(Ag_1, ACT(Ag_1, Ag_2, t, (\alpha, Door(open)))) \equiv$
$Create(Ag_1, PC(Ag_1, Ag_2, t, Want_P(Ag_1, AC(Ag_2, Ag_1, (\alpha, Door(open))))))$

The Ag_1's request is expressed by an action commitment attempt created by Ag_1 towards Ag_2. By asking Ag_2 to open the door, Ag_1 wants that Ag_2 commits to open the door.

Action Occurrences applied to Commitments and related Notions
$M, Pa, s_i \models Withdraw(Ag_1, SC(Ag_1, Ag_2, t, \varphi))$ iff
$\quad \exists \alpha \in Gap(Ag_1, s_i) : M, Pa, s_i \models Happens(\alpha; NPersist(SC(Ag_1, Ag_2, t, \varphi))?)$
$\quad \& [\exists Pa' \in \sigma \& \exists s_j [Pa' : T(s_j) \leq T(s_i) \& Pa' \in Rsc(Ag_1, Ag_2, s_j)$
$\quad\quad \& M, Pa', s_j \models Create(Ag_1, SC(Ag_1, Ag_2, t, \varphi)) \& Pa_{s_j, s_i} = Pa'_{s_j, s_i}$
$\quad\quad \& M, Pa'_{s_j, s_i}, s_j \models \neg\varphi]$

$Pa_{s_j, s_i} = Pa'_{s_j, s_i}$ means that the paths Pa and Pa' are similar on the fragment $s_j, s_{j+1}, \ldots, s_i$. $M, Pa'_{s_j, s_i}, s_j \models \neg\varphi$ means that the content φ is not satisfied on the path Pa' on the fragment $s_j, \ldots, s_i$. The semantics of $NPersist$ formula is defined as follows.

$M, Pa, s_i \models NPersist(SC(Ag_1, Ag_2, t, \varphi))$ iff $\exists s_j : T(s_j) \leq T(s_i)$
$\quad \& M, s_j \models Create(Ag_1, SC(Ag_1, Ag_2, t, \varphi) \& Pa \notin Rsc(Ag_1, Ag_2, s_j)$

The semantics of $Withdraw$ formula indicates that an agent Ag_1 withdraws its commitment about φ at a state s_i along a path Pa iff the following conditions are satisfied: (1) Ag_1 has already created this commitment in the past along a satisfaction path Pa' which is similar to the path Pa since the creation moment of the commitment until the current state s_i; (2) The commitment content is not yet true at the withdrawal moment; (3) Ag_1 performs an action α so that this commitment does not persist at the current moment. A commitment does not persist along a path Pa iff this path does not correspond to some satisfaction paths. The idea of a commitment withdrawal is that the agent performs an action α which changes the path from a satisfaction path Pa' to a path Pa along which the commitment does not persist, and at the withdrawal moment, the commitment content is not yet true. We notice that along the path Pa the commitment content can be true or false. This corresponds to the intuitive idea that the content of a withdrawn commitment may be accidentally true.

Example 10. The formula $Withdraw(Ag_1, SC(Ag_1, Ag_2, t, \varphi))$ is satisfied at the state s_i along the path Pa as illustrated in Fig. 3

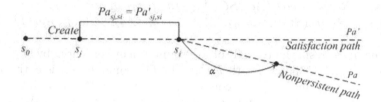

Fig. 3. $Withdraw(Ag_1, SC(Ag_1, Ag_2, t, \varphi))$ at the state s_i along the path Pa

$$M, Pa, s_i \models Active(SC(Ag_1, Ag_2, t, \varphi)) \text{ iff}$$
$$M, Pa, s_i \models \neg Withdraw(Ag_1, SC(Ag_1, Ag_2, t, \varphi))$$
$$U^- Create(Ag_1, SC(Ag_1, Ag_2, t, \varphi))$$

A commitment is active iff this commitment was already created, and until the current moment, the commitment was not withdrawn. Therefore, once the commitment is withdrawn, it becomes inactive.

Example 11. The formula $Active(SC(Ag_1, Ag_2, t, \varphi))$ is satisfied at the state s_i along the path Pa as illustrated in Fig. 4

$$\neg\, Withdraw(Ag_1, SC(Ag_1, Ag_2, t, \varphi))$$
Pa Create
s_0 s_j s_i

Fig. 4. $Active(SC(Ag_1, Ag_2, t, \varphi))$ at the state s_i along the path Pa

$$M, Pa, s_i \models Satisfy(Ag_1, PC(Ag_1, Ag_2, t, p)) \text{ iff}$$
$$M, Pa, si \models Active(PC(Ag_1, Ag_2, t, p)) \ \& \ \exists s_j : T(s_j) \leq T(s_i)$$
$$\& \ M, s_j \models Create(Ag_1, PC(Ag_1, Ag_2, t, p)) \ \& \ M, Pa, s_j \models p$$

$M, Pa, s_i \models Violate(Ag_1, PC(Ag_1, Ag_2, t, p))$ *iff*
$\quad M, Pa, s_i \models Active(PC(Ag_1, Ag_2, t, p))$ & $\exists s_j : T(s_j) \leq T(si)$
$\quad$ & $M, s_j \models Create(Ag_1, PC(Ag_1, Ag_2, t, p))$ & $M, Pa, s_j \models \neg p$

A propositional commitment is satisfied (resp. violated) along a path Pa at a state s_i iff it is active in this state along this path, and it was already created at a state s_j, and along this path from the state s_j the commitment content is true (resp. false). The satisfaction and violation of the other types of commitments can be defined using the satisfaction and violation of propositional commitments. This aspect is detailed in [5].

Action Occurrences applied to Commitment Contents
$M, Pa, s_i \models Accept-cont(Ag_2, SC(Ag_1, Ag_2, t, \varphi))$ *iff*
$\quad M, Pa, s_i \models Active(SC(Ag_1, Ag_2, t, \varphi)) \wedge Create(Ag_2, SC(Ag_2, Ag_1, T(s_i), \varphi))$

$M, Pa, s_i \models Refuse-cont(Ag_2, SC(Ag_1, Ag_2, t, \varphi))$ *iff*
$\quad M, Pa, s_i \models Active(SC(Ag_1, Ag_2, t, \varphi)) \wedge Create(Ag_2, SC(Ag_2, Ag_1, T(s_i), \neg\varphi))$

The acceptance (resp. the refusal) of the commitment content φ by Ag_2 is satisfied in the model M along a path Pa iff: (1) The commitment is active on this path because we cannot act on a commitment content if the commitment is not active; (2) Ag_2 creates a commitment whose content is φ (resp. $\neg\varphi$). Therefore, Ag_2 becomes committed towards the content φ (resp. $\neg\varphi$).

$M, Pa, s_i \models Chal-cont(Ag_2, SC(Ag_1, Ag_2, t, \varphi))$ *iff*
$\exists \alpha \in Gap(Ag_2, s_i) :$
$M, Pa, s_i \models Active(SC(Ag_1, Ag_2, t, \varphi))$
$\quad\quad\quad \wedge Happens(\alpha; Want_J(Ag_2, Justify-cont(Ag_1, SC(Ag_1, Ag_2, t, \varphi)))?)$

The challenge of the commitment content φ by Ag_2 is satisfied in the model M along a path Pa iff: (1) The challenged commitment is active on this path; (2) Ag_2 performs an action so that it wants that Ag_1 justifies its commitment content φ. This semantics highlights the fact that the challenge of a commitment content is an action in itself. The action α corresponds to the production of the utterance that challenges the commitment content. The semantics of the $Want_J$ formula is given in the next subsection.

Argumentation Relations
$M, Pa, s_i \models Justify-cont(Ag_1, PC(Ag_1, Ag_2, t, p), p')$ *iff*
$\quad M, Pa, s_i \models Active(PC(Ag_1, Ag_2, t, p))$
$\quad\quad\quad \wedge Create(Ag_1, PC(Ag_1, Ag_2, T(s_i), p' \therefore p))$

The justification of the commitment content p by Ag_1 using p' is satisfied in the model M on a path Pa iff: (1) This commitment is active on this path; (2) This agent creates on this path a commitment whose content is p' that supports the conclusion p. The fact that the operator $\therefore$ is included in the commitment indicates that Ag_1 is committed that p' is true and then p is true.

$$M, Pa, s_i \models Attack-cont(Ag_2, PC(Ag_1, Ag_2, t, p), p') \text{ iff}$$
$$M, Pa, s_i \models Active(PC(Ag_1, Ag_2, t, p))$$
$$\wedge Justify-cont(Ag_2, PC(Ag_2, Ag_1, T(s_i), \neg p), p')$$

The attack of the commitment content p by Ag_2 is satisfied in the model M along a path Pa iff: (1) This commitment is active on this path; (2) This agent justifies along this path its commitment whose content is $\neg p$.

$$M, Pa, s_i \models Defend-cont(Ag_1, PC(Ag_1, Ag_2, t, p), p') \text{ iff}$$
$$\exists p'' \in L : M, Pa, s_i \models Active(PC(Ag_1, Ag_2, t, p))$$
$$\wedge X^- F^- Attack-cont(Ag_2, PC(Ag_1, Ag_2, t, p), p''))$$
$$\wedge Attack-cont(Ag_1, PC(Ag_2, Ag_1, *, p''), p'))$$

The defense of the commitment content p by Ag_1 is satisfied in the model M along a path Pa iff: (1) This commitment is active on this path; (2) Ag_1 attacks the attacker of the content of its commitment.

$$M, s_i \models Want_J(Ag_1, Justify-cont(Ag_2, PC(Ag_2, Ag_1, t, p))) \text{ iff}$$
$$\exists p' \in L : \forall Pa \ Pa \in Rw(Ag_1, Ag_2, s_i) \Rightarrow \exists s_j [Pa :$$
$$T(s_j) = T(s_i) \ \& \ M, Pa, s_j \models F^+ Justify-cont(Ag_2, PC(Ag_1, Ag_1, t, p), p')$$

This formula means that Ag_1 wants that Ag_2 justifies its commitment content. The formula is satisfied in the model iff along all accessible paths via Rw, Ag_2 justifies in the future this commitment.

4   Discussion and Related Work

Our semantics is useful when designing MAS because unlike mental semantics, this semantics can be verified. The reason is that it is expressed in terms of public commitments and arguments and not in terms of private mental states. The compliance of agents with this semantics can be checked by verifying whether the agents behave in accordance with their commitments and arguments. Our semantic framework is a prescriptive theory serving to establish rules regulating the behavior of agents when communicating. It can be used for specifying agent communication protocols implementing these rules. Equipping these protocols by an operational semantics like the one proposed by [10] will be of a great importance as a framework for designing and implementing normative agent communication.

A number of semantics of agent communication languages have been proposed in the literature. Singh proposes a SC-based semantics in order to stress the importance of conventions and the public aspects of agent interactions [23]. Singh uses CTL to propose a formal language and a formal model in which the notion of commitment is described by using an accessibility relation. Verdic-chio and Colombetti propose a logical model of commitments using CTL* [26]. They introduce a number of predicates in order to represent events and actions. Mallya et al. define some constraints in order to capture some operations on commitments [20]. Our logical model belongs to this class of commitment-based semantics, but it differs from these proposals in the following respects:

a) In our approach the commitment semantics is defined as an accessibility relation that takes into account the satisfaction of the commitment. The com-mitment semantics is defined in terms of the paths along which the commitment must be satisfied. This way is more intuitive than the semantics defined by Singh.

b) We differentiate commitments as static structures evaluated in states from the operations applied to commitments as dynamic structures evaluated on paths. This enables us to describe more naturally the evolution of agent communica-tion as a system of states/transitions. Our logical model allows us to describe the dynamics of agent interactions in terms of the actions that agents apply to commitments, commitment contents and arguments.

c) In our model, the strength of commitments as a basic principle of agent communication does not result only from the fact that they are observable, but also from the fact that they are supported by arguments. The commit-ment notion we formalize is not only a public notion but also a deontic one. The deontic aspect is captured by the fact that commitments are thought of as obligations. The agent is obliged to respect its commitments (i.e to sat-isfy them), to behave in accordance with these commitments and to justify them. The idea is to impose this constraint in the model we are interested in.

d) In our semantics, we capture not only propositional commitments, but the various other types of commitments. This enables us to have a greater ex-pressivity and to capture many different types of speech acts. In addition, all the elements constituting our commitment and argument approach are seman-tically expressed in a clear and unambiguous way using the same logical framework.

As an extension of this work, we plan to specify protocols using the com-mitment and argument semantics and verify the conformance of agents with these protocols using "a priori conformance test" as proposed by Baldoni and his colleagues in [2]. Investigating the computational complexity of our theory including logic-based protocol specification and conformance is another key issue for future work.

Acknowledgements

The first author is supported in part by the Faculty of Engineering & Computer Science at Concordia University. This work is also supported by NSERC and FQRSC (Canada). We would also like to thank the three anonymous reviewers for their interesting comments and suggestions.

References

1. Amgoud, L., Maudet, N., Parsons, S.: An argumentation-based semantics for agent communication languages. 15th European Conf. on AI (2002) 38–42
2. Baldoni, M., Baroglio, C., Martelli, A., Patti, V.: Verification of protocol conformance and agent interoperability. F. Toni, P. Torroni (Eds.), Computational Logic in Multi-Agent Systems. Springer LNAI 3900 (2006) 265–283
3. Belnap, N., Perloff, M.: The way of the agent. Studia Logica 51 (1992) 463–484
4. Belnap, N.: Backwards and towards in the modal logic of Agency. Philosophy and Phenomenological Research 51 (1991) 777–807
5. Bentahar, J.: A pragmatic and semantic unified framework for agent communication. Ph.D. Thesis, Laval University, Canada May (2005)
6. Bentahar, J., Moulin, B., Chaib-draa, B.: Commitment and argument network: a new formalism for agent communication. F. Dignum (Ed.), Advances in Agent Communication. Springer LNAI 2922 (2004) 146–165
7. Bentahar, J., Moulin, B., Meyer, J-J.Ch., Chaib-draa, B.: A computational model for conversation policies for agent communication. J. Leite, P. Torroni (Eds.), Computational Logic in Multi-Agent Systems. Springer LNCS 3487 (2004) 178-195
8. Bentahar, J., Moulin, B., Meyer, J-J.Ch., Chaib-draa, B.: A logical model for commitment and argument network for agent communication. Proc. of the Int. Joint Conf. on AAMAS (2004) 792–799
9. Bentahar, J., Moulin, B., Meyer, J-J.Ch., Chaib-draa, B.: A modal semantics for an argumentation-based pragmatics for agent communication. I. Rahwan, P. Moraitis, C. Reed (Eds.), Argumentation in Multi-Agent Systems. Springer LNAI 3366 (2005) 44–63
10. Moreira, Á.F., Vieira, R., Bordini, R.H.: Extending the operational semantics of a BDI agent-oriented programming language for introducing speech-act based communication. J. Leite, A. Omicini, L. Sterling, P. Torroni (Eds.), Declarative Agent Languages and Technologies. Springer LNAI 2990 (2004) 135-154
11. Chellas, B.F.: Time and modality in the logic of agency. Studia Logica, 51 (1992) 485–518
12. Costantini, S., Tocchio, A.: About declarative semantics of logic-based agent languages. M. Baldoni, U. Endriss, A. Omicini, P. Torroni (Eds.), Declarative Agent Langiages and Technologies III. Springer LNAI 3904 (2006) 106–123
13. Dung, P.M.: On the acceptability of arguments and its fundamental role in non-monotonic reasoning, logic programming and n-person games. Artificial Intelligence 77 (1995) 321–357
14. Elvang-Goransson, M., Fox, J., Krause, P.: Dialectic reasoning with inconsistent information. 9th Conf. on Uncertainty in Artificial Intelligence (1993) 114–121
15. Emerson, E.A., Halpern, J.Y.: Sometimes and not never, revisited: on branching versus linear time temporal logic. Journal ACM 33(1) (1986) 151–178
16. Endriss, U., Maudet, N., Sadri, F., Toni, F.: Protocol conformance for logic-based agents. Proc. of the Int. Joint Conf. on Artificial Intelligence (2003) 679–684
17. Guerin, F., Pitt, J.: Denotational semantics for agent communication languages. Proc. of 5th International Conf. on Autonomous Agents (2001) 497–504
18. Harel, D.: Dynamic logic: axiomatics and expressive power. Ph.D. Thesis, (1979)
19. Kakas, A.C., Miller, R., Toni, F.: An argumentation framework for reasoning about actions and change. Proc. of LPNMR 99, LNCS 1730 (1999) 78–91
20. Mallya, A., Yolum, P., Singh, M.P.: Resolving commitments among autonomous agents. F. Dignum (Ed.), Advances in Agent Communication. Springer LNAI 2922 (2004) 166–182

21. Prakken, H., Vreeswijk, G.: Logics for defeasible argumentation. Handbook of Philosophical Logic (Second Edition) (2000)
22. Sadri, F., Toni, F., Torroni, P.: Dialogues for negotiation: agent varieties and dialogue sequences. 8th Int. Workshop on ATAL. Springer LNCS 2333 (2001) 405–421
23. Singh, M.P.: A social semantics for agent communication language. F. Dignum, M. Greaves (Eds.), Issues in Agent Communication. Springer LNCS 1916 (2000) 31–45
24. Toni, F.: Multi-agent systems in computational logic: challenges and outcomes of the SOCS project. F. Toni, P. Torroni (Eds.), Computational Logic in Multi-Agent Systems. Springer LNAI 3900 (2006) 420-426
25. Torroni, P.: Computational logic in multi-agent systems: recent advances and future directions. J. Dix, J. Leite, K. Satoh (Eds.). Annals of Mathematics and Artificial Intelligence 42(1-3) Kluwer (2004) 293–305
26. Verdicchio, M., Colombetti, M.: A logical model of social commitment for agent communication. Proc. of the Int. Joint Conf. on AAMAS (2003) 528–535
27. Wooldridge, M.: Semantic issues in the verification of agent communication languages. Journal of AAMAS 3(1) Springer (2000) 9–31

Contextual Reasoning in Agent Systems

Stijn De Saeger[1] and Atsushi Shimojima[2]

[1] School of Knowledge Science, Japan Advanced Institute of Science and Technology
stijn@jaist.ac.jp
[2] Faculty of Culture and Information Science, Doshisha University
ashimoji@mail.doshisha.ac.jp

Abstract. This paper makes a case for the importance of a formal theory of context and contextual reasoning in agent systems, and proposes a channel theoretic account for modeling the intricacies of agent reasoning in context. Using an example of reasoning about perspectives we shown that this model fulfills the formal requirements for a theory of context, and offers a nice explanatory account of contextual reasoning in terms of information flow.

1 Context and Agents

Due to the essentially distributed nature of knowledge representation and reasoning in agent systems, the problem of context dependence is hardly a peripheral issue – it concerns the very heart of the enterprise. When tasks and responsibilities of reasoning agents in such distributed systems are not strictly separated and non-overlapping but bear upon a common target or application domain, the complexities of managing "context" as the structured variations in agents' perception, representation and reasoning demand a formal solution.

1.1 The Representation of Context

Seminal work on the problem of generality in artificial intelligence by McCarthy and his group in the 1980's ([16]) kicked off a new research program on the formalization of context in its various guises. Together with his student Guha ([14]) they set the stage for a first formalization, which Buvač and Mason built upon to construct their Propositional Logic of Context ([6]). Some of these early results found their way into Lenat's common sense knowledge base CYC. In the beginning of the 1990's Giunchiglia reformulated the problem of context in terms of *locality of reasoning*, and introduced the idea of bridging mechanisms allowing for the transfer of reasoning between specialized local contexts. The two most visible present day representatives of this tradition are Local Models Semantics ("LMS", Ghidini and Giunchiglia [9]) and MultiContext Systems ("MCS", Giunchiglia and Serafini [12]).

Much around the same time people in the philosophy and linguistics community, notably situation theory (Barwise and Perry, [2]), were dealing with some of

K. Inoue, K. Satoh, and F. Toni (Eds.): CLIMA VII, LNAI 4371, pp. 171–190, 2007.

the same issues in natural language semantics. Many of the philosophical under-pinnings of situation theory were imported later into channel theory (Barwise and Seligman [3]), a mathematical account of information flow in distributed systems, which we draw upon in this paper.

1.2   Connection with Agent Systems

In 2000, a series of papers by Benerecetti, Bouquet and Ghidini ([5,4], henceforth BBG2000) set out to address some foundational issues in the growing field. Building on earlier analyses by Giunchiglia they defined a logic of contextual reasoning to be a logic of the relationships between *partial*, *approximate*, and *perspectival* representations. More precisely: [1]

- **Partiality:** A representation is partial when it describes only a subset of a more comprehensive state of affairs.
- **Approximation:** A representation is approximate when it abstracts away some aspects of a given state of affairs.
- **Perspective:** A representation is perspectival when it encodes a spatio-temporal, logical, and cognitive point of view on a state of affairs.

Partiality is a relative notion rather than a binary yes-no property, and rep-resentations may be more or less partial with respect to the target of the repre-sentation. Typical examples are problem solving contexts, in which most infor-mation irrelevant to the problem at hand is omitted for reasons of conciseness and clarity. Knowledge representation involves (at least) two kinds of partiality: partiality of *truth* and partiality of *expression*. The former supports the intu-ition that the truth of all propositions need not (cannot?) be *decidable* in any given context; the latter says that not all propositions should be *expressible* in any context. As an example, the proposition "Saddam Hussein was involved in 9/11" has no denotation or meaning in the context of the 1990's, while it has no obvious truth value in (most contexts of) the year 2002.

The classic example for reasoning with approximate representations is Mc-Carthy's *above-theory* ([15,17,16] and more), which involves reasoning with var-ious abstractions of some block world, represented at varying degrees of approx-imation. Also, in explaining how to get to my house, I can draw a quick map that is a very approximate representation of the area where I live. This is an important rationale for the way resource-bounded agents (like humans) thrive on contextual reasoning: efficiency in the face of a problem search space that is for all practical purposes infinite. Approximation then, is about economy of representation at the *level of granularity*.

And finally, perspectivity is often just spatio-temporal context dependence, and indeed this will be the case with our working example throughout this paper. Sometimes it can be more subtle though. Think for instance of a software agent crawling internet news sites. Whether it will classify terms like *"Hamas"* as a

---

[1] Definitions taken from BBG2000 ([5]).

terrorist organization, a group of freedom fighters or a humanitarian organization depends on a certain perspective that is highly contextual.[2]

In short, a suitable logic of context must *(i)* allow for such varying representations, and *(ii)* incorporate appropriate reasoning mechanisms for operating on such representations. Contextual reasoning then is characterized in terms of operations on and structured transformations between context-dependent representations thus conceived.

The import of these issues for work on intelligent agent architectures is immediate: integrating and combining data derived from a variety of essentially distributed information sources is considered one of the principal tasks of an intelligent agent system. In this paper we present a channel-theoretic account of contextual reasoning based on the well-known "magic box" example, one of the paradigmatic examples of contextual reasoning ([20], [5] and many others) in the literature. Actually, it may well be the simplest example conceivable that generates the relevant intuitions concerning the various phenomena involved. We will make use of it here to demonstrate a model of contextual reasoning with applications for agent systems, based on key ideas from channel theory (Barwise and Seligman, [3]). There is also a proof of concept implementation of the example in Python, and source code can be obtained from the authors upon request.

1.3   The Magic Box Explained

The example concerns three views (**Side**, **Front** and **Top**) on a partitioned cube, where each partition or sector may or may not contain a ball. The context dependence we are looking to capture is in these perspectives: they represent partial views on reality that, though obviously different, must at least be compatible in some fundamental way, by virtue of referring to the same object – the box. In what follows, we will often implicitly identify views with agents and vice versa. So, we simply talk about agent **Side** when referring to some agent that views the cube from the side. Fig. 1 shows what we mean.

Looking at the magic box in terms of our model, we can represent it quite straightforwardly as a six-dimensional state space Σ_{box}, each dimension representing one partition of the cube (ordered from upper left to lower right). Concretely, for any dimension i of a state $\sigma \in \Sigma$, $\sigma_i = 1$ iff there is a ball in the partition with index i. In other words, let Σ_{box} be the set $\{0,1\}^6 = \{\langle 0,0,0,0,0,0 \rangle, \langle 0,0,0,0,0,1 \rangle, \ldots, \langle 1,1,1,1,1,1 \rangle\}$, with $|\Sigma_{box}| = 64$.

Though not necessarily very interesting in itself, Σ_{box} represents all possible states of affairs of some part of 'reality' under attention, the cube. For conciseness, we will enumerate all possible states in Σ_{box} simply as the alphabet of bitstrings of length 6, while retaining the full generality of the state space semantics. Thus for the purpose of this paper we simply write some state $\langle 1,0,1,1,0,0 \rangle$ as 101100.

The question then arises what Σ_{box} will look like through the eyes of our agents, **Top**, **Side** and **Front**. An agent's *scheme of individuation* is an

---

[2] Example is due to [13].

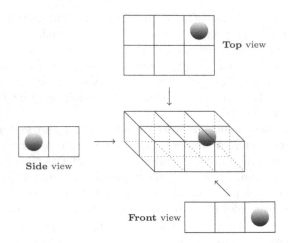

Fig. 1. The magic box

abstraction of the ability of that agent to distinguish semantically relevant patterns in its surroundings. Simply put, this boils down to the agent's capabilities of detecting meaningful patterns in a collection of states. For example, let's assume that the sectors in the magic box are numbered 1 through 6 from upper left to lower right (in the **Top** view). In that case, whether the ball is in sector 1 or 2 is a meaningful pattern for agent **Front** but not for agent **Side**, as it has no way of distinguishing the two. The opposite situation holds for sectors 1 and 4, and so on.

2   Contexts in Channel Theory

Barwise and Seligman ([3]) developed a theory with the explicit aim of analyzing how information flows in distributed settings. This, so we will argue, makes it particularly well-suited to apply to phenomena like contextual reasoning – as distributed and dynamic as any information processing task.

We will introduce the relevant formal machinery from channel theory (*classifications, infomorphisms* and *local logics*) as we go about formalizing the magic box example. This will take up the remainder of this section. In the next section we compare the end product with other logics of context – LMS and MCS – and conclude.

2.1   Agents as Classifiers

We agree with the explicit assumption in LMS/MCS that contexts do not in general share the same representation language, the case where they *do* being the exception rather than the rule. Indeed, the notion of having "a ball on the left" obviously means different things to each agent **Side**, **Front** and **Top**, and arguably some propositions ("a ball in the center") may not mean anything at all (to **Side** for example). We take this idea as our point of departure: a family of *local languages* $\{L_i\}_{i \in I}$, defined over a set of (agent) indices I. Each L_i is defined as the smallest set of sentences obtained from closing a set of atomic propositions P_i under the usual propositional connectives. Formally, define L_i for each $i \in I$ as the set of sentences ϕ such that:

$$\phi := p \in P_i \mid \phi \vee \phi' \mid \phi \wedge \phi' \mid \phi \supset \phi' \mid \neg \phi \tag{1}$$

The notation $i : \phi$ is used to express that ϕ is an L_i-formula, but we omit the label i when no confusion is likely.

Similarly, $\{M_i\}_{i \in I}$ is a class of models for I, such that for each model $m \in M_i$ and sentence $\phi \in L_i$, m satisfies either ϕ or $\neg \phi$ (written $m \models \phi \vee \neg \phi$). This is just the standard notion of satisfaction from propositional logic.

Definition 1 (Satisfaction). *Given an index $i \in I$, we say a model $m \in M_i$ satisfies a sentence $\phi \in L_i$, written $m \models \phi$ iff:*

$$
\begin{array}{ll}
m \models p & \text{iff } p \in P_i \text{ and } m(p) = 1 \\
m \models \neg \phi & \text{iff not } m \models \phi \text{ (written } m \not\models \phi) \\
m \models \phi \vee \psi & \text{iff } m \models \phi \text{ or } m \models \psi \\
m \models \phi \wedge \psi & \text{iff } m \models \phi \text{ and } m \models \psi \\
m \models \phi \supset \psi & \text{iff } m \not\models \phi \text{ or } m \models \psi
\end{array}
$$

In order to make the strong notion of *locality* that is implicit in this setting more formal, we resort to the channel-theoretic notion of a *classification*. Classifications (or their counterparts in formal concept analysis *formal contexts*, [8]) are a mathematical development of the notion of a binary incidence relation between two data sets.

Definition 2 (Classification). *A classification $\mathcal{C}$ is a triple $(\mathcal{O}, \mathcal{A}, \mathcal{I})$ where $\mathcal{O}$ and $\mathcal{A}$ are sets (of objects and attributes), and $\mathcal{I} \subseteq \mathcal{O} \times \mathcal{A}$ represents a relation classifying objects $o \in \mathcal{O}$ as having attributes $a \in \mathcal{A}$.*

Thinking of $\mathcal{O}$ as a set of states (situations, models, worlds, ...) and $\mathcal{A}$ a set of propositions in some suitable formal language, a classification is just a formal representation of some agent's *scheme of individuation*, if you will. This is essentially what the metaphor of "agents as classifiers" amounts to: that cognitive behaviour presupposes a system of classification that characterizes those states of affairs an agent can distinguish in terms of the (formal) language available to the agent.

In terms of the analysis proposed in BBG2000, the classification relation $\mathcal{I}$ of a classification is just *formalized perspective*, a contingent way of classifying world entities or situations. The object set of these structures, $\mathcal{O}$, encodes *partiality of truth*, while the set of attributes $\mathcal{A}$ encodes *partiality of expression*, the sum total of things that can be talked about by agents sharing this particular classification scheme.

Thus we can represent an agent perspective by a classification $(M_i, L_i, \models_i)_{i \in I}$. In terms of the magic box example, let I be an set of agent labels $\{\text{S}, \text{F}, \text{T}\}$, and P_i be the set of atomic propositions of each L_i, for $i \in I$. Specifically:

- $P_\text{S} = \{\texttt{left}, \texttt{right}\}$
- $P_\text{F} = \{\texttt{left}, \texttt{center}, \texttt{right}\}$
- $P_\text{T} = \{\texttt{one}, \texttt{two}, \texttt{three}, \texttt{four}, \texttt{five}, \texttt{six}\}$

Models for the magic box are the state spaces we introduced higher: $\Sigma_\text{S} = \{0,1\}^2$, $\Sigma_\text{F} = \{0,1\}^3$ and $\Sigma_\text{T} = \{0,1\}^6$. Finally, replacing the classification relation $\mathcal{I}$ by the satisfaction definition above we can express that $\langle 01, \neg\texttt{left}\rangle \in \models_\text{S}$, in other words that $01 \models_\text{S} \neg\texttt{left}$ holds in perspective **Side**. From now on, we will refer to **Side** as the classification $(\Sigma_\text{S}, L_\text{S}, \models_\text{S})$, **Front** as $(\Sigma_\text{F}, L_\text{F}, \models_\text{F})$, and so on. Also, for a set of states $S \subseteq \Sigma_i$, the *intent* of S (written $int(S)$) is the set $\{\phi \mid \phi \in L_i \text{ and for all } \sigma \in S : \sigma \models_i \phi\}$. Dually, the *extent* of a set of L_i-sentences Φ is written $ext(\Phi)$ and denotes the set $\{\sigma \mid \sigma \in \Sigma_i \text{ such that for all } \phi \in \Phi : \sigma \models \phi\}$.

Contexts as Local Logics. It is customary to take the notion of a perspective introduced above and to identify contexts with perspectives. Surely, a context encodes a certain perspective, and in turn a perspective can surely be thought of as a sort of context. Arguably though, the relation between the two is a bit more subtle. A single agent or perspective can be host to many different contexts still. For instance, in the magic box we can assume the view of agent **Top**, who has a full unrestricted two-dimensional view of the box – its states decide all six sectors of the box (at this level of approximation). Then clearly we want to be able to talk about different contexts "inside" the perspective of **Top**, for example the context of **Side**'s observations vs. the context of **Front**'s observations. Intuitively **Top** should have access to the information in either one of them, and be able to account for how this information reflects on what is inferrable in the other context. We like to argue that the gain in simplicity in any formalization that equates agents with contexts is lost when faced with the problem of explaining how and why reasoning in one context transfers to another in the way that it does. In such a scenario one is forced to postulate seemingly ad-hoc inference rules between contexts (like MCS' *bridge rules*) to explain how and why a valid piece of reasoning in this context transfers to that context the way it does.

Having suggested that contexts are not perspectives, we must specify what contexts are then. The intuition of contexts as a "partial theory of the world" provides a good enough starting point. To make it formal, we need to introduce the channel theoretic notions of sequents, theories and finally local logics. [3]

Definition 3 (Sequents, Theory). *Given a set S, a sequent of S is a pair $\langle \Gamma, \Delta \rangle$ of subsets of S. A theory T is a pair $\langle S, \vdash \rangle$ consisting of a set S and a set $\vdash$ of sequents on S.*

---

[3] See [3] for a more detailed analysis of these concepts.

Usually notation is simplified to "$p, q \vdash r$" instead of "$\langle \{p,q\}, \{r\} \rangle \in \vdash$", so as to preserve the intuitive link with a Gentzen style sequent calculus. In an attempt to capture the semantics of a consequence relation that remains neutral between model-theoretic and proof-theoretic consequence, Barwise and Seligman are concerned with a special class of theories called *regular* theories. A theory is regular if it satisfies the following structural rules:

Identity: $\{\alpha\} \vdash \{\alpha\}$		for $\alpha \in S$
Weakening: if $\Gamma \vdash \Delta$ then $\Gamma, \Gamma' \vdash \Delta, \Delta'$		for $\Gamma, \Gamma', \Delta, \Delta' \subseteq S$
Global Cut: if $\Gamma, \Sigma_0 \vdash \Delta, \Sigma_1$ for each partition		
$\langle \Sigma_0, \Sigma_1 \rangle$ of Σ, then $\Gamma \vdash \Delta$		for $\Gamma, \Delta, \Sigma \subseteq S$

These regularity conditions express basic structural requirements any theory T needs to satisfy to be internally consistent. The *Identity* requirement should be self-evident. *Weakening* stipulates that the consequence relation $\vdash$ is monotonic. *Global Cut* can be seen as a generalization of the transitivity of consequence.

Sequents are called the *constraints* of a theory, expressing certain regularities that are taken to hold. Given a classification $\mathcal{C}_i = (\Sigma_i, L_i, \models)_{i \in I}$, the *natural theory* of $\mathcal{C}_i$ is the set of all such regularities emerging from and supported by the classification itself, defined as $\left\{ \langle \Gamma, \Delta \rangle \mid \Gamma, \Delta \subseteq P_i, \bigcap_{\gamma \in \Gamma} ext(\gamma) \subseteq \bigcup_{\delta \in \Delta} ext(\delta) \right\}$. In other words, the notion of satisfaction extends straightforwardly to sequents, as a state σ satisfies a sequent $\Gamma \vdash \Delta$ iff when $\sigma \models \gamma$ for all $\gamma \in \Gamma$, then $\sigma \models \delta$ for at least one $\delta \in \Delta$. It is proved in ([3], p.119) that the unique natural theory generated by a classification is regular.

Thinking of L_i-sentences as suitably defined concepts in some ontology language or description logic, the respective conjunctive and disjunctive interpretations of the sequent premise and conclusion allow to express the *disjointness* and *coverage* of concepts. For ϕ, $\psi \in L_i$, saying $\phi, \psi \vdash \emptyset$ means that ϕ and ψ are disjoint concepts – there is no state that satisfies both. Similarly, $\emptyset \vdash \phi, \psi$ means every state is covered by ϕ and ψ. The connection between negation on the one hand and disjointness and coverage on the other is immediate: $\phi, \neg\phi \vdash \emptyset$ and $\emptyset \vdash \phi, \neg\phi$ (for some $\phi \in L_i$) are classical validities in any theory of a classification. *Local logics* then, make the logical connection between regular theories and classifications.

Definition 4 (Local Logics). *A local logic $\mathcal{L} = (\mathcal{C}_i, T, N)$ is a triple consisting of a classification $\mathcal{C}_i$, a regular theory T and a subset $N \subseteq \Sigma_i$ of states satisfying all constraints in T, called its 'normal tokens'.*

When the classification in question is obvious we sometimes omit reference to it, simplifying notation to $\mathcal{L} = (T, N)$. Furthermore we may refer to a local logic $\mathcal{L}$'s T or N components as $T(\mathcal{L})$ or $N(\mathcal{L})$. A local logic $\mathcal{L}$ is said to be *sound* iff $N = \Sigma_i$, and *complete* iff T is the natural theory T_i associated with $\mathcal{C}_i$, i.e. if all constraints satisfied by Σ_i are in T. Furthermore, let's say that a local logic $\mathcal{L}$ is *internally complete* if its theory T contains all sequents satisfied by all normal tokens in N. Computationally, local logics may be logic programs, where sequents $p, q \vdash r$ are represented as horn clauses or rules $r \leftarrow p, q$, and normal tokens N as a set of models (valuations) for the theory.

In [3], the *natural logic* of an agent classification $\mathcal{C}_i$ is defined as the unique sound and complete local logic $\mathcal{L}_i = (\mathcal{C}_i, T_i, \Sigma_i)$ consisting of the classification $\mathcal{C}_i$, its natural theory T_i and the entire set of L_i-models Σ_i is taken to be normal. In other words, $\mathcal{L}_i$ is the most general logic associated with the perspective encoded by $\mathcal{C}_i$, for some $i \in I$. Nevertheless, we can conceive of a whole host of stronger logics on a given $\mathcal{C}_i$, by varying the T and N components. Barwise and Seligman define a partial order over theories and logics of a fixed classification as follows: for regular theories T_1 and T_2, $T_1 \sqsubseteq T_2$ iff every sequent in T_1 is also in T_2. Similarly, for local logics $\mathcal{L}_1$ and $\mathcal{L}_2$, $\mathcal{L}_1 \sqsubseteq \mathcal{L}_2$ iff $T_1 \sqsubseteq T_2$ for their respective theories, and furthermore $N_2 \subseteq N_1$.

Implicitly, we have been talking about our agents' perceptions in terms of this natural logic all along – it is the sound and complete logic generated by the various classifications of agent perspectives. For example, $\mathcal{L}_{\mathbf{s}}$, the natural logic of **Side**, contains such sequents as $\texttt{left}, \texttt{right} \vdash_{\mathcal{L}_{\mathbf{s}}} \texttt{left}$, and all of its states are normal with respect to this sequent. We can now say what contexts are in the model we propose.

Definition 5 (Contexts). *A context is an internally complete local logic $\mathcal{L} = (\mathcal{C}_i, T, N)$ depending on a perspective (classification) $\mathcal{C}_i = (\Sigma_i, L_i, \models_i)$ (for $i \in I$), a theory T expressed in the language L_i of $\mathcal{C}_i$ and a set of normal situations (states) N that satisfy the theory T.*

In what follows, we will freely refer to contexts as local logics and vice versa, generally preferring the latter in technical discussions and the former when talking about the phenomenon itself. This definition of contexts makes the intuition that a context is not itself a perspective, but obviously dependent on one explicit. Conversely, a perspective can itself be regarded as a context, represented in our model by the natural logic $\mathcal{L}_i$ of some perspective $\mathcal{C}_i$, for $i \in I$.

Often though reasoning in $\mathcal{C}_i$ will take place in some *more specific* local logic $\mathcal{L}'$ such that $\mathcal{L}_i \sqsubseteq \mathcal{L}'$. For instance, **Side** might be operating against the background knowledge that there is only one ball present in the magic box. If we call this context $\mathcal{L}'$, it is easy to see that there are certain inferences that hold in $\mathcal{L}'$ that are not valid in $\mathcal{L}_{\mathbf{s}}$ — $\neg\texttt{left} \vdash_{\mathcal{L}'} \texttt{right}$ is one obvious example.

Just like (weak) chain models in LMS, a certain class of local logics is of special interest: those local logics $\langle T, N \rangle$ where $|N| \leq 1$. In case a local logic contains no normal tokens ($|N| = 0$) we say the logic is inconsistent. If we are under the assumption that contexts are internally complete local logics, then every classification has one unique inconsistent local logic, $\mathcal{L}^{\top}$ in which $\Gamma \vdash_{\mathcal{L}^{\top}} \Delta$, for any $\Gamma, \Delta \subseteq L_i$. In case $|N| = 1$, we call this local logic a *state logic*.

Definition 6 (State Logic). *Given a perspective $\mathcal{C}_i = (\Sigma_i, L_i, \models_i)$ (for $i \in I$), a state logic $\mathcal{L}^{\sigma}$ is a local logic $(\mathcal{C}_i, T, N)$ where $N = \{\sigma\}$, for some $\sigma \in \Sigma_i$. $\mathcal{L}^{\sigma}$ is a complete state logic if T is the set:*

$$\left\{ \langle \Gamma, \Delta \rangle \mid \Gamma, \Delta \in \mathcal{P}(L_i),\ \sigma \models \bigwedge \Gamma \implies \sigma \models \bigvee \Delta \right\}$$

To give an example of a state logic, suppose that the magic box as perceived by **Side** contains just one ball in the right sector, as shown in Fig. 1. Then the context of **Side**'s reasoning about this instance of the box can be represented by a state logic $\mathcal{L}_\mathrm{s}^{10}$, and the following is a valid constraint of $\mathcal{L}_\mathrm{s}^{10}$.

$$\vdash_{\mathcal{L}_\mathrm{s}^{10}} \texttt{left} \tag{2}$$

Thus, if $\mathcal{L}_i$ is the most general context associated with a perspective $\mathcal{C}_i$, the collection of state logics $\mathcal{L}^\sigma$ in $\mathcal{C}_i$ are the most "non-partial" consistent contexts conceivable on a given perspective — they effectively decide all propositions, modulo the expressive limitations inherent in the perspective itself. Of course, this still leaves many cases inbetween. As an example, consider the context of **Side**'s observations of the box, as represented by **Top**. Intuitively, it should be possible to devise a local logic in **Top**'s perspective that represents all and only the information about the box that is available to **Side**.

By virtue of the structure of the magic box, there is a straightforward mapping from **Side** observations to **Top** observations. It is this: any state of the box that **Side** classifies as "right", **Top** classifies as "four $\vee$ five $\vee$ six". Whenever "$\emptyset \vdash \texttt{left}$" holds in a given context of from perspective **Side**, "$\emptyset \vdash$ one $\vee$ two $\vee$ three" must hold in the perspective of **Top**, and so on. If we call $\mathcal{L}_\mathrm{s}'$ the context corresponding to $\mathcal{L}_\mathrm{s}$ in **Top**, then it should be clear what the theory of $\mathcal{L}_\mathrm{s}'$ is — it is exactly the theory of $\mathcal{L}_\mathrm{s}$, modulo the following mapping: $\{\texttt{left} \mapsto \text{one} \vee \text{two} \vee \text{three}, \texttt{right} \mapsto \text{four} \vee \text{five} \vee \text{six}\}$. A similar compatibility relation holds obviously between **Top** and **Front**'s perspectives. Ultimately this should allow us to derive inferences like:

$$\frac{\text{S}:\neg\texttt{left} \qquad \text{F}:\texttt{center}}{\text{T}:\texttt{five}} \tag{3}$$

In order to do so, the realization that we can take the *image* of a context in another perspective (under some mapping) is a key insight. *Infomorphisms* are constructs from channel theory ([3]) denoting a mapping between two classifications that preserves certain interesting properties about their information structure.

Definition 7 (Infomorphisms). *For classifications $\mathcal{C}_i = (\Sigma_i, L_i, \models)$ and $\mathcal{C}_j = (\Sigma_j, L_j, \models)$, an infomorphism $f : \mathcal{C}_i \rightleftarrows \mathcal{C}_j$ from $\mathcal{C}_i$ to $\mathcal{C}_j$ is a pair of contravariant functions $\langle f^\wedge : L_i \to L_j, f^\vee : \Sigma_j \to \Sigma_i \rangle$ satisfying the following fundamental property:*

$$\forall \sigma \in \Sigma_j, \ \phi \in L_i : f^\vee(\sigma) \models_{\mathcal{C}_i} \phi \iff \sigma \models_{\mathcal{C}_j} f^\wedge(\phi)$$

A more suggestive way to put this is saying that the diagram in Fig. 2 commutes.

2.2 Information Flow in the Magic Box

The information flow throughout the magic box then emerges as the system-wide logic regulating the system of constraints between the various perspectives. But

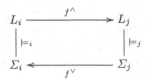

Fig. 2. Infomorphisms Visually

what, or rather, who's context is that? Quite simply, it is the natural logic of the "system-wide" perspective. It seems we can represent this perspective as another classification (say $\mathcal{C}_{box}$) who's role it is to delegate contextual information across all agent representations through a series of infomorphisms, $f : \mathcal{C}_S \rightleftarrows \mathcal{C}_{box}$, $g : \mathcal{C}_T \rightleftarrows \mathcal{C}_{box}$ and $h : \mathcal{C}_F \rightleftarrows \mathcal{C}_{box}$. It may help to think of $\mathcal{C}_{box}$ as a representation of our "external" perspective, standing outside of the model. Representing this global view as just another perspective in the model allows us to reflect on the agents' reasoning from "inside" the model. As the **Top** view essentially coincides with our 3D understanding of the structure of the box — **Top** has access to the complete state of the box — we equip the $\mathcal{C}_{box}$ classification with the same L and Σ components as **Top**. Let $\mathcal{C}_{box}$ therefore be the classification $(\{0, 1\}^6, \{\texttt{one}, \ldots, \texttt{six}\}, \models_{box})$. The picture that emerges can be diagrammed as in Fig. 3.

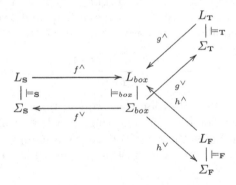

Fig. 3. The Magic Box Channel

We now define the infomorphisms f, g and h. Let's start with the easiest one, the infomorphism $\langle g^\wedge, g^\vee \rangle$ from **Top** to the box classification $\mathcal{C}_{box}$, where:

- $g^\wedge(p) : L_T \rightarrow L_{box} = p$
- $g^\vee(\sigma) : \Sigma_{box} \rightarrow \Sigma_T = \sigma$

Thus, g is just a pair of identity functions on identical classifications. Then g is clearly an infomorphism, as it holds trivially that $\sigma \models_{box} g^\wedge(\phi) \iff g^\vee(\sigma) \models_T \phi$ for $\phi \in L_T$ and $\sigma \in \Sigma_{box}$.

The infomorphism $\langle f^\wedge, f^\vee \rangle$ from **Side** to C_{box} is only slightly more complicated.

- $f^\wedge(p) : L_\mathbf{s} \to L_{box} = q$, where

$$q = \begin{cases} \textbf{one} \vee \textbf{two} \vee \textbf{three} & \text{if } p = \texttt{left} \\ \textbf{three} \vee \textbf{four} \vee \textbf{five} & \text{if } p = \texttt{right} \\ \neg f^\wedge(\psi) & \text{if } \phi = \neg\psi \\ f^\wedge(\psi) \otimes f^\wedge(\psi') & \text{if } \phi = \psi \otimes \psi' \text{ and } \otimes \in \{\wedge, \vee, \supset\} \end{cases}$$

- $f^\vee(\sigma) : \Sigma_{box} \to \Sigma_\mathbf{s} = \mathbf{xy}$ where

$$x = \begin{cases} 1 & \text{if } \sigma_1 + \sigma_2 + \sigma_3 > 0 \\ 0 & \text{otherwise} \end{cases} \qquad y = \begin{cases} 1 & \text{if } \sigma_4 + \sigma_5 + \sigma_6 > 0 \\ 0 & \text{otherwise} \end{cases}$$

Finally, infomorphism h describes how **Front** is related to the C_{box}:

- $h^\wedge(p) : L_\mathbf{F} \to L_{box} = q$, where

$$q = \begin{cases} \textbf{one} \vee \textbf{four} & \text{if } p = \texttt{left} \\ \textbf{two} \vee \textbf{five} & \text{if } p = \texttt{center} \\ \textbf{three} \vee \textbf{six} & \text{if } p = \texttt{right} \\ \neg h^\wedge(\psi) & \text{if } \phi = \neg\psi \\ h^\wedge(\psi) \otimes h^\wedge(\psi') & \text{if } \phi = \psi \otimes \psi' \text{ and } \otimes \in \{\wedge, \vee, \supset\} \end{cases}$$

- $h^\vee(\sigma) : \Sigma_{box} \to \Sigma_\mathbf{F} = \mathbf{xyz}$ where

$$x = \begin{cases} 1 & \text{if } \sigma_1 + \sigma_4 > 0 \\ 0 & \text{otherwise} \end{cases} \quad y = \begin{cases} 1 & \text{if } \sigma_2 + \sigma_5 > 0 \\ 0 & \text{otherwise} \end{cases} \quad z = \begin{cases} 1 & \text{if } \sigma_3 + \sigma_6 > 0 \\ 0 & \text{otherwise} \end{cases}$$

Example. An example might make this a bit more digestible. Recall the configuration of magic box as depicted in Fig. 1. The box contains one ball (in what we called sector 3). Given that **Side**, **Front** and **Top** each have an unconstrained view of the box, their contexts of reasoning will consist of the *state logics* $\mathcal{L}_\mathbf{s}^{10}$, $\mathcal{L}_\mathbf{T}^{001}$ and $\mathcal{L}_\mathbf{T}^{001000}$ respectively. $T(\mathcal{L}_\mathbf{s}^{10})$ is the regular closure of the theory $\langle L_\mathbf{s}, \{\langle \emptyset, \{\texttt{left}\}\rangle, \langle\{\texttt{right}\}, \emptyset\rangle\}\rangle$, representing the state of the box in **Side**'s context. The way infomorphisms are said to capture the information flow from $C_\mathbf{s}$ to C_{box} is in the way they translate the semantic constraints in the context of **Side** into constraints of the magic box itself. Using the infomorphism $f : C_\mathbf{s} \rightleftarrows C_{box}$ as introduced above, we can compute the image context in C_{box} of $\mathcal{L}_\mathbf{s}^{10}$, written $f[\mathcal{L}_\mathbf{s}^{10}]$. To give one example, translating the sequent $\vdash_{\mathcal{L}_\mathbf{s}^{10}} \texttt{left}$ under f gives:

$$\begin{aligned} f^\wedge(\langle\emptyset, \{\texttt{left}\}\rangle) &= \langle f^\wedge(\emptyset), f^\wedge(\{\texttt{left}\})\rangle \\ &= \langle \emptyset, \{f^\wedge(\texttt{left})\}\rangle \\ &= \langle \emptyset, \{\textbf{one} \vee \textbf{two} \vee \textbf{three}\}\rangle \\ &= \vdash_{f[\mathcal{L}_\mathbf{s}^{10}]} \textbf{one} \vee \textbf{two} \vee \textbf{three} \end{aligned} \qquad (4)$$

$f^\wedge(\langle\{\texttt{right}\},\emptyset\rangle)$ is derived similarly. Thus, the image of $T(\mathcal{L}_\texttt{S}^{10})$ under f is the smallest regular theory on C_{box} containing sequents:

$$\emptyset \vdash_{f[\mathcal{L}_\texttt{S}^{10}]} \texttt{one} \vee \texttt{two} \vee \texttt{three}$$

$$\texttt{four} \vee \texttt{five} \vee \texttt{six} \vdash_{f[\mathcal{L}_\texttt{S}^{10}]} \emptyset \tag{5}$$

The normal models of $f[\mathcal{L}_\texttt{S}^\sigma]$ is the maximal set of states $N \subseteq \Sigma_{box}$ such that $f^\vee(N) = \{\texttt{01}\}$, the singleton set of normal models of $\mathcal{L}_\texttt{S}^\sigma$. In this case, $|N| = 7$, as 01 has seven pre-image states in Σ_{box}.

By the same reasoning, we can find the projection of the **Front** view context $\mathcal{L}_\texttt{T}^{001}$ on the magic box. Again, $\mathcal{L}_\texttt{T}^{001}$ is the local logic consisting of the smallest regular theory containing the sequents $\{\langle\emptyset,\{\texttt{right}\}\rangle,\langle\{\texttt{left}\},\emptyset\rangle,\langle\{\texttt{center}\},\emptyset\rangle\}$, and by virtue of being a complete state logic of the box (as far as **Front** is concerned), its normal models are the singleton set $\{\texttt{001}\}$. Projecting this context to the channel core through $h : C_\texttt{F} \rightleftarrows C_{box}$ gives the local logic $h[\mathcal{L}_\texttt{T}^{001}]$ on C_{box}, lifting the current **Front** context to the system-level perspective if you will. By way of example, one sequent holding in **Front**'s context is $\texttt{left} \vdash_{\mathcal{L}_\texttt{T}^{001}}$, implying that no state currently under consideration is of type $\texttt{left}$. The h-image of this sequent becomes:

$$
\begin{aligned}
h^\wedge(\langle\{\texttt{left}\},\emptyset\rangle) &= \langle h^\wedge(\{\texttt{left}\}), h^\wedge(\emptyset)\rangle \\
&= \langle\{h^\wedge(\texttt{left})\},\emptyset\rangle \\
&= \langle\{\texttt{one} \vee \texttt{four}\},\emptyset\rangle
\end{aligned} \tag{6}
$$

And so on for the other sequents. The context of **Front**'s observations in C_{box} is again not a complete state logic of the box – there are three Σ_{box} states the box can be in that correspond to **Front**'s observations – $\{\texttt{001}\}^{-h^\vee} = \{\texttt{001000}, \texttt{000001}, \texttt{001001}\}$.

Interestingly though, joining the contexts $\mathcal{L}_\texttt{S}^{10}$ and $\mathcal{L}_\texttt{T}^{001}$ in the global perspective *does* give a complete state logic of the magic box in C_{box}. As the partial order $\sqsubseteq$ on logics forms a lattice structure, it is straightforward to define meet and join operations of local logics (and thus contexts within a perspective), as shown in [3].

- $\mathcal{L}_1 \sqcup \mathcal{L}_2 =_{def} (T_1 \sqcup T_2, N_1 \cap N_2)$
- $\mathcal{L}_1 \sqcap \mathcal{L}_2 =_{def} (T_1 \sqcap T_2, N_1 \cup N_2)$

Where the join (meet) of theories is defined in terms of the union (intersection) of their sequent sets. To wit, $f[\mathcal{L}_\texttt{S}^{10}] \sqcup h[\mathcal{L}_\texttt{T}^{001}]$ becomes the local logic $\langle C_{box}, T(f[\mathcal{L}_\texttt{S}^{10}]) \sqcup T(h[\mathcal{L}_\texttt{T}^{001}]), N(f[\mathcal{L}_\texttt{S}^{10}]) \cap N(h[\mathcal{L}_\texttt{T}^{001}])\rangle$. As this local logic is supposed to be internally complete, we can just focus on its extent set. Then we have that $\{\texttt{100000}, \texttt{010000}, \texttt{001000}, \texttt{101000}, \texttt{110000}, \texttt{011000}, \texttt{111000}\} \cap \{\texttt{001000}, \texttt{000001}, \texttt{001001}\} = \{\texttt{001000}\}$. This state obviously satisfies the type $\texttt{three}$ ("$\texttt{001000} \models_{box} \texttt{three}$"), and so we get the following valid constraint.

$$\emptyset \vdash_{f[\mathcal{L}_\texttt{S}^{10}] \sqcup h[\mathcal{L}_\texttt{T}^{001}]} \texttt{three} \tag{7}$$

Thus, while the fact that there is a ball in sector 3 is derivable in neither $f[\mathcal{L}_S^{10}]$ nor $h[\mathcal{L}_T^{001}]$, i.e. $\nvdash_{f[\mathcal{L}_S^{10}]}$ **three** nor $\nvdash_{h[\mathcal{L}_T^{001}]}$ **three**, this fact *is* derivable in their *combined* contexts, obtained by computing their join. Moreover, this fact is known in the **Top** perspective, as $\mathcal{C}_{box} = \mathcal{C}_T$ and $g^{-1}[f[\mathcal{L}_S^{10}] \sqcup h[\mathcal{L}_T^{001}]] \sqsubseteq \mathcal{L}_T^{001000}$.

2.3 Properties of Contextual Reasoning

Let's take stock. In the previous section we have freely been moving local logics (i.e. contexts) back and forth over infomorphisms. What do we know about the structural properties of these inference mechanisms? Mapping an L_i-formula ϕ over f into L_{box} gives a straightforward interpretation of i's context from the point of view of other agents. One desirable property of this kind of inter-contextual reasoning is that it offers a formal model of the kind of inferences that can be drawn in the context of an agent $\mathcal{C}$ about the perception of other agents, based on what $\mathcal{C}$ itself knows. How constraints and theories travel across an infomorphism $f : \mathcal{C}_1 \rightleftarrows \mathcal{C}_2$ can be made explicit then by introducing inference rules for inter-contextual reasoning.[4]

$$\frac{\Gamma^{-f} \vdash_{\mathcal{L}_1} \Delta^{-f}}{\Gamma \vdash_{\mathcal{L}_2} \Delta} \; f\text{-Intro} \qquad\qquad \frac{\Gamma^{f} \vdash_{\mathcal{L}_2} \Delta^{f}}{\Gamma \vdash_{\mathcal{L}_1} \Delta} \; f\text{-Elim}$$

As to notation, Γ^f denotes the image of a set of sentences under f. Similarly, Γ^{-f} is the set of $\mathcal{C}_1$ sentences having Γ as its image under f. A natural question then is how f-Intro and f-Elim behave with respect to soundness and completeness of projected inference.

Soundness. With respect to the natural logic of a classification, f-Intro preserves soundness. If some global state $\sigma \in \Sigma_{box}$ were a counterexample to $\Gamma \vdash_{\mathcal{L}_{box}} \Delta$, $f^\vee(\sigma)$ would be a counterexample to $\Gamma^{-f} \vdash_{\mathcal{L}_i} \Delta^{-f}$, for some agent classification $\mathcal{C}_i$ ($i \in I$) such that $f : \mathcal{C}_i \rightleftarrows \Sigma_{box}$. On the contrary, f-Elim does not in general preserve validity. A valid sequent in the logic of the global system classification can be the image of a invalid sequent in one of its component perspectives. This is the case when the counterexample $\sigma \in \Sigma_i$ to $\Gamma^{-f} \vdash_{\mathcal{L}_i} \Delta^{-f}$ is outside the range of $f^\vee$. In other words, f-Elim offers no guarantees in principle concerning the validity of a projected inference in the target context. However, f-Elim *is* sound when $f^\vee$ is surjective. Clearly, in the magic box example $f^\vee$, $g^\vee$ and $h^\vee$ are all surjective, making f-Elim, g-Elim and h-Elim sound inference rules as well. Thus the transfer of inferences along infomorphisms seems to preserve validity.

Completeness. We saw that f-Intro preserves validity of inference, but f-Elim may not. What about non-validity?

As a general result (see [3]), f-Elim preserves non-validity but we may lose completeness with f-Intro. This is just the dual of the soundness results we

---

[4] See [3], p.38.

introduced previously: an invalid inference $\Gamma \vdash_{\mathcal{L}_{box}} \Delta$ cannot be the image of some valid sequent $\Gamma^{-f} \vdash_{\mathcal{L}_i} \Delta^{-f}$, for some $i \in I$. We can think of the natural logic on the channel core $\mathcal{L}_{box}$ as a richer theory of the box, relating those pieces of information that remain constant across perspectives to each other via infomorphisms. The completeness results should be interpreted accordingly.

On the other hand, f-Intro does not preserve non-validity: there can be system-level constraints that are not represented (or indeed representable) in all of the agent perspectives.

In conclusion, f-Intro tells us that any constraint that holds in a component view of the system translates to a valid constraint of the system as a whole. In turn, f-Elim says that system constraints – modulo translation under some infomorphism – reflect on its components, for those perspectives that are part of the system.

2.4   Discussion

> ... Thinking of a context as a theory would not allow us to capture the relationships between different partial, approximate and perspectival representations. This leads to the following idea: *a context is a theory which is 'plugged' into a structure of relationships with other theories.* (BBG2000 ([5]), original emphasis)

In this section we would like to argue that our proposal of local logics as contexts is a straightforward implementation of the idea expressed above. The "theory" role here is played by the concept of local logics; the "structure of" is the (directed) network of interconnected perspectives on some common domain, in this case the magic box.

Before comparing this approach to other formalizations of context, we first argue that contexts thus conceived are indeed partial, approximate and perspectival representations of the magic box.

Partiality.   In the introduction we said a representation is partial when "it describes only a subset of a more comprehensive state of the world". As BBG2000 themselves explain, metaphysically this "more comprehensive state" may be the world, but cognitively, it may be "the totality of what an agent can talk about" ([5], p.9). This meshes well with our original intuition of agents as classifiers, and a classification as some agent's scheme of individuation. Partiality essentially has two faces: partiality of *truth* and *expression*. These follow independently from our separation of *contexts* and *perspectives*. Partiality of expression stems from the fact that contexts live inside perspectives (i.e. local logics on a classification), and thus the expressivity of the host perspective limits the expressivity of any context defined in its terms.

Partiality of truth on the other hand is a property of the contexts themselves: it means contexts do not in general decide every proposition expressible in this perspective. When they do, we called the underlying local logic a complete *state description* $\mathcal{L}^\sigma$, with $|N(\mathcal{L}^\sigma)| = 1$ (0 in the case of inconsistent contexts). More typically though, $N(\mathcal{L}^\sigma)$ will contain a number of states that fit the context, with the partial order $\sqsubseteq$ on local logics as a natural inclusion relation on contexts. Note that the partiality of context has both a semantic reading (the set of possible states N it considers) as well as a proof-theoretic reading: its regular theory T.

Given some local logic $\mathcal{L}$, if we require $\mathcal{L}$ to be sound and complete with respect to its normal tokens (i.e. $\forall \sigma \in N(\mathcal{L})$, $\sigma \models_i p$ iff $\emptyset \vdash_{\mathcal{L}} p$, for any $p \in P_i$) then both readings should yield the same partial context. This tight coupling between a local logic's theory and set of normal tokens is not a requirement in the original definition of a local logic in ([3]). When using local logics to formalize contexts however it seems like a justifiable position, though there may be situations or applications in which this requirement must be relaxed.

Approximation. Any knowledge representation must choose some appropriate level of detail in which to represent the target domain, where the "right" level of approximation is of course a function of the concrete use of the representation. The time-honoured example of this type of context dependence is McCarthy's "above theory" (see [5,15] among others), containing axioms regarding the use of predicates like *on* and *above* (i.e. *above* as the transitive closure of *on*) in some SHRLDU-like block world. At this level of approximation the representation might abstract away from situations and other parameters, yielding sentences like "$\forall xy(on(x,y) \supset above(x,y))$". A more dynamic representation may represent time explicitly, like "$on(x,y,t)$" stating that x is on y at time t. Ideally, a theory of context should have something to say about when and how inferences and regularities in the one representation carry over to the other. For instance, shifting perspectives, assuming that $above(y,z)$ in the more general context from the knowledge that $above(y,z,t_3)$ in the less approximate one may be feasible, whereas the other way around would be harder to justify.

Local logics are quite well-suited to handle these representation shifts. Abusing the magic box example somewhat further, imagine a setting in which a ball travels through the box in discrete time steps $t_1, \ldots, t_n$. As this involves a different representation entirely, we model these respective contexts as the natural logics of two separate classifications – say $\mathcal{L}_s$ (the original **Side** context) and $\mathcal{L}^t$, for some temporal classification $\mathcal{C}_s^t$. The states in the $\mathcal{C}_s^t$ classification then are exactly the states in Σ_s, augmented with a dimension for time. For example, $\langle 1, 0, t_5 \rangle$ might represent the state of the box at time t_5, as seen from **Side**.

Then the natural logic of $\mathcal{C}_s$ and $\mathcal{C}_s^t$ will give rise to different but obviously related patterns of inference, similar to the ones we have been discussing in previous chapters actually. To see how reasoning transfers between $\mathcal{L}_s$ and $\mathcal{L}_s^t$, it suffices to discover an infomorphism $k : \mathcal{C}_s \rightleftarrows \mathcal{C}_s^t$ that will allow us to capture the information flow between the two perspectives. Defining k is straightforward: let $k^\wedge : L_s \to L^t$ be the identity function on sentences, and $k^\vee : \Sigma_s' \to \Sigma^t$ map every state $\sigma = \langle x, y, t \rangle$ to its "timeless" counterpart $\langle x, y \rangle$ in Σ_s, simply "ignoring" the time dimension. Then we can easily integrate $\mathcal{C}_s^t$ (and indeed time dependent versions of other agents) into our picture developed so far.

To summarize, the approximation dimension of a representation can be captured in our model by a hierarchy of logics over n, $n+1$, ..., k-dimensional state spaces Σ, and the infomorphisms that specify their interconnections.

Perspective. If anything, perspectivity is the one property of our model that should be easiest to argue. BBG2000 demonstrate that a context encodes a certain perspective and mention *spatio-temporal* perspective – essentially the kind modeled by the magic box – but also more abstract forms, like the *cognitive* perspective inherent in intensional contexts and the like.

In this paper we made the even stronger claim that perspective is the more primary notion, in terms of which contexts arise ("the" context of a perspective being its natural logic). While the presence of a ball somewhere in the magic box is represented by different states altogether across perspectives, they all find their origin in Σ_{box}, which delegates states σ to their respective images over the 'down' components of the infomorphisms (i.e. $f^\vee$, $g^\vee$, $h^\vee$, ...). The structured differences in perspective can be accounted for then in the way these functions map a given state of the box σ to its various guises in the agent's view on the matter. The net result is that for instance both **Side** and **Front** have ways of talking about a ball being in the left sector ("left") in the context of their respective views, but it is the down-components of infomorphisms having a common domain Σ_{box} that make it possible for **Side** and **Front** to both see a ball in the left sector and still be referring to different states of the box regardless. In conclusion then, the perspectivity of a distributed or contextual representation resides in the way states in a central classification (a *channel*, [3]) are projected to the agent contexts through infomorphisms.

3   Related Work

The literature on contextual reasoning in AI consists mainly of two great traditions. We refer to [1,20,5] for good overviews. One is the school of thought led by McCarthy in Stanford's Formal Reasoning Group. McCarthy's Logic of Context ([15,17]) and subsequent formalizations by Guha ([14]) and Buvač and Mason ([6,18]) pioneered the field, but the proposed formalization was ultimately shown by Serafini and Bouquet in [20] to be unable to deal with certain requirements for contextual reasoning, notably partiality (of both expression and truth).

Instead we focus our attention on the second family of context logics, originating from a group around the university of Trento led by Giunchiglia ([10,12]). Over the years, this tradition gave rise to two related formalisms: Local Model Semantics ("LMS", [9]) and MultiContext Systems ("MCS", [12]).

LMS/MCS sees contextual reasoning as governed by two fundamental principles ([9], [11], [5] et al.): that reasoning is always *local* to some embedding context, using only part of what is potentially available (information, inference rules, ...), and that there exist *compatibility* between facts and reasoning in different contexts. Towards locality then, both LMS and MCS assume a collection of local languages $\{L_i\}_{i \in I}$, for some countable index set I of agents.

Contexts in LMS. Additionally, LMS features a family $\{M_i\}_{i \in I}$ of *local models* for each L_i. A context then is a set of *local models* $\mathbf{c}_i \subseteq M_i$, for $i \in I$. Information flow between contexts is captured in terms of *compatibility sequences*. A compatibility sequence $\mathbf{c}$ for $\{L_i\}$ is a sequence

$$c = \langle \mathbf{c}_0, \mathbf{c}_1, \dots, \mathbf{c}_i, \dots \rangle$$

where each $\mathbf{c}_i$ (for $i \in I$) is a subset of M_i. Then a *compatibility relation* $\mathbf{C}$ is a set of compatibility sequences $\mathbf{c}$. Given such compatibility relation $\mathbf{C}$ such that $\mathbf{C} \neq \emptyset$ and $\langle \emptyset, \emptyset, \dots, \emptyset, \dots \rangle \notin \mathbf{C}$, we say that $\mathbf{C} \models i : \phi$ if for all $\mathbf{c} \in \mathbf{C}$, $\mathbf{c}_i \models \phi$ (where $\mathbf{c}_i \models \phi$ if $m \models_{cl} \phi$, for all $m \in \mathbf{c}_i$ [5]).

In LMS the transfer of reasoning is modeled through *constraints* on the compatibility relation $\mathbf{C}$. One such example is given below, where $\mathbf{c_S}$ and $\mathbf{c_F}$ are sets of local models representing the **Side** and **Front** context, respectively.

$$\forall m_1 \in \mathbf{c_S}, m_2 \in \mathbf{c_F} : m_1 \neq 00 \Leftrightarrow m_2 \neq 000$$

This constraint states that whenever no ball is visible in the one context, this must be true of the other as well. Compatibility between contexts then is enforced through a series of constraints on possible combinations of models across contexts.

Contexts in MCS. In MCS a context C_i is a triple $\langle L_i, \Omega_i, \Delta_i \rangle$ where L_i is a local language like before, Ω_i is a set of facts (axioms), and Δ_i contains local inference rules involving formulas in L_i. In other words, whereas LMS models contexts in terms of models, contexts are proof-theoretical objects in MCS.

A MultiContext system then is a pair $\langle \{C_i\}_{i \in I}, \Delta_{br} \rangle$, where $\{C_i\}_{i \in I}$ is a family of contexts defined over I and Δ_{br} is a set of special-purpose inference rules for reasoning between contexts called "bridge rules". The distinguishing feature of bridge rules is that they support inferences whose premises and conclusion have different context labels, thus allowing reasoning to cross context boundaries.[6]

$$\frac{i_1 : \phi_1 \quad [\dots \quad i_n : \phi_n]}{j : \psi} \, br_{ij} \qquad\qquad \frac{\mathsf{S} : \mathbf{left} \vee \mathbf{right}}{\mathsf{F} : \mathbf{left} \vee \mathbf{center} \vee \mathbf{right}} \, br_{\mathsf{SF}}$$

Fig. 4. Bridge rules in MCS, with an example from the magic box

---

[5] Here $\models_{cl}$ is just the classical satisfaction relation between models and sentences.

[6] There are some obvious constraints on this construction, for example no premise $i : \phi$ may depend on undischarged assumptions in i. ([12]).

Using our previous classification diagram, the transfer of reasoning between contexts in MCS may be represented as follows.

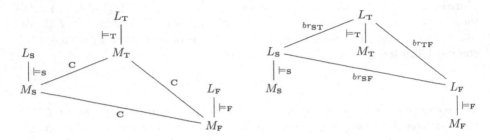

Fig. 5. Information flow between contexts through compatibility relations **C** (LMS, left) and bridge rules Δ_{br} (MCS, right)

It seems then that LMS/MCS formalizes the transfer of reasoning at the *meta-level*. Much of the flexibility of LMS/MCS in dealing with contexts stems from the fact that it is really an interlinked collection of isolated domain theories, where each such theory can be made to "export" theorems to other theories. Though these theories are appropriately referred to as "contexts", their actual *contextuality* crucially derives from manipulations of the compatibility relation **C** between contexts, or the postulation (in terms of bridge rules) of the very correspondence relation between contexts one initially set out to model.

Modeling context through compatibility relations and bridge rules make for powerful tools in the hands of a knowledge engineer, like when faced with the task of integrating information from distributed data sources into one coherent theory about some application domain. As a general *explanatory* account of context though, it leaves some of the more interesting issues concerning the nature of the information flow across contexts unexplored. This point is argued compellingly in the following quote by Edmonds:

> "Most context logics are *external* and *static* formalisms. That is, they attempt to capture the interplay of inference and context from an external (i.e. privileged) standpoint and they formalise what can be inferred given a fixed set of contexts and the corresponding beliefs. This is useful for a designer who might know the appropriate contexts, facts, bridging rules etc. and who wants a framework to bring these elements together. It is much less useful where the context, facts, bridging rules etc. are either not all known, are vague, are too complex or are simply changing too rapidly." (Bruce Edmonds, ([7]))

In this paper, we tried to show how these ontological problems can be avoided in a model that treats contextual reasoning as an instance of the more general phenomenon of *information flow*. To the extent that reasoning about perspectives like in the magic box can be said to exemplify an intelligent agent system, agent *contexts* and agent *perspectives* do not generally coincide, and treating them as one blurs certain important distinctions between the essentially static nature of a perspective and the dynamic nature of the hierarchy of partial contexts that lives inside it. This principled separation of perspectives and contexts allows for partial interpretations of one agent perspective in another, while respecting relations of partiality, approximation and perspectivity among contexts proper. Moreover, by making perspectives first-class entities in the theory one can introduce the external "system-wide" perspective inside the model as well: it is the central classification C_{box} responsible for relating agent perspectives to one another, and thereby regulating the flow of information among contexts.

4 Conclusion

In this paper we have proposed a channel theoretic model of contextual reasoning based on the analysis of the phenomenon in BBG2000, and argued its relevance to the field of multiagent systems.

One final observation before we close. The presented model marks a recent trend (see Schorlemmer and Kalfoglou, [19], among others) where channel theory seems to gradually outgrow the label of esoteric philosophical / mathematical theory to find its way into concrete applications in the field of knowledge representation and knowledge management. We believe this is an exciting development, and look forward to seeing more projects in this area.

References

1. V. Akman and M. Surav. Steps toward formalizing context. *AI Magazine*, 17(3): 55–72, 1996.
2. J. Barwise and J. Perry. *Situations and Attitudes*. MIT Press, Cambridge, MA, 1983.
3. J. Barwise and J. Scligman. *Information Flow. The Logic of Distributed Systems*. Cambridge Tracts in Theoretical Computer Science, Cambridge University Press, 1997.
4. M. Benerecetti, P. Bouquet, and C. Ghidini. On the dimensions of context dependence: Partiality, approximation, and perspective, 1999.
5. M. Benerecetti, P. Bouquet, and C. Ghidini. Contextual reasoning distilled. *JETAI*, 12(3):279–305, 2000.
6. S. Buvac. Propositional logic of context. In R. Fikes and W. Lehnert, editors, *Proceedings of the Eleventh National Conference on Artificial Intelligence*, pages 412–419, Menlo Park, CA, 1993. AAAI Press.
7. B. Edmonds. Inference within a cognitive context. In *Contexts in Logics, Workshop at 2001 CONTEXT Conference*, 2001.
8. B. Ganter and R. Wille. *Formal Concept Analysis – Mathematical Foundations*. Springer Verlag, 1999.
9. C. Ghidini and F. Giunchiglia. Local models semantics, or contextual reasoning = locality + compatibility. *Artificial Intelligence*, 127(2):221–259, 2001.
10. F. Giunchiglia. Contextual reasoning. *Epistemologia*, Special issue on *I Linguaggi e le Macchine*(XVI):345–364, 1993.

11. F. Giunchiglia and P. Bouquet. Introduction to contextual reasoning. an artificial intelligence perspective. *Perspectives on Cognitive Science*, 3:138–159, 1997.
12. F. Giunchiglia and L. Serafini. Multilanguage hierarchical logics or: How we can do without modal logics. *Artificial Intelligence*, 65(1):29–70, 1994.
13. R. Guha, R. McCool, and R. Fikes. Contexts for the semantic web. In S. A. McIlraith, D. Plexousakis, and F. van Harmelen, editors, *Proceedings of the International Semantic Web Conference*, volume 3298 of *Lecture Notes in Computer Science*, November 2004.
14. R. V. Guha. *Contexts: A Formalization and Some Applications*. PhD thesis, Stanford University, 1991.
15. J. McCarthy. Notes on formalizing contexts. In T. Kehler and S. Rosenschein, editors, *Proceedings of the Fifth National Conference on Artificial Intelligence*, pages 555–560, Los Altos, California, 1986. Morgan Kaufmann.
16. J. McCarthy. Generality in artificial intelligence. In V. Lifschitz, editor, *Formalizing Common Sense: Papers by John McCarthy*, pages 226–236. Ablex Publishing Corporation, Norwood, New Jersey, 1990.
17. J. McCarthy and S. Buvač. Formalizing context (expanded notes). In A. Aliseda, R. v. Glabbeek, and D. Westerståhl, editors, *Computing Natural Language*, volume 81 of *CSLI Lecture Notes*, pages 13–50. Center for the Study of Language and Information, Stanford University, 1998.
18. V. B. Sasa Buvač and I. A. Mason. Metamathematics of contexts. *Fundamenta Informaticae*, 23(2/3/4):263–301, 1995.
19. M. Schorlemmer and Y. Kalfoglou. On semantic interoperability and the flow of information, 2003.
20. L. Serafini and P. Bouquet. Comparing formal theories of context in ai, 2004.

An Argumentation-Based Negotiation for Distributed Extended Logic Programs[*]

Iara Carnevale de Almeida[1,2] and José Júlio Alferes[1]

[1] CENTRIA, Universidade Nova de Lisboa
2829-516 Caparica, Portugal
{ica|jja}@di.fct.unl.pt
[2] Department of Computer Science, Universidade de Évora
Colégio Luis Verney; 7000-671 Évora, Portugal
ica@di.uevora.pt

Abstract. The paradigm of argumentation has been used in the literature to assign meaning to knowledge bases in general, and logic programs in particular. With this paradigm, rules of a logic program are viewed as encoding arguments of an agent, and the meaning of the program is determined by those arguments that somehow (depending on the specific semantics) can defend themselves from the attacks of other arguments.

Most of the work on argumentation-based logic programs semantics has focused on assigning meaning to single programs. In this paper we propose an argumentation-based negotiation semantics for distributed knowledge bases represented as extended logic programs that extends the existing ones by considering sets of (distributed) logic programs, rather than single ones. For specifying the ways in which the various logic programs may combine their knowledge we make use of concepts that had been developed in the areas of defeasible reasoning, distributed knowledge bases, and multi-agent setting. In particular, we associate to each program P a cooperation set (the set of programs that can be used to complete the knowledge in P) and the argumentation set (the set of programs with which P has to reach a consensus).

1 Introduction

The ability to view logic programming as a non-monotonic knowledge representation language brought to light the importance of defining clear declarative semantics for logic programs, for which proof procedures (and attending implementations) are then defined. This work is by now well established and consolidated in what concerns the semantics of single logic programs, in particular approaches where the argumentation metaphor is used for providing such clear declarative semantics e.g. [6,11,3,16,15,10]. This metaphor seems adequate too for modelling situations where there are distributed logic programs, each with some 'knowledge about the world', that might negotiate in order to determine the truth value of common conclusions. However, the previous mentioned works do not directly address this issue.

---

[*] The work was partially supported by the Brazilian CAPES, and by the European Commission within the 6th Framework Programme project REWERSE, number 506779.

K. Inoue, K. Satoh, and F. Toni (Eds.): CLIMA VII, LNAI 4371, pp. 191–210, 2007.

In this paper we propose an argumentation-based negotiation semantics for sets of knowledge bases distributed through a multi-agent setting (MAS). In it different agents may have independent or overlapping knowledge bases Kb, each Kb being represented by an extended logic program with denials. If all such agents have complete access to the knowledge bases of all other agents, then they should be able to build arguments using rules of others (cooperate) and would have to defend their arguments against arguments build by the others (argue). In this case, the semantics of argumentation-based negotiation framework should coincide with the semantics of the union of the knowledge bases, viewed as a single one. Here we want to deal with cases where the semantics of multi setting does not necessarily coincide with the union. The basis of our proposal is that agents negotiate by exchanging parts of their knowledge to obtain a consensus concerning the inference of an agent's beliefs. Furthermore, our proposal allows modelling of multi setting with different kinds of purposes. For instance each agent may represent "acquired knowledge" in different periods of time, and we want to know the truth value of some agent's belief in a specific period of time. Another example is when the whole set represents a kind of hierarchy of knowledge such as an organisation where each agent has incomplete (or partial) knowledge of the overall process. Yet another, when we want to "organise" the knowledge about taxonomy into different agents and so represent their natural relation of preferences.

Moreover, a multi-agent setting $\mathcal{A}$ might have the agent's knowledge base physically distributed over a computer network. Therefore, an agent Ag of $\mathcal{A}$ does not need to, and sometimes cannot, argue and/or to cooperate with all agents in $\mathcal{A}$. In our proposal, we state that every agent Ag in $\mathcal{A}$ has associated two sets of agents: the set of agents with which it can cooperate in order to build arguments, and the set of agents with which it must defend from attacks (argue) in order to reach some consensus. In general, little is assumed about these sets: we only impose that every agent argues and cooperates with itself because it would make little sense for an agent neither to access its own knowledge nor to obtain a consensus based upon its own knowledge.

The ability of associating these sets to each agents provides a flexible framework which, besides reflecting the possibly existing physical network, may serve for different purposes as the ones above. For example, for modelling knowledge over a hierarchy where each node of the hierarchy is represented by a Kb that cooperates with all its inferiors, and must argue with all its superiors. Another example is modelling knowledge that evolves. Here the "present" can use knowledge from the "past" unless this knowledge from the past is in conflicting with later knowledge. This can be modelled by allowing any present node to cooperate with its past nodes, and forcing any past node to argue with future nodes. In all these cases, it is important that the knowledge is not flattened, as in the union of all knowledge bases, and that the semantics is parametric on the specific Kb. I.e. it might happens that an argument is acceptable in a given (agent) Kb, and not acceptable in another (agent) Kb of the same system.

As with other argumentation based frameworks (e.g. the ones mentioned above) the semantics is defined based on a notion of acceptable arguments, this notion being itself based on an attacking relation among arguments. Moreover, as in [12], based on acceptability, all arguments are assigned a status: roughly, justified argument are those that are always acceptable; overruled arguments are those that are attacked by a justified argument; other arguments (that may or may not be acceptable but are not attacked by a justified one) are called defensible.

It is also a goal of the proposed framework to be able to deal with mutually inconsistent, and even inconsistent, knowledge bases. Moreover, when in presence of contradiction we want to obtain ways of multi-agent setting reasoning, ranging from consistent (in which inconsistencies lead to no result) to paraconsistent. For achieving this, the agents may exchange strong or weak arguments, as it is made clear below. This also yield a refinement of the possible status of arguments: justified arguments may now be contradictory, based on contradiction or non-contradictory.

In the next section we define the declarative semantics of the proposed framework. The paper continues by showing some properties of the framework, namely properties that relate it to extant work on argumentation and on other semantics for logic programs. We then present a couple of illustrative examples, and end with some conclusions. For lack of space all proofs have been removed from this version of the paper.

2 Declarative Semantics

As motivated in the introduction, in our framework the knowledge bases of agents are modelled by logic programs. More precisely, we use *Extended Logic Program with denials*, itself an extension of Extended Logic Programs [7], for modelling the knowledge bases. Formally:

Definition 1 (Language). *An alphabet B of a language $\mathcal{L}$ is a finite disjoint set of constants and predicate symbols. Moreover, the symbol $\perp \notin B$.*

An atom *over B is an expression of the form $p(t_1, \ldots, t_n)$ where p is a predicate symbol of B and the t_i's are terms. A term over B is either a variable or a constant. An* objective literal *over B is either an atom A or its explicit negation $\neg A$. A default literal over B is of the form $not\ A$ where A is an objective literal. A literal is either an objective literal or a default literal. By $not\ \{L_1, \ldots, L_n\}$ we mean the set of default literals $\{not\ L_1, \ldots, not\ L_n\}$. By (negative) hypothesis of an objective literal L we mean $not\ L$. By explicit complement of an objective literal L we mean $\neg L$ if L is an atom, or A if $L = \neg A$.*

A term (resp. atom, literal) is called ground *if it does not contain variables. By the Extended Herbrand Base $\mathcal{H}$ of B, $\mathcal{H}(B)$, we mean the set of all ground objective literals of B.*

Definition 2 (Extended Logic Program with Denials). *An extended logic program with denials (ELPd) over a language $\mathcal{L}$ is a (finite) set of (ground) rules of the form*

$$L_0 \leftarrow L_1, \ldots, L_l, not\ L_{l+1}, \ldots, not\ L_n \ (0 \le l \le n)$$

or of denials of the form

$$\perp \leftarrow L_1, \ldots, L_l, not\ L_{l+1}, \ldots, not\ L_n \ (0 \le l \le n)$$

where each L_i ($0 \le i \le n$) is an objective literal of $\mathcal{L}$. A rule is ground if all literals are ground. As usual L_0 is called the head, *and $L_1, \ldots, not\ L_n$ the* body *of the rule. If $n = 0$ the rule is called a* fact *and the arrow symbol is omitted.*

Besides the knowledge base, in our framework each argumentative agent Ag in a multi-agent setting $\mathcal{A}$ must have a unique identity of Ag in $\mathcal{A}$, and two sets of agents' identifiers corresponding to argumentative and cooperative agents with Ag, respectively. Moreover, the identity of Ag is in both sets of argumentative and cooperative agents with Ag:

Definition 3 (Argumentative Agent). *An* argumentative agent *(or* agent, *for short) over a language $\mathcal{L}$ and a set of identifiers Ids is a tuple*

$$Ag =< \alpha, \ Kb_\alpha, \ Argue_\alpha, \ Cooperate_\alpha >$$

where $\alpha \in Ids$, Kb_α is an ELPd over $\mathcal{L}$, $Argue_\alpha \subseteq Ids$ and $Cooperate_\alpha \subseteq Ids$ such that $\alpha \in Argue_\alpha$ and $\alpha \in Cooperate_\alpha$.

We denote by $Id(Ag)$ (resp. $Kb_{Id(Ag)}$, $Argue_{Id(Ag)}$ and $Cooperate_{Id(Ag)}$), the 1st (resp. 2nd, 3rd and 4th) position of the tuple Ag, and by $\mathcal{H}(Id(Ag))$ the set of all atoms and explicitly negated atoms of $Kb_{Id(Ag)}$.

Hereafter, we say 'arguments from $Cooperate_{Id(Ag)}$ (or $Argue_{Id(Ag)}$)' instead of 'arguments from agents whose identities are in $Cooperate_{Id(Ag)}$ (or $Argue_{Id(Ag)}$)'.

Definition 4 (Multi-agent argumentative setting). *Let $\mathcal{L}$ be a language, and Ids be a set of identifiers. A* Multi-Agent argumentative setting *(or* Multi-Agent setting, *for short) $\mathcal{A}$ is a set of agents*

$$\mathcal{A} = \{Ag_1, \ldots, Ag_n\}$$

such that all of the Ag_is are agents over $\mathcal{L}$ and Ids, and no two Ag_is have the same identifier. The Extended Herbrand Base of $\mathcal{A}$, $\mathcal{H}(\mathcal{A})$, is the union of all $\mathcal{H}(\alpha_i)$ such that $\alpha_i \in Ids$.

An *argument*, of an agent Ag, for some objective literal L is a *complete well-defined sequence* concluding L over the *set of rules* of Ag's knowledge base. A *complete sequence* of rules means that all required rules are in the sequence. A *well-defined sequence* means a (minimal) sequence of rules concluding some L. For dealing with consistent and paraconsistent reasoning, we define strong and weak arguments, based on strong and weak sets of rules, the former being simply the rules in the Kbs of agents. A *weak set of rules* results from adding to rule bodies the default negation of the head's complement, and of $\bot$, thus making the rules weaker (more susceptible to being contradicted/attacked).

Definition 5 (Strong and Weak Sets of rules). *Let $\mathcal{L}$ be a language, and P be an ELPd over $\mathcal{L}$. The* strong set of rules *of P is $R_P^s = P$ and the* weak set of rules *of P is*

$$R_P^w = \{ \ L \leftarrow Body, not \ \neg L, not \ \bot \mid L \leftarrow Body \in P \ \}$$

We say R_P is a set of rules, if it is either a strong or a weak set of rules of P.

A well-defined sequence for an objective literal L is then built by chaining rules as follows: the head of the last rule in the chain is L; furthermore, if some atom L' (ignoring default literals) appears in the body of a rule then there must be a rule before this one with L' in the head; moreover, the sequence must not be circular and only use rules that are strictly necessary.

Definition 6 (Well-defined Sequence). *Let P be an ELPd, and $L \in \mathcal{H}(P)$. A well-defined sequence for L over a set of (ground) rules S is a finite sequence $[r_1; \ldots; r_m]$ of rules r_i from S of the form $L_i \leftarrow Body_i$ such that:*

- *L is the head of the rule r_m, and*
- *an objective literal L' is the head of a rule r_i $(1 \leq i < m)$ only if L' is not in the body of any r_k $(1 \leq k \leq i)$ and L' is in the body of some r_j $(i < j \leq m)$*

We say that a well-defined sequence for L is complete *if for each objective literal L' in the body of the rules r_i $(1 \leq i \leq m)$ there is a rule r_k $(k < i)$ such that L' is the head of r_k.*

Since we are concerned with modelling knowledge bases distributed over a multi-agent setting, partial arguments of Ag for L must be considered. In fact, an agent alone might not have in its knowledge base enough rules to form a complete argument, but may have part of an argument (a partial argument) that can be complete with knowledge from other agents with which it is able to cooperate. By a partial argument of Ag for L we mean a non-complete well-defined sequence for L, called Seq_L, over the set of rules of Ag's knowledge base. The (both complete and partial) arguments of Ag built only with its own rules are called local arguments of Ag. Since we want to deal with local partial arguments, an argumentation-based semantics with cooperation is proposed. By *argumentation*, we mean the evaluation of arguments to obtain a consensus about a common knowledge; by *cooperation*, we mean the granting of arguments to achieve knowledge completeness.

Definition 7 (Local (Partial or Complete) Argument). *Let $\mathcal{A}$ be a MAS, Ag be an agent in $\mathcal{A}$, $\alpha = Id(Ag)$, Kb_α be the ELPd of Ag, R_α^s (resp. R_α^w) be the strong (resp. weak) set of rules of Kb_α, and $L \in \mathcal{H}(\mathcal{A})$.*

A strong (resp. weak) local partial argument of α for L is a pair (α, Seq_L) such that Seq_L is a well-defined sequence for L over R_α^s (resp. R_α^w). A strong (resp. weak) local complete argument of α for L is any strong (resp. weak) partial local argument (α, Seq_L) such that Seq_L is complete and non-empty. We say that (α, Seq_L) is a k-local argument of α for L, $LA_\alpha^k(L)$, if it is either a local partial argument or a local complete argument over R_L^k of α for L (where k is either s, for strong arguments, or w, for weak ones).

The *set of local arguments* of Ag contains all possible local (complete and partial) arguments over Ag's knowledge base.

Definition 8 (Set of Local Arguments). *Let $\mathcal{A}$ be a MAS, and α be an agent's identity in $\mathcal{A}$. The set of k-local arguments of α is:*

$$LA_\mathcal{A}^k(\alpha) = \bigcup_{L \in \mathcal{H}(\mathcal{A})} LA_\alpha^k(L)$$

where $LA_\alpha^s(L_i)$ (resp. $LA_\alpha^w(L_i)$) is the set of all strong (resp. weak) local arguments of α for L_i. Local arguments of α are

$$LA_\mathcal{A}(\alpha) = LA_\mathcal{A}^s(\alpha) \cup LA_\mathcal{A}^w(\alpha)$$

and we denote by $LA(\mathcal{A})$ the union of all local arguments of agents in $\mathcal{A}$.

Note that an agent Ag in a multi-agent setting $\mathcal{A}$ is able to build arguments for an objective literal L in $\mathcal{H}(\mathcal{A})$ even when Ag has no knowledge about such L (i.e. there is no rule $L \leftarrow Body$ in $Kb_{Id(Ag)}$). This is so because empty sequences are not ruled out by Definition 7. Now, partial arguments of an agent may be completed with the "help" of a sets of (complete and partial) arguments from $Cooperate_{Id(Ag)}$.

To complete a local partial argument of an agent Ag with (partial or complete) arguments from $Cooperate_{Id(Ag)}$, we need first to define an *operator* to concatenate these arguments in terms of well-defined sequences[1].

Definition 9 (Operator +). *Let* $1 \leq i \leq n$, Seq_i *is a well-defined sequence for an objective literal* L_i, *and* R_i *be the set of all rules in* Seq_i.

The concatenation $Seq_1 + \ldots + Seq_n$ *is the set of all well-defined sequences for* L_n *over* $\bigcup_{i=1}^{n} R_i$.

We introduce cooperation by defining a *set of available arguments* of an agent Ag given a set S of (complete or partial) arguments. Every (complete or partial) argument of Ag in S is considered an available argument of Ag. Moreover, if a partial argument for an objective literal L of Ag may be further completed with arguments in S belonging to $Cooperate_{Id(Ag)}$, this further completed argument is also available.

Definition 10 (Set of Available Arguments). *Let* $\mathcal{A}$ *be a MAS and* α *be an agent's identity in* $\mathcal{A}$. *The set of available arguments given a set* S *of arguments,* $Av(S)$, *is the least set such that:*

- *if* $(\alpha, Seq_L) \in S$ *then* $(\alpha, Seq_L) \in Av(S)$, *and*
- *if* $\exists\{(\beta_1, Seq_{L'}), \ldots, (\beta_i, Seq_L)\} \subseteq Av(S)$ *and* $\{\beta_1, \ldots, \beta_i\} \subseteq Cooperate_\alpha$ *then for any* $NSeq_L \in Seq_{L'} + \ldots + Seq_L$, $(\alpha, NSeq_L) \in Av(S)$

where $\alpha, \beta_1, \ldots, \beta_i$ *are agent's identifiers in* $\mathcal{A}$. *Let* $LA(\mathcal{A})$ *be the set of local arguments of* $\mathcal{A}$. *We denote by* $Args(\mathcal{A})$ *the set of available arguments of* $\mathcal{A}$ *given* $LA(\mathcal{A})$, *and dub it the* set of all available arguments in $\mathcal{A}$. *Members of* $Args(\mathcal{A})$ *will be called* arguments.

As mentioned in the Introduction, we are concerned with obtaining ways of reasoning in a multi-agent setting, ranging from consistent to paraconsistent. For this, the agents cooperate and argue by exchanging strong and weak arguments. We assume that every proponent (resp. opponent) agent in a given multi-agent setting exchanges arguments in the same way, i.e. every proposed (resp. opposing) argument is a strong or weak argument. The following two properties reinforce such an assumption. According to the first property, every available argument is of the same kind, strong or weak, as the given set of arguments. From the second property, we see that an agent might have all arguments from its cooperative agents.

Proposition 1. *If* S *is a set of strong (resp. weak) arguments, then* $Av(S)$ *is also a set of strong (resp. weak) arguments.*

---

[1] In short, several distinct well-defined sequences are obtained when concatenating two or more well-defined sequences. Furthermore, we can obtain well-defined sequences that are not in fact complete.

Proposition 2. *Any available argument* (β, Seq_L) *of* β *for* L *is an available argument* (α, Seq_L) *of* α *for* L *iff* $\beta \in Cooperate_{\alpha}$.

The following example illustrates how available arguments are built via operator $+$. This example also depicts available arguments built by agents that are not directly interrelated, i.e. there is an "indirect cooperation" between such agents.

Example 1. Let be $\mathcal{A} = \{Ag_1, Ag_2, Ag_3\}$ such that each agent is

$$
\begin{aligned}
Ag_1 &= \; < 1, \{a \leftarrow b\}, \{1\}, \{1\} > \\
Ag_2 &= \; < 2, \{c \leftarrow not\; b\}, \{2\}, \{1,2\} > \\
Ag_3 &= \; < 3, \{b; d \leftarrow not\; a\}, \{3\}, \{2,3\} >
\end{aligned}
$$

The set of strong local arguments of $\mathcal{A}$ is

$$
LA^s(\mathcal{A}) = \left\{ \begin{array}{c} (1, []), (1, [a \leftarrow b]), \\ (2, []), (2, [c \leftarrow not\; b]), \\ (3, []), (3, [b]), (3, [d \leftarrow not\; a]) \end{array} \right\}
$$

For simplicity, we call $LA^s(\mathcal{A})$ as S. Based on the first condition of Definition 10, every argument in S is an available argument, i.e. $Av(S) = S$. Based on the second condition of Definition 10, we further obtain the following available arguments:

- $(1, [c \leftarrow not\; b])$ because $\{(2, [c \leftarrow not\; b]), (1, [])\} \subset Av(S)$;
- since $\{(3, [b]), (2, [])\} \subset Av(S)$, $(2, [b]) \in Av(S)$.
  Similarly $(2, [d \leftarrow not\; a]) \in Av(S)$, because $\{(3, [d \leftarrow not\; a]), (2, [])\} \subset Av(S)$;
- as a consequence, $(1, [b])$ and $(1, [d \leftarrow not\; a])$ are available arguments because $\{(2, [b]), (1, [])\} \subset Av(S)$ and $\{(2, [d \leftarrow not\; a]), (1, [])\} \subset Av(S)$, respectively;
- because $\{(1, [a \leftarrow b]), (1, [b])\} \in Av(S)$, $(1, [b;\; a \leftarrow b]) \in Av(S)$ [2].

The least set of available arguments of $\mathcal{A}$ given $LA^s(\mathcal{A})$ is

$$
Av(LA^s(\mathcal{A})) = LA^s(\mathcal{A}) \cup \{ \; (1, [c \leftarrow not\; b]), \; (2, [b]), \; (2, [d \leftarrow not\; a]),
$$
$$
(1, [b]), \; (1, [d \leftarrow not\; a]), \; (1, [b; a \leftarrow b]) \; \}
$$

From Definition 10, $Args(\mathcal{A})$ contains all available arguments of an agent Ag built via cooperation with agents in $Cooperate_{Id(Ag)}$. However, some of these arguments might not be acceptable with respect to arguments in $Args(\mathcal{A})$ from $Argue_{Id(Ag)}$. We now describe how a negotiation process should be performed, where cooperation and argumentation are interlaced processes. Initially, assume that an available argument A of Ag is acceptable w.r.t. a set of arguments S if every argument against A from $Argue_{Id(Ag)}$ is attacked by an argument in S. Intuitively, if an agent Ag builds an available argument A by concatenating its local partial argument with arguments from $Cooperate_{Id(Ag)}$,

---

[2] $(1, [b;\; a \leftarrow b])$ can also be obtained from the set of available arguments

$$
\{(1, [a \leftarrow b]), (2, [b])\}
$$

Both ways to complete the local partial argument $(1, [a \leftarrow b])$ of agent Ag_1 are correct, but the former is less intuitive. So, we prefer to illustrate it in the former way.

then A must be evaluated by every argumentative agent in $\mathcal{A}rgue_{Id(Ag)}$. It means that each argumentative agent Ag^a should try to build an available argument CA against A. Two situations may occur:

1. Ag^a argues and cooperates only with itself. If Ag^a cannot build a complete argument CA by itself, and since there is no other agent to cooperate with Ag^a, Ag^a cannot argue against A. On the other hand, if CA is built by Ag^a, Ag^a does not need evaluation of CA by any other agent than itself, and so Ag^a might use its argument against A; or
2. Ag^a argues and/or cooperates with other agents. In such a case, to build a CA may require the concatenation of arguments from $Cooperate_{Id(Ag^a)}$ and then the evaluation of CA by agents in $\mathcal{A}rgue_{Id(Ag^a)}$. The argumentative process for CA of Ag^a finishes when the acceptability of CA with respect to arguments from $\mathcal{A}rgue_{Id(Ag^a)}$ is obtained.

Independently of which situation occurs for each $Ag^a \in \mathcal{A}rgue_{Id(Ag)}$, if there exists at least one acceptable argument CA from $\mathcal{A}rgue_{Id(Ag)}$ against the available argument A of Ag, then A is not acceptable (with respect to $\mathcal{A}rgue_{Id(Ag)}$); otherwise, A is an acceptable argument.

The following example illustrates the above informal description.

Example 2. Let be $\mathcal{A} = \{Ag_1, Ag_2, Ag_3, Ag_4, Ag_5, Ag_6\}$ such that each agent is

$$
\begin{aligned}
Ag_1 &= \; < 1, \{a \leftarrow not\ b, c;\ c\}, \{1,2,3\}, \{1\} > \\
Ag_2 &= \; < 2, \{b \leftarrow not\ d, f\}, \{2,5\}, \{2,4\} > \\
Ag_3 &= \; < 3, \{b \leftarrow d\}, \{3\}, \{3\} > \\
Ag_4 &= \; < 4, \{f\}, \{4\}, \{4\} > \\
Ag_5 &= \; < 5, \{d \leftarrow not\ g\}, \{5,6\}, \{5\} > \\
Ag_6 &= \; < 6, \{g\}, \{6\}, \{6\} >
\end{aligned}
$$

Assume that Ag_1 needs to deduce the acceptability of an argument for a. These are the steps to the solution: Ag_1 should have an argument for the objective literal a and such an argument must be acceptable w.r.t. $\mathcal{A}rgue_1 = \{2,3\}$. Since Ag_1 has an argument $A_1^s(a) = (1, [c; a \leftarrow not\ b, c])$, Ag_2 and Ag_3 should have an argument against $A_1^s(a)$.

1. Ag_3 does not have any argument against $A_1^s(a)$ because it has only a partial argument for b and there is no argument from $Cooperate_3$ to complete it.
2. Ag_2 has a partial argument for b that can be completed by Ag_4's argument for f, i.e. $A_2^s(b) = (2, [f; b \leftarrow not\ d, f]) \in (2, [b \leftarrow not\ d, f]) + (4, [f])$. So, Ag_5 should have an argument against $A_2^s(b)$.
   (a) Ag_5 has the argument $A_5^s(d) = (5, [d \leftarrow not\ g])$, and now agent Ag_6 should have an argument against $A_5^s(d)$.
      i. Ag_6 has the argument $A_6^s(g) = (6, [g])$. The argument $A_6^s(g)$ is, therefore, acceptable because there is no argument from $\mathcal{A}rgue_6$ against it.
   Thus, $A_5^s(d)$ is not acceptable because it is attacked by $A_6^s(g)$.
   Since Ag_5 has no acceptable argument against $A_2^s(b)$, $A_2^s(b)$ is an acceptable argument w.r.t. arguments from $\mathcal{A}rgue_2$.

Finally, $A_1^s(a)$ is not acceptable because there is at least one acceptable argument from $\mathcal{Argue}_1$ against it, viz. $A_2^s(b)$.

We proceed by exposing the required definitions for this informal description. First of all, it is necessary to determine the available arguments that can be used to attack. As expected, only complete arguments in $\mathcal{Args}(\mathcal{A})$ should be considered. These arguments are called *attacking arguments*.

Definition 11 (Attacking Argument). *Let $\mathcal{A}$ be a MAS, α an agent's identity in $\mathcal{A}$, and $S \subseteq \mathcal{Args}(\mathcal{A})$. (α, Seq) is an* attacking argument *given S iff it is a complete argument and belongs to $Av(S)$. If (α, Seq) is either a s-argument or a w-argument, we refer to it by* s-attacking *or* w-attacking argument, *respectively.*

Intuitively, both strong and weak arguments can be attacked in the same way. Since a (weak or strong) argument makes assumptions, other arguments for the complement of one such assumption may attack it. In other words, an argument with $not\ L$ can be attacked by arguments for L. This definition of attack encompasses the case of arguments that are directly conflicting, e.g. an argument for L (with $not\ \neg L$) can be attacked by an argument for $\neg L$. The previous claim that any weak argument $A_\alpha^w(L) = (\alpha, Seq_L^w)$ (and also a strong argument $A_\alpha^s(L) = (\alpha, Seq_L^s)$ which verifies $not\ \bot \in Assump(Seq_L^s)$) can be attacked by every argument for $\bot$. However, it does not make sense to attack arguments for objective literals if they do not lead to *falsity*. By "an objective literal L leads to *falsity*" we mean that there is an argument $A_\alpha(L)$ such that $A_\beta(\bot)$ is built based on such an argument, e.g.

$$A_\beta^s(\bot) : A_\alpha^s(L) + [\bot \leftarrow L, not\ L']$$

We only consider objective literals that are in the body of the rule for $\bot$ because these literals immediately lead to *falsity*. We assume that the involvement of other objective literals are not as strong as those in the body of the denial[3]. Then objective literals are *directly conflicting with* $A_\beta(\bot)$ if the following holds:

Definition 12 (Directly Conflict with $A_\bot$). *Let $A_\beta(\bot)$ be an argument of β for $\bot$, '$\bot \leftarrow Body$' be the rule in $A_\beta(\bot)$ and $\{L_1, \ldots, L_n\}$ be the set of all objective literals in $Body$. The set of objective literals* directly conflicting with $A_\beta(bot)$ *is*

$$DC(Seq_\bot) = \{\bot\} \cup \{L_1, \ldots, L_n\}$$

If an argument of α for L has a default negation $not\ L'$ in it, any argument for L' attacks $A_\alpha(L)$ (by undercut [11]). The other attacking relation (called rebut [11]) states that an argument also attacks another one when both arguments have complementary conclusions (i.e. one concludes L and the other $\neg L$). With strong and weak arguments, *rebut can be reduced to undercut*[4]. So, we can say informally that "an argument of α

---

[3] We further assume they can be detected in a process of "belief revision", e.g. [4]. However, a discussion of this issue is beyond the scope of this proposal.

[4] This simplification has been proposed in [3,5,14]. [3] defines a methodology for transforming non-exact, defensible rules into exact rules with explicit non-provability conditions and shows that this transformation eliminates the need for rebuttal attacks and for dealing with priorities in the semantics. In [14,5], it is proposed that "attacks" can be reduced to "undercut" by considering weaker version of arguments.

for a conclusion L *attacks* an argument of β with an assumption *not* L". Such a "notion of attack" shows that we need to make both the conclusions and the assumptions of an argument precise before defining an attack.

Definition 13 (Conclusions and Assumptions). *Let* $A_\alpha(L) = (\alpha, Seq_L)$ *be an argument of* α *for* L. *The conclusions of* $A_\alpha(L)$, $Conc(Seq_L)$, *is the set of all objective literals that appear in the head of rules in* $A_\alpha(L)$. *The assumptions of* $A_\alpha(L)$, $Assump(Seq_L)$, *is the set of all default literals appearing in the bodies of rules in* $A_\alpha(L)$.

Intuitively, we want to define attack in terms of both attacking and available arguments. However, we still need to determine which attacking arguments can be used to attack available ones. Moreover, to prevent cyclic definitions, an attack is defined only in terms of arguments.

Definition 14 (Attack). *Let* $\mathcal{A}$ *be a MAS,* α *and* β *be agent's identifiers in* $\mathcal{A}$, *and* $Argue_\alpha$ *be the* α's *set of argumentative agents. An argument* (β, Seq_{L_1}) *of* β *for* L_1 *attacks an argument* (α, Seq_{L_2}) *of* α *for* L_2 *iff*

- $\beta \in Argue_\alpha$; *and*
- Seq_{L_1} *is a well-defined sequence over* R_β, *or* $\alpha \in Argue_\beta$ *and*

$$Seq_{L_1} \in Seq_{L_2} + Seq'_{L_1}$$

where Seq'_{L_1} *is a well-defined sequence for* L_1 *over* R_β; *and*
- L_1 *is the symbol* $\perp$, *not* $\perp \in Assump(Seq_{L_2})$ *and* $L_2 \in DC(Seq_{L_1})$, *or* L_1 *is an objective literal different from* $\perp$ *and not* $L_1 \in Assump(Seq_{L_2})$.

Recall that, as with other argumentation based frameworks the semantics is defined based on a notion of acceptable arguments, where a set of arguments is acceptable if any argument attacking it is itself attacked by the set. Now, in this distributed setting, care must be taken about which arguments can be used to attack a set of arguments, and which arguments are available for being used to defend the attacks. Before presenting the definition of acceptable arguments we motivate for the definition in such a distributed setting. Moreover, note that the above definition of attack has a condition that foresees cases where "indirect cooperation" between argumentative agents is needed. The following example illustrates such a situation.

Example 3. Consider $\mathcal{A} = \{Ag_1, Ag_2\}$ where:

$$Ag_1 = \; <1, \{c; a \leftarrow c, not\ b\}, \{1,2\}, \{1\} >$$
$$Ag_2 = \; <2, \{b \leftarrow c; z \leftarrow not\ a\}, \{1,2\}, \{2\} >$$

The set of available arguments of $\mathcal{A}$ given $LA(\mathcal{A})$ is

$$Args(\mathcal{A}) = \{A_1^s(c), A_1^s(a), PA_2^s(b), A_2^s(z)\}$$

Moreover, from Definition 14, the complete argument $A_1^s(a)$ attacks $A_2^s(z)$ and the partial argument $PA_2^s(b)$ attacks $A_1^s(a)$. However, we only want attacking arguments (i.e. complete arguments) to be used to determine the acceptability of an argument w.r.t. $Args(\mathcal{A})$. Then, $PA_2^s(b)$ will not be used and, consequently, $A_2^s(z)$ is not acceptable. Nevertheless, $A_1^s(a)$ has a rule for c that can be used to complete $PA_2^s(b)$. If agent Ag_2 may 'use' such a rule from $A_1^s(a)$ to complete its partial argument $PA_2^s(b)$, Ag_2 has an argument

$$(2, [c; b \leftarrow c])$$

that can be used against $A_1^s(a)$. Therefore, $A_2^s(z)$ is acceptable w.r.t. $Args(\mathcal{A})$.

At this point, it is quite clear that we should evaluate available arguments of a multi-agent setting $\mathcal{A}$ to conclude which of them are acceptable with respect to a set S of arguments (that are already considered acceptable with respect to a set of arguments from $\mathcal{A}$). However, should an argument of an agent Ag be acceptable in $Argue_{Ag}$ if such an argument is to be used in a cooperation process? For instance, consider:

$$Ag_1 = <1, \{q \leftarrow a; c\}, \{1\}, \{1, 2\}>$$
$$Ag_2 = <2, \{a \leftarrow not\ b; b \leftarrow not\ a, not\ c\}, \{2\}, \{2\}>$$

and assume that every argument in $LA(\mathcal{A})$ is a strong argument.

For having an acceptable argument for q in Ag_1, Ag_1 must complete its available argument for q, viz. $PA_1^s(q) = (1, [q \leftarrow a])$. Agent Ag_2 has an available argument for a, $A_2^s(a) = (2, [a \leftarrow not\ b])$. However, Ag_2 has also an attacking argument $A_2^s(b) = (2, [b \leftarrow not\ a, not\ c])$ against $A_2^s(a)$. Two possible approaches can deal with this situation:

1. since both arguments attack each other, neither $A_2^s(a)$ nor $A_2^s(b)$ are acceptable in $Argue_2$, and so $A_2^s(a)$ cannot be used to complete $PA_1^s(q)$; or
2. since there is no acceptable argument in $Argue_2$ attacking $A_1^s(a)$, it is defensible. Furthermore, $A_1^s(a)$ is used to complete $PA_1^s(q)$ and so the resulting available argument is

$$A_1^s(q) = [a \leftarrow not\ b; q \leftarrow a]$$

However, $A_1^s(q)$ should be evaluated by $Argue_1$. Via cooperation, Ag_1 has an attacking argument

$$A_1^s(b) = (1, [b \leftarrow not\ a, not\ c])$$

against $A_1^s(q)$. But Ag_1 has also an attacking argument $A_1^s(c) = (1, [c])$ against $A_1^s(b)$ which no argument attacks. Thus, $A_1^s(c) = (1, [c])$ is acceptable and, consequently, $A_1^s(b)$ is not acceptable (both with respect to arguments from $Argue_1$). Therefore, $A_1^s(q)$ is acceptable with respect to arguments from $Argue_1$.

The second approach allows us to draw more acceptable arguments than the first one. In fact, the arguments evaluated are acceptable if we consider the overall agent's knowledge. Moreover, this approach is more credulous than the first one. Therefore, we follow the latter and define that for a given agent Ag in a multi-agent setting $\mathcal{A}$, an agent $Ag^c \in Cooperate_{Id(Ag)}$ cooperates with an available argument A under one of the following conditions: (i) A is not attacked by any argument from $Argue_{Id(Ag^c)}$, or (ii) A is attacked, but every attacking argument B against A is attacked by some argument from $Argue_{Id(Ag^c)}$. In both cases, A is considered a *defensible argument*. The following operator defines which are the defensible arguments, given a set of available arguments of a multi-agent setting. In the remainder, we use the notation p and o to distinguish the proposed argument from the opposing one, i.e. p (resp. o) is a (strong or weak) proposed (resp. opposing) argument.

Definition 15 (Operator $Def_{p,o}(S)$). *Let $\mathcal{A}$ be a MAS, $Args(\mathcal{A})$ be the set of available arguments of $\mathcal{A}$, $S \subseteq Args(\mathcal{A})$ be a set of p-arguments. $Def_{p,o}(S)$ is the set of all o-arguments of $Args(\mathcal{A})$ that are not attacked by any attacking argument given S. Arguments in $Def_{p,o}(S)$ are called* defensible arguments.

Assume that arguments in the set of defensible arguments are opposing arguments, and every argument in a set of available arguments is a proposed argument. Now we can determine how available p-arguments are acceptable with respect to a set S of p-arguments from $Args(\mathcal{A})$, such that S is a pre-defined set of acceptable arguments. In order to determine the set of acceptable arguments with respect to S, the following steps must be performed:

1. obtain the opposing arguments via $Def = Def_{p,o}(S)$. This encompasses the following two sub-steps:
   (a) get the set $Atts$ of p-attacking arguments given S, i.e. the complete arguments in $Av(S)$. This sub-step also allows p-partial arguments in S to be completed by arguments in S and so new p-arguments are built;
   (b) reject o-arguments in $Args(\mathcal{A})$ that are attacked by arguments in $Atts$.
2. obtain the proposed (partial or complete) arguments given S, i.e. $Av(S)$. This sub-step also allows p-partial arguments to be completed by arguments in S and so new p-arguments are built.
3. determine which are (i) the opposing arguments attacking some proposed argument and (ii) the opposing arguments attacked by arguments in S.

Definition 16 (Acceptable Argument). *Let $\mathcal{A}$ be a MAS, $Args(\mathcal{A})$ be the set of arguments of $\mathcal{A}$, $S \subseteq Args(\mathcal{A})$ be a set of p-arguments, and α, β, and γ be agent's identifiers in $\mathcal{A}$. A p-argument (α, Seq_L) for a literal L is acceptable$_{p,o}$ w.r.t. S iff (i) it is either a local argument, or it belongs to the set of available arguments given S; and (ii) for any o-attacking argument $(\beta, Seq_{L'})$ for a literal L' given $Def_{p,o}(S)$: if $(\beta, Seq_{L'})$ attacks (α, Seq_L) then there exists a complete p-argument $(\gamma, Seq_{L''})$ for a literal L'' in S that attacks $(\beta, Seq_{L'})$.*

We now formalise the concept of acceptable arguments with a fixpoint theory and also define a characteristic function $p \, o$ of multi-agent setting $\mathcal{A}$ over a set of acceptable arguments S as follows:

Definition 17 (Characteristic Function). *Let $\mathcal{A}$ be a MAS, $Args(\mathcal{A})$ be the set of available arguments of $\mathcal{A}$, and $S \subseteq Args(\mathcal{A})$ be a set of p-arguments. The characteristic function $p \, o$ of $\mathcal{A}$ over S is:*

$$F_{\mathcal{A}}^{p,o} : 2^{Args(\mathcal{A})} \to 2^{Args(\mathcal{A})},$$
$$F_{\mathcal{A}}^{p,o}(S) = \{Arg \in Args(\mathcal{A}) \mid A \text{ is acceptable}_{p,o} \text{ w.r.t. } S\}$$

We can see that, if an argument A is $acceptable_{p,o}$ w.r.t. S, A is also $acceptable_{p,o}$ w.r.t. any superset of S. In fact, it can be shown that $Def_{p,o}(S)$ is anti-monotonic, and so $F_{\mathcal{A}}^{p,o}$ is monotonic. Being monotonic, it is guaranteed that $F_{\mathcal{A}}^{p,o}$ always has a least fixpoint (according to the set inclusion ordering over sets of arguments):

Proposition 3. *Define for any $\mathcal{A}$ the following transfinite sequence of sets of arguments:*

$$
\begin{aligned}
S^0 &= \emptyset \\
S^{i+1} &= F_{\mathcal{A}}^{p,o}(S^i) \\
S^\delta &= \bigcup_{\alpha < \delta} S^\alpha \text{ for limit ordinal } \delta
\end{aligned}
$$

1. *$F_{\mathcal{A}}^{p,o}$ is monotonic, and so there must exist a smallest λ such that S^λ is a fixpoint of $F_{\mathcal{A}}^{p,o}$, and $S^\lambda = lfp(F_{\mathcal{A}}^{p,o})$.*
2. *If $F_{\mathcal{A}}^{p,o}$ is finitary then $lfp(F_{\mathcal{A}}^{p,o}) = F_{\mathcal{A}}^{p,o\uparrow\omega}(\emptyset)$.*

By knowing the set S of all acceptable arguments of $\mathcal{A}$, we can split all complete arguments from $Args(\mathcal{A})$ into three classes: justified arguments, overruled arguments or defensible arguments. An argument A is *justified* when A is in S. An argument A is *overruled* when A is attacked by at least one argument in S. Finally, an argument A is *defensible* when A is attacked by an argument $B \in Args(\mathcal{A})$, and neither A nor B are attacked by acceptable arguments.

Definition 18 (Justified, Overruled or Defensible Argument). *Let $\mathcal{A}$ be a MAS, $Args(\mathcal{A})$ be the set of available arguments of $\mathcal{A}$, $S \subseteq Args(\mathcal{A})$, and $F_{\mathcal{A}}^{p,o}$ be the characteristic function p o of $\mathcal{A}$ and over S. A complete p-argument for a literal L of an agent with identity α is:*

- *justified$_{\mathcal{A}}^{p,o}$ iff it is in $lfp(F_{\mathcal{A}}^{p,o})$*
- *overruled$_{\mathcal{A}}^{p,o}$ iff there exists a justified$_{\mathcal{A}}^{o,p}$ o-argument for a literal L' of an agent β in $\mathcal{A}$ attacking it*
- *defensible$_{\mathcal{A}}^{p,o}$ iff it is neither justified$_{\mathcal{A}}^{p,o}$ nor overruled$_{\mathcal{A}}^{p,o}$.*

We denote the $lfp(F_{\mathcal{A}}^{p,o})$ by $JustArgs_{\mathcal{A}}^{p,o}$.

Example 4. Let $\mathcal{A} = \{Ag_1, Ag_2, Ag_3\}$ such that each agent is

$$
\begin{aligned}
Ag_1 &= \; <1, \{\, a \leftarrow not\ b\,\}, \{1,2\}, \{1\}\} > \\
Ag_2 &= \; <2, \{\, b \leftarrow not\ c\}, \{2,3\}, \{2\} > \\
Ag_3 &= \; <3, \{\, c \leftarrow not\ a\,\}, \{2,3\}, \{3\}\} >
\end{aligned}
$$

In this example we show how to obtain $lfp(F_{\mathcal{A}}^{s,s}(\emptyset))$. First of all, we determine the set of strong local arguments of $\mathcal{A}$:

$$
LA^s(\mathcal{A}) = \left\{
\begin{array}{ll}
(1, []), & (1, [a \leftarrow not\ b]), \\
(2, []), & (2, [b \leftarrow not\ c]), \\
(3, []), & (3, [c \leftarrow not\ a])
\end{array}
\right\}
$$

and the set of available arguments of $\mathcal{A}$ given $LA^s(\mathcal{A})$, i.e $Args(\mathcal{A}) = LA^s(\mathcal{A})$

– let $S^0 = \emptyset$. Since $Atts^0 = \emptyset$, the set of opposing arguments is

$$Def^0 = Def_{s,s}(S^0) = \{(1,[a \leftarrow not\ b]),(2,[b \leftarrow not\ c]),(3,[c \leftarrow not\ a])\}$$

The set of proposed arguments is $Av(S^0) = LA^s(\mathcal{A})$. Then we determine the following attacks

opposing argument	proposed argument
$(2,[b \leftarrow not\ c])$	$(1,[a \leftarrow not\ b])$
$(3,[c \leftarrow not\ a])$	$(2,[b \leftarrow not\ c])$
	$(3,[c \leftarrow not\ a])$
	$(1,[]),(2,[]),(3,[])$

So $S^1 = F_{\mathcal{A}}^{s,s}(S^0) = \{(3,[c \leftarrow not\ a]),(1,[]),(2,[]),(3,[])\}$;
– since $Atts^1 = \{(3,[c \leftarrow not\ a])\}$,

$$Def^1 = Def_{s,s}(S^1) = \{(1,[a \leftarrow not\ b]),(3,[c \leftarrow not\ a])\}$$

The set of proposed arguments is $Av(S^1) = S^1$. Despite the opposing argument $A_2^s(b) = (2,[b \leftarrow not\ c])$ attacks the proposed argument $(1,[a \leftarrow not\ b])$, $A_2^s(b)$ is attacked by the acceptable argument $(3,[c \leftarrow not\ a])$, so

$$S^2 = F_{\mathcal{A}}^{s,s}(S^1) = S^1 \cup \{(1,[a \leftarrow not\ b])\}$$

– since $F_{\mathcal{A}}^{s,s}(S^2) = S^2$, the set of justified$_{\mathcal{A}}^{s,s}$ arguments is

$$JustArgs_{\mathcal{A}}^{s,s} = \{(3,[c \leftarrow not\ a]),(1,[a \leftarrow not\ b]),(1,[]),(2,[]),(3,[])\}.$$

Argument $(2,[b \leftarrow not\ c])$ is overruled$_{\mathcal{A}}^{s,s}$ because it is attacked by the justified$_{\mathcal{A}}^{s,s}$ argument $(3,[c \leftarrow not\ a])$. No argument in $Args(\mathcal{A})$ is defensible$_{\mathcal{A}}^{s,s}$.

3   Properties

Here we assume very little about the sets of argumentative and cooperative agents of an agent. By imposing restriction on these sets different properties of the whole setting can be obtained. In particular, as expected, if all agents in a multi-agent setting $\mathcal{A}$ argue and cooperate with all others, then the result is exactly the same as having a single agents with the whole knowledge:

Theorem 1. *Let $\mathcal{A}$ be a MAS over $\mathcal{L}$ and Ids such that for every agent $Ag \in \mathcal{A}$: $Cooperate_{Id(Ag)} = Ids$ and $Argue_{Id(Ag)} = Ids$, and $F_{\mathcal{A}}^{p,o}$ be the characteristic function p o of $\mathcal{A}$. Let $P = \{< \beta, Kb_\beta, \{\beta\}, \{\beta\} >\}$ such that*

$$Kb_\beta = \bigcup_{\alpha_i \in Ids} Kb_{\alpha_i}$$

and $F_P^{p,o}$ be the characteristic function p o of P.
   Then, for every agent $\alpha_i \in Ids$: $(\alpha_i, Seq) \in lfp(F_{\mathcal{A}}^{p,o})$ iff $(\beta, Seq) \in lfp(F_P^{p,o})$.

Corollary 1. *If $\mathcal{A}$ is as in Theorem 1 then for any pair of agents in $\mathcal{A}$, with identifiers α_i and α_j :, $(\alpha_i, Seq) \in lfp(F_{\mathcal{A}}^{p,o})$ iff $(\alpha_j, Seq) \in lfp(F_{\mathcal{A}}^{p,o})$.*

However, the semantics at one agent can different from that of the union, as desired:

Example 5. Consider $\mathcal{A} = \{Ag_1, Ag_2, Ag_3\}$ such that each agent is

$$Ag_1 = <1, \{\, a \leftarrow not\ b\, \}, \{1,2,3\}, \{1,2,3\}\} >$$
$$Ag_2 = <2, \{\, b \leftarrow not\ c\}, \{1,2,3\}, \{1,2,3\} >$$
$$Ag_3 = <3, \{\, c \leftarrow not\ a\, \}, \{1,2,3\}, \{1,2,3\}\} >$$

$Def_{s,s}(\emptyset) = \{(1, []), (2, []), (3, []), (1, [a \leftarrow not\ b]), (2, [a \leftarrow not\ b]), (3, [a \leftarrow not\ b]), (1, [b \leftarrow not\ c]), (2, [b \leftarrow not\ c]), (3, [b \leftarrow not\ c]), (1, [c \leftarrow not\ a]), (2, [c \leftarrow not\ a]), (3, [c \leftarrow not\ a])\}$. The arguments $A^s(a)$, $A^s(b)$, and $A^s(c)$ are attacked[5]. As there is no "counter-attack" to any of those attacks, $lfp(F_{\mathcal{A}}^{s,s}(\emptyset)) = JustArgs_{\mathcal{A}}^{s,s} = \emptyset$. No argument in $Args(\mathcal{A})$ is overruled$_{\mathcal{A}}^{s,s}$, and all of arguments are concluded to be defensible$_{\mathcal{A}}^{s,s}$. However, we obtain a different result if we consider that

$$Ag_1 = <1, \{\, a \leftarrow not\ b\, \}, \{1,2\}, \{1,2\}\} >$$
$$Ag_2 = <2, \{\, b \leftarrow not\ c\}, \{2,3\}, \{2,3\} >$$
$$Ag_3 = <3, \{\, c \leftarrow not\ a\, \}, \{3\}, \{3\}\} >$$

Here $Def_{s,s}(\emptyset) = \{(1, []), (2, []), (3, []), (1, [a \leftarrow not\ b]), (1, [b \leftarrow not\ c]), (1, [c \leftarrow not\ a]), (2, [b \leftarrow not\ c]), (2, [c \leftarrow not\ a]), (3, [c \leftarrow not\ a])\}$, and $lfp(F_{\mathcal{A}}^{s,s}(\emptyset)) = JustArgs_{\mathcal{A}}^{s,s} = \{A_2^s(c), A_3^s(c)\}$. Note here how the result differs also from agent to agent.

Due to space limitations we do not detail here general properties when some other weaker restriction are imposed (e.g. imposing transitivity, symmetry in the cooperation or argumentation set, etc). Instead, we discuss about some properties of $JustArgs_{\mathcal{A}}^{p,o}$ and comparisons. Since p (resp. o) denote the kind of a proposed (resp. an opposing) argument, i.e. strong argument or weak argument, assume that p (resp. o) in $\{s, w\}$. Both $JustArgs_{\mathcal{A}}^{w,w}$ and $JustArgs_{\mathcal{A}}^{w,s}$ are both conflict-free[6] and non-contradictory[7]. Thus, every argument in both $JustArgs_{\mathcal{A}}^{w,w}$ and $JustArgs_{\mathcal{A}}^{w,s}$ is non-contradictory, i.e. it is not related to a contradiction at all. Furthermore, $F_{\mathcal{A}}^{w,w}$ has more defensible arguments than $F_{\mathcal{A}}^{w,s}$. Therefore, we obtain a consistent way of reasoning in a multi-agent setting $\mathcal{A}$ if we apply $F_{\mathcal{A}}^{w,w}$ over $Args(\mathcal{A})$.

In contrast, $JustArgs_{\mathcal{A}}^{s,s}$ and $JustArgs_{\mathcal{A}}^{s,w}$ may be contradictory. However, to evaluate the acceptability of available arguments without considering the presence of *falsity* or both arguments for L and $\neg L$, the proposed arguments should be strong ones, and every opposing argument is a weak argument. Since $F_{\mathcal{A}}^{s,w}$ respects the 'Coherence

---

[5] For simplicity, since every agent argues with every other, we omit agent identity of the arguments.

[6] A set S of arguments is conflict-free if there is no argument in S attacking an argument in S.

[7] A set S of arguments is non-contradictory if neither an argument for *falsity* nor both arguments for L and $\neg L$ are in S.

Principle' of [9,1], i.e. given that every opposing argument is a weak one, it can be attacked by any proposed argument for its explicit negation. Therefore, we obtain a paraconsistent way of reasoning in a multi-agent setting $\mathcal{A}$ if we apply $F_{\mathcal{A}}^{s,w}$ over $Args(\mathcal{A})$. Moreover, a justified$_{\mathcal{A}}^{s,w}$ argument of an agent in $\mathcal{A}$ is related to a contradiction with respect to $JustArgs_{\mathcal{A}}^{s,w}$:

Definition 19 (Relation to a Contradiction). *Let $\mathcal{A}$ be a MAS, α and β be agents' identity in MAS, $\beta \in Argue_\alpha$, and $JustArgs_{\mathcal{A}}^{s,w}$ be the $lfp(F_{\mathcal{A}}^{s,w})$. A justified$_{\mathcal{A}}^{s,w}$ s-argument $A_\alpha^s(L) = (\alpha, Seq_L)$ is:*

- *contradictory$_{\mathcal{A}}^{s,w}$ if L is the symbol $\bot$, or there exists a justified$_{\mathcal{A}}^{s,w}$ s-argument $(\beta, Seq_\bot)$ such that $L \in DC(Seq_\bot)$, or there exists a justified$_{\mathcal{A}}^{s,w}$ s-argument $(\beta, Seq_{\neg L})$; or*
- *based-on-contradiction$_{\mathcal{A}}^{s,w}$ if $A_\alpha^s(L)$ is justified$_{\mathcal{A}}^{s,w}$, it does not exists a justified$_{\mathcal{A}}^{s,w}$ s-argument $(\beta, Seq_{\neg L})$ and $A_\alpha^s(L)$ is also overruled$_{\mathcal{A}}^{s,w}$; or*
- *non-contradictory$_{\mathcal{A}}^{s,w}$, otherwise.*

As already said, any agent's belief should be concluded only with respect to both sets of argumentative and cooperative agents with such an agent. Intuitively, we can conclude that different truth values of a given literal L over a multi-agent setting $\mathcal{A}$ might be obtained. It happens because it depends on which agent the literal L is inferred from, and also on what the specification of both sets of cooperative and argumentative agents is, given the overall agents in $\mathcal{A}$. Then, a truth value of an agent's conclusion in a (consistent or paraconsistent) way of reasoning is as follows:

Definition 20 (Truth Value of an Agent's Conclusion). *Let $\mathcal{A}$ be a MAS, α is an agent's identity of $\mathcal{A}$, $k \in \{s, w\}$, and L be an objective literal or the symbol $\bot$. L over $\mathcal{A}$ is:*

- *false$_\alpha^{k,w}$ iff for all argument of α for L: it is overruled$_{\mathcal{A}}^{k,w}$*
- *true$_\alpha^{k,w}$ iff there exists a justified$_{\mathcal{A}}^{k,w}$ argument of α for L. Moreover, L is*
  - *contradictory$_\alpha^{k,w}$ if L is the symbol $\bot$ or there exists a justified$_{\mathcal{A}}^{k,w}$ argument of α for $\neg L$*
  - *based-on-contradiction$_\alpha^{k,w}$ if it is both true$_\alpha^{k,w}$ and false$_\alpha^{k,w}$*
  - *non-contradictory$_\alpha^{k,w}$, otherwise.*
- *undefined$_\alpha^{k,w}$ iff L is neither true$_\alpha^{k,w}$ nor false$_\alpha^{k,w}$.*

Note that this point that truth is defined parametric of the agent. So, it is only natural that the truth value of a proposition may differ from agent to agent.

Proposition 4. *Let $k \in \{s, w\}$. L is undefined$_\alpha^{k,w}$ iff there is no justified$_{\mathcal{A}}^{k,w}$ argument of α for L and at least one argument of α for L is not overruled$_{\mathcal{A}}^{k,w}$.*

This paraconsistent semantics for multiple logic programs is in accordance with the paraconsistent well-founded semantics $WFSX_p$ [1]. In fact, both coincide if there is a single program (or a set, in case all cooperate and argue with all other, cf. Theorem 1):

Theorem 2 ($WFSX_p$ semantics vs $F_{\mathcal{A}}^{s,w}$). *Let P be an ELP such that $\bot \notin \mathcal{H}(P)$, and let L be an objective literal in $\mathcal{H}(P)$. $L \in WFSX_p(P)$ iff L is true$_{\mathcal{A}}^{s,w}$, not $L \in WFSX_p(P)$ iff L is false$_{\mathcal{A}}^{s,w}$, and $\{L, not\ L\} \cap WFSX_p(P) = \emptyset$ iff L is undefined$_{\mathcal{A}}^{s,w}$.*

Moreover, there is a relation between the consistent reasoning is obtained of $F_{\mathcal{A}}^{w,w}$ and [6]'s grounded (skeptical) extension if the following holds. To show this, we first relate [6]'s definitions of both *RAA-attack* and *g-attack* to our definition of *attack* as follows:

Lemma 1. *Let* P *be an ELP such that* $\perp \notin \mathcal{H}(P)$, (A_L, L) *be an argument for* L, $\{(A_L, L), (A_{L'}, L'), (A_{\neg L}, \neg L)\} \subseteq Args(P)$ *such that not* $L \in A_{L'}$, $\{1, 2, 3\}$ *is a subset of agent's identities of* $\mathcal{A}$, *and* $\{(1, Seq_L^w), (2, Seq_{L'}^w), (3, Seq_{\neg L}^w)\} \in Args(\mathcal{A})$ *such that not* $L \in Assump(Seq_{L'}^w)$.

If (A_L, L) *g-attacks* $(A_{L'}, L')$ *then* $(1, Seq_L^w)$ *attacks* $(2, Seq_L^w)$.

If $(A_{\neg L}, \neg L)$ *RAA-attacks* (A_L, L) *then* $(3, Seq_{\neg L}^w)$ *attacks* $(1, Seq_L^w)$.

Theorem 3 (Grounded extension vs $F_{\mathcal{A}}^{w,w}$). *Let* P *be an ELP such that* $\perp \notin \mathcal{H}(P)$, L *be an objective literal in* $\mathcal{H}(P)$, B *be the Ground Extension's characteristic function of* P, (A_L, L) *be an argument for* L, *and* α *be an agent's identity of* $\mathcal{A}$.

An argument $(A_L, L) \in lfp(B)$ *iff* $\exists(\alpha, Seq_L^w) \in lfp(F_{\mathcal{A}}^{w,w})$.

An argument $(\{not\ L\}, L) \in lfp(B)$ *iff* $\neg\exists(\alpha, Seq_L^w) \in gfp(F_{\mathcal{A}}^{w,w})$.

4 Illustrative Examples

To illustrate the results of the proposed semantics, we present here some examples. The first example illustrates how the framework can be used to model over a hierarchy and in the second to model evolving knowledge.

Example 6 (Business Process Management). This example is derived from ADEPT project[8] which developed negotiating agents for business process management. One such process deals with the provision of customer quotes for networks adapted to the customer's needs. The agents' interaction involves both argumentation and cooperation as follows: *customer service division* (CSD) must not quote if the customer is not credit-worthy which it should assume by default.

So, CSD should obtain an agreement with *vet customer* (VC) which means that VC may counter-argue and give evidence for the credit-worthiness of the customer. In case credit is approved, if CSD does not have a portfolio item for the solicited quote, it needs from *design department* (DD) a quote for it. DD might do this task if *surveyor department* (SD) does not argue that such a task is not important. DD needs information held by CSD.

Considering first the *customer service division*, it knows about the client's equipment (dubbed eq) and its requirements (dubbed req): requirements 2 and 3, and equipments 2 and 3. Furthermore, CSD knows the customer is important. These can be represented as facts: $req(2)$; $req(3)$; $eq(2)$; $eq(3)$; and $important$. Besides these facts about a particular client, CSD has general rules such as requirements 1, 2 and 3 together make up a portfolio and can be quoted if a previous quote exists (otherwise, the DD has to prepare a quote):

$$portofolio \leftarrow req(1), req(2), req(3)$$
$$quote \leftarrow portfolio, previousQuote$$

---

[8] See details in *http://lsdis.cs.uga.edu/Projects/*

CSD does not provide a quote if the client is not credit-worthy:

$$\neg quote \leftarrow not\ creditWorthy$$

The *Vet Customer* knows the client is not credit-worthy: it has a fact $\neg creditWorthy$. The *design department* knows that there is no need to survey the client site if the client has equipments 1, 2 and 3. It can be represented by the rule:

$$\neg need2survey \leftarrow eq(1), eq(2), eq(3)$$

In general, DD assumes that the SD does a survey unless it is busy which can be represented by the rule $survey \leftarrow not\ busySD$. The quote of DD can be obtained by a simple design cost if there was no need survey; otherwise, by a complex design cost:

$$quote \leftarrow \neg need2survey, simpleDesignCost$$
$$quote \leftarrow survey, complexDesigCost$$
$$simpleDesignCos$$
$$complexDesignCost$$

Finally, the knowledge of *Surveyor Department* is fairly simple: its domain is its own busyness and since it is lazy it derives that it is busy unless the customer is important

$$busySD \leftarrow not\ important$$

Since such a system must have consistent conclusions we illustrate the results in a weak-weak reasoning. The truth value of the main conclusions are as follows: $important$ is $true_{csd}^{w,w}$, $complexDesignCost$ and $survey$ are $true_{dd}^{w,w}$, $\neg creditWorthy$ is $true_{vc}^{w,w}$; $busySD$ is $false_{sd}^{w,w}$; both $quote$ and $\neg quote$ are $undefined_{csd}^{w,w}$.

Example 7. In this example we illustrate the usage of the proposed framework to reason about evolving knowledge bases. For it, each argumentative agent represents the knowledge (set of rules) added at a point of time. Moreover, each such agents can cooperate with all agents representing past states, and has to argue with all agents representing future states. Consider a concrete example taken from [2] where initially, in Ag_1:

$$sleep \leftarrow not\ tv\_on$$
$$tv\_on \leftarrow$$
$$watch\_tv \leftarrow tv\_on$$

It is easy to see that with this knowledge in Ag_1, there is a $justified_{\mathcal{A}}^{s,w}$ argument for $watch\_tv$ and that the only argument for $sleep$ is $overruled_{\mathcal{A}}^{s,w}$. The knowledge base is then updated, in Ag_2 by adding the rules:

$$\neg tv\_on \leftarrow power\_failure$$
$$power\_failure \leftarrow$$

The reader can check that, for Ag_2 the previous argument for $watch\_tv$ is now overruled, and that the argument for $sleep$ is $justified_{\mathcal{A}}^{s,w}$. Now if another update comes, e.g stating $\neg power\_failure$, in Ag_3 the argument for $sleep$ is again $overruled_{\mathcal{A}}^{s,w}$, and for $watch\_tv$ $justified_{\mathcal{A}}^{s,w}$, as expected. Note how, in this example, the cooperation is used to inherit rules from the past, and the argumentation to make sure that previous rules in conflict with later ones are overruled.

5 Conclusion and Further Work

We propose an argumentation-based negotiation for agent's knowledge bases. We define a declarative semantics for Argumentation-based Negotiation for a multi-agent setting (MAS). Moreover, every agent Ag in a MAS argues and cooperates with a subset of agents in the MAS, i.e. Ag has a set of argumentative agents and a set of cooperative agents. Then, the semantics for Argumentation-based Negotiation is composed by two interlaced processes, viz. argumentation and cooperation. The former imposes that every agent should argue with other agents to evaluate its knowledge. The latter allows an agent to handle its incomplete knowledge with 'help' of other agents. The Argumentation-based Negotiation proposal allows to model a multi-agent setting with different kinds of representation. Furthermore, any agent in a MAS can be queried regarding the truth value of a conclusion. Moreover, a truth value of an agent's belief depends on which agent such a belief is inferred, and also how is the specification of both sets of cooperative and argumentative agents given the overall agents in the MAS. Nevertheless, such answer is always consistent/paraconsistent with the knowledge base of such agents.

Besides the comparisons above, it is worth mentioning [8], which proposes a negotiation framework to be applied in a context of that an agent is a tuple, consisting of its arguments, its domains[9], and lists of its argumentation and cooperation partners. We differ from the authors when they said that an agent should be aware of its domains. A domain is understood by those authors as the set of predicates defining the agent's domain expertise. We assume that our agent has no explicit knowledge about the multi-agent setting domain but we restrict the agents communication by defining the sets of argumentative and cooperative agents. [13] follows the [8]'s specification of an agent. They propose an operational semantics for argumentation by assuming local and global ancestors to detected loop. However, it is not clear how they detected the global ancestor to prove the truth value of an objective literal L.

For the declarative semantics defined here, we have also defined an operational semantics, based on sets of dialogues trees, and an accompanying distributed implementation. The definition of this operational semantics and implementation is however outside the scope of this paper, and is part of a forthcoming one. Also part of ongoing and future work is the comparison of this approach with approaches for dealing with preferences and also with updates in the context of logics programs. It seems clear that the flexibility offered by the sets of cooperative and argumentative agents allows for giving priority to sets of rules over other sets of rules. This is somehow similar to what is done in preferences in the context of logics programs, and a comparison with these frameworks is in order. Also in order is a comparison with logic programming updates. Example 7 suggests how our framework can be used for modelling updates. In this example, the results coincide with those of [2], but a study on how general this equivalence is ongoing.

We also intend to introduce the capability of the agents to revise their knowledge as consequence of internal or external events. In case of no agreement in a negotiation process the agents would be able to discuss (or negotiate again) how and when they got their knowledge, and try to find a way to get an agreement.

---

[9] A set of predicate names defining the agent's domain expertise.

References

1. J. J. Alferes, C. V. Damásio, and L. M. Pereira. A logic programming system for non-monotonic reasoning. *Journal of Automated Reasoning*, 14(1):93–147, 1995.
2. J. J. Alferes, J. A. Leite, L. M. Pereira, H. Przymusinska, and T. C. Przymusinski. Dynamic updates of non-monotonic knowledge bases. *The Journal of Logic Programming*, 45(1–3):43–70, September/October 2000.
3. A. Bondarenko, P. M. Dung, R. Kowalski, and F. Toni. An abstract, argumentation-theoretic approach to default reasoning. *Journal of Artificial Intelligence*, 93(1–2):63–101, 1997.
4. L. M. Pereira e M. Schroeder C. V. Damásio. Revise: Logic programming and diagnosis. In U. Furbach J. Dix and A. Nerode, editors, *4th International Conference (LPNMR'97)*, volume LNAI 1265 of *Logic Programming and NonMonotonic Reasoning*, pages 353–362. Springer, July 1997.
5. Iara de Almeida Móra and José Júlio Alferes. Argumentative and cooperative multi-agent system for extended logic programs. In F. M. Oliveira, editor, *XIVth Brazilian Symposium on Artificial Intelligence*, volume 1515 of *LNAI*, pages 161–170. Springer, 1998.
6. P. M. Dung. On the acceptability of arguments and its fundamental role in nonmonotonic reasoning, logic programming and n-person games. *Journal of Artificial Intelligence*, 77(2):321–357, 1995.
7. M. Gelfond and V. Lifschitz. Logic programs with classical negation. In Warren and Szeredi, editors, *7th International Conference on LP (ICLP)*, pages 579–597. MIT Press, 1990.
8. S. Parsons, C. Sierra, and N. R. Jennings. Agents that reason and negotiate by arguing. *Journal of Logic and Computational*, 8(8):261–292, 1998.
9. L. M. Pereira and J. J. Alferes. Well founded semantics for logic programs with explicit negation. In *European Conference on Artificial Intelligence (ECAI)*, pages 102–106. John Wiley & Sons, 1992.
10. J. L. Pollock. Defeasible reasoning with variable degrees of justification. *Journal of Artificial Intelligence*, 133:233–282, 2002.
11. H. Prakken and G. Sartor. Argument-based extended logic programming with defeasible priorities. *Journal of Applied Non-Classical Logics*, 7:25–75, 1997.
12. H. Prakken and G. A. W. Vreeswijk. *Handbook of Philosophical Logic*, volume 4, chapter Logics for Defeasible Argumentation, pages 218–319. Kluwer Academic, 2 edition, 2002.
13. M. Schroeder and R. Schweimeier. Arguments and misunderstandings: Fuzzy unification for negotiating agents. *Journal of Computational Logic in Multi-Agent Systems*, 93:1–18, August 2002.
14. Michael Schroeder, Iara de Almeida Móra, and J. J. José Júlio Alferes. Vivid agents arguing about distributed extended logic programs. In Ernesto Costa and Amilcar Cardoso, editors, *Progress in Artificial Intelligence, 8th Portuguese Conference on Artificial Intelligence (EPIA)*, volume 1323 of *LNAI*, pages 217–228. Springer, 1997.
15. R. Schweimeier and M. Schroeder. Notions of attack and justified arguments for extended logic programs. In F. van Harmelen, editor, *15th European Conference on Artificial Intelligence*. IOS Press, 2002.
16. G. A. W. Vreeswijk. Abstract argumentation systems. *Journal of Artificial Intelligence*, 90(1–2):225–279, 1997.

Belief Updating by Communication Channel

Shingo Hagiwara, Mikito Kobayashi, and Satoshi Tojo

School of Information and Science, Japan Advanced Institute of
Science and Technology,
1–1 Asahidai, Nomi, Ishikawa 923-1292, Japan
{s-hagiwa,m-kobaya,tojo}@jaist.ac.jp

Abstract. In this paper, we introduce the notion of communication channel into a multiagent system. We formalize the system in term of logic with Belief modality, where each possible world includes CTL. We represent the channel by a reserved set of propositional variables. With this, we revise the definition of *inform* of FIPA; if the channel exists the receiver agent surely learns the information whereas if not the action fails. According to this distinction, the current state in each world would diverge into two different states. We have implemented a prover, that works also as a model builder. Given a formula in a state in a possible world, the system proves whether it holds or not, while if an *inform* action is initiated the system adds new states with branching paths.

1 Introduction

There have been many logical approaches to multi agent systems. Among them, BDI logic (*Belief, Desire* and *Intention*) together with *CTL* (Computational Tree Logic) has often been employed [1, 2, 3, 4, 5, 6], as its semantics seems useful to represent the changes of knowledge state of each agent.

However in this framework, the formalization of communicability has rather been neglected although the communication seems one of the most important issues of multi agent systems. Van Eijk [7] discussed this issue, but the study still lacks a sound formalization such as axiomatization or proper semantics.

On the other hand, the issue on communication has been well .studied outside the BDI/CTL logic [8, 9, 10]. Especially, ACL (Agent communication Language) of FIPA (Foundation for Intelligent Physical Agents) is important, where *inform* is defined as an action of Dynamic Logic and an agent must satisfy several prerequisites to transfer knowledge to others.

In this paper, we will introduce the notion of *communication channel* to represent communicability formally. With this, we will incorporate the *inform* action of FIPA into BDI/CTL logic. According to the dynamic change of knowledge state of each agent, we need to discuss how the semantics is updated for each *inform* action. We will show the actual procedure, presenting the implementation.

This paper consists of the following sections. In Section 2, we explain how the communication channel is defined, mentioning why it is not a modal operator but a kind of proposition. In Section 3, we propose a formalization in

K. Inoue, K. Satoh, and F. Toni (Eds.): CLIMA VII, LNAI 4371, pp. 211–225, 2007.
© Springer-Verlag Berlin Heidelberg 2007

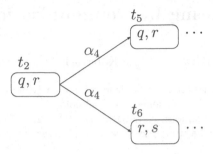

Fig. 1. A branching temporal structure

$B_{CTL/C}$, where we define the syntax and the Kripke semantics, in which we would also suggest how we should update a model, when the inform action is performed. In Section 5, we explain our implementation. In the final section, we discuss some problems of our theory and summarize our contribution of this paper.

2   Communicability and Agent Action

In this section, we discuss an agent action and its execution, and how to formalize communicability.

2.1   An Effect of a Communication Channel on an Agent Action

We regard that an agent can choose only one of those actions available at a given time, because we hypothesize that the agent is a *Rational Agent*[11]. Therefore, she deliberately evaluates a precondition to perform an action and performs it only if the precondition is satisfied.

According to Wooldridge, "the *transitions between states* are *labeled* with actions." However, the result of an action may not be unique; as in Fig.1 the states of t_5 and t_6 show the results of the action. He has explained that "from state t_2, the agent has no choice about what action to perform – it must perform α_4, and either state t_5 or state t_6 will result." This implies that multiple different results may accompany an action.

Accordingly, an agent first recognizes the feasible actions, and then, selects one action from among them, which immediately is executed. As the action may possibly cause multiple results, multiple state transitions occur. When an agent executes a sequence of actions, because of differing results, the state transitions may diverge. Namely, between the belief of an agent and the real situation, the branching structure of the state transitions may become different. We regard that one of the causes of such divergence could be reduced by the existence of the communication channel. For example, let us assume a situation that an agent sends packets to a receiver, via the Internet. As far as the operation has no trouble, the receiver surely would receive them. However, if some router *en route* fails, the operation may not be completed; even worse, the sender may not know whether the packets were successfully received.

Then, instead of the formalization of success/failure in communication, we propose the notion of a secure *communication channel*.

2.2   Why Is Communication Channel Defined as a Proposition?

In this study, we will integrate the communication channel into FIPA's definition, which consists of *Feasibility Precondition* (FP) and *Rational Effect* (RE). FP consists of the preconditions (i.e. one or more propositions) which need to be satisfied before an agent can execute an action, and RE indicates the effects of the action.

Conceivably, there are many choices as to how to formalize a communication channel; (i) a predicate of first order logic, (ii) a modal operator, (iii) a Cartesian product of two agents, and (iv) a proposition. Here, we discuss the pros and cons of each choice.

First, (i) the simplest method may be a predicate of FOL, where a channel predicate has two arguments of indices of the sender and the receiver agents, as $channel(i, j)$. Though this representation seems appropriate at first glance, this method requires the reform of all definitions of FIPA. Also, in this case, the universe of a model must be multiply sorted into a set of individuals and a set of agent indices. If so, we also need to provide quantifiers ($\forall, \exists$) with sort declarations. Thus, we have judged that these issues would reduce the strictness of the preceding theories.

Next, (ii) we have considered regarding the channel as a modality, as $C_{ij}\varphi$, which means that φ could be possibly informed from agent i to j. However, in this case, we should attach the operator C_{ij} to all the propositions to be transferred. In addition, when n agents are given, n^2 operators would be required, which unnecessarily complicates the logic. Moreover, in this case, an agent cannot *inform* the channel itself as a unit of knowledge. The last issue also negates (iii) the formalization by Cartesian product.

The final option, (iv) the formalization by a proposition, has its own problem. Let c_{ij} be a proposition that is the channel from the agent i to j. If c_{ij} is a propositional variable, it could own its truth value regardless of the indices i and j. If the truth value does not concern i nor j, c_{ij} cannot represent the channel between i and j. On the other hand, if we assume that c_{ij} is a propositional constant, then n^2 constants, besides $\top$ and $\bot$, could be assigned to any propositional variables. All things considered, we would like to stick to this final option, as we would like to treat the channel itself as a payload of the *inform* action, defining a reserved set of channel variables. Moreover, since this method is not incompatible with the logic used in action definitions, the logic can be used with a slight modification, that is, the original distinction of propositional variables/constants of FOL becomes three categories; propositional variables, channel variables, and constants.

3 Logic of Branching Time and Epistemic State with Communication Channel

In this section, we introduce a temporal epistemic logic system $B_{CTL/C}$ based on CTL to reason agent's epistemic states on communications. In the logic, an agent's epistemic state is possibly modified by one time step per communication. Generally, when we consider a multiagent model, it is appropriate to include the branching time.

We summarize the formal definition of syntax and semantics of our logic of $B_{CTL/C}$, in the following sections. The objective of the logic is to embed the notion of communication channel into the preceding logical framework of Rao [3, 4], i.e., BDI–CTL. However, as the first step to such integration, we restrict available modal operators only to B (belief) now. Further developments will be discussed in the Conclusion.

3.1 Syntax of $B_{CTL/C}$

All temporal operators are formed by a pair of $(A,\ E)$ and $(F,X,$ etc...$)$.

Definition 1. *(Signature) The language L consists of the following vocabulary*

P	*a set of propositional variables*
Agent	*a set of agents*
C	*a set of communication channel variables, where $C \subseteq Agent \times Agent$*

In addition, the symbols are used as follows:

$\neg, \vee$	*the logical connectives*
$AX, AF, AG,$	*the propositional temporal operators*
B_α	*the propositional epistemic operators, where $\alpha \in Agent$*

Moreover, we define a formula as follows.

Definition 2. *Formula*
Let α be a propositional variable($\alpha \in P$), and c_{ij} be a communication channel variable($c_{ij} \in C$ and $i,j \in Agent$). Then, α, c_{ij} are formulae. Let φ, ψ be formulae. Then, $B_i\varphi$, $AX\varphi$, $AF\varphi$, $AG\varphi$, $EX\varphi$, $EF\varphi$, $EG\varphi$, $\neg\varphi$ and $\varphi \vee \psi$ are formulae.

Finally, we define the abbreviated notations as follows:

$$\varphi \wedge \psi \equiv \neg(\neg\varphi \vee \neg\psi) \quad \varphi \supset \psi \equiv \neg\varphi \vee \psi$$
$$EX\varphi \equiv \neg AX\neg\varphi \qquad EF\varphi \equiv \neg AG\neg\varphi$$
$$EG\varphi \equiv \neg AF\neg\varphi$$

3.2 Semantics of $B_{CTL/C}$

Kripke semantics of $B_{CTL/C}$ is based on Rao's BDI_{CTL}[4, 3], though his model includes epistemic operators D and I which we have omitted.

A Kripke structure $B_{CTL/C}$ is defined as follows:

$$M = \langle W, \{T_w : w \in W\}, \{R_w : w \in W\}, \{B_i : i \in Agent\}, V, C\rangle$$

Here, W is a set of possible worlds, T_w is a set of states for each $w \in W$, R_w is a binary relation ($R_w \subseteq T_w \times T_w$, however seriality is not guaranteed in our model), v is a truth assignment to the primitive proposition, and c is a truth assignment to the communication channel variables. Moreover, B_α is a set of accessibility relations($B_\alpha \subseteq W \times T_w \times W$, e.g. $(w, t, w') \in B_\alpha$), where α is an agent index. Here, if $(w, t, w') \in B_i$ and $t \in T_w$, then $t \in T_{w'}$, i.e. $T_w \subseteq T_{w'}$. The accessibility relation B_i must satisfy the axiom KD45 [1].

A satisfaction relation $\vDash$ is given as follows, where $(w_k, t_l) \vDash \varphi$ means that φ holds at t_l in w_k, for possible world w_k and state t_l. Besides, $Path$ denotes a set of paths in a possible world and $p[i]$ denotes the ith element of p from t, respectively.

$$
\begin{aligned}
(w, t) &\vDash \varphi & &\Longleftrightarrow v(w, t, \varphi) \in V \\
(w, t) &\vDash c_{ij} & &\Longleftrightarrow c(w, t, c_{ij}) \in C, \text{ where } i \text{ and } j \text{ are indices of agents} \\
(w, t) &\vDash \neg\varphi & &\Longleftrightarrow (w, t) \nvDash \varphi \\
(w, t) &\vDash \varphi \vee \psi & &\Longleftrightarrow (w, t) \vDash \varphi \text{ or } (w, t) \vDash \psi \\
(w, t) &\vDash B_j\varphi & &\Longleftrightarrow \forall w'' \in \{w'|(w, t, w') \in B_j\}, (w'', t) \vDash \varphi \\
(w, t) &\vDash AX\varphi & &\Longleftrightarrow \forall p \in Path, (w, p[1]) \vDash \varphi \\
(w, t) &\vDash AF\varphi & &\Longleftrightarrow \forall p \in Path, \exists i \geq 0, (w, p[i]) \vDash \varphi \\
(w, t) &\vDash AG\varphi & &\Longleftrightarrow \forall p \in Path, \forall i \geq 0, (w, p[i]) \vDash \varphi
\end{aligned}
$$

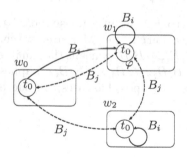

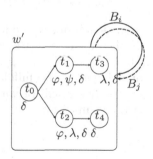

Fig. 2. An example of the operator B

Fig. 3. An example of temporal operators

Example 1. Fig.2 is an example of the operator B. In Fig.2, $(w_0, t_0) \vDash B_i\varphi$, $(w_2, t_0) \nvDash B_i\varphi$ and $(w_0, t_0) \vDash B_j\neg B_i\varphi$. Namely, 'B' is equivalent to the operator

---

[1] For the operator B and an arbitrary formula φ, the following axioms hold.
K : $B(\varphi \supset \psi) \supset (B\varphi \supset B\psi)$, **D** : $B\varphi \supset \neg B\neg\varphi$ (seriality), **4** : $B\varphi \supset BB\varphi$ (transitivity) and **5** : $\neg B\neg\varphi \supset B\neg B\neg\varphi$ (Euclidean).

'□' on the accessibility relations. Moreover, in Fig.3, belief-accessibility relations exist in all of the states in w'. In the figure, $(w', t_0) \vDash AX\varphi$, $(w', t_0) \vDash EX\psi$, $(w', t_0) \vDash AF\lambda$, $(w', t_0) \vDash AG\delta$, and $(w', t_0) \vDash AXB_i\varphi$.

4 *Inform* Action

In this section, we revise FIPA's *inform* action to introduce the communicability. The original definition of *inform* of FIPA[12, 8] is as follows.

Definition 3. *FIPA Inform Act*
$\langle i, inform(j, \varphi) \rangle$

>   *feasibility pre-condition* $: B_i\varphi \wedge \neg B_i(Bif_j\varphi \vee Uif_j\varphi)$
>   *rational effect* $: B_j\varphi$

A formula $B_j\varphi$ means that an agent j believes φ, and a formula $U_j\varphi$ means that an agent j is uncertain about φ, but that the agent supposes that φ is more likely than $\neg\varphi$. Also, $Bif_j\varphi$ and $Uif_j\varphi$ are the abbreviations of $B_j\varphi \vee B_j\neg\varphi$ and $U_j\varphi \vee U_j\neg\varphi$, respectively.

First, we exclude the epistemic operator U from the FIPA's definition, because U has not been strictly formalized in terms of logic. Then, we revise the *inform* action as follows.

Definition 4. *inform Act (Revised)*
$\langle i, inform(j, \varphi) \rangle$

>   *feasibility pre-condition* $: B_i\varphi \wedge \neg B_i(Bif_j\varphi) \wedge B_i c_{ij}$
>   *rational effect* $: (B_iB_j\varphi)$ or $(B_iB_j\varphi \wedge B_j\varphi \wedge B_jB_i\varphi)$

In the revised definition, we added $B_i c_{ij}$ to FP because we supposed that a sender agent should recognize the communication channel. Moreover, we changed FIPA's RE to $(B_iB_j\varphi)$ or $(B_iB_j\varphi \wedge B_j\varphi \wedge B_jB_i\varphi)$. $B_iB_j\varphi$ means that an intended transfer could hopefully be fulfilled, and $B_iB_j\varphi \wedge B_j\varphi \wedge B_jB_i\varphi$ implies that knowledge actually arrived. Because of these two possible cases, the succeeding states bifurcate as in Fig.4.

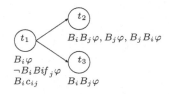

Fig. 4. An example of branching

With regard to B_i-accessibility, we also need to bifurcate states in w_1 to synchronize time as in the right-hand side of Fig.5. If we add states only in w_0, as in the left-hand side of Fig.5, B_i has an accessibility from (w_0, t_1) both to (w_1, t_2) and to (w_1, t_1). In this case, B_i include a relation from (w_0, t_1) to (w_1, t_2), and then B_i must be in $W \times T_w \times T_w \times W$, viz, this violates the definition of $B_i \subseteq W \times T_w \times W$.

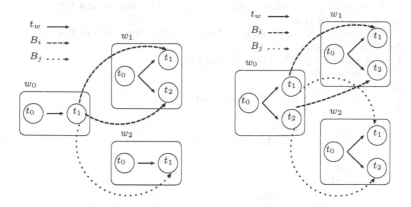

Fig. 5. State bifurcation in $B_{CTL/C}$

Therefore, with using the revised *inform* action, failure and success of the action are represented by states bifurcation which is caused by the communication channel C_{ij}.

5   A Model-Updating System for $B_{CTL/C}$

In this section, we explain the model-updating system of $B_{CTL/C}$, implemented in **SWI-Prolog** [13]. We show that the model-building system evaluates the truth values of logical formulae. Also, it works as a model builder, adding new epistemic states in each world.

5.1   Proof Procedure

First, we give the procedure $prove(w, t, \varphi)$ which proves φ in the given state t and in the possible world w. It returns the result as to whether $(w, t) \models \varphi$ holds or not.

Let W be a set of worlds, T_w a set of states, R_w the relations among states, v truth assignment of propositional variables, c truth assignment of communication channel variables, B_α (α is an index of an agent) a set of belief accessible relations, respectively. Then $w \in W$, $t \in T_w$. In addition, ψ and χ are sub-formulae of φ. The sequence of the procedure is in Algorithm 1.

In this algorithm, each rule just resolves φ into sub-formulae ψ and χ with some operators. Moreover, in a cycle on B_i and R_w, our program does not check nodes which have been checked once already. Therefore, the algorithm halts.

```
input  : w, t, φ
output: YES or NO
prove(w, t, φ)
begin
    if φ ≡ ψ ∧ χ then
    |   if prove(w, t, ψ) =YES and prove(w, t, χ) =YES then  return YES;
    else if φ ≡ ψ ∨ χ then
    |   if prove(w, t, ψ) =YES and prove(w, t, χ) =YES then  return YES;
    else if φ ≡ ¬ψ then
    |   if prove(w, t, ψ) =YES then  return NO;
    |   else  return YES;
    else if φ ≡ ψ ⊃ χ then
    |   if prove(w, t, ¬ψ ∨ χ) =YES then  return YES;
    else if φ ≡ AXψ then
    |   forall (t, w, t') ∈ T_w do
    |   |   if prove(w, t', ψ) =NO then  return NO;
    |   end
    |   return YES;
    else if φ ≡ AGψ then
    |   if prove(w, t, ψ) =YES then
    |   |   T' = {t'|t' is reachable from t with transitivity , t' ∈ T_w};
    |   |   forall t' ∈ T' do
    |   |   |   if prove(w, t', ψ) =NO then  return NO;
    |   |   end
    |   |   return YES;
    |   end
    else if φ ≡ AFψ then
    |   if prove(w, t, ψ) =YES then
    |   |   return YES
    |   else
    |   |   forall (t, w, t') ∈ T_w do
    |   |   |   if prove(w, t', AFψ) =NO then  return NO;
    |   |   end
    |   end
    else if φ ≡ EXψ then
    |   if prove(w, t, ¬AX¬ψ) =YES then  return YES;
    else if φ ≡ EGψ then
    |   if prove(w, t, ¬AF¬ψ) =YES then  return YES;
    else if φ ≡ EFψ then
    |   if prove(w, t, ¬AG¬ψ) =YES then  return YES;
    else if φ ≡ B_iψ then
    |   forall (w, t, w') ∈ B_i do
    |   |   if prove(w', t, ψ) =NO then  return NO;
    |   end
    |   return YES;
    else
    |   if (w, t, φ) ∈ V or (w, t, φ) ∈ C then  return YES;
    end
    return NO;
end
```

Algorithm 1. $prove(w, t, φ)$

5.2   Procedure of Model-Updating

Here, we give the algorithm of the *inform* action as follows. However, in this implementation, φ is restricted to a propositional variable or a communication channel variable, because φ possibly has temporal operators. If φ has temporal operators, then we need to consider additional states which are beyond the next time step in updating the model. Moreover, for $F\varphi$, we cannot determine the state in which φ holds.

Let W be a set of worlds, T_w a set of states, R_w the relations among states, v truth assignment of propositional variables, c truth assignment of communication channel variables, *Agent* a set of indices of agents, and B a set of belief accessible relations, respectively. Also, let FP be our feasible pre-condition formula $B_i\varphi \wedge \neg B_i Bif_j\varphi \wedge B_i c_{ij}$. Then $w \in W$, $t \in T_w$ and $i, j \in Agent$. The procedure is shown in Algorithm 2.

---

input : w, t, i, j, φ
output: $M' = \langle W, T'_w, R'_w, \{B'_i : i \in Agent\}, V', C' \rangle$
$inform(w, t, i, j, \varphi)$
begin
   if $(w, t) \models B_i\varphi \wedge \neg B_i Bif_j\varphi \wedge B_i c_{ij}$ **then**
      forall $w' \in W$ **do**
         $T'_{w'} = T_{w'} \cup \{t', t''\}$;
         $R'_{w'} = R_{w'} \cup \{tR_{w't'}, tR_{w't''}\}$;
      end
      forall $k \in Agent$ **do**
         $B'_k = B_k \cup \{(w, t', w'), (w, t'', w')|(w, t, w') \in B_k\}$
      end
      $W^1 = \{w''|(w, t, w') \in B_i, (w', t, w'') \in B_j\}$;
      $W^2 = \{w'|(w, t, w') \in B_j\}$;
      $W^3 = \{w''|(w, t, w') \in B_j, (w', t, w'') \in B_i\}$;
      if φ *is a proposition* **then**
         $V_1 = \{v(w, t', \varphi), v(w, t'', \varphi)|w \in W^1\}$;
         $V_2 = \{v(w, t', \varphi)|w \in W^2 \cup W^3\}$;
      else
         $C_1 = \{c(w, t', \varphi), c(w, t'', \varphi)|w \in W^1\}$;
         $C_2 = \{c(w, t', \varphi)|w \in W^2 \cup W^3\}$
      end
      $V' = V \cup V_1 \cup V_2$;
      $C' = C \cup C_1 \cup C_2$;
   end
end

Algorithm 2. $inform(w, t, i, j, \varphi)$

This procedure first tries to prove FP as follows.

$? - \mathtt{prove(world, state,} B_i\varphi \wedge \neg B_i(B_j\varphi \vee B_j\neg\varphi) \wedge B_i c_{ij})$

This query evaluates whether the agent i can select (execute) the action. If the result is 'YES', then the system adds two new states, each of which represents a new state dependent on whether knowledge was transferred or not, as in Fig.6 and Fig.7. Then, R_w and B_i for all $i \in Agent$ are copied from t, and new relations on t' and t'' are added. Finally, $B_i B_j \varphi$, $B_j \varphi$ and $B_j B_i \varphi$ are asserted in t', and $B_i B_j \varphi$ is asserted in t''.

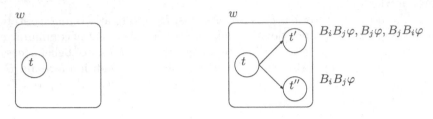

Fig. 6. before the *inform* action   **Fig. 7.** after the *inform* action

Note that t' is the case in which the communication channel exists, whereas in case t'' the channel does not, as shown in Fig.7.

Our model-building system ensures that two new states are added to the current state, although c_{ij} (let i and j be indices of a sender agent and a receiver, respectively) holds in the state from which the action is performed, because c_{ij} is headed by B_i; in our model-building system, a proposition without an epistemic operator is meaningless.

5.3   An Execution Example

We assume a situation where three computers, a sender, a receiver and DNS (Domain Name Server) exist. Here, we show an example of an *inform* action, where indices of s, r and d mean *sender, receiver* and *dns* in this description, and '##', '&&', '=>' and '~' mean $\vee$, $\wedge$, $\supset$ and $\neg$, respectively and 'bel(i, p)' means $B_i p$ in each execution log.

First, the sender tries to send the packet p. However, the sender does not believe in the communication channel from the sender to the receiver, and thus, the action fails (FP is not satisfied). Next, the DNS informs the sender of the existence of the channel. Hence, the sender could inform the receiver of p. Then, only t_1 exists in each world in the initial model shown in Fig.8.

We show some computer screens for examples. When the model-building system reads the file of the model definition, it compiles the definition to the interim data, and checks whether the accessible relations of belief in the model satisfy **KD45**. If the system finds errors, then it outputs the error relations and fixes them automatically. The model-building system could not choose an appropriate serial access because it could not decide the accessibility relation which is defined by '◇' automatically. We intentionally use an incomplete model which does not have belief accessibility relations from w_5 to w_5 and from w_{17} to w_{16}, as shown below.

```
?- model_checking(dns).
Agent = agent(sender) : State = state(1)
axiom D is not satisfied on
 [world(5), world(17)]
axiom 4 OK
axiom 5 is not satisfied on
 [world(14), world(16)]
add relation in AXIOM 4
add relation in AXIOM 5
SYSTEM >data(dns, relation(belief, agent(sender),
    node(state, world(17), state(1)),
    node(state, world(17), state(1))))
SYSTEM >data(dns, relation(belief, agent(sender),
    node(state, world(16), state(1)),
    node(state, world(16), state(1))))
Agent = agent(dns) : State = state(1)
axiom D OK
axiom 4 OK
axiom 5 OK
Agent = agent(receiver) : State = state(1)
axiom D OK
axiom 4 OK
axiom 5 OK
Yes
```

Next, we check the receiver's knowledge about whether she knows p or not as follows.

```
?- prove(world(1),state(1),bel(receiver,p)).
NO
```

In the state t_1 in the world w_1, she does not know p.

Then, we show the *inform* action; the sender agent tries to inform the receiver of p.

```
?- inform(world(1),state(1),sender,receiver,p).
SYSTEM >knowledge is atom, ok
SYSTEM >INFORM: CANNNOT EXECUTE!
YES
```

Since the sender does not believe in a channel from the sender to the receiver, this action fails. Next, DNS informs the sender of the existence of the channel.

```
?- inform(world(1),state(1),dns,sender,channel(sender,receiver)).
SYSTEM >knowledge is atom, ok
SYSTEM >FP bel(dns, channel(sender, receiver))&&
        ~bel(dns, bel(sender, ~channel(sender, receiver))
        ##bel(sender, channel(sender, receiver)))&&
        bel(dns, channel(dns, sender)) is satisfied
SYSTEM >INFORM: AGENT dns -[channel(sender, receiver)]
        -> AGENT sender
```

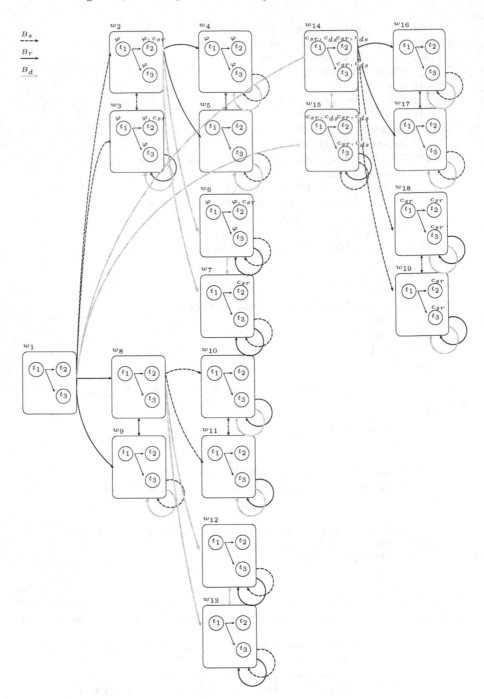

Fig. 8. A model for Example of Section 5.3, after the *inform* action

```
SYSTEM >Effect: bel(dns, bel(sender, channel(sender, receiver)))
SYSTEM >Effect: bel(sender, channel(sender, receiver))
SYSTEM >Effect: bel(sender, bel(dns, channel(sender, receiver)))
Yes
```

Since the *dns* agent believes in the channels from the *dns* to the sender and from the sender to the receiver, the action succeeds. Thus, the states t_2 and t_3 are added to all the worlds, and c_{sr} is added to the state t_2 in the worlds $w_2, w_3, w_6, w_7, w_{19}$ and t_3 in w_{19} in the model of Fig.8. Then, the *dns* agent comes to believe in $B_d B_s c_{sr}$ in the state t_2 and t_3, and the sender comes to believe in $B_s c_{sr}$ and $B_s B_d c_{sr}$ in t_2 in w_1. Therefore, t_2 indicates that the communication channel actually exists, and t_3 means that it does not. If the channel actually exists in the state t_1 in the world w_1, then the model-building system can erase t_3, though we have not implemented the erasing function yet. In future, we are going to revise it so as to prune branches, given the actual data of channels.

Next, the sender retries to inform the receiver of p, as follows.

```
?- inform(world(1),state(2),sender,receiver,p).
SYSTEM >knowledge is atom, ok
SYSTEM >FP bel(sender, p)&& ~bel(sender, bel(receiver, ~p)
  ##bel(receiver, p))&&bel(sender, channel(sender, receiver))
          is satisfied
SYSTEM >INFORM: AGENT sender -[p]-> AGENT receiver
SYSTEM >Effect: bel(sender, bel(receiver, p))
SYSTEM >Effect: bel(receiver, p)
SYSTEM >Effect: bel(receiver, bel(sender, p))
Yes
```

Here, the action succeeds. Then, the states t_4 and t_5 which are accessible from t_2 are added in a similar way to the above action (*ex facto*, t_6 and t_7 also need to be added to t_3; however, in t_3, since c_{sr} was not recognized by the sender agent, we do not need to consider it), and p is added to t_4 in w_5, w_8, w_9, w_{10} and w_{11}, and to t_5 in w_5. Then, $B_s B_r p$ holds in t_4 and t_5 in w_1, and $B_r p$ and $B_r B_s p$ hold in t_4 in w_1.

Finally, we check the receiver's knowledge as follows:

```
?- prove(world(1),state(4),bel(receiver,p)).
Yes
?- prove(world(1),state(1),'EF' bel(receiver,p)).
Yes
```

Therefore, we could confirm that she came to believe p on t_5 in w_1, and this means that communication channels exist on both transitions from t_1 to t_3 and from t_3 to t_5 in w_1.

6   Conclusion

In this paper, we introduced the notion of *communication channel* in BDI–CTL logic, and revised the definition of the *inform* action. We have developed an implementation that proves whether a given formula belongs to $B_{CTL/C}$ or not in a given model. Also, performing the *inform* action, the system updates the model by adding new states and new transitions.

In order to improve the definition of *inform*, we changed the contents of FP and RE. In FP, we introduced the recognition of communication channel $B_i c_{ij}$, and thus the agent could perform actions based on that. In RE, we provided the recognition of $B_i B_j \varphi$ and $B_j B_i \varphi$ for agents; these represent the cognitive states of the agents after communication. RE was denoted by $(B_i B_j \varphi)$, *or* $(B_i B_j \wedge B_j \varphi \wedge B_j B_i \varphi)$; the '*or*' implies that either the channel exists or not. These post-conditions are similar to the operator '$\oplus$' of Wooldridge[14], though our operation is independent of any specific computer system.

As for the formalization of the communication channel, we employed the method of *channel propositional variables*. Thus, we could transfer the channel itself as a piece of knowledge to other agents.

By the way, the *inform* action in the current system can inform only an atomic formula. Otherwise, an agent could inform another agent of $\neg B \varphi \wedge \varphi$, and if $\neg B_j \varphi \wedge \varphi$ was informed from agent i to j then j would believe $B_j (\neg B_j \varphi \wedge \varphi)$; a contradiction. However, since it is meaningless that the agent i informs $B_j \varphi$ to the agent j, we should prohibit such an action.

Because our implementation is to reify our theory and still remains as an experimental system, we could not examine the efficiency. We need to consider an efficient algorithm toward a practical system.

As future work, we need to include the epistemic operators of *Intention* and *Desire* into the logic, for an agent to initiate the *inform* action. With the intention modality, we may be able to represent autonomous communication in agents. Thus far, we have only treated the *inform* action. According to the FIPA, there are many actions in the multiagent system. Among them, we especially need to implement the *request* action. Together with *inform* and *request*, we will be able to represent the *confirm* action where agents can conceive the existence of communication channels between them.

References

[1] A. E. Emerson, J. Srinivasan: Linear time, branching time and partial order in logics and models for concurrency. In J. W. de Bakker, W. P. de Roever, Rozenberg, G., eds.: Branching time temporal logic. (1989) 123–172

[2] A. E. Emerson, J. Y. Halpern: Decision procedures and expressiveness in the temporal logic of branching time. In: Proceedings of the 14th Annual ACM Symposium. (1982) 169–180

[3] A. S. Rao, M. P. Gergeff: Modeling rational agents within a bdi-architecture. In: Proceeding of International Conference on Principles of Knowledge Representation and Reasoning. (1991)

[4] A. S. Rao, M. P. Gergeff: Decision procedures for bdi logics. Journal of Logic and Computation 9(3) (1998) 293–342

[5] A. S. Rao, M. P. Georgeff: BDI-agents: from theory to practice. In: Proceedings of the First Intl. Conference on Multiagent Systems, San Francisco (1995)

[6] M. E. Bratman: Intention, Plans, and Practical Reason. the University of Chicago Press (1999)

[7] R.M. van Eijk, F. S. de Boer, W. van der Hoek, J. J. Ch. Meyer: Process algebra for agent communication: A general semantic approach. In Huget, M., ed.: Communication in Mulitiagent Systems - Agent Communication Languages and Conversation Policies. Volume 2650., Springer-Verlag (2003) 113–128

[8] FIPA. Foundation for Intelligent Physical Agents: Communicative act library specification (2002) http://www.fipa.org.

[9] P. R. Cohen, H. J. Levesque: 8. In: Rational interaction as the basis for communication. MIT Press, Cambridge (1990) 221–255

[10] T. Finin, D. McKay, R. Fritzson, R. McEntire: KQML : An Information and Knowledge Exchange Protocol. In: Knowledge Building and Knowledge Sharing. Ohmsha and IOS Press (1994)

[11] Wooldridge, M.: Reasoning about Rational Agent. The MIT Press (2000)

[12] FIPA Foundation for Intelligent Physical Agents: Fipa 97 part 2 version 2.0: Agent communication language specification (1997) http://www.drogo.cselt.it/fipa.org.

[13] : SWI-Prolog Version 5.6.2. (2006) University of Amsterdam, http://www.swi-prolog.org/.

[14] Wooldridge, M., Fisher, M., Huget, M.P., Parsons, S.: Model checking multi-agent systems with mable. In: AAMAS'02, ACM (2002)

On the Implementation of Global Abduction

Henning Christiansen

Roskilde University, Computer Science Dept.
P.O.Box 260, DK-4000 Roskilde, Denmark
henning@ruc.dk

Abstract. Global Abduction (GA) is a recently proposed logical formalism for agent oriented programming which allows an agent to collect
information about the world and update this in a nonmonotonic way
when changes in the world are observed. A distinct feature of Global
Abduction is that in case the agent needs to give up one plan, it may
start a new one, or continue a suspended plan, while its beliefs learned
about the world in the failed attempts persist. This paper describes an
implementation of GA in the high-level language of Constraint Handling
Rules (CHR). It appears to be a first attempt to a full implementation
of GA, which also confirms CHR as a powerful meta-programming language for advanced reasoning. The construction gives rise a discussion of
important issues of the semantics and pragmatics of Global Abduction,
leading to proposals for a specific procedural semantics and architecture
that seem well suited for real-time applications.

1   Introduction

Global Abduction (GA) is an extended form of logical abduction which has been
proposed recently by Ken Satoh [22,23]. As opposed to traditional Abductive
Logic Programming [19], GA features the reuse of abducibles from one branch
of computation in another branch. Abducibles are here believed properties of a
dynamic world, so that truth of a belief may change due to an observed change
in the world. If an agent follows one plan (i.e., one branch of computation)
that does not give a solution, the beliefs learned are assumed still to be valid
(until contradicting evidence is learned) and should be available when another
plan is tried; this other plan may be a new branch of computation or one that
was previously suspended, but which can be taken up again if it appears to fit
with the new state of beliefs. Interestingly, GA allows not only accumulation
of knowledge but also replacing a belief by its opposite when the circumstances
indicate that this is relevant.

We shall not go into a detailed explanation of GA nor argue for its advantages, but all in all, we find GA a very promising approach which deserves an
implementation so that more experience can be obtained. In the present paper
we describe how it can be implemented using state of the art constraint logic
programming technology represented by the language of Constraint Handling
Rules. However, this paper is not intended as a piece of technical documentation

K. Inoue, K. Satoh, and F. Toni (Eds.): CLIMA VII, LNAI 4371, pp. 226–245, 2007.

only, and the implementation in an appropriate high-level language provides a setting for raising and discussing in a concrete manner, important issues of GA and its use for agent modeling.

The language of Constraint Handling Rules (CHR) [15] is an extension to Prolog designed as a declarative language for writing constraint solvers for CLP systems and is now integrated in several major Prolog versions. Previous work [1,3,5,6,7,8,9,10,26] has shown that CHR is a powerful language for implementing advanced logical reasoning that goes beyond standard logic programming paradigms, and in the present paper we extend these experiences to the implementation of GA. Logic programming languages such as Prolog or CHR provide via their term structure and unification a direct way to represent and manipulate syntax trees of a GA framework; furthermore, we utilize CHR's constraint store as a global resource which holds global beliefs as well as a pool of (active or suspended) processes. Compared to a possible implementation in Prolog, we avoid dragging around these components as explicit arguments to the interpreting predicates, and we do not have to care about search as this is done by the underlying CHR system. However, the greatest advantage of using CHR is the close resemblance of the rules that comprise the implementation to an abstractly specified proof system. All in all, the implementation in CHR provides a transparent and executable representation of GA's operational semantics that lends itself to experimentation with details of and possible extensions to GA. If the goal were ultimate efficiency, other technologies may be considered.

In the present paper we concentrate on the basic mechanisms of GA, but our work is intended to lead to an implementation of GA based on a high-level syntax and which employs the facilities of a full scale Prolog system to have GA programs communicate online with its environment. The code explained below has been developed and tested in SICStus Prolog [27], which provides the *de facto* reference implementation of CHR. Our system is still at a prototype stage with no interesting applications developed so far, but it indicates that full scale implementations are within reach with a reasonable amount of effort.

Section 2 explains the basic notions of GA, and we refer to [23] for a complete description; we define also notions of soundness and completeness for procedures and provide definitions used later for discussing flow of control and floundering. Section 3 gives a brief introduction to CHR with an emphasis on its advantages as meta-programming language for logical reasoning. In section 4 we explain how belief states can be represented and maintained, and explain the implementation of a multiple-process architecture for GA, and section 5 extends with integrity constraints. A proposal for extending GA with real world monitoring and forward reasoning is given in section 6. Section 7 uses the implementation described so far to analyze and give proposals for selection rules and flow of control; we end up advocating range-restricted GA programs with left-to-right execution as a suitable choice that respects the pragmatic considerations underlying GA. We add to section 7 also an explanation of how a cut operator indicated by [22,23] can be added to GA and implemented in the left-to-right-setting. Section 8 provides a comparison with other related paradigms, and a final section provides a summary and indicates future direction.

2   Global Abduction

Disjoint sets of *belief predicates*, *ordinary predicates*, and *equality* and *nonequality predicates* = and $\neq$ are assumed, the latter two having their standard syntactic meaning; we allow positive and negative literals over belief predicates but not over the other categories (for which "literal", thus, indicates "atom" only). We define also *annotated literals* of the form announce(B) and hear(B), where B is a belief literal. A notation of prefix plus and minus is applied for positive and negative belief literals. *Program clauses* are defined as usual, expected to have an ordinary atom as their head and a conjunction of zero or more literals as body. An *integrity constraint* is a clause whose head is false (expressing falsity), and with only belief literals in the body. A *global abductive framework* (GAF) $\langle B, P, IC \rangle$ consists of a sets of belief predicates B, program clauses P, and integrity constraints IC. A *belief set* is a set of ground literals over belief predicates which contains no pair of contradictory literals.

Intuitively, an announcing literal announce(L) for ground belief L means to assert L in a current belief set so that a hearing literal hear(L) becomes satisfied in that belief set. The truth value of a belief literal not in the given belief set is recognized as unknown, and similarly for corresponding annotated literals. We introduce the semantics informally by an example; it anticipates left-to-right execution but it should be stressed that this is not assumed for the declarative semantics of [22].

Example 1. The following program is supposed to help an agent to decide whether or not to cross the street; sS stands for "stop signal" and t for "traffic".

```
decide(walk):- hear(-sS), hear(-t).
decide(wait):- hear(+sS).
check:- announce(-sS), announce(+t).
check:- announce(+sS).
```

The initial query is check, decide(X) which corresponds to a process which may split into two, one for each of the two check clauses.

(1) announce(-sS), announce(+t), decide(X)
(2) announce(+sS), decide(X)

Each process has its own set of *belief assumptions* (BA) which must be consistent with the *current* global *belief state* (CBS) in order to classify as *active*. The BA of a process consists of those beliefs it has applied in getting to its present state; the CBS consists of announced beliefs, maintained in a nonmonotonic way and independently of which processes made the announcements.

Suppose (1) executes the two announcements leading to process

(1′) decide(X) with $BA = \{-sS, +t\}$ and
$CBS = \{-sS, +t\}$.

Process (1') splits into (1'.1) and (1'.2).

(1'.1) `hear(-sS)`, `hear(-t)` with binding `X=walk` and $BA = \{\text{-sS, +t}\}$.
(1'.2) `hear(+sS)` with binding `X=wait` and $BA = \{\text{-sS, +t}\}$.

Process (1'.1) continues with `hear(-sS)` but gets stuck on `hear(-t)` which does not fit with CBS; (1'.2) gets stuck in a similar way. Thus branches $(1\cdots)$ failed to provide a solution, but the CBS persists. Now process (2) may be tried, doing `announce(+sS)`, which results in a revision of CBS:

$$CBS = (\{\text{-sS, +t}\} \text{ revised with +sS}) = \{\text{+sS, +t}\}.$$

Left of (2) is `decide(X)`, which via 2nd clause executes successfully a `hear` and terminates with the binding `X=wait` and the final belief set $\{\text{+sS, +t}\}$.

Example 2. GA as described by [22,23] and in the present paper is in principle a mono-agent system, but the inherent or-parallelism makes it possible to obtain the effect of co-operating agents. The following program simulates two agents co-operating on finding a treasure in a DAG defined by predicates `edge/2` and `origin/1` whose arguments are node identifiers; some nodes may contain a treasure indicated by facts such as `treasureAt(n75,goldBar)`. The agent supposed to locate the treasure (predicate `successPath`) can only traverse secure edges, which it identifies by checking beliefs such `+secure(n17,n38)`. Initially, no such belief exists, and another agent (predicate `secureEdges`) able to pass any edge is checking the graph and announcing its findings. For simplicity, security is determined by facts such as `secureCheck(n30,n32)`.[1] The program is as follows with facts omitted.

```
searchTreasure(T):- origin(O), successPath(O,_,T).
searchTreasure(_):- origin(O), secureEdges(O).

successPath(X,Y,T):-
        edge(X,Y), treasureAt(Y,T), hear(+secure(X,Y)).
successPath(X,Z,T):-
        edge(X,Y), hear(+secure(X,Y)), successPath(Y,Z,T).

secureEdges(X):- edge(X,Y), announceIfSecure(X,Y), secureEdges(Y).

announceIfSecure(X,Y):- secureCheck(X,Y), announce(+secure(X,Y)).
announceIfSecure(_,_).
```

The top level query which initiates the search is `searchTreasure(T)`. Notice that only the `successPath` agent can succeed in contrast to `secureEdges` which has no way of stopping successfully. The latter will traverse that graph with all branches eventually failing but with the important side-effect of producing the beliefs that are necessary for `successPath` to find a treasure.

---

[1] In a realistic system, the judgement of secure edges might involve communication with external sensors.

A declarative semantics for GA is given in [22], based on a three-valued minimal model approach [14,21]. Truth value of a statement ϕ in a GAF $\langle \mathcal{B}, \mathcal{P}, \mathcal{IC} \rangle$ is expressed relative to a belief set Bs, written $\langle \mathcal{B}, \mathcal{P}, \mathcal{IC} \rangle \models_{Bs} \phi$.

By a *proof procedure*, which may exist as an implemented program, we indicate a device which given a GAF and an initial goal G produces zero or more *answers*, each of which is a pair $\langle Bs, \sigma \rangle$ of belief set Bs and substitution σ to the variables of G; a *goal* is a set (or sequence, depending on context) of literals.

Definition 1. *Let a GAF $GA = \langle \mathcal{B}, \mathcal{P}, \mathcal{IC} \rangle$ and an initial goal G be given, and assume a fixed proof procedure.*

- *A* correct answer *for G in GA is one $\langle Bs, \sigma \rangle$ so that $\langle \mathcal{B}, \mathcal{P}, \mathcal{IC} \rangle \models_{Bs} G\sigma\rho$ for any grounding substitution ρ.*
- *A* computed answer *for G in GA is one returned by the proof procedure.*
- *A proof procedure is* sound *whenever any computed answer is also a correct answer.*
- *A proof procedure is* complete *whenever, for any correct answer $\langle Bs, \sigma \rangle$, there exists a computed answer $\langle Bs', \sigma' \rangle$ so that $Bs' \subseteq Bs$ and $\sigma = \sigma'\rho$ for some substitution ρ.*

Example 3. A correct answer for the treasure hunting program of example 2 consists of a set Bs of beliefs of the kind +secure(n_i, n_j) and a substitution such as T=goldBar, where Bs identifies a subgraph of secure edges in which the goldBar is found.

GA has some inherent problems concerning the relationship between correct answers and computed answers not recognized in [22]. We illustrate this with the following queries (variables existentially quantified); the first one is not problematic but the remaining ones are:

1. announce(+b(1)), hear(+b(1))
2. announce(+b(X)), hear(+b(1))
3. announce(+b(1)), hear(+b(X))

No. 1 is clearly satisfied with the belief set {+b(1)} and we would expect any capable implementation to recognize this. No's 2–3 are also satisfiable with {+b(1)} by substitution X $\mapsto$ 1. The procedural semantics of [22] does not recognize the solutions for 2–3 but ends in floundering states.

We may, however, ask whether it is reasonable to expect them to be found. As presented intuitively and illustrated by the examples of [22,23], announce is an event that goes "before" hear, and announce indicates changes in the agent's belief about the world. So producing X $\mapsto$ 1 from case 2 is a bit absurd as this corresponds to an agent for whom an act of Providence modifies the world to fit what it wants to hear. On the other hand, we may suggest an extension that produces the solution for case 3, which seems intuitively correct when considering hear(+b(X)) as a query for information about the current status for belief predicate b/1; we return to this topic in section 7.

We adapt the notion of range-restriction familiar from deductive databases in order to impose restrictions on which GAFs we prefer. Range restriction in a database implies that any query or relation has a well-defined and finite extension derivable from base relations; for a knowledge based system such as GA, these database heuristics appear quite reasonable. We define a left-to-right version of this notion which ensures that every variable achieves a definite value under left-to-right, thus reducing the risk of floundering under left-to-right execution; we end up later concluding that left-to-right fits well with a pragmatic understanding of GA.

Definition 2. *A clause, an integrity constraint, or a query (considered as a clause with empty head) is* range-restricted *(rr) whenever any variable in it appears (as well) in an ordinary literal in its body; it is* **hear** range-restricted *(***hear***-rr) whenever any variable in it appears (as well) in an ordinary or* **hear** *literal in its body; it is* left-to-right range-restricted *(lr-rr) whenever any variable in it has a leftmost occurrence within the body in an ordinary literal; it is* left-to-right **hear** range-restricted *(lr-***hear***-rr) whenever any variable in it has a leftmost occurrence within the body in an ordinary or* **hear** *literal.*

A GAF has one of these properties if all its clauses, integrity constraints, and permitted queries have the property.

Example 4. The following clause is *lr-rr*.

p(X,Y):- q(X), r(Y), announce(+Y).

The next one is *lr-***hear***-rr* but not *lr-rr*.

p(X,Y):- q(X), hear(-Y).

The clauses p(X,Y):- q(X) and p:- announce(+X) have none of these properties.

The primary source on GA, [22], proposes a proof procedure which is not reproduced here. Our implementation is explained below in a self-contained way but for the interested reader, we refer to the steps of that proof procedure writing, e.g., PP3.5 for its case 3.5. We refer to the following central notions: an *execution state* consists of a set of *processes* and a *current belief set*. A *process* is a triplet consisting of a *current goal* (a query), a set of belief literals called its *belief assumptions* that has been used by this process so far, and an answer substitution. A process is *active* if its belief assumptions are true in the current belief set, *suspended* otherwise.

3   Constraint Handling Rules as a Metalanguage for Logic-Based Systems

Constraints of CHR are first-order atoms whose predicates are designated constraint predicates, and a constraint store is a set of such constraints. CHR is integrated with Prolog and when a constraint is called, the constraint solver defined by the programmer takes over control. A constraint solver is defined in terms of rules which can be of the following two kinds.

$$\text{Simplification rules: } c_1, \ldots c_n \text{ <=> } Guard \mid c_{n+1}, \ldots, c_m$$
$$\text{Propagation rules: } c_1, \ldots c_n \text{ ==> } Guard \mid c_{n+1}, \ldots, c_m$$

The c's are atoms that represent constraints, possibly with variables, and a simplification rule works by replacing in the constraint store, a possible set of constraints that matches the pattern given by the *head* $c_1, \ldots c_n$ by those corresponding constraints given by the *body* $c_{n+1}, \ldots, c_m$, however only if the condition given by *Guard* holds. A propagation rule executes in a similar way but without removing the head constraints from the store. The declarative semantics is hinted by the applied arrow symbols (bi-implication, resp., implication formulas, with variables assumed to be universally quantified) and it can be shown that the indicated procedural semantics agrees with this. There is also a hybrid of the two rules, called *simpagation* $cs_1 \backslash cs_2$ <=> $\cdots$ in which cs_1 are kept in the store and cs_2 removed when such a rule applies. Guards should be tests (with no unifications to head variables and no calls to constraints), and rule bodies can, in fact, be any executable Prolog term and is executed as such. Procedurally, CHR is a committed choice language which means that a failure (in Prolog's sense) within the body of a CHR rule means failure of the goal that triggered that rule, but backtracking remains in Prolog constructs as usual. Notice that CHR uses a one-way matching and not unification when a rule applies for a set of constraints.

Example 5. Consider the query ?- p(a), q(a), p(A), q(B), p(C), q(C) to a program consisting of the following simplification rule,

```
p(X), q(X) ==> applied.
```

where all predicates are declared as constraints. The following constraint store is returned

```
applied, p(A), q(B), applied
```

indicating the one-way matching, i.e., the rule is not applied for pairs of p and q whose arguments are unifiable but not identical.

When a constraint is called, rules are tested for applicability in textual order, and when a rule is chosen, its body finishes before the possibly next rule for that constraint is allowed to start.

CHR is more powerful than indicated by its declarative semantics, as the constraint store can be used as a global resource that can be modified in nonmonotonic ways. A simplification rule may, for example, remove a piece of information and replace it with complementary information. In this way we may use the constraint store for, say, a pool of processes and for belief sets. Furthermore, CHR programmers tend to employ their procedural knowledge about the sequential order in which rules are tried, as we do in the following; this has inspired to the formulation of a formal semantics, the so-called refined operational semantics [13], that takes all these aspects into account. There is an interesting analogy between the view of the constraint store as a global resource and a recently proposed semantics for CHR based on linear logic [4]; this relationship, however, has not studied further.

As indicated by [2], CHR makes it possible to combine different control strategies in an easy way, and for GA we need to make use of process delays and breadth-first search. For the latter, we need to be careful in catching Prolog-failures in one branch so they do not destroy other branches; in other words, a process with a failure should be eliminated, i.e., avoid calling a continuation in case of a failure. This can be done in the following way using Prolog's conditional construct (for background of such transformation of CHR rules, see [16]).

Head ==> *Guard* | (*SuccessOrFailure* -> *Continuation* ; true).

In most well-behaved CHR programs, all references to the constraint store are normally made indirectly by the matching in head of rules. However, in some cases (as in our code, below), it may be useful to test explicitly whether a certain constraint is in the store; CHR has a primitive called find_constraint for this purpose.

For the meta-programming task at hand, we need to do renaming of variables which is done using a predicate renameVars/2 which produces a copy of its first argument with all variables consistently replaced by other variables. It is implemented by the one-liner renameVars(A,B):- asserta(dummy(A)), retract(dummy(B)).

Finally, we remind the reader that there is a the risk of confusion due to terminological overlap: a *constraint* of CHR is a single atom, while an *integrity constraint* in general is a complex condition which is some cases can be identified with a *rule* of CHR.

4   Belief States and Processes

GA's belief literals are represented by means of two constraints, indicated by symbols plus and minus (which can be written as prefix operators) for positive and negative literals. A current belief state, then, is represented as the set of such constraints in the store. According to PP3.5, adding a belief literal to the state should remove any possible opposite literal; the complete code necessary for managing the belief state, including rules that remove duplicates, is as follows.

```
constraints + /1, - /1.

+X \ -X#Old <=> true pragma passive(Old).
-X \ +X#Old <=> true pragma passive(Old).
+X \ +X <=> true.
-X \ -X <=> true.
```

The pragma passive syntax indicates that only a call to a predicate matching an occurrence which is *not* marked as passive is able to trigger that rule; see [27] for a detailed explanation. It is applied here to keep only the most recently announced belief in store and to remove a possible earlier contradictory belief. These rules must precede any others so that process rules are never triggered in a state with contradictory beliefs.

Processes are represented in the store by declaring a constraint `process/3` whose arguments are as follows.

    `process(`*Goals*`, `*BeliefAssumptions*`, `*Bindings*`)`

The first argument is a list containing the remaining subgoals to be resolved by that process; 2nd arg. is the process' assumptions given as a list of beliefs; 3rd arg. the bindings of variables of the initial query.

We assume a predicate `inCurrent/1` which given the assumptions of a process tests (using `find_constraint`) whether they hold in the current belief state; this implements GA's test for active processes. This predicate is used as a guard in every rule that describes a computational step of a process. We explain at the end of the section how the binding argument is handled; it can be ignored for the understanding of the overall principles of the procedure. The following rules capture PP1, PP3 except PP3.1; the handling of integrity constraints in PP3.5 is postponed until section 5. The `add` predicate adds an element to a list but avoiding duplicates. The rules below select always the left-most literal for execution, but other alternatives are discussed later.

```
process([],As,Bind) <=> inCurrent(As) | write(Bind), success.

process([(X=Y)|Gs],As,Bind) <=> inCurrent(As) |
    (X=Y -> process(Gs,As,Bind) ; true).

process([(X\=Y)|Gs],As,Bind) <=> ?=(X,Y), inCurrent(As) |
    (X=Y -> true ; process(Gs,As,Bind)).

process([hear(B)|Gs],As,Bind) <=> ground(B) |
    add(B,As,NewAs), process(Gs,NewAs, Bind).

process([announce(B)|Gs],As,Bind) <=> ground(B), inCurrent(As) |
    B, add(B,As,NewAs), process(Gs,NewAs,Bind).
```

The `success` constraint removes (by rules not shown) all other `processes` from the system so that they cannot continue. Thus, after printing the bindings, the final constraint store returned by CHR will consist of exactly the final belief set plus `success`. Failure of the computation in the sense of GA is signified by a final state in which no `success` is present; this principle implements PP3.2; any other final state (with suspended `process` constraints) is "floundering".

The rules for equality and nonequality eliminate processes with Prolog-failure using the technique described in section 3 above. For nonequality, a peculiar SICStus Prolog test `?=(X,Y)` is used [27]. It is satisfied whenever X and Y are either identical or sufficiently instantiated as to tell them different; this makes our procedure go a bit further that Satoh's proof procedure which has to wait until both arguments become ground.

Finally, we implement `hear(B)` by the little trick of adding B to the process' assumptions. In this way, the process needs to wait until consistency of assumptions and B becomes true, and this provides the behaviour of PP3.4.

We will discuss a subtlety of the implementation of `hear` and `announce` inherited from the original proof procedure. In case a process which has, say, `-p` in its belief set executes `hear(+p)` or `announce(+p)`, its updated belief set will contain an inconsistency and the process will, thus, be considered suspended in any belief state. It is straightforward to adjust our implementation so such processes vanish instead of staying uselessly in the constraint store. Furthermore, we may also ask the question whether it will be a better design to stop a process which has `-p` in its belief set before it executes `announce(+p)`, possibly modifying the global belief about `p`.

There is one omission in the procedure presented so far that concerns restarting of once suspended processes. A process is delayed in case the `inCurrent` test tells it passive, but it may happen later that another process changes the belief state in a way that makes the `inCurrent` test succeed.

The basic mechanisms of CHR try a rule r for applicability when either a constraint (which has a matcher in the head of r) is called or when a variable in such a stored constraint is unified. However, CHR does not test for cases where the outcome of a guard changes from false to true in the absence of the other kinds of "triggering events", as is the case with our use of `inCurrent`.[2] We implement a mechanism for this delay-and-retry phenomenon by the following rules.

```
process(Gs,As,Bind) <=> \+ inCurrent(As) |
    delayedProcess(Gs,As,Bind).
```

```
+_ \ delayedProcess(Gs,As,Bind)#Delay <=> inCurrent(As) |
    process(Gs,As,Bind) pragma passive(Delay).
```

```
-_ \ delayedProcess(Gs,As,Bind)#Delay <=> inCurrent(As) |
    process(Gs,As,Bind) pragma passive(Delay).
```

For simplicity of code, these rules perform a check for possible restart whenever the belief state changes. This can be optimized by introducing instead a specialized constraint for restart which is called whenever some process goes passive or vanishes and which locates one other delayed process for restart using a simplification rule of the form `restart, delayedProcess(···)#Delay <=> inCurrent(As) | ···` (replacing the two last rules above). An explicit `restart` constraint will also make it possible to refine the process scheduling strategy in different ways.

In order to handle the goals of ordinary predicates we need to start a new process for each clause whose head unifies with the goal in a breadth-first way. This is done by a compilation of clauses into CHR rules described as follows. Consider a predicate p/k, defined by clauses $p(\overline{t_1}):-B_1, \ldots, p(\overline{t_n}):-B_n$; the expressions $\overline{t_i}$ indicate sequences of k terms, B_i arbitrary bodies, and $\overline{X}$, $\overline{X}_r$ below

---

[2] Such guards are not considered not good style of CHR programming, but are difficult to avoid in the present case. In an attempt to do this by a matching rule head, we would need one specific rule for each possible set of belief assumptions with those assumptions in the head, which of course vary dynamically; hence this approach is impossible.

sequences of k distinct Prolog variables. The ith clause, $i = 1, \ldots, n - 1$ is compiled into the following rule.

```
process([p(X̄)|Gs],As,Bind) ==>
    renameVars(f(X̄,Gs,Bind),f(X̄ᵣ,GsR,BindR)),
    append([X̄ᵣ=t̄ᵢ|Bᵢ],GsR,NewGs),
    (inCurrent(As) -> process(NewGs,As,BindR)
                ; delayedProcess(NewGs,As,BindR)).
```

Clause n is compiled in a similar way, except that the rule is made into a simplification rule, i.e., using <=> instead of ==>. The strategy applied is, thus, that n fresh copies replace the original call $p(\cdots)$, so that the unifications for the different clauses can be done correctly in simultaniety.[3]

Example 6. The definition of predicate successPath in the treasure hunting program of example 2 is compiled into the following CHR rules.

```
process([successPath(X1,Y1,T1)|Gs],As,Bind) ==>
  renameVars(f(X1,Y1,T1,Gs,Bind),f(XR,YR,TR,GsR,BindR)),
  append([(XR,YR,TR)=(X,Y,T),edge(X,Y),
          treasureAt(Y,T),hear(+secure(X,Y))],GsR,NewGs),
  (inCurrent(As) -> process(NewGs,As,BindR)
              ; delayedProcess(NewGs,As,BindR)).

process([successPath(X1,Z1,T1)|Gs],As,Bind) <=>
  renameVars(f(X1,Z1,T1,Gs,Bind),f(XR,ZR,TR,GsR,BindR)),
  append([(XR,ZR,TR)=(X,Z,T),edge(X,Y),hear(+secure(X,Y)),
          successPath(Y,Z,T)],GsR,NewGs),
  (inCurrent(As) -> process(NewGs,As,BindR)
              ; delayedProcess(NewGs,As,BindR)).
```

Execution of the CHR program consisting of all compiled clauses of the program of example 2 and the specific ones mentioned above, respecting their given order, will result in a co-routine-like behaviour. Firstly, process([successPath(*origin*, _,T)], $\cdots$) expands and delays along all edges going out from the *origin*, waiting to hear(+secure($\cdots$)). Then process([secureEdges(*origin*)], $\cdots$) will begin to work and likely produce annuouncements that activate processes for successPath, and control shifts back and forth until either a treasure is found or the whole computation fails.

An initial query such as p(X,Y), q(Y,Z) is given to the system as a process constraints with the following arguments.

```
process([p(X,Y),q(Y,Z)],[],['X'=X,'Y'=Y,'Z'=Z])
```

The first argument is the list containing the query, the 2nd is the (still) empty list of belief assumptions (but default beliefs can be added here), and the 3rd

---

[3] The test for inCurrent(As) made inside the body (instead of as guard) takes care of those cases where, say, the execution if B_i has changed the belief set so that the next inCurrent(As) for B_{i+1} fails.

one represents the bindings. Each "equation" represents an association between a variable (say X at the rhs) and its name ('X' at the lhs, which is a quoted constant that Prolog prints without quotes). Along each branch of computation, the variable will be affected by all unifications and renamings, but its name is not. Thus in the final state, it represents perfectly the binding made to the variable X appearing in the initial query.

5   Integrity Constraints in GA

In [23], integrity constraints are not used and for the examples in that paper, we can do with the implemented system described so far. The integrity constraints of [22] can be handled in a way similar to how we handled consistency of belief sets above. While consistency means that *all* beliefs in a process' assumptions are in the current belief set, a given integrity constraint is satisfied if *not all* beliefs of a certain set are in the current belief set. As for consistency, a process should delay if it violates an integrity constraint and be tested again when the current belief set changes.

Integrity constraints should be tested in the `process` rule for `announce(B)` (cf. PP3.5), and this can be done by adding to its guard an extra test `icHolds(B)`. It succeeds when, for each ground instance of an integrity constraint containing the actual B, the other belief literals in it are not in the current belief set. This can be implemented in a way similar to `inCurrent`, and a suitable delay-and-retry mechanism for `announce process`es can be implemented using the same principles as we used above for the general `inCurrent` test. The extensions to the code are straightforward and omitted.

Readers familiar with earlier work on abductive logic programming (ALP) in CHR (e.g., [1,9]) may wonder why we did not write integrity constraints directly as rules of CHR, e.g., write "`false:- a,b`" as a propagation rule "`+a,+b==>false`" which, then, would fail when, say, `+a` is added to a state including `+b`. It seems possible to adapt the code shown above to this approach as well, but a mechanism to wake up processes that were blocked by failing integrity constraints may become difficult to implement.

Writing integrity constraints as CHR rules works perfectly for ALP in a combination of Prolog and CHR, since in that paradigm more and more abducibles are collected in a monotonic fashion; the indicated failures caused by integrity constraints discard effectively the current branch, and Prolog backtracks neatly to the next one. In GA, on the other hand, control may jump back and forth between different branches and the belief set may be updated in nonmonotonic ways.

6   Proposal for an Extension of AG with Monitor Processes and Forward Reasoning

By a monitor process, we indicate a process which supplies real world data into the global belief set. In this way the agent may adjust its behaviour according to events in the real world. We suggest to have separate mechanisms for defining such processes for the following reasons.

- Monitors should work independently of other processes and not wait until other processes decide to give up the control. This may be implemented by a sort of interrupt technology or, what is easily incorporated into the present CHR implementation, called with regular intervals from the rules that comprise the interpreter.
- Monitor processes should be released from the basic GA restriction of keeping their own belief assumptions consistent with the current (global) belief set. If a normal GA process executes `announce(+a)` followed by `announce(-a)` it blocks forever as its belief assumptions contains {+a,-a} which is inconsistent with any belief state. This is obviously not what we want for a process monitoring real world events.

Current Prolog systems with CHR, such as SICStus [27], provide libraries which can communicate with external state-of-affairs, so we may suggest to add a special syntax as follows.

> `monitor` *code*.

The code can inspect different external sources and perform suitable **announcements** and in this way affect the program execution to change its processes accordingly (the interpreter takes care to call all monitors now and then).

Furthermore, it seems useful to include forward reasoning at the level of the global belief set. This is done simply by writing CHR rules about beliefs, e.g.:

> `+robber, -police ==> +emergency.`

If the combination of beliefs recorded in the head occurs in the current belief set, those in the body are added immediately, and this may affect the GA program, e.g., to switch process.

In the detailed design of a mechanism for forward reasoning, it should be considered whether the programmer is responsible for supplying additional rules to remove conclusions in case their premises disappear, or such additional rules should be produced by an automatic analysis.

7   Details of the Procedural Semantics

The strategies for selection of literal and process for the continuation are important choices from logical as well as pragmatic perspectives.

The procedure outlined above considers only the leftmost literal of a process for possible execution, and when an ordinary literal is expanded by means of a clause, its body is appended to the left, which yields a Prolog-like depth-first, left-to-right execution within each branch of computation. This may cause deadlocks and loss of completeness as illustrated by the following.

> `process([hear(a),announce(a)], ...).`

If desired, the selection of literal can be modified as to search for the leftmost one for which an execution step can apply.

We take the liberty to assume that our implementation is *sound*, independently of selection strategies. We base this claim on the fact that the implementation is modeled over the abstract proof procedure of [22] for which a soundness result is given; the referenced paper does not give completeness results. In fact, it is not complete as we indicated by example queries in section 2.

Our own procedure as well as that of [22] can be extended further for *lr*-**hear**-*rr* programs by adapting the step for **hear** so that in case of a nonground argument, it tries to unify the argument with the different current beliefs in separate processes. Another source for lack of completeness in our procedure is that it does not try out alternative interleavings of different processes. A jump from one process to another takes place only in case the leftmost literal L is blocked, either because the process is suspended as a whole or a specific condition for L is unsatisfied. A detailed analysis can show that when this happens, control will go to one of the delayed processes if any, otherwise it will move upward in the execution tree, searching for the nearest point where an ordinary atom can try an alternative program clause.

It may be possible to obtain a complete procedure, i.e., one that eventually produces (answers that subsume) all correct answers by trying different interleavings on backtracking, or by an approach that keeps track of alternative belief states in parallel. Such implementations, however, are likely not of any practical value due to lack of efficiency. In addition, a backtracking implementation may be problematic for a program with real world monitoring.

However, it is interesting to notice in [23], that the inventor of GA restricts to a version of it that employs a Prolog-like execution strategy and even suggests the addition of a procedural device analogous to Prolog's cut. There may be good reasons for this.

First of all, GA is really about resources, **announce** *creates* a new resource, and **hear** *applies* it. The papers about GA [22,23] apply usages that indicate an implicit notion of time (which is reflected in our paper as well), so it is reasonably to assume that a GA programmer has an understanding of a sequential execution. I.e., the bodies in a clause are executed from left-to-right, possible halting or interleaved with other branches, but never right-to-left or any other order.

Under these considerations, it is reasonable to restrict programs to be *lr*-**hear**-*rr*, which provides a good intuitive reading of programs with beliefs states as well as the implicit time moving from left to right.

Thinking of GAFs as a practical programming language for developing complex but fairly efficient agents, we may suggest to fix a deterministic execution strategy which makes it possible for the programmer to foresee – and optimize – the procedural behaviour of the program. This is the way things are done, and programmers tend to think, in logic program languages such as Prolog and CHR (as we have demonstrated fully above!). The execution strategy implemented in our system seems to be a good candidate for a fixed strategy, and this may conveniently be combined with a check that rejects GAFs that are not *lr*-**hear**-*rr*.

A Note on the Implementation of Cut

Cut in a breadth-first context works differently from cut in Prolog and it is not obvious how it should work. We show an example; assume a predicate p is defined by a set of clauses as follows.

$$p(\cdots) :- B_1, \ !, \ B_2, \ !, \ B_3.$$
$$p(\cdots) :- B_4, \ !, \ B_5.$$
$$p(\cdots) :- B_6.$$

In case, say, p(a) can unify with the heads of all these clauses, a process for each clause may become active, and when one of them reaches its cut, the other two should be eliminated. Assumes, as an example, that this happens in the first clause. But at this point in time, the processes for all three clauses may have multiplied into several ones each. A voting among logic programmers will likely indicate a majority for the proposal that all processes arising from the two last clauses should be eliminated. It is less clear for the different processes that arise during the processing of B_1, all having "the same" cut in their query arguments that represent their continuations.

We will take the solution that only the particular subprocess that gets to the cut first should survive. To obtain this, we associate a unique key with the particular call to p, which is attached to each of the three derived processes so that any process in the state keeps a list of keys referring to split-points involving cuts that may endanger it.

The split-point's key is also attached to the visible cut operators so when one of those is executed, it knows which processes to eliminate. The winning process, i.e., the one to be the first to reach a cut, can be handled as follows.

```
process([cut(N)|Gs],As,Bind,Cuts) <=> inCurrent(As) |
    eliminate(N), process(Gs,As,Bind,Cuts).
```

Elimination of the relevant processes can be done by the following CHR rules.

```
eliminate(N) \ process(_,_,_,Cuts)#X <=> member(N,Cuts) | true
    pragma passive(X).
eliminate(_) <=> true.
```

(A rule similar to the first one should also be added for delayedProcesses.) To see that it works, notice that the winning process is outside the pool when eliminate makes its harvest. The eliminate constraint triggers the simpagation rule as many times as possible to eliminate processes referring to the given cut, and finally it eliminates itself by the last rule; after that, the winner can safely enter the pool again.

For the above to work correctly, cut numbers must be distributed in a consistent way to all expansions of a given call to an ordinary predicate *p* whose definition contains one or more cuts. One way to do this obtain this is by

1. creating a new cut number to be added as a new head to the cut list at each point in the interpreter, where a recursive call to **process** occurs with a *changed* continuation (this excludes the rules for process re-activation), and
2. in the expansion rule for a given body, using the head of the current cut list to annotate the cuts in that body.

We indicate the expansion rule compiled for a clause $p(\overline{t_i}):\text{-}B_i$, in which both principles 1 and 2 are applied. Assume that **nextInt/1** is a Prolog predicate that returns the next unused integer number.

```
process([p(X̄)|Gs],...,[N|Cuts]) ==>
    renameVars(...),
    annotateCuts(N,Bᵢ,BiWithCutNos),
    append([X̄ᵣ=t̄ᵢ| BiWithCutNos],...,NewGs),
    nextInt(M),
    (inCurrent(...) -> process(NewGs,...,[M,N|Cuts])
                    ; delayedProcess(NewGs,...,[M,N|Cuts])).
```

With this technique, it is ensured that the elimination process described above will catch all relevant **process** constraints, independently of whether or not the first literal has been expanded.

An encoding of cut by means of **announce** and an integrity constraint is exemplified in [22] but it is difficult to compare this idea with our general proposal.

8   Comparison with Other Paradigms

It is interesting to compare with Assumptive Logic Programming [28,12] which can be understood as Prolog extended with operators to manage global resources (called assumptions), which include counterparts to **announce** and **hear**. The specification of that language explicitly says that the operations affect the state given to the continuation, defined in the standard Prolog way. It is possible to announce linear hypothesis, meaning that they can used once (i.e., consumed), or intuitionistic ones which can be applied infinitely many times. It is also possible to refer to "timeless" assumptions which can be requested before they are announced; this is useful because assumptions and requests are matched by unification, and it is shown to have relevant applications for linguistic phenomena. Assumptive Logic Programming does not include the possibility of jumping from branch to branch and reusing beliefs, but may be interesting to propose an extension of GA with the full repertoire of Assumptive Logic Programming's operators which provides a high flexibility for working with beliefs.

The reader may wish to compare the architecture described in the present paper with a CHR based implementation of Assumptive Logic Programming with integrity constraints and combined with traditional Abductive Logic Programming, as done in the the HYPROLOG system [8,9].

It may, in fact, be questioned whether a more appropriate name for GA would be Global Assumptive Programming, as GA as well as Assumptive Logic Programming share the property that new knowledge is explicitly announced with specific operators and explicitly consulted with others. In traditional Abductive Logic Programming [19], on the other hand, there is no explicit creation of knowledge: when the program refers to a particular piece of information, for the first or the nth time, the system provides an illusion that it was there already from the beginning.

Furthermore, it seems fairly straightforward and relevant to extend GA to describe systems of multiple cooperating agents. Each agent has its own program clauses and can execute them as described, including jumping from branch to branch, and the current belief state could be shared between all such agents. Alternatively, distinctions can be made between an agent's private beliefs and common beliefs. Implementationwise, each agent may run on its own physical processor, or parallelism can be simulated. Such a system seems to be useful for coordinating agents which access different external sources simultaneously in order to solve a given task.

A subset of GA can be executed within the speculative computation framework of [24,25] which is reported to be implemented in Prolog; the same goes for another speculative framework [18] for which a Java implementation is reported. The mentioned frameworks as well as the agent-oriented logic programming languages of [11,20], just to mentioned a few, may also seem interesting to approach with implementations in CHR. The primary papers on GA [22,23] situate the formalism within other work on (multi-) agent programming systems, and we refer the interested reader to these papers for more references.

In the speculative computations of [24,25], a belief state is updated by outside events in a way which is not specified, and our proposal of monitor processes can be a way to implement such facilities. GA extends these speculative computations by allowing a program dynamically to update its belief state by announcements.

A proof method called Dynamic SLDNF [17] has been applied for implementing an agent-oriented architecture which allows arbitrary clauses to be removed and added; a representation of the proof tree is maintained in an incremental way when the program changes, and it is not obvious that CHR should provide special advantages here.

As we have indicated, CHR is a powerful meta-programming language for advanced reasoning demonstrated mostly by our own work [1,6,7,8,9]; we may also refer to [3,26]. The present paper shows that a rule-based approach to constraint programming fits well also for implementation of process-oriented languages.

9   Conclusion

We have suggested an implementation of Satoh's Global Abductive Frameworks using the high-level programming language of Constraint Handling Rules. We have described the basic principles applied in a prototype version and shown how the different aspects of the formalism can be implemented, including cut. It appears that a well-structured implementation in CHR exposes the abstract principles of an operational semantics as well as subtle details of control, and it provides a workbench for experimenting with alternative choices of design. We have learned several important things from this exercise:

- We have been able to analyze and compare different execution strategies and advocate one which we claim fits with realistic implementations as well as applications in real-time environments.
- The implementation principles are described in so much detail as to indicate that a full instrumented version with a high-level syntax[4] is within reach with a reasonable amount of effort.
- We have compared with other systems, and we have provided a catalogue of interesting and implementable extensions to Global Abduction.

Acknowledgement. This work is supported by the CONTROL project, funded by Danish Natural Science Research Council.

References

1. Slim Abdennadher and Henning Christiansen. An experimental CLP platform for integrity constraints and abduction. In *Proceedings of FQAS2000, Flexible Query Answering Systems: Advances in Soft Computing series*, pages 141–152. Physica-Verlag (Springer), 2000.
2. Slim Abdennadher and Heribert Schütz. Chr^V: A flexible query language. In Troels Andreasen, Henning Christiansen, and Henrik Legind Larsen, editors, *FQAS*, volume 1495 of *Lecture Notes in Computer Science*, pages 1–14. Springer, 1998.
3. Marco Alberti, Federico Chesani, Marco Gavanelli, and Evelina Lamma. The CHR-based implementation of a system for generation and confirmation of hypotheses. In Armin Wolf, Thom W. Frühwirth, and Marc Meister, editors, *W(C)LP*, volume 2005-01 of *Ulmer Informatik-Berichte*, pages 111–122. Universität Ulm, Germany, 2005.
4. Hariolf Betz and Thom W. Frühwirth. A linear-logic semantics for constraint handling rules. In Peter van Beek, editor, *CP*, volume 3709 of *Lecture Notes in Computer Science*, pages 137–151. Springer, 2005.
5. Henning Christiansen. Automated reasoning with a constraint-based metainterpreter. *Journal of Logic Programming*, 37(1-3):213–254, 1998.
6. Henning Christiansen. Abductive language interpretation as bottom-up deduction. In Shuly Wintner, editor, *Natural Language Understanding and Logic Programming*, volume 92 of *Datalogiske Skrifter*, pages 33–47, Roskilde, Denmark, July 28 2002.

---

[4] Our experiences with other systems implemented in a combination of CHR and Prolog [7,9] demonstrate that high-level syntax is fairly straightforward to implement as soon as the underlying mechanics is in place, using operator declarations and the `term_expansion` primitive; see [27].

7. Henning Christiansen. CHR Grammars. *Int'l Journal on Theory and Practice of Logic Programming*, 5(4-5):467–501, 2005.
8. Henning Christiansen and Veronica Dahl. Assumptions and abduction in Prolog. In Elvira Albert, Michael Hanus, Petra Hofstedt, and Peter Van Roy, editors, *3rd International Workshop on Multiparadigm Constraint Programming Languages, MultiCPL'04; At the 20th International Conference on Logic Programming, ICLP'04 Saint-Malo, France, 6-10 September, 2004*, pages 87–101, 2004.
9. Henning Christiansen and Verónica Dahl. HYPROLOG: A new logic programming language with assumptions and abduction. In Maurizio Gabbrielli and Gopal Gupta, editors, *ICLP*, volume 3668 of *Lecture Notes in Computer Science*, pages 159–173. Springer, 2005.
10. Henning Christiansen and Davide Martinenghi. Symbolic constraints for meta-logic programming. *Applied Artificial Intelligence*, 14(4):345–367, 2000.
11. Stefania Costantini and Arianna Tocchio. A logic programming language for multi-agent systems. In Sergio Flesca, Sergio Greco, Nicola Leone, and Giovambattista Ianni, editors, *JELIA*, volume 2424 of *Lecture Notes in Computer Science*, pages 1–13. Springer, 2002.
12. Verónica Dahl, Paul Tarau, and Renwei Li. Assumption grammars for processing natural language. In *ICLP*, pages 256–270, 1997.
13. Gregory J. Duck, Peter J. Stuckey, Maria J. García de la Banda, and Christian Holzbaur. The refined operational semantics of Constraint Handling Rules. In Bart Demoen and Vladimir Lifschitz, editors, *Logic Programming, 20th International Conference, ICLP 2004, Saint-Malo, France, September 6-10, 2004, Proceedings*, volume 3132 of *Lecture Notes in Computer Science*, pages 90–104. Springer, 2004.
14. Melvin Fitting. A deterministic prolog fixpoint semantics. *J. Log. Program.*, 2(2):111–118, 1985.
15. Thom Frühwirth. Theory and practice of constraint handling rules, special issue on constraint logic programming. *Journal of Logic Programming*, 37(1–3):95–138, October 1998.
16. Thom W. Frühwirth and Christian Holzbaur. Source-to-source transformation for a class of expressive rules. In Francesco Buccafurri, editor, *APPIA-GULP-PRODE*, pages 386–397, 2003.
17. Hisashi Hayashi. *Computing with Changing Logic programs*. PhD thesis, Imperial College of Science, Technology and Medicine, University of London, 2001.
18. Katsumi Inoue and Koji Iwanuma. Speculative computation through consequence-finding in multi-agent environments. *Ann. Math. Artif. Intell.*, 42(1-3):255–291, 2004.
19. A.C. Kakas, R.A. Kowalski, and F. Toni. The role of abduction in logic programming. *Handbook of Logic in Artificial Intelligence and Logic Programming*, vol. 5, Gabbay, D.M, Hogger, C.J., Robinson, J.A., (eds.), Oxford University Press, pages 235–324, 1998.
20. João Leite and Luís Soares. Enhancing a multi-agent system with evolving logic programs. In Katsumi Inoue, Ken Satoh, and Francesca Toni, editors, *Seventh Workshop on Computational Logic in Multi-Agent Systems (CLIMA-VII)*, 2006. To appear.
21. Teodor C. Przymusinski. The well-founded semantics coincides with the three-valued stable semantics. *Fundam. Inform.*, 13(4):445–463, 1990.
22. Ken Satoh. "All's well that ends well" - a proposal of global abduction. In James P. Delgrande and Torsten Schaub, editors, *NMR*, pages 360–367, 2004.

23. Ken Satoh. An application of global abduction to an information agent which modifies a plan upon failure - preliminary report. In João Alexandre Leite and Paolo Torroni, editors, *CLIMA V*, volume 3487 of *Lecture Notes in Computer Science*, pages 213–229. Springer, 2004.
24. Ken Satoh, Katsumi Inoue, Koji Iwanuma, and Chiaki Sakama. Speculative computation by abduction under incomplete communication environments. In *ICMAS*, pages 263–270. IEEE Computer Society, 2000.
25. Ken Satoh and Keiji Yamamoto. Speculative computation with multi-agent belief revision. In *AAMAS*, pages 897–904. ACM, 2002.
26. Christian Seitz, Bernhard Bauer, and Michael Berger. Multi agent systems using Constraint Handling Rules for problem solving. In Hamid R. Arabnia and Youngsong Mun, editors, *IC-AI*, pages 295–301. CSREA Press, 2002.
27. Swedish Institute of Computer Science. SICStus Prolog user's manual, Version 3.12. Most recent version available at http://www.sics.se/isl, 2006.
28. Paul Tarau, Verónica Dahl, and Andrew Fall. Backtrackable state with linear assumptions, continuations and hidden accumulator grammars. In John W. Lloyd, editor, *Logic Programming, Proceedings of the 1995 International Symposium*, page 642. MIT Press, 1995.

Adding Evolving Abilities to a Multi-Agent System

João Leite and Luís Soares

CENTRIA, Universidade Nova de Lisboa, Portugal
jleite@di.fct.unl.pt, luizsoarez@gmail.com

Abstract. This paper reports on a fertile marriage between madAgents, a Java and Prolog based multi-agent platform, and EVOLP, a logic programming based language to represent and reason about evolving knowledge.

The resulting system, presented with a formal semantic characterisation and implemented using a combination of Java, XSB Prolog and Smodels, provides an improvement of madAgents, allowing for the implementation of a richer agent architecture where agents' beliefs and behavior, as well as their evolution, are specifiable in EVOLP. It inherits the merits of Answer Set Programming (e.g., default negation for reasoning about incomplete knowledge, a semantics based on multiple answer-sets for reasoning about several possible worlds, etc.) on top of which we add all the specific merits of EVOLP for specifying evolving knowledge. At he same time, the resulting system provides a proof of principle that EVOLP can easily be adopted by existing MAS, to represent an evolving belief base, or also to represent the agent's evolving behavior.

1   Introduction

This paper reports on what we believe to be a fertile marriage between madAgents (Multimedia Deductive Agents) [28], a Java based multi-agent platform, and EVOLP [2], a computational logic language to represent and reason about evolving knowledge.

We have recently seen an increase in the cross fertilisation between the areas of Multi-Agent Systems (MAS) and Computational Logic (CL). On the one hand, CL provides a rigorous, general, integrative and encompassing framework for systematically studying computation, be it syntax, semantics, procedures, or implementations, tools, and standards. On the other hand, MAS provides a rich and demanding environment populated with problems that challenge Computational Logic. Examples of this cross fertilisation include CL based MAS such as IMPACT [29,16], 3APL [20,15], Jason [9], DALI [14], ProSOCS [12], FLUX [30] and ConGolog [19], to name a few. For a survey on some of these systems, as well as others, see [26,11,10].

While CL, and Logic Programming in particular, can be seen as a good representation language for static knowledge, if we are to move to a more open and dynamic environment, typical of the agency paradigm, we must consider ways and means of representing and integrating knowledge updates from external as well as internal sources. In fact, an agent should not only comprise knowledge about each state, but also knowledge about the transitions between states. The latter may represent the agent's knowledge about the environment's evolution, coupled to its own behaviour and evolution. The lack of rich mechanisms to represent and reason about dynamic knowledge

K. Inoue, K. Satoh, and F. Toni (Eds.): CLIMA VII, LNAI 4371, pp. 246–265, 2007.

and agents i.e. represent and reason about environments where not only some facts about it change, but also the rules that govern it, and where the behaviours of agents also change, is common to the above mentioned systems.

To address this issue the paradigm of Evolving Logic Programming (EVOLP) was introduced in [2]. EVOLP generalizes Answer-set Programming [18] to allow for the specification of a program's own evolution, in a single unified way, by permitting rules to indicate assertive conclusions in the form of program rules. Such assertions, whenever belonging to a model of the program P, can be employed to generate an updated version of P. Furthermore, EVOLP also permits, besides internal or self updates, for updates arising from the environment. The resulting language, EVOLP, provides a simpler, and more general, formulation of logic program updating, running close to traditional LP doctrine, setting itself on a firm formal basis in which to express, implement, and reason about dynamic knowledge bases, opening up several interesting research topics.

Indeed, EVOLP can adequately express the semantics resulting from successive updates to logic programs, considered as incremental specifications of agents, and whose effect can be contextual. In contradistinction to other approaches, it automatically and appropriately deals, via its update semantics [23], with the possible contradictions arising from successive specification changes and refinements. Furthermore, the EVOLP language can express self-modifications triggered by the evolution context itself, present or future. Additionally, foreseen updates not yet executed can automatically trigger other updates, and moreover updates can be nested, so as to determine change both in the next state and in other states further down an evolution strand.

In this paper, we report on the enhancement of the Java based Multi-Agent Platform madAgents [28] with EVOLP, aiming at serving two objectives:

1. provide a *de facto* improvement of madAgents, allowing for the implementation of a richer agent architecture where agents' beliefs and behaviour, as well as their evolution, are specifiable in EVOLP. This allows for the inheritance of all merits of Answer Set Programming (e.g., default negation for reasoning about incomplete knowledge; semantics based on multiple answer-sets for reasoning about several possible consistent worlds; a number of extensions such as preferences, revision, abduction, etc - see [32] for more on this subject) on top of which we add all the specific merits of EVOLP for specifying evolving knowledge.
2. provide a proof of principle that EVOLP can easily be adopted by existing MAS, to represent an evolving belief base, or also to represent the agent's evolving behaviour.

The paper is organised as follows: in Section 2 we briefly overview the Multi-Agent Platform madAgents; in Section 3 we define the EVOLP based agent architecture and its semantics, and illustrate with a small example. In Section 4 we elaborate on some aspects related to the implementation. In Section 5 we compare with other related proposals to conclude in Section 6.

2   Multi-Agent Platform

Our implementation is based on the madAgents [28] platform for logic-based agents, that serves as a base to the development of multi-agent systems, freeing the developer from tasks specific to the distributed systems areas. The main purpose of this platform is to provide a flexible and customisable basis for the development and deployment of multi-agent systems, so that most effort can be focused on the artificial intelligence dimension of the problem.

The platform is implemented with Java[1] and XSB Prolog[2], and includes a set of classes and Prolog files from which to extend the application and build the agents. Prolog is used to handle all Knowledge Representation and Reasoning, connecting to Java modules through InterProlog[3] interface. The semantics of this platform is simple, defined by a set of interactions between agents and other software modules. This way the platform supports an agent architecture that can be easily extended to integrate other modules or functionalities, while the meaning of the resulting application is only dependent on the nature of the modules, the actions of the agents and their reasoning rules. The platform's main functionalities include:

- A communication system built over TCP/IP, allowing agents to control the sending and receiving of messages. Message handling is automatically managed by the system which checks for messages arriving at the inbox and sends messages added to the outbox. Message preprocessing can also be handled by this module, which can be tuned to any specific agent communication language or a developer-defined language. Furthermore, the final destination of the messages, i.e., if they call Java methods or if they are asserted to the agent's knowledge base, is also handled by this module;

- Support for local and RMI-based actions. Actions, can be more than just sending messages and, in some cases, executing a method can be more expressive than requesting such in a message. Local method execution was already possible because of the InterProlog interface. But it could also be the case that an agent could provide methods for other agents to call remotely. This can be easily accomplished with the use of Java's Remote Method Invocation capabilities. The madAgents architecture already provides templates of RMI-based actions that can be called remotely from other agents, thus helping in the development of applications based on this technology.

- Synchronous or asynchronous agent execution. Agents can be synchronised with the platform manager, making their execution cycle dependent on a certain message from the platform manager. Only after receiving this message can the agent go on with its reasoning cycle (deciding which actions to execute and executing them). But agents can also be implemented so as to function like an asynchronous distributed system, where there is no global clock and the reasoning speed of the agents may differ. In this case, the multi-agent application has a non-deterministic execution. To further improve this sense of non-determinism, the agents' reasoning speed can also be defined, providing the application with agents of different reactive nature.

---

[1] Available at http://java.sun.com

[2] Available at http://xsb.sourceforge.net

[3] Available at http://www.declarativa.com/InterProlog

The madAgents platform is used extensively in the current version of the MulE Game Engine [6], an architecture for the development of online multiplayer role-playing games with enhanced realism, to implement several different types of agents, some of them more active in the game (monsters, artificial players) while others are more limited in their actions (non-player characters). It is also used in a video annotation server for personalisation purposes [8]. This server uses madAgents-based agents to perform audiovisual personalisation based on the analysis of the video's semantic data associated with video notes, then suggesting a set of preferential videos to the user.

3 Agent Architecture

In this section we describe the agent architecture. We start by presenting the language of Evolving Logic Programs (EVOLP), and its semantics, as it constitutes the basis for our architecture. Then, we proceed by showing how the language and its semantics can be used to support an architecture for mental agents whose epistemic specification may dynamically change, without loosing its fine theoretical character.

In a nutshell, EVOLP [2] is a simple though quite powerful extension of logic programming, which allows for modeling the dynamics of knowledge bases expressed by programs, be it caused by external events, or by internal requirements for change. From the syntactical point of view, evolving programs are just generalized logic programs (i.e. extended LPs plus default negation in rule heads), extended with (possibly nested) assertions, whether in heads or bodies of rules. This is in clear contrast with earlier proposals to this effect (e.g. LUPS [5], EPI [17] and KABUL [23]) since EVOLP was designed, above all, with the desire to add as few new constructs to traditional logic programming as possible. From the semantical point of view, a model-theoretic characterization is offered of the possible evolutions of such programs. These evolutions arise both from self (i.e. internal to the agent) updating, and from external updating originating in the environment (including other agents).

3.1 Language

We start with the usual preliminaries. Let $\mathcal{A}$ be a set of propositional atoms. An objective literal is either an atom A or a strongly negated atom $\neg A$. A default literal is an objective literal preceded by not. A literal is either an objective literal or a default literal. A rule r is an ordered pair $H(r) \leftarrow B(r)$ where $H(r)$ (dubbed the head of the rule) is a literal and $B(r)$ (dubbed the body of the rule) is a finite set of literals. A rule with $H(r) = L_0$ and $B(r) = \{L_1, \ldots, L_n\}$ will simply be written as $L_0 \leftarrow L_1, \ldots, L_n$. A generalized logic program (GLP) P, in $\mathcal{A}$, is a finite or infinite set of rules. If $H(r) = A$ (resp. $H(r) = not\,A$) then $not\,H(r) = not\,A$ (resp. $not\,H(r) = A$). If $H(r) = \neg A$, then $\neg H(r) = A$. By the expanded generalized logic program corresponding to the GLP P, denoted by $\mathbf{P}$, we mean the GLP obtained by augmenting P with a rule of the form $not\,\neg H(r) \leftarrow B(r)$ for every rule, in P, of the form $H(r) \leftarrow B(r)$, where $H(r)$ is an objective literal. Two rules r and r' are conflicting, denoted by $r \bowtie r'$, iff $H(r) = not\,H(r')$.

An interpretation M of $\mathcal{A}$ is a set of objective literals that is consistent i.e., M does not contain both A and $\neg A$. An objective literal L is true in M, denoted by $M \vDash L$, iff $L \in M$, and false otherwise. A default literal $not\ L$ is true in M, denoted by $M \vDash not\ L$, iff $L \notin M$, and false otherwise. A set of literals B is true in M, denoted by $M \vDash B$, iff each literal in B is true in M.

An interpretation M of $\mathcal{A}$ is an answer set of a GLP P iff

$$M' = least\,(\mathbf{P} \cup \{not\ A \mid A \notin M\})$$

where $M' = M \cup \{not\_A \mid A \notin M\}$, A is an objective literal, and $least(.)$ denotes the least model of the definite program obtained from the argument program by replacing every default literal $not\ A$ by a new atom not_A.

In order to allow for logic programs to evolve, we first need some mechanism for letting older rules be supervened by more recent ones. That is, we must include a mechanism for deletion of previous knowledge along the agent's knowledge evolution. This can be achieved by permitting default negation not just in rule bodies, as in extended logic programming, but in rule heads as well[25]. Furthermore, we need a way to state that, under some conditions, some new rule should be asserted in the knowledge base[4]. In EVOLP this is achieved by augmenting the language with a reserved predicate $assert/1$, whose sole argument is itself a full-blown rule, so that arbitrary nesting becomes possible. This predicate can appear both as rule head (to impose internal assertions of rules) as well as in rule bodies (to test for assertion of rules). Formally:

Definition 1. *Let $\mathcal{A}$ be a set of propositional atoms (not containing $assert/1$). The extended language $\mathcal{A}_{assert}$ is defined inductively as follows:*

- *All propositional atoms in $\mathcal{A}$ are propositional atoms in $\mathcal{A}_{assert}$;*
- *If r is a rule over $\mathcal{A}_{assert}$ then $assert(r)$ is a propositional atom of $\mathcal{A}_{assert}$;*
- *Nothing else is a propositional atom in $\mathcal{A}_{assert}$.*

An *evolving logic program over a language $\mathcal{A}$*[5] *is a (possibly infinite) set of generalized logic program rules over $\mathcal{A}_{assert}$.*

Example 1. Examples of EVOLP rules are:

$$assert\,(not\ a \leftarrow b) \leftarrow not\ c.$$
$$a \leftarrow assert\,(b \leftarrow).$$
$$assert\,(assert\,(a \leftarrow) \leftarrow assert\,(b \leftarrow not\ c)\,, d) \leftarrow not\ e.$$

Intuitively, the first rule states that, if c is false, then the rule $not\ a \leftarrow b$ must be asserted in the agent's knowledge base; the 2nd that, if the fact $b \leftarrow$ is going to be asserted in the agent's knowledge base, then a is true; the last states that, if e is false, then a rule must be asserted stating that, if d is true and the rule $b \leftarrow not\ c$ is going to be asserted then the fact $a \leftarrow$ must be asserted.

---

[4] Note that asserting a rule in a knowledge base does not mean that the rule is simply added to it, but rather that the rule is used to update the existing knowledge base according to some update semantics, as will be seen below.

[5] Here we extend EVOLP for LPs with both strong and default negation, unlike in [2] where only LP's without strong negation were used.

This language alone is enough to model the agent's knowledge base, and to cater, within it, for internal updating actions that change it. But self-evolution of a knowledge base is not enough for our purposes. We also want the agent to be aware of events that happen outside itself, and desire the possibility too of giving the agent update "commands" for changing its specification. In other words, we wish a language that allows for influence from the outside, where this influence may be: observation of facts (or rules) that are perceived at some state; assertion commands directly imparting the assertion of new rules on the evolving program. Both can be represented as EVOLP rules: the former by rules without the assert predicate in the head, and the latter by rules with it. Consequently, we shall represent outside influence as a sequence of EVOLP rules:

Definition 2. *Let P be an evolving program over the language $\mathcal{A}$. An* event sequence *over P is a sequence of evolving programs over $\mathcal{A}$.*

3.2 Semantics

In general, we have an EVOLP program describing an agent's initial knowledge base. This knowledge base may already contain rules (with asserts in heads) that describe some forms of its own evolution. Besides this, we consider sequences of events representing observation and messages arising from the environment. Each of these events in the sequence are themselves sets of EVOLP rules, i.e. EVOLP programs. The semantics issue is thus that of, given an initial EVOLP program and a sequence of EVOLP programs as events, to determine what is true and what is false after each of those events.

More precisely, the meaning of a sequence of EVOLP programs is given by a set of *evolution stable models*, each of which is a sequence of interpretations or states. The basic idea is that each evolution stable model describes some possible evolution of one initial program after a given number n of evolution steps, given the events in the sequence. Each evolution is represented by a sequence of programs, each program corresponding to a knowledge state.

The primordial intuitions for the construction of these program sequences are as follows: regarding head asserts, whenever the atom $assert(Rule)$ belongs to an interpretation in a sequence, i.e. belongs to a model according to the stable model semantics of the current program, then $Rule$ must belong to the program in the next state; asserts in bodies are treated as any other predicate literals.

The sequences of programs are treated as in Dynamic Logic Programming [23,3,1], a framework for specifying updates of logic programs where knowledge is given by a sequence of logic programs whose semantics is based on the fact that the most recent rules are set in force, and previous rules are valid (by inertia) insofar as possible, i.e. they are kept for as long as they do not conflict with more recent ones. In DLP, default negation is treated as in answer-set programming [18]. Formally, a *dynamic logic program* is a sequence $\mathcal{P} = (P_1, \ldots, P_n)$ of generalized logic programs and its semantic is determined by (c.f. [23,1] for more details):

Definition 3. *Let $\mathcal{P} = (P_1, \ldots, P_n)$ be a dynamic logic program over language $\mathcal{A}$. An interpretation M is a (refined) dynamic stable model of $\mathcal{P}$ at state s, $1 \leq s \leq n$ iff*

$$M' = least\left(\left[\rho_s\left(\mathcal{P}\right) - Rej_s(M)\right] \cup Def_s(M)\right)$$

where:

$$Def_s(M) = \{not\ A \mid \nexists r \in \rho(\mathcal{P}), H(r) = A, M \models B(r)\}$$
$$Rej_s(M) = \{r \mid r \in \mathbf{P}_i, \exists r' \in \mathbf{P}_j, i \leq j \leq s, r \bowtie r', M \models B(r')\}$$

and A is an objective literal, ρ_s ($\mathcal{P}$) denotes the multiset of all rules appearing in the programs $\mathbf{P}_1, ..., \mathbf{P}_s$, and M' and least(.) are as before.

Intuitively, given an interpretation M, the set $Rej_s(M)$ contains those rules which are overridden by a newer conflicting rule whose body is true according to the interpretation M. The set $Def_s(M)$ contains default negations $not\ A$ of all unsupported atoms A, i.e., those atoms A for which there is no rule, in any program, whose body is true according to the interpretation M, which can thus be assumed false *by default*.

Before presenting the definitions that formalize the above intuitions of EVOLP, let us show some illustrative examples.

Example 2. Consider an initial program P containing the rules

> $a.$
> $assert(not\ a \leftarrow) \leftarrow b.$
> $c \leftarrow assert(not\ a \leftarrow).$
> $assert(b \leftarrow a) \leftarrow not\ c.$

and that all the events are empty EVOLP programs. The (only) answer set of P is $M = \{a, assert(b \leftarrow a)\}$ and conveying the information that program P is ready to evolve into a new program (P, P_2) by adding rule $(b \leftarrow a)$ at the next step, i.e. to P_2. In the only dynamic stable model M_2 of the new program (P, P_2), atom b is true as well as atom $assert(not\ a \leftarrow)$ and also c, meaning that (P, P_2) evolves into a new program (P, P_2, P_3) by adding rule $(not\ a \leftarrow)$ at the next step, i.e. in P_3. This negative fact in P_3 conflicts with the fact in P, and the older is rejected. The rule added in P_2 remains valid, but is no longer useful to conclude b, since a is no longer valid. So, $assert(not\ a \leftarrow)$ and c are also no longer true. In the only dynamic stable model of the last sequence both a, b, and c are false.

This example does not address external events. The rules that belong to the i-th event should be added to the program of state i, and proceed as in the example above.

Example 3. In the example above, suppose that at state 2 there is an external event with the rules, r_1 and r_2, $assert(d \leftarrow b) \leftarrow a$ and $e \leftarrow$. Since the only stable model of P is $I = \{a, assert(b \leftarrow a)\}$ and there is an outside event at state 2 with r_1 and r_2, the program evolves into the new program obtained by updating P not only with the rule $b \leftarrow a$ but also with those rules, i.e. $(P, \{b \leftarrow a;\ assert(d \leftarrow b) \leftarrow a;\ e \leftarrow\})$. The only dynamic stable model M_2 of this program is $\{b, assert(not\ a \leftarrow), assert(d \leftarrow b), e\}$.

If we keep with the evolution of this program (e.g. by subsequent empty events), we have to decide what to do, in these subsequent states, about the event received at state 2. Intuitively, we want the rules coming from the outside, be they observations or assertion commands, to be understood as events given at a state, that are not to persist by inertia.

I.e. if rule r belongs to some set E_i of an event sequence, this means that r was perceived, or received, after $i - 1$ evolution steps of the program, and that this perception event is not to be assumed by inertia from then onward. In the example, it means that if we have perceived e at state 2, then e and all its possible consequences should be true at that state. But the truth of e should not persist into the subsequent state (unless e is yet again perceived from the outside). In other words, when constructing subsequent states, the rules coming from events in state 2 should no longer be available and considered. As will become clear below, making these events persistent can be specified in EVOLP.

Definition 4. *An* evolution interpretation *of length n of an evolving program P over $\mathcal{A}$ is a finite sequence $\mathcal{I} = (I_1, I_2, \ldots, I_n)$ of interpretations $\mathcal{A}_{assert}$. The* evolution trace *associated with evolution interpretation $\mathcal{I}$ is the sequence of programs $(P_1, P_2, \ldots, P_n)$ where:*

- $P_1 = P$;
- $P_i = \{r \mid assert(r) \in I_{i-1}\}$, *for each* $2 \leq i \leq n$.

Definition 5. *An evolution interpretation $(I_1, I_2, \ldots, I_n)$, of length n, with evolution trace $(P_1, P_2, \ldots, P_n)$ is an* evolution stable model *of an evolving program P given a sequence of events $(E_1, E_2, \ldots, E_k)$, with $n \leq k$, iff for every i ($1 \leq i \leq n$), I_i is a dynamic stable model at state i of $(P_1, P_2 \ldots, (P_i \cup E_i))$.*

Notice that the rules coming from the outside do not persist by inertia. At any given step i, the rules from E_i are added and the (possibly various) I_i obtained. This determines the programs P_{i+1} of the trace, which are then added to E_{i+1} to determine the models I_{i+1}. The definition assumes the whole sequence of events given a priori. In fact this need not be so because the events at any given step n only influence the models in the evolution interpretation from n onward:

Proposition 1. *Let $M = (M_1, \ldots, M_n)$ be an evolution stable model of P given a sequence of events $(E_1, E_2, \ldots, E_n)$. Then, for any sets of events $E_{n+1}, \ldots, E_m$ ($m > n$), M is also an evolution stable model of P given $(E_1, \ldots, E_n, E_{n+1}, \ldots, E_m)$.*

EVOLP programs may have various evolution models of given length, or none:

Example 4. Consider P with the following two rules, and 3 empty events:

$$assert\,(a \leftarrow) \leftarrow not\,assert\,(b \leftarrow), not\,b.$$
$$assert\,(b \leftarrow) \leftarrow not\,assert\,(a \leftarrow), not\,a.$$

The reader can check that there are 2 evolution stable models of length 3, each representing one possible evolution of the program after those empty events:

$$M_1 = \langle\{assert(a \leftarrow)\}, \{a, assert(a \leftarrow)\}, \{a, assert(a \leftarrow)\}\rangle$$
$$M_2 = \langle\{assert(b \leftarrow)\}, \{b, assert(b \leftarrow)\}, \{b, assert(b \leftarrow)\}\rangle$$

Since various evolutions may exist for a given length, evolution stable models alone do not determine a truth relation. A truth relation can be defined, as usual, based on the intersection of models:

Definition 6. *Let P be an evolving program, $\mathcal{E}$ an event sequence of length n, both over the language $\mathcal{A}$, and M an interpretation over $\mathcal{A}_{assert}$. M is a* Stable Model of P *given $\mathcal{E}$ iff $(M_1, \dots, M_{n-1}, M)$ is an evolution stable model of P given $\mathcal{E}$ with length n, for some interpretations $M_1, \dots, M_{n-1}$. We say that propositional atom A of $\mathcal{A}$ is:* true given $\mathcal{E}$ *iff A belongs to all stable models of P given $\mathcal{E}$;* false given $\mathcal{E}$ *iff A does not belong to any stable models of P given $\mathcal{E}$;* unknown given $\mathcal{E}$ *otherwise.*

A consequence of the above definitions is that the semantics of EVOLP is, in fact, a proper generalization of the answer-set semantics, in the following sense:

Proposition 2. *Let P be a generalized (extended) logic program (without predicate assert/1) over a language $\mathcal{A}$, and $\mathcal{E}$ be any sequence with $n \geq 0$ of empty EVOLP programs. Then, M is a stable model of P given $\mathcal{E}$ iff the restriction of M to $\mathcal{A}$ is an answer set of P (in the sense of [18,25]).*

The possibility of having various stable models after an event sequence is of special interest for using EVOLP as a language for reasoning about possible evolutions of an agent's knowledge base. Like for answer-set programs, we define the notion of categorical programs as those such that, for any given event sequence, no "branching" occurs, i.e. a single stable model exists[6].

Definition 7. *An EVOLP program P is* categorical *given event sequence $\mathcal{E}$ iff there exists only one stable model of P given $\mathcal{E}$.*

3.3   Agent Architecture

We now turn our attention to the agent architecture. Each agent is conceptually divided into three layers as depicted in Figure 1.

- The Platform Layer deals with all the necessary platform specific protocols such as registration, coordination, control, etc.
- The Physical Layer is responsible for interfacing the agent with the environment, providing an actuator responsible for executing actions in the environment as well as an inbox and outbox to process the all incoming and outgoing events.
- The Mental Layer is responsible for maintaining the agent's beliefs, behaviour and capabilities and deliberation processes.

In this section we will describe in greater detail the Mental Layer. Lack of space prevents us from presenting details concerning the other two layers.

The Mental Layer can be seen as being divided into three main components, namely the Beliefs, Capabilities and Deliberation, even though each may provide for more than one aspect. The Beliefs module is specified in EVOLP, thus specifying not only the beliefs of the agent but also its behaviour and evolution. The Capabilities module contains information regarding the actions that the agent can perform, together with their epistemic effects, in the form of updates both to the agent's own Beliefs as well as to other

---

[6] The definition of conditions over programs and sequences ensuring that a program is categorical is beyond the scope of this paper.

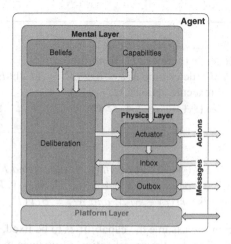

Fig. 1. Agent Architecture

agent's beliefs. The Deliberation Module executes the common observe-think-act cycle
[21], implementing some specific semantics. Formally, an agent initial specification is
defined as follows:

Definition 8. *Let* $\mathcal{N} = \{\alpha_1, ..., \alpha_n\}$ *be a set of agent names and* $\mathcal{A}$ *a propositional
language[7]. An agent* (α_i) *initial specification, or an agent* α_i *at state 1, is a tuple*
$\langle \alpha_i, \mathcal{C}, Sel(\cdot), \mathcal{P}_1 \rangle$ *where:*

- $\mathcal{C}$ *is a pair* $(\mathcal{A}_\mathcal{C}, \mathcal{E}_\mathcal{F})$ *representing the capabilities of the agent where* $\mathcal{A}_\mathcal{C}$ *is a set
  of propositions, each representing an action that agent* α_i *is capable of preforming
  and* $\mathcal{E}_\mathcal{F}$ *is a set of predicates of the form* effects $(Action, \alpha_j, Effect)$ *with* $Action \in$
  $\mathcal{A}_\mathcal{C}$, $\alpha_j \in \mathcal{N}$ *and* Effect *is an EVOLP program over language* $\mathcal{A} \cup \mathcal{A}_\mathcal{C}^{\alpha_j}$ *(where*
  $\mathcal{A}_\mathcal{C}^{\alpha_j}$ *is the set of actions that agent* α_j *is capable of preforming) representing the
  epistemic effects, on* α_j, *of agent* α_i *performing action* Action *i.e., after* Action *is
  performed,* Effect *should be added to agent's j next event;*
- $Sel(\cdot)$ *is some selection function that selects one dynamic stable model given a
  dynamic logic program;*
- $\mathcal{P}_1 = (P_1)$ *is a dynamic logic program consisting of just one evolving logic program,* P_1, *over language* $\mathcal{A} \cup \mathcal{A}_\mathcal{C}$, *representing the agent's initial beliefs and behaviour specification.*

According to the execution mode specified in the Platform Layer (e.g. synchronous,
asynchronous, etc) an agent evolves into the next state as per the following observe-
think-act cycle and definition:

---

[7] Without loss of generality, we are assuming that all agents share a common language.

$$cycle\left(s, \langle \alpha_i, (\mathcal{A}_C, \mathcal{E}_{\mathcal{F}}), Sel\left(\cdot\right), \mathcal{P}_s\rangle\right)$$
$$observe \text{ (percieve } E_s \text{ from inbox)}$$
$$think \text{ (determine } M_s = Sel\left(\mathcal{P}_{s-1}, (P_s \cup E_s)\right))$$
$$act \text{ (execute actions } M_s \cap \mathcal{A}_C)$$
$$cycle\left(s+1, \langle \alpha_i, (\mathcal{A}_C, \mathcal{E}_{\mathcal{F}}), Sel\left(\cdot\right), \mathcal{P}_{s+1}\rangle\right)$$

Definition 9. *Let $\langle \alpha_i, C, Sel\left(\cdot\right), \mathcal{P}_s\rangle$ be agent α_i at state s and E_s the events perceived by agent α_i at state s. Agent α_i at state $s+1$ is $\langle \alpha_i, C, Sel\left(\cdot\right), \mathcal{P}_{s+1}\rangle$ where[8] $\mathcal{P}_{s+1} = (\mathcal{P}_s, P_{s+1})$, $P_{s+1} = \{r \mid assert(r) \in M_s\}$, and $M_s = Sel\left(\mathcal{P}_{s-1}, (P_s \cup E_s)\right)$.*

In the previous definition, we assume the capabilities to be fixed. However, it needs not be so as we can easily allow for the specification of updates to this component if we wish to have the agent, for example, learn new capabilities.

Unlike its original inductive definition, we employ a constructive view of EVOLP. The main difference relates to the existence of the selection function that trims some possible evolutions when selecting one stable model, corresponding to the commitment made when some set of actions is executed, and not another. This commitment is obtained by fixing the trace, instead of simply storing the initial program, sequence of events and choices made. The resulting simplicity, obtained by using a constructive definition, is due to the fact that the agent no longer has to deal with past possible choices that were not taken. The commitment made at each step means that there is no need to keep other alternatives for that state. Note, however, that this does not mean that, due to this commitment, some alternative action that was not chosen at some state cannot be executed at the subsequent state. If this action is still an option after the initial commitment it will still be present is some model of the subsequent state.

The following result relates both views of EVOLP:

Theorem 1. *Let $\langle \alpha, C, Sel\left(\cdot\right), \mathcal{P}_s\rangle$ (where $\mathcal{P}_s = (P_1, P_2, \ldots, P_s)$) be agent α at state s resulting from the initial specification $\langle \alpha, C, Sel\left(\cdot\right), (P_1)\rangle$ and the sequence of events $\mathcal{E} = (E_1, E_2, \ldots, E_s)$. Let M_s be an interpretation. Then:*

- *If M_s is a dynamic stable model of $\mathcal{P}_s$ then M_s is a stable model of P_1 given $\mathcal{E}$;*
- *If P_1 is* categorical *given $\mathcal{E}$, then, M_s is a stable model of P_1 given $\mathcal{E}$ iff M_s is a dynamic stable model of $\mathcal{P}_s$.*

3.4 Illustrative Example

In this section we present a small illustrative example. In this example we consider two agents, *teacher* and *student*. The student will want to know how to get a PhD, and will ask the teacher for as along as he does not know how. He knows that people that are

---

[8] If $\mathcal{P} = (P_1, \ldots, P_s)$ is a DLP and P a GLP, by $(\mathcal{P}, P)$ we mean the DLP $(P_1, \ldots, P_s, P)$.

not smart do not get PhDs. The teacher will tell the student to study, in case the student has not told the teacher he has already studied. The student, however, when requested to study, may chose between studying or not. When the student finally tells the teacher that he has studied, then the behaviour of the teacher will be updated, and he will, from then onwards, reply to the student's subsequent requests by teaching him one of two rules, both regarding ways to get a PhD (either by having a good advisor or doing good work). Teaching the rule amounts to sending it as an assertion event to the student agent, which will be used to update the student's beliefs.

The tuple $\langle teacher, (\mathcal{A}_\mathcal{C}^t, \mathcal{E}_\mathcal{F}^t), Sel^t(\cdot), (P_1^t) \rangle$ is the teacher's initial specification, where:

$$P_1^t = \{tell\_study \leftarrow ask, not\ studied, not\ study.$$
$$assert\,(studied) \leftarrow study.$$
$$assert\,(teach\_r1 \leftarrow not\ teach\_r2,\ ask.) \leftarrow study.$$
$$assert\,(teach\_r2 \leftarrow not\ teach\_r1,\ ask.) \leftarrow study.\}$$

$$\mathcal{A}_\mathcal{C}^t = \{tell\_study, teach\_r1, teach\_r2\}$$

$$\mathcal{E}_\mathcal{F}^t = \{effects\,(teach\_r1, student, \{assert\,(phd \leftarrow good\_advisor.)\})$$
$$effects\,(teach\_r2, student, \{assert\,(phd \leftarrow good\_work.)\})$$
$$effects\,(tell\_study, student, \{tell\_study.\})\}$$

and a non-deterministic random choice function $Sel^t(\cdot)$. The first rule in P_1^t specifies that any event $study$ should make $tell\_study$ true in case there is no evidence that the student has studied (in the past or present). When the teacher receives an event E_i with $study$, $assert\,(studied)$ is part of the model and $studied$ is used to update the beliefs by becoming part of P_{i+1}^t so that it becomes persistent. Furthermore, the assertions specified by the last two rules also cause an update, rendering their argument rules "active". Any subsequent event E_i with ask is replied to with either $teach\_r1$ or $teach\_r2$ as it generates two stable models, each of which with one of those actions. The initial program P_1^t only defines the mental dimension of actions, i.e., it defines which action to perform but not its concrete effects. This amounts to the clear separation between reasoning about actions and action execution. Note that we can include a rule of the form $effect \leftarrow action$ in the program where $effect$ is the epistemic effect of deciding to perform $action$. For example, to have the teacher only performs actions $teach\_r1$ and $teach\_r2$ once, we could include the rules $assert\,(taught\_r1) \leftarrow teach\_r1.$ and $assert\,(taught\_r2) \leftarrow teach\_r2.$ and add $not\ taught\_r1$ and $not\ taught\_r2$, respectively, to the bodies of the two rules asserted, as follows:

$$teach\_r1 \leftarrow not\ teach\_r2, not\ taught\_r1, ask.$$
$$teach\_r2 \leftarrow not\ teach\_r1, not\ taught\_r2, ask.$$

Let us now pay attention to the student. $\langle student, (\mathcal{A}_\mathcal{C}^s, \mathcal{E}_\mathcal{F}^s), Sel^s(\cdot), (P_1^s) \rangle$ is it's initial specification, where $Sel^s(\cdot)$ is a non-deterministic random choice function and

$$P_1^s = \{study \leftarrow not \neg study, tell\_study.$$
$$\neg study \leftarrow not \, study, tell\_study.$$
$$not \, phd \leftarrow not \, smart.$$
$$ask \leftarrow not \, phd.$$
$$good\_advisor.\}$$

$$\mathcal{A}_C^s = \{ask, study\}$$

$$\mathcal{E}_{\mathcal{F}}^s = \{ \, effects \, (ask, teacher, \{ask.\}) \,,$$
$$effects \, (study, teacher, \{study.\}) \}$$

We will now illustrate a possible run of this system, assuming a synchronous mode of operation. Initially, the teacher's only stable model is $M_1^t = \{\}$. The student has one dynamic stable model, namely $M_1^s = \{ask, good\_advisor\}$, which has the effect of sending the event $\{ask\}$ to the teacher agent, i.e. $E_2^t = \{ask\}$. At state 2, the teacher will have one dynamic stable model $M_2^t = \{ask, tell\_study.\}$, as he does not know the student has studied. This will send the event $\{tell\_study\}$, i.e. $E_3^s = \{tell\_study\}$. Meanwhile, since at state 2 the student still does not know how to obtain a PhD, he asks again (we cannot say he is very polite), sending the appropriate event to the teacher i.e. $E_3^t = \{ask\}$.

At state 3, the teacher will have one dynamic stable model $M_3^t = \{ask, tell\_study.\}$, as he still does not know the student has studied, and thus $E_4^s = \{tell\_study\}$. Meanwhile, the student has just received the $tell\_study$ event and has two dynamic stable models, $M_3^s = \{tell\_study, ask, study\}$ and $M_3^{s\prime} = \{tell\_study, ask, \neg study\}$. If the student chooses $M_3^{s\prime}$, this story will just go on as before. Eventually, the student will choose M_3^s, sending the events $E_4^t = \{study, ask\}$ to the teacher. After this set of events is finally sent, the teacher, at state 4, will have one dynamic stable model $M_4^t = \{assert \, (teach\_r2 \leftarrow not \, teach\_r1, \; ask.), assert \, (teach\_r1 \leftarrow not \, teach\_r2, !ask.), ask, study, assert \, (studied)\}$. Having this model will cause the fact $studied$ and the rules $teach\_rule1 \leftarrow not \, teach\_r2, \; ask.$, and $teach\_rule2 \leftarrow not \, teach\_r1, \; ask.$ to belong to P_5^t. Furthermore, the teacher will not send any events to the student since none of the elements of M_4^t is one of its actions.

To cut this story short, after the next ask by the student, the teacher will have two dynamic stable models (of the DLP $(P_1^t, ..., P_5^t)$ where $P_2^t = P_3^t = P_4^t = \emptyset$), one with $teach\_rule1$ true and another with $teach\_rule2$ true. The teacher's selection function chooses one of them and either executes $teach\_rule1$ or $teach\_rule2$, causing either of $assert \, (phd \leftarrow good\_advisor.)$ and $assert \, (phd \leftarrow good\_work.)$ to be sent to the student. If the student receives the event $assert \, (phd \leftarrow good\_advisor.)$, he will stop asking because he can conclude phd, even though $not \, smart$ is still true, since the newly accquired rule will serve, as per the DLP semantics, to reject the rule $not \, phd \leftarrow not \, smart$. As long as the teacher keeps sending the event $assert \, (phd \leftarrow good\_work.)$, since the student cannot prove $good\_work$ (besides impolite he is also lazy), he will keep asking the teacher until the teacher eventually selects the action $teach\_rule1$, sends $assert \, (phd \leftarrow good\_advisor.)$, and the student will stop bothering the teacher.

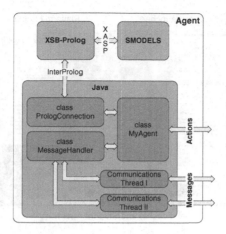

Fig. 2. Agent Implementation Architecture

4 Implementation

In this section we briefly elaborate on some issues related to the implementation of a generic agent. As depicted in Figure 2, the implementation employs five different technologies, namely Java, XSB Prolog, Interprolog, XASP (package provided by XSB), Smodels[9]. In the madAgents platform, the agents' execution is controlled from the Java component, where each agent is represented by a Java Thread. Each agent has an instance of a `MessageHandler` class, which handles all communication and a `PrologConnection` class which interfaces with XSB-Prolog. Interfacing between the Java and Prolog components is handled by InterProlog. The Java component also provides a Graphical User Interface, shown in Figure 3.

The agent's execution cycle proceeds as follows:

1. Wait for the agent's reasoning delay to exhaust, or wait for a synchronisation message to arrive from the platform manager;
2. Check for new messages and process them. Message processing can be the assertion of the message in the agent's knowledge base or the direct execution of a certain method. Messages may originate in other agent's, in the platform manager or encode outside events. Communication is implemented so as to provide a transparent message exchange mechanism to the agents, where they only have to call methods to add messages to their inbox or outbox and the `MessageHandler` class does all the rest. This class also contains a simple "address book", allowing the agent to know the host and port where to contact a certain agent;
3. Select one dynamic stable model which will encode the actions to execute. Determining the set of dynamic stable models is performed in two steps: first the DLP is syntactically transformed into a single logic program, written in an extended language, whose answer-sets are in a one-to-one correspondence with the dynamic

---

[9] Available at http://www.tcs.hut.fi/Software/smodels.

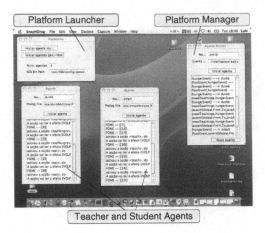

Fig. 3. Graphical User Interface

stable models of the initial DLP, following the results in [23]; subsequently, Smodels is invoked from within XSB, using the interface XASP, to determine the stable models of the transformed program. Finally, the Selection function is used to select one of these models. If the selection function chooses randomly, we can have Smodels determine one model only, thus saving computational time;

4. Execute the chosen actions. Action execution may include method calling or message sending;

5. Determine the next program in the trace and cycle again. Since the transformation mentioned above is incremental, the agent effectively keeps the transformed program, adding just the rules corresponding to the new part of the trace. The newly added required methods were encapsulated in the `PrologConnection` class. This class now includes methods for setting up the Prolog environment, calling non-deterministic goals, and calculating the new EVOLP trace and program transformation.

5 Related Work

Other systems exist that, to some extent, are related to the one we presented. Each has some specific characteristics that make them more appropriate for some applications, although none has the rich update characteristics of EVOLP.

3APL [20,15] is a logic based programming language for implementing agents with beliefs, goals, and plans as mental attitudes, that can generate and revise plans to achieve goals, and are capable of interaction. Actions can be external, communication, or internal mental ones, resembling actions and their effects in our system. 3APL supports the integration of Prolog and Java. MadAgents does not have an explicit goal base nor plan library, although answer set programming can be used for planning purposes, and goals can be represented by integrity constraints without requiring a language extension or, as explored elsewhere in [27], by means of DLP to obtain extra expressivity. 3APL lacks the ability to deal with updates such as our system.

Jason [9] is a Java written interpreter for an extended version of AgentSpeak(L), a BDI-styled logic-based agent-oriented programming language. It provides features such as speech-act based communication, customisable selection and trust functions, and overall agent architecture (perception, belief-revision, inter-agent communication, and acting), and easy extensibility through user-defined "internal actions". A detailed comparison with Jason is subject for future work. A first impression shows that both systems use default negation for knowledge representation and, as others, Jason does not provide the ability to deal with updates such as our system.

IMPACT [29,16] is a system developed with the main purpose of providing a framework to build agents on top of heterogeneous sources of knowledge. It provides the notion of an agent program written over a language of so-called code-calls, encapsulations of whatever the legacy code is. Code-calls are used in clauses, that form agent programs, determining constraints on the actions that are to be taken by agents. Agent programs and their semantics resemble logic programs extended with deontic modalities. The semantics is given by the notion of a rational status sets, which are similar to the notion of stable models used in our system. While IMPACT is at a far more advanced stage of development than our system, we believe that our system, namely due to its use of EVOLP, has the potential to meet IMPACT standards, while providing an added value in what concerns the ability to represent evolutions.

MINERVA [24,23] uses KABUL (Knowledge and Behaviour Update Language) to specify agents' behaviour and their updates. MINERVA is conceptually close to our system concerning its knowledge representation mechanism. One difference is that MINERVA uses KABUL whereas our system uses EVOLP. Even though KABUL has some extra features that allow for more elaborate forms of social knowledge, EVOLP is a simpler and more elegant language that has all the features required for this application. Furthermore madAgents provides with a full fledged multi-agent platform.

DALI [14] is an Active Logic Programming Language, somehow related to MINERVA and our present system, designed for executable specification of logical agents. It uses plain Horn Clauses and its semantics is based on Least Herbrand Models. Three main differences are noticed when comparing our system with DALI: our semantics is based on ASP, with default negation while DALI uses plain Horn Clauses and the semantics is based on Least Herbrand Models; DALI is implemented in PROLOG while our system uses a combination of Java, XSB and Smodels; DALI does not allow for evolving specifications such as the ones provided by EVOLP.

Another multi-agent system that somehow relates to our proposal is PROSOCS [12]. PROSOCS, Programming Societies of Computees, is implemented with Sicstus Prolog, Java and JXTA, a Java-based peer to peer system. PROSOCS has the main motivations of the madAgents platform, namely to allow for a simple implementation of multi-agent systems based on an already implemented set of functionalities, namely those related with communication and interaction between the agents and the environment, as well as those related with the most basic reasoning capabilities. Also, as in the madAgents platform, PROSOCS agents are based on an agent template which already has a set of sensors and actuators which function as the interface to the environment. Differences arise in the fact that PROSOCS agents use a peer to peer system for implementing the whole agent discovery and communication processes, and end up making the agents dependent on this system. Additionally, PROSOCS agents also use a different mental model – Logic Programming with Priorities and Abductive Logic Programming with Abductive Event Calculus. They do not provide any way of specifying how the knowledge of a certain agent evolves, this accounting for another difference between PROSOCS and our proposal, which defines this concept with a precise semantics. PROSOCS agents have explicit planning capabilities whereas our agents only have those capabilities through the use of the expressive power of Answer-Set Programming. In summary, besides the implementation choices (Sicstus Prolog vs. XSB, Jasper vs. Interprolog, JXTA vs. madAgents communication system) the main differences reside in the difference between the capabilities of representing knowledge evolution, which is the central point of our proposal.

6   Concluding Remarks

In this paper we presented a platform and architecture that resulted from combining madAgents with EVOLP.

Being a paper that describes the theory of the underlying the system, its implementation, and some examples, it necessarily lacks some deeper explanations concerning other important issues. Some of the issues that were left out concern open problems and a deeper comparison with the other related systems, while others refer to issues that were addressed, often representing non-trivial challenges, such as for example the details concerning the implementation of the transformation into a program to be sent to Smodels because of its restricted use of variables. However, we had to leave something out and this is the result of our choice. Before we end, in this final section, we re-elaborate on some of the main points of our system.

Using default negation allows for reasoning with incomplete information, important in open environments. In this paper, we additionally extended EVOLP to also allow for strong negation. By combining both forms of negation, the programmer can obtain the full expressivity of answer-set programming.

The stable model based semantics, assigning a set of models at each state, allows for reasoning about possible worlds. The inclusion of the selection function allows for meta-reasoning about these possible worlds using any paradigm chosen by the programmer. However, some preference based semantics, specifiable in logic programming (c.f. [13,4]), can be directly programmed in the agent's EVOLP program to allow for the specification of preferences.

Even though we only presented the stable model based semantics, the architecture allows for the use of a well founded three valued semantics that allows for more efficient, though less expressive, top down proof procedures [31,7].

The architecture effectively separates the notions of reasoning about actions and acting, even though this was not exemplified in detail in this paper. The agent reasons about actions, choosing which ones to execute. These will be executed, resulting (or not) in changes to the environment which can be monitored and may produce new inputs to the agent in the form of events. In parallel, the execution of each action will have an epistemic effect reflected by the (self)-update of the agent's knowledge, in the form of a set of events to be included in the agent's input, which can be seen as the effects of knowing that the action was executed, different from those of the action itself.

The possibility of having several different modes of execution, namely time-driven, event driven, synchronous and asynchronous, allows for the specification of different types of agents, as well as incorporating different coordination policies, specifiable in logic programming.

The specification language EVOLP, being based on logic programs with the stable model semantics (aka. answer set programming), and properly extending these, directly supports the representation, specification and reuse of the grand number of results produced by those working in answer-set programming for knowledge representation and reasoning (see [32] for references).

Most of all, we believe to have achieved both main goals i.e. to provide an improvement of madAgents, allowing for the implementation of a richer agent architecture where agents' beliefs and behaviour, as well as their evolution, is specifiable in EVOLP, and to provide a proof of principle that EVOLP can easily be adopted by existing MAS, to represent an evolving belief base, or also to represent the agent's evolving behaviour.

Researchers working in computational logic for multi-agent systems, have often been criticized for not carrying their theoretical results to the implementation stage. Even though our platform and architecture are evolving proposals and in constant development, they are fully implemented while enjoying a well defined formal semantics.

We are currently working on several directions, both on applications of the current system, as well as on extensions of EVOLP with direct applicability in the context of Multi-Agent Systems. On the application side, we would like to mention that we are re-designing the MulE Game Engine [6] to benefit from our enhanced system. Initial results can be found in [22]. Regarding extensions of EVOLP, we are already working on using EVOLP to represent and reason about declarative goals (preliminary results can be found in [27]) and plans, as well as enriching EVOLP with the possibility to deal with complex events, through the definition of a suitable event algebra. Preliminary explorations regarding the introduction of probabilities in the EVOLP framework are also being pursued.

Overall, on the development side, we believe that this is just the initial result of a constantly evolving ongoing project which we believe to be very promising.

References

1. J. J. Alferes, F. Banti, A. Brogi, and J. A. Leite. The refined extension principle for semantics of dynamic logic programming. *Studia Logica*, 79(1):7–32, 2005.
2. J. J. Alferes, A. Brogi, J. A. Leite, and L. M. Pereira. Evolving logic programs. In S. Flesca, S. Greco, N. Leone, and G. Ianni, editors, *Proceedings of the 8th European Conference on Logics in Artificial Intelligence (JELIA'02)*, volume 2424 of *LNAI*, pages 50–61. Springer, 2002.
3. J. J. Alferes, J. A. Leite, L. M. Pereira, H. Przymusinska, and T. Przymusinski. Dynamic updates of non-monotonic knowledge bases. *Journal of Logic Programming*, 45(1-3):43–70, 2000.
4. J. J. Alferes and L. M. Pereira. Updates plus preferences. In M. Ojeda-Aciego, I. P. de Guzmán, G. Brewka, and L. M. Pereira, editors, *Procs. of the 7th European Workshop on Logics in Artificial Intelligence (JELIA'00)*, volume 1919 of *LNAI*, pages 345–360. Springer, 2000.

5. J. J. Alferes, L. M. Pereira, H. Przymusinska, and T. Przymusinski. LUPS : A language for updating logic programs. *Artificial Intelligence*, 138(1-2):87–116, 2002.

6. P. Assunção, L. Soares, J. Luz, and R. Viegas. The mule game engine - extending online role-playing games. In *Proceedings of the 9th Annual Conference on Innovation and Technology in Computer Science Education (ITiCSE'05)*. ACM, 2005.

7. F. Banti, J. J. Alferes, and A. Brogi. Well founded semantics for logic program updates. In C. Lemaître, C. A. Reyes, and J. A. González, editors, *Procs of the 9th Ibero-American Conference on Artificial Intelligence (IBERAMIA'04)*, volume 3315 of *LNAI*, pages 397–407. Springer, 2004.

8. M. Boavida, S. Cabaço, N. Folgôa, F. Mourato, F. Sampayo, and A. Trabuco. Video based tools for sports training. In *Proceedings of the 5th International Symposium Computer Science in Sport, IACSS'05*, 2005.

9. R. Bordini, J. Hübner, and R. Vieira. Jason and the Golden Fleece of agent-oriented programming. In Bordini et al. [11], chapter 1.

10. R. H. Bordini, L. Braubach, M. Dastani, A. El F. Seghrouchni, J. J. Gomez-Sanz, J. Leite, G. O'Hare, A. Pokahr, and A. Ricci. A survey of programming languages and platforms for multi-agent systems. *Informatica*, 30(1):33–44, 2006.

11. R. H. Bordini, M. Dastani, J. Dix, and A. El Fallah Seghrouchni, editors. *Multi-Agent Programming: Languages, Platforms and Applications*. Number 15 in Multiagent Systems, Artificial Societies, and Simulated Organizations. Springer, 2005.

12. A. Bracciali, N. Demetriou, U. Endriss, A. Kakas, W. Lu, and K. Stathis. Crafting the mind of a prosocs agent. *Applied Artificial Intelligence*, 20(4-5), 2006.

13. G. Brewka and T. Eiter. Preferred answer sets for extended logic programs. *Artificial Intelligence*, 109(1-2):297–356, 1999.

14. S. Costantini and A. Tocchio. A logic programming language for multi-agent systems. In S. Flesca, S. Greco, N. Leone, and G. Ianni, editors, *Proceedings of the 8th European Conference on Logics in Artificial Intelligence (JELIA'02)*, volume 2424 of *LNAI*, pages 1–13. Springer, 2002.

15. M. Dastani, M. B. van Riemsdijk, and J.-J. Ch. Meyer. Programming multi-agent systems in 3APL. In Bordini et al. [11], chapter 2.

16. J. Dix and Y. Zhang. IMPACT: a multi-agent framework with declarative semantics. In Bordini et al. [11], chapter 3.

17. T. Eiter, M. Fink, G. Sabbatini, and H Tompits. A framework for declarative update specifications in logic programs. In B. Nebel, editor, *Proceedings of the seventeenth International Conference on Artificial Intelligence (IJCAI'01)*, pages 649–654. Morgan Kaufmann, 2001.

18. M. Gelfond and V. Lifschitz. Logic programs with classical negation. In D. Warren and P. Szeredi, editors, *Proceedings of the 7th international conference on logic programming*, pages 579–597. MIT Press, 1990.

19. G. De Giacomo, Y. Lesprance, and H.J. Levesque. Congolog, a concurrent programming language based on the situation calculus. *Artificial Intelligence*, 121(1-2):109–169, 2000.

20. K. Hindriks, F. de Boer, W. van der Hoek, and J.-J. Ch. Meyer. Agent programming in 3APL. *Int. J. of Autonomous Agents and Multi-Agent Systems*, 2(4):357–401, 1999.

21. R. Kowalski and F. Sadri. From logic programming towards multi-agent systems. *Annals of Mathematics and Artificial Intelligence*, 25(3-4):391–419, 1999.

22. J. Leite and L. Soares. Evolving characters in role playing games. In R. Trappl, editor, *Cybernetics and Systems, Proceedings of the 18th European Meeting on Cybernetics and Systems Research (EMCSR 2006)*, volume 2, pages 515–520. Austrian Society for Cybernetic Studies, 2006.

23. J. A. Leite. *Evolving Knowledge Bases*. IOS Press, 2003.

24. J. A. Leite, J. J. Alferes, and L. M. Pereira. Minerva - a dynamic logic programming agent architecture. In J.-J. Ch. Meyer and M. Tambe, editors, *Intelligent Agents VIII*, volume 2333 of *LNAI*, pages 141–157. Springer, 2002.

25. V. Lifschitz and T. Woo. Answer sets in general non-monotonic reasoning (preliminary report). In B. Nebel, C. Rich, and W. Swartout, editors, *Proceedings of the Third International Conference on Principles of Knowledge Representation and Reasoning (KR'92)*, pages 603–614. Morgan Kaufmann, 1992.

26. V. Mascardi, M. Martelli, and L. Sterling. Logic-based specification languages for intelligent software agents. *Theory and Practice of Logic Programming*, 4(4):429–494, 2004.

27. V. Nigam and J. Leite. A dynamic logic programming based system for agents with declarative goals. In U. Endriss and M. Baldoni, editors, *Procs. of the 4th International Workshop on Declarative Agent Languages and Technologies (DALT'06).*, LNAI. Springer, 2006. to appear.

28. L. Soares, P. Assunção, J. Luz, and R. Viegas. Madagents - an architecture for logic-based agents. submitted, 2006.

29. V. S. Subrahmanian, P. Bonatti, J. Dix, T. Eiter, S. Kraus, F. Ozcan, and R. Ross. *Heterogeneous Agent Systems*. MIT Press, 2000.

30. M. Thielscher. *Reasoning Robots: The Art and Science of Programming Robotic Agents*. Springer, 2005.

31. A. van Gelder, K.A. Ross, and J.S. Schlipf. Unfounded sets and well-founded semantics for general logic programs. *Journal of the ACM*, 38(3):620–650, 1991.

32. Working group on Answer-Set Programming. http://wasp.unime.it.

The Second Contest on Multi-Agent Systems Based on Computational Logic

Mehdi Dastani[1], Jürgen Dix[2], and Peter Novák[2]

[1]Utrecht University
P.O.Box 80.089, 3508 TB Utrecht, The Netherlands
mehdi@cs.uu.nl
[2]Clausthal University of Technology
Julius-Albert-Str. 4, 38678 Clausthal-Zellerfeld, Germany
dix@tu-clausthal.de, peter.novak@in.tu-clausthal.de

Abstract. The second edition of the contest on *Multi-Agent Systems based on computational logic* was held in conjunction with the CLIMA '06 workshop in Hakodate, Japan. Based on the experiences from the first edition of this contest ([8]), we decided to improve the setting of the first edition. In particular, we built a server to simulate the multi-agent system environment in which the agents from different groups can sense the environment and perform their actions. In this way, different multi-agent systems can compete with each other for the same resources. This allows for much more objective evaluation criteria to decide the winner. Three groups from Brazil, Spain and Germany did participate in this contest. The actual contest took place prior to the CLIMA workshop and the winner, the group from Brazil, was announced during CLIMA '06.

1 Introduction

Multi-agent systems are a promising paradigm in software engineering. Various multi-agent system development methodologies have been proposed each of which focuses on specific stages of the software development process. For example, Gaia focuses on the specification and design stages assuming that other stages such as requirement and implementation are similar to corresponding stages of other software development paradigms. Therefore, the designers of Gaia propose models to specify and design multi-agent systems, but they ignore the implementation models.

Moreover, there is a growing number of agent-oriented programming languages that are proposed to facilitate the implementation of multi-agent systems. These programming languages introduce programming constructs that can facilitate efficient and effective implementation of multi-agent systems. On the other hand, many aspects involved in multi-agent systems require logical representation and reasoning: to represent agent's knowledge and actions and to reason about them. In the last decades, research on computational logic has resulted in numerous implementable methods and techniques that can be used to model such aspects.

K. Inoue, K. Satoh, and F. Toni (Eds.): CLIMA VII, LNAI 4371, pp. 266–283, 2007.

The development of multi-agent systems requires efficient and effective solutions for different problems which can be divided into three classes: the problems related to

1. the development of individual agents,
2. the development of mechanisms to manage the interactions between individual agents, and
3. the development of the shared environment in which agents perform their actions.

Typical problems related to individual agents are how to specify, design and implement issues such as *autonomy, pro-active/reactive behaviour, perception and update of information, reasoning and deliberation,* and *planning.* Typical problems related to the interaction of individual agents are how to *specify, design and implement* issues such as *communication, coordination, cooperation* and *negotiation.* Finally, typical problems related to the development of their environment are how to *specify, design and implement* issues such as *resources and services,* agents' access to *resources,* active and passive *sensing* of the environment, and realizing the *effects of actions.*

This competition is an attempt to stimulate research in the area of multi-agent systems by

1. *identifying key problems during MAS development, and*
2. *evaluating state-of-the-art techniques and approaches from both computational logic and multi-agent systems.*

While there already exist several competitions in various areas of artificial intelligence (theorem proving, planning, Robo-Cup, etc.) and, lately, also in specialized areas in agent systems (Trading Agent Competition (TAC) [1] and AgentCities competitions [2]), the emphasis of this contest is on the use of *computational logic* in the development of multi-agent systems. We believe that approaches and techniques of computational logic are essential for the development of multi-agent systems ([3,7,4] for at least two reasons:

1. logical approaches have proven to be very useful for specifying and modeling multi-agent systems in a precise manner, and
2. the specification and models can be executed.

We tried to encourage participants to use existing methods and techniques from computational logic research, as well as existing development methodologies and programming languages for multi-agent systems. However, in order to evaluate how computational logic based implementations will perform in a head-to-head competition with other systems, we decided to open the contest also to non-logic based submissions.

2   Scenario Description

The competition task consisted of developing a multi-agent system to solve a cooperative task in a dynamically changing environment. The environment of the multi-agent system was a grid-like world where agents could move from one cell to a neighbouring cell if there was no agent or obstacle already in that cell. In this environment, gold could appear in the cells. Participating agent teams were expected to explore the environment, avoid obstacles and compete with another agent team for the gold. The agents of each team could coordinate their actions in order to collect as much gold as they could and to deliver it to the depot where the gold can be safely stored. Agents had only a local view on their environment, their perceptions could be incomplete, and their actions could fail. The agents were able to play different roles (such as explorer or collector), communicate and cooperate in order to find and collect gold in an efficient and effective way.

Each team competed against all other teams in a series of matches. Each match between two competing teams consisted of five simulations. A simulation between two teams was a competition between them with respect to a certain starting configuration of the environment. Winning a simulation yielded three points for the team, a draw was worth one point and a loss resulted in zero points. The winner of the whole tournament was evaluated on the basis of the overall number of collected points in the matches during the tournament.

2.1   Technical Description of the Scenario

In this contest, the agents from each participating team were executed locally (on the participant's hardware) while the simulated environment, in which all agents from competing teams performed their actions, was run on the remote contest simulation server. The interaction/communication between agents from one team had to be managed locally, but the interaction between individual agents and their environment (run on the simulation server) was done via Internet. Participating agents had to connect to the simulation server that provided the information about the environment. Each agent from each team did connect and communicate to the simulation server using one TCP connection.

After the initial phase[1], during which agents from all competing teams connected to the simulation server, identified themselves and got a general match information, the competition started. The simulation server controlled the competition by selecting the competing teams and managing the matches and simulations. In each simulation, the simulation server provided in a cyclic fashion sensory information about the environment to the participating agents and expected agent's reaction within a given time limit. Each agent had to react to the received sensory information by indicating which action (including the skip action) it wanted to perform in the environment. If no reaction was received from the agent within the given time limit, the simulation server assumed that the agent has performed the skip action.   After a finite number of steps the

---

[1] The contest organizers contacted participants before the actual tournament and provided them the IDs necessary for identification of their agents for the tournament.

simulation server stopped the cycle and participating agents received a notification about the end of a match.

2.2 Team, Match, and Simulation

An agent team consisted of four software agents with distinct IDs. There were no restrictions on the implementation of agents, although we encouraged the use of computational logic based approaches. The tournament consisted of three matches. Each match was a sequel of five simulations during which two teams of agents competed in several different settings of the environment. For each match, the server 1) picked two teams to play it and 2) started the first simulation of the match. Each simulation in a match started by notifying the agents from the participating teams and distributing them the details of the simulation. These included for example the size of the grid, depot position, and the number of steps performed by the simulation. A simulation consisted of a number of simulation steps. Each step consisted of 1) sending a sensory information to agents (one or more) and 2) waiting for their actions. In the case that an agent had not responded within a timeout (specified at the beginning of the simulation) by a valid action, it was considered to perform the skip action in the given simulation step.

2.3 Environment Objects

The (simulated) environment was a rectangular grid consisting of cells. The size of the grid was specified at the start of each simulation and was variable (not more than 100x100 cells). The [0,0] coordinate of the grid was in the top-left corner (north-west). The simulated environment contained one depot, which served for both teams as a location of delivery of gold items. The environment could contain the following objects in its cells:

- obstacle (a cell with an obstacle could not be visited by an agent),
- gold (an item which could be picked from a cell),
- agent,
- depot (a cell to which gold items were to be delivered in order to earn a point in a simulation), or
- mark (a string data with a maximum of 5 characters which could be read / written / rewritten / removed by an agent)

There could be only one object in a cell, except that an agent could enter cells containing gold, depot or mark, and a gold item could be in a marked cell visited by an agent. At the beginning of a simulation the grid contained obstacles, gold items and agents of both teams. Distribution of obstacles, gold items and initial positions of agents could be either hand crafted for the particular scenario, or completely random. During the simulation, gold items could appear randomly (with a uniform distribution) in empty cells of the grid. The frequency and probability of gold generation was simulation specific, however not known to neither agents, nor participants.

Perception. Agents were located in the grid and the simulation server provided each agent with the following information:

- absolute position of the agent in the grid,
- the content of the cells surrounding the agent and the content of the cell in which the agent was currently standing in (9 cells in total).

If two agents were standing in each other's field of view, they could recognize whether they were an enemy, or whether they belong to the same team. However an agent was not able to recognize whether the other agent carries a gold item or not. If there was a mark in a cell, which was in an agent's field of view, it received also the information about its content.

Actions. Agents were allowed to perform one action in a simulation step. The following actions were allowed:

- **skip:** The execution of the skip action does not change the state of the environment (under the assumption that other agents do not change it).
- **movements (east, north, west, south):** An agent can move in four directions in the grid. The execution of move east, move north, move west, and move south changes the position of the agent one cell to the left, up, right, and down, respectively. A movement action succeeds only when the cell to which an agent is about to move does not contain another agent or obstacle. Moving to and from the depot cell is regulated by additional rules described later in this description.
- **pick, drop:** An agent can carry only one gold item which it successfully picked up before. An agent can pick up a gold item if 1) the cell in which an agent stands in contains gold, and 2) the agent is not carrying another gold item. An agent can drop the gold item it is carrying only in the cell it is standing in. The result of a successful pick action is that in the next simulation step the acting agent was considered to carry a gold item and the cell, it is standing in, does not contain the gold item any more. The result of a drop action is that the acting agent is not carrying the gold item anymore and that the cell it is standing in contains the gold item in the next simulation step. Dropping a gold item to a depot cell does increase the score of the agent's team by one point. The depot cell does never contain a gold item that can be picked by an agent.
- **mark, unmark:** An agent is allowed to mark a cell it is standing in by a string data with a maximum of 5 characters. The result of a mark action was that the cell in which an agent was located, contained a string in the next simulation step. The depot cell, and cells containing an obstacle could not be marked. By marking a previously marked cell, the old mark was removed and replaced by the new one. If the cell in which an agent was located, contains a mark, then the agent received the string in the perception information from the simulation server. An agent is also allowed to unmark the marked cell it is standing in. The result of an unmark action is that the cell does not contain a mark in the next simulation step. Agents do not get immediate

feedback on their actions, but can learn about the effects of their actions (and the actions of other agents) from the perception information that is sent to them in the next simulation step.

All actions, except the skip action, could fail. The result of a failed action was the same as the result of the skip action. An action could fail either because the conditions for its successful execution were not fulfilled, or because of the information distortion (described later in this text).

Depot cell. There are strong conditions imposed on the depot cell:

1. an agent not carrying a gold item is unable to enter the depot cell (the result of such an action is the same as if the depot were an obstacle)
2. an agent which enters the depot cell should drop the gold item as the very next action it is executing
3. after dropping the gold item in a cell, an agent must leave the cell in the first subsequent simulation step, when he is able to move (i.e. when there is an empty cell around at the time of agent's move action).

If an agent does not leave the depot in the first possible opportunity, or does not drop the gold item as the very next action after entering the depot, the simulation server punishes it by "teleporting" it away (it is moved to a random cell not containing another agent, or obstacle in the grid by the environment simulator).

Timeout, Information Distortion, and Final Phase. The agents had to inform the simulation server which actions they want to perform within a timeout specified at the beginning of the simulation. The contest organizers did not take any responsibility for the speed of the Internet connection between the server and participating agents. Timeouts were set reasonably high, so that even participants with a slow network connection, or using a time demanding deliberation, were able to communicate with the server in an efficient way.

A ping interface was provided by the server in order to allow participating agents to test the speed of their connection during the whole duration of the tournament.

Agents could receive incomplete information about the environment from the simulation server. The simulation server could omit information about particular environment cells. However, this happened only with a certain probability, guaranteed to be not higher than 20 percent and fixed for each simulation.

In the final phase, the simulation server sent a message to each agent allowing them to disconnect from the server ending the tournament.

2.4   General Agent-2-Server Communication Principles

Agents communicated with the contest server by exchanging XML messages and using standard TCP/IP stack with socket session interface. Messages were XML documents that could be analyzed by standard XML parsers available for many programming languages. The Internet coordinates (IP address and port) of the contest server (and a dedicated test server) were communicated to the participants via the official CLIMA VII Contest mailing list.

Communication Protocol. The tournament was divided into three phases. During the initial phase, agents connected to the simulation server and identify themselves by user-name and password (AUTH-REQUEST message). Credentials for each agent were distributed in advance via e-mail. As a response, agents received the result of their authentication request (AUTH-RESPONSE message) which could either succeed or fail. After successful authentication, agents had to wait until the first simulation of the tournament started.

At the beginning of each simulation, agents of the two participating teams were notified (SIM-START message) and received simulation specific information: simulation ID, opponent's ID, grid size, number of steps the simulation last and the depot position.

In each simulation step an agent received a perception about its environment (REQUEST-ACTION message) and it had to respond by performing an action (ACTION message). Each request-action message contained information about 9 neighbouring cells around agent (including the one agent stands on), its absolute position in the grid, simulation step number and a deadline for its response. Agent had to deliver its response within the given deadline. The action message had to contain the identifier of the action and action parameters, if required.

When the simulation was finished, participating agents received the notification about it (SIM-END message) which included the information about the number of gold items collected by the team agent and the information about the result of the simulation (whether the team won, or lost the simulation).

All agents that did not participate in a simulation had to wait until the simulation server notified them about either 1) the start of a simulation, they are going to participate in, or 2) the end of the tournament.

At the end of the tournament, all agents received the notification (BYE message). Subsequently the simulation server terminated the connection to the agent.

Reconnection. When an agent lost its connection to the simulation server, the tournament proceeded without disruption, only all the actions of a disconnected agent were considered to be empty. Agents were themselves responsible for maintaining the connection to the simulation server and in a case of connection disruption, they were allowed to reconnect.

Agents reconnected by performing the same sequence of steps as at the beginning of the tournament. After establishing the connection to the simulation server, it could send AUTH-REQUEST message and receive AUTH-RESPONSE. After successful authentication, the server could send a SIM-START message to an agent. If an agent participated in a currently running simulation, the SIM-START message was delivered immediately after AUTH-RESPONSE. Otherwise an agent had to wait until a next simulation in which it participates started. In the next subsequent step when the agent was picked to perform an action, it received the standard REQUEST-ACTION message containing the perception of the agent at the current simulation step and simulation proceeded in a normal mode.

Ping Interface. The simulation server provided a ping interface in order to allow agents to test their connection to the simulation server. Agents could send a PING message containing a payload data (ASCII string up to 100 characters) and receive PONG message with the same payload. As all messages contained a timestamp, agents could also use ping interface to synchronize their time with the server.

Protocol Sequence Diagram (UML Like Notation)

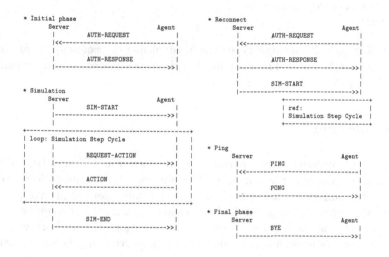

XML Messages Description. XML messages exchanged between server and agents were zero terminated UTF-8 strings. Each XML message exchanged between the simulation server and agent consisted of three parts:

- Standard XML header: Contained the standard XML document header `<?xml version="1.0" encoding="UTF-8"?>`
- Message envelope: The root element of all XML messages was `<message>`. It had attributes: the timestamp and a message type identifier.
- Message separator: Each message is a UTF-8 zero terminated string. Messages are separated by null byte.

Timestamp is a numeric string containing the status of the simulation server's global timer at the time of message creation. The unit of the global timer is milliseconds and it is the result of standard system call "time" on the simulation server (measuring number of milliseconds from January 1, 1970 UTC). Message type identifier is one of the following values: `auth-request`, `auth-response`, `sim-start`, `sim-end`, `bye`, `request-action`, `action`, `ping`, `pong`.

Messages sent from the server to an agent contained all attributes of the root element. However, the timestamp attribute could be omitted in messages sent from an agent to the server. In the case it was included, server silently ignored it. Example of a server-2-agent message:

```
<message timestamp="1138900997331" type="request-action">
    <!-- optional data -->
</message>
```

Example of an agent-2-server message:

```
<message type="auth-request">
    <!-- optional data -->
</message>
```

According to the message type, the root element `<message>` can contain simulation specific data. These simulation data are described and explained in the official CLIMA VII webpage[2].

3   Submission

A submission consisted of two parts. The first part was a description of analysis, design and implementation of a MAS for the above application. We have encouraged submissions that specify, design and implement multi-agent systems using existing agent-oriented methodologies such as Gaia [12], Prometheus [9] and Tropos [6]. For the description of the implementation, the authors were asked to explain how their design is implemented. In particular, they were asked to explain which computational logic techniques (e.g. logic programming, formal calculi, etc.) are used to implement aspects of the multi-agent system such as mental states (e.g., goals, beliefs, plans, and roles) of individual agents, communication, coordination, negotiation, and dialogue. Although we emphasized the use of computational logic techniques, we did not exclude submissions that were based on other approaches (e.g. based on machine learning, neural nets, etc.) and programming paradigms.

The second part was the participation in the contest tournament by means of an (executable) implementation of a multi-agent system. The source code together with instructions on how to install it, including precise instructions on software and hardware requirements, had to be submitted just before the competition started.

---

[2] `http://cig.in.tu-clausthal.de/fileadmin/user_upload/_temp_/c7c-protocol.txt`

3.1 Received Submissions

We have received three submissions for this edition of the CLIMA contest. From the received submissions, two submissions used an existing multi-agent development methodology to specify, design, and implement a running multi-agent system. The use of computational logic techniques was explicitly discussed in two of the submissions. The use of computational logic in the third submission emerged mostly from using Prolog as the programming language for implementing the multi-agent system.

The submission from R.H. Bordini, J.F. Hübner, and D.M. Tralamazza uses Prometheus [9] as the multi-agent development methodology to specify and design their multi-agent system. Using this methodology, the multi-agent system is designed by means of a System Overview Diagram that describes the interaction between miner (searching) and courier agents. These agents are subsequently specified and designed in terms of Goal Overview Diagram and Agent Overview Diagrams describing their specific knowledge, goals and plans. Their designed system is then implemented in Jason [5], which is an interpreter of an extension of the agent-oriented programming language AgentSpeak [10]. As it was required by the contest, their multi-agent system consisted of four individual agents. These agents follow a general strategy according to which each agent is responsible for one quadrant of the grid environment. Each agent can then play two roles: carrying gold or searching for gold. The agents from the team can communicate to help each other. For example, a searching agent that finds some gold can ask a courier agent to transport the gold to the gold depot. The use of computational logic techniques in this submission emerges mostly from the use of computational logic techniques in AgentSpeak language and its Jason interpreter.

The submission from C. Cares, X. Franch, and E. Mayol uses a goal-oriented development methodology which is based on a combination of antimodels (a requirement engineering technique) and an extension of Tropos [6]. This methodology is used to specify and design a multi-agent system for the Gold mining scenario of the contest. They specify the goals of the multi-agent system, analyze possible attacks on these goals (e.g., the goal of the competitor team), and propose adequate responses to such attacks. Based on the resulting specification, they identify possible involved agents and design their strategies. Their extension of Tropos enables them to generate a Prolog implementation of the identified agents and their designed strategies. The fact that the implementation is based on Prolog seems to be the only use of computational logic in their system.

The final submission from S. Schiffel and M. Thielscher does not use any specific multi-agent system development methodology. The focus on this submission is rather on the use of computational logic techniques in implementing the Gold mining scenario. In particular, they implement their multi-agent system in FLUX [11], which is a programming language based on constraint logic programming. The agent implemented in FLUX can reason logically about their sense information and actions in the presence of incomplete knowledge. Each agent builds a mental model of the environment by sensing the environment and performing actions. A FLUX agent program consists of a kernel (the reasoning capability of the agent), a domain-specific background theory (the model of the environment), and a strategy (the behaviour of the agent). The mental model of the agents is defined in terms of fluents that represent the position of agents, the position of the gold depot, the position of the obstacles, and the fact that an agent carries gold. The strategies of the agents are defined in terms of the actions that are proposed in the contest description. In this system, all FLUX agents share the same background theory, and each agent acts according to its individual strategy and the role it plays

4   Technical Infrastructure

In order to run the competition, we developed a multi-agent system environment simulation server MASSim. Briefly, the server's architecture consists of

1. *simulation plug-in* - a replaceable module providing the logics of the environment simulation,
2. *agent session manager* - responsible for holding the sessions between the server and individual agents and en/de-coding of XML messages of the protocol,
3. *visualization library* - which produced the SVG records from each time frame of the simulation environment state,
4. *contest webinterface* - providing a public view and interface to the MASSim server, and
5. MASSim core module - managing the tournament scheme and providing the connection between the simulation plug-in, agent session manager and webinterface.

Most of the software components were implemented in Java 1.5.0. The webinterface module, running as a set of Java servlets under Apache webserver with Tomcat application server, was loosely connected to the core simulation server via Java RMI (Remote Method Invocation) protocol so, that if a need arose due to high CPU load, we could run the webinterface and the core simulation server on different computers.

The whole MASSim server architecture was designed with the following requirements in mind:

1. *high versatility* - the core system (MASSim simulation server) should depend on the most standard software today so that contest participants are able to download and install the system without a hassle. It should be easily deployable on standard configurations using Linux OS, Apache webserver and Tomcat application server;
2. *open and reusable* - we designed the server so that it can accommodate vast range of discrete-time simulation scenarios which can be easily connected to the core server API;

3. *component based design* - each MASSim simulation server component communicates with other components using a well-defined API such that we are able to replace it quickly on the ground of changing requirements (e.g. different tournament structure, different network communication protocol, or a visualization technology)

The system, including a documentation which is still partly a work in progress, is published on the official Contest website: `http://cig.in.tu-clausthal.de/ CLIMAContest/`.

4.1   Contest Preparation

Several days before the start of the competition, the contest organizers contacted participants via e-mail with details on time and Internet coordinates (IP addresses/ports) of the simulation server. Participants received also agent IDs necessary for identification of their agents for the tournament. Agents had to communicate with the simulation server using TCP protocol and by means of messages in XML format. The details about communication protocol and message format was specified and provided to participants long enough before the actual competition.

The MASSim simulation server system proved to be a reliable and successful platform for the CLIMA VII Contest. During the first testing phase (05.02.2006–15.03.2006), we published the system on the Contest website. The participants could download it and use it for development and debugging of their multi-agent systems. Together with the simulation server, we published also a sample implementation of an agent team. The contest participants could copy our full-fledged working contest protocol implementation written in Java. This should speed up the agent team development and participants could focus more on the scenario strategy rather than the technical issues.

The main testing phase of the contest was run between March 15th and April 27th 2006. During this period we ran the MASSim simulation server on our network infrastructure with a slightly modified tournament structure implementation. Participants had to subscribe for a testing account and after receiving valid credentials for each of their agents they could start using the test server. Agents could connect to our test MASSim server running at `agentmaster. in.tu-clausthal.de` port 12300 and participate in a test match against our *CLIMABot* agent team. We did not allow agents of different teams compete against each other as this should happen exclusively during the tournament itself.

For completeness, we give a short description of our own *CLIMABot* team. The agents are completely on their own, there is no communication, no lobal map building. An agent can be in two modes:

Mode 1: the agent moves randomly in its environment and looks for gold. It remembers all gold positions and stores them in a list. This list is updated while it is wandering around.

Mode 2: if an agent wants to get to a target at the position (X,Y) it tries the
shortest way to get there. If there are more shortest ways (as the grid is
rectangular and in the case when there are no obstacles directly around it)
it chooses the shortest path randomly.

If on the direct way to the target it bumps into an obstacle so that it
cannot proceed further in the desired direction it pushes the current direction
it wants to go to the stack, then it turns clockwise (to the right) and tries
to go in the new direction each step checking whether it is not possible to
turn into the desired direction (top of the stack). If on this way the agent
bumps into another obstacle it just pushes the current direction onto the
stack, again turns clockwise and proceeds. It does this thing until the stack
is empty. Otherwise the stack is just filled with stuff forever.

If, being in mode 1, an agent finds a piece of gold, it picks it and switches
to mode 2. In the case it finds another piece of gold on its way to the depot it
remembers its position in a list. Once it delivered the piece of gold, it picks the
nearest known piece of gold from the list and goes to it applying the algorithm
in mode 2. If the list is empty, it switches to mode 1.

4.2   Tournament

The CLIMA VII Contest tournament was scheduled for Thursday, April 27th
2006, 15:00 CEST (GMT+2). However, because of last-minute technical difficulties of the Spanish team, we had to postpone the start of the tournament
for a couple of minutes so the tournament finally started at 15:26 the same
day. First, we let all the participating teams to compete against our *CLIMABot*
agent team and then real tournament matches followed in the following order
Germany:Spain, Brazil:Spain and Brazil:Germany. The tournament finished on
April 27th at 21:58 after 9 hours and 32 minutes. Matches took from 27 minutes
(Germany:CLIMABot) to 1 hour 48 minutes (Spain:CLIMABot).

During the tournament itself, the current tournament status could be watched
in real-time using our webinterface at http://agentmaster.in.tu-clausthal.
de/. Throughout the whole tournament we have not observed any technical
problems. All the results, together with the SVG recordings of all the matches
and the official DVD ISO image with a mirror-copy of the whole tournament
website can be downloaded from http://agentmaster.in.tu-clausthal.de/.

4.3   Simulation Instances

The teams competed in matches each consisting of 5 simulations with identifiers
Random1, *Random2*, *Labyrinth1*, *Labyrinth2* and *Labyrinth*. As the names suggest, the first two simulation instances *Random1* (Figure 1) and *Random2* were
randomly generated simulations differing in the parameters while the last three
were handcrafted mazes.

Labyrinth1 (Figure 2) was a maze of rows of obstacles with gates at the very
ends. This simulation instance proved to be the most difficult for the participating agent teams, because a random exploration of the grid did not lead to

satisfactory results. In order to collect gold items in this simulation instance agents had to implement a systematic search of the environment.

Labyrinth2 and *Labyrinth* (Figure 3) were inverted versions (w.r.t. initial position of agent teams) of the same simulation instance consisting of a simple rectangular maze with some holes in the structure and the depot in the middle. In order to succeed in this simulation instance, agents had to develop an internal representation of the environment, but a systematic exploration of the environment was not a hard requirement.

The following is a detailed description of simulation instances:

simulation ID:	Random1	Random2	Labyrinth1	Labyrinth2	Labyrinth
grid size:	25x25	25x25	35x35	30x30	30x30
depot position:	random	random	(10,17)	(14,14)	(14,14)
number of obstacles:	20	40	305	126	126
initial number of gold items:	75	20	60	45	45
information distortion probability:	10%	10%	3%	1%	1%
action failure probability:	2%	2%	2%	2%	2%
gold generation frequency:	3sec	3 sec	3 sec	3 sec	3 sec
number of generated gold items:	1	1	1	1	1
number of simulation steps:	500	500	500	500	500

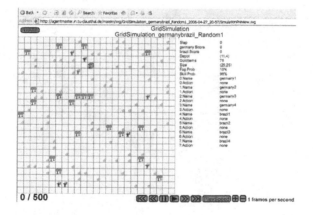

Fig. 1. Simulation instance *Random1* with a screenshot of the visualization interface

5   Contest Results

The winner of the CLIMA VII Contest was the team from Brazil with the highest number of points: 25. The second team was from Spain with 14 points followed by the team from Germany with 4 points. The summary of the whole tournament is summarized in the Table 1. All the partial summaries of the matches can be found in Tables 2, 3 and 4.

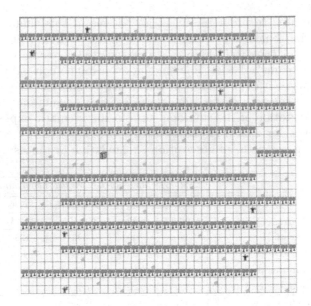

Fig. 2. Simulation instance *Labyrinth1*

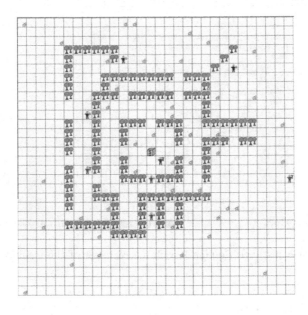

Fig. 3. Simulation instance *Labyrinth2*

We did not include the results of our *CLIMABot* team. In fact, had our team attended the contest, it would have been the winner. This is interesting because it shows that not a lot of logic or strategies are needed to win the whole contest.

Our team has been written by our students in just 2 days. We are still not sure why such a simple strategy turned out to be superior to all other contestants.

Table 1. Final tournament results

Rank	Team	Score	Points
1.	brazil	265 : 125	25
2.	spain	225 : 176	14
3.	germany	79 : 268	4

Table 2. Summary of the match between team Germany and the team Spain

Simulation/Score	germany	spain
Random1	36	33
Random2	6	10
Labyrinth	2	36
Labyrinth1	0	0
Labyrinth2	3	53

Table 3. Summary of the match between team Brazil and the team Spain

Simulation/Score	brazil	spain
Random1	33	33
Random2	3	4
Labyrinth	41	22
Labyrinth1	15	2
Labyrinth2	37	32

Table 4. Summary of the match between team Brazil and the team Germany

Simulation/Score	brazil	germany
Random1	23	18
Random2	11	9
Labyrinth	50	2
Labyrinth1	11	0
Labyrinth2	41	3

6   Conclusion

The major motivations behind organizing the CLIMA Contest are the following:

- to foster the research and development of practically oriented approaches to programming multi-agent systems,
- to evaluate the state-of-the-art techniques in the field, and
- to identify key problems using these techniques.

After successfuly organizing two editions of the CLIMA Contest we still cannot give a full account of the impact of our Contest to the research in MAS. However we can briefly summarize what we believe are the major contributions of the Contest.

Finding bugs: Apart from growing attention, we learned from participants of the CLIMA Contest that they gathered a lot of practical experience in programming agent teams for the contest. We consider this already a major success: It helps to deepen the understanding of practical aspects of using tools, approaches and languages. Participating in the CLIMA Contest already helped to discover several bugs in prominent agent programming language interpreters and thus to improve the overall quality of the tool.

Classroom use: In the meantime, the technical infrastructure we developed for the CLIMA Contest, is already used in teaching processes of at least two universities in Germany and Australia. The advantage of using our simulation server in MAS lectures is its versatility and simplicity of the Contest scenario. Practical experience of students with programming simple multi-agent systems using our simulation server also helps to raise general awareness about multi agent research and applications of it.

Objective evaluation: A difficulty with the previous edition of this contest was the lack of an objective evaluation criterion by means of which the winner of the contest could be decided. In fact, the evaluation of the last contest edition was partially based on the performance of the agent teams in grid-like environments that were built by the participating groups themselves. As a consequence, different agent teams could not compete with each other in one and the same shared environment. Therefore, we decided for this contest edition to build an environment server in order to create equal conditions for the participating agent teams. Moreover, this environment server enables agent teams to focus on computational techniques and methods to implement gold mining strategies (using local communication technologies and hardware) by taking off the burden of implementing the simulation environment from the participants' shoulders.

As the whole software infrastructure is already developed and the feedback from the CLIMA VII Contest was in favour of keeping the current competition scenario, we are only planning to slightly modify and improve our scenario and simulation instances. As far as the contest management concerns, we learned a lot during the CLIMA VII Contest, especially with respect to managing the contest infrastructure, mailing lists and contest schedule planning and announcements. As the size of the last tournament in terms of number of participants was rather low, we did not consider to divide participating teams into groups and execute the tournament in several eliminating rounds.

We are currently finalizing and improving the documentation of our software packages. They will be freely made available and can be used by interested colleagues.

Acknowledgements

We are very thankful to our students in the Department of Informatics of Clausthal University of Technology. They worked hard in order to meet all the deadlines and deliver high-quality code. In particular, our thanks go to

- *Bernd Fuhrmann* for the core server component, contribution to the overall architecture and the code repository management,
- *Michael Köster* for the CLIMA VII Contest simulation plug-in, deployment scripts and the run-time server configuration,
- *David Mainzer* for the SVG visualization component, and
- *Dominik Steinborn* for the webinterface, its connection with the core server and his care for the testing and run-time server deployment.

We also thank all the contest participants who contributed to its success.

References

1. http://www.sics.se/tac.
2. http://www.agentcities.org/EUNET/Competition.
3. R. Bordini, M. Dastani, J. Dix, and A. E. Fallah-Seghrouchni. *Multi-Agent Programming: Languages, Platforms, and Applications*. Number 15 in MASA. Springer, Berlin, 2005.
4. R. Bordini, M. Dastani, J. Dix, and A. E. Fallah-Seghrouchni. *Programming Multi-Agent Systems*, volume 3346. LNAI, Springer Verlag, 2005.
5. R. H. Bordini and J. F. Hübner. BDI Agent Programming in AgentSpeak Using *Jason* (Tutorial Paper). In F. Toni and P. Torroni, editors, *CLIMA VI*, volume 3900 of *Lecture Notes in Computer Science*, pages 143–164. Springer, 2005.
6. J. Castro, M. Kolp, and J. Mylopoulos. Towards requirements-driven information systems engineering: the TROPOS project. *Information Systems*, 27:365–389, 2002.
7. M. Dastani, J. Dix, and A. E. Fallah-Seghrouchni. *Programming Multi-Agent Systems*, volume 3067. LNAI, Springer Verlag, 2004.
8. M. Dastani, J. Dix, and P. Novak. The First Contest on Multi-Agent Systems based on Computational Logic. In F. Toni and P. Torroni, editors, *Proceedings of CLIMA '05, London, UK*, volume 3900 of *Lecture Notes in Artificial Intelligence*, pages 373–384. Springer, Berlin, 2006.
9. L. Padgham and M. Winikoff. Prometheus: A methodology for developing intelligent agents. In *Agent-Oriented Software Engineering III: Third International Workshop (AOSE'02)*. Springer, LNAI 2585, 2003.
10. A. S. Rao. AgentSpeak(L): BDI agents speak out in a logical computable language. In W. V. de Velde and J. W. Perram, editors, *MAAMAW*, volume 1038 of *Lecture Notes in Computer Science*, pages 42–55. Springer, 1996.
11. M. Thielscher. FLUX: A logic programming method for reasoning agents. *CoRR*, cs.AI/0408044, 2004.
12. F. Zambonelli, N. R. Jennings, and M. Wooldridge. Developing multiagent systems: The Gaia methodology. *ACM Transactions on Software Engineering and Methodology (TOSEM)*, 12(3):317–370, 2003.

Using Antimodels to Define Agents' Strategy

Carlos Cares[1,2], Xavier Franch[1], and Enric Mayol[1]

[1] Dept. Llenguatges i Sistemes Informàtics - Universitat Politècnica de Catalunya,
Jordi Girona, 1-3 08034 Ph +34 934137839, Barcelona, Spain
{ccares,franch,mayol}@lsi.upc.edu
[2] Dept. Ingeniería de Sistemas, Universidad de La Frontera,
Av. Francisco Salazar 01145, Ph +56 45325000, Temuco, Chile

Abstract. Antimodels constitute a goal-oriented technique to reformulate a software system at the requirements stage mainly for security concerns. This technique recognizes external goals that conflict with the system's goals. In addition Tropos is one of the most relevant agent-oriented software development methodologies which uses the $i*$ modelling language. Tropos covers the software development from the early stage of requirements to implementation. In this paper we propose the use of antimodels to identify risk situations and we use an antigoal resolution taxonomy to reformulate agents' roles and goals. We test our approach in the context of the Second Computational Logic on Multi-Agent Systems contest where we have used Tropos to implement the proposed collecting agent problem. Combining antimodels, the antigoal resolution taxonomy and the Tropos extension to obtain Prolog implementations, we have obtained a competitive solution.

1 Introduction

Agent orientation has been recognized as the "new" paradigm in software engineering [1-3]. It means that the conceptual framework based on agent concepts has been used more than for building software products, it has been used as a design metaphor and, moreover, as the conceptual framework to elicit and to specify requirements. There are many agent-oriented software development methodologies which use the agent's conceptual framework to complete the stages of the software process. One the most referenced is Tropos [4, 5], which achieves the stages from early requirements elicitation to detailed design. $i*$ [6] is the modelling language of Tropos, which has been recognized as agent- and goal-oriented and in this way, the focus of the modelling stage is both the identification of agents and the design of their goals. Thus the aim of the detailed design is to specify how agents can achieve, in a coordinate and cooperative way, their goals using a specific set of tasks and resources.

The $i*$ framework [6] proposes the use of two models: the Strategic Dependency (SD) model to represent organizational actors with their social dependencies, and the second model is the Strategic Rationale Model used to represent the internal agent's rationale. In any case, depending on the focus, both aspects could be represented in the same diagram. At the actor level there are constructs for different actor

K. Inoue, K. Satoh, and F. Toni (Eds.): CLIMA VII, LNAI 4371, pp. 284–293, 2007.

specializations (*role*, *position* and *agent*) and their relationships (*is-a*, *is-part-of*, *covers*, *plays* and *occupies*). The actors can have social dependencies between them that are characterized by a resource, task, goal and *softgoal*. A *softgoal* represents a goal, which can be partially satisfied, or a goal that requires additional agreement about how it is satisfied. They have usually been used for representing non-functional requirements and quality concerns. The SR models the internal actors' *tasks*, *resources* and *goals* and their relationships such as *means-end* (to relate tasks and resources with goals), *contributions* (to represent how softgoals are satisfied) and *decompositions* (to represent how tasks are decomposed).

From the requirements engineering discipline, we have considered the concept of antimodels, which have been proposed as a security technique [7]. This is based on identifying threats for each system's goal. These are called antigoals and are goals from external agents which might want to prevent the accomplishment of the system's goals. The antimodel analysis involves eliminating, reducing or tolerating the identified threats. In spite of antimodels being used in the context of KAOS methodology [8], we claim that antimodels can be used to improve the rationality behind goals' achievement, beyond security concerns and the KAOS's modelling language.

With this aim, we propose specifying antimodels at the requirements stage as a mechanism oriented to supporting the agents' strategy definition. We frame this proposal within the topic of knowledge reuse at requirements stage; in fact, the suggested procedure for antigoals resolution is based on a small resolution taxonomy proposed in [9] and, furthermore, taxonomic representation of knowledge has been acknowledged as a reuse topic [10].

On the other hand, Tropos [4, 5] covers software process from early requirements to implementation with a different focus on each stage: (1) Early Requirements focuses on social context; (2) Late Requirements focuses on the system-to-be; (3) Architectural Design, focuses on systems components; and (4) Detailed Design and (5) Implementation, both focus on software agents. In [11] we have proposed a method to extend Tropos with the aim of obtaining predicate-based implementation solutions. In this paper we call it Tropos-PL. Therefore we rely on Tropos-PL for both testing our technique for defining agents' strategy and for obtaining a logic-based implementation. To test the approach we have participated in the Second Computational Logic in Multi-Agent Systems (CLIMA) Contest where we have obtained a good performance [12]. In order to overview our proposal in the next section we introduce antimodels, we extend the procedure for obtaining them and, moreover, we sustain that the $i*$ framework is suitable for both: representing antimodels, and representing the requirements organizational procedure to obtain them. In section 3 we describe the relevant context of the collecting problem presented at the CLIMA contest and we show how the antimodel concept helps us to define the agents' strategy. We also describe how part of this strategy has been implemented in Prolog. In section 4 we present the refined guidelines to get the Prolog code. Finally, in section 5 we summarize the proposed process remarking on the diverse contributions of this approach.

2 Representing Antimodels in the *i** Framework

Antimodels have been proposed in [7] as a way to deal with security requirements. This technique is used within a goal-oriented approach and has the aim of building a model where security threats are represented as goals from attacking agents. The proposal is based on both the possibility of decomposing goals that provide KAOS [8] and an antigoal resolution taxonomy. In figure 1 we present a summary of the antigoal resolution procedure originally proposed in [9], and the associated antigoal resolution taxonomy [7].

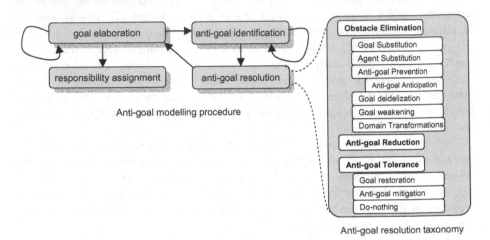

Fig. 1. Summary of Lamsweerde and Letier's antigoal based modelling [7, 9]

We can appreciate that the proposed procedure is strongly centred on the system's goals. We think that it is possible to get good results also using an agent perspective. Therefore we propose an extension oriented to the identification of attacking or threatening agents, and considering their goals as possible antigoals. We prefer to use the *i** framework for both purposes: to represent the software process as proposed in [13] and supported in [14], and to model the multi-agent system as proposed by Tropos [4, 5], but using the Tropos-PL's extension presented in [11].

In figure 2 we show the procedure's extension to the antigoal based modelling. This approach includes the agent identification considering both the own agent and attacking or threatening agents. Thus we think that agent nature can also help to identify new goals. If the new goals belong to the agent then we use these to look for antigoals. Therefore we have additional cycles for recognizing and identifying antigoals. Moreover we have represented these activities inside the requirement engineer's boundary which means that we perceive this process as a requirements problem. Additionally, we have added the previously identified antigoal resolution taxonomy as a necessary resource for antigoal resolution.

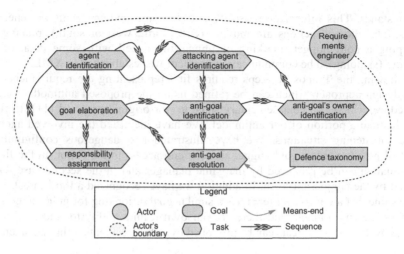

Fig. 2. Proposed antigoal modelling

To represent some threat or attack we have introduced a new construct which we have called antigoal attack. This construct sets a relationship between two goals of different agents. We think that this construct preserves the semantic of a recognized external threat which probably becomes material in an attack. We could have two alternatives within the *i** framework for the antigoal attack construct. The first is negative contributions; however these are preferred for internal concerns or some kind of system equilibrium used mainly for softgoals achievement analysis. The second is the *threat* construct proposed in [15]. However, this threats' representation is not associated with any agent and also affects quality concerns. An example of our antigoal attack construct can be found in figure 3.

We claim that this defence taxonomy and the procedure of antigoal based modelling are useful to design agent's strategy. We examine the collection agent problem formulated in the Second CLIMA contest [12] and we apply the above model to get the general design of agents' behaviour.

3 Applying Tropos-PL for the Collecting Agent Problem

The formulated problem in the Second CLIMA Contest [12] was to collect the maximum numbers of *gold nuggets* in a simulated environment which could be a grid of a maximum of 100x100 cells on a remote server. The competition is a set of two team games. Each team can have only 4 agents in this space and the simulation environment controls the situation on the grid. Moreover there is a depot cell where the gold nuggets should be deposited. There can only be one agent in a cell, and an agent can enter cells containing gold, the depot or a mark. At the beginning of a simulation the grid contains obstacles and gold items randomly set, and the agents of both teams. The environment provides the perception of the cells surrounding each agent represented by information such as absolute position of the agent in the grid, the contents of the cells surrounding the agent and the contents of the cell in which the agent stands. This information also describes if surrounding agents are enemies or allies. The allowed actions are moving (east, north, west or south), picking up or dropping a gold nugget, marking or unmarking a cell with some data, or doing nothing (skipping). The communication protocol was established in XML.

Following the Tropos-PL steps requires first representing the requirements, and a first design approach which can be refined using the proposed antimodel modelling procedure, which is a complementary stage to our original proposal [11]. In figure 3 we illustrate a portion of our antimodel. We have identified the involved agents and some threatening situations. We have illustrated two dangerous configurations: a blocked path towards a gold nugget and difficult access to the depot. In the first case the situation can be produced by the game manager and in the second case it can be caused by the competitor team. In addition we have recognized a third threat, because we assume that a competitor team has a similar goal of looking for gold nuggets which changes the environment and therefore our own team's ability to find gold nuggets. This show how some threats can be provoked by software agents or human agents.

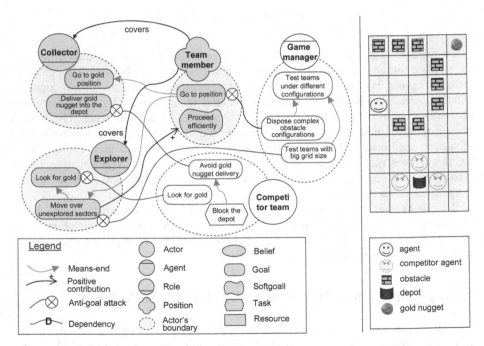

Fig. 3. Collecting antimodel and dangerous configurations

In order to refine our initial design we inspect the antigoal resolution taxonomy (figure 1) looking for adequate responses. In the case of the goal *go to position* and *deliver gold nugget into the depot* we have decided that it is feasible to apply the category *goal deidelization*. This means that we have to improve our ideal assumption of directly reaching a position, either a gold nugget or the depot position. Therefore, according the above procedure, we have elaborated a new set of goals, such as: *register blocked positions* and *find the shortest, unblocked and unexplored path*.

Now we analyze the attack against the goal *move over unexplored sectors* and hence against the softgoal *proceed efficiently*. The large size of the grid together with the allowance of only rectangular movements means that, for example, the goal *move over unexplored sectors* is difficult to achieve. If we suppose that an agent is inside the depot and that it believes that there is a set of gold nugget positions, and it has the goal of *moving along unexplored (disjoint) paths*, then the problem corresponds to the Eulerian disjoint paths problem in grid graphs, which is NP-complete [16]. For example, if an agent is in the position (10,10) and it wishes to go to the position (18,18), there are 12870 different paths to reach it. To handle this situation we have formulated a combination of two strategies: first using the *agent substitution* mechanism, and second using the *goal weakening* mechanism, both coming from the taxonomy. In the first case we made the decision to separate the team into two types of agents, *field agents* and *strategy agents*, because the rules allow for other types of agents to exist outside the grid environment. Therefore the first step was to separate the team and then, according to the procedure, to assign the responsibility to a new role: the *coach*. In the second case, the *goal weakening* involved relaxing the goal and defining a heuristic oriented to achieve it. Thus we revise the original goal to *try to move over unexplored sectors*.

The last identified attack is concerned with competing to find the *gold nuggets*. Thus finding and picking up a *gold nugget* means that the opposing team loses this possibility. In this case we have used the *antigoal mitigation* option. Given that agents closer to the depot take less time in reaching it, we have planned to mitigate the above opposition looking for gold nuggets in the positions closer to the depot, at least in the first competing seconds. Hence we have also formulated the alternative goal *go to depot's nearest gold position*.

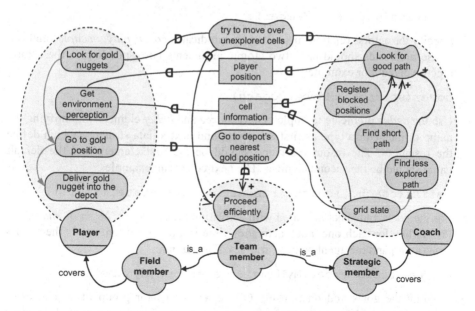

Fig. 4. Refined model after the anti-goal analysis

Moreover, given that we have a new agent configuration we also revise the initial roles of collector and explorer because the process of *responsibility assignment* (figure 1), has meant that few actions are assigned to both these roles. Additionally, we take the non performance difference using collectors and explorers as separate roles [11], so we combine them under the role *player*. In figure 4 we partially illustrate the resulting design after the antigoal analysis.

4   Obtaining the Prolog Code

In [11] we have proposed five suggestions to translate the detailed design to Prolog code. However, within our participation in the second CLIMA contest, we also have included a refining for the original translating suggestions. Thus, we refine the five original suggestions in a procedure of 9 steps. We have used SWI Prolog [17], therefore some specific Prolog codifications should be verified under other interpreters. The refined procedure is:

1. Generate the instantiation of agents by using the *agent* predicate. The name of the agent should be a Prolog atom and it should appear like the unique argument, for example:

   ```
   agent(carlos).
   ```

2. Specify the generic actors using the predicates *position* and *role*. The name of these positions and roles should be a Prolog atom and they should appear like the unique argument of these predicates, for example:

   ```
   position(strategicMember).
   ```

3. Specify the actors' relationships using the predicates *cover*, *play*, *occupies* and *isa*. These predicates should have two atomic arguments corresponding to the actor's type involved. For example:

   ```
   cover(strategicMember,coach).
   ```

4. Use the *define* predicate to implement *resource* and *belief* elements, identifying the name of the actor's type as first argument, and next a data structure which define the resources. The resource's name should be the first element and the default value should be the second element. The next code is an example.

   ```
   define(coach,[[coach][resources,[gridState,[]],]]).
   ```

5. For the goals and tasks indicated with activation times *always*, *begin* or *end*, add a Prolog line for each one. Each activation time is a predicate that needs the actor's type (atom) and the agent name (variable). For example:

   ```
   always(fieldMember,MyName):- stepDone(MyName).
   ```

6. Program the goals and plans using OR separators (|) for group of sequences of *means-end* and AND separators (,) for *task-decompositions*. The assumed semantic

is that any *means* is enough to accomplish the specified *end*. It is recommended that use a first argument with a variable containing the name of the agent. For example:

```
goal22(MyName):-  means1(MyName) | means2(MyName).
```

7. Program the undecomposed goals or tasks updating or taking action about resources using *updateResource* or *getResource* predicates. Verify that the access is allowed using the *amI* predicate.

```
goForRemoteGN(MyName):- amI(MyName,fieldMember),
   thread_peek_message(goldNugget(MyName,GNPosition)),
   updateResource(MyName,gnPosition,GNPosition).
```

8. Use the predicates *thread_peek_message* for dependencies which allow that the agent continues its execution and, *thread_get_message* for dependencies where the agent should wait an answer. On the other hand, it is necessary to use the *thread_send_message* predicate for generating answer messages. In the above example we illustrate an invocation to the *thread_peek_message* predicate.
9. Write the main program and call the predicates *runBegin, runEnd,* and *runAlways* (without parameters). For example:

```
main:-runBegin,runAlways,runEnd.
```

However, beyond this set of suggestions, it is necessary to consider the extra code which is needed for running the program. The first part is the small library of predicates which has been created with the aim that the above suggestions take effect in the designed way. This library has three components: (a) the threads control, which allows that, the agents being executed on independent threads, (b) the data structure access, which allows accessing the defined resources and beliefs of the agents, and, (c) the deduction predicates to heritage the agents' structures when there are *covers, is-a,* and *occupies* relationships.

The another code portion is related with the specific technical solution, thus, in the case of the collecting example it was necessary to set the stop condition on the *always* predicate and set the communication with the server which simulates the collecting environment. Although we tried some XML parsing libraries, we finally had to implement our own set of predicates for parsing and creating the messages of the established communication protocol.

During the contest the team had a good performance in all previewed situations. However we had some problems with hard labyrinths. In figure 5 we illustrate a part of a match that we lost against the winner team.

We consider that our designing approach was right despite this because we assumed a random disposition of obstacles and, as the antimodels technique suggested, we considered the most probable threats. We obtained a good performance in the contest, thus we consider that the antimodels technique as a refining process for agents' strategy, complemented with the procedure to obtain a predicative-based implementation, forms a good approach for tackling the overall process of developing a computational logic multi-agent application.

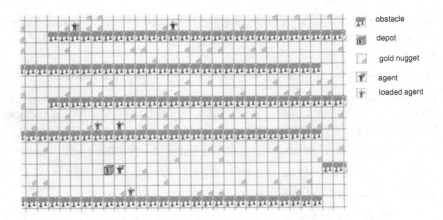

Fig. 5. Portion of a problematic scenario for our team

5 Conclusions

To summarize, we have used antimodels to identify threats represented as external goals (antigoals) and the resolution taxonomy proposed in [9] to refine the architectural and detailed design of a Tropos-based software process. In this way we present a goal-oriented requirement technique in the context of an agent-oriented software development, guided by an agent-oriented software development methodology. This combination has been possible because $i*$, the modelling language of Tropos, allows the representation of agent's and actor's goals. Moreover we have proposed a specific symbol to represent antigoals into $i*$ models. In this way we have formulated a specific security technique to support the design of the agents' strategy in the context of an agent-oriented software development.

We think that this work contributes to software engineering for several reasons. First, it extends the antimodel technique, considering additional cycles for recognizing antigoals. Second, it supports the use of antimodels not only with goal modelling but also agent modelling. Third, it supports the use of antimodels in refining agents' strategy. Fourth it constitutes an additional case for testing the Tropos-PL and allows its refinement. Finally, we think that this work is a particular case of reusing knowledge at the software process. Furthermore, we remark that the process has presented a minor complexity because we have reused our original winning design of the First CLIMA Contest [11]; we have used antimodels and an existing taxonomy to improve the original design. This design has allowed to prevent the most of the possible threat situations and to have specific answers for them. Therefore we have applied not only agent-oriented engineering techniques in our predicate-based approach but also the classical software engineering reuse principle. In fact this constitutes the main focus of our future work. Furthermore, we think that the suggested procedures of refining the agents' strategies, of reusing $i*$ design, and of using taxonomic knowledge, could be supported by CASE tools.

Acknowledgements

This work has been done in the framework of the research project UPIC, ref. TIN2004-07461-C02-01, supported by the Spanish Ministerio de Ciencia y Tecnología. Carlos Cares has been partially supported by the MECE-SUP FRO0105 Project of the Chilean government and University of La Frontera.

References

1. Giorgini P.: Agent-Oriented Software Engineering Report on the 4th AOSE Workshop (AOSE 2003). *SIGMOD Record*, **32** (2003) 117-118
2. Jennings N. R.: On agent-based software engineering. *Art. Intelligence*, **117** (2000) 277-296
3. Yu E.: Agent-Oriented Modelling: Software versus the World. *AOSE 2001. LNCS*, **2222** (2002) 206-225
4. Castro J., Kolp M., Mylopoulos J.: A Requirements-Driven Development Methodology. *Advanced Information Systems Engineering: 13th International Conference, CAiSE 2001,Interlaken, Switzerland*, (2001) 108-123
5. Giunchiglia F., Mylopoulos J.,Perini A.: The Tropos Software Development Methodology: Processes, Models and Diagrams. *AOSE 2002 LNCS*, **2585** (2003) 162-173
6. Yu E.: *Modelling Strategic Relationships for Process Reengineering*. University of Toronto, Toronto (1995)
7. Lamsweerde A. v.: Elaborating Security Requirements by Constructing of Intentional Anti-models. *Proc. of the 26th Int. Conference on Software Engineering (ICSE'04)*, Edinburgh, Scotland, UK, May 23-28 (2004)
8. Dardenne A., Fickas S., Lamswerdee A. v.: Goal-directed Concept Acquisition in Requirements Elicitation. *Proceedings of the 6th International Workshop on Software Specification and Design*, Como, Italy, Oct 25-26 (1991) 14-21
9. Lamsweerde A. v., Letier E.: Handling obstacles in goal-oriented requirements engineering. *IEEE Transactions on Sofware Engineering*, **26** (2000) 978-1005
10. Cybulski J. L.,Reed K.: Requirements Classification and Reuse: Crossing Domain Boundaries. *LNCS*, **1844** (2000) 190-210
11. Cares C., Franch X., Mayol E.: Extending Tropos for a Prolog Implementation: A Case Study Using the Food Collecting Agent Problem. *6th Int. Workshop on Computational Logic in Multi-Agent Systems (CLIMA VI). LNCS*, **3900** (2006) 396-405
12. Dastani M., Dix J.,Novak P.: *Tournament CLIMA Contest VII*, Accessed July 2006 2006 at http://agentmaster.in.tu-clausthal.de/massim/clima/data/20060429191348/index .html
13. Yu E.,Mylopoulos J.: Understanding "why" in software process modelling, analysis, and design. *Proceedings of the 16th international Conference on Software Engineering*, Sorrento, Italy, May 16 - 21 (1994) 159-168
14. Cares C., Franch X., Mayol E.,Alvarez E.: Goal-Driven Agent-Oriented Software Processes. *32nd Euromicro Conference on Software Engineering and Advanced Applications (SEAA)*, Cavtat/Dubrovnik, Croatia, Aug-Sept (2006) 336-343
15. Mouratidis H., Giorgini P., Manson G.,Philp I.: A Natural Extension of Tropos Methodology for Modelling Security. *Proceedings of the Agent Oriented Methodologies Workshop (OOPSLA 2002). Seattle, USA*, November (2002)
16. Marx D.: Eulerian disjoint paths problem in grid graphs is NP-Complete. *Discrete Applied Mathematics*, **143** (2004) 336-341
17. Wielemaker J.: *SWI-Prolog 5.1: Reference Manual*. SWI, U. of Amsterdam, (2003)

Multi-Agent FLUX for the Gold Mining Domain (System Description)

Stephan Schiffel and Michael Thielscher

Dresden University of Technology, 01062 Dresden, Germany
{stephan.schiffel,mit}@inf.tu-dresden.de

Abstract. FLUX is a declarative, CLP-based programming method for the design of agents that reason logically about their actions and sensor information in the presence of incomplete knowledge. The mathematical foundations of FLUX are given by the fluent calculus, which provides a solution to the fundamental frame problem in classical logic. We show how FLUX can be readily used as a platform for specifying and running a system of cooperating FLUX agents for solving the Gold Mining Problem.

1 Introduction

Research in Cognitive Robotics [1] addresses the problem of how to endow agents with the high-level cognitive capability of reasoning. Intelligent agents rely on this ability when they draw inferences from sensor data acquired over time, when they act under incomplete information, and when they exhibit plan-oriented behavior. For this purpose, a mental model of the environment is formed, which an agent constantly updates to reflect the changes it has effected and the sensor information it has acquired. The fluent calculus [2] is a knowledge representation language for actions that extends the classical situation calculus [3,4] by the concept of a state, which provides an effective solution to the fundamental frame problem [5]. FLUX [6,7] has recently been developed as a high-level programming method for the design of intelligent agents that reason about their actions on the basis of the fluent calculus. In this paper, we show how FLUX can be readily used as a platform for specifying and running a system of cooperating agents for solving the Gold Mining Problem.

Based on constraint logic programmin, FLUX comprises a method for encoding incomplete states along with a technique of updating these states according to a declarative specification of the elementary actions and sensing capabilities of an agent. Incomplete states are represented by lists (of fluents) with variable tail, and negative and disjunctive state knowledge is encoded by constraints. FLUX programs consist of three parts: a *kernel*, which provides the general reasoning facilities by means of an encoding of the foundational axioms in the fluent calculus; a domain-specific *background theory*, which contains the formal specification of the environment, including effect axioms for the actions of the agent; and a

K. Inoue, K. Satoh, and F. Toni (Eds.): CLIMA VII, LNAI 4371, pp. 294–303, 2007.
© Springer-Verlag Berlin Heidelberg 2007

Name	Type	Meaning
At	N × N ↦ FLUENT	position of the agent
Depot	N × N ↦ FLUENT	location of the depot
Obstacle	N × N ↦ FLUENT	cells containing a static obstacle
CarriesGold	FLUENT	agent carries gold

Fig. 1. The fluents for the Gold Mining domain

strategy, which specifies the intended behavior of an agent. We present the specification of a system of multiple FLUX agents which use identical background knowledge but act autonomously using individual strategies.

2   A Fluent Calculus Specification of the Gold Mining Domain

The fluent calculus is a method for representing knowledge of actions and change in classical logic. The calculus provides the formal foundation for agents to maintain an internal, symbolic model of their environment and to reason about the effects of their actions.

2.1   Fluents and States

In the fluent calculus, the various states of the environment of an agent are axiomatized on the basis of atomic components, called *fluents*. These are formally defined as functions into the pre-defined sort FLUENT. The table in Figure 1 lists the fluents used by each individual agent in the Gold Mining domain. We assume uniqueness-of-names for all fluents $\mathcal{F} = \{At, Depot, Obstacle, CarriesGold\}$, that is,

$$\bigwedge_{\substack{F, G \in \mathcal{F} \\ F \neq G}} F(\overline{x}) \neq G(\overline{y}) \ \wedge \ \bigwedge_{F \in \mathcal{F}} F(\overline{x}) = F(\overline{y}) \supset \overline{x} = \overline{y}$$

A distinctive feature of the fluent calculus is that it provides an explicit representation of *states*. Informally speaking, a state is a complete collection of fluents that are true. Formally, every term of sort FLUENT is also of the special sort STATE, representing a singleton state in which just this fluent holds. The special function ∘ : STATE × STATE ↦ STATE is used to compose sub-states into a state in which each fluent from either of the sub-states holds. The special constant ∅ : STATE denotes the empty state.

A fluent is then defined to hold in a state just in case the latter contains it:[1]

$$Holds(f : \text{FLUENT}, z : \text{STATE}) \stackrel{\text{def}}{=} (\exists z')\, z = f \circ z' \tag{1}$$

---

[1] Throughout the paper, variables of sort FLUENT and STATE will be denoted by the letters f and z, respectively, possibly with sub- or superscript.

This definition is accompanied by the foundational axioms of the fluent calculus, by which, essentially, states are characterized as non-nested sets of fluents. In the following, free variables are assumed to be universally quantified.

1. Associativity and commutativity,

$$(z_1 \circ z_2) \circ z_3 = z_1 \circ (z_2 \circ z_3) \qquad z_1 \circ z_2 = z_2 \circ z_1$$

2. Empty state axiom,
$$\neg Holds(f, \emptyset)$$

3. Irreducibility and decomposition,

$$Holds(f_1, f) \supset f_1 = f$$
$$Holds(f, z_1 \circ z_2) \supset Holds(f, z_1) \vee Holds(f, z_2)$$

4. State existence,
$$(\forall P)(\exists z)(\forall f) \, (Holds(f, z) \equiv P(f))$$

where P is a second-order predicate variable of sort FLUENT.

This very last axiom guarantees the existence of a state term for all combinations of fluents. Note, however, that this does not imply that any combinations of fluents may correspond to a physically possible state. For example, in the Gold Mining domain a state containing $At(1, 1) \circ At(1, 2)$ as sub-state will be defined as impossible; see Section 2.2.

Semantically, a state always describes a complete state of affairs, since fluents not contained in a state are false by the definition of $Holds$ (cf. (1)). On the other hand, the rigorous axiomatic definition allows for specifying incomplete state knowledge. As an example, let Z_0 denote the initial state, then the agent may know the following:

$$(\exists a_x, a_y) \, (Holds(At(a_x, a_y), Z_0) \wedge \neg Holds(Obstacle(a_x, a_y), Z_0))$$
$$(\exists d_x, d_y) \, (Holds(Depot(d_x, d_y), Z_0) \wedge \neg Holds(Obstacle(d_x, d_y), Z_0))$$
$$\neg Holds(CarriesGold, Z_0)$$

With the help of the foundation axioms, along with uniqueness-of-names, this specification can be rewritten to

$$(\exists z)(\exists a_x, a_y, d_x, d_y) \, (\, Z_0 = At(a_x, a_y) \circ Depot(d_x, d_y) \circ z \, \wedge$$
$$\neg Holds(Obstacle(a_x, a_y), z) \, \wedge$$
$$\neg Holds(Obstacle(d_x, d_y), z) \, \wedge \qquad \qquad (2)$$
$$\neg Holds(CarriesGold, z) \,)$$

2.2   Actions and Situations

Adopted from the situation calculus [3,4], actions are modeled in the fluent calculus by functions into the pre-defined sort ACTION. The actions of each individual agent in the Gold Mining domain are defined in Figure 2. Action

Name	Type	Meaning
Skip	ACTION	do nothing
Move	$\{East, \ldots, South\} \mapsto$ ACTION	move to the neighboring cell
Pick	ACTION	pick up gold
Drop	ACTION	drop gold
Mark	MARKING $\mapsto$ ACTION	mark a cell
Unmark	MARKING $\mapsto$ ACTION	unmark a cell

Fig. 2. The actions for the Gold Mining domain

Mark allows to place a marker at the current location. Markers provide a simple form of communication because they can be read by other agents upon entering the cell. Our agents, however, do not use this functionality because markers can also be set, read, and erased (via action *Unmark*) by the opponents.

Sequences of actions are represented by so-called *situations*, which are axiomatized as terms of the special sort SIT. The constant S_0 : SIT denotes the initial situation, and the function Do : ACTION $\times$ SIT $\mapsto$ SIT denotes the successor situation reached by performing an action in a situation.

Situations and states are related by the pre-defined function $State$: SIT $\mapsto$ STATE. This allows to extend the *Holds*-expression to situation arguments:[2]

$$Holds(f : \text{FLUENT}, s : \text{SIT}) \overset{\text{def}}{=} Holds(f, State(s))$$

This allows to define so-called *domain constraints*, which restrict the set of all states to those that can actually occur. The Gold Mining domain is characterized by the following domain constraints:

$$(\forall s)\,(\exists a_x, a_y)\,(Holds(At(a_x, a_y), s) \wedge \neg Holds(Obstacle(a_x, a_y), s))$$
$$(\forall s)\,(\forall a_x, a_y, a'_x, a'_y)\,(Holds(At(a_x, a_y), s) \wedge Holds(At(a'_x, a'_y), s) \supset$$
$$a_x = a'_x \wedge a_y = a'_y)$$
$$(\forall s)\,(\exists d_x, d_y)\,(Holds(Depot(d_x, d_y), s) \wedge \neg Holds(Obstacle(d_x, d_y), s))$$
$$(\forall s)\,(\forall d_x, d_y, d'_x, d'_y)\,(Holds(Depot(d_x, d_y), s) \wedge Holds(Depot(d'_x, d'_y), s) \supset$$
$$d_x = d'_x \wedge d_y = d'_y) \tag{3}$$

Put in words, the agent is always at a unique location, which cannot contain a static obstacle; and there is a unique location for the team's depot, which too is free of an obstacle.

2.3   Preconditions and State Update Axioms

Similar to the classical situation calculus, the executabilty of actions is axiomatized with the help of the predicate $Poss$: ACTION $\times$ STATE. In the Gold Mining

---

[2] Throughout the paper, variables of sort ACTION and SIT will be denoted by the letters a and s, respectively, possibly with sub- or superscript.

domain, we have the following precondition axioms, where the auxiliary predicate $Adjacent(a_x, a_y, d, a'_x, a'_y)$ defines (a'_x, a'_y) to be adjacent to cell (a_x, a_y) in direction d.

$$Poss(Skip, z) \equiv \top$$
$$Poss(Move(d), z) \equiv (\exists a_x, a_y, a'_x, a'_y)\,(\,Holds(At(a_x, a_y), z) \wedge$$
$$Adjacent(a_x, a_y, d, a'_x, a'_y) \wedge$$
$$\neg Holds(Obstacle(a'_x, a'_y), z)\,) \qquad (4)$$
$$Poss(Pick, z) \equiv \top$$
$$Poss(Drop, z) \equiv Holds(CarriesGold, z)$$
$$Poss(Mark, z) \equiv \top$$
$$Poss(Unmark, z) \equiv \top$$

Note that picking up gold is always possible by definition; if the respective cell does not contain gold, the action will have no effect (see below).

Effects of actions are specified in the fluent calculus on the basis of two macros defining the removal and addition of fluents:

$$z_1 - f = z_2 \stackrel{\text{def}}{=} (z_2 = z_1 \vee z_2 \circ f = z_1) \wedge \neg Holds(f, z_2)$$
$$z_1 + f = z_2 \stackrel{\text{def}}{=} z_2 = z_1 \circ f$$

These macros generalize to removal and addition of finitely many fluents in a straightforward way. The *hauptsatz* of the fluent calculus says that these two functions provide an effective solution to the frame problem (see, e.g., [7]):

Theorem 1. *The foundational axioms of the fluent calculus entail*

$$z_2 = z_1 - f_1 - \ldots - f_m + g_1 + \ldots + g_n \supset$$
$$[\,Holds(f, z_2) \equiv \bigvee_i (f = g_i) \vee [Holds(f, z_1) \wedge \bigwedge_j (f \neq f_j)]\,]$$

On this basis, so-called state update axioms define the effects of an action a in a situation s as the difference between the current $State(s)$ and its successor $State(Do(a, s))$. The state update axioms in the Gold Mining domain are as follows:

$$Poss(Skip, s) \supset State(Do(Skip, s)) = State(s)$$

$$Poss(Move(d), s) \supset$$
$$(\exists a_x, a_y, a'_x, a'_y)\,(\,Holds(At(a_x, a_y), s) \wedge Adjacent(a_x, a_y, d, a'_x, a'_y) \wedge$$
$$State(Do(Move(d), s)) = State(s) - At(a_x, a_y) + At(a'_x, a'_y)\,)$$

$$Poss(Pick, s) \supset State(Do(Pick, s)) = State(s) + CarriesGold$$
$$\vee State(Do(Pick, s)) = State(s) \qquad (5)$$

$$Poss(Drop, s) \supset State(Do(Drop, s)) = State(s) - CarriesGold$$

$$Poss(Mark, s) \supset State(Do(Mark, s)) = State(s)$$

$$Poss(Unmark, s) \supset State(Do(Unmark, s)) = State(s)$$

Note that the state update axioms for action *Pick* is *nondeterministic*, that is, it does not entail whether the agent will actually be successful in trying to pick up gold. By its control strategy, however, an agent will only attempt this action in a situation where it has sensed the presence of gold in its current cell. Furthermore, the sensor information received immediately after such an action will inform the agent about its success. Since our agents do not make use of markers, these are not represented in their world model and, hence, the two actions *Mark* and *Unmark* do not change the state.

Sensor information provides additional knowledge of the environment. We represent the result of sensing in the Gold Mining domain with the help of situation-dependent predicates like *ObstacleSensed* : $\mathbb{N} \times \text{SIT}$ such that an instance *ObstacleSensed*(d, s) is true if an obstacle has been sensed in direction d (where d encodes the eight directions north, north-east, ...). For the sake of simplicity, and in accordance with the specification of the Gold Mining challenge, we assume that knowledge of the sensing predicates is given to the agent after any of its actions.[3] Thus, if the agent is informed about an obstacle in its vicinity, then this provides additional knowledge of the state at the current situation:

$$ObstacleSensed(s) \equiv (\exists x, y, x', y', d) \, (\, Holds(At(x,y), s) \, \wedge$$
$$Adjacent(x, y, d, x', y') \, \wedge$$
$$Holds(Obstacle(x', y'), s) \,)$$

3   A Multi-Agent FLUX System

FLUX [6,7] is a high-level programming method for the design of intelligent agents that reason about their actions on the basis of the fluent calculus. Using the paradigm of constraint logic programming, FLUX comprises a method for encoding incomplete states along with a technique of updating these states via a declarative specification of the elementary actions and sensing capabilities of an agent.

Figure 3 depicts the general architecture of a FLUX control program. The kernel P_{kernel}, which endows agents with general reasoning facilities, is the same for all programs. It has been formally verified against the foundational axioms of the fluent calculus. The second part, P_{domain}, of a FLUX agent program contains encodings of the axiomatization of a particular application domain. In our system of agents for the Gold Mining domain, all agents use the same background theory. On top of this, the intended behavior of an individual agent is defined via a control program $P_{strategy}$.

3.1   State Encoding

Incomplete states are represented by lists of (possibly non-ground) fluents and a variable tail, that is, $Z = [F1,...,Fk \mid \_\,]$. It is assumed that the arguments

---

[3] This is conceptually simpler than the use of an extension of the fluent calculus which is based on an explicit model of the knowledge of an agent and which allows to explicitly reason about the effects of sensing actions [8].

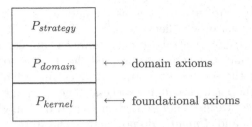

Fig. 3. The three components of a FLUX program

of fluents are encoded by integers or symbolic constants, which enables the use of a standard arithmetic solver for constraints on partially known arguments. Further state knowledge is expressed by the following *state constraints* [6,9]:

constraint	semantics
not_holds(F,Z)	$\neg Holds(f, z)$
not_holds_all(F,Z)	$(\forall \overline{x}) \neg Holds(f, z)$, $\overline{x}$ variables in f
or_holds([F1,...,Fn],Z)	$\bigvee_{i=1}^{n} Holds(f_i, z)$
if_then_holds(F,G,Z)	$Holds(f, z) \supset Holds(g, z)$
all_holds(F,Z)	$(\forall \overline{x}) Holds(f, z)$, $\overline{x}$ variables in f

These state constraints have been carefully designed so as to be sufficiently expressive while allowing for efficient constraint solving. As an example, the following clause encodes the specification of state Z_0 of Section 2.1 (cf. (2)) along with additional knowledge that follows from domain constraints (cf. (3)):

```
init(Z0) :- Z0 = [at(AX,AY),depot(DX,DY) | Z],
            not_holds_all(at(_,_), Z),
            not_holds_all(depot(_,_), Z),
            not_holds(obstacle(AX,AY), Z),
            not_holds(obstacle(DX,DY), Z),
            not_holds(carries_gold, Z).
```

The FLUX kernel includes an efficient solver for the various state constraints using Constraint Handling Rules [10], which have been formally verified against the fluent calculus [6,9].

3.2   State Update in FLUX

The second part, P_{domain}, of a FLUX agent program contains encodings of the domain axioms. These include action precondition axioms, which are straightforward encodings of the corresponding fluent calculus axioms (cf. (4)), and state update axioms. For encoding the latter, the FLUX kernel provides the definition of a predicate update(Z1,[G1,...,Gn],[F1,...,Fm],Z2), which encodes the equation $z_2 = z_1 - f_1 - \ldots - f_m + g_1 + \ldots + g_n$ of the fluent calculus.

Interaction with the Environment

The physical effects of actions are straightforwardly specified in FLUX in accordance with the state update axioms. In addition, the update of the world model requires to account for the interaction of an agent with its environment, possibly including communication with other agents. To this end, effects of actions are encoded in FLUX by clauses which define the predicate state_update(Z1,A,Z2,Y) in such a way that performing action a in state z_1 and receiving sensor information $\bar{y}$ yields updated state z_2. The following encoding shows how the physical effects (cf. axioms (5) in Section 2.3) as well as the interaction with the environment can be specified for the Gold Mining agents:

```
state_update(Z, skip, Z, []).

state_update(Z1, move(D), Z2, [Obst]) :-
   holds(at(AX,AY), Z1), adjacent(AX, AY, D, AX1, AY1),
   update(Z1, [at(AX1,AY1)], [at(AX,AY)], Z2),
   obstacles_sensed(Obst, Z2).

state_update(Z1, pick, Z2, [Gold]) :-
     Gold = true,  update(Z1, [carriesGold], [], Z2)
   ; Gold = false, Z1 = Z2.

state_update(Z1, drop, Z2, []) :-
   update(Z1, [], [carriesGold], Z2).

state_update(Z, mark, Z, []).

state_update(Z, unmark, Z, []).
```

According to this definition, the execution of the action $Move(d)$ is assumed to return a sensing vector Obst of binary values indicating which of the surrounding cells house a static obstacle. Auxiliary predicate obstacles_sensed(Obst,Z2) is then defined in such a way as to extend the incomplete state z_2 with this knowledge. The execution of action $Pick$ is assumed to return a sensing value indicating whether picking up the gold was actually successfully. This allows to resolve the nondeterminism in the corresponding state update axiom.[4] In the same fashion, information received through communication can be added to the specification of state updates in FLUX [11].

3.3 FLUX Strategies

While the FLUX agents for the Gold Mining problem share the same background theory, each one of them acts according to its individual strategy, depending on

---

[4] The specification of the Gold Mining challenge says that a $Move(d)$ action, too, may fail with a small likelihood. This can be incorporated into the corresponding state update axiom in a similar way.

the role it plays. The agents communicate acquired knowledge of the obstacles in the environment. As a high-level programming language, FLUX allows to define complex strategies by which the agents systematically explore the environment and cooperate in transporting collected gold items to their depot.

The basic strategy of each agent is defined by the following clause, which defines the next action of an agent based on the current state z:

```
getNextAction(Action, Z) :-
  holds(at(X, Y), Z), holds(depot(DepotX, DepotY), Z),
  ( holds(carries_gold, Z) ->
    ( (X = DepotX, Y = DepotY) -> Action = drop
      ;
      direction(X, Y, DepotX, DepotY, Z, Action) )
    ;
    ( holds(gold(X,Y),Z) -> Action = pick
      ;
      gotoNextGold(X, Y, Z, Action) ) ).
```

First the agent determines its own and the depot's position. Which action to take depends on whether the agent carries gold or not. If the agent carries a gold item and is currently at the depot then the obvious action to take is dropping the gold. In case the agent is not at the depot it determines the direction it has to take to reach the depot. This might involve path planning to avoid obstacles and other agents and also to explore unknown territory on the way to the destination in order to find new gold. For the exploration of the environment, the agents also maintain a list of choicepoints along with the current path in order to be able to backtrack if necessary.

In case the agent does not carry gold at the moment it goes to a location that contains a gold item and picks up gold there. This involves deciding which known gold location to go to or which unknown territory to explore to find new gold. Our agents usually head for the nearest gold item unless another agent, which is also aiming at this cell, is closer. This condition makes sure that teammates do not compete but cooperate in collecting gold items. If there is no known gold item nearby, or all known gold items will be taken by the other agents, the agent heads to the nearest unexplored location.

For efficient calculation of the agents' actions, any plan that an agents devises is stored in the state and followed unless new knowledge is obtained which makes replanning necessary or favorable. Depending on the plan this can include failure of actions; previously unknown obstacles, or other agents, blocking the way; discovery of new gold; or teammates taking the gold the agent is heading for.

4   Discussion

The purpose of this study was to demonstrate that FLUX can be readily used for the high-level control of multiple cooperating agents in a competitive environment. Unfortunately, the team of FLUX agents did not perform very well at the actual CLIMA-06 competition. The problem, however, was entirely due to a suboptimal strategy and did not show up in any of our preceding experiments with smaller environments.

The closest work related to FLUX is the programming language GOLOG [1] for dynamic domains, which is based on successor state axioms as a solution to the frame problem. The main differences are, first, that with its underlying constraint solver, FLUX provides a natural way of representing and reasoning with incomplete states as well as nondeterministic actions. Second, the logic programs for GOLOG described in the literature all apply the principle of *regression* to evaluate conditions in agent programs, whereas FLUX is based on the *progression* of states. While the former is efficient for short action sequences, the computational effort increases with the number of performed actions. With the progression principle, FLUX programs scale up well to the control of agents over extended periods.

For future work, we intend to develop a formal model of cooperation and competition in multiagent settings based on the fluent calculus and FLUX.

References

1. Lespérance, Y., Levesque, H., etal: A logical approach to high-level robot programming—a progress report. In Kuipers, B., ed.: Control of the Physical World by Intelligent Agents, Papers from the AAAI Fall Symposium, New Orleans, LA (1994) 109–119
2. Thielscher, M.: From situation calculus to fluent calculus: State update axioms as a solution to the inferential frame problem. Artificial Intelligence **111** (1999) 277–299
3. McCarthy, J.: Situations and Actions and Causal Laws. Stanford Artificial Intelligence Project, Memo 2, Stanford University, CA (1963)
4. Reiter, R.: Knowledge in Action. MIT Press (2001)
5. McCarthy, J., Hayes, P.J.: Some philosophical problems from the standpoint of artificial intelligence. Machine Intelligence **4** (1969) 463–502
6. Thielscher, M.: FLUX: A logic programming method for reasoning agents. Theory and Practice of Logic Programming **5** (2005) 533–565
7. Thielscher, M.: Reasoning Robots: The Art and Science of Programming Robotic Agents. Volume 33 of Applied Logic Series. Kluwer (2005)
8. Thielscher, M.: Representing the knowledge of a robot. In: Proceedings of KR (2000) 109–120
9. Thielscher, M.: Handling implicational and universal quantification constraints in flux. In: Proceedings of CP. Volume 3709 of LNCS, Springer (2005) 667–681
10. Frühwirth, T.: Theory and practice of constraint handling rules. Journal of Logic Programming **37** (1998) 95–138
11. Narasamdya, I., Martin, Y., Thielscher, M.: Knowledge of Other Agents and Communicative Actions in the Fluent Calculus. In: Proceedings of KR (2004) 623–633

Using *Jason* to Implement a Team of Gold Miners

Rafael H. Bordini[1], Jomi F. Hübner[2], and Daniel M. Tralamazza[3]

[1] Department of Computer Science
University of Durham
Durham DH1 3LE, U.K.
R.Bordini@durham.ac.uk
[2] Departamento de Sistemas e Computação
Universidade Regional de Blumenau
Blumenau, SC 89035-160, Brazil
jomi@inf.furb.br
[3] School of Computer & Communication Sciences
Ecole Polytechnique Fédérale de Lausanne
CH-1015 Lausanne, Switzerland
daniel.tralamazza@epfl.ch

Abstract. This paper describes a team of agents that took part in the second CLIMA Contest. The team was implemented in a logic-based language for BDI agents and was run in a Java-based interpreter that makes it easy for legacy code to be invoked from within the agents' practical reasoning. Even though the implementation was not completely finished in time, the team won the competition, and the experience also allowed us to improve various aspects of the interpreter.

1 Introduction

In this paper, we describe the development of a team of agents created to enter the second CLIMA Contest, which took place with CLIMA VII. We quote bellow the general description of the scenario (Figure 1 shows a screenshot).

> Recently, rumours about the discovery of gold scattered around deep Carpathian woods made their way into the public. Consequently hordes of gold miners are pouring into the area in the hope to collect as much of gold nuggets as possible. Two small teams of gold miners find themselves exploring the same area, avoiding trees and bushes and competing for the gold nuggets spread around the woods. The gold miners of each team coordinate their actions in order to collect as much gold as they can and to deliver it to the trading agent located in a depot where the gold is safely stored.
>
> (http://cig.in.tu-clausthal.de/CLIMAContest/)

The first important characteristic of the team described here is that the agents were programmed in AgentSpeak, an agent-oriented programming language based on logic programming and suitable for (BDI) reactive planning systems (the language is briefly explained in Section 2). An interpreter for an extended version of AgentSpeak called *Jason* was used to run the agents (see Section 3). Section 4 presents the overall team specification and Section 5 gives further details of the implementation.

K. Inoue, K. Satoh, and F. Toni (Eds.): CLIMA VII, LNAI 4371, pp. 304–313, 2007.
© Springer-Verlag Berlin Heidelberg 2007

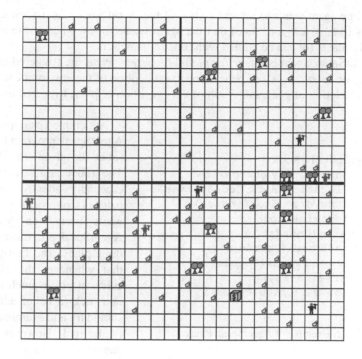

Fig. 1. The Contest Scenario and the Quadrants Used by our Team

2   AgentSpeak

The AgentSpeak(L) programming language was introduced in [7]. It is based on logic programming and provides an elegant abstract framework for programming BDI agents. The BDI architecture is, in turn, the predominant approach to the implementation of *intelligent* or *rational* agents [8], and a number of commercial applications have been developed using this approach.

An AgentSpeak agent is defined by a set of *beliefs* giving the initial state of the agent's *belief base*, which is a set of ground (first-order) atomic formulæ, and a set of plans which form its *plan library*. An AgentSpeak plan has a *head* which consists of a triggering event (specifying the events for which that plan is *relevant*), and a conjunction of belief literals representing a *context*. The conjunction of literals in the context must be a logical consequence of that agent's current beliefs if the plan is to be considered *applicable* when the triggering event happens (only applicable plans can be chosen for execution). A plan also has a *body*, which is a sequence of basic actions or (sub)goals that the agent has to achieve (or test) when the plan is triggered. *Basic actions* represent the atomic operations the agent can perform so as to change the environment. Such actions are also written as atomic formulæ, but using a set of *action symbols* rather than predicate symbols. AgentSpeak distinguishes two types of *goals*: achievement goals and test goals. Achievement goals are formed by an atomic formulæ prefixed with the '**!**' operator, while test goals are prefixed with the '**?**' operator. An *achievement goal* states that the agent wants to achieve a state of the world where the associated atomic formulæ is true. A *test goal* states that the agent wants to test whether the associated atomic formulæ is (or can be unified with) one of its beliefs.

An AgentSpeak agent is a *reactive planning system*. Plans are triggered by the *addition* ('+') or *deletion* ('-') of beliefs due to perception of the environment, or to the addition or deletion of goals as a result of the execution of plans triggered by previous events.

A simple example of an AgentSpeak program for a Mars robot is given in Figure 2. The robot is instructed to be especially attentive to "green patches" on rocks it observes while roving on Mars. The AgentSpeak program consists of three plans. The first plan says that whenever the robot perceives a green patch on a certain rock (a belief addition), it should try and examine that particular rock. However this plan can only be used (i.e., it is only applicable) if the robot's batteries are not too low. To examine the rock, the robot must retrieve, from its belief base, the coordinates it has associated with that rock (this is the reason for the test goal in the beginning of the plan's body), then achieve the goal of traversing to those coordinates and, once there, examining the rock. Recall that each of these achievement goals will trigger the execution of some other plan.

```
+green_patch(Rock)
   : not battery_charge(low)
   <- ?location(Rock,Coordinates);
      !traverse(Coordinates);
      !examine(Rock).
+!traverse(Coords)
   : safe_path(Coords)
   <- move_towards(Coords).
+!traverse(Coords)
   : not safe_path(Coords)
   <- ...
```

Fig. 2. Example of AgentSpeak Plans

The two other plans (note the last one is only an excerpt) provide alternative courses of action that the rover should take to achieve a goal of traversing towards some given coordinates. Which course of action is selected depends on its beliefs about the environment at the time the goal-addition event is handled. If the rover believes that there is a safe path in the direction to be traversed, then all it has to do is to take the action of moving towards those coordinates (this is a basic action which allows the rover to effect changes in its environment, in this case physically moving itself). The alternative plan (not shown here) provides an alternative means for the agent to reach the rock when the direct path is unsafe.

3   *Jason*

The *Jason* interpreter implements the operational semantics of AgentSpeak as given in, e.g., [4]. *Jason* [1] is written in Java, and its IDE supports the development and execution of distributed multi-agent systems [3,2]. Some of the features of *Jason* are:

---

[1] *Jason* is *Open Source* (GNU LGPL) and is available from http://jason.sourceforge.net

- speech-act based inter-agent communication (and annotation of beliefs with information sources);
- the possibility to run a multi-agent system distributed over a network (using SACI or some other middleware);
- fully customisable (in Java) selection functions, trust functions, and overall agent architecture (perception, belief-revision, inter-agent communication, and acting);
- straightforward extensibility and use of legacy code by means of user-defined "internal actions" implemented in Java;
- clear notion of *multi-agent environments*, which can be implemented in Java (this can be a simulation of a real environment, e.g., for testing purposes before the system is actually deployed).

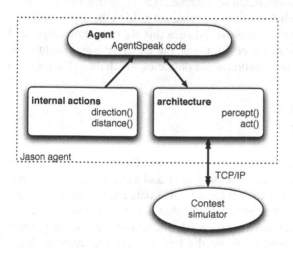

Fig. 3. Agent Extensibility and Customisation

To implement our agent team, two of these features were specially useful: architecture customisation and internal actions (see Figure 3). A customisation of the agent architecture is used to interface between the agent and its environment. The environment for the CLIMA Contest was implemented by the contest organisers in a remote server that simulates the mining field, sending perception to the agents and receiving requests for action execution. Therefore, when an agent attempts to perceive the environment, the architecture sends to it the information provided by the simulator, and when the agent chooses an action to be performed, the architecture sends the action execution request to the simulator. For example, the plan

```
+pos(X,Y) : Y > 0 <- up.
```

is triggered when the agent perceives its position and its current line in the world grid is greater than zero. The +pos(X,Y) percept is produced by the architecture from the messages sent by the simulator, and up is an action that the architecture sends to the simulator.

Although most of the agent is coded in AgentSpeak, some parts were implemented in Java, in this case because we wanted to use legacy code, in particular, we already had a Java implementation of the A* search algorithm, which we used to find paths in instances of the simulated scenario (it is interesting to note that in one of the "maze" scenarios used in the competition, our team was the only to successfully find a path to the depot). This algorithm was made accessible to the agents by means of *internal actions*. These were used in AgentSpeak plans as shown in the example below:

```
+gold(X,Y): pos(X,Y) & depot(DX,DY) & carrying_gold
     <- pick; jia.direction(X,Y,DX,DY,Dir); Dir.
```

In this plan, when the agent perceives some gold in its current position, it picks up the gold and calls the `direction` internal action of the `jia` library. This internal action receives two locations as parameters ($\langle$X,Y$\rangle$ and $\langle$DX,DY$\rangle$), computes a path between them using A* (using the Manhattan distance as heuristic, as usual in scenarios such as this), and instantiates `Dir` with the first action (`up`, `down`, `left`, or `right`) according to the path it found from the first to the second coordinate. The plan then says that the agent should perform the action instantiated to variable `Dir`. Note that this plan is illustrative, it does not generate the behaviour of carrying the gold to the depot; only one step towards it is performed in the excerpt above. Also, as this is a cooperative team and each agent has only a partial view of the environment, the underlying architecture ensures that the agents share all the information about obstacles which the A* algorithms uses for navigation.

4   Overall Team Strategy

The team is composed of two roles enacted by five agents. The miner role is played by four agents who will have the goal of finding gold and carrying it to the depot. The team also has one agent playing the leader role; its goals are to allocate agents' quadrants and allocate free agents to a piece of gold that has been found. The leader agent helps the team, but each team must have exactly four miner agents that log into the simulation server as official contestants, so the leader is not registered with the server. The diagrams in Figures 4, 5, and 6 give an overview of the system and the two roles using the Prometheus methodology [6].

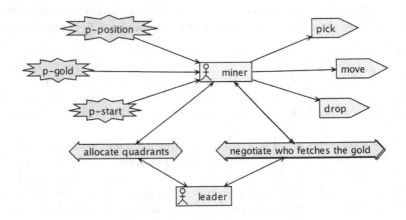

Fig. 4. System overview diagram

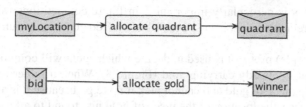

Fig. 5. Leader agent specification

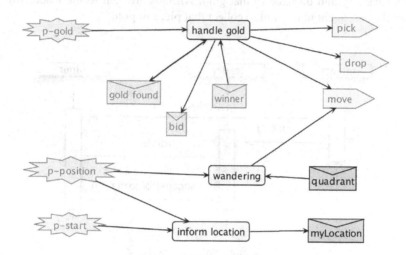

Fig. 6. Miner agent specification

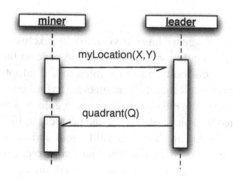

Fig. 7. Quadrant allocation protocol

The overall strategy of the *Jason* team is as follows. Each miner is responsible for systematically (rather than randomly) searching gold *within* one quadrant of the environment (see Figure 9). Since the initial positions of the agents are only known when the game starts, the allocation of the agents to quadrants depends on such positions. The team uses the protocol in figure 7 for the leader to allocate each agent to a quadrant. At the beginning of each game, the four miner agents send their location to the leader agent, the leader allocates each quadrant to an agent by checking which agent is nearest to that quadrant, and sends a message to each agent saying which quadrant they have been allocated. We have decided to centralise some decisions in a leader agent so as to decrease the number of required messages in a distributed negotiation; even though all agents were run in the same machine in the actual competition, this is particularly important if in future competitions we decide to run agents in different machines, in case agents become too elaborate to run them all in one machine.

Another (simple) protocol is used to decide which agent will commit to gold found by a miner that is already carrying gold (Figure 8). When a miner (e.g., miner1 in Figure 8) sees a piece of gold and cannot pick it up (e.g., because it is already carrying gold), it broadcasts the location of the piece of gold just found to all agents. The other agents bid to take on the task of fetching that piece of gold; such bid is computed based on its availability and distance to that gold. All bids are sent to the leader who then chooses the best agent to commit to collect that piece of gold.

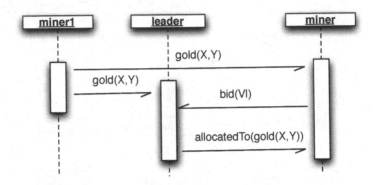

Fig. 8. Gold Allocation Protocol

5   Implementation in *Jason*

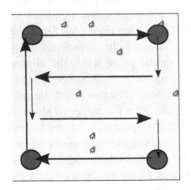

Fig. 9. Miner's Search Path Within its Quadrant

The miner agents have two mutually exclusive goals: "find gold" or "handle gold". Whenever the agent has currently no other intention, it adopts the goal of exploring its own quadrant to find gold. When the agent either perceives some gold or was allocated to a piece of gold by the protocol in Figure 8, it gives up the "find gold" goal and commits to the goal of handling that particular piece of gold. When this latter goal is achieved, the agent commits again to the "find gold" goal.

To systematically find gold in its quadrant, the miner "scans" its quadrant as illustrated in Figure 9. The plans for achieving this goal determine that the agent should start from the place where it last stopped searching for gold, or start from the position in its quadrant which is closest to the depot. As the agent can perceive gold in all neighbouring cells, it can skip three lines when moving vertically.

When a miner sees a piece of gold, three relevant plans can be selected as applicable depending on the following conditions (the AgentSpeak code is shown in Figure 10):

1. The first plan is applicable when the miner is not carrying gold and is free. [2] The plan execution consist of removing the belief that it is free, adding a belief that there is gold at that location, and creating a goal to handle that gold.
2. The second plan is applicable when the miner is also not carrying gold but is not free because it is going to position OldX, OldY to collect some gold there. In this case, it prefers the gold just found, so the agent: (i)drops the previous intention; (ii) announces the availability of gold at the "old" location to the other agents (this will trigger again the allocation protocol in Figure 7); and (iii) creates a goal to handle the piece of gold it has just found.
3. If none of the above plans is applicable (i.e., the agent is carrying gold), the third alternative plan is used to announce the gold location to others agents, starting the allocation protocol (shown in Figure 7).

The last three plans in Figure 10 implement part of the allocation protocol. When the agent receives a message with some gold position, if it is free, it sends a bid based on its Manhattan distance to the gold; otherwise, it sends a very high bid. When some gold is allocated by the leader to the agent, it handles this gold if it is still free. Note that this is not an optimal strategy: we have not as yet dealt with the possibility that reallocating tasks to the agents that are already committed (i.e., no longer free) might lead to a better overall task allocation; in the future, we might use some DCOP (Distributed Constraint Optimisation Problem) algorithm for this.

The plan to achieve the goal of handling a found piece of gold[3] is shown in Figure 11. The plan initially drops the goal of finding gold (exploration behaviour), moves the agent to the gold position, picks the gold, announces to others that the gold was collected so they do not try to fetch this gold (to avoid agents moving to pieces of gold that are no longer there), retrieves the depot location from the belief base, moves the agent to the depot, drops the gold, and finally chooses another gold to pursue. In case the handle-gold plan fails (e.g., because the gold disappeared due to the environment being dynamic), the event -!handle(G) is created and the second plan is selected. This plan just removes the information about that gold location from the belief base and chooses another piece of gold to be collected. The choose_gold plans find the nearest known gold and create a gold to handle it; if no gold location is known, the agent is free and resumes the gold-searching behaviour.

It is important to note that AgentSpeak is the language used to define the high-level (practical) reasoning of the agents. The use of internal actions facilitates keeping the agent language at the right level of abstraction, even when legacy code needs to be invoked.

---

[2] The agent maintains a belief stating whether it is currently "free" or not. Being free means that the agent is not committed to handling any piece of gold.

[3] Note that only the most important plans are included here; the complete code is available in the *Jason* web site.

```
+cell(X,Y,gold) : not carrying_gold & free
  <- -free; +gold(X,Y);
     !handle(gold(X,Y)).
+cell(X,Y,gold) : not carrying_gold & not free &
                     .desire(handle(gold(OldX,OldY))) &
  <- +gold(X,Y);
     .dropIntention(handle(gold(_,_)));
     .broadcast(tell,gold(OldX,OldY));
     !handle(gold(X,Y)).
+cell(X,Y,gold) : not committed(gold(X,Y))
  <- +gold(X,Y);
     .broadcast(tell,gold(X,Y)).

+gold(X1,Y1)[source(A)] : A \== self & free & pos(X2,Y2)
  <- jia.dist(X1,Y1,X2,Y2,Dist);
     .send(leader,tell,bidFor(gold(X1,Y1),Dist)).
+gold(X1,Y1)[source(A)] : A \== self
  <- .send(leader,tell,bidFor(gold(X1,Y1),1000)).

+allocatedTo(Gold,Me)[source(leader)]
  :  .myName(Me) & free // I am still free
     <- -free; !handle(Gold).
```

Fig. 10. Relevant Plans for When Gold is Perceived or Allocated

```
+!handle(gold(X,Y)) : true
  <- .dropIntention(explore(_,_));
     !pos(X,Y);     !ensure(pick);
     .broadcast(tell,picked(gold(X,Y)));
     ?depot(_,DX,DY);
     !pos(DX,DY); !ensure(drop);
     -gold(X,Y);    !choose_gold.

-!handle(Gold) : true  <- -Gold; !choose_gold.

+!choose_gold : not gold(_,_) <- +free.
+!choose_gold : gold(_,_)
  <- .findall(gold(X,Y),gold(X,Y),LG);
     !calcGoldDistance(LG,LD);
     // LD is a list of terms d(Distance,gold(X,Y))
     !min(LD,d(Distance,NewGold));
     !handle(NewGold).

+!pos(X,Y) : pos(X,Y) <- true.
+!pos(X,Y) : not pos(X,Y) & pos(AgX,AgY)
  <- jia.getDirection(AgX, AgY, X, Y, D);
     D; !pos(X,Y).
```

Fig. 11. Plans to Handle a Piece of Gold

6   Conclusion

The AgentSpeak code for the team of gold miners, in our opinion, is a quite elegant solution, being declarative, goal-based (based on the BDI architecture), and also neatly allowing agents to have long term goals while reacting to changes in the environment. The *Jason* interpreter provided good support for high-level (speech-act based) communication, transparent integration with the contest server, and for use of existing Java code (e.g., for the A* algorithm). Although not a "purely" declarative, logic-based approach, the combination of both declarative and legacy code was quite efficient without compromising the declarative level (i.e., the agent's practical reasoning which is the specific level for which AgentSpeak is an appropriate language).

On the other hand, using a new programming paradigm [1] is never easy, and we also faced difficulties with *Jason* being a new platform that had some features that had never been thoroughly tested before. The development of a *Jason* team was a good experience not only in the result of the competition but also for experimenting with multi-agent programming and the improvements of the *Jason* platform that ensued. The scenarios where our team did not do so well were the ones with highest uncertainty; we still need more work and experience taking this type of scenario into consideration. In future versions of this team, we plan to avoid the use of centralised negotiation (which has the leader as a single point of failure) and to use $\mathcal{M}$oise+ [5] to create an organisation with the specification of the roles in the system. In our original strategy, there was yet another role which was that of the "courier"; in case the depot happens to be in a position too far from the some of the quadrants, the courier would help carry to the depot pieces of gold from agents that are in the more distant quadrants. We also plan to experiment with DCOP algorithms for optimal allocation of agents to collect pieces of gold.

References

1. R. H. Bordini, M. Dastani, J. Dix, and A. El Fallah Seghrouchni, editors. *Multi-Agent Programming: Languages, Platforms and Applications*. Springer, 2005.
2. R. H. Bordini, J. F. Hübner, et al.   *Jason*, manual version 0.8, Mar 2006. http://jason.sourceforge.net/.
3. R. H. Bordini, J. F. Hübner, and R. Vieira. *Jason* and the golden fleece of agent-oriented programming. In Bordini et al. [1], chapter 1, pages 3–37.
4. R. H. Bordini and Á. F. Moreira. Proving BDI properties of agent-oriented programming languages: The asymmetry thesis principles in AgentSpeak(L). *Annals of Mathematics and Artificial Intelligence*, 42(1–3):197–226, Sept. 2004.
5. J. F. Hübner, J. S. Sichman, and O. Boissier. Using the Moise+ for a cooperative framework of MAS reorganisation. In *Proc. of 17th SBIA*, LNAI 3171, pages 506–515. Springer, 2004.
6. L. Padgham and M. Winikoff. *Developing Intelligent Agent Systems: A Practical Guide*. John Wiley and Sons, 2004.
7. A. S. Rao. AgentSpeak(L): BDI agents speak out in a logical computable language. In *Proc. of MAAMAW'96*, LNAI 1038, pages 42–55. Springer 1996.
8. M. Wooldridge. *Reasoning about Rational Agents*. The MIT Press, Cambridge, MA, 2000.

Author Index

Lecture Notes in Artificial Intelligence (LNAI)

Vol. 4160: M. Fisher, W. van der Hoek, B. Konev, A. Lisitsa (Eds.), Logics in Artificial Intelligence. XII, 516 pages. 2006.

Vol. 4155: O. Stock, M. Schaerf (Eds.), Reasoning, Action and Interaction in AI Theories and Systems. XVIII, 343 pages. 2006.

Vol. 4149: M. Klusch, M. Rovatsos, T.R. Payne (Eds.), Cooperative Information Agents X. XII, 477 pages. 2006.

Vol. 4140: J.S. Sichman, H. Coelho, S.O. Rezende (Eds.), Advances in Artificial Intelligence - IBERAMIA-SBIA 2006. XXIII, 635 pages. 2006.

Vol. 4139: T. Salakoski, F. Ginter, S. Pyysalo, T. Pahikkala (Eds.), Advances in Natural Language Processing. XVI, 771 pages. 2006.

Vol. 4133: J. Gratch, M. Young, R. Aylett, D. Ballin, P. Olivier (Eds.), Intelligent Virtual Agents. XIV, 472 pages. 2006.

Vol. 4130: U. Furbach, N. Shankar (Eds.), Automated Reasoning. XV, 680 pages. 2006.

Vol. 4120: J. Calmet, T. Ida, D. Wang (Eds.), Artificial Intelligence and Symbolic Computation. XIII, 269 pages. 2006.

Vol. 4118: Z. Despotovic, S. Joseph, C. Sartori (Eds.), Agents and Peer-to-Peer Computing. XIV, 173 pages. 2006.

Vol. 4114: D.-S. Huang, K. Li, G.W. Irwin (Eds.), Computational Intelligence, Part II. XXVII, 1337 pages. 2006.

Vol. 4108: J.M. Borwein, W.M. Farmer (Eds.), Mathematical Knowledge Management. VIII, 295 pages. 2006.

Vol. 4106: T.R. Roth-Berghofer, M.H. Göker, H.A. Güvenir (Eds.), Advances in Case-Based Reasoning. XIV, 566 pages. 2006.

Vol. 4099: Q. Yang, G. Webb (Eds.), PRICAI 2006: Trends in Artificial Intelligence. XXVIII, 1263 pages. 2006.

Vol. 4095: S. Nolfi, G. Baldassarre, R. Calabretta, J.C.T. Hallam, D. Marocco, J.-A. Meyer, O. Miglino, D. Parisi (Eds.), From Animals to Animats 9. XV, 869 pages. 2006.

Vol. 4093: X. Li, O.R. Zaïane, Z. Li (Eds.), Advanced Data Mining and Applications. XXI, 1110 pages. 2006.

Vol. 4092: J. Lang, F. Lin, J. Wang (Eds.), Knowledge Science, Engineering and Management. XV, 664 pages. 2006.

Vol. 4088: Z.-Z. Shi, R. Sadananda (Eds.), Agent Computing and Multi-Agent Systems. XVII, 827 pages. 2006.

Vol. 4087: F. Schwenker, S. Marinai (Eds.), Artificial Neural Networks in Pattern Recognition. IX, 299 pages. 2006.

Vol. 4068: H. Schärfe, P. Hitzler, P. Øhrstrøm (Eds.), Conceptual Structures: Inspiration and Application. XI, 455 pages. 2006.

Vol. 4065: P. Perner (Ed.), Advances in Data Mining. XI, 592 pages. 2006.

Vol. 4062: G.-Y. Wang, J.F. Peters, A. Skowron, Y. Yao (Eds.), Rough Sets and Knowledge Technology. XX, 810 pages. 2006.

Vol. 4049: S. Parsons, N. Maudet, P. Moraitis, I. Rahwan (Eds.), Argumentation in Multi-Agent Systems. XIV, 313 pages. 2006.

Vol. 4048: L. Goble, J.-J.C.. Meyer (Eds.), Deontic Logic and Artificial Normative Systems. X, 273 pages. 2006.

Vol. 4045: D. Barker-Plummer, R. Cox, N. Swoboda (Eds.), Diagrammatic Representation and Inference. XII, 301 pages. 2006.

Vol. 4031: M. Ali, R. Dapoigny (Eds.), Advances in Applied Artificial Intelligence. XXIII, 1353 pages. 2006.

Vol. 4029: L. Rutkowski, R. Tadeusiewicz, L.A. Zadeh, J.M. Zurada (Eds.), Artificial Intelligence and Soft Computing – ICAISC 2006. XXI, 1235 pages. 2006.

Vol. 4027: H.L. Larsen, G. Pasi, D. Ortiz-Arroyo, T. Andreasen, H. Christiansen (Eds.), Flexible Query Answering Systems. XVIII, 714 pages. 2006.

Vol. 4021: E. André, L. Dybkjær, W. Minker, H. Neumann, M. Weber (Eds.), Perception and Interactive Technologies. XI, 217 pages. 2006.

Vol. 4020: A. Bredenfeld, A. Jacoff, I. Noda, Y. Takahashi (Eds.), RoboCup 2005: Robot Soccer World Cup IX. XVII, 727 pages. 2006.

Vol. 4013: L. Lamontagne, M. Marchand (Eds.), Advances in Artificial Intelligence. XIII, 564 pages. 2006.

Vol. 4012: T. Washio, A. Sakurai, K. Nakajima, H. Takeda, S. Tojo, M. Yokoo (Eds.), New Frontiers in Artificial Intelligence. XIII, 484 pages. 2006.

Vol. 4008: J.C. Augusto, C.D. Nugent (Eds.), Designing Smart Homes. XI, 183 pages. 2006.

Vol. 4005: G. Lugosi, H.U. Simon (Eds.), Learning Theory. XI, 656 pages. 2006.

Vol. 4002: A. Yli-Jyrä, L. Karttunen, J. Karhumäki (Eds.), Finite-State Methods and Natural Language Processing. XIV, 312 pages. 2006.

Vol. 3978: B. Hnich, M. Carlsson, F. Fages, F. Rossi (Eds.), Recent Advances in Constraints. VIII, 179 pages. 2006.

Vol. 3963: O. Dikenelli, M.-P. Gleizes, A. Ricci (Eds.), Engineering Societies in the Agents World VI. XII, 303 pages. 2006.

Vol. 3960: R. Vieira, P. Quaresma, M.d.G.V. Nunes, N.J. Mamede, C. Oliveira, M.C. Dias (Eds.), Computational Processing of the Portuguese Language. XII, 274 pages. 2006.

Vol. 3955: G. Antoniou, G. Potamias, C. Spyropoulos, D. Plexousakis (Eds.), Advances in Artificial Intelligence. XVII, 611 pages. 2006.

Vol. 3949: F.A. Savacı (Ed.), Artificial Intelligence and Neural Networks. IX, 227 pages. 2006.

Vol. 3946: T.R. Roth-Berghofer, S. Schulz, D.B. Leake (Eds.), Modeling and Retrieval of Context. XI, 149 pages. 2006.

Vol. 3944: J. Quiñonero-Candela, I. Dagan, B. Magnini, F. d'Alché-Buc (Eds.), Machine Learning Challenges. XIII, 462 pages. 2006.

Vol. 3937: H. La Poutré, N.M. Sadeh, S. Janson (Eds.), Agent-Mediated Electronic Commerce. X, 227 pages. 2006.